Pro Windows 8 Development with HTML5 and JavaScript

Adam Freeman

Apress®

Pro Windows 8 Development with HTML5 and JavaScript

ISBN-13 (pbk): 978-1-4302-4404-1

ISBN-13 (electronic): 978-1-4302-4402-8

President and Publisher: Paul Manning
Lead Editor: Ewan Buckingham
Technical Reviewers: Fabio Claudio Ferracchiati and Andy Olsen
Editorial Board: Steve Anglin, Mark Beckner, Ewan Buckingham, Gary Cornell, Louise Corrigan, Morgan Ertel, Jonathan Gennick, Jonathan Hassell, Robert Hutchinson, Michelle Lowman, James Markham, Matthew Moodie, Jeff Olson, Jeffrey Pepper, Douglas Pundick, Ben Renow-Clarke, Dominic Shakeshaft, Gwenan Spearing, Matt Wade, Tom Welsh
Coordinating Editor: Christine Ricketts
Copy Editors: Antoinette Smith, Lori Cavanaugh, and Nancy Sixsmith
Compositor: SPi Global
Indexer: SPi Global
Artist: SPi Global
Cover Designer: Anna Ishchenko

Distributed to the book trade worldwide by Springer Science+Business Media New York, 233 Spring Street, 6th Floor, New York, NY 10013. Phone 1-800-SPRINGER, fax (201) 348-4505, e-mail orders-ny@springer-sbm.com, or visit www.springeronline.com. Apress Media, LLC is a California LLC and the sole member (owner) is Springer Science + Business Media Finance Inc (SSBM Finance Inc). SSBM Finance Inc is a Delaware corporation.

For information on translations, please e-mail rights@apress.com, or visit www.apress.com.

Apress and friends of ED books may be purchased in bulk for academic, corporate, or promotional use. eBook versions and licenses are also available for most titles. For more information, reference our Special Bulk Sales–eBook Licensing web page at www.apress.com/bulk-sales.

Any source code or other supplementary materials referenced by the author in this text is available to readers at www.apress.com. For detailed information about how to locate your book's source code, go to www.apress.com/source-code/.

Dedicated to my lovely wife, Jacqui Griffyth.

Contents at a Glance

Contents

■ ■ ■

PART 1

Getting Started

I begin this book by setting the scene for the content and style, putting Windows 8 development in context and showing you how easily you can build on existing knowledge of web app development to create a simple Windows 8 app.

CHAPTER 1

■ ■ ■

Putting Windows 8 in Context

Windows 8 represents Microsoft's desire to break out of the traditional desktop computing market and make an impact in the mobile world, which has been dominated by Android devices and, of course, Apple products.

Microsoft's plan is to offer the user consistency across devices, allowing the same apps to operate on the user's data irrespective of which device, or which kind of device, the user has at hand. This is attractive to many users and it leverages Microsoft's greatest asset—the leading position in the desktop computing market—to drive sales, acceptance, and credibility in the tablet and smart-phone markets.

The traditional Windows desktop isn't a good model for consistency across different types of devices, and attempts to add touch support and rework the interface for smaller screens have not ended well. Trying to extend the old Windows model to small devices is part of the reason Microsoft's previous forays into the mobile world have fared so badly.

And that's where Windows apps come in. Rather than perpetuate its existing application model, Microsoft has decided to create a new one. Windows Store applications, more commonly known as *apps*, are available on every device that can run Windows 8 and its derivatives (Windows Phone 8, Windows RT, etc.). More important, Windows apps run as well on large-screen desktop machines with a mouse and keyboard as they do on a moderately sized touch-screen tablet. Windows Store apps are a big departure from regular Windows desktop apps: they fill the screen, don't have title bars and buttons, and have a completely different look and feel.

Another big departure for Microsoft is that you can use web technologies to create apps, which is the reason I have written this book and, most likely, the reason you are reading it. By embracing HTML, CSS, and JavaScript, Microsoft has embraced a completely new community of developers, who can take their knowledge of web app development and apply it to Windows app development.

■ **Note** Microsoft uses the term Windows Store App, which I find awkward and I can't bring myself to use it throughout this book. Instead, I'll refer to *Windows apps* and, often, just plain *apps*. I'll leave you to mentally insert the official Microsoft names as you see fit.

Putting App Development in Context

Windows apps are at the heart of Microsoft's effort to present a consistent user experience across a range of different device types, including traditional desktop PCs, tablets, and smart phones. Windows apps offer fast and fluid user interactions, support touch and keyboard/mouse input, and integrate tightly into Microsoft's cloud services, allowing users to replicate their data everywhere they work and on every device they use.

Apps are very different from traditional Windows desktop applications. Windows 8 apps fill the screen by default, are *chromeless* (which means there is no surrounding window, title bar, or buttons), and can't be resized or overlapped the way desktop apps can. Users don't close apps and there are no Close or Exit buttons. Only one app is displayed at a time, so there is no need for windows or title bars.

Key dialogs that require input from the user, such as file pickers, are also full screen and are like mini-apps in their own right. In fact, they look and feel a lot like apps you might see on an iPhone, iPad, or Android device—which is, of course, no accident. With Windows 8, Microsoft aims to gain some of the lucrative smart-phone and tablet market and hopes to leverage its dominance in the desktop world by making apps available across a wide range of platforms, including regular PCs.

Apps benefit from a range of integration services, known as *contracts*, which make it easy to create apps that are tightly integrated into the Windows platform and can share data with other apps. If you have just installed Windows 8 and have been wondering what some of the icons on Charm Bar are for, then wonder no more. Apps use contracts to provide services to the user through the Charm Bar. It may seem like an awkward tool when you are new to Windows, but it becomes second nature pretty quickly.

Developing Windows Apps with JavaScript and HTML

One of the biggest departures for Microsoft with Windows 8 has been making JavaScript and HTML first-class citizens for app development. This is a big deal for two reasons: the first is that Microsoft has invested heavily in the .NET platform over the years and has been reluctant to open up Windows development for tools and languages that are not part of the .NET family, such as C#. That has changed completely with Windows 8.

The second reason is that Microsoft has stuck to the standards. The JavaScript and HTML that you have used to write web apps is the same JavaScript and HTML that you use to write Windows apps. There are still new libraries and techniques to learn—hence this book—but if you have developed a web app, then you already have a big chunk of the knowledge and experience you will need for app development. I demonstrate this in Chapter 3, where I show you how to create your first app using little more than regular JavaScript and HTML. This web-driven theme runs deep: apps written in JavaScript/HTML are executed using Internet Explorer 10 (although this isn't evident to the user, who won't be able to tell which technology family you have used to create your app). You don't get to change which browser is used to execute your app, but after a while, you won't really want to—IE10 turns out to be pretty good and has some good support for the new HTML5 and CSS3 features. (There are some Microsoft-specific extensions, but they occur when the W3C standard is still being developed or where the feature is very app-specific.)

Developing Apps with Visual Studio

Unlike with regular web development, you can't choose your own development tools when writing apps using JavaScript and HTML: you must use Visual Studio 2012, which is the same tool required for development targeting any Microsoft platform. So, the bad news is that you have to learn a new development environment, but the good news is that Visual Studio is excellent and Microsoft has taken the time to make the JavaScript and HTML support as good as any of the tools and editors I use for regular web development. I have to admit, though, that I already had a soft spot for Visual Studio from my time writing C# apps and services, and you may find that the learning curve is steep as you grapple with a new set of tools *and* a new kind of application development. This isn't a book about Visual Studio, but in Chapter 2 I give you a quick tour of the essential features to help get you started.

Publishing Windows Apps

Most Windows apps are sold through the *Windows Store*. The exception is apps written for the enterprise, which can be installed like traditional desktop apps (although this is available only in the Windows 8 versions targeted at corporations). The Windows Store is much like any other app store—users can search for apps, see rankings of successful apps, and get updates for their apps. And, like any other app store, the Windows Store operates by taking a cut from your app sales. I'll explain how you use the Windows Store as a developer in Part IV of this book, but it will be helpful if you bear in mind that publishing via the Windows Store is the ultimate goal of app development.

What Is in This Book?

In this book, I show you how to use your knowledge of web app technologies and techniques and apply them to create rich, fluid, and dynamic Windows apps. I start by showing you these web technologies can be used to create a simple app using the same approach that you would encounter in regular web app deployment and then show you the different techniques, libraries, and features available to take advantage of Windows 8 and the app environment.

Who Is This Book For?

You are an experienced web developer who already knows the basics of JavaScript, HTML, and CSS and who wants to develop apps for Windows 8. You want to build on your web experience to create apps that go beyond the browser and take advantage of the Windows platform features in a way that regular web apps can't offer.

What Do I Need to Know Before I Read This Book?

You need to know how to write a simple web app, using HTML, CSS, and JavaScript. You need to understand HTML elements and attributes, CSS styles, and JavaScript concepts such as functions and events. You don't have to be an expert in any of these technologies, but you do need some experience. I don't provide an introduction to web development in this book, and you will struggle to follow the examples if you are new to the world of web technologies.

Windows app development uses HTML5 and CSS3, but it isn't critical if you are up to speed with the latest drafts of the HTML5 specifications. The new features in HTML5 and CSS3 are largely evolutionary, and a good understanding of HTML4 will give you enough of a foundation to figure out what you don't know.

■ **Tip** The HTML5-related features I use most often in this book are actually the new CSS3 layout features, which make it easy to create fluid interfaces. You *can* use the new elements and APIs, but for the most part you don't need to, and some key features are exposed more conveniently through the app-specific APIs.

What If I Don't Have That Experience?

You may still get some benefit from this book, but you will find it very hard going and you'll have to figure out a lot of the basic techniques required for app development on your own. I have written a couple of other books you might find useful. If you are new to HTML, read *The Definitive Guide to HTML5*. This explains everything you need to create regular web content and basic web apps. I explain how to use HTML markup and CSS3 (including the new HTML5 elements) and how to use the DOM API and the HTML5 APIs (including a JavaScript primer if you are new to the language). If you want to learn more about practical web app development, then read *Pro jQuery*. jQuery is a very popular JavaScript library that simplifies web app development. I don't use jQuery in this book, but you will improve your understanding of all aspects of web development by learning how to use jQuery effectively (and since you *can* use jQuery for Windows app development, the time you spend will stand you in good stead later). For more advanced topics, read *Pro JavaScript for Web Apps*, in which I describe the development tricks and techniques I use in my own web development projects. All three of these books are published by Apress.

What Don't I Need to Know?

You don't need to have any experience in Windows desktop development or other Microsoft technologies (such as C#, XAML, or the .NET framework). Developing apps with web technologies builds on what you already use for web app development, and while there is a lot to learn, you don't have to worry about other programming languages or markups.

But Don't I Have to Know C# for the Advanced Features?

No, honestly. Microsoft has done a pretty good job of putting JavaScript on a par with C# and the other .NET languages and making HTML a good alternative to XAML (which is the way user interfaces are defined in most .NET apps). When you get deep into app development, you will become aware that you are using libraries of JavaScript objects that are shared with the .NET languages. This is evident only because some of the object and property names are a bit odd—in all other respects you won't even know that other languages are supported.

I have been writing Windows apps in both HTML/JavaScript and XAML/C# for a while and I have yet to find any feature available to .NET programmers that is unavailable to web technology programmers. HTML and JavaScript are first-class technologies in the world of app development.

What Tools and Technologies Do I Need?

You need two things for app development: a PC running Windows 8 and Visual Studio 2012. If you get serious about app development, you'll need to buy a copy of Windows 8, but if you are just curious, you can get a 90-day trial from Microsoft—I'll explain how later in Chapter 2.

Visual Studio 2012 is Microsoft's development environment. The good news is that Microsoft makes a basic version of Visual Studio, available free of charge, and that's the version I'll be using throughout this book. It has the catchy name of Visual Studio 2012 Express for Windows 8 and I'll tell you how to get it later in this chapter.

Paid versions of Visual Studio are available, and you can use any of the different Visual Studio editions with this book. Microsoft tends to charge for features such as enterprise integration, version control, and test management, and while they are all useful features, none of them are essential for app development and I don't rely on them in any way.

What Is the Structure of This Book?

In this chapter, I introduce you to Visual Studio and show you how to create a simple project. I give you a quick tour of the key parts of the Visual Studio interface, explain what each of the files in a Windows app development project looks like, and show you how to run and test an app using the app simulator tool, which is included with Visual Studio.

In Chapter 3, I show you how to build your first app. I focus on using basic HTML, CSS, and JavaScript features to demonstrate how much of your existing web app development knowledge can be applied directly to Windows app development. You'll be pleasantly surprised by just how much you can do. Of course, you didn't buy a Pro-level book for the basics, and most of the rest of the book shows you the different techniques and features that transform a basic app into one that provides a first-class app experience. In the sections that follow, I briefly describe what you will learn in the other parts of the book.

Part II: Core Development

There are some core features that almost all apps benefit from using. In this part of the book, I explain these fundamentals techniques, showing you how to let the user navigate through your app's content, how to adapt your app layout to the capabilities and configuration of the device it is running on, and how to make best use of the extensive asynchronous programming support that runs through pretty much all of the Windows app development libraries. By the time you finish this part of the book, you'll know how to create an app that is dynamic, adaptive, and responsive.

Part III: UI Development

You can create the UI for a app, known as the *layout*, using the standard HTML elements, such as button and input, but you also have access to the WinJS UI library, which contains the interface controls that give Windows apps their distinctive look and feel. In this part of the book, I take you on a tour of the controls, explain when they should be used and how they are applied to regular HTML elements, and give you many, many examples so you can see them in operation. By the time you have finished this part of the book, you will know how to apply the distinctive Windows look and feel to create pretty, pretty apps.

Part IV: Platform Integration

Once you have your application structure and layout in place, you can start to integrate your app into the features and services that Windows provides. This includes making your app part of the file and data search process, working with the file system, telling Windows that your app supports different types of file and protocol, printing, and sharing data between apps. I cover all of these topics in this part of the book and also show you how to create different kinds of notifications for your apps, including low-key *live tiles* and more intrusive *toast notifications*. By the time you finish this part of the book, you will know how to make your app a first-class Windows citizen that is fully integrated into the wider platform and your user's workflow.

Part V: Selling Apps

In the final part of this book, I show you how to prepare an app and go through the process for publishing it in the Windows Store. By the end of this part of the book, you will have seen the complete life of a Windows app, from an initial basic implementation through to advanced features and, finally, its release to the world.

Are There Lots of Examples in This Book?

There are *loads* of examples in this book and I demonstrate every key feature you'll need to create first-rate apps. In some cases, I go back and combine different features to show you how they work together, the benefits of these combinations, and on occasion, the problems that can arise. There are so many examples in this book that I had trouble fitting all of the code into the chapters. To help fit everything in, I list JavaScript code and HTML markup in two ways. The first time I introduce a new file, I show you the complete contents. You can see an example of this in Listing 1-1, which is code taken from Chapter 6.

Listing 1-1. A complete listing of a new file

```
(function () {
    "use strict";

    WinJS.Namespace.define("ViewModel.State", {
        appBarElement: null,
        navBarContainerElement: null,
        navBarControlElement: null
    });

    WinJS.Namespace.define("ViewModel.UserData", {

    });
})();
```

When I make a change to a file, I tend to show only the part that is being changed, similar to Listing 1-2. The code in bold shows the changes I have made that are relevant to the technique or feature I am demonstrating.

Listing 1-2. A partial listing of a modified file

```
...
WinJS.Namespace.define("ViewModel.UserData", {
    word: null,
    wordLength: {
        get: function() {
            return this.word ? this.word.length : null;
        }
    }
});
...
```

What If I Want to Follow the Examples Myself?

You can download the complete code for every example in this book from Apress.com. The code is organized by chapter and each project shows the completed state of each app, so you can see what the finished result looks like and follow along if you wish. You can use the code in your own projects or create new apps using the examples as templates.

Creating the Visual Studio Project

To create a new app project, you can either click on the New Project link on the Visual Studio Start page (which is displayed when you first start Visual Studio 2012) or select New Project from the File menu.

■ **Note** Actually, it is the FILE menu, because Microsoft has decided to display the menus in Visual Studio in capital letters, even though this gives the impression that your development tool is shouting at you. I will just refer to the menus in regular case.

You will see the New Project dialog windows, as shown in Figure 2-1. Visual Studio includes templates to get you started on different kinds of projects, and these are displayed on the left side of the dialog. The set of available templates differs based on the Visual Studio edition you are using. The figure shows the templates available for Visual Studio Express 2012 for Windows, which supports four programming languages for creating apps. For each language there are templates that are prepopulated to some extent, for creating different projects.

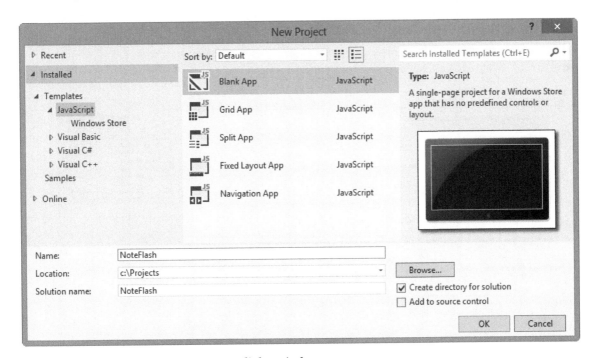

Figure 2-1. The Visual Studio New Project dialog window

I understand why Microsoft includes these templates, but they are pretty useless. It can be a bit alarming for new programmers to be faced with an empty project and a blinking cursor, but the code they put into these templates isn't very good and is rarely the kind of thing you will want for anything but the simplest and most trivial projects.

Tip   Visual Studio supports colored themes. The default for most Visual Studio editions is the dark theme, which is predominantly black and doesn't show up well in screen shots. I have switched to the light theme, which is why the New Project dialog in the figure looks different from what you can see on your screen. I changed the theme by selecting Options from the Tools menu and changing the Color Theme setting in the Environment section.

Navigate to the Blank App template in the Templates > JavaScript section. The Blank Template creates an almost empty project with just the files that are required to let you run an app without generating any errors. This is the template I will use throughout the book, and when I say I created a new project, this will always be the template I have used.

Enter NoteFlash in the name field. This is the name of the first app you will create in Chapter 3. I am not going to do any serious development at this point, but by the end of the chapter you'll understand what the moving parts in a Windows 8 app project are and then you can see how they are used in Chapter 3.

Next, click the Browse button to select a location for your project. It doesn't matter where you save the files, as long as you can find them again later. Finally, click the OK button to create the project. Visual Studio will grind away for a moment as it generates the files and configures the content, and then you'll see the initial view of the project, as shown in Figure 2-2.

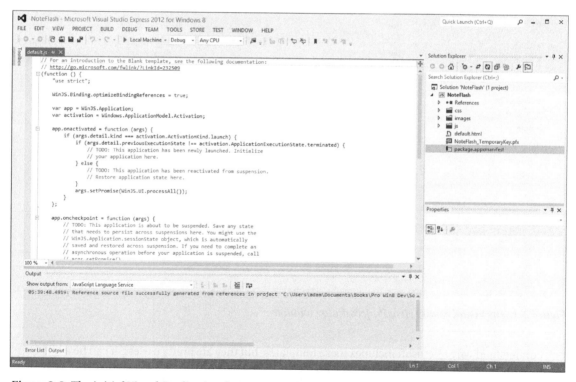

Figure 2-2. The initial Visual Studio view for a new project

In the sections that follow, I'll show you the most important Visual Studio features that you'll use in app development. Some of this will be a little obvious, but stick with me, because Visual Studio offers a tightly integrated development environment and it is useful to know how the parts all work together.

Running the Project

The best place to start with a new project is to run it and see how it looks. You have three choices when it comes to running your apps during development. The first is to run the app on the same PC you are using to write the code, the local machine. The second is to run the app in a simulator that is included with Visual Studio. The final option is to run the app on another device.

Of the three options, the simulator is most useful. The problem with running the app on the device you are working on is that Windows 8 apps are full-screen and they cover Visual Studio and the rest of the desktop. You can toggle between your app and the desktop, but it is a clumsy process, especially when you are trying to debug some kind of problem or error.

Running the app on another device can be very useful. You'll need to download and install the Remote Tools for Visual Studio 2012 on the device, which you can get from Microsoft at `http://msdn.microsoft.com/en-gb/windows/apps/br229516`. I find the ability to run an app remotely to be useful when I want to test how a feature or problem relates to a hardware capability that my development machine doesn't have—a touch screen, for example. I don't use it for regular development because it takes a few seconds for Visual Studio to package up and transmit the app to the remote device, and this becomes tiresome after a while.

■ **Tip** You can't just copy an app onto another device as you would with a traditional Windows desktop application. Microsoft is very keen on the use of the Windows Store to deploy apps, and until you are ready to publish, the easiest way to test on a device is with the remote tools.

This leaves the third option: the Visual Studio simulator. This is how I test my apps during development, and I recommend you do the same. The simulator is a reasonably faithful re-creation of a real Windows 8 device, and you can use it to simulate some important device characteristics, including device orientation, GPS locations, touch-and-gesture input, and different screen sizes and resolutions. It isn't perfect, however, and there are some app features that you can't properly test in the simulator. I'll point out these features in the appropriate chapters so you will know to use one of the other ways to run the app.

You select the way you want to run your app using the Visual Studio menu bar. By default Visual Studio will run a new project on the local machine, but you can change this by clicking on the arrow next to the button shown in Figure 2-3. The text displayed by this button reflects the choice you have made, so it might not match the figure exactly—but you can't miss the button, because it has a large green arrow next to it. (The arrow you need to click to change the setting is the small down arrow to the right of the button text—not the green one).

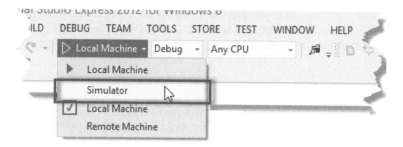

Figure 2-3. *Selecting the way Visual Studio will run the app*

Pick the Simulator option from the drop-down menu, as highlighted in the figure. Once you have made your choice, click on the green arrow or the button text to start the app. Visual Studio will launch the simulator, install your app, and start running it. The Blank App Visual Studio template you used to create the project really does generate just the basic structure of an app, so there isn't a lot to see at the moment—just a black screen with small text in the top left corner that says Content goes here. Ignore the app for the moment and look at the buttons on the right edge of the simulator window, which I have shown in Figure 2-4. You can also start the app by selecting Start Debugging from the Visual Studio Debug menu—the effect is the same. I'll come back to the Visual Studio debugger later in this chapter.

■ **Note**   When I tell you to start the app, I mean that you should select the Start Debugging menu item or click the button on the toolbar so the debugger is used. There are a couple of features that need to be tested without the debugger, but I'll make this clear when you get to them. In all other cases, you should make sure the debugger is running.

Figure 2-4. *The Visual Studio simulator*

■ **Tip** There is one file shown by the `Solution Explorer` that I haven't mentioned: the `NoteFlash_TemporaryKey.pfx` file. This file contains a digital certificate used to automatically sign the app package during development. You replace this file with a real certificate during the publishing process, which I describe in Part 5 of this book.

The Visual Studio Tools

In this section, I'll give a brief tour of the different parts of Visual Studio you will use to develop apps. I don't go into detail, because Visual Studio is like any other IDE and you will have used a text editor and debugger countless times before. This section of the chapter shows you how to find the major IDE building blocks and points out the useful features that you may not have readily discovered on your own.

The Visual Studio Editor

You open the editor by double-clicking on a file in the `Solution Explorer` window. The editor does all of the things you would expect. The editor adapts to the file format so you can edit HTML, CSS, and JavaScript files seamlessly, and it does autocomplete for all three types. It color codes the syntax and it knows that you can embed CSS and JavaScript inside HTML files and responds accordingly. It is a very good programmer's editor, and it does everything that every other programmer's editor does.

You can configure how each language is handled in the editor by selecting `Tools` from the Visual Studio `Options` menu. Expand the `Text Editor` section and you will see a `General` item that applies to all languages and a set of per-language items. You can control color coding, indentation, autocomplete, and many other features to tailor the editor to your preferences.

One feature worth pointing out is the Visual Studio editor's excellent text search capabilities. Typing `Control+F` opens an in-editor search box you can use to locate items in the current file. Each editor window can be searched independently with its own search box or you can click the down arrow to expand the scope of a search. I use the search feature a lot and I miss it when I am using other IDEs or editors.

The JavaScript Console

The Visual Studio interface changes when you start the app. One of the changes is that the `JavaScript Console` window will appear. (If it isn't visible or if you inadvertently close it, you can manually open this window from the `Windows` item on the `Visual Studio Debug` menu, but only while the app is running with the debugger.)

The `JavaScript Console` window is one of the most useful Visual Studio features for tracking down problems in your app and performs several different roles. If you make calls to the `console.log` method from your JavaScript code, the strings you specify will be displayed in the `JavaScript Console` window, just as you would expect.

You can also execute arbitrary JavaScript code and explore the variables and functions that your app defines. As a simple example, I am going to change the `default.html` file so that the p element has an `id` attribute, as shown in Listing 2-4.

Listing 2-4. Adding an id attribute to the p element

```
<!DOCTYPE html>
<html>
```

```
<head>
    <meta charset="utf-8" />
    <title>NoteFlash</title>

    <!-- WinJS references -->
    <link href="//Microsoft.WinJS.1.0/css/ui-dark.css" rel="stylesheet" />
    <script src="//Microsoft.WinJS.1.0/js/base.js"></script>
    <script src="//Microsoft.WinJS.1.0/js/ui.js"></script>

    <!-- NoteFlash references -->
    <link href="/css/default.css" rel="stylesheet" />
    <script src="/js/default.js"></script>
</head>
<body>
    <p id="paraElem">Content goes here</p>
</body>
</html>
```

I have highlighted the element I modified. Start the app and find the JavaScript Console window and type the following into the text box at the bottom of the window:

```
paraElem.style.fontSize = "40pt"
```

If you hit return, you will see that what is displayed in the simulator window is resized to 40 points, as shown in Figure 2-9.

Figure 2-9. Using the JavaScript Console window to locate and configure an HTML element

There are a couple of key points to note in this simple example. The first is that the JavaScript Console provides you with access to the live state of your app. You can call any function, read or modify any variable, and change any style. The only limitation is that JavaScript variables and functions need to be part of the global namespace—a topic I return to in Chapter 3.

The second point is that Internet Explorer allows you to locate HTML elements by treating the value of their id attributes as global variables. This is not a standard feature, although some other browsers do similar things. I use this feature a lot in this book and it means that I don't have to use the verbose DOM API (although to be clear, you *can* use the DOM API if you prefer, both in your app code and in the JavaScript Console window). The paraElem variable returns the DOM object that represents the p element in the HTML document, and I am able to use the standard HTMLElement objects and properties to manipulate the element—in this case, changing the value of the style.fontSize property to increase the size of the text.

USING BROWSER QUIRKS IN APP DEVELOPMENT

Being able to locate HTML elements by their `id` attribute values is very useful, but it is not a standard DOM feature and so it is classified as a *browser quirk*. In web app development, you will have learned to avoid browser quirks because you need to support a wide array of browsers and you don't want to tie your app to browser-specific features.

Things are different in the world of app development. The only browser that will be used to run a JavaScript Windows 8 app is Internet Explorer, and installing a new browser, such as Chrome or Firefox, will have no effect on Windows 8 apps.

This means that you can use Internet Explorer's quirks without fear, although you may question whether doing so is good practice. I have gone back and forth on this issue for some months. Initially I stuck to the standard DOM API, even though I find it verbose and annoying. I made life easier for myself by using the `WinJS.Utilities` feature, which is like a simplified version of jQuery. (You can use jQuery in app projects, but I don't in this book—and I must admit, I don't tend to use it in my Windows 8 app projects in general. There just isn't much of a need, even though I am a huge jQuery fan—see my Pro jQuery book, published by Apress, if you have any doubts about my jQuery fan-boy status.)

In the end, though, I decided I was missing an important point: Windows 8 app development *isn't* web app development, even though it shares common roots and technologies. I was avoiding the convenient and time-saving quirks out of habit, rather than because they cause problems. In fact, some quirks help avoid problems—for example, I find locating elements using global variables to be less error-prone than using the DOM API.

You are free to choose whichever approach suits you best—but I suggest that you examine your decision to make sure you are not being needlessly dogmatic, as I was when I began Windows 8 app development.

Throughout this book, I locate elements by their global properties—with two exceptions. I use the DOM API when I want to make it very clear that I am locating an HTML element in an example, and I use the jQuery-like `WinJS.Utilities` feature (which I introduce in Chapter 3 and describe fully in Chapter 18) when I want to select multiple elements with a CSS selector so I can perform an operation on all of them in a single step.

The DOM Explorer

One of the other windows that appear when you start the app is the DOM Explorer. This allows you to explore the HTML structure of the app, look at the box layout properties of individual elements, and trace how CSS precedence rules have been applied to determine style for elements. The DOM Explorer window appears as a tab in the editor area of Visual Studio. I find myself inadvertently closing the DOM Explorer window quite often—if you do the same, you can reopen it from the Windows item of the Visual Studio Debug menu.

The feature I find most useful is being able to locate an element in the HTML document by clicking on it in the app. This is something that is pretty standard in web app development tools, and it is nice to be able to use in app development as well. At the top of the DOM Explorer window is the Select Element button, which I have highlighted in Figure 2-10.

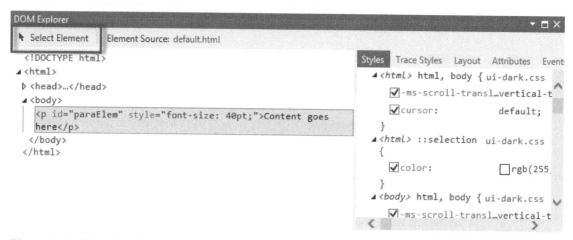

Figure 2-10. Using the Select Element feature of the DOM Explorer window

Click this button and switch to the simulator window. You will see elements highlighted as you move over them, and their details are displayed in the DOM Explorer window. Click on the element you are interested in and use the DOM Explorer to see all of its characteristics, layout details, and CSS styles.

The Debugger

Visual Studio contains my favorite debugger. I find it faster and more reliable than any other debugger I have used, and I like the way it integrates so nicely into the rest of Visual Studio. I am not going to give you a detailed tutorial on debugging, because you already know how to use a debugger from your web app projects, but in the sections that follow I'll show you the useful additions Visual Studio provides.

Setting Breakpoints in Your Own Code

If you want to set a breakpoint in code that you can modify (as opposed to one of the Microsoft JavaScript files), the simplest way is to use the JavaScript debugger keyword, as shown in Listing 2-5, where I have added this kind of breakpoint to the default.js file.

Listing 2-5. Using the debugger keyword to create a breakpoint

```
// For an introduction to the Blank template, see the following documentation:
// http://go.microsoft.com/fwlink/?LinkId=232509
(function () {
    "use strict";

    WinJS.Binding.optimizeBindingReferences = true;

    var app = WinJS.Application;
    var activation = Windows.ApplicationModel.Activation;

    app.onactivated = function (args) {
        if (args.detail.kind === activation.ActivationKind.launch) {
            if (args.detail.previousExecutionState !==
```

and Visual Studio will create a small window that displays the current value. Type F5 to resume execution and wait until the next loop iteration triggers the debugger again. You'll see that the value window is updated to show you the current value of the variable, as illustrated by Figure 2-12.

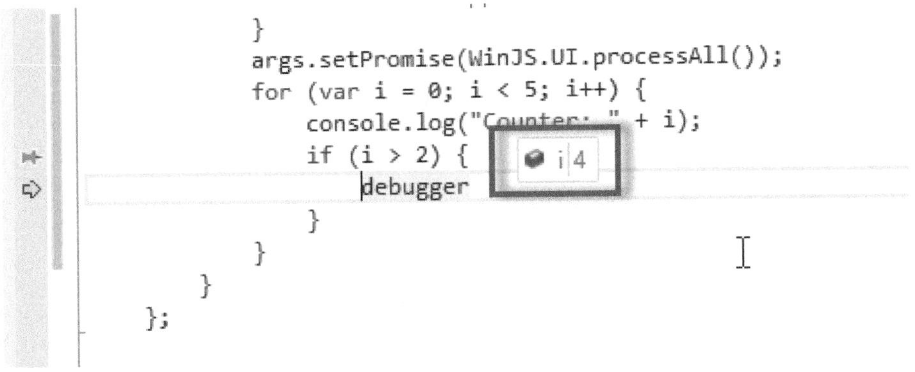

Figure 2-12. Monitoring the value of a variable using Visual Studio

If you click on the value in the window, a text box will appear that will let you change the value assigned to the variable. When you type F5 to resume execution, the new value will be used.

Using the JavaScript Console

The JavaScript Console window is also very useful when debugging. While the execution of the app is halted, the scope for the JavaScript Console is the context of the breakpoint. This means that you can refer to variables and call functions that are defined locally and not just globally. As an example, start the app, wait for the debugger to take control, and type the letter i into the text box at the bottom of the JavaScript Console window and press Enter. You'll see the current value displayed. If you assign a value to the variable using the console (e.g., entering i = 5 and pressing Enter), your value will be used when the execution of the app is resumed.

The JavaScript Console can also be used to explore complex objects. As an example, type args into the textbox and press Enter. Click on the arrow to the left of the response and you will see the properties and functions defined by the args object, which is passed to the function in which I placed the debugger keyword. Don't worry about this object for the moment—I explain its significance in detail in Part 19. You can see in Figure 2-13 the way the JavaScript Console displays the object.

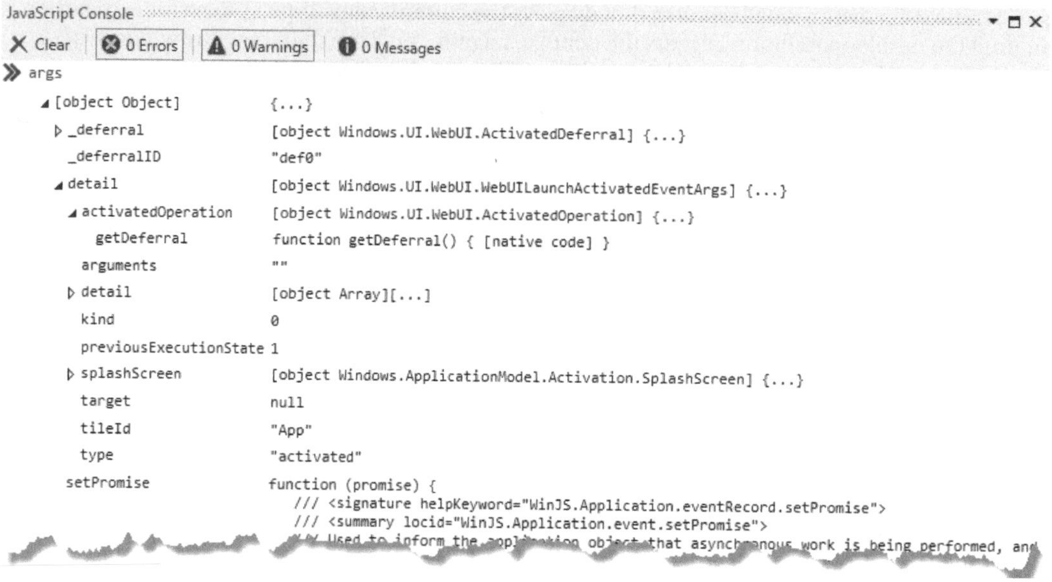

Figure 2-13. *Exploring an object with the JavaScript Console window*

I use this feature a lot. It doesn't allow you to modify values by clicking on them, but you can enter in JavaScript statements that assign new values to the object or its properties—and you can execute its functions as well.

Summary

In this chapter, I created an initial Visual Studio project and used it to show you the structure of an app under development, highlighting the references to the Microsoft libraries and the default HTML, JavaScript, and CSS files. I also gave you a very quick tour of the key Visual Studio features you will use in app development. Visual Studio is a big and complex tool, but the parts I showed you will put you in good standing as you begin Windows 8 app development. In the next chapter, I build on the project I created to demonstrate how far you can get in app development with your existing web app development skills and knowledge.

■ **Tip** The initial page for an app doesn't have to be this simple—you can mix local elements with those from other pages in any combination that suits your app. I tend to use this page for content that is common across the entire app, which you'll see in Chapter 7 when I add a Windows 8-specific control called an *AppBar*.

Defining the Code

As I explained in Chapter 2, Visual Studio creates the js/default.js file when it creates a new project and adds a script element to the default.html file that ensures this file is loaded when the app starts. Throughout this book, I'll use the default.js file as my main JavaScript file, and this chapter is no exception.

You can see in Listing 3-2 the changes I have made to the default.js file. I have simplified the code to remove some features that I won't describe until later in the book and removed the comments.

Listing 3-2. The revised default.js file

```
(function () {
    "use strict";

    var app = WinJS.Application;
    var activation = Windows.ApplicationModel.Activation;

    window.$ = WinJS.Utilities.query;

    window.showPage = function (url, options) {
        WinJS.Utilities.empty(pageFrame);
        WinJS.UI.Pages.render(url, pageFrame, options);
    };

    app.onactivated = function (args) {
        showPage("/pages/selectorPage.html");
    };

    app.start();
})();
```

There is a lot to explain about this code, even though there are just a few statements. Since this is the first real Windows app JavaScript file I have shown you, I'll start by explaining the structure and content of this file in the following sections.

Dealing with the Global Namespace

One of the most commonly encountered problems in JavaScript development is *global namespace collisions*. By default, any JavaScript variable created outside a function or defined without the var keyword is a *global variable*, meaning that it is accessible throughout the JavaScript code in an app. This is as true for web apps as it is for Windows apps. There are only so many sensible variable names, and it is just a matter of time before two variables called something like data or user are defined and problems arise, especially when an app relies on libraries from different programmers. Different sections of code end up with different expectations about the value and meaning of the contested variable, and the result can be anything from slightly odd behavior to data corruption.

Using Self-Executing Functions

In Listing 3-2 you can see two of the three conventions for Windows apps that are intended to reduce namespace pollution. The first is that all of the JavaScript statements are contained within a *self-executing function*. By placing a function between parentheses and then adding another pair of parentheses afterward, a function is executed immediately after it is defined:

```
(function() {
    // ... statements go here ...
})();
```

The benefit of using a self-executing function is that any variables defined within the function are local to the scope of the function and will be deleted when the function has completed, keeping the global namespace clear. Self-executing functions are added to any JavaScript file that Visual Studio creates for you, and I use them extensively in this book. I recommend that you adopt this practice in your own code because it is one of the simplest ways to help reduce global namespace problems.

Using Strict Mode

The second convention that helps keep the global namespace clear is the use of *strict mode*, which is enabled by placing "use strict" in a function, like this:

```
(function() {
    "use strict";
    // ... statements go here ...
})();
```

Strict mode enforces some restrictions on the way you can use JavaScript. One such restriction is that you can't implicitly create global variables by omitting the var keyword:

```
...
var color1 = "blue";   // OK–scope is local to function
color2 = "red";        // Not OK–this is a global variable
...
```

The Windows JavaScript runtime will generate an error if you define a variable that is implicitly global when strict mode is used. Using strict mode is optional, but it is good practice and it disables some of the more confusing and odd JavaScript behaviors. You can get full details of the changes that strict mode enforces by reading Appendix C of the ECMAScript Language Specification at www.ecma-international. org/publications/files/ECMA-ST/Ecma-262.pdf.

Understanding Windows App Namespaces

Now that you know that managing the global namespace is important, the first of the regular statements in Listing 3-2 will start to make sense:

```
...
window.$ = WinJS.Utilities.query;
...
```

This statement is just a convenience. If you have read my *Pro jQuery* book, you know I am a big fan of jQuery and I am accustomed to being able to query the document for elements using the $ shortcut. The WinJS API (application programming interface), which I introduce in the *Understanding the Windows APIs* sidebar, contains the WinJS.Utilities.query method, which does a CSS-selector-based query of the current document and supports some basic jQuery-like actions. It isn't jQuery, but it is close enough for most simple tasks and I'll use it throughout this book.

■ **Tip**   You can go ahead and use jQuery (or any of your favorite JavaScript libraries) for your Windows apps. I keep things simple in this book and use just the built-in facilities, but since JavaScript Windows apps are executed using Internet Explorer 10, just about any well-written JavaScript library will work fine. Just watch out for areas where Windows 8 does something different from web apps. A good example is the set of events used to signal the life cycle of a Windows app. You should use these in preference to the ready function that jQuery defines, for example, because they allow you to properly integrate into the operating system. I explain these events in Chapter 19. You may also want to look at the WinJS UI controls that I describe in Part 3 of this book—some of them depend on other WinJS features and if you use other jQuery libraries for those features, you won't get the best UI experience.

I want my $ shortcut to be available globally, so I have to explicitly define it as a property of the window object (a little-known fact is that all JavaScript global objects are actually window properties). By assigning the WinJS.Utilities.query function to window.$, I keep within the constraints of the self-executing function and strict mode—neither of these conventions is intended to stop you from deliberately defining global variables, only to prevent you from doing it accidentally.

In addition to self-executing functions and strict mode, the third way that Microsoft helps to reduce global namespace pollution is to support *namespaces*, such as WinJS.Utilities:

```
...
window.$ = WinJS.Utilities.query;
...
```

Namespaces allow you to group together related objects and functions in a structured way. In Chapter 4 I'll show you how to create your own namespaces. The WinJS namespace contains the entirety of the WinJS API, which includes a child namespace called Utilities, which is the home for the jQuery-like objects and methods for DOM manipulation. The Utilities namespace contains, among other things, the query method, which lets me locate HTML elements using CSS selectors. Namespaces create hierarchies of objects that are grouped by purpose or common functionality.

Unlike namespaces in languages such as C#, Windows app JavaScript namespaces don't restrict access to the code they contain—all of the functions and data values are available globally through the namespace. Windows app JavaScript namespaces are all about using structure to keep the global namespace clear.

UNDERSTANDING THE WINDOWS APIS

You have access to a number of different APIs when you write a Windows 8 app using HTML and JavaScript. The first, and most obvious, are the DOM and standard JavaScript APIs. These are available because a JavaScript Windows app is run using Internet Explorer 10, and this means you have access to all the facilities of a web browser (at least the ones provided by IE10, anyway). You'll see as I build out the NoteFlash app in this chapter that you can create a basic Windows app using little more than standard HTML elements and regular JavaScript.

You also have access to the Windows API. These are the objects accessed through namespaces that begin with Windows. The objects in this API are the same ones available to C#, Visual Basic, and C++ programmers, but are presented so that they can be used easily in JavaScript. Microsoft has done a pretty decent job of making JavaScript a first-class language for Windows app development, and the Windows API is at the heart of this feature.

The final API is WinJS, which contains objects that are specific to Windows apps written using HTML and JavaScript. In some cases, these objects make it easier to use the Windows API, but mostly they provide features that are required only by JavaScript programmers. A good example is the additional UI controls that augment the standard HTML elements (which I describe in Part 3). These are specific to JavaScript because the other languages use the Extensible Application Markup Language (XAML) instead. You can read the source code for the WinJS API by opening the References section of your Visual Studio project. (The source code for the Windows API isn't available.)

Defining a Global Navigation Function

My default.html document contains the pageFrame element into which I will insert other pages. I want to expose the ability to navigate to other pages as a global function, as follows:

```
...
window.showPage = function (url, options) {
    WinJS.Utilities.empty(pageFrame);
    WinJS.UI.Pages.render(url, pageFrame, options);
};
...
```

I have defined the showPage function as a property of the window object so that it is available globally. The benefit of this function is that it allows me to avoid hard-coding the pageFrame element name into each content page I create. The arguments to the showPage function are the URL of the page I want to display and any state information that should be passed to the page.

■ **Tip**   In Chapter 7 I introduce the *Navigation* feature, which simplifies this technique.

Inside this function, you can see some WinJS API calls. I want to replace, rather than add to, any content in the pageFrame element. I call the WinJS.Utilities.empty method, which removes any children of the element passed as its argument. I refer to the pageFrame element as a global variable, which is the Internet Explorer feature I describe in Chapter 2 when discussing the issue of using browser-specific features.

Once I have removed any existing content, I call the WinJS.UI.Pages.render method. This method is part of the larger *Pages* feature, which offers some useful behaviors above and beyond using an iframe element, for example. At its heart, though, the render method is a wrapper around the XMLHttpRequest object that is commonly used in web app Ajax requests.

■ **Tip**   I'll show you some of the features that WinJS.UI.Pages provides when I add pages to the app later in this chapter, and I cover this part of the API in depth in Chapter 5. You can read about the WinJS.Utilities API in Chapter 18.

Displaying the Initial Page

The last step in setting up the app is to display the initial page in the `pageFrame` element, by using my `showPage` global function:

```
...
var app = WinJS.Application;

app.onactivated = function (eventObject) {
    showPage("/pages/selectorPage.html");
};
app.start();
...
```

The `WinJS.Application` object provides the basic foundation for a Windows app—including defining events that describe the app life cycle. I'll explain the life cycle fully in Chapter 19, but by adding a handler function to the `onactivated` property, I express interest in the `activated` event, which is sent when the application is launched. This gives me the opportunity to perform any one-time initialization tasks—including displaying my initial page using the `showPage` function. You can ignore the final statement in this fragment—the call to the `app.start` method. All you need to know at the moment is that the handler function for the `activated` event is where you initialize your app (I explain the `start` method in Chapter 19, but you don't need to know how it works until then, just that it is required to trigger the function assigned to the `onactivated` property).

Adding the Musical Note Font

For the `NoteFlash` app, I need to be able to display musical notes. The simplest way I found is to use a font called `MusiQwik`, created by Robert Allgeyer, which I have included in the source code download for this book. You can download the font directly from `luc.devroye.org/allgeyer/allgeyer.html` if you prefer.

I need to make the font part of the Visual Studio project. I created a project folder called `resources` and copied the `MusiQwik.ttf` file from the font download file into it. Since this is the first time I have added a folder to the project, I'll give you step-by-step instructions.

First you must ensure that the debugger isn't running, because the `Solution Explorer` won't let you modify the project structure when it is. Stop the app by clicking the Stop button on the toolbar (the one with the red square icon) or by selecting `Stop Debugging` from the Debug menu.

Right click on the bold `NoteFlash` entry in the `Solution Explorer` window and select `Add New Folder` from the pop-up menu. A new folder will be added to the project and its name will be selected so that you can easily change it—to `resources` in this case. Hit Enter to confirm the name and you will have created and named the folder. You can now copy the `MusiQwik.ttf` file from the source code download into the folder.

Defining the App-Wide CSS

The next step is to write the CSS that will make the music font available for use in my HTML files. Internet Explorer 10, which is used to execute JavaScript Windows apps, supports the CSS3 *web fonts* feature, which allows for the definition of custom font faces. Listing 3-3 shows the CSS I added to the `css/default.css` file that defines the font face and related styles. I removed the default styles and `media` rules that Visual Studio adds (and which you saw in Chapter 2).

Listing 3-3. The contents of the css/default.css file

```css
@font-face {
    font-family: 'Music';
    font-style: normal;
    font-weight: normal;
    src: url('/resources/MusiQwik.ttf');
}

*.music {
    font-family: Music, cursive;
    font-size: 200px;
    letter-spacing: 0px;
}

*.musicSmall {
    font-size: 100px;
}

*.musicDisabled {
    color: #808080;
}

#pageFrame {
    height: 100%;
}
```

This is all standard CSS3. I use the @font-face rule to define a new font face, using the MusiQwik.ttf as the source of the font. This rule produces a new font face called Music.

I use the new font face in style for the music class, which allows me to have the text in any element appear as a series of notes. The musicSmall and musicDisabled classes are common styles that I use throughout this app. I will combine them with the music class to create specific effects.

I define the font-face rule and the associated styles in the default.css file because anything I define here will automatically be available to each of the individual pages that are loaded and inserted into the default.html file. This isn't Windows-specific magic—it works because Visual Studio adds a link element to default.html when it creates the file that imports the css/default.css file:

```html
...
<link href="/css/default.css" rel="stylesheet">
...
```

The styles defined in default.css will be applied to the elements from other pages that I insert into default.html, which makes default.css especially well-suited for defining app-wide styles and rules.

I don't want to labor this point too much, but this is a good example of how much the JavaScript Windows app model depends on web standards and, as a consequence, how far your knowledge of HTML, CSS, and JavaScript can get you along the path toward app development. Even when I start to add more Windows-specific features, the app will still be driven by the underlying web technologies and standards.

Adding the Selector Page

Now that the navigation master page and common styles are in place, I can add the app's content pages. I will start with the selector page, which allows the user to select which group of notes she will be tested on.

I like to keep my content pages grouped together in the Visual Studio project, so I have added a pages folder to the project. Into this folder I have added selectorPage.html by right-clicking the newly added pages folder in the Solution Explorer, selecting Add ➤ New Item from the pop-up menu and using the Page Control item template.

The Page Control template is a convenient Visual Studio feature that creates an HTML file, a JavaScript file, and a CSS file in a single step. The HTML file contains a link element for the CSS file and a script element for the JavaScript file, so that the code and styles are loaded automatically when the HTML is used.

The JavaScript and CSS files are created in the same folder as the HTML file and are named automatically, which means that my project contains three new files: pages/selectorPage.html, pages/selectorPage.css, and pages/selectorPage.js. You can see in Figure 3-4 how these files are shown in the Solution Explorer.

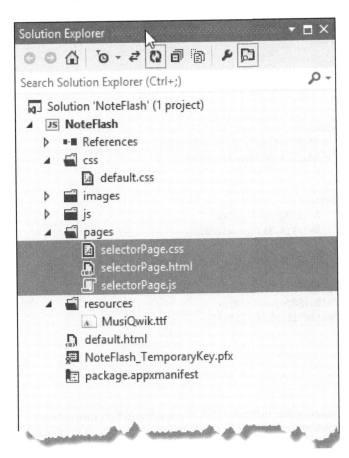

Figure 3-4. Using the Page Control template to create a linked set of HTML, CSS, and JavaScript files

The new CSS and JavaScript files allow me to differentiate between styles and code that are specific to a particular page and those that apply to the entire app (and are defined in the default.css and default.js files). Listing 3-4 shows the content of my selectorPage.html file, which contains the HTML markup that will be presented to the user.

Listing 3-4. The contents of the selectorPage.html file

```
<!DOCTYPE html>
<html>
<head>
    <meta charset="utf-8" />
    <title>selectorPage</title>

    <!-- WinJS references -->
    <link href="//Microsoft.WinJS.1.0/css/ui-dark.css" rel="stylesheet" />
    <script src="//Microsoft.WinJS.1.0/js/base.js"></script>
    <script src="//Microsoft.WinJS.1.0/js/ui.js"></script>

    <link href="selectorPage.css" rel="stylesheet" />
    <script src="selectorPage.js"></script>
</head>
<body>
    <div id="selectorFrame">
        <h1 id="prompt">Select Notes</h1>

        <div id="leftHand" class="musicButton">
            <div class="music musicSmall musicDisabled">'&======!</div>
            <div class="music musicSmall">'&#175;==&#70;===!</div>
            <h2 class="">Left Hand</h2>
        </div>
        <div id="bothHands" class="musicButton">
            <div class="music musicSmall">'&==&#70;===!</div>
            <div class="music musicSmall">'&#175;==&#70;===!</div>
            <h2 class="">Both Hands</h2>
        </div>

        <div id="rightHand" class="musicButton">
            <div class="music musicSmall">'&==&#70;===!</div>
            <div class="music musicSmall musicDisabled">'&#175;======!</div>
            <h2 class="">Right Hand</h2>
        </div>
    </div>
</body>
</html>
```

I have highlighted the link and script elements that bring the CSS and JavaScript files into context and the changes I have made to the file. Windows apps really are like web apps and there is no magic that associates the files that Visual Studio creates with the HTML page—you are responsible for making sure everything you need is linked to the HTML, although Visual Studio helps a lot when it creates files from its templates.

Defining the Selector Page JavaScript Code

The elements in the selectorPage.html markup are styled to look like buttons, but they are just div elements. To make them *behave* like buttons, I need to use a combination of CSS and JavaScript code. You have already seen the CSS—in Listing 3-5, I defined the div.musicButton and div.musicButton:hover styles to set the foundation style and to respond when the pointer is moved into the screen area occupied by one of the three div elements.

To supplement this basic behavior, I have to switch to JavaScript, which I have defined in the pages/selectorPage.js file so as to follow the Windows app convention. You can see the code in Listing 3-6.

Listing 3-6. The contents of the selectorPage.js file

```
(function () {
    "use strict";

    function handleMusicButtonEvents(e) {
        switch (e.type) {
            case "mousedown":
                this.style.backgroundColor = "#6B997A";
                break;
            case "mouseup":
                this.style.backgroundColor = "";
                break;
            case "click":
                showPage("/pages/flashCardsPage.html", this.id);
                break;
        }
    };

    WinJS.UI.Pages.define("/pages/selectorPage.html", {
        ready: function (element, options) {
            var buttons = WinJS.Utilities.query("div.musicButton");
            ["mouseup", "mousedown", "click"].forEach(function (eventType) {
                buttons.listen(eventType, handleMusicButtonEvents);
            });
        }
    });
})();
```

In this file, you can see the other half of the navigation model. In the default.js file, I used the WinJS.UI.Pages.render method to display pages, such as selectorPage.html. In selectorPage.js, I use the WinJS.UI.Pages.define method to respond when the page is displayed.

The arguments to the define method are the URL of the page and an object that defines handler functions for different events. In this example, I have defined a handler for the ready event, which is invoked each time the page is displayed. (I explain both parts of this feature in detail in Chapter 5.)

There is some subtlety to the way this method operates, and it is hinted at by the first argument: the page URL. You don't have to register your event handler functions in the JavaScript file associated with the page. You can put them in any JavaScript code that has been incorporated into the app—for my simple app, that means default.js or creating a new file and using a script element to import the code. I go in depth into the define method in Chapter 5, but for the moment, it is enough to know this this is the

Windows app pattern for defining code that should be executed when markup in the specified file has been loaded into the app.

OPTIMIZING AND LOADING JAVASCRIPT

When writing a regular web app, there is a lot of incentive to take direct control of loading your JavaScript code. You start by minifying or minimizing the code so that it requires less bandwidth, you concatenate multiple files together to reduce the number of HTTP connections the browser has to make, and you use content Delivery networks (CDNs) to get ahold of popular JavaScript libraries in the hope of improving performance or, ideally, benefitting from a previously downloaded version of common libraries you require.

If you are serious about web app performance, you start looking at using a JavaScript loader to bring in your JavaScript code asynchronously. The two loaders I use in web apps are YepNope and RequireJS. Used carefully, a good JavaScript loader can really reduce the amount of time the user has to stare at a loading screen and, in the case of a conditional loader like YepNope, avoid downloading script files that are not needed for a particular user, browser, or platform.

You *can* apply these same techniques to your JavaScript Windows apps, but there isn't any benefit in doing so—and, worse, you just make your app harder to test and debug.

Windows 8 apps are deployed locally, which means that your script files are loaded very quickly—so quickly that it is unlikely that you will need to defer execution to address perceptions of performance. Equally, since JavaScript files are loaded locally, there is no need to minify your code to reduce bandwidth consumption.

There are some important WinJS features and conventions that implicitly rely on synchronous script execution, including the define method I showed you in the previous section. That's not to say that you can't work around these situations—but you should stop and ask yourself what problem you are trying to solve before doing so. I have been writing Windows apps since the earliest release versions of Windows 8 and I have yet to encounter any problem that would have been solved by adding a JavaScript loader. There may be very specific situations in which a loader is useful and that I haven't encountered yet, but these are likely to occur so infrequently that you shouldn't automatically add a loader to your Windows app project just because it is part of your development workflow for web apps.

Handling the Button Clicks

In my handler for the ready event, I register the handleMusicButtonEvents function as a handler for the click, mousedown, and mouseup events. I am not using button elements in the markup, so I respond to the mousedown and mouseup events by applying and removing a background color. These are the standard DOM events that you encounter during web app development, and you handle them in exactly the same way you would a regular HTML page.

I located the elements that I wanted using the WinJS.Utilities.query method, which is the one that I aliased to $ in the default.js file earlier. I have used the method name explicitly in this file so you can clearly see what's happening. The query method takes a CSS selector and returns a collection of standard DOM HTMLElement objects that represent the matching elements in the page (this is the *entire* markup of the app at the point when the method is called, not just the content in the content HTML file). The collection of matching elements can be treated like a regular array, but is actually a WinJS.Utilities. QueryCollection object, which defines a number of useful methods. One of these methods is listen, which takes an event name and a handler function and calls the addEventListener method on each of the HTMLElements in the collection. If you are a jQuery user, you will recognize the degree to which the WinJS. Utilities namespace is inspired by the jQuery API. (I'll introduce you to various WinJS.Utilities features as I use them and I discuss the namespace in detail in Chapter 18.)

■ **Tip** You will notice that I am using the standard DOM events to handle user interaction. This works perfectly well (and I use these events throughout this book), but if you want to deal with touch and gesture input, you need to use events that are Microsoft-specific. I explain in Chapter 17 what these events are and how they work. For regular input, such as dealing with buttons, the regular DOM events will work, even if the user has touched the screen rather than used a mouse.

When the user clicks or touches one of the elements, I call the global showPage navigation function I created in the default.js file earlier, passing in the id of the selected element, like this:

```
...
showPage("/pages/flashCardsPage.html", this.id);
...
```

In this showPage function, this argument is passed to the WinJS.UI.Pages.render method, like this:

```
...
window.showPage = function (url, options) {
    var targetElem = document.getElementById("pageFrame");
    WinJS.Utilities.empty(targetElem);
    WinJS.UI.Pages.render(url, targetElem, options);
};
...
```

This is a simple technique to pass information from one page to another, but it requires prior knowledge and coordination between pages. It is fine for simple apps like this one but is problematic in real projects. In Part 2 of this book I show you various techniques and features to help remove these dependencies and create apps made up of loosely coupled components, which make apps easier to write and easier to maintain.

You can see how the app appears in Figure 3-5: the button-like div elements that allow the user to select the notes she wants to be tested on are neatly displayed on the layout grid and respond to basic mouse interaction (although the page they load when clicked doesn't exist yet).

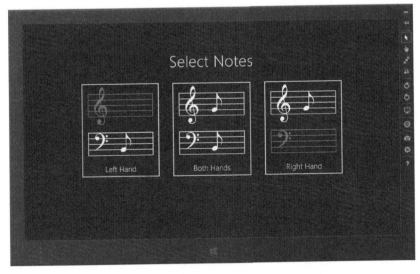

Figure 3-5. Allowing the user to select a set of notes

It doesn't look like much at the moment, but most of this chapter has been about the context and background for Windows app development. So far, the app itself consists of just a few short files and some basic JavaScript. The pace will pick up in the next chapter and you'll see the rest of the app functionality quickly fall into place.

Summary

The example app doesn't do much at the moment, but in getting to this point you have learned some of the most essential concepts in Windows app development. You have also learned about the conventions and features that Windows provides to help you manage the global namespace. Windows app development is *not* web app development, but your existing skills give you an excellent foundation for creating rich and fluid Windows apps. In this chapter, you saw how I used standard HTML and CSS to create the structure and layout for the app, including the CSS3 web fonts and the grid layout (albeit using a vendor-specific prefix) and standard DOM events like click and mouseover. In the next chapter, I'll add to the example app and build out the functionality.

CHAPTER 4

■ ■ ■

Completing the App

In this chapter, I will complete the basic version NoteFlash example app that I started in Chapter 3. I continue to use approaches and techniques that have a lot in common with regular web app development, but I also start to mix in more Windows-specific functionality that is available through the WinJS API. I provide a brief overview of each Windows app feature as I use it and explain where in the book you can get more details.

Revisiting the Example App

In this chapter, I will build directly on the NoteFlash project from Chapter 3. As you will recall, I put the basic structure of the app in place, defined a navigation function, and defined the styles that will be applied throughout the app. I also used the Page Control item template to generate a set of related HTML, CSS, and JavaScript files I used to create the content that allows the user to select the notes to be tested on. You can see how that turned out in Figure 4-1. In this chapter, I'll create additional content that will perform the testing based on the user's selection.

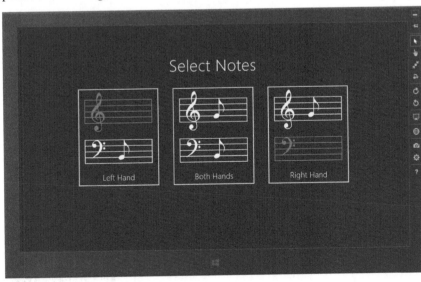

Figure 4-1. The NoteFlash selector page

Defining the Notes Data

The next step in building out the example app is to define the notes the user will be tested on. To do this, I have added a new JavaScript file to the js folder called notes.js, the content of which you can see in Listing 4-1. (Right-click on the js folder in the Solution Explorer, select Add ➤ New Item, and use the JavaScript File item template.)

■ **Tip** Add a JavaScript file by right-clicking on the js folder in the Solution Explorer window and selecting Add ➤ New Item from the pop-up menu. Select JavaScript File from the list of file types, set the name of the file to be notes.js, and click the Add button.

Listing 4-1. Defining the note data

```
(function () {
    "use strict";

    var Note = WinJS.Class.define(function (note, character, hand) {
        this.note = note;
        this.character = character;
        this.hand = hand;
    });

    WinJS.Namespace.define("Notes", {
        leftHand: [
                new Note('C', 80, "left"), new Note('D', 81, "left"),
                new Note('E', 82, "left"), new Note('F', 83, "left"),
                new Note('G', 84, "left"), new Note('A', 85, "left"),
                new Note('B', 86, "left"), new Note('C', 87, "left"),
                new Note('D', 88, "left"), new Note('E', 89, "left"),
                new Note('F', 90, "left"), new Note('G', 91, "left"),
                new Note('A', 92, "left"), new Note('B', 93, "left"),
                new Note('C', 94, "left")
        ],
        rightHand: [
                new Note('C', 82, "right"), new Note('D', 83, "right"),
                new Note('E', 84, "right"), new Note('F', 85, "right"),
                new Note('G', 86, "right"), new Note('A', 87, "right"),
                new Note('B', 88, "right"), new Note('C', 89, "right"),
                new Note('D', 90, "right"), new Note('E', 91, "right"),
                new Note('F', 92, "right"), new Note('G', 93, "right"),
                new Note('A', 94, "right"),
        ],
    });

})();
```

This file requires some explanation. I have employed two useful features from the WinJS API: *classes* and *namespaces*. I explain each of them in the following sections.

Windows JavaScript Classes

JavaScript is a *prototype-based* object-oriented language, which means that inheritance works by cloning existing objects (these objects are known as *prototypes*). All of the other languages that can be used for Windows app development use *class-based* inheritance, where the capabilities of objects are defined in separate classes. Objects are created as instances of these classes. Most mainstream programming languages use class-based inheritance, and if you have written software using C# or Java, for example, you will have already encountered classes.

The WinJS API includes support for creating classes in JavaScript. The WinJS.Class.define method takes up to three arguments: a function that is the class constructor, an object that contains the class instance members, and an object that contains the class static members. The WinJS.Class.derive method lets you create new classes by deriving from existing ones.

■ **Tip** Microsoft has said that class-based inheritance offers performance benefits over the standard JavaScript prototype-based approach, but I suspect it relates more to the way the Windows API has to be exposed to both JavaScript *and* languages that support classes natively.

In the notes.js file, I define a basic class called Note, like this:

```
...
var Note = WinJS.Class.define(function (note, character, hand) {
    this.note = note;
    this.character = character;
    this.hand = hand;
});
...
```

I have defined only the constructor for this class and it takes three arguments—the musical note (such as C), the character that represents the note in the music font, and which hand the note relates to (because, of course, both hands are used when playing the piano—something that is causing me much difficulty in my music lessons).

Once you have defined a class, you can create new instances using the new keyword, like this:

```
...
var myNote = new Note('C', 80, "left");
...
```

This statement creates a Note object that represents the note C for the left hand, represented by character code 80 in the music font I added to the project in Chapter 3.

The new keyword is a standard part of JavaScript, but it isn't widely used in web app development. The classes that the WinJS.Class.define method creates are pretty basic and they lack most of the features you would expect of classes in other languages. The main benefit of this approach is that it provides a mechanism for exposing the Windows API in a way that can be consumed within JavaScript.

You don't have to use classes in your own JavaScript, but it is important to understand this feature because Microsoft has used it extensively in the WinJS API and you'll encounter it as soon as you use the debugger to step through that code. I rarely use classes in my own code because I think they add a lot of the problems of class-based inheritance without any of the benefits.

Creating Namespaces

As I explained in Chapter 3, *namespaces* are among the techniques for reducing pollution of the global namespace in Windows apps (the other two are *self-executing functions* and *strict mode*). The idea behind namespaces is that you create a single global variable and attach data values and functions to it, rather than make each individual value and function global.

You have already seen how Microsoft structures the API using namespaces, such as WinJS.Utilities and WinJS.UI.Pages. If you want to use the query method to search for elements in the HTML, you call WinJS.Utilities.query. The query method is part of the WinJS.Utilities namespace, and that namespace contains lots of other useful functions.

Namespaces can be hierarchical. The Utilities namespace is part of the WinJS namespace. WinJS contains lots of child namespaces and Utilities is just one of them. In the previous section I used the WinJS.Class.define method—this method is in the WinJS.Class namespace, and Class is a peer to Utilities. By using namespaces, Microsoft has packed a huge amount of functionality into two global namespace objects: WinJS and Windows.

And that's all namespaces are: global objects. Listing 4-2 shows how you could use regular JavaScript objects to re-create the WinJS.Utilities.query method, for example.

Listing 4-2. A namespace as a hierarchy of objects

```
...
var WinJS = {
    Utilities: {
        query: function (someArguments) {
            // ...implementation goes here...
        }
    }
};
...
```

The hierarchical nature of namespaces means that you can reuse names for variables and methods at different points in the namespace hierarchy. A (hypothetical) WinJS.Database.query method, for example, is entirely separate from WinJS.Utilities.query, even though the methods are both called query. This is one of the benefits of namespaces. If all methods were global, I'd end up with names like queryHTMLById and queryHTMLByTagName, which are the same kind of verbose names you see in the DOM API, in which all methods are peers. Using namespaces to add structure to code means that a method *name* can be meaningful while the context in which the method operates comes from its *namespace*.

You can use the WinJS API to create your own namespaces, using the features of the WinJS.Namespace namespace, which I used in the notes.js file as follows:

```
...
WinJS.Namespace.define("Notes", {
    leftHand: [
        new Note('C', 80, "left"), new Note('D', 81, "left"),
        // ...other notes removed for brevity...
    ],
    rightHand: [
        new Note('C', 82, "right"), new Note('D', 83, "right"),
        // ...other notes removed for brevity...
    ],
});
...
```

I have highlighted the most important part of the CSS file: the use of the flexbox layout, which is the other CSS3 layout I use a lot in this book (the first being the grid layout I showed you in Chapter 3. The other properties I have used in the flashCardsPage.css are commonly used, but the flexbox layout is new and not that widely adopted yet—in part because the specification is still being developed, which is why I have to use vendor-specific property names.

Understanding the Flex Box Layout

The *flexible box layout*, which is usually referred to as *flexbox*, provides a fluid layout that responds well when the screen size changes. This is important in Windows apps because the user can reorient the device or change the amount of the screen that is allocated to the app (I discuss both of these features and show you how to adapt to them in Chapter 6).

■ **Tip**   I tend to use the grid layout when I need to divide up the screen space precisely and the flexbox layout when I am more concerned with fluidity and centering elements.

You enable the flexbox layout by setting the display property to –ms-flexbox, just as I did in the listing. The most important property is –ms-flex-direction, which specifies which way the child elements are laid out. I have listed the supported values for this property in Table 4-1.

Table 4-1. The Values for the –ms-flex-direction Property

Value	Description
Row	Child elements are laid out left to right in the order defined in the HTML
Column	Child elements are laid out top to bottom in the order defined in the HTML
Row-reverse	Child elements are laid out right to left, where the first element defined in the HTML is right-most
Column-reverse	Child elements are laid out bottom to top, where the first element defined in the HTML is bottom-most

In the listing I specified the column value, which means that my elements will be laid out from top to bottom in the order they are defined in the HTML.

The –ms-flex-pack property specifies how elements are aligned along the axis specified by the –ms-flex-direction property (along the vertical axis for the column values and the horizontal axis for the row values). I have listed the values for this property in Table 4-2.

Table 4-2. The Values for the –ms-flex-pack Property

Value	Description
Start	The child elements are stacked up at the start of the axis
End	The child elements are stacked up at the end of the axis
Justify	The child elements are spaced out so that they occupy the container height/width

In the listing I have used the justify property, which means that the elements in the flashContainer element will be spaced out so that they occupy the full height of the element.

The `-ms-flex-align` property specifies the alignment of elements along the axis that is not being used by the `-ms-flex-direction` property—that is, 90 degrees from the axis along which the elements are laid out, known as the *orthogonal axis*. The values for this property are shown in Table 4-3.

Table 4-3. The Values for the –ms-flex-align Property

Value	Description
Start	The elements are stacked to the leading edge of the orthogonal axis
End	The elements are stacked up at the trailing edge of the orthogonal axis
Center	The elements are aligned to the center of the container elements
Stretch	The elements are stretched so that they fill the full length of the orthogonal axis

You can build a lot of fluidity into a layout using these three properties, but there are others that I don't use in this book (and very often don't find useful). You can see the complete list at `http://msdn.microsoft.com/en-us/library/windows/apps/hh453474.aspx`.

■ **Tip** I value the flexbox layout most for easily letting me center elements in a layout, without having to mess around with absolute positions and other nonsense. Just set the `-ms-flex-align` property to `justify` and `-ms-flex-pack` properties to `center` and the child elements will be laid out in the center of the element.

In the listing I specified the `center` value, which means that my elements will be aligned to the center of the flashContainer element. Combined with the other values I specified, the child elements of the flashContainer element will be laid out vertically, distributed so that they occupy the full height of the element and positioned in the center of the element. You can see the layout of the page in Figure 4-2.

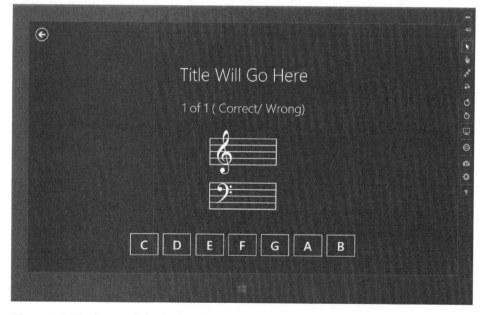

Figure 4-2. The layout of the flash card page

I haven't defined the JavaScript code to control these elements yet, but you can already see the main building blocks for the functionality: the placeholder for details of the user's correct and incorrect responses, the staves required to show notes in the left and right hand, and the set of buttons the user will click or touch to identify a note.

Defining the Code for the Flash Card Page

Listing 4-6 shows the contents of the flashCardsPage.js file. There isn't a huge amount of code, but there is some interesting stuff going on, which I'll explain in the following sections.

Listing 4-6. The flashCardsPage.js file

```
(function () {
    "use strict";

    var appState = WinJS.Binding.as({
        title: "", mode: null, leftNote: "=",
        rightNote: "=", currentIndex: 0, noteCount: 0,
        notes: [], currentNote: null,
        results: {
            numberCorrect: 0,
            numberWrong: 0
        },
    });

    WinJS.UI.Pages.define("/pages/flashCardsPage.html", {
        ready: function (element, options) {

            WinJS.Binding.processAll(document.body, appState);

            backButton.addEventListener("click", function (e) {
                showPage("/pages/selectorPage.html");
            });
            $("#noteButtons button").listen("click", handleButtonClick);

            setState(options);
            selectAndDisplayNote();
        }
    });

    function setState(mode) {

        appState.mode = mode;
        switch (mode) {
            case "leftHand":
                appState.title = "Left Hand Notes";
                break;
            case "rightHand":
                appState.title = "Right Hand Notes";
                break;
```

```
            case "bothHands":
                appState.title = "All Notes";
                break;
        }

        appState.notes = [];
        if (mode == "leftHand" || mode == "bothHands") {
            Notes.leftHand.slice().forEach(function (item) {
                appState.notes.push(item);
            });
        }
        if (mode == "rightHand" || mode == "bothHands") {
            Notes.rightHand.slice().forEach(function (item) {
                appState.notes.push(item);
            });
        }
        appState.currentIndex = 0;
        appState.results.numberCorrect = 0;
        appState.results.numberWrong = 0;
        appState.noteCount = appState.notes.length;
    }

    function selectAndDisplayNote() {
        if (appState.notes.length > 0) {
            var index = Math.floor((Math.random() * appState.notes.length));
            var note = appState.notes.splice(index, 1)[0];
            appState.leftNote = (note.hand == "left" ? "&#"
                + note.character + ";" : "=");
            appState.rightNote = (note.hand == "right" ? "&#"
                + note.character + ";" : "=");
            appState.currentNote = note;
            appState.currentIndex++;
        } else {
            $("#noteButtons button").forEach(function (item) {
                item.style.display = "none";
            });
            $("#noteButtons button[id]").setAttribute("style", "");
        }
    }

    function handleButtonClick(e) {
        if (this.id == "restart") {
            showPage("/pages/flashCardsPage.html", appState.mode);
        } else if (this.id == "back") {
            showPage("/pages/selectorPage.html");
        } else {
            $("button[data-note].correct").removeClass("correct");
            $("button[data-note=" + appState.currentNote.note + "]")
                .addClass("correct");

            if (this.innerText == appState.currentNote.note) {
```

```
    if (mode == "leftHand" || mode == "bothHands") {
        Notes.leftHand.slice().forEach(function (item) {
            appState.notes.push(item);
        });
    }
    if (mode == "rightHand" || mode == "bothHands") {
        Notes.rightHand.slice().forEach(function (item) {
            appState.notes.push(item);
        });
    }
    appState.currentIndex = 0;
    appState.results.numberCorrect = 0;
    appState.results.numberWrong = 0;
    appState.noteCount = appState.notes.length;
}
...
```

The argument to this function is the value received by the ready event handler, which indicates which set of notes the user wants to be tested on: the left-hand notes, the right-hand notes, or both. I set the value of the appState.title property in the data object based on this value, which triggers an update to one of the HTML data bindings:

```
...
<h1 id="title" data-win-bind="innerText: title"></h1>
...
```

The next part of the function clears the appState.notes array and repopulates it with values from the Notes namespace (which I created earlier in this chapter). The final set of notes in the appState.notes array depends on which button the user clicked in the selectorPage.

Resetting the Other State Values

The rest of this function resets the remaining values in the appState object. All of these values are used in data bindings:

```
...
<h1 class="subhead" id="currentNote">
    <span data-win-bind="innerText: currentIndex">1</span> of
    <span data-win-bind="innerText: noteCount">1</span>
    (<span data-win-bind="innerText: results.numberCorrect">
    </span> Correct/
    <span data-win-bind="innerText: results.numberWrong"></span> Wrong)
</h1>
...
```

Resetting the values for these properties has the dual effect of clearing the app state and resetting the user interface. Without data bindings, I would have had to reset the contents of elements manually, making sure to locate all of the instances where each data value is displayed—this would be reasonably simple for such a basic app as this one, but it quickly becomes a painful and error-prone process for more complex apps. I'll come back to this topic in Chapter 8, when I revisit data binding in more depth and introduce view models.

I call the setState function whenever I receive the WinJS.UI.Pages.ready event, as follows:

```
...
WinJS.UI.Pages.define("/pages/flashCardsPage.html", {
    ready: function (element, options) {
        // ...other statements removed for brevity...
        setState(options);
        selectAndDisplayNote();
    }
});
...
```

This ensures that I reset the app state and clean up the data binding values each time the page is displayed.

Showing the Flash Cards

The selectAndDisplayNote function is responsible for picking a note at random from the set contained in the appState.notes array and displaying it to the user:

```
...
function selectAndDisplayNote() {
    if (appState.notes.length > 0) {
        var index = Math.floor((Math.random() * appState.notes.length));
        var note = appState.notes.splice(index, 1)[0];
        appState.leftNote = (note.hand == "left" ? "&#"
            + note.character + ";" : "=");
        appState.rightNote = (note.hand == "right" ? "&#"
            + note.character + ";" : "=");
        appState.currentNote = note;
        appState.currentIndex++;
    } else {
        $("#noteButtons button").forEach(function (item) {
            item.style.display = "none";
        });
        $("#noteButtons button[id]").setAttribute("style", "");
    }
}
...
```

This is achieved using standard JavaScript code. If no notes are left with which to test the user, then I make a layout change—the code for which I have marked in bold. These statements hide the answer buttons and display additional navigation buttons. You can see the alternate set of buttons in Figure 4-5. Notice that I have used the WinJS.Utilities.query method, which I aliased to $ earlier, to locate button elements using their id attribute values.

Figure 4-5. The additional navigation buttons

I defined these buttons alongside the regular answer buttons but set the value of the CSS `display` property to `none`, so they are not initially visible. I defined the buttons in this way to emphasize once again how the standard HTML and CSS features are available in Windows apps:

```
...
<div id="noteButtons">
    <button data-note="C">C</button>
    <button data-note="D">D</button>
    <button data-note="E">E</button>
    <button data-note="F">F</button>
    <button data-note="G">G</button>
    <button data-note="A">A</button>
    <button data-note="B">B</button>
    <button id="back" style="display: none">Back</button>
    <button id="restart" style="display: none">Again</button>
</div>
...
```

As a related benefit, all of the buttons—answer and navigation—were matched by my search for elements using the $ alias and were configured to call the `handleButtonClick` function when they are clicked.

Handling the Answer and Navigation Button Events

The last piece of the app functionality is contained in the `handleButtonClick` function, which is executed when any of the answer buttons or the additional navigation buttons is clicked:

```
...
function handleButtonClick(e) {
    if (this.id == "restart") {
        showPage("/pages/flashCardsPage.html", appState.mode);
    } else if (this.id == "back") {
        showPage("/pages/selectorPage.html");
    } else {
        $("button[data-note].correct").removeClass("correct");
        $("button[data-note=" + appState.currentNote.note + "]")
            .addClass("correct");

        if (this.innerText == appState.currentNote.note) {
            appState.results.numberCorrect++;
        } else {
            appState.results.numberWrong++;
        }
        selectAndDisplayNote();
    }
}
...
```

The function uses standard JavaScript techniques for the most part, but there are a couple of aspects that are worth drawing your attention to and that I describe in the following sections. Notice how I add and remove CSS classes to and from the answer buttons:

```
...
$("button[data-note]").removeClass("correct").removeClass("normal");
$("button[data-note=" + appState.currentNote.note + "]")
    .addClass("correct").addClass("normal").removeClass("correct");
...
```

The correct CSS class applies a green background color to a button. When the user clicks a button, I remove the correct class from any button it is applied to and then reapply it to the correct button for the currently displayed note. This allows me to create a simple visual cue that indicates the correct answer.

Relying on Data Bindings to Disseminate Data Updates

I want to draw your attention to the way in which the dynamic data bindings are used:

```
...
if (this.innerText == appState.currentNote.note) {
    appState.results.numberCorrect++;
} else {
    appState.results.numberWrong++;
}
...
```

I increment data values in the appState object each time I assess the answer the user provides, keeping a tally of the number of right and wrong answers.

What's important is what I *don't* have to do: I don't have to manually update the HTML elements to display the updated information. This happens automatically because the values I am updating are observable and the elements in the layout display the data through the data binding system.

Not only is this a more convenient approach, but it also creates a more scalable and maintainable application structure. I can change the layout of the HTML elements and I can display the same data values in many places around the application—but when I need to make an update, I have to assign a new value only to the data object, just like in the code fragment. This is an important concept in any app that has a UI, but it is especially important in Windows app development and I will return to this topic in Chapter 8.

You can see the completed app in Figure 4-6, showing the notes being displayed to the user, along with information about which group of notes is being tested, the user's progress, and the color cue that indicates the correct answer.

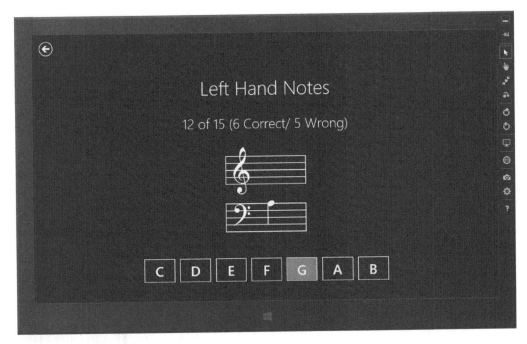

Figure 4-6. The completed NoteFlash app

As I mentioned before, this isn't the final version of the NoteFlash app, but the basic functionality is complete and the user can test his sight-reading abilities. In later chapters, I'll return to this app and add further features.

Updating the App Manifest

Although I have completed the HTML, CSS, and JavaScript components of the app, there is still a little work to be done. If you go to the Start screen and locate the tile for the NoteFlash app, you'll see that the way the app is presented to the user is rather basic, as shown in Figure 4-7.

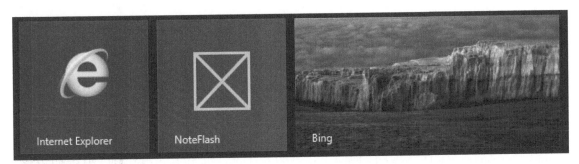

Figure 4-7. The default tile for the NoteFlash app

By default, Visual Studio assigns a default icon to the app tile and uses the project as the app name. We can improve the way the app is presented to the user by making some simple changes to the manifest.

Double-click the package.appxmanifest file in the Solution Explorer window and navigate to the Application UI tab in the manifest editor. This page contains the basic settings for the app.

Setting the Tile Images and Color

The first change I am going to make is the image and color used for the app tile. Windows apps use images of different sizes for a range of purposes. There is an image for the square tile, like the one shown in Figure 3-7, and this must be 150 pixels by 150 pixels.

Tiles can also be wide (right-click on a tile and select the Larger button), which requires an image that is 310 pixels by 150 pixels. There is a small icon, 30 by 30 pixels, which is used when the app is displayed as part of a list, and finally, a 620-pixel by 300-pixel image that is used as the splash screen when the app is launched.

For this app, I created a series of images and placed them in the images folder of the Visual Studio project. These files show the treble clef symbol, but since I have used a white icon and a transparent background, I can't show you the images on the printed page—but you'll be able to see them when it is applied to the app. (And they are in the source code download for this chapter, of course.)

In the Application UI tab of the manifest editor, there are a number of text fields so that you can specify the images for the tile, as shown in Figure 4-8.

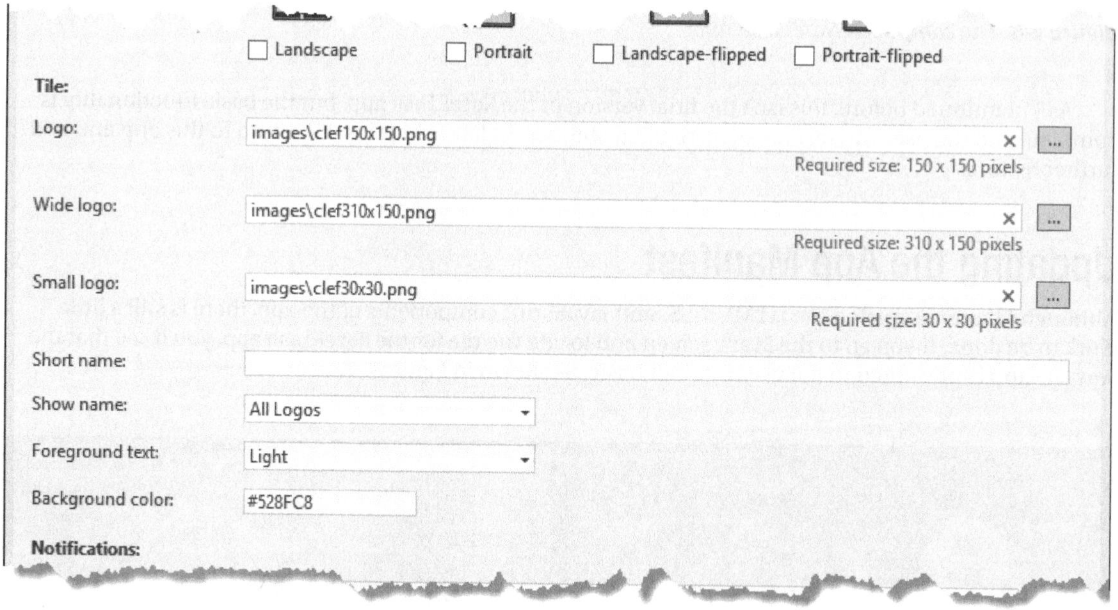

Figure 4-8. Setting the images for the tile

The names of my image files start with clef and then detail the resolution—clef30x30.png, for example. You can see how I have set the image names for the various fields in the manifest. The images are not scaled and you won't be able to use an image if it is not the right size.

Also notice that I have set a value for the Background color option. This is used to set the color of the tile—for this app, I have picked a shade of blue, specified by the hex code #528FC8.

■ **Tip**   Although it is not shown in the figure, I have also set the image for the splash screen.

Setting the App Name

I also want to change the name that is displayed on the tile, which is taken from the Display name field in the manifest. I have changed this to Note Flash, as shown in Figure 4-9.

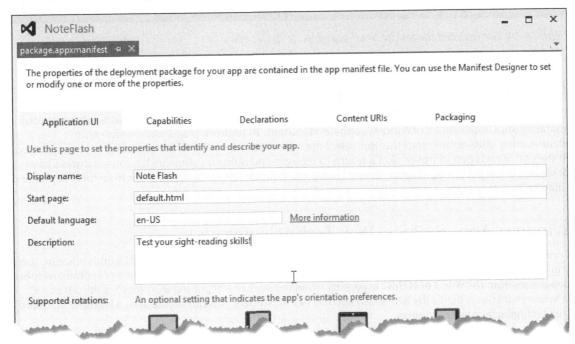

Figure 4-9. Changing the display name for the app

I have also changed the Description field, which provides the user with a summary of the app. The result of changing the display name and applying the images is the tile shown in Figure 4-10, presenting the user with a much more polished tile for the app.

■ **Tip**   This is a *static tile*, which shows just the image and the app name. In Chapter 27, I show you how to create *live tiles*, which display useful information to the user.

Figure 4-10. The updated tile for the NoteFlash app

Testing the Completed App

That's all there is to the NoteFlash app. It is a simple piece of software, but it demonstrates some essential characteristics and features of Windows app development. To improve your basic musical note identification skills, simply start the app, select the notes you want to be tested on, and give your answers. At the end of each part of this book, I'll return to this app and refine it using the Windows features I have described in the preceding chapter. Before I move on, I want to recap the key themes from this chapter and Chapter 3.

Windows Apps Build on Web Technologies

I can't emphasize this point enough: if you are developing Windows apps using HTML and JavaScript, then you are building on the skills you already have for regular web app development. There are some pretty big departures from the world of HTML, especially when it comes to integrating with some of the advanced Windows 8 features, but as the NoteFlash app has demonstrated, you can accomplish a lot using standard web technologies and techniques.

Windows Apps Are Not Web Apps

Although your web app development experience is extremely useful, you won't deliver the full potential of your app without using the platform features and following the Microsoft conventions. You have already seen key areas where Windows apps differ from web apps—in the core navigation model—and I'll show you many more throughout the rest of the book.

Data Binding Simplifies App Development

I am a big fan of data binding in both web and Windows apps, and I cover this topic in depth in Chapter 8. Windows apps can get pretty complex, and you should embrace every possible technique that keeps your code and markup manageable, including data binding. You can manually set the content of HTML elements if you prefer, but you'll make life harder for yourself, especially when it comes to maintaining or enhancing your app.

The WinJS API Is Written in JavaScript

The WinJS API is a bridge between the worlds of regular web app and Windows app development. Best of all, you can read through the WinJS code to see how Microsoft has implemented different features and apply the debugger to track down difficult problems. This isn't the case for the Windows API, but you'll find that you spend most of your time using WinJS features as you get up to speed with Windows app development.

Summary

In this chapter I showed you how to complete the functionality of the NoteFlash app and, in doing so, introduced more of the core WinJS functionality. Of particular note are the WinJS support for classes, namespaces, and data binding. Now that you have seen how a basic Windows app is created, it is time to start to dig into the details. In Part II of this book, I show the core features from the WinJS API that you use to create the structure of a good Windows app.

PART 2

Core Development

In this part of the book, I introduce you to the core development features and techniques which underpin Windows 8 development. This includes creating layouts that adapt to the way the Windows device is being used, allowing the user to navigate around an app and using data binding and templates to create dynamic app layouts. I also introduce the Promise object, which is a key building block in the asynchronous programming model which is used throughout Windows app development.

CHAPTER 5

■ ■ ■

The Single-Page Model

When I created the NoteFlash app, I briefly introduced the idea of the single-page navigation model. In this chapter, I will dive into this topic in depth. The basic idea behind the single-page model is that there is one HTML page (often referred to as the master page or main page) that is always displayed to the user and that is responsible for importing other content into its structure as the state of the app changes.

This model provides the basis for allowing the user to navigate your app. You import content into the main page in response to user input and interactions, often replacing content that you have previously displayed. The WinJS API provides the tools and features you need to import and display your app's content and navigate around it. In this chapter, I will show you how to perform these actions and explain the different models for handling navigation operations. This isn't the most exciting of topics, but the single-page model is at the heart of a Windows app, and getting it right makes every other aspect of app development simpler and easier—it might be a little dull, but it is worth paying attention. Table 5-1 provides the summary for this chapter.

Table 5-1. Chapter Summary

Problem	Solution	Listing
Create the foundations for the single-page model	Define an HTML master page that contains an element into which you will import content	5-1–5-3
Import static content declaratively	Use the WinJS.UI.HtmlControl control	5-4, 5-6
Activate the declarative WinJS UI controls in an HTML document	Call the WinJS.UI.processAll method	5-5
Avoid CSS import issues	Ensure that the CSS styles you define in imported content are scoped to affect only local elements	5-7
Import static content programmatically	Apply the HtmlControl control from JavaScript	5-8–5-11
Import dynamic content	Use the WinJS.UI.Pages.render method	5-12
Register a callback for imported content	Use the WinJS.UI.Pages.define method	5-13
Control the order in which content is imported	Use the WinJS.Promise object returned by the WinJS.UI.Pages.render method	5-14, 5-15
Add flexible navigation to an app	Use the WinJS.Navigation API	5-16–5-19

Creating the Single-Page Project

To demonstrate the techniques that underpin the single-page model, I have created an example Visual Studio project called SinglePageNav using the Blank Application template (this is the same one I used in Chapter 2 for the NoteFlash app and the one I use throughout this book). For my foundation for importing other content, I will use the default.html file that Visual Studio creates. You can see the starting point for default.html in Listing 5-1.

Listing 5-1. The initial version of the default.html file in the SinglePageNav project

```
<!DOCTYPE html>
<html>
<head>
    <meta charset="utf-8">
    <title>SinglePageNav</title>

    <!-- WinJS references -->
    <link href="//Microsoft.WinJS.1.0/css/ui-dark.css" rel="stylesheet" />
    <script src="//Microsoft.WinJS.1.0/js/base.js"></script>
    <script src="//Microsoft.WinJS.1.0/js/ui.js"></script>

    <!-- SinglePageNav references -->
    <link href="/css/default.css" rel="stylesheet">
    <script src="/js/default.js"></script>
</head>
<body>
    <div id="gridContainer">
        <div id="left">
            <h1 class="colHeader">Content Controls</h1>
            <button id="button1">Button One</button>
            <button id="button2">Button Two</button>
        </div>

        <div id="topRight" class="contentBlock">
            <h1 class="colHeader">Top Right</h1>
            <div class="message">This is part of default.html</div>
            <div class="contentTarget message">
                This is where the content will go
            </div>
        </div>

        <div id="bottomRight" class="contentBlock">
            <h1 class="colHeader">Bottom Right</h1>
            <div class="message">This is part of default.html</div>
            <div class="contentTarget message">
                This is where the content will go
            </div>
        </div>
    </div>
</body>
</html>
```

The three elements that define the structure of the layout for this app are the div elements with the ids of left, topRight, and bottomRight. The left element contains some button elements that I'll use later in this chapter to import content in response to user input. The topRight and bottomRight elements provide the structure in which I'll display the imported content.

Defining the Initial CSS

I have used the CSS grid layout to position the elements, using the styles I defined in the css/default.css file, which you can see in Listing 5-2.

Listing 5-2. The default.css file

```css
#gridContainer {
    height: 100%;
    display: -ms-grid;
    -ms-grid-columns: 1fr 1fr;
    -ms-grid-rows: 1fr 1fr;
}

#left {
    -ms-grid-row-span: 2;
    background-color: black;
    padding: 10px;
}

#topRight {
    -ms-grid-column: 2;
    background-color: #617666;
}

#bottomRight {
    -ms-grid-column: 2;
    -ms-grid-row: 2;
    background-color: #767676;
}

div.contentBlock {
    border: medium solid white;
    padding: 5px; margin: 2px;
}

div.message {
    font-size: 30px;
}

button {
    font-size: 30px; margin: 10px;
}

#frameTarget {
```

```
        width: 100%;
        height: 100%;
}
```

I have highlighted the CSS properties that relate to the grid layout. These properties create a grid with two rows and two columns. The left element spans two rows, and since I have not explicitly specified a position, it will be in the first column and row. The topRight and bottomRight elements are in the second column, one in each of the rows. You can see the effect of the grid layout in Figure 5-1.

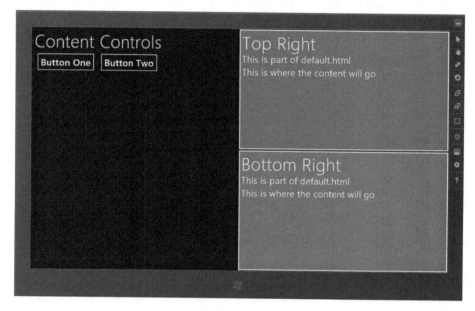

Figure 5-1. The initial layout of the example project

Defining the Initial JavaScript

My initial JavaScript code in the js/default.js file is shown in Listing 5-3. Aside from creating the $ alias I like for the WinJS.Utilities.query method, the code locates the button elements inside the div element called left and registers a callback function for the click event.

Listing 5-3. The initial contents of the js/default.js file

```
(function () {
    "use strict";

    var app = WinJS.Application;
    window.$ = WinJS.Utilities.query;

    app.onactivated = function (eventObject) {
        $('#left button').listen("click", function (e) {
            // button handler code will go here
        });
    };
```

```
    app.start();
})();
```

I'll add the code to handle the `click` event later in this chapter.

Importing Content Declaratively

The simplest way to bring content into your single-page app is to do so declaratively, which simply means applying a mechanism to the HTML elements in the `default.html` file. Listing 5-4 shows how to apply the declarative technique to one of the container elements in the example app layout.

Listing 5-4. Importing content declaratively

```
...
<div id="topRight" class="contentBlock">
    <h1 class="colHeader">Top Right</h1>
    <div class="message">This is part of default.html</div>
    <div class="contentTarget message"
        data-win-control="WinJS.UI.HtmlControl"
        data-win-options="{uri: 'contentBasic.html'}">
        This is where the content will go
    </div>
</div>
...
```

A major part of the WinJS API is a set of UI controls. These are enhancements that are applied to standard HTML elements to provide app-specific features. To import content into my app declaratively, I have used a very basic control called `HtmlControl`.

I apply `HtmlControl` to the `div` element where I want the imported content inserted. Applying the control means setting the `data-win-control` attribute to the full name of the control object in the WinJS API, which is `WinJS.UI.HtmlControl`.

I have to configure the control, to specify the name of the file that I want imported. The format is to include a fragment of JSON, where the `uri` property defines the file name, which in this example is `contentBasic.html`. I don't like embedding JSON into HTML like this, but it is required for declarative imports.

■ **Tip**   I will not get too far into the mechanics of the WinJS UI controls in this chapter. I cover them in detail in Part 3 of this book.

The final step is to activate the controls, which requires a JavaScript method call. This undermines the declarative nature of this example somewhat, but this is a single call that activates any controls you have added to the HTML. You can see the required method call, which I have added to `default.js`, in Listing 5-5.

Listing 5-5. Activating the controls in the HTML markup

```
(function () {
    "use strict";
```

```
    var app = WinJS.Application;
    window.$ = WinJS.Utilities.query;

    app.onactivated = function (eventObject) {
        $('#left button').listen("click", function (e) {
            // button handler code will go here
        });
        WinJS.UI.processAll();
    };

    app.start();
})();
```

The Windows runtime doesn't automatically search the DOM to find elements with the data-win-
control attribute. I must explicitly request this search, which is what the WinJS.UI.processAll method
does. The last step is to define the content that I want to import. Listing 5-6 shows the contents of the
contentBasic.html file.

■ **Tip**   I created the contentBasic.html file by right-clicking on the project entry in the Solution Explorer window,
selecting Add New Item from the pop-up menu, and using the HTML Page item template. This template creates a
single HTML page. This is different from the Page Control item template that I used previously, which creates the
HTML file, a CSS file, and a JavaScript file (and adds link and script elements in the HTML file). The Page
Control template is there just for convenience and doesn't confer any special attributes on the files it creates. In
fact, I prefer to create my files individually as I need them and rarely use the Page Control template in my own
projects.

Listing 5-6. The contentBasic.html file

```html
<!DOCTYPE html>
<html>
    <head>
        <title>Basic Content</title>
        <style type="text/css">
            div.message {
                font-family: serif;
                text-align: right;
            }
        </style>
    </head>
    <body>
        <div class="message">
            Hello from the contentBasic.html file
        </div>
    </body>
</html>
```

This is a simple HTML file that contains an inline `style` element and some basic HTML. If you start the example app, you will see the effect of the declarative import, which is shown in Figure 5-2. I have highlighted the imported content in the figure.

Notice that the content that was already in the `div` element is still there. Importing content doesn't replace any existing child elements—you have to explicitly remove the contents of the target element if you want only the imported content (which I'll do shortly).

Figure 5-2. Importing content declaratively

Understanding the Import Mechanism

If you run the example or look at Figure 5-2, you will notice that all the text in the right column is now aligned to the right of the parent element, when it previously was aligned to the left edge (as shown in Figure 5-1). This happened because of the way content is processed when it is imported into an app.

This example uses the `HtmlControl`, but the same thing happens with the Pages feature I describe later in this chapter. To understand what is happening, consider the CSS in the example app. The `default.css` file contains a style for the `message` class, like this:

```
...
div.message {
    font-size: 30px;
}
...
```

The `contentBasic.html` file contains a `style` element that *also* defines a style for the `message` class:

```
...
div.message {
    font-family: serif;
    text-align: right;
}
...
```

When a file is imported, the `script` elements it contains are added to the head element of the master HTML document. CSS in Windows applications follows the same rules of precedence as for a web app. This means that the style applied to the elements in the `message` class is the combined set of properties from both files, and since the `script` element is added to the head of the master document, this combined set of properties will affect all of the `message` elements and not just those that have been imported.

■ **Tip** CSS precedence takes into account the order in which properties are defined. This means that properties in imported content override those defined in the master file.

The easiest way to ensure that your styles affect elements in only one document is to make sure you narrow the scope of your CSS styles so they affect only imported elements. You can see how I have done this for `contentBasic.html` in Listing 5-7.

Listing 5-7. Narrowing the focus for CSS styles in imported content

```
<!DOCTYPE html>
<html>
    <head>
        <title>Basic Content</title>
        <style type="text/css">
            #contentBasicTop div.message {
                font-family: serif;
                text-align: right;
            }
        </style>
    </head>
    <body>
        <div id="contentBasicTop">
            <div class="message">
                Hello from the contentBasic.html file
            </div>
        </div>
    </body>
</html>
```

I have added a `div` element that acts as the parent for the elements that will be imported into the document. The `div` doesn't change the appearance or structure of the imported content, but it does allow me to narrow the focus for my styles so they don't leak into the rest of the layout. You can see the effect of this change in Figure 5-3. Notice that the content from the `default.html` file is no longer affected by the right alignment.

Figure 5-3. The effect of narrowing the focus for CSS styles in imported content

Importing Content Programmatically

The declarative `HtmlControl` is the simplest way to import content, but some limitations come with that simplicity. The first is that there is no way to change the content once it has been loaded—using JavaScript to change the value of the `data-win-options` attribute doesn't load new content. The second limitation is that you'll almost certainly encounter problems if you import content that contains `script` elements—the `HtmlControl` works reliably only with simple, static content, like the kind I used in the previous example.

The issue with JavaScript depends on the code itself. When content is imported, `script` elements are dealt with in the same way as `style` elements and added to the head element of the master document. The content of the `script` element is executed as soon as it is inserted into the head element, which happens before the HTML elements are imported. Since the elements you want to operate on don't yet exist, the code will fail. You can't rely on DOM events or tricks like the jQuery ready method because the underlying events are fired when Internet Explorer loads the master document. By the time the content is imported, the browser has fired its ready events and moved on.

JavaScript code that operates only on the elements that are already in the master document will work, but it is counterintuitive to put that kind of code into a file you are going to import. Doing so creates a *tight coupling* between the master layout and the imported code—something I'll get into in more detail in the next section but that is generally a bad idea.

That doesn't mean that using the `HtmlControl` declaratively isn't useful, but it is pretty basic. If you want to break your app layout into manageable pieces and load them at runtime, then the declarative `HtmlControl` is perfect, simple, and reliable. If you want something more complex, you should look at the programmatic alternatives, which I describe in the following section.

Using HtmlControl Programmatically

The next step up in flexibility is to use `HtmlControl` programmatically. This switches the use of the `HtmlControl` so that it all happens in the JavaScript code and is no longer embedded into the HTML. Now, I must say that I don't use the `HtmlControl` in this way in my projects—it lacks the simplicity of the declarative approach and doesn't have the flexibility of the Pages feature that I describe later. The main reason I am showing you this technique is to demonstrate a common pitfall: the tight-coupling concept I mentioned. Let me start by showing the programmatic use. First, I need to reset my HTML elements in the `default.html` file to remove the declarative attributes, as shown in Listing 5-8.

Listing 5-8. Removing the declarative HtmlControl attributes

```
...
<div id="topRight" class="contentBlock">
    <h1 class="colHeader">Top Right</h1>
    <div class="message">This is part of default.html</div>
    <div class="contentTarget message">
        This is where the content will go
    </div>
</div>
...
```

I can now add statements to my JavaScript code in the `default.js` file to use `HtmlControl` programmatically, which I do in Listing 5-9.

Listing 5-9. Using HtmlControl programatically

```
(function () {
    "use strict";

    var app = WinJS.Application;
    window.$ = WinJS.Utilities.query;

    app.onactivated = function (eventObject) {
        $('#left button').listen("click", function (e) {
```

```
        var targetElem;
        if (this.id == "button1") {
            targetElem = $('#topRight div.contentTarget')[0];
        } else {
            targetElem = $('#bottomRight div.contentTarget')[0];
        }
        WinJS.Utilities.empty(targetElem);
        new WinJS.UI.HtmlControl(targetElem, {uri: 'contentBasic.html'});
    });
    WinJS.UI.processAll();
    };
    app.start();
})();
```

I have added the new code to the click handler function for the button controls. Each button locates a different target element in the document and assigns it to the targetElem variable.

■ **Note**   This is a basic form of content *navigation*, in that I am providing a way for the user to change the composition of the layout. Using regular HTML elements and events for navigation is perfectly permissible in a Windows app, but there also are some app-specific UI controls and APIs dedicated to navigation, which I describe in Chapter 7.

I use the WinJS.Utilities.empty method to remove the existing content in the target element and then create a new HtmlControl object to import the contentBasic.html file. The two constructor arguments for an HtmlControl object are the target HTML element and an object that contains the configuration information in the same format I used declaratively in the previous section. You can obtain the target element using the standard DOM API methods (such as document.getElementById), using the IE feature of treating id attribute values as variables, or, as I have done in this example, the WinJS.Utilities.query method. This is the method I have aliased to $ and it returns an array of the elements that match a CSS query string, even when there is only one matching element. This is why I have to extract the element I want by appending [0] to the method call.

■ **Tip**   The configuration information for a programmatically created HtmlControl is an object—not a JSON string. You must remember not to encase the argument in quotes.

The result of these changes is that no content is imported until one of the buttons in the left panel is clicked. Both buttons import the same content—the contextBasic.html file—but the element into which the content is imported differs. These actions work independently of each other, by which I mean that if you click both buttons, the contents of the contentBasic.html file will be imported into two locations in the document, as shown in Figure 5-4.

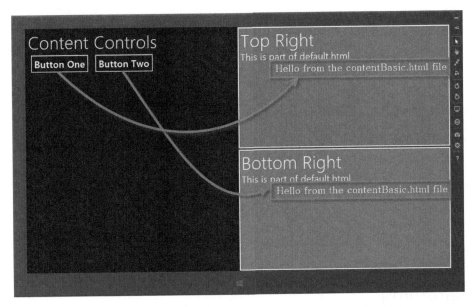

Figure 5-4. Programmatically importing the same content into two locations

Using HtmlControl programmatically addresses some of the shortfalls that the declarative use has. For a start, I gain control over when the content is imported—in this example, I import the content in response to a button click. Second, I can change the content that is displayed by removing any content that exists in the target element and creating another HtmlControl object. This is a big step forward and it lets me decompose my app into manageable chunks that I can compose and display to the user on demand, reusing part of the layout to import and display content based on the changing state of the app.

The Perils of Importing Interactive Content

Even when used programmatically, HtmlControl doesn't cope with script elements in a useful way—they are still added to the head element of the master document and executed before the regular HTML elements are imported. However, the HtmlControl object constructor takes an optional argument of a callback function that will be executed when the content has been imported. This provides the timing signal that I didn't have previously, allowing me to create code that can operate on the newly added elements. At least, that's how it looks initially—but it is a trap and caution is required. I am going to work through the use of the callback function and show you the problem it creates. First, I need some content that requires JavaScript to make it useful. Listing 5-10 shows the contents of a new file that I added to the root project folder, called contentButton.html.

Listing 5-10. The contentButton.html file

```
<!DOCTYPE html>
<html>
    <head>
        <title>Button Content</title>
    </head>
    <body>
        <div id="contentBasicTop">
```

91

```
            <div class="message">
                <button id="contentButton">Press Me</button>
            </div>
        </div>
    </body>
</html>
```

This is a regular HTML file that contains a button element. This presents me with a problem, because I need to set up a handler function so I can respond to the button's events. In Listing 5-11, you can see how I have used the third HtmlControl argument in the default.js file to provide a function that finds the button and wires it up.

Listing 5-11. Using the HtmlControl callback function to process imported elements

```
(function () {
    "use strict";

    var app = WinJS.Application;
    window.$ = WinJS.Utilities.query;

    function loadLowerContent() {
        var targetElem = $('#bottomRight div.contentTarget')[0];
        WinJS.Utilities.empty(targetElem);
        new WinJS.UI.HtmlControl(targetElem, { uri: "contentBasic.html" });
    }

    app.onactivated = function (eventObject) {
        $('#left button').listen("click", function (e) {
            var targetElem = $('#topRight div.contentTarget')[0];
            WinJS.Utilities.empty(targetElem);

            new WinJS.UI.HtmlControl(targetElem, { uri: "contentButton.html" },
                function () {
                    contentButton.addEventListener("click", loadLowerContent);
                });
        });
        WinJS.UI.processAll();
    };
    app.start();
})();
```

I locate the button element by its id attribute value and set up an event handler using the addEventListener method.

This all works as you'd expect: if buttons on the left side of the app layout are pressed, the contentButton.html file is loaded and the elements it contains are added to the layout. My callback function is then invoked and my button is configured. To see the effect, start the app and click Button One in the left panel. You will see that the contents of the contentButton.html file are imported into the top-right panel, including the button element. Click the newly imported button and the contents of the contentBasic.html file are imported into the lower right panel.

There are two problems with this approach. One is visible and reasonably easy to sort out. The other is invisible, but much more important and requires time and attention to understand and resolve.

Understanding the CSS Issue

The visible issue is a variation on the CSS scope problem I described earlier. I want to revisit this because it emphasizes the importance of narrowing the scope of your CSS selectors when importing content.

If you run the example app and click Button One, the contentButton.html file is loaded. The Press Me button that appears is aligned with the left edge of its parent container. If you click the Press Me button, the contentBasic.html file is imported into the layout and the Press Me button's alignment is shifted to the right side of the parent. You can see the effect in Figure 5-5, which shows the app before and after the button is clicked.

Figure 5-5. The delayed movement of a button driven by imported CSS

The cause of this change is the additional properties defined for the message style in the contentBasic. html file. The button in the contentButton.html file is contained inside of a div element that is part of the message class, and both files share the same element structure and naming pattern. When the contentBasic.html file is imported, the CSS styles I defined are applied more widely than I intended.

The fact that the problem is triggered by a sequence of interactions makes it much harder to spot during development and testing (and most problems of this nature are more subtle than a button suddenly shifting position).

Understanding the Tight-Coupling Issue

The more serious problem is that I have created a tight coupling between the default.js and contentButton.html files. Tight coupling means simply that a change to one component in an app will require me to make one or more changes elsewhere—that is, the code in the default.js file is dependent on the contents of the contentButton.html file. So, for example, if I change the id of the button element in the contentButton.html file or replace it with a different kind of element, I have to update the default.js file so that the HtmlControl callback function reflects these changes as well.

This is a much more serious problem than it may sound. For a simple example app, the additional work that arises from managing the dependencies between tightly coupled components doesn't amount to much. But for a real app, with real users and real schedules and real test plans, it becomes a serious burden. Every change requires tracking down all of the places in the app that are affected, correctly applying an update, and then testing the entire app. This is such a painful process, and has such a detrimental effect on software quality and developer productivity, that it is important to avoid tight coupling where possible.

For my example, I need to remove the knowledge about the content and structure of the contentButton.html file from default.js. This means making contentButton.html a self-contained unit that default.js can treat like a black box, and that means fixing the imported script element execution issue I explained earlier so that imported content can include code. Next I explain how the WinJS Pages feature provides the solution I am looking for.

Using the WinJS Pages Feature

The WinJS Pages feature provides the tools I need to solve my content import problem without creating coupling issues. Because the Pages feature addresses the JavaScript timing issue, it is suitable for importing all kinds of content. This makes it useful for breaking an app into manageable chunks of static content and for creating JavaScript code that operates on the elements in the imported document. This flexibility comes at the cost of complexity—there is no declarative support for the Pages feature and there are at least two steps to importing content. As you'll see, the first step requires adding code to import the content. This happens in the default.js file. The second step is to add code to the file that is being imported, following a specific pattern so that I am notified when imported elements have been added to the DOM.

The functionality for the Pages feature is contained in the WinJS.UI.Pages namespace. In the following sections, I show you how to use this namespace to implement the import process (and an optional step that can make it easier to import content in a specific order).

Importing the Content

The first step is, of course, to import the content through the WinJS.UI.Pages.render method. There is no declarative support for this, so any content import relies on the render method. You can see the changes to the default.js file to use the render method in Listing 5-12.

Listing 5-12. Using the WinJS.UI.Pages.render method to import content

```
(function () {
    "use strict";

    var app = WinJS.Application;
    window.$ = WinJS.Utilities.query;

    app.onactivated = function (eventObject) {
        $('#left button').listen("click", function (e) {
            var targetElem = $('#topRight div.contentTarget')[0];
            WinJS.Utilities.empty(targetElem);

            var buttonTargetElem = $('#bottomRight div.contentTarget')[0]

            WinJS.UI.Pages.render("contentButton.html", targetElem,
                { content: "contentBasic.html", target: buttonTargetElem });
        });
        WinJS.UI.processAll();
    };
    app.start();
```

```
})();
```

The first two arguments to the render method specify the content to import and the target element into which the content will be inserted. The third argument, which is optional, is more interesting. This argument allows you to specify an arbitrary data object, which is made available to the code in imported content. This is a nice feature, because it allows you to create complex blocks of functionality that you can reuse in different ways by passing in different data values. There is no required format for the data object—you can pass anything from a simple string to a complex object. In the example, I have used an object whose properties specify the information the button in the contentButton.html file requires—the content that should be imported when it is clicked and the element into which the content should be inserted.

Registering the Callback

The Pages feature doesn't change the way the content is loaded. Any script elements in the imported file are still added to the head element and executed immediately. The Pages feature adds a callback mechanism that notifies me when my content has been inserted into the document, which means that I can defer execution of JavaScript code until the elements I want to operate on have been added to the DOM. The handler for the callback is set up using the WinJS.UI.Pages.define method, and you can see how I have used this method in the script element of the contentButton.html file in Listing 5-13.

Listing 5-13. Using the WinJS.UI.Pages.define method to register a callback function

```
<!DOCTYPE html>
<html>
    <head>
        <title>Button Content</title>
        <script>
            WinJS.UI.Pages.define("contentButton.html", {
                ready: function (element, data) {
                    document.getElementById("contentButton").addEventListener("click",
                        function (e) {
                            new WinJS.UI.HtmlControl(data.target,{ uri: data.content });
                        });
                }
            });
        </script>
    </head>
    <body>
        <div id="contentButtonTop">
            <div class="message">
                <button id="contentButton">Press Me</button>
            </div>
        </div>
    </body>
</html>
```

The define method takes two arguments. The first is the name of the file that you want to be notified about—in this scenario, this is always the name of the current file, since I want to be notified when the HTML elements have been imported.

The second argument is more complex—it is an object whose properties specify callback functions that will be executed in response to different parts of the content life cycle. The set of properties is defined by the `WinJS.UI.Pages.IPageControlMembers` interface and covers the various stages in the life cycle.

■ **Note**   JavaScript doesn't support *interfaces*, but the other Windows app programming languages do. Without getting bogged down in the details, for JavaScript Windows apps an interface defines either the set of methods and properties an object has to define to be used in a certain situation or, as in this case, a set of supported values or property names. The idea of interfaces doesn't fit well into JavaScript, but it is part of the cost of having the language treated as a first-class Windows app citizen and having access to the Windows API.

The set of supported property names is `error`, `init`, `load`, `processed`, and `ready`, and they can be used to monitor particular files when they are imported.

When you use the `define` method inside of an imported file, the property that is most useful is `ready` and the function you assign to this property is executed when the content has been loaded and inserted into the master layout. The `ready` property is the timing signal I needed to support JavaScript code that operates on the HTML elements of the imported file.

The function you assign to the `ready` property is passed two arguments when it is executed. The first argument is the element into which the content will be inserted. The second argument is the data object that was passed to the `render` method.

In the example, I use the `target` and `content` properties from the data object to configure the way the `click` event from the `Press Me` button is handled. By passing in the information in this way, I ensure that the code in the `contentButton.html` isn't dependent on the structure of the elements in the `default.html` file.

■ **Tip**   This technique isn't quite perfect, because the imported file needs to know its own path in the Visual Studio project—meaning that moving or renaming the file requires a code change. I have not found a way around this issue, but the result is still preferable to having the kind of deep dependencies I started with.

Ensuring the Content Order

Many of the methods in the WinJS and Windows APIs work *asynchronously*. This means that when you call a method, the work it needs to do is scheduled to be performed later. The method returns control to your code immediately so that the next statement in your script can be executed. If there is a result from this method, it is usually handled through a callback function that you pass to the method when you invoke it.

You can spot asynchronous methods in the API documentation because they return a `WinJS.Promise` object. A `Promise` represents an undertaking to perform some work at some point in the future and defines all of the functionality you need to set up your callback functions when the `Promise` is fulfilled (i.e., the work has been done). I explain the workings of the `Promise` object in Chapter 9, but I need to introduce some basic usage now to show you how to deal with some content import issues.

The reason Microsoft has used asynchronous methods so widely is to force developers to create responsive apps. In particular, Microsoft wants to avoid a problem that has plagued previous versions of Windows, where the UI of an application freezes because it is performing some long-lived activity in the foreground, such as waiting for a connection to a server or saving a large amount of data. By driving

Promise objects throughout the API, Microsoft ensures that Windows app UIs rarely fall into this trap, albeit at the cost of making life slightly more complicated for the developer.

I say slightly more complicated because you are probably already familiar with the idea of asynchronous programming from web app development. Ajax requests a perfect example of an operation that is performed in the background and whose results are signaled using callback functions. And if you are a jQuery fan, you will be pleased to learn that the jQuery Deferred Object feature is based on the same CommonJS Promises/A specification as the Windows Promise object (you can read more about this at http://wiki.commonjs.org/wiki/Promises/A).

The reason that Promises are important in this chapter is that the WinJS.UI.Pages.render method is asynchronous. When you call this method, the content you specify isn't loaded immediately but is scheduled to be loaded later. That's fine if you are filling your target element with a single piece of content, as I have been doing so far in this chapter, but it can cause problems when you are importing several items into the same element.

The issue is that there is no guarantee that the background tasks are performed in the order in which they were scheduled. The Windows runtime is free to fulfill Promises in any order it likes (a common approach in asynchronous programming), and content is inserted as soon as it is available (which means that content that takes longer to process can be inserted later than simpler items, even if processing of the longer content starts first).

In Listing 5-14, I have shown the first of the two approaches to importing multiple content items into a single element. When the button whose id is button1 is clicked, I call the render method three times and ignore the Promise objects that the method calls return. This is the approach you take when you don't care about the order in which they are inserted. The listing shows the contents of the default.js file.

Listing 5-14. Using the Promise returned by the render method to order content

```
(function () {
    "use strict";

    var app = WinJS.Application;
    window.$ = WinJS.Utilities.query;

    app.onactivated = function (eventObject) {
        $('#left button').listen("click", function (e) {
            var targetElem = $('#topRight div.contentTarget')[0];
            WinJS.Utilities.empty(targetElem);

            if (this.id == "button1") {
                WinJS.UI.Pages.render("contentButton.html", targetElem)
                WinJS.UI.Pages.render("contentBasic.html", targetElem);
                WinJS.UI.Pages.render("contentButton.html", targetElem);
            }
        });
        WinJS.UI.processAll();
    };
    app.start();
})();
```

The order that I called the render method suggests a content order of contentButton.html, contentBasic.html, and then contentButton.html once again. But since I have ignored the WinJS.Promise objects, I am effectively leaving the order to be determined at runtime. If you run the example and click Button One, you will see the result shown in Figure 5-6.

Figure 5-6. *The unmanaged order of content*

As you can see in the figure, the order in which the content was imported doesn't match the order in which I called the render method. There are lots of reasons this can happen, but the most significant impact on ordering comes from the fact that the render method caches content. The second call to load the contentButton.html file completes very quickly because the result of the first call is cached.

■ **Tip**   Although the caching makes a big difference in this example, you still can't rely on a particular order when you discard the Promise objects returned by the render method. And because so many things affect the order in which background work is performed, you can't rely on getting the same result even when you call the same set of methods a second time—every time can be different.

Forcing a Content Order with Promises

Promise objects define a method called then, which you use to specify a function to be executed when the Promise is fulfilled (i.e., when the background work has been completed). The then method lets you chain functions together and so defer the scheduling of one background task until another has been completed. Listing 5-15 shows how I have used Promise.then to force the order in which my content is imported when the button labeled Button Two is clicked.

Listing 5-15. *Using the Promise returned by the render method to order content*

```
(function () {
    "use strict";

    var app = WinJS.Application;
    window.$ = WinJS.Utilities.query;

    app.onactivated = function (eventObject) {
        $('#left button').listen("click", function (e) {
            var targetElem = $('#topRight div.contentTarget')[0];
            WinJS.Utilities.empty(targetElem);

            if (this.id == "button1") {
```

```
            WinJS.UI.Pages.render("contentButton.html", targetElem)
            WinJS.UI.Pages.render("contentBasic.html", targetElem);
            WinJS.UI.Pages.render("contentButton.html", targetElem);
        } else {
            WinJS.UI.Pages.render("contentButton.html", targetElem)
            .then(function () {
                return WinJS.UI.Pages.render("contentBasic.html", targetElem);
            }).then(function () {
                return WinJS.UI.Pages.render("contentButton.html", targetElem);
            });
        }
    });
    WinJS.UI.processAll();
};
app.start();
})();
```

Notice that I return the Promise object I got from the render method as the result of the function I pass to the then method. This ensures that subsequent functions are not executed until the Promise is fulfilled. I'll show you different ways of orchestrating Promises in Chapter 9, but you can see the effect of this arrangement by starting the app and clicking on Button Two. Figure 5-7 shows the result—as you would expect, the content has been imported in the same order in which I called the render method.

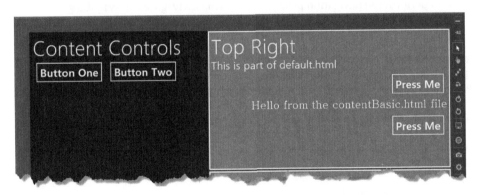

Figure 5-7. Forcing the order in which content is imported

The benefit of this approach is that the content is in the order I want. The drawback is that I have denied the runtime the opportunity to load and process multiple items at once, which is one of the main benefits of asynchronous programming. When it comes to ordering the content in layouts, the performance penalty is usually worth paying to get the result you need.

Using the Navigation API

I still have one problem in my example app: the details of where the user can navigate must be included in every page. This can be limiting when you want to present the user with different routes to navigate to the same content. Imagine, for example, a page that displays data in a particular way and can be reached through two other pages—you'd like to offer a way for the user to return to the page he came from, but there is no way to know which page that is.

You can solve this problem using the WinJS Navigation API, which is contained in the WinJS.Navigation namespace. The Navigation API helps you keep track of the navigation changes you make in your application and use that data to create more flexible layouts. In the following sections, I'll show you how to use this API. The Navigation API doesn't actually do any navigation—it just acts as a broker between parts of the app that require navigation services and code you provide that implements your preferred navigation policy. As navigation requests are created and completed, the Navigation API maintains a navigation history, which you can use to create more flexible navigation in your content.

Handling the Navigation Events

The first thing you must do when using the Navigation API is register callback functions for at least one of the *navigation events*. These events are triggered when navigation requests are made (which I'll demonstrate in the next section). Three navigation events occur in sequence for every navigation request—I have summarized these events in Table 5-2. There are no built-in handlers for these events and so you can interpret them as makes most sense in the content of your app. I tend to handle the navigating event and ignore the others.

Table 5-2. The WinJS.Navigation Events

Name	Description	Convenience Property
beforenavigate	Use to prepare your content for navigation	WinJS.Navigate.onbeforenavigate
navigating	Use to perform the navigation process	WinJS.Navigate.onnavigating
navigated	Use to indicate that navigation is complete	WinJS.Navigate.onnavigated

You can register a handler function for each event with the WinJS.Navigate.addEventListener method or the convenience properties I have shown in the table. The Navigation API is a self-assembly navigation system, so the way you interpret these events in your app is entirely up to you. For my example app, I will register a handler for the navigating event and respond by using the Pages API to import content into the app layout. You must arrange to register your event handler functions as part of the initial setup of the app so that you respond to all navigation requests. In Listing 5-16, you can see the event handler I have added to the default.js file: placing the code in this file means that my event handler will be registered when the app loads my HTML master file.

Listing 5-16. Handling the navigation events

```
(function () {
    "use strict";

    var app = WinJS.Application;
    window.$ = WinJS.Utilities.query;

    app.onactivated = function (eventObject) {

        WinJS.Navigation.addEventListener("navigating", function (e) {
            var targetElem = $('#topRight div.contentTarget')[0];
            WinJS.Utilities.empty(targetElem);

            var content = e.detail.location == "basic"
                ? "contentBasic.html" : "contentButton.html";
```

```
            WinJS.UI.Pages.render(content, targetElem);
        });
    };
    app.start();
})();
```

In this listing I have registered a handler function for the navigating event. When I receive this event, I locate and empty a target element in the layout and then use the render method to import content, just as I did in the previous examples. (I am importing only one item, so I am ignoring the Promise object that the render method returns.)

My handler function receives an Event object as an argument. The detail.location property provides me with the navigation location that has been requested. One of the advantages of using the Navigation API is that your content doesn't have to know the name of the file that it wants to navigate to—it can request anything, using any naming mechanism you create. In my example, navigating to basic will import the contentBasic.html file and navigating to button will import the contentButton.html file.

■ **Tip** This may seem like a minor feature, but it is a useful idea. Every explicit file name that you embed in content has to be updated if the structure of the project changes. By separating the name of the location that is requested from the name of the file that is imported, you put the code that needs to be kept in sync with the project structure in a single place. When the project structure changes, you just have to update your navigation event handler.

Calling the Navigate Method

The navigate method is at the heart of the Navigate API. You call this method when you want to navigate to another part of your app. The Navigation API triggers the events I described in the previous section, which in turn executes the navigation code you have set up in your event handler function.

The arguments to the navigate method are the location you are requesting and an optional state object with which you can pass information to the content you navigate to. Listing 5-17 shows how I have used the navigate method in the default.js file.

Listing 5-17. Using the navigate method in the default.js file

```
(function () {
    "use strict";

    var app = WinJS.Application;
    window.$ = WinJS.Utilities.query;

    app.onactivated = function (eventObject) {

        WinJS.Navigation.addEventListener("navigating", function (e) {
            var targetElem = $('#topRight div.contentTarget')[0];
            WinJS.Utilities.empty(targetElem);

            var content = e.detail.location == "basic"
                ? "contentBasic.html" : "contentButton.html";
```

```
            WinJS.UI.Pages.render(content, targetElem);
        });

        $('#left button').listen("click", function (e) {
            if (this.id == "button1") {
                WinJS.Navigation.navigate("basic", "Hello from default.js");
            } else {
                WinJS.Navigation.navigate("button");
            }
        });
        WinJS.UI.processAll();
    };
    app.start();
})();
```

It looks a bit odd to call the navigate method in the same code block that defines the navigation event handler function, but the pattern starts to make more sense as I continue to adopt the Navigation API in the rest of the example app. Listing 5-18 shows the changes to the contentButton.html file so that clicking the button element calls the navigate method.

Listing 5-18. Using the navigate method in the contentButton.html file

```
<!DOCTYPE html>
<html>
    <head>
        <title>Button Content</title>
        <script>
            WinJS.UI.Pages.define("contentButton.html", {
                ready: function (element, data) {
                    document.getElementById("contentButton")
                        .addEventListener("click", function (e) {
                            WinJS.Navigation.navigate("basic");
                        });
                }
            });
        </script>
    </head>
    <body>
        <div id="contentButtonTop">
            <div class="message">
                <button id="contentButton">Press Me</button>
            </div>
        </div>
    </body>
</html>
```

Now I have some content that can request navigation to the basic content without needing to know what the content file is called or where in the layout the content will be inserted. The responsibility for handling the navigation resides with the navigation event handler function, which provides a service to the rest of the app. Notice that there is no direct relationship between the caller of the navigate method and the event handler function. When you call the navigate method, you rely on the Navigation API to send the event and expect that there is a handler function that is willing and able to perform the navigation on your behalf. (This is why it is important to ensure that your handler function is registered when the app first starts.)

Using the Navigation History

At this point, I have a working navigation system that allows me to reach the contentBasic.html file in two ways. I can click Button One, which navigates directly to the content, or I can click Button Two, which takes me to contentButton.html, and then click Press Me. Now that I have established two routes to the same content, I can use the other features of the Navigation API to ensure that the user gets a consistent navigation experience. For my simple example app, this means that I can set up the Back button so that it returns to the page that the user came from. I have modified the contentBasic.html file to use the Navigation API, as Listing 5-19 illustrates.

Listing 5-19. Using the Navigation API in the contentBasic.html file

```
<!DOCTYPE html>
<html>
    <head>
        <title>Basic Content</title>
        <style type="text/css">
            #contentBasicTop {
                border: medium solid white;
                margin: 10px;
                padding: 10px;
                font-family: serif;
            }
        </style>
        <script>
            WinJS.UI.Pages.define("/contentBasic.html", {
                ready: function () {
                    var backButton = document.getElementById("back");

                    if (!WinJS.Navigation.canGoBack) {
                        backButton.disabled = true;
                    } else {
                        backButton.addEventListener("click", function (e) {
                            WinJS.Navigation.back();
                        });
                    }

                    if (WinJS.Navigation.state) {
                        $("#contentBasicTop div.message")[0].innerText
                            = WinJS.Navigation.state;
                    }
                }
            });
        </script>
    </head>
    <body>
        <div id="contentBasicTop">
```

```
        <div class="message">
            No Message
        </div>
        <button id="back">Back</button>
    </div>
  </body>
</html>
```

The important element in this document is the button. When my ready handler is executed, I find the button element by its id and use the Navigation API to configure it. The Navigation API maintains a history of the locations that have been navigated to. If it is possible to return to the previous location, then the WinJS.Navigation.canGoBack property returns true.

In my listing, I disable the button if I can't go back, and set up a handler function for the click event if I can. My handler calls the WinJS.Navigation.back method if you click the button while it is enabled. This causes the Navigation API to emit the navigation events using the last-visited location, providing a neat way for my content to be able to unwind the navigation sequence. There are equivalent members in the Navigation API for moving forward and determining the current location, just like when you use the browser's history API in a web app.

The other part of the Navigation API that I have included in the listing is the state object. In the default.js file, I called the navigate method with a simple string as the state object argument. This object is available through the WinJS.Navigation.state property. If a state object is available, I use it to set the content of the div element in the imported content.

■ **Tip** The state object is available to the navigation event handler functions through the detail.state property of the Event object.

You can see the effect of navigating to contentBasic.html by clicking Button One in Figure 5-8. If you navigate in this way when the app has just been started, there is no navigation history and so the canGoBack property returns false, which means that the Back button will be disabled. Although there is no history, there is a state object available and you can see the message displayed in the layout.

Figure 5-8. Navigating to contentBasic.html by clicking Button One

By way of contrast, you can see the effect of navigating to contentBasic.html by clicking on Button Two and then the Press Me button in Figure 5-9. There is navigation history available, so the Back button is enabled and clicking it will navigate back to contentButton.html (and, of course, the point here is that there are no references to contentButton.html in the code or markup of the contentBasic.html file). I don't pass a state object argument to the navigate method in this navigation sequence, which is reflected in the message.

Figure 5-9. *Navigating to contentBasic.html by clicking Button One and Press Me*

AVOIDING THE BROWSER NAVIGATION FEATURES

Now that you have seen how the Navigation API works, you might be wondering why you wouldn't just use the browser's built-in history and location objects. The problem is that these objects don't let you tailor navigation to an app's single-page content model. A JavaScript Windows app *can* navigate away from the master page to a new top-level page, but when that happens all of the state and content in the app is lost (since it is maintained using simple JavaScript objects). This is particularly problematic when using view models, which I introduce in Chapter 8.

You need to be careful not to use the navigation features built into the browser—if you do, you will break out of the single-page model. Doing this won't kill the app, but you'll lose any data that is built on regular global JavaScript objects and variables, including navigation history and custom namespace, for example. This data is lost once you navigate to another top-level page, and navigating back to your master page won't restore it.

The most frequent cause of inadvertent top-level navigation in my projects has been when I use a elements for navigation and forget to override the default click behavior. If you use a elements in your projects, you must be sure to handle the click event, call the preventDefault method on the event, and use the WinJS Navigation API to request a navigation change.

Summary

In this chapter I have shown you one of the fundamental building blocks for a Windows app: the single-page layout. This kind of layout is becoming popular for web apps, but making it work properly in an app requires the use of some WinJS features. I showed you how to import simple static content using HtmlControl, how to import and manage more complex content using the WinJS.UI.Pages API, and finally, how to use the WinJS.Navigation API to create flexible navigation within your app.

The Windows app approach to the single-page layout model is complicated and there is a lot to take in. But don't worry—it quickly becomes second nature and you'll soon be at home with the features and techniques I have described. In the next chapter, I show you how to make your app adapt and respond to different layouts and orientations, which is important if you want to present your users with a first-class Windows experience.

CHAPTER 6

■ ■ ■

Creating an Adaptive Layout

In Chapter XXX, I showed you how to create a layout for your app using the Metro support for the single-page content model. In this chapter, I show you how to make that layout adapt to different views and orientations. Views are available on most Windows 8 devices and allow the user to select different ways to interact with an app—including having two Metro apps run side by side. Orientations arise on devices that can be held in different positions or are easily rotated and that are equipped with a sensor to report on their state. You need to think carefully about how you will accommodate different views and orientations in your app to create a first-class Metro experience.

I also show you how to deal with high–pixel density displays. These displays are increasingly common on tablet and phone platforms and present the user with a crisper display than is possible with traditional hardware. For the most part, Windows 8 takes care of pixel density for you, but there is one key exception that requires attention: bitmap images. I explain how Windows 8 approaches pixel density and show you the Metro features that help you present the right resolution bitmap for the hardware being used. Table 6-1 provides the summary for this chapter.

Table 6-1. Chapter Summary

Problem	Solution	Listing
Adapt to Metro views using CSS	Use media rules with the -ms-view-state property.	6-1–6-4
Adapt to Metro views using JavaScript	Handle the resize event emitted by the DOM window object and read the current view from the Windows.UI.ViewManagement. ApplicationView.value property	6-5, 6-6
Adapt to view changes in imported content	Listen for the resize event in the ready handler for the WinJS.UI. Pages.define method and use CSS media rules with the -ms-view-state property.	6-7, 6-8
Break out of the snapped view	Call the Windows.UI.ViewManagement.ApplicationView.tryUnsnap method	6-9
Adapt to device orientation using JavaScript	Handle the orientationchanged event emitted by the Windows. Graphics.Display.DisplayProperties object.	6-10, 6-11
Adapt to device orientation using CSS	Use media rules with the orientation property.	6-12
Set and override orientation preferences.	Set the initial preferences in the app manifest and override them using the Windows.Graphics.Display.DisplayProperties object.	6-13, -6-14

Creating the Example Project

I have created an example project called AppViews so that I can demonstrate the different features in this chapter. Once again, I have used the Visual Studio Blank App project template. You can see the additions I have made to default.html, which I will use as my HTML master page, in Listing 6-1.

Listing 6-1. The contents of the default.html file in the AppViews Project

```
<!DOCTYPE html>
<html>
<head>
    <meta charset="utf-8">
    <title>AppViews</title>

    <!-- WinJS references -->
    <link href="//Microsoft.WinJS.1.0/css/ui-dark.css" rel="stylesheet" />
    <script src="//Microsoft.WinJS.1.0/js/base.js"></script>
    <script src="//Microsoft.WinJS.1.0/js/ui.js"></script>

    <!-- AppViews references -->
    <link href="/css/default.css" rel="stylesheet">
    <link href="/css/views.css" rel="stylesheet">
    <script src="/js/default.js"></script>
</head>
<body>
    <div id="gridContainer">
        <div id="topLeft">Top Left</div>
        <div id="topRight">Top Right</div>
        <div id="bottomLeft">Bottom Left</div>
        <div id="bottomRight">Bottom Right</div>
    </div>
</body>
</html>
```

I used the CSS grid feature to create a master layout that is a 2-by-2 grid. The grid will be contained in the div element whose id is gridContainer, and each of the child elements contains a label to indicate its position. You can see the CSS properties I have used to create the layout in Listing 6-2, which shows the css/default.css file. There is a second CSS file linked to default.html—this file is called views.css. It is currently empty, and I'll come back to it later in this chapter.

Listing 6-2. The default.css file

```css
#gridContainer {
    display: -ms-grid;
    -ms-grid-rows: 1fr 1fr;
    -ms-grid-columns: 1fr 1fr;
    height: 100%;
    font-size: 40pt;
}

#gridContainer > div {
    border: medium solid white;
    padding: 10px; margin: 1px;
}

#topLeft {
    -ms-grid-row: 1; -ms-grid-column: 1;
    background-color: #317f42;
}

#topRight {
    -ms-grid-row: 1; -ms-grid-column: 2;
    background-color: #5A8463;
}

#bottomLeft {
    -ms-grid-row: 2; -ms-grid-column: 1;
    background-color: #4ecc69;
}

#bottomRight {
    -ms-grid-row: 2; -ms-grid-column: 2;
    background-color: #46B75E;
}

span, button, img {
    font-size: 25pt;
    margin: 5px;
    display: block;
}

#testImg {
    width: 100px;
    height: 100px;
}
```

■ **Tip** I have left the js/default.js file as it was created by Visual Studio. I'll come back to this file and show you its content later in the chapter.

These files produce a simple app that has four colored quadrants, as shown in Figure 6-1. I'll use this app in the rest of this chapter to explain the different views in which an app can be displayed and how you can adapt to them.

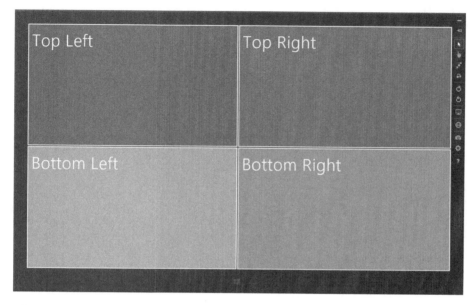

Figure 6-1. The example app shown in the default view

Understanding the Metro Views

A Metro app can be displayed in one of four views. Figure 6-1 shows the app in the full-screen landscape view, where the entire display is dedicated to the example app and the longest edges of the screen are at the top and bottom of the device. There are three other views you need to deal with: *full-screen portrait*, *snapped*, and *filled*.

In the *full-screen portrait view*, your app occupies the entire screen, but the longest edges are at the left and right of the device. In the *snapped view*, the app is displayed in a 320 pixel–wide strip at the left or right edge of the screen. In the *filled view*, the app is displayed on the entire screen except the 320-pixel strip that a snapped app occupies. Snapped and filled views are supported only if the horizontal resolution of the display is 1366 pixels or greater. For most of today's devices, this means that the filled and snapped views are available only when the device is in the landscape orientation—but this is not a requirement, and with a large enough screen, a device would be able to snap and fill in both landscape and portrait orientations. You can see the example app in the snapped and filled views in Figure 6-2.

■ **Tip**   The easiest way to cycle between the filled and snapped views is to press Win+. (the period key).

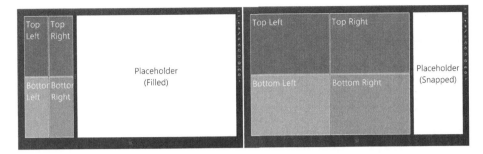

Figure 6-2. The example app in the snapped and filled views

As you can see, the default behavior for a Metro app is just to fit into whatever space is available. In the case of my example app, this means that the available space is evenly allocated across the columns in my grid. This generally isn't so bad when your app is in the filled view, because 320 pixels isn't a huge loss of screen real estate. It can have a greater impact when your app is in the snapped view because, well, 320 pixels isn't much room at all. As the figure shows, my example is squashed into the available space and doesn't display its text fully.

■ **Note**   The other app in the figure reports its current view. I have included the app in the source-code download for this book just in case you might find it useful—the app is called `PlaceHolder` and it is in the folder for this chapter. It uses the same features and functionality that I describe in this chapter, which is why I have not listed the code.

The user decides which view he wants and when he wants it. You can't create an app that works only in certain views, and so you need to make sure that you take the time to make your app layout adapt in a meaningful way for each view. There are different ways of adapting to the views, and I'll take you through them in the sections that follow.

■ **Note**   The best way to understand this chapter is to follow along and build the app out as I do. This will allow you to see the way the app responds to view changes, which the static screenshots can't properly capture.

Adapting to Views Using CSS

The first way to adapt to the different views is to use CSS. Microsoft has defined some Metro-specific CSS media rules that are applied when the app moves from one view to another. You can see the four rules in Listing 6-3, which shows the `css/views.css` file I mentioned earlier.

Listing 6-3. Responding to view changes in the views.css file

```
@media screen and (-ms-view-state: fullscreen-landscape) {
}

@media screen and (-ms-view-state: fullscreen-portrait) {
```

```
}

@media screen and (-ms-view-state: filled) {
    #topLeft {
        -ms-grid-column-span: 2;
    }

    #topRight {
        -ms-grid-row:  2;
    }

    #bottomRight {
        display: none;
    }
}

@media screen and (-ms-view-state: snapped) {
    #gridContainer {
        -ms-grid-columns: 1fr;
    }
}
```

This is, to my mind at least, one of the nicest touch points between Metro and the standard web technologies that underpin it. CSS media rules are simple and elegant, and by defining a small number of Metro-specific properties, Microsoft has made it very easy to respond to the different views.

I often struggle with Microsoft and what I see as its tendency to ignore or distort accepted standards, but I have to give the company credit for the lighter touch it has taken with Metro. I have defined properties for two of the media rules, which I'll explain in the following sections.

When Visual Studio creates a CSS file as part of a new project, it adds four media rules that correspond to the four views. This is usually in the default.css file, but it suited me for this project to move them to views.css. The styles you define in each rule are active only when your app is being displayed in the corresponding view. The usual CSS precedence rules apply, which means that the rules are usually defined as the last items in your project's CSS files. If you use a separate file to define the rules, as I have done for the example project, then you need to make sure that the link element that imports the CSS comes last, as I have done in the default.html file:

```
...
<!-- AppViews references -->
<link href="/css/default.css" rel="stylesheet">
<link href="/css/views.css" rel="stylesheet">
<script src="/js/default.js"></script>
...
```

Adapting to the Filled View

Most apps can tolerate losing 320 pixels of the screen without too many problems. In the event that you create an app whose layout won't adapt on its own, you can define styles in the media rule that is applied when the -ms-view-state property value is filled. To demonstrate adapting to the filled view, I have redefined some of the CSS grid properties applied to the div elements that fill each quadrant in the default landscape view:

```
...
@media screen and (-ms-view-state: filled) {
    #topLeft {
        -ms-grid-column-span: 2;
    }

    #topRight {
        -ms-grid-row:  2;
    }

    #bottomRight {
        display: none;
    }
}
...
```

The combination of the CSS grid layout and the media rules make it easy to apply sweeping changes when you adapt to a specific view. For this view, I have changed the layout so that three of the four div elements are visible, extended one div element so that it spans two columns, and repositioned a third element to a different location in the grid. You can see the effect in Figure 6-3.

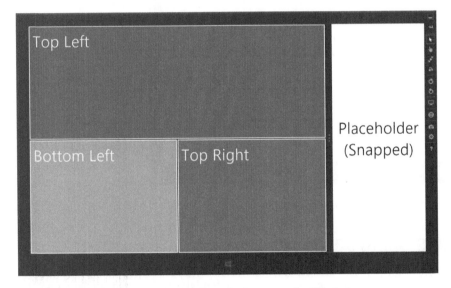

Figure 6-3. Using the CSS grid to adapt the layout to the filled view

Adapting to the Snapped View

The snapped view usually requires more thought. You need to put something useful in that 320-pixel strip, but the whole of your app's layout usually won't fit. My preferred approach is to switch to an information-only view of the app while it is in the snapped view and break out of this view as soon as the user interacts with my app. I'll show you how to change your app's view later in this chapter.

Whatever your approach, you have to deal with the fact that you have a relatively small amount of space compared to the overall screen size. In my example app, I respond by altering my CSS grid so that it has only one column—this has the effect of hiding the content in the rest of the grid, using the property shown in Listing 6-4.

Listing 6-4. Adapting to the snapped view

```
...
@media screen and (-ms-view-state: snapped) {
    #gridContainer {
        -ms-grid-columns: 1fr;
    }
}
...
```

You can see the result in Figure 6-4.

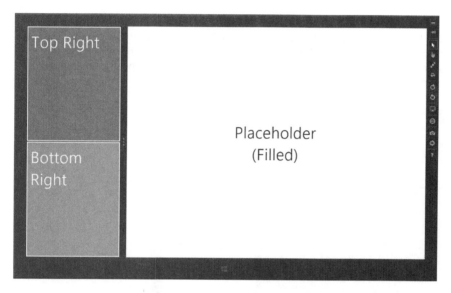

Figure 6-4. Using the CSS grid to adapt to the snapped view

Adapting to Views Using JavaScript

I like the CSS approach for adapting to views, but it only gets me so far—I can't use it to change the content of elements, for example. For more extensive changes, you can supplement your CSS media rules with some JavaScript code. The view-related functionality is contained in the Windows.UI.ViewManagement namespace. This is the first time in this book that I have used functionality from the Windows API, rather than the WinJS, API. The Windows API is shared between HTML/JavaScript Metro apps and those written in Microsoft .NET technologies, such as XAML/C#. As a consequence, some of the method and event naming can be a little awkward. In the sections that follow, I'll show you how to detect the current view and receive notifications when the view changes.

Detecting the Current View

You can find out in which view the application is currently displayed by reading the value of the `Windows.UI.ViewManagement.ApplicationView.value` property (as I said, some of the naming in the Windows API is a little odd). This property returns an integer that corresponds to a value in the `Windows.UI.ViewManagement.ApplicationViewState` enumeration, as shown in Table 6-2.

■ **Tip** Metro *enumerations* are a bit like namespaces and interfaces. They don't really make much sense in JavaScript, but they make it possible to consume the objects in the Windows API as peers to other Metro languages such as C#. In JavaScript, they are presented as objects whose properties define a set of expected or supported values.

Table 6-2. Values describing the current view

Numeric Value	Enumeration Value	View
0	fullScreenLandscape	The device is in the landscape orientation and the app occupies the entire screen
1	filled	The app is displayed in the filled view
2	snapped	The app is displayed in the snapped view
3	fullScreenPortrait	The device is in the portrait orientation and the app occupies the entire screen

I have added some code to the `default.js` file so that one of the grid elements displays the current orientation, as shown in Listing 6-5.

■ **Tip** I don't want to keep typing out `Windows.UI.ViewManagement` in my code, so I have created a variable called view as an alias to the namespace—you can see the statement that does this emphasized in the listing.

Listing 6-5. Obtaining and displaying the current orientation in JavaScript

```
(function () {
    "use strict";

    var app = WinJS.Application;
    var view = Windows.UI.ViewManagement;

    app.onactivated = function (eventObject) {
        topRight.innerText = getMessageFromView(view.ApplicationView.value);
    };

    function getMessageFromView(currentView) {
        var displayMsg;
        switch (currentView) {
            case view.ApplicationViewState.filled:
```

```
                    displayMsg = "Filled View";
                    break;
                case view.ApplicationViewState.snapped:
                    displayMsg = "Snapped View";
                    break;
                case view.ApplicationViewState.fullScreenLandscape:
                    displayMsg = "Full - Landscape";
                    break;
                case view.ApplicationViewState.fullScreenPortrait:
                    displayMsg = "Full - Portrait";
                    break;
            }
            return displayMsg;
        }

    app.start();
})();
```

In this listing, I get the current view and use the ApplicationViewState enumeration to map from the numeric string to a message I can display to the user. I then use this message to set the innerText property of the object representing the topRight element in the DOM.

Receiving View Change Events

The code in the previous listing gets the view when the app starts, but it doesn't keep the UI up to date when the user switches to a different view. To create an app that adapts fluidly to the different views, I need to listen for the view change events, which are signaled through the resize event of the DOM window object. You can see how I have handled these events in the default.js file in Listing 6-6.

Listing 6-6. Handling view change events

```
(function () {
    "use strict";

    var app = WinJS.Application;
    var view = Windows.UI.ViewManagement;

    app.onactivated = function (eventObject) {

        topRight.innerText = getMessageFromView(view.ApplicationView.value);
        window.addEventListener("resize", function () {
            topRight.innerText = getMessageFromView(view.ApplicationView.value);
        });
    }

    function getMessageFromView(currentView) {
        var displayMsg;
        switch (currentView) {
            case view.ApplicationViewState.filled:
                displayMsg = "Filled View";
                break;
```

```
            case view.ApplicationViewState.snapped:
                displayMsg = "Snapped View";
                break;
            case view.ApplicationViewState.fullScreenLandscape:
                displayMsg = "Full - Landscape";
                break;
            case view.ApplicationViewState.fullScreenPortrait:
                displayMsg = "Full - Portrait";
                break;
        }
        return displayMsg;
    }

    app.start();
})();
```

The resize event signals a change in the view, but to figure out which view the user has selected, I have to read the ApplicationView.value property once again. I then pass the value to the getMessageFromView function to create a string I can display in the top-right panel of the app layout.

You can see the result of my additions to the example app in Figure 6-5. The example app responds to view changes using CSS media rules to control the layout and JavaScript to alter the content (albeit making simple changes in both cases). You could, of course, do everything in JavaScript, but I find that this approach becomes pretty unwieldy and hard to test. A good mix of CSS for the layout and JavaScript for the content works best for me.

Figure 6-5. Adapting to views by using JavaScript to change element content

Adapting to View Changes in Imported Content

There is no special mechanism to disseminate information about the view to content you have imported into your layout, but you can use the CSS media rules and respond to the resize event just as for the master page. Listing 6-7 shows a simple example of an all-in-one page I have added to the project called content. html. (An all-in-one page contains the script and styles in the same file as the markup—I use these throughout the book to add self-contained demonstrations to example apps.)

Listing 6-7. Responding to view changes in imported content

```
<!DOCTYPE html>
<html>
    <head>
        <title></title>
        <script>
```

```
        var view = Windows.UI.ViewManagement;

        function setButtonContent(viewState) {
            if (viewState == view.ApplicationViewState.snapped) {
                button1.innerText = "Change View";
            } else {
                button1.innerText = "Button One";
            }
        }

        WinJS.UI.Pages.define("/content.html", {
            ready: function () {
                setButtonContent(view.ApplicationView.value);

                window.addEventListener("resize", function () {
                    setButtonContent(view.ApplicationView.value);
                });
            }
        });
    </script>
    <style type="text/css">
        button {
            font-size: 30px;
        }
        @media screen and (-ms-view-state: snapped) {
            #button1 {
                font-size: 40px;
                font-family: serif;
            }
            #button2 {
                display: none;
            }
        }
    </style>
</head>
<body>
    <div>
        <button id="button1">Button One</button>
        <button id="button2">Button Two</button>
    </div>
</body>
</html>
```

I have imported this content using the WinJS.UI.Pages.render method in the default.js file, as shown in Listing 6-8. See Chapter XXX for more details of this method. The content is imported into the element with the id of bottomRight, which occupies the lower right part of the grid layout.

Listing 6-8. Importing the content.html file to the bottomRight element

```
...
app.onactivated = function (eventObject) {
```

```
topRight.innerText = getMessageFromView(view.ApplicationView.value);
window.addEventListener("resize", function () {
    topRight.innerText = getMessageFromView(view.ApplicationView.value);
});
WinJS.UI.Pages.render("/content.html", document.getElementById("bottomRight"));
}
...
```

The content.html document contains two button elements. When the app is displayed in the snapped view, I hide one of the buttons from view and change the content and style of the other. Notice that I check the current view in addition to responding to the change events—this is important because you can't make assumptions about which view the app is being displayed in when the content is loaded. You can see the two states for the button elements in Figure 6-6.

Figure 6-6. Using the view change events and CSS media rules in imported content

This is exactly the same set of techniques I used for the master content, but I wanted to emphasize that you need to apply them throughout your app, including any content you import. If you don't apply these techniques rigorously, you end up with an app that appears odd to the user when certain app states and views are combined.

■ **Tip** You may see references to an updateLayout property used with the WinJS.UI.Pages.define method being used to respond to view changes. This is something used by the Visual Studio Navigation Application project template to combine the view events with the Pages feature. It isn't part of the WinJS or Windows APIs and it relies on all sorts of stuff that, frankly, I don't like or recommend. I suggest you handle the change events and use CSS media rules in your content as I have shown in this section.

Breaking Out of the Snapped View

Depending on the approach you take to the snapped view, you may want the option to break out into a larger layout. I mentioned earlier that I tend to favor an information-only layout in the snapped view and so, for example, I would want to switch to a larger view when the user interacts with my app so he can see the controls for creating and editing data. You can request that your app be unsnapped by calling the ApplicationView.tryUnsnap method. Listing 6-9 shows the use of this method in the content.html file.

Listing 6-9. Unsnapping an app from the snapped view

```
...
<script>
    var view = Windows.UI.ViewManagement;

    function setButtonContent(viewState) {
        if (viewState == view.ApplicationViewState.snapped) {
            button1.innerText = "Change View";
        } else {
            button1.innerText = "Button One";
        }
    }

    WinJS.UI.Pages.define("/content.html", {
        ready: function () {
            setButtonContent(view.ApplicationView.value);

            window.addEventListener("resize", function () {
                setButtonContent(view.ApplicationView.value);
            });

            button1.addEventListener("click", function (e) {
                var unsnapped = view.ApplicationView.tryUnsnap();
                button1.innerText = unsnapped ? "Unsnapped" : "Failed";
            });
        }
    });
</script>
...
```

The tryUnsnap method works only when the app is in the snapped view and is in the foreground (i.e., being displayed to the user). The method returns true if the unsnapping works and false if it doesn't. Unsnapping the app causes the view change events to be triggered and the CSS media rules to be applied, just as though the user had changed the view, so you don't have to use the result from the tryUnsnap method to reconfigure the app directly.

Adapting to Device Orientation

Many Windows 8 devices are portable and equipped with orientation sensors. Windows 8 will automatically change its orientation to match the way the device is being held. There are four orientations: landscape, portrait, landscape-flipped, and portrait-flipped. Orientations and views are closely related—when the device is in the landscape orientation, for example, your app can be shown in the full screen, snapped, and filled views. The flipped orientations are achieved by rotating the device 180 degrees from the corresponding regular orientation—essentially inverting the device.

Devices have two orientations. The current orientation of a device is, as you would expect, the present orientation and is one of the four orientations I listed. Devices also have a native orientation, which is where the orientation sensor is at zero degrees. The native orientation is only ever landscape or portrait and is typically where the hardware buttons of the device match the orientation of the display.

Not all devices will change orientation, and some will change orientation only very rarely. A good example is desktop devices, where monitors are generally fixed in position and reorienting them requires an explicit configuration change. In the sections that follow, I'll show you how to handle device orientations to create a flexible and adaptable Metro app.

Determining and Monitoring the Device Orientation

The Windows.Graphics.Display namespace provides the means to determine the current orientation and to receive notification when the orientation changes. I have added elements to the default.html file, as shown in Listing 6-10, so that I can easily display the view and the orientation.

Listing 6-10. Adding elements to default.html to display the view and the orientation

```
...
<div id="gridContainer">
    <div id="topLeft">Top Left</div>
    <div id="topRight">
        <span id="view"></span>
        <span id="currentOrientation"></span>
        <span id="nativeOrientation"></span>
    </div>
    <div id="bottomLeft">Bottom Left</div>
    <div id="bottomRight">Bottom Right</div>
</div>
...
```

Listing 6-11 shows how I use these elements and demonstrates how to get the orientation values and listen for changes in the default.js file.

Listing 6-11. Determining and monitoring the device orientation

```
(function () {
    "use strict";

    var app = WinJS.Application;
    var view = Windows.UI.ViewManagement;
    var display = Windows.Graphics.Display;

    app.onactivated = function (eventObject) {

        view.innerText = getMessageFromView(view.ApplicationView.value);

        window.addEventListener("view", function () {
            topRight.innerText = getMessageFromView(view.ApplicationView.value);
        });

        displayOrientation();

        display.DisplayProperties.addEventListener("orientationchanged", function (e) {
            displayOrientation();
        });
```

```
        WinJS.UI.Pages.render("/content.html", document.getElementById("bottomRight"));
    };

    function displayOrientation() {
        var msg = getStringFromValue(display.DisplayProperties.currentOrientation);
        currentOrientation.innerText = "Current: " + msg;

        msg = getStringFromValue(display.DisplayProperties.nativeOrientation);
        nativeOrientation.innerText = "Native: " + msg;
    }

    function getStringFromValue(value) {
        var result;
        switch (value) {
            case display.DisplayOrientations.landscape:
                result = "Landscape";
                break;
            case display.DisplayOrientations.landscapeFlipped:
                result = "Landscape Flipped";
                break;
            case display.DisplayOrientations.portrait:
                result = "Portrait";
                break;
            case display.DisplayOrientations.portraitFlipped:
                result = "Portrait Flipped";
                break;
        }
        return result;
    }

    function getMessageFromView(currentView) {
        var displayMsg;
        switch (currentView) {
            case view.ApplicationViewState.filled:
                displayMsg = "Filled View";
                break;
            case view.ApplicationViewState.snapped:
                displayMsg = "Snapped View";
                break;
            case view.ApplicationViewState.fullScreenLandscape:
                displayMsg = "Full - Landscape";
                break;
            case view.ApplicationViewState.fullScreenPortrait:
                displayMsg = "Full - Portrait";
                break;
        }
        return "View: " + displayMsg;
    }

    app.start();
```

```
})();
```

The `Windows.Graphics.Display.DisplayProperties` object provides access to the device orientation. The `currentOrientation` and `nativeOrientation` values return integers that correspond to values from the `DisplayOrientations` enumeration. I have listed these values in Table 6-3.

Table 6-3. Values Describing the Current and Native Orientations

Numeric Value	Enumeration Value	Orientation
0	none	No orientation information is available
1	landscape	The device is oriented so that the width of the display is greater than the height.
2	portrait	The device is oriented 90 degrees clockwise to the landscape orientation such that the height of the display is greater than the width
4	landscapeFlipped	The device is oriented 180 degrees relative to the landscape orientation
8	portraitFlipped	The device is oriented 270 degrees clockwise relative to the landscape orientation

The `nativeOrientation` property will return only the `landscape` or `portrait` values and set the baseline from the other values are relative. In the listing I read the values of the `currentOrientation` and `nativeOrientation` properties and display them in the layout. I also create a handler function for the `orientationchanged` event, which is emitted by the `DisplayProperties` object. This event is triggered when either the current or the native orientation is changed. The `Event` object passed to the handler function doesn't include information about which value has changed, which means that you have to read the property values and figure out what you need to do in the context of your app. Figure 6-7 shows how the orientation information is displayed in the example app (the values you see, of course, will depend on the device orientation). I have left the code that displays the current view to emphasize that you need to manage the combination of orientation and views to create an app that has a fully responsive layout.

Figure 6-7. Displaying the current and native orientation

You can use the Visual Studio simulator to test orientations and you can change the orientation by using the two buttons highlighted in the figure. The native orientation for the simulator is the landscape orientation, and in the figure I have rotated the simulator through 180 degrees (you might be able to make out that the small Microsoft logo is at the top of the simulator window).

Using CSS to Adapt to Device Orientation

You can also use CSS media rules to respond to the device orientation, but only in terms of whether the device is in a landscape or portrait orientation—the difference between the standard and flipped views cannot be expressed through CSS. The key rule property is orientation and the supported values are landscape and portrait. Listing 6-12 shows how I have added a media rule to the css/views.css file to make the app layout adapt to orientation changes.

Listing 6-12. Using a CSS media rule to adapt to device orientation

```
@media screen and (-ms-view-state: fullscreen-landscape) {
}

@media screen and (-ms-view-state: fullscreen-portrait) {
}

@media screen and (-ms-view-state: filled) {
    #topLeft {
        -ms-grid-column-span: 2;
    }

    #topRight {
        -ms-grid-row:  2;
    }

    #bottomRight {
        display: none;
    }
}

@media screen and (-ms-view-state: snapped) {
    #gridContainer {
        -ms-grid-columns: 1fr;
    }
}

@media screen and (orientation: portrait) {
    #topLeft {
        background-color: #eca7a7;
    }
}
```

My addition changes the background color of one of the div elements in the layout when the device is in a portrait orientation. This style is applied when the device is in the portrait or portrait-flipped orientations. You can see the effect in Figure 6-8 (if you are reading the printed version of this book, with black-and-white images, you will need to run the example).

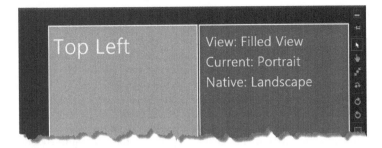

Figure 6-8. Changing the color of an element in response to an orientation change

It may seem that this kind of `orientation` media rule property duplicates the functionality of the `-ms-view-state` I showed you earlier in the chapter, but actually they work together nicely. I find the `orientation` property useful when I want to apply styles when the device is in landscape orientation, irrespective of whether it is in the full screen, snapped, or filled view, for example.

Expressing Your Device Orientation Preferences

Not all apps are able to offer their full user experience in all orientations, and so you can request that your app not be rotated as the device moves between orientations. You can declare your long-term preferences using the app's manifest. You saw the manifest in Chapter XXX when I added tile icons to the `NoteFlash` app, and it contains the configuration information that the runtime needs to execute your app. To open the manifest, double-click on the `package.appxmanifest` file in the `Solution Explorer` window. Visual Studio opens a nice editor for the manifest by default, but the manifest is just an XML file and you can edit the text directly if you prefer. I rather like the editor, since it covers all of the configuration options using a nice UI. To change the orientation settings, click on the `Application UI` tab and check the orientations you want to support in the `Supported Rotations` section, as shown in Figure 6-9.

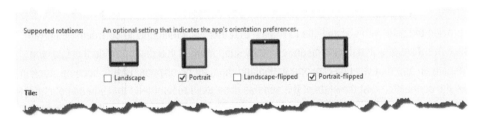

Figure 6-9. Using the manifest editor to select the supported orientations for an app

When you set the orientations you want to support, you are expressing a preference and nothing more. In the figure, I have stated that my example app works best in the portrait and portrait-flipped orientations and that, if possible, Windows should display my app only in those orientations.

■ **Tip** Not checking any of the options signals that your app is happy to be displayed in all of them.

Not checking an option doesn't prevent your app from being displayed in that orientation. Windows will try to accommodate your wishes, but only if it makes sense on the device running your app. As an example, my portrait-only preference doesn't make sense on a landscape-only desktop device and so Windows will show my app in landscape, because to do otherwise would be useless for the user.

You can't use orientation preferences to avoid implementing dealing with the snapped and filled views. If your app really can't work in a specific combination of orientation and view, then you need to handle this by listening for the view and orientation change events and displaying a message to the user that explains the problem and encourage him to switch your app to the preferred permutation.

For devices where the preferences do make sense, Windows will honor your preferred orientations. For my example app, this means that if you start the app in a landscape orientation, the app will be started in portrait mode, even though it means that the layout will be at 90 degrees—the idea is that this will encourage the user to reorient the device to suit your app. It works nicely and for tablet devices it is a natural and seamless reaction.

■ **Note**   A screenshot doesn't do much to illustrate the effect, since it would just show the layout displayed at 90 degrees from the regular orientation. You really need to experiment with the example to understand the effect. Unfortunately, you will need a device with an accelerometer for testing because the Visual Studio simulator ignores orientation preferences. I use a Dell Inspiron Duo for this kind of testing—it is a little underpowered, but reasonably priced, and it has the hardware required for orientation changes.

Overriding Manifest Orientation Preferences

You can change the orientation preferences of your app while it is running, which has the effect of temporarily overriding the settings in the manifest. I say temporarily, because the next time your app is started, the manifest preferences will take effect again. Being able to override the orientation preference is useful if your app has distinct modes, some of which can't be meaningfully expressed in certain orientations. As the user navigates through the app content and layout, you can keep Windows informed about which orientations you would like to support at any given moment.

■ **Caution**   You must provide the user with a visual cue to explain that there is a relationship between the current state of your app and the current set of orientations you are currently supporting. If you don't provide this cue, you will confuse the user, creating an app that will enter an orientation and then, for no obvious reason, become stuck in it. The user will not make the connection that the state of the app has changed. I recommend that you do not change orientation preferences dynamically—instead, support all orientations and adapt your layout to explain why certain app states don't work in certain orientations.

The orientation preferences can be changed dynamically through the autoRotationPreferences property of the Windows.Graphics.Display.DisplayProperties object. You use the JavaScript bitwise OR operator (expressing using the | character) to combine values from the DisplayOrientations enumeration to specify which orientations you are willing to support. To demonstrate this feature, I have added a button element labeled Lock to the default.html file, as shown in Listing 6-13. This button overrides the orientation preferences and prevents the orientation from changing.

Listing 6-13. Adding a button to the default.html file

```
...
<div id="gridContainer">
    <div id="topLeft">Top Left
        <button id="lock">Lock</button>
    </div>
    <div id="topRight">
        <span id="view"></span>
        <span id="currentOrientation"></span>
        <span id="nativeOrientation"></span>
    </div>
    <div id="bottomLeft">Bottom Left</div>
    <div id="bottomRight">Bottom Right</div>
</div>
...
```

Listing 6-14 demonstrates how I change the preferred orientations of my app in the default.js file in response to the button element being clicked.

Listing 6-14. Changing orientation preferences dynamically

```
(function () {
    "use strict";

    var app = WinJS.Application;
    var view = Windows.UI.ViewManagement;
    var display = Windows.Graphics.Display;

    app.onactivated = function (eventObject) {

        view.innerText = getMessageFromView(view.ApplicationView.value);

        window.addEventListener("view", function() {
            topRight.innerText = getMessageFromView(view.ApplicationView.value);
        });

        displayOrientation();

        display.DisplayProperties.addEventListener("orientationchanged", function (e) {
            displayOrientation();
        });

        lock.addEventListener("click", function (e) {
            if (this.innerText == "Lock") {
                display.DisplayProperties.autoRotationPreferences =
                    display.DisplayOrientations.landscape |
                    display.DisplayOrientations.landscapeFlipped;
                this.innerText = "Unlock";
            } else {
                display.DisplayProperties.autoRotationPreferences = 0;
                this.innerText = "Lock";
```

```
        }
    });

    WinJS.UI.Pages.render("/content.html", document.getElementById("bottomRight"));
    };

    // ... code removed for brevity

    app.start();
})();
```

This is another example that you can't test in the simulator—you need to use a device with an orientation sensor. When the button is clicked, I restrict my preferences to the landscape and landscape-flipped orientations. When the button is clicked again, I set the autoRotationPreferences property to zero, indicating that I have no orientation preferences.

■ **Note**   Windows will immediately rotate your app if you change the preferences so that the current orientation isn't one of your preferred options. You should use this behavior carefully and never force an orientation change unless it is explicitly in response to a clearly described user interaction. Triggering an orientation change without user direction is annoying and confusing and it will undermine your user's confidence in your app.

Adapting to Pixel Density

There is a trend toward displays with a greater number of pixels per inch. This was initially made popular by Apple and its "retina" displays, but this kind of hardware has become more widespread and is used in Windows 8 devices as well. The effect of a greater pixel density is to break the link between the number of pixels in a display and the display's size, creating a high-resolution display that is physically small.

Traditionally, when the resolution of a display increased, the size of the screen increased as well. The goal was to be able to display more on the screen—more UI controls, more windows, more rows in a table, and so on.

With a high–pixel density display, the goal is to display the same amount as for a low–pixel density display of the same size and to use the additional pixels to make the image crisper and sharper. To achieve this, Windows scales up Metro applications—if this isn't done, you end up with text that is too small to read and UI controls that are too small to touch or click. Table 6-4 shows the three scaling levels that Windows 8 applies to Metro apps based on the density of the pixels in the display.

Table 6-4. The Windows 8 Scaling Levels for Metro Apps

Scaling	DPI	Description
100%	Up to and including 134 dots per inch (dpi)	This is the default scaling level for standard density displays
140%	From 135 to 173 dpi	This is the scaling level for intermediate density displays
180%	174 dpi and greater	This is the scaling level for high density displays

Windows scales a Metro app automatically and will always scale to one of the levels in the table. You don't have to worry about scaling up your layouts, even if they contain absolute dimensions—Windows will translate the number of CSS pixels you specify, for example, into the scaled-up number of display pixels behind the scenes. And when you query the size of an element in the DOM, you will get back CSS pixels and not the scaled value. All of this makes it very easy to create Metro apps that look good on high- and low-pixel densities.

The one thing that doesn't work well in this arrangement is a bitmap image, where the quality of the display degrades as the pixel density increases. The effect on a high-density display is that bitmap images appear blurred and have jagged edges, as shown in Figure 6-10. The image on the left shows what happens when the image is scaled up and the image on the right shows the crisp edges you should aim for.

Figure 6-10. The blurring effect that arises when bitmap images are scaled up on a high–pixel density display

The best way to address this problem is to use vector image formats, like SVG. That's easier to say than do because a lot of design packages lack good SVG support. A more practical solution is to create a bitmap scaled for each of the Windows 8 scaling levels and ensure that the most appropriate image is used to match the pixel density of the display. To demonstrate this approach I have created three image files. You can see them in Figure 6-11.

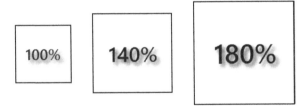

Figure 6-11. The images for demonstrating Metro support for high–pixel density displays

In a real project, you would create three versions of the same image. Since I want to make it clear which image is being displayed, I have created three separate images. Each image shows the scaling factor that I want to use it for and the image sizes match that scale: the first image is 100 x 100 pixels, the second is 140 x 140 pixels, and the last one is 180 x 180 pixels. In the sections that follow, I'll show you how to use these images in a Metro app.

Using Automatic Resource Loading

The simplest approach is to follow a naming convention and let the Metro runtime load the right file for the scaling factor in use. To demonstrate this, I have added copies of the test images to the images folder in the example project using the following file names:

- `img.scale-100.png`
- `img.scale-140.png`
- `img.scale-180.png`

By inserting scale-XXX before the file suffix, where XXX is the scaling percentage, you tell the Metro runtime that these files are variations of an image for use at different densities. You exclude the scaling information when you use these files in your HTML, as you can see in Listing 6-15, which shows an img element I have added to the default.html file.

■ **Caution**   It isn't enough just to copy the image files into the images folder on the disk. You also need to right-click the images folder in the Visual Studio Solution Explorer window and select Add Existing Item from the pop-up menu. Select the image files and click the Add button.

Listing 6-15. Using an image from a set of scaled files

```
...
<div id="gridContainer">
    <div id="topLeft">Top Left
        <button id="lock">Lock</button>
    </div>
    <div id="topRight">
        <span id="view"></span>
        <span id="currentOrientation"></span>
        <span id="nativeOrientation"></span>
    </div>
    <div id="bottomLeft">Bottom Left
        <img id="testImg" src="images/img.png" />
    </div>
    <div id="bottomRight">Bottom Right</div>
</div>
...
```

Testing Image Selection

Testing this feature is tricky without a range of devices with different pixel-density displays. The Visual Studio simulator supports switching between different screen resolutions and densities, but it doesn't handle images properly and shows them at their native size, which defeats the point of the simulation. The simulator does, however, load the correct images to reflect the simulated density, so I can get the effect I want by constraining the size of the img element, which I have done using one of the styles I defined in the default.css file, shown by Listing 6-16. This is not something you need to do for real devices and real projects.

Listing 6-16. Fixing the size of an image element to illustrate pixel-density support

```
...
#testImg {
    width: 100px;
    height: 100px;
}
...
```

One of the buttons at the edge of the simulator window changes the screen dimension and density, as shown in Figure 6-12. The most useful settings are for the 10.6-inch display, which can be emulated with four different resolutions, covering the different scale levels that Windows 8 supports.

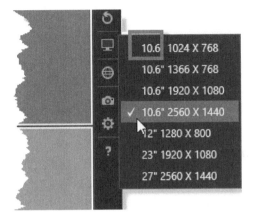

Figure 6-12. Changing the screen characteristics in the Visual Studio simulator

To test this technique, start the app and switch between the available pixel densities. You will see that the image targeted for the pixel density is displayed automatically.

■ **Tip** You will have to reload the app in the debugger after each change to see the right image—the mapping between the requested image name (img.png) and the scaled version (img.scaled-XXX.png) seems to be cached.

Adapting to Pixel Density Using JavaScript

You can get details of the pixel density and the zoom factory through the Windows.Graphics.Display. DisplayProperties object. To demonstrate how this works, I have added copies of the image files to the project images folder using the names img100.png, img140.png and img180.png. I have created these copies so that they are not subject to the scaling naming scheme I described in the previous section. In addition, I have removed the src attribute from the img element in the default.html file, as shown in Listing 6-17.

Listing 6-17. Removing the src attribute from the img element in the default.html file

```
...
<div id="gridContainer">
    <div id="topLeft">Top Left
        <button id="lock">Lock</button>
    </div>
    <div id="topRight">
        <span id="view"></span>
        <span id="currentOrientation"></span>
        <span id="nativeOrientation"></span>
```

```
        </div>
        <div id="bottomLeft">Bottom Left
            <img id="testImg" />
        </div>
        <div id="bottomRight">Bottom Right</div>
    </div>
...
```

The information I want is available through the DisplayProperties.resolutionScale property, which returns a value that corresponds to the Windows.Graphics.Display.ResolutionScale enumeration. The values in this enumeration are scale100Percent, scale140Percent, and scale180Percent. In Listing 6-18, you can see how I set the value of the src attribute for the img element based on the value from the resolutionScale property in the default.js file.

Listing 6-18. Explicitly selecting images based on the display scale factor

```
(function () {
    "use strict";

    var app = WinJS.Application;
    var view = Windows.UI.ViewManagement;
    var display = Windows.Graphics.Display;

    app.onactivated = function (eventObject) {

        switch (display.DisplayProperties.resolutionScale) {
            case display.ResolutionScale.scale100Percent:
                testImg.src = "images/img100.png";
                break;
            case display.ResolutionScale.scale140Percent:
                testImg.src = "images/img140.png";
                break;
            case display.ResolutionScale.scale180Percent:
                testImg.src = "images/img180.png";
                break;
        };

        // ...code removed for brevity...
    };

    app.start();
})();
```

Note You can also adapt to pixel density using CSS media rules, but there is no convenient scale mapping and you have to work with the pixel density value directly. This is problematic with the Visual Studio simulator because it rounds the pixel-density numbers the wrong way, so the simulated resolutions don't fall into the proper categories. Further, since you need to adapt bitmap images only to pixel density, which you can't do using CSS, there is little value in this technique. If you do find yourself adapting any other part of your layout to pixel density, there is something wrong with your approach. Remember: Windows will scale everything else in your app for you.

Summary

In this chapter, I have shown you the different ways in which you need to make your app layout adapt to the device—adapting to views, adapting to orientation, and adapting to pixel density. Making sure that your app adapts in a meaningful way is important in creating a fluid and high-quality user experience that blends nicely with the device and operating system capabilities. If you don't think through your approach to adaptions or, worse, skip them entirely, you'll create an app that behaves oddly and doesn't really mesh with the Metro experiences. My advice is to take the time to consider what the best response your app can make will be, especially when it comes to the snapped-view and the portrait-view orientations.

In the next chapter, I'll introduce some UI controls that are a distinctive part of Metro and that you can use to provide consistent and easy navigation around your app's functionality.

CHAPTER 7

■ ■ ■

Commands & Navigation

In Chapter 5, I showed you how to use the single-page layout to create the foundation for a Windows app. As I did this, I used button and anchor (a) elements to navigate around the content, much as I would have done in a regular web app. In this chapter, I'll show you the app-specific controls that are dedicated to offering the commands to navigate around the app and to manipulate the data or objects that it presents: the *AppBar* and the *NavBar*. These controls provide a big part of the distinctive visual style and interaction model of a Windows app and are present in most apps (the exception seems to be games, where nonstandard interfaces are common). In this chapter, I'll show you how to create and apply these controls and, in doing so, provide more detail about the WinJS control model, which I touched on in Chapter 5 when I used HtmlControl to import content. Table 7-1 provides the summary for this chapter.

Table 7-1. Chapter Summary

Problem	Solution	Listing
Defining an AppBar	Apply the WinJS.UI.AppBar control to a div element and populate it with div elements to which the WinJS.UI.AppBarCommand control has been applied.	7-1- 7-6
Responding to AppBar commands	Handle the click event emitted by the div element to which the WinJS.UI.AppBar control has been applied. Determine which command has been selected by reading the id value of the HTMLElement that originated the event.	7-7
Adapting the AppBar commands	Use the showOnlyCommands, showCommands, or hideCommands method to select the command presented to the user.	7-8
Soliciting further information from the user when a command is selected	Use a Flyout control containing the elements that you need to capture the required information from the user.	7-9–7-11
Defining a NavBar	Apply the WinJS.UI.AppBar control to a div element, setting the placement option to top.	7-12–7-16
Using a custom layout for a NavBar	Set the layout option to custom.	7-17–7-20
Animating the navigation to new content	Use the methods in the WinJS.UI.Animation namespace.	7-21

Creating the Example Project

The example project for this chapter, which I created using the `Blank App` template and called `AppBars`, follows the single-page navigation model. This chapter is about navigation, and so I have created a project that has a master page and two content files, which I'll show you shortly. I import one of the content files when the app starts and then, later in the chapter, I will add some Windows app UI controls to navigate to and from the other content. The `default.html` file will act as the master page and is shown in Listing 7-1.

Listing 7-1. The default.html master page for the AppBars project

```
<!DOCTYPE html>
<html>
<head>
    <meta charset="utf-8">
    <title>AppBars</title>

    <!-- WinJS references -->
    <link href="//Microsoft.WinJS.1.0/css/ui-dark.css" rel="stylesheet" />
    <script src="//Microsoft.WinJS.1.0/js/base.js"></script>
    <script src="//Microsoft.WinJS.1.0/js/ui.js"></script>

    <!-- AppBars references -->
    <link href="/css/default.css" rel="stylesheet">
    <script src="/js/default.js"></script>
</head>
<body>
    <div id="contentTarget"></div>
</body>
</html>
```

This will be my master page and I will import content into the `div` element whose `id` attribute is `contentTarget`. In all other respects, I have left this file just as it was created by Visual Studio when I used the `Blank Application` project template.

Defining and Loading the Content

I start with one content file in this project, which I have called `page1.html` (which I have added to the root project folder, alongside `default.html`). As you can see in Listing 7-2, this file contains an `h1` element that makes it clear which file has been loaded and some `span` elements (I'll use these when I explain commands, later in this chapter).

Listing 7-2. The content of the page1.html file

```
<!DOCTYPE html>
<html>
    <head>
        <title></title>
    </head>
    <body>
        <div id="page1Container" class="container">
            <h1>This is Page 1</h1>
```

```
            <span>Command: <span id="command">None</span></span>
        </div>
    </body>
</html>
```

Defining the JavaScript

I have used the WinJS.Navigation API to handle requesting and loading content in the js/default.js file, which you can see in Listing 7-3. My handler for the navigating event clears the target element in the master page and uses the WinJS.UI.Pages.render method to load the specified content. I will be using the name of the file directly to request content in this app. The starting position for the app is to load page1. html and I'll use the navigation controls to switch to other content later in the chapter.

Listing 7-3. Loading the initial content in the default.js file

```
(function () {
    "use strict";

    var app = WinJS.Application;

    WinJS.Navigation.addEventListener("navigating", function (e) {
        WinJS.Utilities.empty(contentTarget);
        WinJS.UI.Pages.render(e.detail.location, contentTarget);
    });

    app.onactivated = function (eventObject) {
        WinJS.Navigation.navigate("page1.html");
    };

    app.start();
})();
```

Defining the CSS

The final file in this project is the css/default.css file, which I have used to define styles for both the master page and the separate content files. You can see the CSS styles in Listing 7-4.

Listing 7-4. The contents of the default.css file

```
#contentTarget, div.container {
    width: 100%;
    height: 100%;
    text-align: center;
    display: -ms-flexbox;
    -ms-flex-direction: column;
    -ms-flex-align: center;
    -ms-flex-pack: center;
}

#page1Container {
```

```
        background-color: #317f42;
}

#page2Container {
        background-color: #5A8463;
}

div.container span {
        font-size: 30pt;
}
```

I have used the flexbox layout to arrange the elements, as you can see in Figure 7-1, which shows the initial appearance of the example app.

Figure 7-1. The initial appearance of the AppBars example app

Creating Application Commands

The AppBar appears at the bottom of the screen and provides the user with access to *commands*. A command performs some function on the data or objects that are currently in scope, which typically means that your commands should be relevant to the content you are currently presenting to the user.

The AppBar is an essential part of the Windows app user experience. It provides a consistent and familiar anchor point for critical interactions and allows you to move UI controls away from the main layout of your app so that you use the screen real estate to give users access to more of their data. In this section, I am going to get into the detail of the AppBar, showing you how to create, populate, and manage the UI control and how to respond to user commands, and tell you everything you need to know to get the best from AppBars in your app. The place to start is, naturally enough, by creating an AppBar, which is done through the WinJS.UI.AppBar object. The easiest way to create an AppBar is to do so declaratively, by adding data attributes to standard HTML elements. AppBars are typically added to the master page so that you don't have to set them up again each time you import new content. With this in mind, Listing 7-5 shows the addition of an AppBar to the default.html file.

■ **Note** The WinJS.UI.AppBar object is an example of a WinJS UI control. The ones I cover in this part of the book are related to the fundamental layout and structure of an app. In Part 3 of this book, I cover the more general UI control objects and show you how to apply them.

Listing 7-5. Adding an AppBar to the default.html file

```html
<!DOCTYPE html>
<html>
<head>
    <meta charset="utf-8">
    <title>AppBars</title>

    <!-- WinJS references -->
    <link href="//Microsoft.WinJS.1.0/css/ui-dark.css" rel="stylesheet" />
    <script src="//Microsoft.WinJS.1.0/js/base.js"></script>
    <script src="//Microsoft.WinJS.1.0/js/ui.js"></script>

    <!-- AppBars references -->
    <link href="/css/default.css" rel="stylesheet">
    <script src="/js/default.js"></script>
</head>
<body>
    <div id="contentTarget"></div>

    <div id="appbar" data-win-control="WinJS.UI.AppBar">

        <button data-win-control="WinJS.UI.AppBarCommand"
            data-win-options="{id:'cmdBold', label:'Bold', icon:'bold',
                section:'selection', tooltip:'Bold', type: 'toggle'}">
        </button>

        <button data-win-control="WinJS.UI.AppBarCommand"
            data-win-options="{id:'cmdFont', label:'Font', icon:'font',
                section:'selection', tooltip:'Change Font'}">
        </button>

        <hr data-win-control="WinJS.UI.AppBarCommand"
            data-win-options="{type:'separator', section:'selection'}" />

        <button data-win-control="WinJS.UI.AppBarCommand"
            data-win-options="{id:'cmdCut', label:'Cut', icon:'cut',
                section:'selection', tooltip:'Cut'}">
        </button>

        <button data-win-control="WinJS.UI.AppBarCommand"
```

```
        data-win-options="{id:'cmdCut', label:'Paste', icon:'paste',
            section:'selection', tooltip:'Paste'}">
    </button>

    <button data-win-control="WinJS.UI.AppBarCommand"
        data-win-options="{id:'cmdRemove',label:'Remove', icon:'remove',
            section:'global', tooltip:'Remove item'}">
    </button>

    <button data-win-control="WinJS.UI.AppBarCommand"
        data-win-options="{id:'cmdAdd', label:'Add', icon:'add',
            section:'global', tooltip:'Add item'}">
    </button>
    </div>
</body>
</html>
```

There is a lot going on in these elements, which I'll break down step by step. Figure 7-2 shows the AppBar that these elements create, which gives you some context as I explain how the various parts fit together. I have cut out the middle of the AppBar in the figure to make it easier to see the individual buttons.

■ **Tip**   The AppBar won't appear if you run the example at this point. You need to apply the changes shown in Listing 7-6 first.

Figure 7-2. The AppBar created by the elements in Listing 7-5

Declaring the AppBar Control

The starting point for an AppBar is to create a WinJS.UI.AppBar object, which I do using the data-win-control attribute on a div element, like this:

```
...
<div id="appbar" data-win-control="WinJS.UI.AppBar">
    // ...elements removed for brevity
</div>
...
```

This is the same UI control pattern that I used in the previous chapters and that is used throughout WinJS. You take a regular HTML element, a div element in the case of AppBars, and use the data-win-control attribute to indicate which user control you want to create. As I mentioned previously, the

Windows runtime doesn't search for these attributes automatically, which is why I have added a call to the `WinJS.UI.processAll` method in the `default.js` file, as shown in Listing 7-6. Without the call to the `processAll` method, the AppBar control won't be applied to the `div` element and the AppBar won't pop up when the user right-clicks or swipes.

Listing 7-6. Calling the processAll method to apply WinJS UI controls

```
(function () {
    "use strict";

    var app = WinJS.Application;

    WinJS.Navigation.addEventListener("navigating", function (e) {
        WinJS.Utilities.empty(contentTarget);
        WinJS.UI.Pages.render(e.detail.location, contentTarget);
    });

    app.onactivated = function (eventObject) {
        WinJS.UI.processAll().then(function() {
            WinJS.Navigation.navigate("page1.html");
        });
    };
    app.start();
})();
```

The `processAll` method processes the elements in the background and returns a `WinJS.Promise` object that is fulfilled when the processing is finished and all of the UI controls have been created. I introduced the `Promise` object in Chapter 5 and spoke briefly about using the then method to defer an operation until the `Promise` has been fulfilled. I cover the `Promise` object in depth in Chapter 9.

■ **Tip** Notice that I don't have to handle the swipe or right-click to show the AppBar control myself. This is wired up by default in an app so that the AppBar (and the NavBar, which I introduce later in the chapter) appear automatically.

I have put the to the `WinJS.Navigation.navigate` method in a function that I pass to the then method of the `Promise` returned by the `processAll` method. This is important. Although I set up the AppBar in the master page, I want to manage and control it from within the content page (I'll explain why and show you how to do this later in this chapter). I have no way to signal to imported content that the HTML elements in the master page have been processed and converted into WinJS UI controls, which is significant because I don't want the code in that content to start accessing control features before they are ready (this would cause exceptions to be thrown). The solution is to ensure that the `processAll` method has finished its work before importing the content, and that means using the WinJS `Promise`, as shown in the code.

■ **Tip** I say that WinJS controls are created from or applied to HTML elements, but all that's really happening is that WinJS formats the HTML elements with some CSS and, in some cases, adds some new elements. The technique is very similar to JavaScript-based UI libraries, such as jQuery UI and jQuery Mobile. I don't want to give you the impression that there is some kind of magic going on—for the most part, the WinJS controls are standard HTML and CSS. In some cases, the JavaScript code uses some Windows API calls, but that is pretty rare, and these are the same Windows APIs that you can use in your code (and that I describe throughout this book).

Adding Buttons to the AppBar

You present commands to the user by adding button elements to the AppBar with a data-win-control value of WinJS.UI.AppBarCommand, like this:

```
...
<button data-win-control="WinJS.UI.AppBarCommand"
    data-win-options="{id:'cmdBold', label:'Bold', icon:'bold',
        section:'selection', tooltip:'Bold', type: 'toggle'}">
</button>
...
```

You supply the configuration for the AppBar button through the data-win-options attribute, using a JSON string that contains the configuration information. The properties in the JSON string correspond to properties in the WinJS.UI.AppBarCommand object. I have summarized these configuration properties in Table 7-2 and I describe each of them in the sections below. Understanding these options is the key to getting the most out of AppBars.

Table 7-2. Configuration Properties for the AppBarCommand Control

Property	Description
id	Identifies the command that the button relates to
label	Sets a text label displayed under the button icon
icon	Sets the icon using a value from the AppBarIcon enumeration
section	Specifies whether the button is part of the selection or global sections of the AppBar
tooltip	Specifies a pop-up tool tip that is displayed when the mouse hovers over the button
type	Specifies the command type

Setting the Command ID

The id property identifies the command that the button relates to. There are no predefined commands, so you are free to assign id values that make sense in the context of your app. There are two uses for this property. First, when responding to user interaction, you use the id property to determine which command has been requested. Second, you use the ids to tell the AppBar which commands to display when you import content. I demonstrate both uses in the Responding to Commands section later in this chapter.

Configuring the Appearance of the Command Button

The icon, label, and tooltip properties define the appearance of the button. The icon property specifies the glyph used in the button. Glyphs are produced by displaying a character from the Segoe UI Symbol font, which is part of Windows 8. You can see the range of icons in the font using the Character Map tool that is included in Windows 8.

The value for the icon property is usually a value from the WinJS.UI.AppBarIcon enumeration, which provides a convenient mapping scheme for character codes. The bold value assigned to the button I showed you previously equates to the WinJS.UI.AppBarIcon.bold property, which is defined in the base.js file added to apps by Visual Studio as:

```
...
bold:              "\uE19B"
...
```

(You can see the contents of base.js by expanding References in the Solution Explorer Window.) You don't need to specify the namespace or object name for the character that you want—just bold will do. If you want to use a character for which there isn't a value in the enumeration, you can simply use the font character code instead of the name (i.e., \uE19B instead of bold).

■ **Tip** If you can't find an icon that suits your needs, you can set the icon property to the name of a PNG file that contains a custom icon.

The label and tooltip properties specify the string that is displayed beneath the icon in the button and the string that is displayed when the mouse hovers over a button or when the user slides his finger over the button without releasing it. The value of these properties is not inferred automatically based on the icon value and you are free to use any text that makes sense in your app. However, it is important that you don't assign new meanings to well-known icons, because the values you assign to the label and tooltip properties won't always be displayed to the user. In the button I showed you in the code fragment, I set icon to bold and label and tooltip both to Bold, which produced the buttons shown in Figure 7-3.

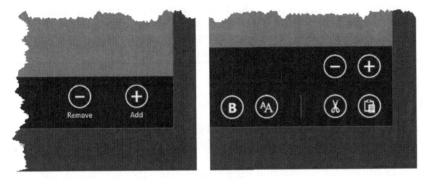

Figure 7-3. Configuring the appearance of command buttons in the AppBar

The left side of the figure shows part of the AppBar as it is displayed in the full-screen landscape view, where the label text is displayed (I have shown only one side of the AppBar and the other buttons are off to the side). The right side of the figure shows the AppBar in the snapped view. The label text isn't displayed in this view because the AppBar has adapted to the reduced screen space by omitting the label and packing and stacking the icons closer together. You can't rely on the tooltip value to help the user figure out what a button will do, either, because they are not shown on touch-only devices. You can rely on the clarity of the icon *only* to communicate the meaning of a button—which makes it important to make an appropriate selection and respect the convention associated with widely known icons.

■ **Tip** If you find yourself struggling to communicate a command via an icon, you may want to stop and think about the design of your app. The Windows app user experience is about interactions being immediate and obvious, and it may be that you are trying to pack too much meaning into a single command. You may be able to create a better experience for your users by breaking the action into a sequence of commands or using context menus (which I describe in Part 3 of this book).

Grouping and Separating Buttons

There are two sections in the AppBar: The *selection* section occupies the left-hand side of the AppBar and contains commands that apply to the data or object the user has selected. The *global* section occupies the right-hand side of the AppBar and contains commands that are always available and are not affected by individual selections. The section property determines which section a button is assigned to, and the supported values are, as you might expect, selection and global.

When you create an AppBar, you populate each section with all of the commands that your app supports in all situations. You then change the set of commands and the state of individual commands to match the state of the app—I'll show you how to do this shortly.

SELECTING LOCATIONS FOR GLOBAL COMMANDS

Microsoft has defined some rules for how some global commands are located on the AppBar. If your app has a New or Add command, then it should be placed as the right-most global command and it should be displayed with the add glyph (and this glyph should not be used for any other command).

The command placed to the left of New or Add should be the counterpart. If your app deals with data or objects that have a life outside of the app (such as photos, which reside on device storage and can be accessed by other apps), then you must use a Delete command (a label value of Delete and an icon value of delete). If your app deals only with its own data, then you should use a Remove command (a label value of Remove and an icon value of remove). If the action will delete multiple items, then you should use a Clear command (a label value of Clear and an icon value of clear).

Setting the Command Type

There are four types of command that can be added to the AppBar, as specified by the type property—these types correspond to the values button, toggle, separator, and flyout. If you don't explicitly set a value for the type property, then the button value is used.

The button and toggle types create regular buttons that trigger events when they are clicked. The difference between them is that the toggle type creates a toggle button that has on and off states. The Bold button that I focused on earlier is a toggle command and you can see how the off and on states are displayed in Figure 7-4. I'll show you shortly how to check and change the toggle state programmatically.

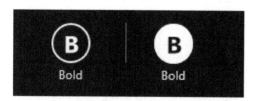

Figure 7-4. The different states of a toggle command shown with a separator

The figure also shows the third kind of command you can add to an AppBar: the separator type. (This can be hard to make out on the page—the separator is a slim vertical bar and is best seen by running the example.) The other three command types are created from button elements, but you create a separator from an hr element, like this:

```
...
<hr data-win-control="WinJS.UI.AppBarCommand"
    data-win-options="{type:'separator', section:'selection'}" />
...
```

Commands are added to their section in the AppBar in the order they are defined in HTML, so you can simply add separators between the button elements that represent other types of commands as you define them. The final command type, flyout, is used to associate a command with a pop-up. I'll show you how to use this kind of command in the Using Flyouts section later in this chapter.

Responding to Commands

You respond to commands from the AppBar by registering a handler function for the click event on the AppBar HTML element. The best place to handle the click event is in the content that you import into the master page—this allows you to respond to commands appropriately for different content without resorting to tight-coupling. Listing 7-7 shows the addition of a script element to the page1.html file that responds to the commands in the AppBar.

Listing 7-7. Responding to commands in the page1.html file

```
<!DOCTYPE html>
<html>
    <head>
        <title></title>
        <script>
            WinJS.UI.Pages.define("page1.html", {
                ready: function () {
                    appbar.addEventListener("click", function (e) {
                        command.innerText = e.target.winControl.label;
                    });
                }
            });
        </script>
    </head>
    <body>
        <div id="page1Container" class="container">
            <h1>This is Page 1</h1>
            <span>Command: <span id="command">None</span></span>
        </div>
    </body>
</html>
```

I use the addEventListener method to register a handler function for the click event to the div element to which the AppBar control has been applied. This relies on the way that DOM events are propagated up through the hierarchy of elements in a document and means that I can avoid having to find individual command button elements and deal with them directly. The important statement in the script element in the listing is this one:

```
...
document.getElementById("command").innerText = e.target.winControl.label;
...
```

This statement takes the value of the label property of the command that was clicked and uses it to set the innerText property of the span element in the markup. When the WinJS.UI.processAll method processes an element with a data-win-control attribute, it attaches a winControl property to the object that represents the element in the DOM. The winControl property returns an object that allows you to work with the features and capabilities of the UI control.

■ **Tip**   Notice that I have used e.target to locate the element that the click event originated from. The event comes from the command, rather than the AppBar, so you need to be sure to work on the correct element.

The object returned by the winControl property is the one specified by the data-win-control attribute. In the case of an AppBar command, the winControl is a WinJS.UI.AppBarCommand object, and I can access all of the properties and methods that are defined by this object. In this case, I have read the label property to get the text string displayed under the command button.

The AppBarCommand object is pretty simple and most of the members it defines correspond to the configuration options I described earlier in the chapter (id, icon, section, type, and so on). There are some additional properties and I have described them in Table 7-3, although I don't explain a couple of them in detail until later in the chapter.

Table 7-3. Additional Properties for the AppBarCommand Object

Property	Description
disabled	Gets or sets the disabled status for the button
element	Returns the HTMLElement that the AppBarCommand was applied to (the button or hr element with the data-win-control attribute)
hidden	Returns true if the command is hidden
selected	For toggle commands, returns true if the command is toggled on and false otherwise

Adapting the AppBar to Specific Content

When declaring your AppBar, you add all the commands that you will need in your app and then specify which ones are shown to the user when you import content into the master page. This allows you to have one set of consistent elements for the AppBar and still adapt to the state of your app so that the capabilities of imported content are reflected in the commands in the AppBar.

It is important to differentiate between commands that are *disabled* and those that are *hidden*. Disabled commands are still present on the AppBar, but the command button is grayed out, indicating that the command is not applicable now but that it might be later—perhaps when the user has selected an object or data item, for example.

A hidden command is removed from the AppBar entirely—you hide commands when there are no circumstances in which the command is applicable for the current content. You hide and disable commands using the winControl object of the element to which the WinJS.UI.AppBar control was applied. In Listing 7-8, I have added to the page1.html file to configure the AppBar commands.

Listing 7-8. Tailoring the AppBar commands to match the capabilities of imported content

```
<!DOCTYPE html>
<html>
    <head>
        <title></title>
```

```
<script>
    WinJS.UI.Pages.define("page1.html", {
        ready: function () {

            appbar.winControl.showOnlyCommands(["cmdBold", "cmdFont", "cmdAdd"]);
            appbar.winControl.getCommandById("cmdBold").disabled = true;

            appbar.addEventListener("click", function (e) {
                command.innerText = e.target.winControl.label;
            });
        }
    });
</script>
</head>
<body>
    <div id="page1Container" class="container">
        <h1>This is Page 1</h1>
        <span>Command: <span id="command">None</span></span>
    </div>
</body>
</html>
```

Using the winControl property, I am able to access the methods and properties of the WinJS.UI.AppBar control. In this listing, I have used two of the methods available: the showOnlyCommands method takes an array of command id values and hides all of the commands that are not specified in the array. I use this method to hide all but the cmdBold, cmdFont, and cmdAdd commands.

The getCommandById accepts an id value and returns the corresponding AppBarCommand object. In the listing, I locate the AppBarCommand object for the cmdBold command and set the disabled property to true (which, as I described in the previous section, keeps the button on the AppBar but prevents it from being used). You can see the effect of these methods on the AppBar in Figure 7-5.

Figure 7-5. Tailoring the AppBar to imported content

I like using the showOnlyCommands method because it means that I provide a definitive list of the commands I want to be displayed, but there are other methods in the AppBar object that you can use to prepare the AppBar for your content. In Table 7-4 I have described the complete set of methods that you can use to show, hide, and locate commands.

Table 7-4. WinJS.UI.AppBar Methods for Tailoring Commands

Methods	Description
getCommandById(id)	Returns the AppBarCommand object that corresponds to the command id passed as the argument
hideCommands(idArray)	Hides the commands specified in the array of command id values.
showCommands(idArray)	Shows the commands specified in the array of command id values.
showOnlyCommands(idArray)	Shows only the commands specified in the array of command id values and hides all of the other commands in the AppBar

Using Flyouts

Basic commands can be handled with the button or toggle command types, but for complex commands you need to use the flyout type, which links the command with a pop-up window known as a *flyout*. Flyouts are created using WinJS.UI.Flyout UI control, and in this section I'll show you how to create and use flyouts and how to associate them with your AppBar commands.

■ **Tip**   In this section, I explain how to use the Flyout control with AppBars, but you can also use the Flyout to create general-purpose pop-ups. See Chapter 12 for more details and examples.

Declaring the Flyout

The best place to declare your flyouts is in your master page so that the same set of elements is available throughout the app. Flyouts are applied to div elements by setting the data-win-control attribute to WinJS.UI.Flyout. You can set the content of the div element as you see fit to accommodate the needs of your app—the role of the Flyout UI control is to handle the pop-up window, and there are no constraints on what you present to the user. Listing 7-9 shows a simple flyout that I added to the default.html file.

Listing 7-9. Adding a flyout to the default.html file

```
<!DOCTYPE html>
<html>
<head>
    <meta charset="utf-8">
    <title>AppBars</title>

    <!-- WinJS references -->
    <link href="//Microsoft.WinJS.1.0/css/ui-dark.css" rel="stylesheet" />
    <script src="//Microsoft.WinJS.1.0/js/base.js"></script>
    <script src="//Microsoft.WinJS.1.0/js/ui.js"></script>

    <!-- AppBars references -->
    <link href="/css/default.css" rel="stylesheet">
    <script src="/js/default.js"></script>
</head>
<body>
    <div id="contentTarget"></div>
```

```html
<div id="appbar" data-win-control="WinJS.UI.AppBar">
    <button data-win-control="WinJS.UI.AppBarCommand"
        data-win-options="{id:'cmdBold', label:'Bold', icon:'bold',
            section:'selection', tooltip:'Bold', type: 'toggle'}">
    </button>

    <button data-win-control="WinJS.UI.AppBarCommand"
        data-win-options="{id:'cmdFont', label:'Font', icon:'font',
            section:'selection', tooltip:'Change Font', type: 'flyout',
            flyout: 'fontFlyout'}">
    </button>

    <!-- other commands removed for brevity -->

</div>

<div id="fontFlyout" data-win-control="WinJS.UI.Flyout">
    <h3>Select a Font</h3>
    <select id="fontSelect">
        <option>First Font</option>
        <option>Second Font</option>
        <option>Third Font</option>
    </select>
</div>
</body>
</html>
```

In this listing I have defined a flyout that contains a simple header and a select element with three option elements. To associate the flyout with a command, I set the command's type property to flyout and the flyout property to the id of the div element to which the WinJS.UI.Flyout control has been applied.

The elements that form the flyout are hidden until the user clicks or touches the associated command button. At that point, the flyout is displayed above the button, as shown in Figure 7-6. Flyouts are *lightly dismissed*, meaning that they will be hidden again if the user clicks outside the area of the screen that the flyout occupies. This means that you don't have to add any kind of cancel button to remove the flyout.

 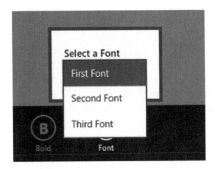

Figure 7-6. Using a flyout with an AppBar command

Styling Flyouts

The default style for flyouts is pretty plain. If you want to make your flyouts fit in with the visual theme of the rest of your app, you can override the CSS win-flyout class. Listing 7-10 shows how I have overridden this style in the default.css file to change the background color and apply a border. You will need to add these styles to the default.css file if you are following this example.

Listing 7-10. Styling flyouts through the win-flyout class

```
...
div.win-flyout {
    background-color: #4FCB6A;
    border: thick solid black;
}

div.win-flyout select {
    border: medium solid black;
}
...
```

Responding to Flyout Interactions

Declaring and displaying flyouts is only part of the process. You also need to respond to the user's interaction with the elements you add to the flyout. The best place to handle the flyout interaction is in the JavaScript code for the master page—this allows you create a consistent treatment for a flyout that is applied irrespective of the content that is being displayed.

However, you need to use a *view model* and *data binding* to make this approach work without creating a tight-coupling problem between the master page and the imported content. I don't describe view model and data binding until Chapter 8, so I am going to accept the need for the master page to have detailed knowledge of the content so I can demonstrate handling the flyout and show you how to resolve the tight-coupling problem later in the book. Listing 7-11 shows the additions to the default.js file to respond to the flyout.

Listing 7-11. Responding to a flyout

```
(function () {
    "use strict";

    var app = WinJS.Application;

    WinJS.Navigation.addEventListener("navigating", function (e) {
        WinJS.Utilities.empty(contentTarget);
        WinJS.UI.Pages.render(e.detail.location, contentTarget);
    });

    app.onactivated = function (eventObject) {

        WinJS.UI.processAll().then(function() {
            WinJS.Navigation.navigate("page1.html");

            fontSelect.addEventListener("change", function (e) {
```

```
                command.innerText = this.value;
                fontFlyout.winControl.hide();
            });
        });
    };
    app.start();
})();
```

I have handled the change event from the `select` element just as I would in a regular web app, and I set the `innerText` property of the `span` element defined in page1.html to the value the user has selected. This is the tightly coupled part—the code in the `default.js` file should not know about the structure and nature of the content in the page1.html (but as I say, you can address this using a view model and data binding, which I describe in Chapter 8).

The key part of this example is this statement:

```
...
fontFlyout.winControl.hide();
...
```

Once I have processed the user interaction, I locate the element to which the `Flyout` control has been applied and call the `hide` method through the `winControl` property. The flyout light-dismiss feature applies only when the user clicks outside the pop-up and not when the user has performed an action using the controls it contains. This means that you must explicitly remove the pop-up from the display (using the `hide` method) at the completion of a successful interaction.

For this simple flyout, I can respond as soon as the user makes a selection using the `select` element, but for more complex interactions you can rely on an `OK` button or some other kind of explicit signal that the user is done.

Creating Navigation Commands

The NavBar slides down from the top of the screen and acts as a counterpoint to the AppBar. Whereas the AppBar provides the commands that operate on the data and objects in the current content, the NavBar provides the means to move around the different areas of the app. NavBars are created using the same `WinJS.UI.AppBar` UI control as AppBars, but you have more flexibility in the way that you present commands to the user. In this section, I'll show you how to add and manage a NavBar in your app. To demonstrate navigation controls, I have added two new files to the project, called page2.html and page3.html. You can see page2.html in Listing 7-12.

Listing 7-12. The page2.html file

```
<!DOCTYPE html>
<html>
    <head>
        <title></title>
    </head>
    <body>
        <div id="page2Container" class="container">
            <h1>This is Page 2</h1>
        </div>
    </body>
</html>
```

These files will initially be used to demonstrate navigation, but later in the chapter I'll use the page2.html file to demonstrate how to create a custom set of navigation controls. You can see the contents of page3.html in Listing 7-13.

Listing 7-13. The page3.html file

```
<!DOCTYPE html>
<html>
    <head>
        <title></title>
    </head>
    <body>
        <div class="container">
            <h1>This is Page 3</h1>
        </div>
    </body>
</html>
```

Using a Standard NavBar

Although I find it easier to define the AppBar in the master page, I tend to take a different approach when it comes to the NavBar. I create a separate file that contains the NavBar elements and import it into each content file using the WinJS.UI.Pages namespace, employing the techniques I described in Chapter 5. In this section, I am going to show you a standard NavBar, which follows the same command-based approach as I used for the AppBar. Listing 7-14 shows the contents of the standardNavBar.html file that I added to the example project using the Visual Studio HTML Page item template. (Later in this chapter, I'll show you a different NavBar design.)

Listing 7-14. The contents of the standardNavbar.html file

```
<!DOCTYPE html>
<html>
    <head>
        <title></title>
        <script>
            WinJS.UI.Pages.define("standardNavBar.html", {
                ready: function () {
                    navbar.addEventListener("click", function (e) {
                        var navTarget = e.target.winControl.id
                            == "cmdPage2" ? "page2.html" : "page3.html";
                        WinJS.Navigation.navigate(navTarget);
                    });
                }
            });
        </script>
    </head>
    <body>
        <div id="navbar" data-win-control="WinJS.UI.AppBar"
            data-win-options="{placement:'top'}">

            <button data-win-control="WinJS.UI.AppBarCommand"
```

```
            data-win-options="{id:'cmdPage2', label:'Page 2', icon:'\u0032',
                section:'selection', tooltip:'Page2'}">
        </button>

        <button data-win-control="WinJS.UI.AppBarCommand"
            data-win-options="{id:'cmdPage3', label:'Page 3', icon:'\u0033',
                section:'selection', tooltip:'Page3'}">
        </button>
    </div>
    </body>
</html>
```

The NavBar follows the command pattern I used for the AppBar with two buttons that navigate to the page2.html and page3.html files. When you use a WinJS.UI.AppBar control as a NavBar, you must set the placement property to top using the data-win-options attribute, as I did in the listing.

The placement property is how you differentiate between WinJS.UI.AppBar controls being used as AppBars and those being used as NavBars. When the user clicks or touches one of the command buttons, I receive the click event and use the command's id property to work out which page the user wants to navigate to and pass this to the WinJS.Navigation.navigate method.

Applying a Standard NavBar

I want to use the standard NavBar in the page1.html file and you can see how I do this in Listing 7-15.

Listing 7-15. Using the standard NavBar in the page1.html file

```
<!DOCTYPE html>
<html>
    <head>
        <title></title>
        <script>
            WinJS.UI.Pages.define("page1.html", {
                ready: function () {

                    appbar.winControl.showOnlyCommands(["cmdBold", "cmdFont", "cmdAdd"]);
                    appbar.winControl.getCommandById("cmdBold").disabled = true;
                    appbar.addEventListener("click", function (e) {
                        command.innerText = e.target.winControl.label;
                    });
                    WinJS.UI.Pages.render("standardNavBar.html", navBarContainer);
                }
            });
        </script>
    </head>
    <body>
        <div id="page1Container" class="container">
            <h1>This is Page 1</h1>
            <span>Command: <span id="command">None</span></span>
        </div>
    </body>
</html>
```

This is the standard use of the render method, with the exception that the element I am importing the content into is not defined in the page1.html file. I am going to use multiple styles of NavBar in this example app, and that requires some shuffling of elements, the first of which is to have a common element in the master page into which content can load its required NavBar. You can see how I have added this element to the default.html file in Listing 7-16. (And let me stress again that I demonstrate some much better techniques for handling this kind of situation when I introduce view models in Chapter 8.)

Listing 7-16. Adding a common element to default.html into which the NavBar will be imported

```
...
<body>
    <div id="contentTarget"></div>
    <div id="navBarContainer"></div>
    <div id="appbar" data-win-control="WinJS.UI.AppBar">

        <!-- commands removed for brevity -->

    </div>

    <div id="fontFlyout" data-win-control="WinJS.UI.Flyout">
        <h3>Select a Font</h3>
        <select id="fontSelect">
            <option>First Font</option>
            <option>Second Font</option>
            <option>Third Font</option>
        </select>
    </div>
</body>
...
```

When the page1.html file is imported, it will import the contents of the standardNavBar.html file and insert them into the common element in the default.html file. You can see the effect in Figure 7-7. The NavBar is shown at the same time as the AppBar and in response to the same interactions. Once again, I don't need to handle any events to make the NavBar appear—this is wired up automatically when the control is applied and both NavBar and AppBar are shown when the user swipes or right-clicks.

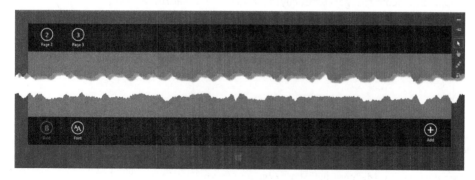

Figure 7-7. Adding a NavBar to the example app

The detail can be hard to make out in the figure, but you can see the two command buttons I added close-up in Figure 7-8. There are no predefined icons for numerals, so I set the icon values for the commands to be the character codes from the Segoe UI Symbol font (\u0032 and \u0033). Clicking on the commands will navigate to the corresponding page.

Figure 7-8. The commands on the standard NavBar buttons

Using a Custom NavBar

Using a series of buttons to represent commands on a NavBar doesn't always make sense. In these situations, you can define a custom layout for the WinJS.UI.AppBar control. Listing 7-17 shows the contents of the customNavBar.html file, which I added to the project using the Visual Studio HTML Page item template.

Listing 7-17. The contents of the customNavBar.html file

```
<!DOCTYPE html>
<html>
    <head>
        <title></title>
        <script>
            WinJS.UI.Pages.define("customNavBar.html", {
                ready: function (element, title) {
                    navBarTitle.innerText = title;
                    navBarBack.addEventListener("click", function () {
                        WinJS.Navigation.back();
                    });
                }
            });
        </script>
    </head>
    <body>
        <div id="navbar" data-win-control="WinJS.UI.AppBar"
            data-win-options="{placement:'top', layout:'custom'}">
            <div id="navBarContent">
                <button id="navBarBack" class="win-backbutton"></button>
                <h1 id="navBarTitle">Page Title</h1>
            </div>
        </div>
    </body>
</html>
```

This is another self-contained NavBar with the HTML elements and the code that responds to them defined in the same file. The difference is that I have set the layout property to custom in the data-win-options attribute. The `custom` value tells the `WinJS.UI.AppBar` control that you don't want the standard command-based layout and that you will provide and manage the elements in the NavBar yourself.

■ **Caution**   You *can* use custom layouts with AppBars as well as NavBars—but it is generally a bad idea. The navigation structures of apps can vary and the user will expect the NavBars to reflect the distinct characteristics of your app. Commands, on the other hand, should be consistent and be applied using the conventions I described earlier. The user will expect commands in the AppBar and for them to be laid out and respond in a manner that is consistent with all other Windows apps. There is something wrong with your design if you have to express the unique nature of your app using a nonstandard AppBar.

As the listing shows, I have populated the NavBar with a `button` and an `h1` element. I have used a convenient Windows CSS class called `win-backbutton`, which creates a button with an arrow contained in a circular border. The elements in the NavBar are contained within a `div` element. I adopted this structure so that I can easily style the elements—you can see the styles I added to the `default.css` file in Listing 7-18.

Listing 7-18. Styles in the default.css file for the custom NavBar layout

```
...
#navBarContent {
    display: -ms-flexbox;
    -ms-flex-direction: row;
    -ms-flex-align: start;
    width: 100%;
    height: 80px;
}

#navBarBack {
    margin-top: 18px;
    margin-left: 20px;
}

#navBarTitle {
    padding-top: 3px;
    margin-left: 20px;
}
...
```

I have used a CSS flexbox layout to position the elements. As you will have realized, I use this layout often, because it fits very well with the general style of a Windows app, where controls flow along a common axis—you'll see this visual theme more clearly when I describe the semantic zoom concept in Chapter 16.

Applying a Custom NavBar

The process of applying a NavBar with a custom layout is just the same as for a regular NavBar, except you must ensure that the elements in the layout are properly configured and prepared. For my custom NavBar layout, I need to set the content of the `h1` element, which I do by passing a data object through the render method so that it can be used by the ready function defined in the customNavBar.html file. Listing 7-19 shows the page2.html file, which uses the custom NavBar.

Listing 7-19. The contents of the page2.html file

```
<!DOCTYPE html>
<html>
    <head>
        <title></title>
        <script>
            WinJS.UI.Pages.define("page2.html", {
                ready: function () {
                    WinJS.UI.Pages.render("customNavBar.html", navBarContainer,
                        "Page 2");
                }
            });
        </script>
    </head>
    <body>
        <div id="page2Container" class="container">
            <h1>This is Page 2</h1>
        </div>
    </body>
</html>
```

I don't need to listen for the click event for the button in the NavBar because it is handled in the customNavPage.html file using the WinJS.Navigation API.

■ **Tip**   I have also added page3.html to the project, but it is essentially the same as page2.html and so I won't waste space by listing the contents.

Tweaking the NavBar and AppBar Behavior

The WinJS API expects there to be only one NavBar in an app. When the WinJS.UI.processAll method processes an element to which the WinJS.UI.AppBar control has been applied, it moves it out of its original place in the DOM so that it isn't affected by changes in the imported content. This is a problem for my example, because I want to switch freely between NavBars to reflect the content I am displaying.

I have a second issue to resolve as well. The AppBar and NavBar are not hidden automatically when the user navigates to another part of the app. I am going to remove the NavBar, so I don't have to worry about hiding it—but I do need to make sure the AppBar is hidden; otherwise, it will just be lingering around the screen and obscure my newly imported content.

To resolve both of these problems, I have added some code to the function in the default.js file that responds to navigation requests. You can see the changes in Listing 7-20.

Listing 7-20. Removing the NavBar and hiding the AppBar in response to a navigation event

```
(function () {
    "use strict";
```

```
    var app = WinJS.Application;

    WinJS.Navigation.addEventListener("navigating", function (e) {

        if (window.navbar) {
            window.navbar.parentNode.removeChild(navbar);
        }

        if (window.appbar) {
            window.appbar.winControl.hide();
        }

        WinJS.Utilities.empty(contentTarget);
        WinJS.UI.Pages.render(e.detail.location, contentTarget);
    });

    app.onactivated = function (eventObject) {
        WinJS.UI.processAll().then(function () {
            WinJS.Navigation.navigate("page1.html");

            fontSelect.addEventListener("change", function (e) {
                command.innerText = this.value;
                fontFlyout.winControl.hide();
            });
        });
    };
    app.start();
})();
```

Before I navigate to the requested content, I remove the element whose id is navbar and hide the appbar element via its winControl. This gives me the app state I require so that the new content can load its own NavBar and isn't obscured by the AppBar. You can see the effect created by the NavBars in Figure 7-9.

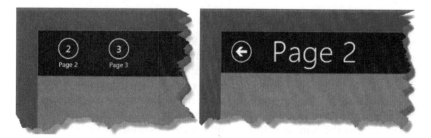

Figure 7-9. Using two styles of NavBar in an app

Animating the Navigation Transition

The last thing I am going to do in this chapter is to animate the transition from one page of content to another. The WinJS.UI.Animation namespace defines a number of animations that you apply to elements at key transitions in app state. I'll show you these animations as I describe the functionality they relate to—in this chapter, the relevant animations are applied when a content page leaves the display and when another arrives. I explain the animations fully in Chapter 18, but I just want to provide a quick overview here.

Content transitions in an app can happen so quickly that the human eye won't always detect them—especially if the two content pages involved share common visual cues, such as color and typography. You want your user to be aware that the content has changed as a result of clicking or touching a navigation command. If it isn't obvious, you will break the fluid interaction model that good apps possess and cause the user to take a second to check that the action he expected has been performed.

You let the user know that there has been a change with visual signals. I have used different background colors for the content pages in the example, which can be a very useful and powerful signal, especially if colors are used consistently throughout an app to indicate different functional areas. Another powerful visual signal is an animation. Listing 7-21 shows how I have added animations to the navigation event handler function in the default.js file—applying the animations in this function means that they will be applied consistently throughout the app.

Listing 7-21. Applying navigation animations to the example app

```
(function () {
    "use strict";

    var app = WinJS.Application;

    WinJS.Navigation.addEventListener("navigating", function (e) {

        if (window.navbar) {
            window.navbar.parentNode.removeChild(navbar);
        }

        if (window.appbar) {
            window.appbar.winControl.hide();
        }

        // These statements are commented out
        //WinJS.Utilities.empty(contentTarget);
        //WinJS.UI.Pages.render(e.detail.location, contentTarget);

        WinJS.UI.Animation.exitPage(contentTarget.children).then(function () {
            WinJS.Utilities.empty(contentTarget);
            WinJS.UI.Pages.render(e.detail.location, contentTarget).then(function () {
                return WinJS.UI.Animation.enterPage(contentTarget.children)
            });
        });
    });

    app.onactivated = function (eventObject) {
        WinJS.UI.processAll().then(function () {
            WinJS.Navigation.navigate("page1.html");
        });
    };

    app.start();
})();
```

The two animation methods that I have used in this listing are `exitPage` and `enterPage`. The names explain what each animation is intended for, and the argument for both methods is one or more elements that require animation. For simplicity, I pass the result of the `children` property of the element that hosts the imported content in the master page.

Notice that there are no options to configure the style or duration for these animations. By using these methods, you apply the standard page transition animations, which are the same for all Windows apps. This is a great approach because a lot of developers who are perfectly sensible and rational people go a little crazy when given an animation library to play with and tend to forget that animations are to help the user.

I can't show you the animations in screenshots, so you should run the example app to see the effect. The animations triggered by the `exitPage` and `enterPage` methods are brief, simple, and effective. They are simple enough and quick enough that they don't annoy the user when they see the animations for the 100th time, but they are substantial enough to trigger the realization that the content in the app has changed.

Summary

In this chapter, I have shown you how to use the `WinJS.UI.AppBar` control to create AppBars and NavBars. These are essential elements in the Windows user experience and they bring consistency and clarity to the interactions the user has with your app. That's not to say that using AppBars and NavBars should be constraining—even with the conventions that Microsoft has set out, there are many different ways to structure the command you present the user, and you have the option of using a custom NavBar layout to tailor the navigation experience you offer.

In the next chapter, I introduce the topics of *view models* and *data binding*. Now that we have looked at the fundamental structure of the layout and navigation of a Windows app, it is time to consider how you can take the same approach to structuring and displaying your app's data.

CHAPTER 8

■ ■ ■

View Models & Data Binding

In this chapter, I am going to introduce you to *view models* and *data binding*. These are two essential techniques that allow you create apps which scale well, are easy to develop and maintain, and respond fluidly to data changes.

You may already be familiar with models and view models from design patterns such as Model-View-Controller (MVC), Model-View-ViewModel (MVVM and Model-View-View Controller (MVVC). I am not going to get into the details of these patterns in this book. There is a lot of good information about MVC, MVVM and MVVC available, starting with Wikipedia, which has some very balanced and insightful descriptions.

I find the benefits of using a view model to be enormous and well worth considering for all but the simplest app projects, and I recommend you seriously consider following the same path. I am not a pattern zealot, and I firmly believe in taking the parts of patterns and techniques that solve real problems and adapting them to work in specific projects. To that end, you will find that I take a pretty liberal view of how a view model should be used.

The WinJS features that I describe in this chapter underpin some of the fundamental interaction models that Windows app support. To make sure I set a solid foundation for the more advanced features, I start this chapter slowly and gradually introduce the key concepts. Understanding these features is a precursor to getting the best out of advanced UI controls and concepts such as semantic zoom, which I describe in Chapter 16. Table 8-1 provides the summary for this chapter.

Table 8-1. Chapter Summary

Problem	Solution	Listing
Define and consume a view model	Create a globally available object using the WinJS.Namespace.define method and refer to the object properties as the authoritative source of data.	1-10
Create observable objects	Use the WinJS.Binding.as method.	11
Receive change notifications from observable objects	Use the bind method (which is added to the object by the as method)	12
Manually orchestrate updates for calculated properties in an observable object	Use the notify method to signal a change	13-15
Activate declarative bindings	Call the WinJS.Binding.processAll method	16

Problem	Solution	Listing
Create a declarative binding	Apply the data-win-bind attribute to an HTML element	17
Create observable arrays	Use the WinJS.Binding.List object	18
Receive change notifications from observable arrays	Listen for the iteminserted, itemchanged, itemremoved and itemmoved events.	19
Create reusable binding templates	Use the WinJS.Binding.Template control	20-21
Convert a view model value so that it can be used by a binding property	Use a binding converter	22-23
Create a binding converter that can adapt its result	Use an open binding converter	24

Revisiting the Example App

In this chapter, I continue to build on the AppBars project that I created in the previous chapter. As a reminder, this app introduced NavBars and AppBars and contained a number of simple content pages. I'll build on this foundation to show new app features.

Decoupling App Components

I am going to start by applying a view model to fix some of the shortcomings of the example app from Chapter 7. In doing this, I will show you my preferred structure for view model objects and demonstrate how simple a view model can be while still making the life of the developer easier.

■ **Note** As I said before, I take a very liberal position on what constitutes a view model and that includes data which is not presented to the user directly.

Defining the View Model

The most important characteristics of a view model are global availability and consistency. In a Windows app, the easiest way to create a basic view model is to use the WinJS.Namespace feature (which I introduced in Chapters 3 and 4) to create and export a view model object to the global namespace. Listing 8-1 shows the contents of the viewmodel.js file, which I added to the js folder of the AppBars example project.

Listing 8-1. The contents of the viewmodel.js file

```
(function () {
    "use strict";

    WinJS.Namespace.define("ViewModel.State", {
        appBarElement: null,
        navBarContainerElement: null,
        navBarControlElement: null
    });
```

```
WinJS.Namespace.define("ViewModel.UserData", {

    });
})();
```

I like to create a top-level namespace called ViewModel which contains nested namespaces that represent each broad category of data that I want to work with. In the example, I have defined two namespaces. ViewModel.State is where I define data about the app's state, which I would loosely define as the data that one part of the app needs to know in order to work smoothly with some other part of the app. This namespace contains three properties which I will use to address the lingering tight-coupling issues I introduced into the example app in Chapter 7.

The second namespace I defined in ViewModel.UserData. I use this namespace to store the data that the user cares about. This varies from app to app, but it includes any values that the user has entered and any data I have derived from those values. This is the front-of-house data, as opposed to the behind-the-scenes data I put in the ViewModel.State namespace. There are no properties in this namespace initially, but I'll add some later in this chapter.

■ **Tip**   JavaScript is a dynamic language, which means that I don't need to define properties in the view model before I assign values to them. I do so anyway because I want my view model definition to be the canonical reference for the data it contains; and, in my mind, that means defining properties and assigning null to them, rather than creating the properties elsewhere in the app at the point where I first use them.

My Windows apps generally have a view model that contains these two namespaces. I add others depending on which *contracts* my app supports. I explain contracts in Part IV of this book, but these two are the basic ones that I use most often. I separate out state data from user data because I find it makes it easier to determine which data to store persistently; something that I discuss further in Chapter 20.

Importing and Populating the View Model

The view mode is defined in a self-executing JavaScript function, so all I have to do to use it in the example app is to import the code with a script element and set the values for the properties the view model contains. I want the view model to be available from the moment the app starts and to be available irrespective of which content has been imported and displayed, which means that the script element needs to be placed in the default.html file in its role as the master page for the example app. Listing 8-2 shows the addition of the script element.

Listing 8-2. Using a script element to load the view model code

```
...
<head>
    <meta charset="utf-8">
    <title>AppBars</title>

    <!-- WinJS references -->
    <link href="//Microsoft.WinJS.1.0/css/ui-dark.css" rel="stylesheet" />
    <script src="//Microsoft.WinJS.1.0/js/base.js"></script>
    <script src="//Microsoft.WinJS.1.0/js/ui.js"></script>
```

```
    <!-- AppBars references -->
    <link href="/css/default.css" rel="stylesheet">
    <script src="/js/viewmodel.js"></script>
    <script src="/js/default.js"></script>
</head>
...
```

I have added the script element for the viewmodel.js file *before* the one for default.js, which gives me the opportunity to refer to the view model as I initialize the app. In the example app, I want to set values for the elements that will contain the AppBar and NavBar controls in the default.js file, as shown in Listing 8-3.

Listing 8-3. Populating the view model

```
(function () {
    "use strict";

    var app = WinJS.Application;

    WinJS.Navigation.addEventListener("navigating", function (e) {

        var navbar = ViewModel.State.navBarControlElement;
        if (navbar) {
            navbar.parentNode.removeChild(navbar);
        }

        if (ViewModel.State.appBarElement) {
            ViewModel.State.appBarElement.winControl.hide();
        }

        //WinJS.Utilities.empty(contentTarget);
        //WinJS.UI.Pages.render(e.detail.location, contentTarget);

        WinJS.UI.Animation.exitPage(contentTarget.children).then(function () {
            WinJS.Utilities.empty(contentTarget);
            WinJS.UI.Pages.render(e.detail.location, contentTarget).then(function () {
                return WinJS.UI.Animation.enterPage(contentTarget.children)
            });
        });
    });

    app.onactivated = function (eventObject) {
        WinJS.UI.processAll().then(function () {

            ViewModel.State.appBarElement = appbar;
            ViewModel.State.navBarContainerElement = navBarContainer;

            WinJS.Navigation.navigate("page1.html");

            fontSelect.addEventListener("change", function (e) {
                command.innerText = this.value;
```

```
                fontFlyout.winControl.hide();
            });
        });
    };
    app.start();
})();
```

Consuming the View Model

I set the values in the view model so that detail of the element structure in the default.html file isn't spread throughout the app. If I change the default.html file, I only have to reflect those changes in the default.js file and not hunt down and find all of the instances that the appbar and navBarContainer values are used. In the code contained in the content files, I can import the NavBar I want into the element listed in the view model, as illustrated by Listing 8-4 which shows the content of the page2.html file.

Listing 8-4. Using the view model to locate the element into which the NavBar is loaded

```
<!DOCTYPE html>
<html>
<head>
    <title></title>
    <script>
        WinJS.UI.Pages.define("page2.html", {
            ready: function () {
                WinJS.UI.Pages.render("customNavBar.html",
                    ViewModel.State.navBarContainerElement, "Page 2");
            }
        });
    </script>
</head>
<body>
    <div id="page2Container" class="container">
        <h1>This is Page 2</h1>
    </div>
</body>
</html>
```

Only two of the properties in the ViewModel.State namespace are set in the default.js file. The third property, navBarControlElement, is set by the code that sets up each style of NavBar used by the app, as illustrated in Listing 8-5, which shows the script element from the customNavBar.html file—this allows me to have a globally available property which is set to reflect the currently imported content.

Listing 8-5. Setting view model property values from within NavBar code

```
...
<script>
    WinJS.UI.Pages.define("customNavBar.html", {
        ready: function (element, title) {

            ViewModel.State.navBarControlElement = navbar;
```

```
        navBarTitle.innerText = title;
        navBarBack.addEventListener("click", function () {
            WinJS.Navigation.back();
        });
    }
});
</script>
...
```

This property is used in the navigation event handler function in default.js, and it means that NavBar controls don't have to be applied to an element whose id is navbar. Finally, I have applied the same change to the standardNavBar.html file, as shown in Listing 8-6.

Listing 8-6. Setting view model property values from within NavBar code

```
...
<script>
    WinJS.UI.Pages.define("standardNavBar.html", {
        ready: function () {

            ViewModel.State.navBarControlElement = navbar;

            navbar.addEventListener("click", function (e) {
                var navTarget = e.target.winControl.id
                    == "cmdPage2" ? "page2.html" : "page3.html";
                WinJS.Navigation.navigate(navTarget);
            });
        }
    });
</script>
...
```

The result of these changes is that the view model acts as a repository of information about the state and structure of the app, allowing the various components to work together without having prior knowledge of each other. When I make changes in my markup or code, I only need to make sure that the view model properties reflect the changes, rather than hunt down all of the dependencies and make the changes manually.

Separating Data from the Layout

The most value in a view model comes from separating the data in an app from the HTML, which presents it to the user. By combining a view model with *data binding*, you can make your app easier to develop, easier to test, and easier to maintain. I'll explain how data binding works later in this section, but first I am going to show you the problem that I am setting out to fix. Before I get started, I need to add some new CSS styles to the project for the elements that I am going to add in this chapter. To this end, I have created a new file called /css/extrastyles.css, the contents of which you can see in Listing 8-7. There are no new techniques in this CSS, and I am listing the new styles so you can see all aspects of the project.

Listing 8-7. The contents of the extrastyles.css file

```css
#page2BoxContainer {
    display: -ms-flexbox;
    -ms-flex-direction: row;
    -ms-flex-align: stretch;
    -ms-flex-pack: justify;
    margin-top: 20px;
}

div.page2box {
    width: 325px;
    padding: 10px;
    margin: 5px;
    border: medium solid white;
    background-color: gray;
    display: -ms-flexbox;
    -ms-flex-direction: column;
    -ms-flex-pack: center;
}

div.page2box * {
    display: block;
    margin: 4px;
    font-size: 18pt;
}
```

The classes and id attribute values referred to in these styles are for elements that I'll add shortly. To bring the contents of the file into the scope of the project, I added a link element to the default.html file as follows:

```html
...
<head>
    <meta charset="utf-8">
    <title>AppBars</title>

    <!-- WinJS references -->
    <link href="//Microsoft.WinJS.1.0/css/ui-dark.css" rel="stylesheet" />
    <script src="//Microsoft.WinJS.1.0/js/base.js"></script>
    <script src="//Microsoft.WinJS.1.0/js/ui.js"></script>

    <!-- AppBars references -->
    <link href="/css/default.css" rel="stylesheet">
    <link href="/css/extrastyles.css" rel="stylesheet">
    <script src="/js/viewmodel.js"></script>
    <script src="/js/default.js"></script>
</head>
...
```

Demonstrating the Problem

Without a view model, the authoritative source for an item of data is an HTML element; that is, when you want a data value, you have to locate the element that contains it in the DOM and read the value from the appropriate HTMLElement object. As a demonstration, I have made some changes to the page2.html file, as shown in Listing 8-8.

Listing 8-8. Using elements in the layout as the authoritative source of data values

```
<!DOCTYPE html>
<html>
    <head>
        <title></title>
        <script>
            WinJS.UI.Pages.define("page2.html", {
                ready: function () {
                    WinJS.UI.Pages.render("customNavBar.html",
                        ViewModel.State.navBarContainerElement, "Page 2");

                    wordbutton.addEventListener("click", function (e) {
                        var word = wordinput.value;
                        wordspan.innerText = word;
                        lengthspan.innerText = word.length;
                    });
                }
            });
        </script>
    </head>
    <body>
        <div id="page2Container" class="container">
            <h1>This is Page 2</h1>

            <div id="page2BoxContainer">
                <div id="p2left" class="page2box">
                    <input id="wordinput" placeholder="Enter a word">
                    <button id="wordbutton">OK</button>
                </div>

                <div id="p2middle" class="page2box">
                    <span>The word is:</span>
                    <span id="wordspan">????</span>
                </div>

                <div id="p2right" class="page2box">
                    <span>The length is:</span>
                    <span id="lengthspan">????</span>
                </div>
            </div>
        </div>
    </body>
</html>
```

This is a simple example. I have added three div elements to the layout. I have positioned them using the CSS flexbox layout and applied the classes I defined in the extrastyles.css file.

You can see the effect of the new markup and code in Figure 1. You enter a word into the input element in the left-hand panel and click on the OK button. The word you entered is displayed in the middle panel, and the length of the word is displayed in the right-hand panel. In the figure, I have entered the word *Apress*.

Figure 8-1. Adding three panels to the page2.html layout

The input element in this example is the authoritative source of the data that the user has entered. I need to read the value property of the HTMLElement object that represents the input element in the DOM if I want the word entered by the user. This approach had the benefit of simplicity, but it introduces some profound problems.

One problem is that the input element isn't *really* authoritative. You can be reasonably confident that the input element contains the user's data at the *precise moment* when the button is clicked, but at all other times the user could be in the process of changing the value. You can't be sure that you have useful data if you read the value property at any other moment except when the button is clicked.

The more serious problem is that the data value isn't persistent when used in the single-page content model. The Windows app runtime discards the input element and its content when the user navigates to a new page. New elements are generated when the user navigates back to this page, and any data the user entered before the navigation is lost.

Applying the View Model

The solution is, of course, to use the view model. Listing 8-9 shows the addition of two new properties in the viewmodel.js file, representing the two data items I display to the user. Since I am working with data that the user has entered, I have defined these properties in the ViewModel.UserData namespace.

Listing 8-9. Defining a property in the view model for the user's data

```
(function () {
    "use strict";

    WinJS.Namespace.define("ViewModel.State", {
        appBarElement: null,
        navBarContainerElement: null,
        navBarControlElement: null
    });

    WinJS.Namespace.define("ViewModel.UserData", {
        word: null,
        wordLength: {
```

```
        get: function() {
            return this.word ? this.word.length : null;
        }
    }
});
})();
```

The word property will contain the value that the user enters. There is no default value for this data item, so I have assigned null to the property.

The wordLength property is known as a *derived value* or *computed value*, meaning that the value it returns is based on some other value in the view model. To create this property, I have used a relatively new JavaScript feature called a *getter*. Getters, and their counterpart, *setters*, allow you to use functions to create complex properties. In this example, I have only defined a getter, which means that the value can be read but not modified.

■ **Tip**   The benefit of using computed values in the view model is that the logic to generate the value is kept in one place, rather than embedded in each script element that needs to display the value. If I need to change the wordLength property later, perhaps to count only vowels, then I only have to change the view model. This is another aspect of adding structure to the app so that the code responsible for configuring the HTML elements isn't responsible for generating those values as well.

The use of getters and setters is invisible to the consumer of the view model, who obtains the wordLength value by reading ViewModel.UserData.wordLength, just as though it were a regular property. Having defined these properties, I need to make two sets of changes to page2.html, as shown in Listing 8-10.

Listing 8-10. Using the view model to store and retrieve data

```
...
<script>
    function updateDataDisplay() {
        var word = ViewModel.UserData.word;
        var wordLength = ViewModel.UserData.wordLength;
        if (word) {
            wordspan.innerText = word;
        }
        if (wordLength) {
            lengthspan.innerText = wordLength;
        }
    };

    WinJS.UI.Pages.define("page2.html", {
        ready: function () {
            WinJS.UI.Pages.render("customNavBar.html",
                ViewModel.State.navBarContainerElement, "Page 2");

            wordbutton.addEventListener("click", function (e) {
                ViewModel.UserData.word = wordinput.value;
                updateDataDisplay();
```

```
        });
    }
});
</script>
...
```

I respond to the button being clicked by updating the property in the view model, which I do like any other JavaScript assignment. At this point, the view model object has no special powers or features, other than I have made it the authoritative source for my data:

```
...
ViewModel.UserData.word = wordinput.value;
...
```

The other change is to update the middle and right-hand panels using the view model when the value of the ViewModel.UserData.word property changes. I have moved the statements that update the panels into a function called updateDataDisplay, which uses the view model to obtain the word and wordLength data values. The functionality of the app is the same, but now the view model acts as the data repository and as an intermediary between the code that updates the property and the code that responds to those updates.

Using Data Binding

At this point I have achieved my goal but not in a helpful way. For example, although I have separated the update code into its own function and used the view model data for the updates, I still have to trigger the update directly from the click event handler function associated with the button element.

The next stage in structuring the app is to break the link between the update function and the click event handler. I am going to do this with *data binding*, which is where two data items are linked together and kept in sync.

For Windows apps, data binding is provided through the WinJS.Binding namespace. The process for setting up data binding requires two steps: making a data item *observable* and then *observing* the data item so that you receive notifications when the value of that data item changes. I show you both steps in the sections that follow.

Making Objects Observable

An *observable object* emits an event whenever the value of one of its properties is changed. This event allows interested parties to monitor the property value and respond accordingly. You make an object observable by using the WinJS.Binding.as method, and you can see how I have applied this method to the viewmodel.js file in Listing 8-11.

Listing 8-11. Making part of the view model observable

```
(function () {
    "use strict";

    WinJS.Namespace.define("ViewModel.State", {
        appBarElement: null,
        navBarContainerElement: null,
        navBarControlElement: null
    });
```

```
WinJS.Namespace.define("ViewModel", WinJS.Binding.as({
    UserData: {
        word: null,
    }
}));

WinJS.Namespace.define("ViewModel.UserData", {
    wordLength: {
        get: function () {
            return this.word ? this.word.length : null;
        }
    }
});
})();
```

Creating an observable view model isn't entirely straightforward, and you can see this reflected in the structural changes I have made in the view model. These changes are required to work around a series of conflicts and limitations in the WinJS API. I'll walk you through each of them in detail so that you understand what's going on and can recognize them if you encounter them in your own code.

Resolving the Namespace versus Binding Conflict

The WinJS.Binding.as method works by replacing the properties in your object with getters and setters. This allows you to keep using the properties without having to worry about how they are implemented and allows the observable object to seamlessly emit events when new values are set. The result is an object that is observable but which remains compatible with the code that uses it.

To support this approach, the WinJS.Binding.as method creates some private members using the JavaScript convention of prefixing the member name with an underscore character (_).

But when the WinJS.Namespace.define method exports an object into the global namespace, it hides any object members whose names begin with an underscore. The idea is, I assume, to enforce some rigor and prevent consumers of your namespaces accessing your private variables and methods.

The problem comes when you use the WinJS.Binding.as method to create an observable object that you want to export using the WinJS.Namespace.define method—the private members added by the as method are hidden by the define method, breaking the object. The result is that you can't simply apply the as method to the object you want to export to the namespace, like this:

```
...
WinJS.Namespace.define("ViewModel.UserData",
    WinJS.Binding.as({
        word: null
    })
);
...
```

The define method only hides the private members from the top-level of the object it is passed, which means you can work around the problem by structuring the namespace differently, like this:

```
...
WinJS.Namespace.define("ViewModel", WinJS.Binding.as({
    UserData: {
        word: null,
    }
```

```
}));
...
```

The UserData part of the namespace is passed to the as method, which solves the problem. There are a few places where the different parts of the WinJS API don't work together as well as they should, and this is the one that is most often encountered by new Windows app developers.

Resolving the Getter Conflict

The WinJS.Binding.as method transforms the simple value properties in an object so that they become observable. It doesn't operate on functions, but it does cause problems with values which use getters and setters. It is for this reason that I have moved the definition of the wordLength property into a separate call to the WinJS.Namespace.define method:

```
...
WinJS.Namespace.define("ViewModel.UserData", {
    wordLength: {
        get: function () {
            return this.word ? this.word.length : null;
        }
    }
});
...
```

The define method is *additive*, meaning that I can define properties or functions and they will be added to any existing namespace objects that I have already defined with the same name (rather than replacing them). In this case, my wordLength property is added to the ViewModel.UserData namespace but isn't passed through the WinJS.Binding.as method, which means that my computed view model property works properly and returns a value derived from the word property in the same namespace.

Consuming Observable Object Events

The result of the somewhat tortured setup process is that the word property in my ViewModel.UserData namespace is observable. When I change the value of the word property, the ViewModel.UserData object will send an event to any interested parties.

You register interest in a property using the bind method on the observable object. In Listing 8-12, you can see how I have used this method in the script element of the page2.html file.

Listing 8-12. Using the WinJS.Binding.bind method to receive property value change events

```
...
<script>
    function updateDataDisplay(newValue) {
        wordspan.innerText = newValue;
        lengthspan.innerText = ViewModel.UserData.wordLength;
    };

    WinJS.UI.Pages.define("page2.html", {
        ready: function () {
            WinJS.UI.Pages.render("customNavBar.html",
                ViewModel.State.navBarContainerElement, "Page 2");
```

```
                ViewModel.UserData.bind("word", updateDataDisplay);

                wordbutton.addEventListener("click", function (e) {
                    ViewModel.UserData.word = wordinput.value;
                });
            }
        });
    </script>
    ...
```

The `bind` method is added to the observable object when I call the `WinJS.Binding.as` method. The arguments to `bind` are a string containing the name of the property you want to observe and a function that will handle events sent when the value of the property changes. In my case, I have called the `bind` method on the `ViewModel.UserData` object, specifying that I want to observe the `word` property and that change events will be handled by the `updateDataDisplay` function.

The event handler function is passed two arguments - the new value and the old value for the property being observed (mu example only has one argument because I don't care about the previous value). In this listing, I have modified the `updateDataDisplay` function so that the middle panel in the layout is set using the new value argument and update the right-hand panel to reflect the word length.

Using the `bind` method creates a programmatic binding (i.e. the binding is defined in JavaScript code). I am able to use programmatic bindings to simplify my code and ensure that the different parts of my app are automatically kept in sync with one another, using the view model as a broker or intermediary.

Refactoring the Observable Properties

I still have one problem to resolve with my data binding, which is that the `wordLength` property isn't observable. The effect of this is that a consumer of values from the view model has to know that the `wordLength` property is computed from the `word` property and use events from the latter property as a trigger to check for changes in the former.

Fixing this is reasonably simple and requires some mild slight-of-hand in the `viewmodel.js` file, as shown in Listing 8-13.

Listing 8-13. Manually sending update events to make properties observable

```
(function () {
    "use strict";

    WinJS.Namespace.define("ViewModel.State", {
        appBarElement: null,
        navBarContainerElement: null,
        navBarControlElement: null
    });

    WinJS.Namespace.define("ViewModel", WinJS.Binding.as({
        UserData: {
            word: null,
            wordLength: null
        }
    }));

    ViewModel.UserData.bind("word", function (newVal) {
```

```
        if (newVal) {
            ViewModel.UserData.wordLength = newVal ? newVal.length : null;

        }
    });
})();
```

In this listing I have used the `bind` method to make the view model observe itself. This allows me to move the logic that computes values for the `wordLength` property out of the `ViewModel.UserData` object, which means that the `wordLength` property becomes observable in its own right.

This isn't a perfect technique, because there is the potential for a consumer of the view model to receive a change event for the `word` property and to read the `wordLength` property before it has been updated. For most projects, however, this is a perfectly reasonable approach and requires only a small amount of work to avoid some of the problems in the WinJS data binding support; I'll show you an alternative approach shortly for those apps where the timing issue is unacceptable.

By making both properties observable, I enable consumers of the view model to receive notifications when either changes. Listing 8-14 shows the `script` element from `page2.html`, which shows change events being handled for both the `word` and `wordLength` properties.

Listing 8-14. Binding to multiple view model properties

```
...
<script>
    function updateWordDisplay(newValue) {
        if (newValue) {
            wordspan.innerText = newValue;
        }
    };

    function updateLengthDisplay(newValue) {
        if (newValue) {
            lengthspan.innerText = newValue
        }
    };

    WinJS.UI.Pages.define("page2.html", {
        ready: function () {
            WinJS.UI.Pages.render("customNavBar.html",
                ViewModel.State.navBarContainerElement, "Page 2");

            ViewModel.UserData.bind("word", updateWordDisplay);
            ViewModel.UserData.bind("wordLength", updateLengthDisplay);

            wordbutton.addEventListener("click", function (e) {
                ViewModel.UserData.word = wordinput.value;
            });
        }
    });
</script>
...
```

The handler function for bind events isn't passed details of which property has changed, which means that the easiest way to handle the change events is with a function dedicated to a single property. You can see this in the listing, where I have split the updateDataDisplay function into two separate functions, one for each of the observable properties. The result is that observers of the wordLength property don't need to know that the property is derived from the word property.

Solving the Problem Entirely

Before I move on, I want to show you a different approach to making the view model observable which doesn't have the potential timing issues from the previous section. You only need to use this approach is you are using computed properties *and* it is imperative that all related property values are updated before any change events are sent. For all other situations, you should use the approach I showed you in Listing 8-14, which is simpler and easier to work with. Listing 8-15 shows the more advanced approach needed to solve the update issue entirely.

Listing 8-15. Solving the update ordering issue in the viewmodel.js file

```
(function () {
    "use strict";

    WinJS.Namespace.define("ViewModel.State", {
        appBarElement: null,
        navBarContainerElement: null,
        navBarControlElement: null
    });

    WinJS.Namespace.define("ViewModel", WinJS.Binding.as({
        UserData: {
            // no properties defined here
        }
    }));

    WinJS.Namespace.define("ViewModel.UserData", {
        _wordValue: null,
        wordLength: null,
        word: {
            get: function() {
                return this._wordValue;
            },
            set: function (newVal) {
                var oldWordVal = this._wordValue;
                var oldLengthVal = this.wordLength;
                this._wordValue = newVal;
                this.wordLength = newVal ? newVal.length : null;
                this.notify("word", newVal, oldWordVal);
                if (this.wordLength != oldLengthVal) {
                    this.notify("wordLength", this.wordLength, oldLengthVal);
                }
            }
        }
    }
```

```
    });
})();
```

Setting up the view model in this way requires two steps. The first is to use `WinJS.Binding.as` method to create an observable object that contains no properties. This sets up the observable functionality in the object, but doesn't replace any of the properties with getters and setters.

The second step is to manually define the properties that require synchronized updates using just the define method so that they are added to the object you exported as a namespace in the first step.

You use getters and setters to define the property from which the other values are derived. In the setter, you perform the calculations for the derived properties and then use the `notify` method to issue the updates for the changes properties, like this:

```
...
this.notify("word", newVal, oldWordVal);
if (this.wordLength != oldLengthVal) {
    this.notify("wordLength", this.wordLength, oldLengthVal);
}
...
```

The `notify` method was added to the `ViewModel.UserData` object when I called the `WinJS.Bind.as` method, as was the `bind` method that observers need to use to register for events. The arguments for the `notify` method are the name of the property that has changes, the new value, and the old value. The `notify` method is the same mechanism used internally by observable objects, and it allows you to gain complete control over the way that your view model emits change events. In the listing, by ensuring that the `notify` method isn't called until all of the property values have been updated, I am able to ensure that the change events for the `word` and `wordLength` properties are not sent until I have updated both values.

Let me reiterate that you only need to go to these lengths under very specific circumstances. I have shown you this technique because those circumstances arise surprisingly often and because it allows you to get more of a detail about how the WinJS data binding mechanism fits together.

Using Declarative Bindings

In the examples I have shown you so far, the values in the view model have been consumed using *programmatic* bindings, meaning that I receive the notification of the property value change in my JavaScript code and I respond by updating the contents of one or more of the elements in the app's HTML. I can optimize this process by using *declarative bindings*, wherein I include details of the data binding as part of the HTML element declaration and allow WinJS to manage the update process for me.

Processing the Document

The precursor to using declarative bindings is to make a call to the `WinJS.Binding.processAll` method, which locates the bindings in the HTML and activates them. When using the single-page content model, it is important to place the call to this method in your navigation event handler function so that the declarative bindings in your pages are processed when you import content; otherwise, your bindings won't be activated. In my example app, the navigation event handler is in the `default.js` file, and you can see the `processAll` method call in Listing 8-16.

Listing 8-16. Calling the WinJS.Binding.processAll method in the navigation event handler function

```
(function () {
    "use strict";
```

```
WinJS.Binding.optimizeBindingReferences = true;

var app = WinJS.Application;

WinJS.Navigation.addEventListener("navigating", function (e) {

    var navbar = ViewModel.State.navBarControlElement;
    if (navbar) {
        navbar.parentNode.removeChild(navbar);
    }

    if (ViewModel.State.appBarElement) {
        ViewModel.State.appBarElement.winControl.hide();
    }

    WinJS.UI.Animation.exitPage(contentTarget.children).then(function () {
        WinJS.Utilities.empty(contentTarget);
        WinJS.UI.Pages.render(e.detail.location, contentTarget)
            .then(function () {
                return WinJS.Binding.processAll(document.body, ViewModel);
            }).then(function() {
                return WinJS.UI.Animation.enterPage(contentTarget.children)
            });
    });
});

app.onactivated = function (eventObject) {
    WinJS.UI.processAll().then(function () {

        ViewModel.State.appBarElement = appbar;
        ViewModel.State.navBarContainerElement = navBarContainer;

        WinJS.Navigation.navigate("page1.html");

        fontSelect.addEventListener("change", function (e) {
            command.innerText = this.value;
            fontFlyout.winControl.hide();
        });
    });
};
app.start();
})();
```

■ **Note**   When you use declarative bindings, you should always set the value of the `WinJS.Binding.optimizeBindingReferences` property to true, as I have done in the example. Although I have not encountered any problems, Microsoft warns that omitting this step creates the risk that memory leaks will result from binding operations. I don't apply this property in some of the examples in this book because I want to keep them as focused as possible on the feature at hand, but for real projects you should take Microsoft's advice.

You need to fit the call to the WinJS.Binding.processAll method into the chain of Promise.then calls so that the bindings are processed after the content has been imported with the WinJS.UI.Pages.render method but before it is shown to the user. The processAll method returns a Promise object, so it is easy to get the sequence right, although the chain of nested then calls can become pretty deep.

■ **Tip** I cover the WinJS.Promise object in depth in Chapter 9.

The arguments to the WinJS.Binding.processAll method are the starting element for the processing and the source of data values. I have set the starting element to be document.body, which ensures that the entire layout is processed. For the source of the data values, I have specified the ViewModel object.

Declaring the Bindings

Once you have arranged to have the bindings processed with the processAll method, you can move on to declaring bindings in your HTML. To demonstrate declarative bindings, I have updated the panels in the page2.html file, as shown in Listing 8-17.

Listing 8-17. Using decalrative bindings in the page2.html file

```
<!DOCTYPE html>
<html>
    <head>
        <title></title>
        <script>
            WinJS.UI.Pages.define("page2.html", {
                ready: function () {
                    WinJS.UI.Pages.render("customNavBar.html",
                        ViewModel.State.navBarContainerElement, "Page 2");

                    wordbutton.addEventListener("click", function (e) {
                        ViewModel.UserData.word = wordinput.value;
                    });
                }
            });
        </script>
    </head>
    <body>
        <div id="page2Container" class="container">
            <h1>This is Page 2</h1>

            <div id="page2BoxContainer">
                <div id="p2left" class="page2box">
                    <input id="wordinput" placeholder="Enter a word">
                    <button id="wordbutton">OK</button>
                </div>

                <div id="p2middle" class="page2box">
                    <span>The word is:</span>
                    <span id="wordspan"
```

```
                          data-win-bind="innerText: UserData.word">????</span>
            </div>

            <div id="p2right" class="page2box">
                <span>The length is:</span>
                <span id="lengthspan"
                    data-win-bind="innerText: UserData.wordLength">????</span>
            </div>
          </div>
        </div>
      </body>
</html>
```

First, notice that I have removed the programmatic bindings from the script element—I no longer call the bind method or update the content of the span elements in code. Instead, I have added data-win-bind attributes to the span elements. This attribute is at the heart of the declarative binding feature, and it allows you to specify how values for one or more properties on an HTMLElement object are set.

WinJS declarative bindings operate on the HTMLElement object that represents an element in the DOM. This means that if you want to set the text content of an element, you specify that the innerText property be set to the UserData.word property of the object you passed to the processAll method, like this:

```
...
<span id="wordspan" data-win-bind="innerText: UserData.word"></span>
...
```

A colon character (:) separates the name of the property from the data property name. Declarative bindings are automatically kept up-to-date if the data item they relate to is observable. Both of the declarative bindings in this listing relate to observable data items, and so my layout is kept in sync with my view model. This is a nice alternative to using programmatic bindings when you just need to display values to the user.

■ **Tip** You can bind multiple properties in a single **data-win-bind** attribute by separating bindings with a semi-colon (;).

Creating Observable Arrays

As I mentioned earlier, the WinJS.Binding.as method only makes simple value properties observable. It will ignore objects, functions, dates, and arrays (although in the case of objects, it will look for nested simple value properties and make them observable). In this section, I'll show you how to create observable arrays. Not only are observable arrays useful, but they form an important foundation for some of the UI controls that I describe in Part III of this book.

Creating an Observable Array

You create observable arrays by creating new WinJS.Binding.List objects. You can see how I have added such an object to the viewmodel.js file in Listing 8-18. I will use this List to keep a simple history of the words entered by the user.

Listing 8-18. Adding an observable array to the view model

```
(function () {
    "use strict";

    WinJS.Namespace.define("ViewModel.State", {
        appBarElement: null,
        navBarContainerElement: null,
        navBarControlElement: null
    });

    WinJS.Namespace.define("ViewModel", WinJS.Binding.as({
        UserData: {
            word: null,
            wordLength: null,
        }
    }));

    ViewModel.UserData.wordList = new WinJS.Binding.List();

    ViewModel.UserData.bind("word", function (newVal) {
        if (newVal) {
            ViewModel.UserData.wordLength = newVal ? newVal.length : null;
            ViewModel.UserData.wordList.push(newVal);
        }
    });
})();
```

The WinJS.Binding.List object is affected by the way that the WinJS.Namespace.define method removes properties and functions whose name start with an underscore—the solution is to add the List object to the namespace manually, as shown in the listing.

▪ **Tip**   Notice that I have returned to the simpler form of the view model in the listing. The techniques I describe in the rest of the chapter can be applied to either approach, but this simpler view model makes it easier for me to illustrate the changes I make.

The List object is not a direct replacement for a JavaScript array. It implements many of the methods and properties that you find on an array, including the push method that I used in the listing to add an item to the List when the word property is updated. The main difference is that the there are no array indexers (like myArray[0]) and you have to use the getAt and setAt methods (myArray.getAt(0)) instead. You get used to it pretty quickly, and on the positive side, the List object supports some nice features for sorting and filtering its contents. Table 8-2 summarizes the most important methods defined by the List object.

Table 8-2. Useful methods defined by the List object

Method	Description
every(callback, context)	Uses the callback function to evaluate every item in the List and returns true if the callback returns true every time. The context object is passed to the function each time it is called.

Method	Description
filter(callback, context)	Uses the callback function to evaluate every item in the List and returns an array containing those items for which the callback returns true.
forEach(callback, context)	Executes the callback function on each item in the List. This method does not return a result.
getAt(index)	Returns the object at the specified index. Use this method instead of an array index.
indexOf(item, from)	Returns the index of the specified item. The optional from argument can be used to start the search from a particular index.
move(index, newIndex)	Moves the position of an item from index to newIndex.
pop()	Removes and returns the last item in the List.
push(newItem)	Adds a new item to the end of the List.
reverse()	Reverses the order of the items in the List. This operation is performed on the List items in situ and doesn't create a new list.
setAt(index, newItem)	Replaces the item at the specified index with a new item.
shift()	Removes and returns the first item in the List.
unshift(newItem)	Adds a new item to the start of the List.

These are just the basic methods, and I recommend you take some time to look at the API documentation and explore the List object capabilities in more detail.

■ **Tip** Many of the capabilities supported by the List object are required by its role as a data source for some of the WinJS UI controls. You can learn more about data sources and the controls that use them in Part III.

In Listing 8-18, I created an empty List object, but you can pre-populate a List if you pass a JavaScript array to the constructor. You can also pass an optional configuration object, which supports the properties shown in Table 8-3.

Table 8-3. The configuration properties for the WinJS.Binding.List object

Property	Description
binding	When true, each item in the List will be made observable by being passed to the WinJS.Binding.as method. See the Making Objects Observable section earlier in this chapter for details. The default value is false.
proxy	When true, the array passed as the first argument to the constructor is used as the storage for the List. The default is false, which means that the contents of the array are copied into storage which is private to the List object. Be careful when using true because the List object will not know when you modify the contents of the array directly.

You apply these options as follows:

```
...
var myArray = ["Apple", "Orange", "Cherry"];
var myList = new WinJS.Binding.List(myArray, {
```

```
    proxy: true,
    binding: false
});
...
```

I have yet to use either of these options in a real project. The proxy property is dangerous, and the binding option requires some very careful coding in the handler functions for the events emitted by the List to prevent observing objects that are no longer part of the collection (and in the cases where this has been useful, I have preferred to take care of making the objects observable myself).

Observing a List

As you might expect, the List object emits events whenever the contents of the collection are changed. There are several events, the most useful of which are iteminserted, itemchanged, itemremoved and itemmoved. The significance of each event is evident from its name, and you can get details of what has been inserted, changed, removed, or moved by looking at the detail property of the event passed to the event handler function.

■ **Tip** These events are emitted when the set of objects contained by the List are changed—for example, when a new item is added to the List or when an item is removed. Changing the value of a property of an object in the List won't cause the events to be triggered.

To demonstrate observing a List object, I have added a new panel to the layout defined by page2.html and added some new code to the script element. You can see the changes in Listing 8-19.

Listing 8-19. Observing a WinJS.Binding.List object

```
<!DOCTYPE html>
<html>
<head>
    <title></title>
    <script>
        WinJS.UI.Pages.define("page2.html", {
            ready: function () {
                WinJS.UI.Pages.render("customNavBar.html",
                    ViewModel.State.navBarContainerElement, "Page 2");

                wordbutton.addEventListener("click", function (e) {
                    ViewModel.UserData.word = wordinput.value;
                });

                ViewModel.UserData.wordList.addEventListener("iteminserted", function(e){
                    var newDiv = document.createElement("div");
                    newDiv.innerText = e.detail.value;
                    WinJS.Utilities.addClass(newDiv, "word");
                    wordList.appendChild(newDiv);
                });
            }
        });
```

```
            </script>
    </head>
    <body>
        <div id="page2Container" class="container">
            <h1>This is Page 2</h1>

            <div id="page2BoxContainer">
                <div id="p2left" class="page2box">
                    <input id="wordinput" placeholder="Enter a word">
                    <button id="wordbutton">OK</button>
                </div>

                <div id="p2middle" class="page2box">
                    <span>The word is:</span>
                    <span id="wordspan"
                        data-win-bind="innerText: UserData.word">????</span>
                </div>

                <div id="p2right" class="page2box">
                    <span>The length is:</span>
                    <span id="lengthspan"
                        data-win-bind="innerText: UserData.wordLength">????</span>
                </div>
            </div>

            <div id="wordListContainer" class="page2box">
                <span>Word List:</span>
                <div id="wordList"></div>
            </div>
        </div>
    </body>
</html>
```

You observe a List object by calling the addEventListener method, specifying the event type you are interested in and the callback function that will handle the change events. In this listing, I respond to the iteminserted event by creating a new div element, assigning it to the CSS word class, and adding it to the new layout panel. I set the innerText property to the detail.value property of the Event object passed to the handler function. The Event.detail object also defines the index property for newly added items so you can tell where in the List the item has been added. You can see the result in Figure 8-2: a new element is added each time the user enters a word and clicks the OK button, creating a simple history.

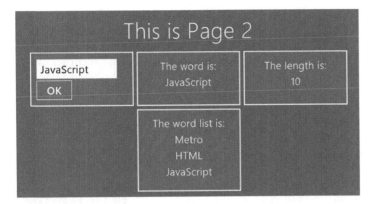

Figure 8-2. Observing a List object to create a simple history display

You'll notice that I have only shown programmatic bindings for the List object. There are some declarative bindings available, but they are wrapped up in some WinJS UI controls. I'll introduce these controls and explain how they can be used with List objects in Part III of this book.

Using Templates

In the previous example, I ended up creating a series of div elements to represent the history of words entered by the user. I did this using the DOM API, which works but is awkward to use and is error-prone. Fortunately, WinJS provides some basic template support which is linked to the data binding feature and which makes it easier to create elements based on data in the view model. Listing 8-20 shows the elements that I created by using JavaScript for the previous example—these will serve as the (simple) goal for my templates.

Listing 8-20. The code-generated elements from the word history list

```
...
<div class="page2box" id="wordListContainer">
    <span>Word List:</span>
    <div id="wordList">
        <div class="word">HTML</div>
        <div class="word">CSS</div>
        <div class="word">JavaScript</div>
    </div>
</div>
...
```

Defining and Using the Template

You denote an element that will be a template by setting the data-win-control attribute to WinJS.Binding.Template. When the document is processed by the WinJS.UI.processAll method, the element is removed from its place in the DOM and prepared for use as a template. Since this is a regular WinJS control, a winControl property is added to the HTMLElement object that represents the host element in the DOM. Listing 8-21 shows the addition of a template to the page2.html file and the JavaScript code that uses it.

Listing 8-21. Declaring and using a template

```
<!DOCTYPE html>
<html>
<head>
    <title></title>
    <script>
        WinJS.UI.Pages.define("page2.html", {
            ready: function () {
                WinJS.UI.Pages.render("customNavBar.html",
                    ViewModel.State.navBarContainerElement, "Page 2");

                wordbutton.addEventListener("click", function (e) {
                    ViewModel.UserData.word = wordinput.value;
                });

                ViewModel.UserData.wordList.addEventListener("iteminserted",
                    function (e) {
                        wordTemplate.winControl.render({ wordValue: e.detail.value },
                            wordList);
                });
            }
        });
    </script>
</head>
<body>
    <div id="wordTemplate" data-win-control="WinJS.Binding.Template">
        <div class="word" data-win-bind="innerText: wordValue"></div>
    </div>

    <div id="page2Container" class="container">
        <h1>This is Page 2</h1>

        <div id="page2BoxContainer">
            <div id="p2left" class="page2box">
                <input id="wordinput" placeholder="Enter a word">
                <button id="wordbutton">OK</button>
            </div>

            <div id="p2middle" class="page2box">
                <span>The word is:</span>
                <span id="wordspan"
                    data-win-bind="innerText: UserData.word">????</span>
            </div>

            <div id="p2right" class="page2box">
                <span>The length is:</span>
                <span id="lengthspan"
                    data-win-bind="innerText: UserData.wordLength">????</span>
            </div>
        </div>
```

```
        <div id="wordListContainer" class="page2box">
            <span>Word List:</span>
            <div id="wordList"></div>
        </div>
    </div>
</body>
</html>
```

You apply the WinJS.Binding.Template control to an element which contains your template. You need to define an id attribute for the template element so you can locate it later. Within the container element, you define the template content using the data-win-bind attribute to refer to the data values you want applied in the template.

You pass the data object that will supply values for the binding directly to the render method template control, which means that the data items don't have to be part of the view model. In the listing, my template consists of a single div element, matching the pattern I used when generating the element in code. I have used the data-win-bind attribute to specify that the innerText property will be set using the wordValue property from the data object passed to the template:

```
...
<div id="wordTemplate" data-win-control="WinJS.Binding.Template">
    <div class="word" data-win-bind="innerText: wordValue"></div>
</div>
....
```

To use the template, you locate the template container element in the DOM and use the winControl property to access the WinJS.Binding.Template object. The template object defines the render method which takes two arguments— the data to be applied to the template and the element to which the content generated from the template will be inserted. You need to make the data values line up with what the template is expecting, so I have created a data object that maps the new value added to the WinJS.Binding.List object to the wordValue property, which I then pass to the render method:

```
...
wordTemplate.winControl.render({ wordValue: e.detail.value }, wordList);
...
```

The result is that my elements are generated from markup, rather purely in code. I like the template approach, and I use templates extensively in my web apps. In Windows apps, some of the more advanced UI controls rely on templates to display data, and I'll show you how they operate (and the role they play) in Part III.

Using Value Converters

I want to go back and tidy up slightly. With the use of data bindings to an observable view model value, I have introduced a slight cosmetic problem, which you can see in Figure 8-3.

Figure 8-3. The initial state of the layout

I set the value of the word and wordLength properties in the view model to null so that the properties are defined and to indicate that no value has been set yet. The problem is that the null value is displayed to the user in the layout, which isn't pretty.

To fix this problem, I am going to use a WinJS *binding converter*, which is a JavaScript function that acts as an intermediary between a view model value and a data binding. You can see how I have created my converter in Listing 8-22, which shows some additions to the viewmodel.js file. You don't have to put your converters in your view model file, but I take a kitchen-sink approach and lump everything together.

Listing 8-22. Adding a binding converter to the viewmodel.js file

```
(function () {
    "use strict";

    WinJS.Namespace.define("ViewModel.State", {
        appBarElement: null,
        navBarContainerElement: null,
        navBarControlElement: null
    });

    WinJS.Namespace.define("ViewModel", WinJS.Binding.as({
        UserData: {
            word: null,
            wordLength: null,
        }
    }));

    ViewModel.UserData.wordList = new WinJS.Binding.List();

    ViewModel.UserData.bind("word", function (newVal) {
        if (newVal) {
            ViewModel.UserData.wordLength = newVal ? newVal.length : null;
            ViewModel.UserData.wordList.push(newVal);
        }
    });

    WinJS.Namespace.define("ViewModel.Converters", {
        defaultStringIfNull: WinJS.Binding.converter(function (val) {
            return val ? val : "<No Word>";
        })
    });
})();
```

I have created a new namespace called ViewModel.Converters and defined a converter called defaultStringIfNull. A converter is a regular JavaScript function that takes a single argument and returns the converted value. This function is passed to the WinJS.Binding.converter method, which returns an object that can be consumed in data bindings. In this example, my converter returns the value it was passed unless it is null, in which case <No Word> is returned.

You put the name of the converter after the view model property in the declarative bindings. Listing 8-23 shows how I have updated the bindings in the page2.html file to use the defaultStringIfNull converter.

Listing 8-23. Applying a value converter

```
...
<div id="p2middle" class="page2box">
    <span>The word is:</span>
    <span id="wordspan"
        data-win-bind="innerText: UserData.word
            ViewModel.Converters.defaultStringIfNull">????</span>
</div>

<div id="p2right" class="page2box">
    <span>The length is:</span>
    <span id="lengthspan"
        data-win-bind="innerText: UserData.wordLength
            ViewModel.Converters.defaultStringIfNull">????</span>
</div>
...
```

You must specify the full path to the converter, which must be available through the global namespace. For my example app, this means that I must refer to the converter as ViewModel.Converters. defaultStringIfNull. You can see the result in Figure 8-4, where a more meaningful value is presented to the user when the word or wordLength properties are null.

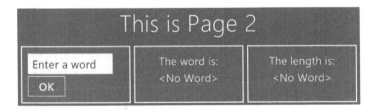

Figure8- 4. Using a binding converter to avoid displaying null to the user

Using an Open Value Converter

The value converter I created using the WinJS.Binding.converter method in the previous section doesn't know where the value it is working on comes from or anything about the element that the converted value will be applied to. This is a *closed value converter* because it always produces the same conversion result for a given input value. You can see the effect of this in Figure 8-4—both places where I use the converter result in <No Word> being displayed, and there is no way that I can tailor the result to better match the target element. The only way I can get different converted values is to create multiple converters, which isn't ideal because most of the converter code would be very similar and lead to needless duplication.

A more advanced alternative is an *open converter*, which gets to see the full details of the binding request. This kind of converter is harder to create, but it means that you can tailor the kind of result your converter produced based on the data value that has been requested or the element to which the converted value will apply. In Listing 8-24, I have replaced the converter in the viewmodel.js file from the previous example with an open converter that adapts the value displayed in the markup based on the data property that is being converted.

■ **Caution**   This is an advanced technique, and for most situations closed bindings will be perfectly adequate. Only use open bindings if you have a situation in which you would be duplicating a lot of code in multiple bindings to generate only slightly different results.

Listing 8-24. Applying an open data converter

```
(function () {
    "use strict";

    WinJS.Namespace.define("ViewModel.State", {
        appBarElement: null,
        navBarContainerElement: null,
        navBarControlElement: null
    });

    WinJS.Namespace.define("ViewModel", WinJS.Binding.as({
        UserData: {
            word: null,
            wordLength: null,
        }
    }));

    ViewModel.UserData.wordList = new WinJS.Binding.List();

    ViewModel.UserData.bind("word", function (newVal) {
        if (newVal) {
            ViewModel.UserData.wordLength = newVal ? newVal.length : null;
            ViewModel.UserData.wordList.push(newVal);
        }
    });

    WinJS.Namespace.define("ViewModel.Converters", {
        defaultStringIfNull: function (src, srcprop, dest, destprop) {
            var srcObject= src;
            var targetObject = dest;

            srcprop.slice(0, srcprop.length -1).forEach(function (prop) {
                srcObject = srcObject[prop] != undefined ? srcObject[prop] : null;
            });

            destprop.slice(0, destprop.length -1).forEach(function (prop) {
```

```
                    targetObject = targetObject[prop] == undefined ? null:
                        targetObject[prop];
                });

                srcObject.bind(srcprop[srcprop.length - 1], function (val) {
                    var value = val != null ? val :
                        srcprop[srcprop.length - 1] == "wordLength" ? "-" : "<No Word>";
                    targetObject[destprop[destprop.length - 1]] = value;
                });
            }
        });

        ViewModel.Converters.defaultStringIfNull.supportedForProcessing = true;
```

```
})();
```

You don't need to call any of the WinJS.Binding methods to create an open converter. Instead, you just create a function which takes four arguments. Your function will be called upon to convert data values, and you can use the arguments to figure out what is being asked for and where it will be applied. To explain the arguments, I'll base my description on the following declarative binding from the example app:

```
...
<span id="lengthspan" data-win-bind="innerText: UserData.wordLength
    ViewModel.Converters.defaultStringIfNull">????</span>
...
```

The first argument is the data object which was passed to the WinJS.Binding.processAll method—for the example, this will be the ViewModel object. The second argument is the data value that is being requested, presented as array of names. In the example binding, I want the UserData.wordLength property which will be presented in the second argument as ["UserData", "wordLength"].

The third argument is the target for the binding. For my example, this will be the span element whose id is lengthspan. The final argument is the property to which the converted value will be applied—this is another array of names, and so my function will receive the array ["innerText"] for the example binding.

Most of the code in this converter deals with the arrays of names so that I am in a position to obtain the data values and apply them to the target object.

You don't just return a value from an open converter. Instead, you have to set up a programmatic binding so that the target is kept up to date as the data values change. I do this using the bind method, just as I described earlier. In the example, I return different values from the conversion, depending on which property has been requested, as follows:

```
...
srcObject.bind(srcprop[srcprop.length - 1], function (val) {
    var value = val != null ? val : srcprop[srcprop.length - 1] ==
        "wordLength" ? "N/A" : "<No Word>";
    targetObject[destprop[destprop.length - 1]] = value;
});
...
```

This technique is an odd mix of programmatic bindings being used to support declarative bindings, and it is a lot more work than either technique on their own. But the flexibility is sometimes worth the effort.

■ **Tip** Notice that I don't make any decisions based on the target element being used—doing so is the path to tight coupling because knowledge of the markup structure will be embedded in the converter. If you must tailor your converted result based on where it will be applied, then limit yourself to making decisions based on the element type or the classes to which it belongs.

By default, functions cannot be called from markup unless you have explicitly set the supportedForProcessing property to true, like this:

```
...
ViewModel.Converters.defaultStringIfNull.supportedForProcessing = true;
...
```

When you create closed converters, this property is set for you automatically, but since open converters are so much more manual, you are responsible for setting it yourself. If you forget, the app will terminate when the converter function is executed.

Summary

In this chapter, I have shown you how to introduce a view model into your Windows app, how to make it observable, and how to respond to updated data values using both programmatic and declarative data bindings. I also showed you how to create observable arrays and how they can be used to drive simple templates.

By applying a view model, you separate the data from the markup, ensure that your data is available throughout the app, and make long-term development and maintenance simplified and easier. By applying data bindings to the view model, you create an app which responds fluidly to data changes. In the next chapter, I will dig into the detail of the WinJS.Promise object and show you how to use it to get the most from the WinJS and Windows APIs.

CHAPTER 9

Using Promises

The basic premise of asynchronous programming in a Windows app is simple. You call a method and the work it performs is scheduled for later execution. At some point in the future, the work is performed and you are notified of the result by means of a callback function.

Asynchronous programming is well-established in JavaScript. You have probably already encountered asynchronous programming when you made an Ajax request in a web app. You wanted to load some content from the server, but didn't want to prevent the user interacting with the app while this was happening. So, you made a method call using the XMLHttpRequest object (or a wrapper library such as jQuery that makes the XMLHttpRequest object easier to use) and provided a function that was executed when the server content arrived. If you hadn't used Ajax, the web app would not have responded to user interaction until the data came back from the server, creating the appearance of a stuck or stalled app.

Asynchronous programming in a Windows app works in the same way and is used for the same reason – to allow the user to interact with the app while other operations are being performed. Windows apps use asynchronous programming more widely than just Ajax requests, which is why there is a general purpose object to represent asynchronous operations: the WinJS.Promise object.

The term *promise* represents a commitment to perform a task and return a result sometime in the future. When this happens, the promise is said to be *fulfilled*. Table 9-1 provides the summary for this chapter.

■ **Tip** The WinJS.Promise object is an implementation of the CommonJS Promises/A specification, which you can read about at http://commonjs.org. This is becoming the standard for JavaScript asynchronous programming and got a huge boost in popularity when the jQuery library adopted it as the foundation for its Deferred Objects feature.

Table 9-1. Chapter Summary

Problem	Solution	Listing
Obtain a Promise for an Ajax request	Use the WinJS.xhr function	1-4
Receive information about the outcome of a Promise	Register callback functions using the Promise.then method.	5
Create a sequence of tasks	Chain together calls to the then method.	6-7

Problem	Solution	Listing
Defer execution of a Promise in a chain	Make sure to return the Promise as the result of the first function passed to the then method.	8
Request cancelation of a Promise	Call the cancel method	9-10
Pass a data value along a chain of Promise objects	Return the value from the function you pass to the then method	11-12
Perform a task when any one of a set of Promises is fulfilled	Use the Promise.any method	13
Perform a task when all of the Promises in a set are fulfilled	Use the Promise.join method	14
Create a Promise that can be used to delay execution of a chain	Use the timeout method with a single argument	15
Arrange for a Promise to be canceled automatically if it is not fulfilled within a specified period	Use the timeout method with two arguments	16
Apply the same set of callback functions to multiple Promise objects	Use the theneach method	17
Create a custom Promise object	Use the WinJS.Promise constructor	18-19
Schedule execution of a task for when any outstanding events and UI updates have been performed	Use the setImmediate method	20
Implement cancelation in a custom Promise	Pass a second function to the Promise constructor which will be invoked when the cancel method is called	21
Create synthetic Promise objects	Use the wrap and wrapError methods	22-24

Creating the Example Project

The best way to get started with asynchronous programming is to jump right in. To build on something familiar, I am going to use the WinJS.xhr function which wraps the XMLHttpRequest object with a WinJS. Promise. To demonstrate this feature, I have created a new project called Promises using the Visual Studio Blank App template. Listing 9-1 shows the contents of the default.html file.

Listing 9-1. The contents of the default.html file

```
<!DOCTYPE html>
<html>
<head>
    <meta charset="utf-8" />
    <title>Promises</title>

    <!-- WinJS references -->
    <link href="//Microsoft.WinJS.1.0/css/ui-dark.css" rel="stylesheet" />
    <script src="//Microsoft.WinJS.1.0/js/base.js"></script>
    <script src="//Microsoft.WinJS.1.0/js/ui.js"></script>
```

```
    <!-- Promises references -->
    <link href="/css/default.css" rel="stylesheet" />
    <script src="/js/viewmodel.js"></script>
    <script src="/js/default.js"></script>
</head>
<body>
    <div class="container">
        <div id="left" class="panel">
            <div>
                <label>1st Zip:</label>
                <input id="zip1" data-win-bind="value: State.zip1" />
            </div>
            <div>
                <label>2nd Zip:</label>
                <input id="zip2" data-win-bind="value: State.zip2" />
            </div>
            <div>
                <button id="go">Go</button>
                <button id="cancel">Cancel</button>
            </div>
            <div id="messages"></div>
        </div>
        <div id="middle" class="panel">Content will go here</div>
        <div id="right" class="panel">Content will go here</div>
    </div>

    <div id="messageTemplate" data-win-control="WinJS.Binding.Template">
        <div class="message" data-win-bind="innerText: message"></div>
    </div>

    <div id="zipTemplate" data-win-control="WinJS.Binding.Template">
        <div><label>Zip:</label><span data-win-bind="innerText: Zipcode"></span></div>
        <div><label>City:</label><span data-win-bind="innerText: City"></span></div>
        <div><label>State:</label><span data-win-bind="innerText: State"></span></div>
        <div><label>Lat:</label><span data-win-bind="innerText: Latitude"></span></div>
        <div><label>Lon:</label><span data-win-bind="innerText: Longitude"></span></div>
    </div>
</body>
</html>
```

This app performs web searches for zip codes. The layout split into three panels, which you can see in Figure 9-1. The left-most panel contains a pair of input elements which allow you to enter the zip codes, alongside the Go and Cancel button. There is also an area where I will display messages about the Ajax request I make.

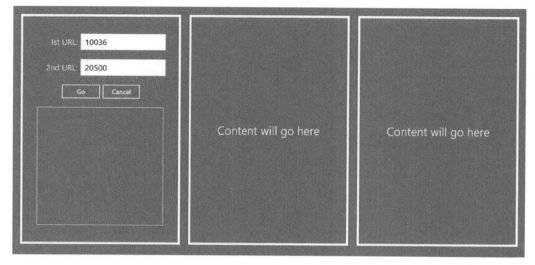

Figure 1. The initial layout of the Promises app

The middle and right panels are where the results of the searches are displayed. As you can see in the listing, I have defined a template for displaying the search results, using the techniques I described in Chapter 8.

You can see the CSS I used to create this layout in Listing 9-2, which shows the css/default.css.

Listing 9-2. The contents of the default.css

```
body {
    display: -ms-flexbox;
    -ms-flex-direction: column;
    -ms-flex-align: center; -ms-flex-pack: center;
    background-color: #5A8463; color: white;
}

div.container {
    display: -ms-flexbox; -ms-flex-direction: row;
    -ms-flex-align: center; -ms-flex-pack: center;
}

div.panel {
    width: 25%; border: thick solid white;
    margin: 10px; padding: 10px; font-size: 14pt;
    height: 500px; width: 350px;
    display: -ms-flexbox; -ms-flex-direction: column;
    -ms-flex-align: center; -ms-flex-pack: center;
}

#left > div { margin: 10px 0;}
#left input {font-size: 14pt; width: 200px;}
div.panel label {display: inline-block; width: 100px; text-align: right;}
div.panel span {display: inline-block; width: 200px;}
```

```
#messages {width: 80%; height: 250px; padding: 10px; border: thin solid white;}
#middle, #right {font-size: 20pt;}
#middle label, #right label {color: darkgray; margin-left: 10px;}
```

As you might expect, I have defined a simple view model for this app. Listing 9-3 shows the contents of the view model, which I created in a file called js/viewmodel.js.

Listing 9-3. The view model for the Promises app

```
(function () {
    WinJS.Namespace.define("ViewModel", WinJS.Binding.as({
        State: {
            zip1: "10036", zip2: "20500",
        }
    }));

    ViewModel.State.messages = new WinJS.Binding.List();
})();
```

Finally, Listing 9-4 shows the contents of the js/default.js file. This file contains the code to locate and set up event handler functions for the button and input elements in the layout, but it doesn't contain the code that will actually make the requests to the web service – I'll add this code later in the chapter.

Listing 9-4. The default.js file

```
(function () {
    "use strict";

    var app = WinJS.Application;
    var $ = WinJS.Utilities.query;

    function requestData(zip, targetElem) {
        ViewModel.State.messages.push("Started for " + zip);
        // ...code will go here...
    }

    app.onactivated = function (args) {

        $('input').listen("change", function (e) {
            ViewModel.State[this.id] = this.value;
        });

        $('button').listen("click", function (e) {
            if (this.id == "go") {
                var p1 = requestData(ViewModel.State.zip1, middle);
                var p2 = requestData(ViewModel.State.zip2, right);
            };
        });

        ViewModel.State.messages.addEventListener("iteminserted", function (e) {
                messageTemplate.winControl.render({ message: e.detail.value }, messages);
            });
```

```
        WinJS.UI.processAll().then(function () {
            return WinJS.Binding.processAll(document.body, ViewModel);
        });
    };

    app.start();
})();
```

At this point the basic structure of the app is complete. You can enter zip codes into the input elements you can click the buttons – all that I lack is the code to do the actual work, and that's what I'll focus on for the rest of this chapter.

This example app makes network connections to request data from a remote server. This requires a *capability* to be enabled in the app's manifest, which lets Windows and the user know that your app is capable of making such requests. This allows Windows to enforce a security policy (apps without the capability won't be allowed to initiate requests) and it allows the user to make an assessment of the risk your app presents when they are considering purchasing it from the Windows Store (although it is clear that user's don't actually pay much attention to this kind of information).

Visual Studio automatically enables this particular capability for you when you create a new app development project. To see the capability, double click on the package.appxmanifest file in the Solution Explorer and navigate to the Capabilities tab. You will see that Internet (Client) is checked, as shown in Figure 9-2, telling Windows that your app is capable of initiating outbound network connections.

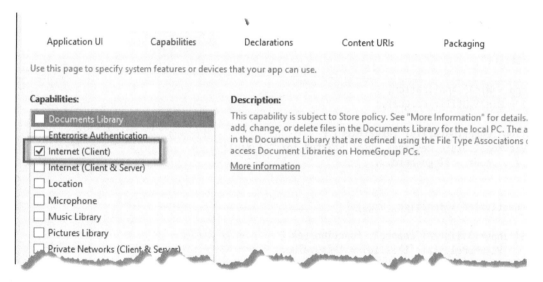

Figure 9-2. Enabling the capability to make outgoing network connections

Dealing with the Basic Asynchronous Programming Flow

You can tell when you are dealing with an asynchronous operation because the method you call will return a WinJS.Promise object. Methods that return a Promise will schedule their work to take place at some point in the future and the outcome of that work will be signaled through the Promise.

Scheduled isn't the most useful word in this context, because it implies some fixed time in the future. In fact, all you know is that the work will be done—you have no influence over when it will be performed and no indication about how long it might be before the task is started. *Deferred* might be a better word— and the one adopted by the jQuery team—but scheduled is the term which is used most widely.

Using asynchronous methods is a trade-off. The benefit is that your app can perform background tasks while remaining responsive to the user. The downside is that you lose direct control over the execution of the task and you don't know when your task will be performed.

For the most part, however, you don't have a choice. Windows uses asynchronous programming throughout the WinJS and Windows API and you can't create a first-class app without embracing the Promise object and the approach to programming that it represents.

Using Asynchronous Callbacks

The Promise object provides you with information about the outcome of the asynchronous task using callback functions. You register these functions using the then method. The then method accepts up to three callback functions as arguments. The first function is called if the task completes successfully (the *success callback*), the second function is called if the task encounters an error (the *error callback*) and the third function is called to signal progress information during the execution of the task (the *progress callback*).

To demonstrate the Promise object, I have used the WinJS.xhr method, which is a wrapper around the standard XMLHttpRequest object that you use in web apps to make Ajax requests. The WinJS.xhr method accepts an object that contains properties that correspond to the properties defined by the XMLHttpRequest, including url, type, user, password and data, all of which are passed unmodified to the XMLHttpRequest object.

■ **Tip** You may have used a convenience wrapper from a library such as jQuery to manage your requests and not have used the XMLHttpRequest object directly. You don't need to understand the workings of XMLHttpRequest to follow this chapter, but if you want more information, then the W3C specification is a good place to start: http://www.w3.org/TR/XMLHttpRequest

---

You can see how I have used WinJS.xhr method and the then function on the Promise that it returns in Listing 9-5, which shows how I have implemented the requestData function in the default.js file. As the listing shows, I use the success callback function to display the data from the server and the error callback to display details of any problems with the request.

Listing 9-5. Using the WinJS.Promise.then method

```
...
function requestData(zip, targetElem) {

    ViewModel.State.messages.push("Started for " + zip);

    var promise = WinJS.xhr({
        url: "http://gomashup.com/json.php?fds=geo/usa/zipcode/" + zip
    }).then(function (xhr) {
        ViewModel.State.messages.push(zip + " Complete");
        var dataObject = JSON.parse(xhr.response.slice(1, -1)).result;
        WinJS.Utilities.empty(targetElem);
        zipTemplate.winControl.render(dataObject[0], targetElem);
    }, function (xhr) {
```

```
        WinJS.Utilities.empty(targetElem);
        targetElem.innerText = "Error: " + xhr.statusText;
    });
    return promise;
}
...
```

The object I pass to the `WinJS.xhr` method has a `url` property which specifies the URL I want to request. The `WinJS.xhr` method returns a `Promise` object and I use the `then` method to register functions for the success and error callbacks.

■ **Tip** You don't *have* to use the `then` method. If you don't care about the outcome of the asynchronous task, just discard or ignore the `Promise` that the method returns to create a fire-and-forget task.

The `WinJS.xhr` method returns immediately and the Ajax request will be performed at some unspecified point in the future. I have no control over when the request will be started and I will only know when the request has finished when one of my callback functions is executed.

If my success callback function is executed, I know I have a response from the server, which I process and display in the layout. If my error callback function is executed, then I know something went wrong and I display details of the error. You can see the result in Figure 9-3, which illustrates the layout of the app after the Go button has been clicked and the `Promise` objects that are created have been fulfilled.

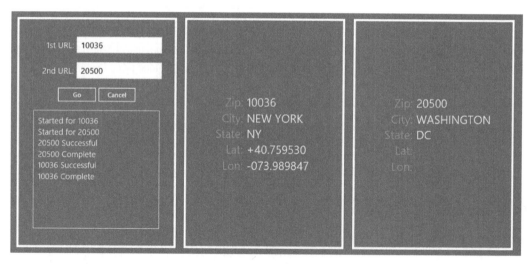

Figure 9-3. Using callback handlers to respond to fulfilled Promises

Most of the asynchronous methods in the WinJS and Windows APIs tend to be more granular than `WinJS.xhr` and pass some kind of result object to the success callback and a descriptive string message to the error function (the progress callback isn't used that often, although you can see a demonstration later in this chapter when I show you how to create your own `Promises`.).

USING THE GOMASHUP ZIP CODE SERVICE

The web service that I use in this example is from GoMashup.com, who offer a number of useful data services. I selected GoMashup because their services are quick, reliable and don't require any developer keys to be included in the request, which makes them ideal for demos. If I want information about the zip code 10036, for example, I make a query with the following URL:

```
http://gomashup.com/json.php?fds=geo/usa/zipcode/10036
```

I get back a string like this:

```
({"result":[{

    "Longitude" : "-073.989847",

    "Zipcode" : "10036",

    "ZipClass" : "STANDARD",

    "County" : "NEW YORK",

    "City" : "NEW YORK",

    "State" : "NY",

    "Latitude" : "+40.759530"

}]})
```

The GoMashup services are intended to be used with JSONP, where a function is invoked to insert the data into the app. This means that I need to strip out the first and last characters of the string to get a valid JSON string that I can parse to create a JavaScript object.

Creating Chains

One of the interesting aspects of the then method is that it returns a Promise which is fulfilled when the callback function has been executed.

This means that the Promise I return from the requestData function isn't the one that is fulfilled when the Ajax request is complete. Instead, it is a Promise which is fulfilled when the Ajax request has been completed *and* either the success or error callback has been executed as well.

Using the then method to create sequences of actions is known as *chaining* and it allows you to gain control over the order in which tasks are performed. As an example, I can change the structure of the requestData function to make it more useful. At the moment, I only add a message to the ViewModel. State.messages object if my request is successful, but with the then method I can differentiate between the fulfillment of the Ajax request and the fulfillment of the initial set of callbacks, as shown in Listing 9-6.

Listing 9-6. Chaining actions together using the then method

```
...
function requestData(zip, targetElem) {

    ViewModel.State.messages.push("Started for " + zip);
```

```
    var promise = WinJS.xhr({
        url: "http://gomashup.com/json.php?fds=geo/usa/zipcode/" + zip
    }).then(function (xhr) {
        ViewModel.State.messages.push(zip + " Successful");
        var dataObject = JSON.parse(xhr.response.slice(1, -1)).result;
        WinJS.Utilities.empty(targetElem);
        zipTemplate.winControl.render(dataObject[0], targetElem);
    }, function (xhr) {
        ViewModel.State.messages.push(zip + " Failed");
        WinJS.Utilities.empty(targetElem);
        targetElem.innerText = "Error: " + xhr.statusText;
    });

    return promise.then(function () {
        ViewModel.State.messages.push(zip + " Complete");
    });

}
...
```

You can see the sequence of these messages in Figure 9-4, which shows the result of clicking the Go button.

Figure 9-4. Using the then method to control the sequence of asynchronous tasks

One of the drawbacks of the Promise object and the then method is that you can end up with code which is hard to read. More specifically, it can be hard to figure out the sequence in which the chain of tasks will be performed. To help make this clear in Listing 9-6, assigned the Promise to a variable called promise and then, separately, to use the then method to create a chain. Usually, however the then method is applied more directly as shown in Listing 9-7.

Listing 9-7. Creating a chain using the then method directly on a Promise

```
function requestData(zip, targetElem) {

    ViewModel.State.messages.push("Started for " + zip);
```

```
var promise = WinJS.xhr({
    url: "http://gomashup.com/json.php?fds=geo/usa/zipcode/" + zip
}).then(function (xhr) {
    ViewModel.State.messages.push(zip + " Successful");
    var dataObject = JSON.parse(xhr.response.slice(1, -1)).result;
    WinJS.Utilities.empty(targetElem);
    zipTemplate.winControl.render(dataObject[0], targetElem);
}, function (xhr) {
    ViewModel.State.messages.push(zip + " Failed");
    WinJS.Utilities.empty(targetElem);
    targetElem.innerText = "Error: " + xhr.statusText;
}).then(function () {
    ViewModel.State.messages.push(zip + " Complete");
});

    return promise;
}
```

Because the then method returns a Promise object, the result from the requestData method is a Promise which is fulfilled when the Ajax request has been completed *and* one of the callback functions has been executed *and* the function which writes the Complete message has been executed. Chains are an easy way to combine Promises, but they can be hard to read.

■ **Tip** The Promise.done method is the complement to the then method. The done method must be used as the last method in a chain because it doesn't return a result. Any unhandled exceptions in the chain are thrown when they reach the done method (whereas they are simply reflected in the state of the Promise by the then method). Throwing an exception like this is not especially useful, because the execution of your app code will have moved on by the time the done method is invoked. A better approach is to make sure you handle any exceptions by using error callback functions in your chains.

Chaining Promises

Notice that the messages shown in Figure 9-4 are intermingled. This is because IE10 is able to perform more than one request concurrently and each request moves through its lifecycle independently. There is no coordination between the requests, which is why the messages are interleaved and why you might have seen different results when you ran the example. This makes sense when you see how I call the requestData function in the event handler for the Go button like this:

```
...
var p1 = requestData(ViewModel.State.zip1, middle);
var p2 = requestData(ViewModel.State.zip2, right);
...
```

I receive the Promise objects that the requestData function returns, but I don't do anything with them and so the requests are scheduled independently. This is fine for my example app, because each request updates a different part of the layout and I have no need to coordinate the results.

In many situations, however, you will want to defer one task until another has completed. You can do this using the then method to create a chain, but you must take care to return the Promise object from the second request as the result of your callback function, as shown in Listing 9-8 which shows the changes I have made to the default.js file to ensure that the requests are performed in sequence.

Listing 9-8. Chaining Promises

```
...
$('button').listen("click", function (e) {
    if (this.id == "go") {
        requestData(ViewModel.State.zip1, middle).then(function () {
            return requestData(ViewModel.State.zip2, right);
        });
    };
});
...
```

This is really important. If you return the Promise object from the callback function, then any subsequent actions in the chain won't be scheduled until that Promise has been fulfilled. That means that the code in Listing 8 creates the following effect:

1. Schedule the first request
2. Wait until the Promise from the first request has been fulfilled
3. Schedule the second request
4. Wait until the Promise from the second request has been fulfilled
5. Add a message to the ViewModel.State.messages object

This is usually the effect that is required – don't schedule an activity until the previous one has been completed. However, if you omit the return keyword, you get a very different effect:

1. Schedule the first request
2. Wait until the Promise from the first request has been fulfilled
3. Schedule the second request
4. Add a message to the ViewModel.State.messages object

If you don't return a Promise from a callback, then subsequent activities will be scheduled as soon as the execution of your callback function has completed – which, when you call an asynchronous method, is as soon as the task has been scheduled and *not* when the task has completed.

The difference is easy to spot in my example app because I am writing out messages throughout the life of the requests. Figure 9-5 shows the sequence of messages in both situations – the left panel shows the effect with the return keyword and the right panel shows the effect without it. The telltale is where the All Requests Complete message appears in the sequence of events.

It isn't always a mistake to omit the return keyword. If you want to defer some task until a predecessor has completed, but don't care about the outcome of that task, then omitting the return keyword is entirely appropriate. Just make sure you know what effect you are aiming for and include or omit return as required.

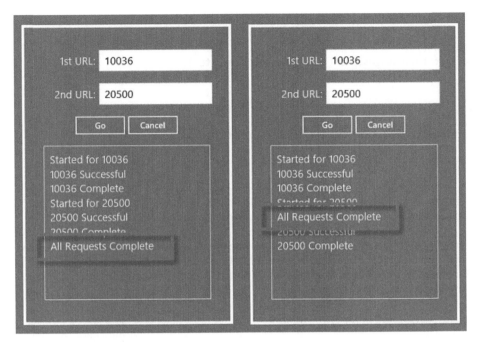

Figure 9-5. The effect of omitting the return keyword from a then callback function

Cancelling Promises

You can request that a Promise be cancelled by calling the Cancel method. This isn't as useful as it might sound because Promises are not required to support cancellation and, if they do, cancellation is a request and the Promise will almost certainly complete its current item of work before checking for cancellation (you can see how this works when I show you how to create your own Promises later in this chapter).

The Promise returned by the WinJS.Xhr function *does* support cancellation, which is one of the reasons why I have used it in this chapter. There is no way to discover the unfulfilled Promise objects in your app, so you need to keep references to the Promises like you would any variable you want to refer to again. You can see how I have wired up the Cancel button and kept references to the Promise objects I create in Listing 9-9.

Listing 9-9. Canceling Promises

```
...
var p1;
var p2;

$('input').listen("change", function (e) {
    ViewModel.State[this.id] = this.value;
});

$('button').listen("click", function (e) {
    if (this.id == "go") {
        p1 = requestData(ViewModel.State.zip1, middle);
        p1.then(function () {
```

```
            p2 = requestData(ViewModel.State.zip2, right);
            return p2;
        }).then(function () {
            ViewModel.State.messages.push("All Requests Complete");
        });
    } else {
        p1.cancel();
        p2.cancel();
        ViewModel.State.messages.push("All Requests Canceled");
    }
});
...
```

When the Cancel button is pressed, I call the cancel method on each of the Promise objects I created when the Go button was pressed. This signals the Promise objects that I want to terminate the requests to the server.

When you cancel a Promise, the error callback is invoked. The object passed to the function has three properties (name, message and description) all of which are set to the string Canceled. You can see how I have handled this situation in the callback function in Listing 9-10. I display the statusText value if there is one and the value of the message property otherwise.

Listing 9-10. Dealing with cancelation in the error callback

```
...
function requestData(zip, targetElem) {

    ViewModel.State.messages.push("Started for " + zip);

    var promise = WinJS.xhr({
        url: "http://gomashup.com/json.php?fds=geo/usa/zipcode/" + zip
    }).then(function (xhr) {
        ViewModel.State.messages.push(zip + " Successful");
        var dataObject = JSON.parse(xhr.response.slice(1, -1)).result;
        WinJS.Utilities.empty(targetElem);
        zipTemplate.winControl.render(dataObject[0], targetElem);
    }, function (xhr) {
        ViewModel.State.messages.push(zip + " Failed");
        WinJS.Utilities.empty(targetElem);
        targetElem.innerText = "Error: "
            + (xhr.statusText != null ? xhr.statusText : xhr.message);
    }).then(function () {
        ViewModel.State.messages.push(zip + " Complete");
    });

    return promise;
}
...
```

The easiest way to test this feature is to restart (rather than refresh the app), click the Go button and then immediately click the Cancel button. Restarting is important because it means that no aspect of the request is cached, giving you just enough time to perform the cancellation. You can see the effect in Figure 9-6.

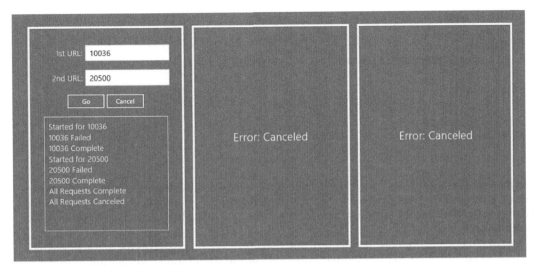

Figure 9-6. The effect of cancelling the requests

Passing a Result from a Promise

You can see in Figure 9-6 that the chained tasks that write the `Complete` message for each request and the overall `All Requests Complete` message are still executed when the `Promises` that make the requests are cancelled tasks are cancelled.

Sometimes, this is exactly what you will want: a task that is performed irrespective of what happened in the preceding `Promise`, but often you will want to be selective about how you proceed in the face of an error. In Listing 9-11, you can see the changes that I made to the `requestData` function in the `default.js` file to present the `Complete` messages from being displayed when the requests are cancelled, which I do by returning a result from my `Promise` functions.

Listing 9-11. Passing a result from a Promise

```
...
function requestData(zip, targetElem) {

    ViewModel.State.messages.push("Started for " + zip);

    var promise = WinJS.xhr({
        url: "http://gomashup.com/json.php?fds=geo/usa/zipcode/" + zip
    }).then(function (xhr) {
        ViewModel.State.messages.push(zip + " Successful");
        var dataObject = JSON.parse(xhr.response.slice(1, -1)).result;
        WinJS.Utilities.empty(targetElem);
        zipTemplate.winControl.render(dataObject[0], targetElem);
        return true;
    }, function (xhr) {
        ViewModel.State.messages.push(zip + " Failed");
        WinJS.Utilities.empty(targetElem);
        targetElem.innerText = "Error: "
            + (xhr.statusText != null ? xhr.statusText : xhr.message);
```

207

```
                return false;
        }).then(function (allok) {
            if (allok) {
                ViewModel.State.messages.push(zip + " Complete");
            }
            return allok;
        });

    return promise;
}
...
```

When the Promise returned by the WinJS.xhr function is fulfilled, either my success or error handler functions will be executed. I have changed the success handler so that it returns true, indicating that the request completed. I changed the error handler to return false, indicating that something went wrong or the request was canceled.

The true or false value from the handler function that is executed is passed as the argument to the next then function in the chain. In this example, I use that value to see if I should display the Complete message for the request.

You can pass any object along the chain of Promise objects in this way, and each then function can return a different result or even a different kind of result. In the listing, I return the same value from my then function that I received as the argument, when I then use elsewhere in the default.js file, as shown in Listing 9-12.

Listing 9-12. Passing the result farther along the chain

```
...
$('button').listen("click", function (e) {
    if (this.id == "go") {
        p1 = requestData(ViewModel.State.zip1, middle);
        p1.then(function () {
            p2 = requestData(ViewModel.State.zip2, right);
            return p2;
        }).then(function (allok) {
            if (allok) {
                ViewModel.State.messages.push("All Requests Complete");
            }
        });
    } else {
        p1.cancel();
        p2.cancel();
        ViewModel.State.messages.push("All Requests Canceled");
    }
});
...
```

Remember that the Promise object returned by the requestData function is the one returned by the final then function, so the result I return from that function will be passed as the argument to the next function in the chain – which is the one shown in the listing. I use the true/false value to determine if I should display the All Requests Complete message to the user. This is a simple example of data flowing through a chain of Promises, but it neatly demonstrates how flexible this technique can be. You can see the reduced set of messages displayed to the user when the Cancel button is clicked in Figure 9-7.

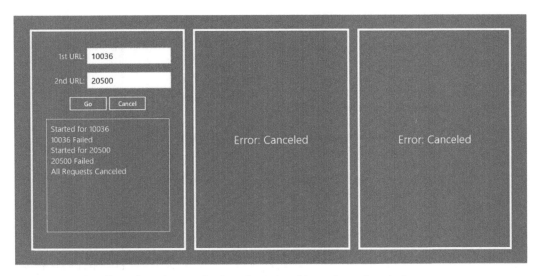

Figure 9-7. The effect of passing results from Promise objects through a chain

Coordinating Promises

The then function isn't the only method available to coordinate asynchronous tasks. The Promise object supports several other methods that can be used to create specific effects or make it easier to work with multiple Promise objects. I summarize these methods in Table 9-2 and demonstrate their use below.

Table 9-2. Coordination methods defined by the WinJS.Promise object

Method	Description
any([])	Accepts an array of Promise objects and returns a Promise which is fulfilled when *one* of the Promises in the array is fulfilled.
join([])	Accepts an array of Promise objects and returns a Promise which is fulfilled when *all* of the Promises in the array are fulfilled.
timeout(time, promise)	Cancels the Promise if it isn't fulfilled in the specified period.
theneach([], functon, function, function)	Applies the same set of callback functions to an array of Promise objects.

Using the any method

The any method accepts an array of Promises and returns a Promise as its result. The Promise returned by the any method is fulfilled when *any* one of the Promise objects in the argument array is fulfilled. You can see the any method in use in Listing 9-13.

Listing 9-13. Using the any method

```
...
var p1, p2;
```

```
$('button').listen("click", function (e) {
    if (this.id == "go") {
        p1 = requestData(ViewModel.State.zip1, middle);
        p2 = requestData(ViewModel.State.zip2, right);

        WinJS.Promise.any([p1, p2]).then(function (complete) {
            complete.value.then(function (result) {
                if (result) {
                    ViewModel.State.messages.push("Request " + complete.key
                        + " Completed First");
                } else {
                    ViewModel.State.messages.push("Request " + complete.key
                        + " Canceled or Error");
                }
            });
        });

    } else {
        p1.cancel();
        p2.cancel();
        ViewModel.State.messages.push("All Requests Canceled");
    }
});
...
```

If you use the then method to set up a callback on the Promise returned by the any method, your function will be passed an object that has two properties. The key property returns the index of the Promise in the argument array that was fulfilled (and which caused the any Promise to be fulfilled as a consequence). The value property returns a Promise which, when fulfilled, passes on the result from the task chain. You can see how I use both of these values to write a message to the layout which reports on which request completed first and its result. You can see the output that this example generates in Figure 9-8.

Figure 9-8. Using the any method to report which Promise is fulfilled first

■ **Tip**   The `Promise` returned by the any method is fulfilled as soon as one of the underlying `Promises` is fulfilled. The any `Promise` doesn't wait until all of the `Promises` are fulfilled and then tell you which was first. The other `Promise` objects may still be unfulfilled the moment when the any `Promise` is fulfilled.

Using the join method

The join method is similar to the any method, but the `Promise` it returns isn't fulfilled until *all* of the `Promise` objects in the argument array have been fulfilled. You can see the `join` method in use in Listing 9-14. The argument passed to the then callback is an array containing the results for all of the original `Promise` objects, arranged in the order of the original array.

Listing 9-14. Using the join method

```
...
var p1, p2;

$('button').listen("click", function (e) {
    if (this.id == "go") {
        p1 = requestData(ViewModel.State.zip1, middle);
        p2 = requestData(ViewModel.State.zip2, right);

        WinJS.Promise.any([p1, p2]).then(function (complete) {
            complete.value.then(function (result) {
                if (result) {
                    ViewModel.State.messages.push("Request " + complete.key
                        + " Completed First");
                } else {
                    ViewModel.State.messages.push("Request " + complete.key
                        + " Canceled or Error");
                }
            });
        });

        WinJS.Promise.join([p1, p2]).then(function (results) {
            ViewModel.State.messages.push(results.length + " Requests Complete");
            results.forEach(function (result, index) {
                ViewModel.State.messages.push("Request: " + index + ": " + result);
            });
        });

    } else {
        p1.cancel();
        p2.cancel();
        ViewModel.State.messages.push("All Requests Canceled");
    }
});
...
```

Notice that I am able to use the any and join methods on the same set of Promise objects. A Promise is able to support multiple calls to the then method and will correctly execute multiple sets of callbacks. You can see the effect of using the any and then methods in Figure 9-9.

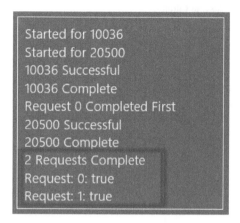

Figure 9-9. The messages displayed as a result from the any and join methods

Working with Timeouts

The Promise.timeout method has two uses, which do very different things. The simplest form of the timeout method takes a single numeric argument and returns a Promise that is fulfilled after the specified period. This may seem a little odd, but it can be useful when you want to defer the scheduling of a chain of Promises. You can see how this works in Listing 9-15.

Listing 9-15. Using the timeout method to defer Promises

```
...
var p1, p2;

$('button').listen("click", function (e) {
    if (this.id == "go") {

        WinJS.Promise.timeout(3000).then(function () {
            p1 = requestData(ViewModel.State.zip1, middle);
            p2 = requestData(ViewModel.State.zip2, right);

            WinJS.Promise.any([p1, p2]).then(function (complete) {
                complete.value.then(function (result) {
                    if (result) {
                        ViewModel.State.messages.push("Request "
                            + complete.key + " Completed First");
                    } else {
                        ViewModel.State.messages.push("Request "
                            + complete.key + " Canceled or Error");
                    }
                });
            });
        });
```

```
            WinJS.Promise.join([p1, p2]).then(function (results) {
                ViewModel.State.messages.push(results.length + " Requests Complete");
                results.forEach(function (result, index) {
                    ViewModel.State.messages.push("Request: " + index + ": " + result);
                });
            });
        });
    } else {
        p1.cancel();
        p2.cancel();
        ViewModel.State.messages.push("All Requests Canceled");
    }
});
...
```

In this listing, I create a delay of three seconds. Once that period has elapsed, the Promise returned by the timeout method is automatically fulfilled and the callback function I set up with the then method is invoked – in this case, the effect is that my requests to the server for the zip code data are not started until three seconds after the Go button is clicked.

Setting Timeouts for Promises

The other use of the timeout method is to set an expiry for a Promise. To use this version of the method, you pass in a timeout value and the Promise you want it to be applied to. You can see how this form of the timeout method used in Listing 9-16.

Listing 9-16. Using the timeout method to automatically cancel Promises

```
...
var p1, p2;

$('button').listen("click", function (e) {
    if (this.id == "go") {

        WinJS.Promise.timeout(250, p1 = requestData(ViewModel.State.zip1, middle));
        WinJS.Promise.timeout(2000, p2 = requestData(ViewModel.State.zip2, right));

        WinJS.Promise.any([p1, p2]).then(function (complete) {
            complete.value.then(function (result) {
                if (result) {
                    ViewModel.State.messages.push("Request "
                        + complete.key + " Completed First");
                } else {
                    ViewModel.State.messages.push("Request "
                        + complete.key + " Canceled or Error");
                }
            });
        });
    } else {
        p1.cancel();
        p2.cancel();
```

```
                ViewModel.State.messages.push("All Requests Canceled");
    }
});
...
```

In this listing, I use the `timeout` method to set a maximum duration of 250 milliseconds for one request and 2 second for the other. If the requests complete in those times, then nothing special happens. However, if the `Promise` objects are not fulfilled at the end of the period, they will be `cancelled` automatically (which is performed by calling the cancel method I demonstrated earlier in this chapter). For this to be useful, you need to make sure that the `Promise` objects you are using support cancelation.

Applying the Same Callback Functions to Multiple Promises

The `theneach` method is a convenient way of applying the same set of callback functions to an array of `Promise` objects. This method doesn't change the order in which the `Promises` are scheduled, but it does return a `Promise` which is equivalent to calling the `join` method for all of the `Promises` returned by the callback functions. Listing 9-17 shows the `theneach` method in use.

Listing 9-17. Using the theneach method

```
...
var p1, p2;

$('button').listen("click", function (e) {
    if (this.id == "go") {

        p1 = requestData(ViewModel.State.zip1, middle);
        p2 = requestData(ViewModel.State.zip2, right);

        WinJS.Promise.thenEach([p1, p2], function (data) {
            ViewModel.State.messages.push("A Request is Complete");
        }).then(function (results) {
            ViewModel.State.messages.push(results.length + " Requests Complete");
        });

    } else {
        p1.cancel();
        p2.cancel();
        ViewModel.State.messages.push("All Requests Canceled");
    }
});
...
```

I have specified only a success function, but you can specify error and progress callbacks as well. There is no context information passed to the callbacks to indicate which `Promise` is being dealt with, which makes the theneach method less useful than it could otherwise be.

Creating Custom Promises

There are two ways to create asynchronous methods. The first, which you have already seen, is to build on existing asynchronous methods, manipulate the Promise objects that they return and return the result. The requestData function from the first example app in this chapter is a good example of an asynchronous method that is created this way.

The other approach is to implement your own Promise and create a custom task to be performed at some point in the future. This is the approach that you take when you want to create an asynchronous method from scratch. In this section, I'll show you how to create your own Promise objects. I have created a Visual Studio project called CustomPromise, where all of the markup, code and CSS are contained in a single file. You can see the content of this file, default.html, in Listing 9-18.

■ **Caution** This is an advanced topic which you won't need for most apps. That said, even if you don't need to use this technique immediately, quickly skimming through this section will help you understand how the Promise objects returned by the methods in the WinJS and Windows namespaces work.

Listing 9-18. The default.html file

```html
<!DOCTYPE html>
<html>
<head>
    <meta charset="utf-8" />
    <title></title>
    <link href="//Microsoft.WinJS.1.0/css/ui-dark.css" rel="stylesheet" />
    <script src="//Microsoft.WinJS.1.0/js/base.js"></script>
    <script src="//Microsoft.WinJS.1.0/js/ui.js"></script>
    <style>
        body {
            display: -ms-flexbox; -ms-flex-direction: column;
            -ms-flex-align: center; -ms-flex-pack: center;
        }
        body, button { font-size: 30pt; margin: 5px}
        #output { margin: 20px; }
    </style>
    <script>
        function displayMessage(msg) {
            output.innerText = msg;
        };

        function calculateSum(count) {
            var total = 0;
            for (var i = 1; i < count; i++) {
                total += i;
            }
            return total;
        };

        WinJS.Application.onactivated = function (args) {
            WinJS.Utilities.query("button").listen("click", function (e) {
```

```
                displayMessage("Starting");
                var total = calculateSum(10000000);
                displayMessage("Done: " + total);
            });
        };
        WinJS.Application.start();
    </script>
</head>
<body>
    <button>Go</button>
    <div id="output">
        Output will appear here
    </div>
</body>
</html>
```

This simple app is perfect for demonstrating how to create custom `Promises`. You can see the layout in Figure 9-10.

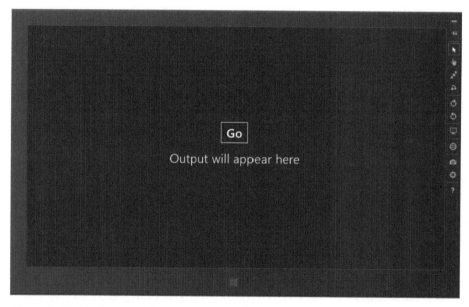

Figure 9-10. *The layout of the CustomPromise app*

When the Go button is clicked, I call the `calculateSum` function which generates the sum of the first 10,000,000 integers. This task takes several seconds to complete, during which the app is *unresponsive*. When an app is unresponsive, the UI won't respond to user interaction. For this simple example, you can tell there is a problem because the `button` element doesn't return to its un-pressed state after it has been clicked until the sum calculation has completed. This is because the `click` event is triggered and processed before the CSS changes are applied, meaning that the calculation blocks any UI updates until it is done. This is the problem that an asynchronous method will solve.

■ **Tip** The value of 10,000,000 works nicely for my PC, but you may need to increase it if you have a faster system or reduce it for a slower one. To get the essence of the problem (and the solution), you want the task to take about 5-10 seconds.

Implementing the Promise

The first step is to create the Promise object, which you do by passing a function to the Promise object constructor. You can see how I have done this in Listing 9-19.

Listing 9-19. Creating a Promise object

```
...
<script>
    function displayMessage(msg) {
        output.innerText = msg;
    };

    function calculateSum(count) {
        return new WinJS.Promise(function (fDone, fError, fProgress) {
            if (count < 5000) {
                fError("Count too small");
            } else {
                var total = 0;
                for (var i = 1; i < count; i++) {
                    total += i;
                }
                fDone(total);
            }
        });
    };

    WinJS.Application.onactivated = function (args) {
        WinJS.Utilities.query("button").listen("click", function (e) {

            displayMessage("Starting");

            calculateSum(10000000).then(function (total) {
                displayMessage("Done: " + total);
            }, function (err) {
                displayMessage("Error: " + err.message);
            });
        });
    };

    WinJS.Application.start();
</script>
...
```

The function that you pass to the Promise constructor takes three arguments, each of which is a function. The first argument is the one you call when you have completed your task and want to return a result. You call the second argument if you want to report an error. The final argument is called when you want to make a progress report.

You can see that I have added support for reporting an error in this listing. If the count argument for the calculateSum function is less than 5000, I call the fError function to indicate a problem. For other values, I calculate the sum and return the result via the fDone function. (Ignore, if you will, the fact that the target is fixed – the calculateSum function doesn't know this).

When you create an asynchronous method, you return Promise object so that the caller can use the then method to receive the result of the task or create a chain. You can see how I do just this in the example in order to get the result from the Promise returned by the calculateSum method.

Deferring Execution

I have implemented a Promise, but I still have a problem: the app is still unresponsive when I click the Go button. Creating a Promise doesn't automatically defer the execution of the task, which is a commonly-encountered pitfall. To make a truly asynchronous method, I have to take an additional step and explicitly schedule the work. I have done this using the setImmediate function, as shown in Listing 9-20.

Listing 9-20. Deferring execution of the task

```
...
<script>
    function displayMessage(msg) {
        output.innerText = msg;
    };

    function calculateSum(count) {
        return new WinJS.Promise(function (fDone, fError, fProgress) {
            if (count < 5000) {
                fError("Count too small");
            } else {
                var total = 0;
                var blocks = 50;
                function calcBlock(start, blockcount, blocksize) {
                    for (var i = start; i < start + blocksize; i++) {
                        total += i;
                    };

                    if (blockcount == blocks) {
                        fDone(total);
                    } else {
                        fProgress(blockcount * 2);
                        setImmediate(function () {
                            calcBlock(start + blocksize, ++blockcount, blocksize)
                        });
                    }
                };

                setImmediate(function () {
```

```
                    calcBlock(0, 1, count / blocks), 1000
                });
            }
        });
    };

    WinJS.Application.onactivated = function (args) {
        WinJS.Utilities.query("button").listen("click", function (e) {

            displayMessage("Starting");

            calculateSum(10000000).then(function (total) {
                displayMessage("Done: " + total);
            }, function (err) {
                displayMessage("Error: " + err.message);
            }, function (progress) {
                displayMessage("Progress: " + progress + "%");
            });
        });
    };

    WinJS.Application.start();
</script>
...
```

There are two basic rules to creating a good asynchronous method. The first rule is to break the task into small subtasks that take only a short period of time to complete. The second rule is to schedule only schedule one subtask at a time. If you deviate from either rule, then you will end up with a non-responsive app *and* the expense involved in creating and managing a Promise.

The best way to create subtasks will vary based on the kind of work being done. For my example, I just have to perform the calculation in smaller chunks, each of which is handled by a call to the inline calcBlock function in the listing.

I have scheduled my subtasks using the setImmediate method, which is defined as part of the IE10 support for JavaScript. This is a relatively new method which is intended to complement the commonly used setTimeout. When you pass a function to setImmediate, you are asking for it to be executed as soon as all the pending events and UI updates have been completed.

The reason that you need to use subtasks is that any new events and UI updates will build up once the JavaScript runtime has started executing your function. You give the JavaScript runtime a chance to clear the event and update backlog by breaking the work into subtasks and only calling setImmediate when each task has completed. Between finishing executing one subtask and starting the next, the runtime is able to respond to user input and keep the app responsive.

Since I have broken up the work into subtasks, I take the opportunity to call the fProgress function at the end of each set of calculations to report progress to any interested listeners. You can see that I have added a third function to my then call to receive and display this information.

PARALLELISM IN WINDOWS APPS

If you have paid close attention to this chapter, you will notice that I don't use the word *parallel*. JavaScript is executed in a single-threaded runtime, which is why there are no keywords to ensure atomic updates or create critical sections, as you would find in languages like C# and Java. You don't create a new thread when you create an asynchronous method and implement the background task; instead, you are simply deferring the task until the main (and only) thread is able and willing to execute it.

However, it *is* possible to create truly parallel apps in JavaScript, where different tasks are performed concurrently by different threads. One way is to build on asynchronous functionality which is written in native code. You have already seen an example of this when I used an XMLHttpRequest object to make Ajax requests. The XMLHttpRequest object is part of the browser and is able to create and manage multiple concurrent requests. This parallelism is hidden from the JavaScript code and notifications for callbacks are marshaled to the main JavaScript thread for simple processing. The Windows API is also written in native code and your calls will often lead to the creation and execution of multiple threads, even if that complexity is hidden away from you as the JavaScript programmer.

If you want to create a truly parallel app in JavaScript, then you should look at the Web Workers specification. This is one of the specifications associated with HTML5 and it is supported by IE10. Web workers are relatively expensive to create and maintain, which means that they are only suited for long-lived tasks and should be used sparingly. I don't get into the Web Workers specification in this book because it is not an app-specific feature, but you can read more about the IE10 support at `http://msdn.microsoft.com/en-us/library/windows/apps/hh767434.aspx`.

Implement Cancelation

You don't have to implement support for cancelation in your custom Promises but it is a good idea to do so, especially for long-lived or resource intensive tasks.

This is because calling the cancel method will trigger the error callbacks to signal the cancelation even if your Promise doesn't support cancelation. This means that your Promise will keep scheduling work (and consuming resources as it does so) even though the callback functions have been called and the app has moved on. As the final insult, the result from your task will be quietly discarded.

To implement cancelation, you pass a second function to the Promise constructor. If the cancel method is called on the Promise object, then your function will be executed. You can see how I have added cancelation support to my example in Listing 9-21.

Listing 9-21. Adding support for cancelation in a custom Promise

```
<!DOCTYPE html>
<html>
<head>
    <meta charset="utf-8" />
    <title></title>
    <link href="//Microsoft.WinJS.1.0/css/ui-dark.css" rel="stylesheet" />
    <script src="//Microsoft.WinJS.1.0/js/base.js"></script>
    <script src="//Microsoft.WinJS.1.0/js/ui.js"></script>
    <style>
        body {
            display: -ms-flexbox; -ms-flex-direction: column;
            -ms-flex-align: center; -ms-flex-pack: center;
        }
        body, button { font-size: 30pt; margin: 5px;}
        #output { margin: 20px; }
    </style>
    <script>
        function displayMessage(msg) {
```

```
        output.innerText = msg;
};

function calculateSum(count) {
    var canceled = false;
    return new WinJS.Promise(function (fDone, fError, fProgress) {
        if (count < 5000) {
            fError("Count too small");
        } else {
            var total = 0;
            var blocks = 50;
            function calcBlock(start, blockcount, blocksize) {
                for (var i = start; i < start + blocksize; i++) {
                    total += i;
                };

                if (blockcount == blocks) {
                    fDone(total);
                } else if (!canceled) {
                    fProgress(blockcount * 2);
                    setImmediate(function () {
                        calcBlock(start + blocksize, ++blockcount, blocksize)
                    });
                }
            };

            setImmediate(function () {
                calcBlock(0, 1, count / blocks), 1000
            });
        }
    }, function () {
        canceled = true;
    });
};

var promise;

WinJS.Application.onactivated = function (args) {
    WinJS.Utilities.query("button").listen("click", function (e) {
        if (this.innerText == "Go") {
            displayMessage("Starting");

            promise = calculateSum(5000000)

            promise.then(function (total) {
                displayMessage("Done: " + total);
            }, function (err) {
                displayMessage("Error: " + err.message);
            }, function (progress) {
                displayMessage("Progress: " + progress + "%");
            });
```

```
                    } else {
                        if (promise != null) {
                            promise.cancel();
                        }
                    }
                });
            };

        WinJS.Application.start();
    </script>
</head>
<body>
    <button>Go</button>
    <button>Cancel</button>
    <div id="output">
        Output will appear here
    </div>
</body>
</html>
```

I added a Cancel button to the HTML in default.html and clicking this button calls the cancel method of the Promise created when the Go button was clicked. Notice that I am careful to cancel the Promise returned by the calculateSum function and not the Promise returned by the then method – it is important to cancel the Promise that is doing the work, not the Promises that will be started subsequently.

■ **Tip** Note that you don't have to check for cancelation constantly. I find that performing a check before scheduling the next subtask is a reasonable approach, striking a good balance between responsiveness and complexity.

Creating Synthetic Promises

You will find that the WinJS.Promise object is used so widely in the Windows APIs that there are times when you need to create a Promise that acts as a wrapper around a data value that you already have to hand. There are some helpful methods defined by the WinJS.Promise object that can help in this situation. I have described these methods in Table 9-3 and demonstrate the two most useful in the sections below.

Table 9-3. *Other WinJS.Promise methods*

Method	Description
as(object)	If the argument is a Promise it is returned unmodified. If the argument is not a Promise, then the result is as though the object were passed to the wrap method.
is(object)	Returns true if the argument is a Promise object (this will return true for any object which defines a then method).
wrap(value)	Returns a Promise that is immediately fulfilled and returns value as its result.
wrapError(error)	Creates a Promise that signals an error using the argument.

I have updated the CustomPromise app so that there is a function which accepts a Promise and use the then method to set up the callbacks which will display information to the user. You can see the script element for this example in Listing 9-22 (the HTML and CSS have not changed).

Listing 9-22. Creating a function which accepts a Promise

```
...
<script>
    function displayMessage(msg) {
        output.innerText = msg;
    };

    function displayResults(promise) {
        promise.then(function (total) {
            displayMessage("Done: " + total);
        }, function (err) {
            displayMessage("Error: " + err.message);
        }, function (progress) {
            displayMessage("Progress: " + progress + "%");
        });
    };

    function calculateSum(count) {
        var canceled = false;
        return new WinJS.Promise(function (fDone, fError, fProgress) {
            if (count < 5000) {
                fError("Count too small");
            } else {
                var total = 0;
                var blocks = 50;
                function calcBlock(start, blockcount, blocksize) {
                    for (var i = start; i < start + blocksize; i++) {
                        total += i;
                    };
                    if (blockcount == blocks) {
                        fDone(total);
                    } else if (!canceled) {
                        fProgress(blockcount * 2);
                        setImmediate(function () {
                            calcBlock(start + blocksize, ++blockcount, blocksize)
                        });
                    }
                };
                setImmediate(function () {
                    calcBlock(0, 1, count / blocks), 1000
                });
            }
        }, function () {
            canceled = true;
        });
    };
```

```
    var promise;

    WinJS.Application.onactivated = function (args) {
        WinJS.Utilities.query("button").listen("click", function (e) {
            if (this.innerText == "Go") {
                displayMessage("Starting");
                promise = calculateSum(10000000)
                displayResults(promise);
            } else {
                if (promise != null) {
                    promise.cancel();
                }
            }
        });
    };
    WinJS.Application.start();
</script>
...
```

In this arrangement, my hands are tied if I want to display data that is not in a Promise. I could, of course, rewrite the function to be more flexible, but that isn't always possible, especially when working with someone else's code. The solution is to create a Promise whose sole purpose is to return a value or error. There is no asynchronous aspect to such a Promise, which is why they are referred to as *synthetic* Promises.

Writing Your Own Synthetic Promise

The best way to understand how this works is to start by writing your own synthetic Promise. For this example, I want to address two new situations in my code. I want to display an error if the user clicks the Cancel button before clicking the Go button and I want optimize the app so that I don't perform the calculation if I already know the result (i.e. if the user clicks the Go button twice in sequence). You can see the additions I need to make to the script element in Listing 9-23.

Listing 9-23. Creating custom synthetic Promise objects

```
...
<script>
    function displayMessage(msg) {
        output.innerText = msg;
    };

    function displayResults(promise) {
        promise.then(function (total) {
            displayMessage("Done: " + total);
        }, function (err) {
            displayMessage("Error: " + err.message);
        }, function (progress) {
            displayMessage("Progress: " + progress + "%");
        });
    };
```

```
var lastResult;
var lastCount = 0;

function calculateSum(count) {
    var canceled = false;

    if (count == lastCount && lastResult != null) {
        return new WinJS.Promise(function (fDone, fError, fProg) {
            fDone(lastResult + " (Cached)");
        });
    } else {
        return new WinJS.Promise(function (fDone, fError, fProgress) {

            if (count < 5000) {
                fError("Count too small");
            } else {
                var total = 0;
                var blocks = 50;
                function calcBlock(start, blockcount, blocksize) {
                    for (var i = start; i < start + blocksize; i++) {
                        total += i;
                    };

                    if (blockcount == blocks) {
                        lastResult = total;
                        lastCount = count;
                        fDone(total);
                    } else if (!canceled) {
                        fProgress(blockcount * 2);
                        setImmediate(function () {
                            calcBlock(start + blocksize, ++blockcount, blocksize)
                        });
                    }
                };
                setImmediate(function () {
                    calcBlock(0, 1, count / blocks), 1000
                });
            }
        }, function () {
            canceled = true;
        });
    }
};

var promise;

WinJS.Application.onactivated = function (args) {
    WinJS.Utilities.query("button").listen("click", function (e) {
        if (this.innerText == "Go") {
            displayMessage("Starting");
            promise = calculateSum(10000000)
```

```
                    displayResults(promise);

              } else {
                    if (promise != null) {
                        promise.cancel();
                    } else {
                        var sPromise = new WinJS.Promise(function (fDone, fError, fProg) {
                            fError({message: "Nothing to Cancel"});
                        });
                        displayResults(sPromise);
                    }
              }
          });
    };
    WinJS.Application.start();
</script>
...
```

The Promises I create in this listing just return a result – there are no tasks and no calls to
setImmediate. In each case, I just call one of the functions to indicate that my Promise is fulfilled or
encountered an error.

Using the Wrapper Methods

The problem with the synthetic Promise objects I created in the last section is that the WinJS API doesn't
know I am just using them as adapters so I can use the displayResults function. There is a lot of plumbing
to set up when a Promise is created and I incur the cost of setting everything up just to discard it a moment
later. To address this, the Promise object defines the wrap and wrapError methods, which create light-
weight Promise objects. This means that they are explicitly intended to be used as adaptors and are less
complex and expensive to create. You use the wrap method when you want to create a Promise that is
fulfilled with a predetermined result and the wrapError method when you want to package up an error
message. Listing 9-24 shows the application of these methods to the example app.

Listing 9-24. Using the wrap and wrapError methods

```
...
<script>
    // ... code omitted for brevity...

    function calculateSum(count) {
        var canceled = false;

        if (count == lastCount && lastResult != null) {
            return WinJS.Promise.wrap(lastResult + " (Cached)");
        } else {
            return new WinJS.Promise(function (fDone, fError, fProgress) {
                // ... code omitted for brevity...
            }, function () {
                canceled = true;
            });
        }
```

```
        };

        var promise;

        WinJS.Application.onactivated = function (args) {
            WinJS.Utilities.query("button").listen("click", function (e) {
                if (this.innerText == "Go") {
                    displayMessage("Starting");
                    promise = calculateSum(10000000)
                    displayResults(promise);

                } else {
                    if (promise != null) {
                        promise.cancel();
                    } else {
                        displayResults(WinJS.Promise.wrapError({
                            message: "Nothing to Cancel"
                        }));
                    }
                }
            });
        };
        WinJS.Application.start();
    </script>
    ...
```

You should use the `wrap` and `wrapError` methods in preference to creating your own synthetic `Promise` objects. Not only are they less expensive, but they make for code which is less convoluted and, therefore, easier to read and maintain.

Summary

In this chapter, I have shown you the detail behind the `WinJS.Promise` object. There are a lot of asynchronous methods in the WinJS and Windows APIs and a good understanding of their mechanics is essential for writing complex apps. It is important to remember that JavaScript code in a Windows app is executed on a single thread, along with the event handlers and UI updates. When you create a custom asynchronous method, you are managing the scheduling of work on that single thread, rather than creating multiple parallel threads. If you get into trouble with asynchronous operations in an app, it will usually be because you are treating the code as though it were multi-threaded. In Part 3 of this book, I show you the WinJS UI controls which you can use to enhance your app and create a look-and-feel which is consistent with other Windows apps.

UI Development

In this part of the book, I show you the UI controls that you can use to build a richer Windows 8 user experience. These controls are used in conjunction with standard HTML elements and provide fluid touch and mouse interactions and support for creating data-driven app layouts.

CHAPTER 10

■ ■ ■

Creating the UI Controls Example Framework

In the chapters of this part of the book, I show you the WinJS UI controls. These are an important part of the WinJS UI and they are a useful supplement to the standard HTML elements that I have been using so far in the example apps. Not only do these controls provide a richer experience for users, but they also provide part of the distinctive look and feel of a Metro app.

There is wide variety of controls and I show them all to you. Each control has a number of configuration options which change their appearance and behavior and to make understanding these features as easy as possible, I want to be able to show you the effects they have on the control live in an example, rather than just describing them.

The amount of markup and code required to demonstrate each control is significant and to treat each one individually would require endless pages of listings for each chapter, which is as unappealing for me to write as it would be for you to read.

Instead, I have built a framework that I can use to easily and concisely generate the examples I need for of each of the UI controls and I use this framework in the chapters that follow. In this chapter, I introduce this framework and show you how it operates so that you'll understand what the smaller listings that I do provide mean. One benefit of this approach is that I have used the same WinJS features and techniques I described in the earlier chapters to create this example, so you can see how they can be applied in a more significant app.

■ **Note** You don't need to follow this chapter in detail to understand the chapters that follow and the descriptions of the WinJS UI controls they contain. I have included this chapter so you can see how I created the examples. There is a lot of code and markup in this chapter and it can be hard going, so you may want to skim through this material and return and read in more depth after you have built your first few Metro apps.

Understanding the Final App

It will help understand the app if you can see the result I am aiming for. My goal is to present you with a simple initial layout with a NavBar containing commands for each of the UI controls. You can see this initial layout in Figure 10-1, which shows the NavBar commands.

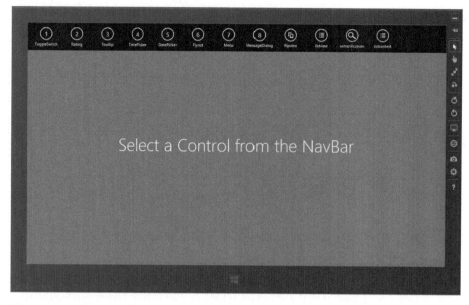

Figure 10-1. The initial layout of the app and the NavBar with a single command

There is one button for each of the NavBar commands and clicking on it will produce a page which contains two panels. The left panel will contain the UI control that I am demonstrating. The right panel will contain other UI controls that you can use to change the settings for the control in the left panel. You can see an example in Figure 10-2, which shows how I demonstrate the FlipView control (which I describe in Chapter 14).

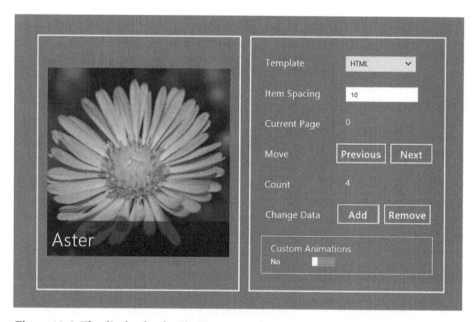

Figure 10-2. The display for the FlipView control

Each of the controls in the right panel lets you view or change a property of the control in the left panel. In creating the example framework, my goal is to be able to generate this markup and the code that drives it as concisely as possible. In Figure 10-2, you can see the different types of control that I will need to generate:

- A select element to let the user select from a fixed range of values
- An input element to let the user enter an unconstrained value
- A span element do display a read-only value to the user
- A set of button elements to let the user perform actions
- A ToggleSwitch control that lets the user select an boolean value

The ToggleSwitch control is one of the WinJS UI controls and I describe it in Chapter 11. You may want to read Chapter 11 and then return here, but my emphasis in this chapter is generating the markup I require and I don't go into the detail of the controls.

■ **Note**   Although the overall result is more concise than long and duplicative listings, the framework itself is quite complex and this chapter contains a lot of code, much of it related to dealing with templates, which I described in Chapter 8.

Creating the Basic Project Structure

To get started, I am going to create the basic structure of the app so that the initial message is displayed to the user and the NavBar is in place. I'll also add the navigation mechanism and put the code files in place that I'll use for the view model and to keep a list of the details of each set of configuration controls that I require. I start by creating a new Visual Studio project call UIControls using the Blank App template and making some basic additions to the default.html file, as shown in Listing 10-1.

Listing 10-1. The initial default.html file from the UIControls project

```
<!DOCTYPE html>
<html>
<head>
    <meta charset="utf-8">
    <title>UIControls</title>

    <!-- WinJS references -->
    <link href="//Microsoft.WinJS.1.0/css/ui-dark.css" rel="stylesheet" />
    <script src="//Microsoft.WinJS.1.0/js/base.js"></script>
    <script src="//Microsoft.WinJS.1.0/js/ui.js"></script>

    <!-- UIControls references -->
    <link href="/css/default.css" rel="stylesheet">
    <script src="/js/viewmodel.js"></script>
    <script src="/js/templates.js"></script>
    <script src="/js/controls.js"></script>
    <script src="/js/default.js"></script>
```

```
</head>
<body>
    <div id="navBarCommandTemplate" data-win-control="WinJS.Binding.Template">
        <button data-win-control="WinJS.UI.AppBarCommand"
            data-win-options="{section:'selection'}"
            data-win-bind="winControl.label: name; winControl.icon: icon">
        </button>
    </div>

    <div id="contentTarget">
        <h1 class="message">Select a Control from the NavBar</h1>
    </div>

    <div id="navbar" data-win-control="WinJS.UI.AppBar"
        data-win-options="{placement:'top'}"></div>
</body>
</html>
```

The script elements I added refer to code files that I'll add shortly.

The templates.js file will contain the code required to generate the elements I need using WinJS templates. These are the same kind of templates that I introduced in Chapter 8 and I'll be defining them in the default.html file. In fact, you can already see the first of the templates in the listing – the element whose id is navBarCommandTemplate will be used to generate the commands for the NavBar, allowing the user to navigate to the content pages in the app, each of which will showcase a single WinJS UI control.

The controls.js file will contain details of the configuration controls I need to generate in order to demonstrate each WinJS UI control. The viewmodel.js file will contain other bits and pieces I need, such binding value converters and data sets for the WinJS UI controls which are driven by data.

Adding the Template Generation Code

My next step was to create the js/templates.js file and populate it with the code required to generate the NavBar commands. You can see the initial version of this file in Listing 10-2, and I'll be adding to this file throughout the chapter as I add support for creating the different kinds of configuration control I require.

Listing 10-2. The initial version of the templates.js file

```
(function () {

    var navBarCommands = [
        { name: "AppTest", icon: "target" },
        { name: "ToggleSwitch", icon: "\u0031" },
        { name: "Rating", icon: "\u0032" },
        { name: "Tooltip", icon: "\u0033" },
        { name: "TimePicker", icon: "\u0034" },
        { name: "DatePicker", icon: "\u0035" },
        { name: "Flyout", icon: "\u0036" },
        { name: "Menu", icon: "\u0037" },
        { name: "MessageDialog", icon: "\u0038" },
        { name: "FlipView", icon: "pictures" },
        { name: "ListView", icon: "list" },
        { name: "SemanticZoom", icon: "zoom" },
```

```
        { name: "ListContext", icon: "list" },
    ];

    WinJS.Namespace.define("Templates", {

        generateNavBarCommands: function (navBarElement, templateElement) {
            navBarCommands.forEach(function (commandItem) {
                templateElement.winControl.render(commandItem, navBarElement);
            });
        },

    });
})();
```

The navBarCommands array contains details of each command that I want to create. Each item in the array has name and icon properties, which I use in the navBarCommandTemplate template I defined in the default.html file.

I will remove the first of these items, the one whose name property is AppTest, when I am done creating the framework. I have added it solely so that I can demonstrate the example framework as I create it and it won't be used in the rest of the chapters in this part of the book.

I have used the WinJS.Namespace.define method to create a new namespace called Templates. This namespace will contain the functions I need to generate elements from the templates I define in the default.html file. There is only one function to start with, which corresponds to the single template I have already defined. The generateNavBarCommands function takes two arguments: the first argument is the NavBar element into which the generated command elements will be inserted and the second argument is the template to use to generate those elements. The function enumerates the elements in the navBarCommands array and uses the WinJS.Binding.Template.render method to generate elements from the array item and insert them into the NavBar element.

UNDERSTANDING THE WINCONTROL PROPERTY

I introduced the winControl property in Chapter 8 when I showed you how to use templates, but it is a more general characteristic of WinJS and particularly important when it comes to the UI controls. As you'll soon see, WinJS UI controls are applied to regular HTML elements, most typically div elements. WinJS creates the controls by adding child elements, CSS styles and event listeners to the underlying element – a technique that is shared by web app UI libraries such as jQuery UI.

When WinJS creates the control, it adds the winControl property to the HTMLElement object representing the underlying element and sets the value of this property to an object from the WinJS.UI namespace. The object that you get back from the winControl property gives you access to the properties, methods and events defined by the WinJS.UI object and you can use them to configure the control or respond to user interaction. You'll see me use the winControl property a lot in this chapter and the chapters that follow to set up and then manage the WinJS controls that I create.

The WinJS.Binding.Template object follows the same pattern. I create a template by applying the data-win-control attribute set to the name of the control I want to create, which is this case is WinJS.Binding.Template. There is no visual component to a Template, but WinJS still creates the control and sets up the winControl property. The WinJS.Binding.Template control defines the render method and so to access this method, I locate the element which has the data-win-control attribute and call the render method on the object returned by the winControl property. This is a pattern you will see for all of the WinJS controls.

Adding the Navigation Code

In the /js/default.js file I have added the code that handles the WinJS.Navigation.navigating event and registers a listener function for the click event from the NavBar. I also call the ViewModel.Templates.generateNavBarCommands method to populate the NavBar with commands that will navigate the app to the content pages for individual UI controls (although I have not created these files yet, and therefore clicking on a NavBar command will result in an error). You can see the code in the default.js file in Listing 10-3.

Listing 10-3. The contents of the /js/default.js file

```
(function () {
    "use strict";

    var app = WinJS.Application;
    window.$ = WinJS.Utilities.query;
    WinJS.Binding.optimizeBindingReferences = true;

    WinJS.Navigation.addEventListener("navigating", function (e) {
        WinJS.UI.Animation.exitPage(contentTarget.children).then(function () {
            WinJS.Utilities.empty(contentTarget);
            WinJS.UI.Pages.render(e.detail.location, contentTarget)
                .then(function () {
                    return WinJS.Binding.processAll(contentTarget, ViewModel.State)
                        .then(function () {
                            return WinJS.UI.Animation.enterPage(contentTarget.children)
                        });
                });
        });
    });

    app.onactivated = function (eventObject) {
        WinJS.UI.processAll().then(function () {

            Templates.generateNavBarCommands(navbar, navBarCommandTemplate);

            navbar.addEventListener("click", function (e) {
                var navTarget = "pages/" + e.target.winControl.label + ".html";
                WinJS.Navigation.navigate(navTarget);
                navbar.winControl.hide();
            });
        })

        //.then(function() {
        //    return WinJS.Navigation.navigate("pages/AppTest.html");
        //})
    };

    app.start();
})();
```

The handler for the `navigating` event animates the transition from one content page to another using the `WinJS.UI.Animation` namespace, which I describe in Chapter 18. I have used it here because the transition between content can be too quick to notice and the animations help draw the user's eye to the fact that the content has changed.

The `click` event handler for the NavBar gets the value of the `label` property from command button that was used (via the `winControl` property) and uses this to navigate to a corresponding HTML file in the pages directory (which I'll create shortly). This follows the same navigation and content management pattern I introduced in Chapter 5 and which I have used in several example apps since.

The JavaScript in the `default.html` file is pretty simple because the heavy lifting will be performed by code which I'll add to the `templates.js` and `viewmodel.js` files. For this app, the default.html file is responsible only for setting up navigation and the NavBar.

■ **Tip** You will notice that there are some statements commented out in the listing. These are a useful shortcut to automatically display a given page of content when the app first loads, which is useful when you are testing and debugging the pages in the example app (otherwise you have to use the NavBar, which quickly becomes tiresome if you use short code-and-then-test cycles, as I do).

Adding the Other JavaScript Files

I want to get the basic structure of the app in place before I start adding pages of content, so I am going to add the `viewmodel.js` file and the `controls.js` files now, even though they will only contain code to create their namespaces. Listing 10-4 shows the content of the `js/controls.js` file, which creates a namespace called `App.Controls`. I will use this namespace to contain details of the controls I need to generate for each content page.

Listing 10-4. The contents of the controls.js file

```
(function () {

    WinJS.Namespace.define("App.Controls", {
        // ...details of configuration controls will go here
    });

})();
```

The initial version `js/viewmodel.js` file is shown in Listing 10-5 and at the moment it just creates a namespace called `ViewModel`.

Listing 10-5. The initial contents of the js/viewmodel.js file

```
(function () {
    "use strict";

    WinJS.Namespace.define("ViewModel", {
        // ...code for view model will go here
    });

})();
```

I won't be using the `viewmodel.js` file in this chapter, but I'll need it when I come to some of the more complex WinJS UI controls like `FlipView` and `ListView` (which I described in Chapters 14 and 15).

Adding the CSS

In the `css/default.css` file I have defined the common styles that I'll use to display the different UI controls. There are some controls which need some additional CSS, but I'll deal with this when I show you how the control works. You can see the contents of the `default.css` file in Listing 10-6. I have shown this file for completeness, but there are no new techniques in these styles and, for simplicity, I have not added support for responding to changes in the app view or orientation.

Listing 10-6. The contents of the css/default.css file

```
body {
    background-color: #5A8463; display: -ms-flexbox; -ms-flex-direction: column;
    -ms-flex-align: center; -ms-flex-pack: center; }

.inputContainer, .selectContainer, .spanContainer {
    width: 100%;}

h2.controlTitle {
    margin: 10px 0px; color: white; font-size: 20px; display: inline-block;
    padding: 10px; font-weight: bolder; width: 140px;}

.controlPanel .win-toggleswitch { width: 90%; margin: 15px; padding-left: 20px;}
.win-toggleswitch .win-title { color: white; font-size: 20px;}

div.flexContainer { display: -ms-flexbox;  -ms-flex-direction: row;
    -ms-flex-align: stretch; -ms-flex-pack: center; }

.controlPanel {
    display: -ms-flexbox; -ms-flex-direction: column; -ms-flex-align: center;
    -ms-flex-pack: center;     border: medium white solid;
    margin: 10px; padding: 20px; min-width: 300px;}

[data-win-control="WinJS.UI.ToggleSwitch"] {
    border: thin solid white; margin: 5px; padding: 10px;width: 250px;}

input.controlInput, select.controlSelect, span.controlSpan  {
    width: 150px;display: inline-block; margin-left: 20px;}

span.controlSpan {
    white-space: nowrap; text-overflow: ellipsis; overflow: hidden; font-size: 14pt;}

div.buttonContainer button {margin: 5px; font-size: 16pt;}

.textPara { display: inline-block; width: 200px; font-size: 18pt;}
.win-tooltip { background-color: #8ED09C; color: white;
    border: medium solid white; font-size: 16pt;}
```

If you run the app at this point you will see something similar to Figure 10-3. The NavBar is displayed on two lines in the figure because there are too many buttons for the standard Visual Studio Simulator resolution – you won't have this problem if the simulator is set to a larger resolution (which I described in Chapter 6). At the end of this chapter, I'll remove the AppTest button from the NavBar which will put the commands onto a single line. The AppTest button will navigate to the pages/Apptest.html file, which I only used to develop and demonstrate the example framework app.

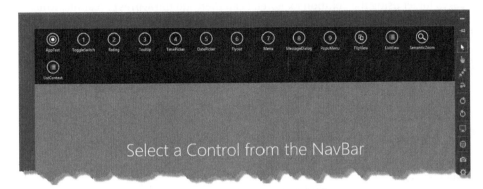

Figure 10- 3. The initial state of the example app

Creating the Test Content Page

The basic structure of the app is in place, which means I can turn my attention to creating the test content page and the code that is required to populate it. Once again, it will be easier to show you the finished content and then work back to show you how I created it. You can see the result of clicking the AppTest button on the NavBar in Figure 10-4.

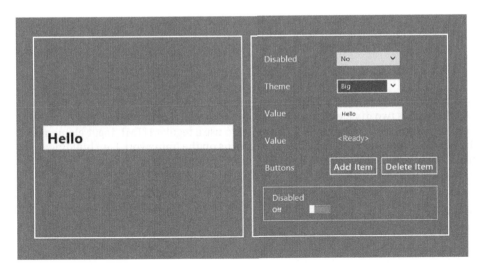

Figure 10-4. The finished content shown when the AppTest button is clicked on the NavBar

In the sections that follow, I'll walk you through the process I used to create this content and the code that generates a lot of its content.

Creating the Content page

Clicking one of the NavBar buttons loads a page of content from the project pages folder, so my first step is to actually create the pages folder using the Solution Explorer. I can then add the AppTest.html file, which is the file that will be loaded when the AppTest button on the NavBar is clicked. You can see the initial contents of this file in Listing 10-7.

Listing 10-7. The initial content of the AppTest.html page

```
<!DOCTYPE html>
<html>
<head>
    <title></title>
    <script>
        WinJS.UI.Pages.define("/pages/AppTest.html", {
            ready: function () {
                Templates.createControls(rightPanel, inputElem, "apptest");
            }
        });
    </script>
</head>
<body>
    <div class="flexContainer">

        <div class="controlPanel">
            <input id="inputElem"/>
        </div>

        <div id="rightPanel" class="controlPanel"></div>
    </div>
</body>
</html>
```

This file shows the standard pattern that I will follow to demonstrate each WinJS UI control. The HTML markup in the file contains two div elements. The first contains the UI control that I am demonstrating. To keep things simple in this chapter, I am going to use a regular HTML input element, rather than one of the WinJS UI controls – this will allow me to focus on the framework I am building without having to dive into the details of the WinJS controls. For this example, I have assigned the input element an id value of inputElem, as follows:

```
...
<div class="controlPanel">
    <input id="inputElem"/>
</div>
...
```

The other div element will contain the elements that will let the user configure the control being demonstrated. This is the main focus of this chapter – the process of describing the elements that I need and generating them from templates, so that I don't have to duplicate a ton of markup and code in subsequent chapters. The id of the target div element is rightPanel, named because it is the right-most panel in the layout:

```
...
<div id="rightPanel" class="controlPanel"></div>
...
```

The most important part of the content page is the JavaScript contained in the script element. I use the WinJS Pages feature from Chapter 5 to register a ready function that will be executed when the content page is loaded. The critical statement is the call to the Templates.createControls method, as follows:

```
...
Templates.createControls(rightPanel, inputElem, "apptest");
...
```

This is the method that generates the configuration elements I require. The arguments to this method are:

- The target element, which will contain the configuration controls that are created
- The UI control element that is being demonstrated
- A key which identifies the set of controls to generate

For the AppTest.html file, the target element is the one whose id is rightPanel. The input element is the one being demonstrated and the key I have used is apptest. You will see how these values are put to use in the next section.

Creating the Template System

Now that I have a test content page to work with, I can begin to build out the code that will generate the elements I require to demonstrate some of the features of the input element which, as you will recall, is acting as a simple stand-in for a real WinJS UI control. In the sections that follow, I'll show you how I describe the set of configuration elements that are required and the means by which I create them.

I am going to start by creating just a single configuration element. It will be a select element which can be used to disable or enable the input element. You can see how this select element will look when it is created in Figure 10-5. It is pretty straight-forward and is a good place for me to start describing the different parts of the code.

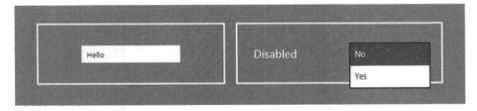

Figure 10-5. Generating a select element to configure the input element

Describing a Select Element

I have to start by describing the select element that I want to generate. I do this in the /js/controls.js file and you can see the additions I have made in Listing 10-8. The select element has two options – No and Yes, which will set the value of the disabled property of the input element to the empty string ("") when the No value is selected and to disabled when the Yes value is selected.

■ **Note**   It may seem odd that I am going to such lengths to generate a simple select element that can be written using four lines of HTML markup. The problem that I am trying to solve is that I have a lot of these select elements to generate and that I don't want to have to list out what is essentially the same markup over and over again in the other chapters in this part of the book. In addition, you'll soon see that I do more than just generate the element – I also create the event handlers that allow the configuration element to operate on the UI control that I am demonstrating – this is another very repetitive code block that I won't have to list out in each chapter. Overall, putting the effort into creating the framework in this chapter will allow me to spend more time focusing on the WinJS UI controls and their features in the chapters that follow.

Listing 10-8. The initial definition for the select element

```
(function () {

    WinJS.Namespace.define("App.Controls", {

        apptest: [{
            type: "select",
            id: "disabled",
            title: "Disabled",
            values: ["", "disabled"],
            labels: ["No", "Yes"]
        }]
    });

})();
```

You can see that I have created an array in the App.Controls namespace with the name apptest – this is the key passed to the Templates.createControls method from the AppTest.html file. This array will contain a series of *definition objects* that describe each of the configuration elements that I need to create. There is only one object at the moment and it describes the select element you can see in Figure 10-4.

■ **Tip**   In later chapters, I'll be listing the definition objects more concisely. I have used displayed each property on its own line in this example to make it easy to understand how these objects work.

I'll explain each of the properties in the object shortly, but first I am going to add the template I'll use to generate select elements to the default.html file, as shown in Listing 10-9. As I go through this chapter, I'll be adding a template for each kind of configuration element that I support in this framework.

Listing 10-9. Adding a template for generating select elements to the default.html file

```
...
<body>
```

```
<div id="navBarCommandTemplate" data-win-control="WinJS.Binding.Template">
    <button data-win-control="WinJS.UI.AppBarCommand"
        data-win-options="{section:'selection'}"
        data-win-bind="winControl.label: name; winControl.icon: icon">
    </button>
</div>

<div id="selectTemplate" data-win-control="WinJS.Binding.Template">
    <div class="selectContainer">
        <h2 class="controlTitle" data-win-bind="innerText: title"></h2>
        <select class="controlSelect"></select>
    </div>
</div>

<div id="contentTarget">
    <h1 class="message">Select a Control from the NavBar</h1>
</div>

<div id="navbar" data-win-control="WinJS.UI.AppBar"
    data-win-options="{placement:'top'}"></div>
</body>
...
```

The structure of the template I'll be using will help me explain the purpose of the properties of the definition object in Listing 10-8, which I have listed in Table 10-1.

■ **Tip**   This table explains the meaning of the properties for a definition object for a select element. Each *type* of definition object has some additional or different properties, which I'll explain as I generate that kind of element later in this chapter.

Table 10-1. The property names of the definition object for a select element

Name	Description
type	The type of configuration element that this definition object represents. This value can be select, input, span, buttons or toggle.
id	The value that should be assigned to the id attribute of the element that is created and which is also the name of the property on the UI control that this configuration element operates on.
title	The content that will be displayed in the h2 element in the template.
values	The values that will be assigned to the option elements contained in the select element
labels	(Optional) The labels for the option elements. If this property is omitted, then the values property will be used for the labels instead.

If you look back to Listing 10-8, you can see how the values I have assigned to the properties correspond to the result shown in Figure 10-4. The type property is set to select, indicating that I want a select element; the id property is set to disabled, which corresponds to the input element property that I want to manage; the title property is set to Disabled so that the user knows what effect changing the configuration element will have on the UI control being demonstrated.

Finally, I have used the values *and* labels properties because the values that are allowed for the input.disabled property are not suitable to be displayed to the user. By supplying values for both properties, I create a mapping between what is presented to the user and the value which is assigned to the UI control property.

Adding the Element Generation Code

I have the definition of the select element and I have a template for generating select elements. All I need now is the code that will bring these together – and I have added the structure for doing this to the /js/ templates.js file, as shown in Listing 10-10.

Listing 10-10. Code to create element using definitions and templates in the templates.js file

```
(function () {

var navBarCommands = [
        { name: "AppTest", icon: "target" },
];

WinJS.Namespace.define("Templates", {

    generateNavBarCommands: function (navBarElement, templateElement) {
        navBarCommands.forEach(function (commandItem) {
            templateElement.winControl.render(commandItem, navBarElement);
        });
    },

    createControls: function (container, uiControl, key) {
        var promises = [];

        App.Controls[key].forEach(function (definition) {
            var targetObject = uiControl.winControl ? uiControl.winControl : uiControl;
            promises.push(Templates["create" + definition.type](container,definition,
                targetObject));
        });

        return WinJS.Promise.join(promises).then(function () {
            $("*[data-win-bind]", container).forEach(function (childElem) {
                childElem.removeAttribute("data-win-bind");
            });
        });
    },

    createtoggle: function (containerElem, definition, uiControl) {
        // ...code to create ToggleSwitch element will go here
    },

    createinput: function (containerElem, definition, uiControl) {
```

```
        // ...code to create input element will go here
    },

    createselect: function (containerElem, definition, uiControl) {
        // ...code to create select element will go here

    },

    createspan: function (containerElem, definition, uiControl) {
        // ...code to create span element will go here
    },

    createbuttons: function (containerElem, definition, uiControl) {
        // ...code to create button elements will go here
    }
});

})();
```

The additions I have made to this file are center around the createControls method, which is the one I called from the AppTest.html file to create the configuration controls I wanted. The createControls method is simpler than it looks, but it is at the heart of the approach I have taken in building this framework, so I am going to talk you through it in detail and relate the way that the code works to the example select element I described in the previous section.

The arguments to the method are: the container into which the configuration controls should be placed when they are created, the UI control which is going to be configured by the newly created controls, and the key which refers to the set of definition objects in the controls.js file. For the select element, these arguments will be the rightPanel element and the input element from the markup in the AppTest. html file and the value apptest, which corresponds to the array containing the definition for the select element I showed you in Listing 10-8.

Processing the Definition Objects

I obtain the array of definition objects associated from the App.Controls namespace using the key I have received. There is only one key at the moment (apptest) and the array I get back contains only one definition object (for my select element), but I'll be adding more definitions later in this chapter (and more keys in subsequent chapters).

I use the forEach method to enumerate the items in the array. The first thing I do is establish the target object that I am working on. In later chapters, I will be using WinJS controls, all of which define the winControl property (see the *Understanding the winControl Property* sidebar for details), but for this chapter, I will be using an input element which doesn't have a winControl property. I figure out what I am working with like this:

```
...
var targetObject = uiControl.winControl ? uiControl.winControl : uiControl;
...
```

This is important because I create event handlers that will apply change the value of properties of the target object when I create the configuration element. When I am working with WinJS controls, I want to operate on the control and not the underlying HTML element to which it has been applied. In this chapter, there is no WinJS control and the HTML element is all I have to work with.

Having identified my target, I call one of the other methods in the `Templates` namespace, based on the value of the type property of the current definition object, like this:

```
...
promises.push(Templates["create" + definition.type](container,definition, targetObject));
...
```

I only have one definition object at the moment and its type property has a value of select, which means that the `Templates.createSelect` method will be called. The other methods in the `Templates` namespace are responsible for creating one kind of element and are passed the container into which the element should be inserted, the current definition object and the target object. I'll implement the first of these methods shortly to demonstrate how they work.

The element creation methods return a `Promise`, which I add to an array called promises. I use the `Promise.join` method (which I described in Chapter 9) on the promises array to create a `Promise` that is fulfilled when all of the individual element have been created, added to the container element and configured.

Cleaning up the Results

The last step in the in the `createObjects` method is to use the `then` method to specify a function that will be executed when all of the individual `Promise` objects are fulfilled. In this function I remove the `data-win-bind` attribute from all of the elements that have it. I'll explain why this is a useful thing to do in detail Chapter 14 when I introduce the `FlipView` element, but the short version is that leaving the `data-win-bind` attribute on elements you have generated can cause problems if the `WinJS.Binding.processAll` method is called after the generated `elements` are added to the document. By removing the attribute I ensure that this doesn't happen.

Generating a Select Element

Everything is now in place for me to generate my select element, which I will do by implementing the createselect method in the templates.js file. You can see how I have done this in Listing 10-11.

Listing 10-11. Generating a select element

```
...
createselect: function (containerElem, definition, uiControl) {
    return selectTemplate.winControl.render(definition).then(function (newElem) {

        var selectElem = WinJS.Utilities.query("select", newElem)[0];
        selectElem.id = definition.id;
        definition.values.forEach(function (value, index) {
            var option = selectElem.appendChild(document.createElement("option"));
            option.innerText = definition.labels ? definition.labels[index] : value;
            option.value = value;
        });

        selectElem.addEventListener("change", function (e) {
            setImmediate(function () {
                uiControl[definition.id] =
                    selectElem.options[selectElem.selectedIndex].value;
```

```
            });
        });
        containerElem.appendChild(newElem.removeChild(newElem.children[0]));
        uiControl[definition.id] = selectElem.options[0].value;
    });
},
...
```

Since this is the first type of element I am generating, I am going to walk through the code in steps and explain how I create the result.

Rendering the Template

I start by using the template I added to the `default.html` file to generate a new set of elements, like this:

```
...
createselect: function (containerElem, definition, uiControl) {
    return selectTemplate.winControl.render(definition).then(function (newElem) {
        // ...code removed for brevity...
},
...
```

The `Promise` you receive when you call the `render` method on a `WinJS.Binding.Template` object with only one argument yields the elements that have been created when it is fulfilled and the elements are not inserted into the app layout. In this listing, I pass the definition object from the `controls.js` file to the render method, which allows the details contained in the definition to be used to populate the template. As a reminder, here is the template I am using (and which I have located in the code using the `id` attribute value):

```
...
<div id="selectTemplate" data-win-control="WinJS.Binding.Template">
    <div class="selectContainer">
        <h2 class="controlTitle" data-win-bind="innerText: title"></h2>
        <select class="controlSelect"></select>
    </div>
</div>
...
```

When the `WinJS.Binding.Template` object has finished rendering the element, I am with some detached elements generated from the template. Detached elements are not yet part of the apps content and the elements look like this:

```
<div class="win-template">
    <div class="selectContainer">
        <h2 class="controlTitle" data-win-bind="innerText: title">Disabled</h2>
        <select class="controlSelect">
        </select>
    </div>
</div>
```

Configuring & Populating the Select Element

At this point I have the elements I need, but they are only partially complete. My next step is to finish off the select element and add the option elements that represent the choices that the user can make, like this:

```
...
createselect: function (containerElem, definition, uiControl) {
    return selectTemplate.winControl.render(definition).then(function (newElem) {

        var selectElem = WinJS.Utilities.query("select", newElem)[0];
        selectElem.id = definition.id;
        definition.values.forEach(function (value, index) {
            var option = selectElem.appendChild(document.createElement("option"));
            option.innerText = definition.labels ? definition.labels[index] : value;
            option.value = value;
        });

        // ...code removed for brevity...
    });
},
...
```

I use the WinJS.Utilities.query method to locate the select element from the set of elements passed to my function from the render method.

My first action is to set the id attribute to the value specified by the definition object. I then use the values and labels arrays from the definition object to create a series of option elements, which I append as children to the select element. This gives me the following HTML:

```
<div class="win-template">
    <div class="selectContainer">
        <h2 class="controlTitle" data-win-bind="innerText: title">Disabled</h2>
        <select class="controlSelect" id="disabled">
            <option value="">No</option>
            <option value="disabled">Yes</option>
        </select>
    </div>
</div>
```

Creating the Event Handler

I want to update the value of the property on the target object when the user picks the on option of the options in the select element. To ensure that this happens, I use the addEventListener method to register a handler function for the change event, as follows:

```
...
createselect: function (containerElem, definition, uiControl) {
    return selectTemplate.winControl.render(definition).then(function (newElem) {

        var selectElem = WinJS.Utilities.query("select", newElem)[0];

        // ...code removed for brevity...
```

```
        selectElem.addEventListener("change", function (e) {
            setImmediate(function () {
                uiControl[definition.id] =
                    selectElem.options[selectElem.selectedIndex].value;
            });
        });

        // ...code removed for brevity...
    });
},
...
```

When the change event is triggered, I update the property on the target object to match the picked value from the select element. Notice that I use the setImmediate method to defer the property change – this allows the select element to finish its transition to the newly-picked value before the property of the UI control is changed. Without the call to setImmediate, the app becomes momentarily unresponsive since the property change on the control will be performed before the select element finishes responding to the user picking a value.

Finishing Up

When I generate the elements from the template, I end up with an outer div element which I don't want to add to the app's layout. To this end, after I have set up the event handler, I select the first child element and add it to the app layout, using the container argument passed to the method, like this:

```
...
createselect: function (containerElem, definition, uiControl) {
    return selectTemplate.winControl.render(definition).then(function (newElem) {

        // ...code removed for brevity...

        containerElem.appendChild(newElem.removeChild(newElem.children[0]));
        uiControl[definition.id] = selectElem.options[0].value;
    });
},
...
```

The very last step is to set the property on the UI control to match the initial value of the select menu – this ensures that the select control and the state of the UI control being demonstrated are in sync.

You can test these additions by starting the app and selecting the AppTest command from the NavBar. You will be able to enable and disable the input element in the left-hand panel by picking values from the select element in the right-hand panel.

Using a Proxy Object

Not all of the features I want to show you in later chapters can be demonstrated simply by setting a property value. In these situations, I need to use a proxy object so that I can respond to changes made to the configuration elements in a useful way. In this section, I'll show you how I added this feature to the example framework.

Adding the Definition Object

First, I am going to add a new definition object to the controls.js file, which will offer a configuration option which cannot be translated into a simple property change. You can see this new definition in Listing 10-12.

Listing 10-12. Adding a new definition object to the controls.js file

```
(function () {

WinJS.Namespace.define("App.Controls", {

    apptest: [
        { type: "select", id: "disabled", title: "Disabled",
            values: ["", "disabled"], labels: ["No", "Yes"] },
        { type: "select", id: "theme", title: "Theme", values: ["Small", "Big"],
            useProxy: true },
    ]
});

})();
```

This definition specifies another select element, with Small and Big options. The important addition is the useProxy property, which I have set to true. This will indicate that when the user picks an option from the select element, the new value should be applied to a proxy, rather than directly to the UI control being demonstrated.

Creating the Proxy Object

I create the proxy object in the script element of the content page, as shown in Listing 10-13, which illustrates the additions I have made to the AppTest.html file. I have created an observable object called proxyObject and passed this as an argument to the createControls method. I create the observable object using the WinJS.Binding.as method, which I described in Chapter 8.

Listing 10-13. Adding a proxy object to the AppTest.html file

```
<!DOCTYPE html>
<html>
<head>
    <title></title>
    <script>
        WinJS.UI.Pages.define("/pages/AppTest.html", {
            ready: function () {

                var proxyObject = WinJS.Binding.as({
                    theme: "Big"
                });

                Templates.createControls(rightPanel, inputElem, "apptest", proxyObject);
            }
        });
```

```
        </script>
    </head>
    <body>
        <div class="flexContainer">

            <div class="controlPanel">
                <input id="inputElem"/>
            </div>

            <div id="rightPanel" class="controlPanel"></div>
        </div>
    </body>
</html>
```

Detecting and Using the Proxy Object

Next, I need to update the createControls method in the templates.js file so that it can receive the proxy object and use it when required to do so by the definition object. You can see the changes I have made to support this in Listing 10-14.

Listing 10-14. Adding support for proxy objects in the createControls method

```
...
createControls: function (container, uiControl, key, proxy) {
    var promises = [];

    App.Controls[key].forEach(function (definition) {
        var targetObject = definition.useProxy ? proxy : uiControl.winControl ?
            uiControl.winControl : uiControl;
        promises.push(Templates["create" + definition.type](container,definition,
            targetObject));
    });

    return WinJS.Promise.join(promises).then(function () {
        $("*[data-win-bind]", container).forEach(function (childElem) {
            childElem.removeAttribute("data-win-bind");
        });
    });
},
...
```

The change is relatively simple – I just have to expand the statement that selected the target for the configuration control changes to take into account the proxy object.

The effect of this addition is that when a definition object specifies that the proxy object should be used, the event handler for the select element generated from the template will change the value of the specified property on the proxy, rather than on the winControl property or the HTML element itself.

251

Responding to Proxy Object Property Changes

The final step is to return to the script element in the AppTest.html file and add some code to monitor the observable proxy object for changes. You can see how I have done this in Listing 10-15.

Listing 10-15. Observing the proxy object for changes

```
...
<script>
    WinJS.UI.Pages.define("/pages/AppTest.html", {
        ready: function () {

            var proxyObject = WinJS.Binding.as({
                theme: "Big"
            });

            Templates.createControls(rightPanel, inputElem, "apptest", proxyObject);

            proxyObject.bind("theme", function (val) {
                inputElem.style.fontSize = val == "Big" ? "25pt" : "";
                inputElem.style.fontWeight =  val == "Big" ? "bold" : "";
            });
        }
    });
</script>
...
```

The theme property in the proxy object will be changed when the user picks a value using the new select element. I observe the theme property using the bind method, which I described in Chapter 8, and change two CSS properties to create different visual effects. This is a simple demonstration of how I can use my example framework to bind configuration elements with more complex UI control features – something that I'll use often in the chapters that follow. You can see the result of picking the Big and Small value in Figure 10-6.

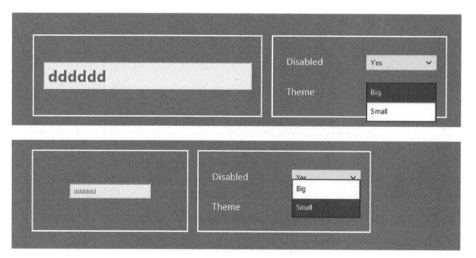

Figure 10-6. Using a proxy object to support more complex configurations

Generating the Other Element Types

You have seen all of the complexity in the example framework now. All that remains is to add the remaining templates for the different element types and to implement the methods that use them in the controls.js files. In the sections that follow, I'll finish off the framework and create a new definition object that demonstrates the remaining types of configuration elements. There are no new techniques in the remainder of this chapter, so I am just going to list the template and code required for each type of element and show you an example of the definition objects that generate each element type.

Generating an Input Element

I use input elements to allow the user to enter an unconstrained value. You can see the definition object for an input configuration element in Listing 10-16.

Listing 10-16. A definition object for an input configuration element

```
(function () {

WinJS.Namespace.define("App.Controls", {

    apptest: [
        { type: "select", id: "disabled", title: "Disabled", values: ["", "disabled"],
            labels: ["No", "Yes"] },
        { type: "select", id: "theme", title: "Theme", values: ["Small", "Big"],
            useProxy: true },
        { type: "input", id: "value", title: "Value", value: "Hello" },
    ]
});

})();
```

You can see the meaning of the properties in this definition object in Table 10-2.

Table 10-2. The property names of the definition object for an input element

Name	Description
type	As for a select element – see Table 1
id	As for a select element – see Table 1
title	As for a select element – see Table 1
value	Specifies the initial content of the input element

You can see the template from the default.html file that I use to generate input elements in Listing 10-17.

Listing 10-17. The input element template from the default.html file

```
...
<div id="inputTemplate" data-win-control="WinJS.Binding.Template">
    <div class="inputContainer">
```

```
            <h2 class="controlTitle" data-win-bind="innerText: title"></h2>
            <input class="controlInput" data-win-bind="value: value"/>
        </div>
    </div>
    ...
```

You can see the implementation of the createinput method in the controls.js file in Listing 10-18.

Listing10- 18. The implementation of the createinput method in the controls.js file

```
...
createinput: function (containerElem, definition, uiControl) {
    return inputTemplate.winControl.render(definition).then(function (newElem) {
        WinJS.Utilities.query("input", newElem).forEach(function (elem) {
            elem.id = definition.id;
            elem.addEventListener("change", function (e) {
                setImmediate(function () {
                    uiControl[elem.id] = elem.value;
                });
            });
            uiControl[definition.id] = elem.value;
        });
        containerElem.appendChild(newElem.removeChild(newElem.children[0]));
    });
},
...
```

The value you enter into the input configuration element I have created in this section updates the value of the input element in the left-hand panel of the layout, which is where the WinJS UI controls will be in later chapters. Note that the relationship is one-way only – which is to say that entering text into the input element in the left-hand panel doesn't update the contents of the input element in the right-hand panel.

Generating a Span Element

I use span elements to display some read-only characteristic of the UI control, usually in support of demonstrating some other feature. I don't create event listeners when I generate span elements and, instead, update the contents from the script element of the content page. Listing 10-19 shows the addition of a span definition object to the controls.js file.

Listing 10-19. Adding a span definition object to the controls.js file

```
(function () {

WinJS.Namespace.define("App.Controls", {
    apptest: [
        { type: "select", id: "disabled", title: "Disabled", values: ["", "disabled"],
            labels: ["No", "Yes"] },
        { type: "select", id: "theme", title: "Theme", values: ["Small", "Big"],
            useProxy: true },
        { type: "input", id: "value", title: "Value", value: "Hello" },
        { type: "span", id: "value", value: "<Ready>", title: "Value" },
```

```
    ]
});

})();
```

You can see the meaning of the properties in this definition object in Table 10-3.

Table 3. The property names of the definition object for a span element

Name	Description
type	As for a select element – see Table 1
id	As for a select element – see Table 1
title	As for a select element – see Table 1
value	Specifies the content of the span element

You can see the template from the default.html file that I used to generate span elements in Listing 10-20.

Listing 10-20. The span template from the default.html file

```
...
<div id="spanTemplate" data-win-control="WinJS.Binding.Template">
    <div class="spanContainer">
        <h2 class="controlTitle" data-win-bind="innerText: title"></h2>
        <span class="controlSpan" data-win-bind="innerText: value"></span>
    </div>
</div>
...
```

You can see the implementation of the createinput method in the templates.js file in Listing 10-21.

Listing 10-21. The implementation of the createspan method in the templates.js file

```
...
createspan: function (containerElem, definition, uiControl) {
    return spanTemplate.winControl.render(definition).then(function (newElem) {
        WinJS.Utilities.query("span", newElem).forEach(function (elem) {
            elem.id = definition.id;
        });
        containerElem.appendChild(newElem.removeChild(newElem.children[0]));
    });
},
...
```

Generating Button Elements

I use button configuration elements to let the user trigger some kind of action – typically adding or removing items from a data source, which I introduce you to in Chapter 14. You can see a definition object for button elements in Listing 10-22.

Listing 10-22. A definition object for button elements

```
(function () {

WinJS.Namespace.define("App.Controls", {

    apptest: [
        { type: "select", id: "disabled", title: "Disabled", values: ["", "disabled"],
            labels: ["No", "Yes"] },
        { type: "select", id: "theme", title: "Theme", values: ["Small", "Big"],
            useProxy: true },
        { type: "input", id: "value", title: "Value", value: "Hello" },
        { type: "span", id: "value", value: "<Ready>", title: "Value" },
        { type: "buttons", title: "Buttons", labels: ["Add Item", "Delete Item"] },
    ]
});

})();
```

You can see the meaning of the properties in this definition object in Table 10-4.

Table 10-4. The property names of the definition object for a span element

Name	Description
type	As for a select element – see Table 1
title	As for a select element – see Table 1
labels	The array of labels. One button will be created for each value in the array.

I don't use a template to generate the button elements and I leave the event handlers to the content pages, which means that the implementation of the createbuttons method in the templates.js file, shown in Listing 10-23, is especially simple.

Listing 10-23. The implementation of the createbuttons method in the templates.js file

```
...
createbuttons: function (containerElem, definition, uiControl) {
    var newDiv = containerElem.appendChild(document.createElement("div"));
    WinJS.Utilities.addClass(newDiv, "buttonContainer");
    if (definition.title) {
        var titleElem = newDiv.appendChild(document.createElement("h2"))
        titleElem.innerText = definition.title;
        WinJS.Utilities.addClass(titleElem, "controlTitle");
    }
    definition.labels.forEach(function (label) {
        var button = newDiv.appendChild(document.createElement("button"));
        button.innerText = label;
    });
}
...
```

Generating ToggleSwitch Controls

The `WinJS.UI.ToggleSwitch` control lets the user pick a true/false value. I demonstrate this control in detail in the next chapter, so I don't want to get into any detail in this chapter. I will present the definition object, the template and the code as-is, and they will make sense after you have read Chapter 11. You can see a definition object for a `ToggleSwitch` control in Listing 10-24.

Listing 10-24. A definition object for a ToggleSwitch control

```
(function () {

WinJS.Namespace.define("App.Controls", {

    apptest: [
        { type: "select", id: "disabled", title: "Disabled", values: ["", "disabled"],
            labels: ["No", "Yes"] },
        { type: "select", id: "theme", title: "Theme", values: ["Small", "Big"],
            useProxy: true },
        { type: "input", id: "value", title: "Value", value: "Hello" },
        { type: "span", id: "value", value: "<Ready>", title: "Value" },
        { type: "buttons", title: "Buttons", labels: ["Add Item", "Delete Item"] },
        { type: "toggle", id: "disabled", title: "Disabled", value: false},
    ]
});

})();
```

You can see the meaning of the properties in this definition object in Table 10-5.

Table 10-5. The property names of the definition object for a ToggleSwitch control

Name	Description
type	As for a select element – see Table 1
id	As for a select element – see Table 1
title	As for a select element – see Table 1
value	Specifies the initial control setting

You can see the template from the `default.html` file that I use to create `ToggleSwitch` controls in Listing 10-25.

Listing 10-25. The template for generating ToggleSwitch controls

```
...
<div id="toggleSwitchTemplate" data-win-control="WinJS.Binding.Template">
    <div data-win-control="WinJS.UI.ToggleSwitch"
        data-win-bind="winControl.checked: value; winControl.title: title">
    </div>
</div>
...
```

And, finally, you can see the implementation of the `createtoggle` method in Listing 10-26. I'll explain the properties I set via the `winControl` property in Chapter 11.

Listing 10-26. The implementation of the createtoggle method in the templates.js file

```
...
createtoggle: function (containerElem, definition, uiControl) {
    return toggleSwitchTemplate.winControl.render(definition).then(function (newElem) {
        var toggle = newElem.children[0];
        toggle.id = definition.id;
        if (definition.labelOn != undefined) {
            toggle.winControl.labelOn = definition.labelOn;
            toggle.winControl.labelOff = definition.labelOff;
        }
        toggle.addEventListener("change", function (e) {
            setImmediate(function () {
                uiControl[definition.id] = toggle.winControl.checked;
            });
        });
        containerElem.appendChild(newElem.removeChild(toggle));
        uiControl[definition.id] = toggle.winControl.checked;
    });
},
...
```

If you run the example app with all of these definition objects, templates and method implementations, you will see the layout shown in Figure 10-4.

Cleaning Up

All that remains now is to remove the AppTest command button from the NavBar so that I have a clean project to work on in the next chapter. You can see the final modification to this project, which I have made to the templates.js file, in Listing 10-27.

Listing 10-27. Removing the test button from the NavBar

```
...
var navBarCommands = [
        //{ name: "AppTest", icon: "target" },
        // ...other commands omitted for brevity...
];
...
```

Summary

In this chapter, I have explained how I created the framework which I'll use to demonstrate the WinJS UI controls in the remaining chapters in this part of the book. Although this framework is reasonably lengthy to explain in its own right, it allows me to avoid spending the first ten pages of each chapter listing out largely identical code and markup. This project has had the additional benefit of demonstrating how some core WinJS features can be combined in more complex ways to create richer effects. In the chapters that follow, I'll take you on a tour of the UI controls that you can use in your Metro apps to provide a richer experience and to present your users with a look-and-feel which is consistent with other Metro apps.

CHAPTER 11

■ ■ ■

Using the ToggleSwitch, Rating and Tooltip Controls

In this chapter, I start to describe the WinJS UI controls in detail, using the framework app that I created in Chapter 10. These UI controls are important building blocks for creating apps which are consistent with the broader Windows visual theme and are worth studying in detail.

The mechanics of WinJS UI controls are similar to those of other JavaScript UI toolkits you may have used, such as jQuery UI. You apply a control to an element and additional elements, styles and event handlers are applied to create a rich visual effect.

You could easily use jQuery UI or a similar library in your Windows app, but you would end up with an odd-looking result and you would miss out on the tight integration that some of the controls have with other WinJS features such as data binding. Throughout this chapter and the ones that follow, I describe each control in turn. I tell you how to apply and configure the control, when you should use the control and how to observe user interactions with the control.

I start with three relatively simple controls in this chapter: the ToggleSwitch, Rating and Tooltip controls. These are the most basic controls and, while they can be useful, they are not that interesting or different from what you might have encountered with other JavaScript UI toolkits. Table 11-1 provides the summary for this chapter.

Table 11-1. Chapter Summary

Problem	Solution	Listing
Use the ToggleSwitch UI control	Apply the data-win-control attribute to a div element with a value of WinJS.UI.ToggleSwitch.	1-3
Declaratively configure a UI control	Use the data-win-options attribute	4
Style a ToggleSwitch	Define styles for the win-toggleswitch CSS class	5
Receive a notification when the state of the ToggleSwitch is changed by the user	Listen for the change event	6
Use the Rating control	Apply the data-win-control attribute to a div element with a value of WinJS.UI.Rating.	7-9
Style a Rating	Define styles for the win-rating CSS class	10
Receive a notification when the state of the Rating changes	Listen for the change, cancel and previewchange events	11

Problem	Solution	Listing
Use the Tooltip Control	Apply the data-win-control attribute to a div or span element with a value of WinJS.UI.Tooltip.	12-14
Set the content of a Tooltip	Set the value of the innerHTML property on the winControl property (not the containing element)or the contentElement property	15-17
Style a Tooltip	Define styles for the win-tooltip CSS class	18

Using the ToggleSwitch Control

I am going to start with the WinJS.UI.ToggleSwitch control. This is a good control to begin with because it is simple and because I use this control in the framework app I created in Chapter 10 to demonstrate features of other controls in this, and subsequent, chapters.

As the name suggests, the ToggleSwitch control lets the user toggle between an on and an off state. Mouse users can click on the empty part of the ToggleSwitch to change the state and touch users can slide the switch left or right. The ToggleSwitch control performs a brief animation as it transitions from one state to the other. You can see how the ToggleSwitch appears in Figure 11-1. I'll show you the additions I made to the example framework to create this layout shortly.

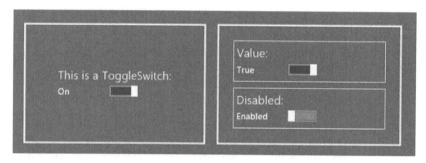

Figure 11-1. The ToggleSwitch controls in the example app

When to use the ToggleSwitch Control

You should use the ToggleSwitch control when you need to present the user with a binary decision. The sliding motion to change the value is very touch friendly and is much easier to use than a regular HTML checkbox or a select element with Yes and No options. I use this control a lot for letting the user configure app settings (which I describe in Chapter 20).

■ **Tip**   If you are displaying several ToggleSwitch controls in a column, make sure that you have all of the true/on values on the same side - it only confuses the user if some switches need to be in the right-hand position to enable a feature and others in the left-hand position.

Demonstrating the ToggleSwitch Control

To demonstrate the ToggleSwitch control, I have added a new HTML file to the pages folder of the UIControls project from Chapter 10. You can see the contents of this file, called ToggleSwitch.html, in Listing 11-1.

Listing 11-1. The contents of the /pages/ToggleSwitch.html file

```
<!DOCTYPE html>
<html>
<head>
    <title></title>
    <script>
        WinJS.UI.Pages.define("/pages/ToggleSwitch.html", {
            ready: function () {
                Templates.createControls(rightPanel, mainToggle, "toggleSwitch");
            }
        });
    </script>
</head>
<body>
    <div id="toggleSwitchContainer" class="flexContainer">

        <div class="controlPanel">
            <div id="mainToggle" data-win-control="WinJS.UI.ToggleSwitch"
                data-win-options="{title:'This is a ToggleSwitch:'}"></div>
        </div>

        <div id="rightPanel" class="controlPanel">
        </div>
    </div>
</body>
</html>
```

You can see from the listing that I have used the key toggleSwitch to locate the definition objects in the controls.js file. You can see those definition objects in Listing 11-2.

Listing 11-2. The definition objects for the ToggleSwitch control

```
(function () {

WinJS.Namespace.define("App.Controls", {

    toggleSwitch: [
        { type: "toggle", id: "checked", title: "Value", value: true },
        { type: "toggle", id: "disabled", title: "Disabled", value: false }],
    });

})();
```

Finally, I added the command to the NavBar by making the addition to the templates.js file shown in Listing 11-3.

261

Listing 11-3. Adding the ToggleSwitch.html file to the NavBar

```
...
var navBarCommands = [
        //{ name: "AppTest", icon: "target" },
          { name: "ToggleSwitch", icon: "\u0031" },
];
...
```

Applying and Configuring the ToggleSwitch Control

The ToggleSwitch control is applied to div elements by setting the data-win-control attribute to WinJS. UI.ToggleSwitch. As I explained in Chapter 10, the underlying HTML element is assigned a winControl property when it is processed by the WinJS.UI.processAll method (either because you have explicitly called the method or because the content has been loaded using the WinJS.UI.Pages.render method, which calls processAll for you).

The winControl property returns the control object specified by the data-win-control attribute and this allows you to call methods and set properties defined by the control in your code. As a convenience, you can set the values for properties declaratively in HTML using the data-win-options attribute, specifying a JSON fragment that contains name/value pairs.

For the left-hand ToggleSwitch, I have set a value for the title property, which is used for the text that is displayed above the control, as shown in Listing 11-4.

Listing 11-4. Setting the title property using the data-win-options attribute

```
...
<div class="controlPanel">
    <div id="mainToggle" data-win-control="WinJS.UI.ToggleSwitch"
        data-win-options="{title:'This is a ToggleSwitch:'}"></div>
</div>
...
```

Table 11-2 describes the configuration properties defined by the ToggleSwitch, all of which can be set using the data-win-options attribute or in your JavaScript code.

Table 11-2. The configuration properties for the ToggleSwitch control

Property	Description
checked	Gets or sets the status of the switch. When true, the switch is "on" and when false the switch is "off".
disabled	Gets or sets the state of the switch. When true, the switch is disabled and cannot be moved by the user. When false, the user can move the switch position.
labelOn	Gets or sets the text displayed when the switch is in the "on" position.
labelOff	Gets or sets the text displayed when the switch is in the "off" position.
title	Gets or sets the text displayed above the switch.

In the code that demonstrates the ToggleSwitch control, I have created configuration controls that change the checked and disabled properties. You can see how I use JavaScript to set other properties by looking at the createtoggle method in the templates.js file, which I showed you at the end of Chapter 10. I use values from the definition objects to set the labelOn, labelOff and title properties.

Styling the ToggleSwitch Control

WinJS UI controls can be styled using a set of CSS classes. This is one of the nice things about working with WinJS controls and one of the reasons that I have yet to feel the need to use jQuery UI in any of my Windows app projects (which is saying something, because I *love* jQuery and jQuery UI). I have listed and described the set of classes supported by the ToggleSwitch control in Table 11-3.

Table 11-3. The CSS classes supported by the ToggleSwitch control

Class	Description
win-toggleswitch	This class can be used to style the entire ToggleSwitch control
win-title	This class can be used to style the title shown above the switch (which is set using the title configuration property)
win-switch	This class can be used to style the switch
win-label-off	This class can be used to style the text displayed when the switch is in the "off" position (which is set using the labelOff configuration property)
win-label-on	This class can be used to style the text displayed when the switch is in the "off" position (which is set using the labelOn configuration property)

Because I use the ToggleSwitch controls to help demonstrate many of the other WinJS UI controls, I have added some CSS styles to the /css/default.css file which apply use the classes in Table 11-3. You can see these styles in Listing 11-5.

■ **Caution**   Don't get carried away styling UI controls. You want to keep your app consistent with the general Windows look and feel. To this end, you should only style controls so that they are legible and corresponds to the color scheme used in your layout.

Listing 11-5. Applying styles to the ToggleSwitch control

```
...
.controlPanel .win-toggleswitch {
    width: 90%;
    margin: 15px;
    padding-left: 20px;
}

.win-toggleswitch .win-title {
    color: white;
    font-size: 20px;
}
...
```

You must use the win-toggleswitch class whenever you override a style for the ToggleSwitch control, even when you are overriding a sub-style such as win-title. If you don't, then the styles defined by the default CSS in the Visual Studio project (in the ui-light.css and ui-dark.css files, which I described in Chapter 2) will have a greater specificity and your custom values won't have an effect.

For the styles in the default.css file, I have applied a border and some margin and padding to the ToggleSwitch controls that I use as configuration controls and changed the text size and color of the title for all ToggleSwitch controls.

■ **Tip**   It can be hard to figure out just what effect custom styles have. You can see how WinJS UI controls are structured by running your app in the debugger, switching to the Visual Studio DOM `Explorer` window, clicking the `Select Element` button and clicking on the control in the layout. You will be able to see the HTML elements that have been created around the element to which the `data-win-control` attribute was applied and see how the underlying components have been styled.

Handling the ToggleSwitch Control Event

The `ToggleSwitch` control emits the change event when the position of the switch is changed by the user (the event is not emitted when the value of the property is changed programmatically). I am going to list out the events for each control in turn and to make it easier to find this information when you need it and you are flicking through the chapter. Table11- 4 describes the change event, even though there is only one and it is pretty basic.

Table 11-4. The events supported by the ToggleSwitch control

Event	Description
change	Emitted when the switch position is changed

I have added a handler to the `ToggleSwitch.html` file which responds to the change event by updating the checked value of one of the configuration controls in the right-hand panel, making the relationship between these controls bi-directional. You can see the event handler in Listing 11-6.

Listing 11-6. Adding a handler for the ToggleSwitch change event

```
<!DOCTYPE html>
<html>
<head>
    <title></title>
    <script>
        WinJS.UI.Pages.define("/pages/ToggleSwitch.html", {
            ready: function () {
                Templates.createControls(rightPanel, mainToggle, "toggleSwitch")
                    .then(function () {
                        mainToggle.addEventListener("change", function () {
                            checked.winControl.checked = mainToggle.winControl.checked;
                        });
                    });
            }
        });
    </script>
</head>
<body>
    <div id="toggleSwitchContainer" class="flexContainer">

        <div class="controlPanel">
            <div id="mainToggle" data-win-control="WinJS.UI.ToggleSwitch"
```

```
                    data-win-options="{title:'This is a ToggleSwitch:'}"></div>
        </div>

        <div id="rightPanel" class="controlPanel">
        </div>
    </div>
</body>
</html>
```

I use the then method to ensure that the configuration controls have been created by the Templates. createControls method and set up the handler using the addEventListener method. Note that I set up the event listener directly on the div element to which the ToggleSwitch control has been applied, but I get the state of the control by reading the winControl.checked value. This is the pattern for all of the WinJS UI controls – events are issued from the underlying HTML element, but the state of the control is accessed through the winControl property.

To test the event handler, start the example app, click the ToggleSwitch button on the NavBar and toggle the ToggleSwitch control in the left-hand layout panel. You will see that the state of the Value configuration control in the right-hand panel changes in sync. The relationship works in reverse as well, but that's because I set up a listener for the change event in the Templates.createtoggle method, which I described in Chapter 10.

■ **Tip** The user cannot move the switch position when a ToggleSwitch is disabled, but the switch will correctly reflect a change if the winControl.checked property is modified programmatically.

Using the Rating Control

The WinJS.UI.Rating control allows the user to express an opinion by providing a star rating. You can see how the Rating control appears in the left panel in Figure 11-2. The user can specify a rating by clicking or touching a star and change a rating my dragging the mouse or a finger up and down the array of stars. I'll show you the additions I made to the example project to create this layout shortly.

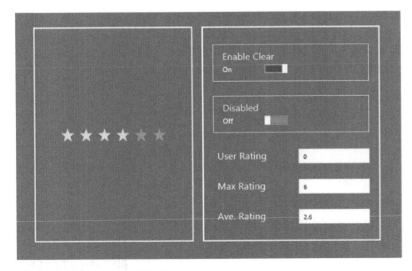

Figure 11-2. A WinJS.UI.Rating control

When to use the Rating Control

The idea of expressing an opinion or rating as a number of stars is so deeply ingrained that you shouldn't use this control for any other purpose. If you want to solicit a number from the user, then use a regular input element with the type attribute set to number.

If you *do* want the user's opinion, then the Rating control is ideal. Try to use a common number of stars (3, 5, and 10 are frequently used), stick with that number throughout your app and make sure that you use the opportunity to express both negative and positive views. Make sure that each star rating has the same meaning whenever the Rating control is used.

Demonstrating the Rating Control

To demonstrate the Rating control, I have added a new HTML file to the pages folder of the UIControls project. You can see the contents of this file, called Rating.html, in Listing 11-7.

Listing11- 7. The contents of the /pages/Rating.html file

```
<!DOCTYPE html>
<html>
<head>
    <title></title>
    <style>
        .win-rating .win-star.win-user.win-full {
            color: yellow;
        }
        .win-rating .win-star.win-average.win-full {
            color:  #000;
        }
        .win-rating .win-star.win-average.win-full,
        .win-rating .win-star.win-tentative.win-full {
            color:  white;
        }
    </style>
    <script>
        WinJS.UI.Pages.define("/pages/Rating.html", {
            ready: function () {
                Templates.createControls(rightPanel, rating, "rating");

                rating.winControl.tooltipStrings = ["Terrible", "Pretty Bad",
                    "Not So Good", "Reasonable", "Good", "Excellent"];
            }
        });
    </script>
</head>
<body>
    <div id="ratingContainer" class="flexContainer">

        <div class="controlPanel">
            <div id="rating" data-win-control="WinJS.UI.Rating"></div>
        </div>
```

266

```
        <div id="rightPanel" class="controlPanel"></div>
    </div>
</body>
</html>
```

This file contains some CSS styles which are specific to the Rating control (and which I describe shortly). Listing 11-8 shows the definition objects I added to the controls.js file to create the configuration elements in the right-hand panel shown in Figure 11-2.

Listing11- 8. The definition objects for the Rating controls

```
...
rating: [
    { type: "toggle", id: "enableClear", title: "Enable Clear", value: true },
    { type: "toggle", id: "disabled", title: "Disabled", value: false },
    { type: "input", id: "userRating", title: "User Rating", value: 0 },
    { type: "input", id: "maxRating", title: "Max Rating", value: 6 },
    { type: "input", id: "averageRating", title: "Ave. Rating", value: 2.6 }],
...
```

So that the user can navigate to the Rating.html page, I made the addition to the templates.js file that is shown by Listing 11-9.

Listing 11-9. Adding the Rating.html file to the NavBar

```
...
var navBarCommands = [
    //{ name: "AppTest", icon: "target" },
    { name: "ToggleSwitch", icon: "\u0031" },
    { name: "Rating", icon: "\u0032" },
];
...
```

Applying and Configuring the Rating Control

The Rating control is applied to div elements by setting the data-win-control attribute to WinJS.UI. Rating. The properties that I manage with the configuration controls are described in Table 11-5 and are accessible through the winControl property.

Table 11-5. The configuration properties for the Rating control

Property	Description
disabled	When true, the control is disabled and the user cannot set a rating.
enableClear	When true, allows the user to remove their rating from the control. If false, then the control will display a rating of at least 1.
averageRating	Gets or sets an average rating which is displayed when there is no user rating available.
maxRating	Gets or sets the maximum allowed rating
userRating	Gets or sets the rating which the user has selected
tooltipStrings	Gets or sets an array of strings which are used as tooltips for the stars in the control

The configuration controls that I defined for the Rating control allow you to experiment with changing all of these properties except tooltipStrings, which I set in the script element of the Rating.html page (and which I explain below).

Managing the Rating

There is a specific interaction between the averageRating, maxRating and userRating properties that you need to work within to get the right effect from a Rating control.

The maxRating property specifies the number of stars that the Rating shows and effectively sets the upper limit for the rating that can be selected using this control. The number of stars shown is a whole number.

The averageRating property can be used to show a rating from elsewhere. Common uses for the average are to show what other users' ratings or ratings from the current user provided on previous occasions. You can specify the averageRating value as a real number (like 4.2) and partial stars will be displayed. The userRating property represents the value that the user has selected. This is another whole number value.

The averageRating value will only be displayed if the userRating property is zero. As soon as the user provides a rating (or the userRating property is set externally), the averageRating value is hidden and the userRating value is displayed. I have added controls to the example for the Rating control that let you specify values for these properties and you can see the transition from the averageRating to the userRating value in Figure 11-3.

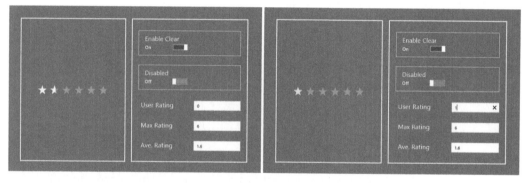

Figure 11-3. Replacing the averageRating with the userRating value

If the enableClear property is true, then the user can drag or slide to the left of the Rating control and clear the userRating value. When this happens, the averageRating value is displayed again. If the enableClear property is false, then the control can't be cleared. Use this setting sparingly because it traps the user into making an irreversible rating. If you do set enableClear to false, then you should provide a nearby and obvious control that sets the userRating property back to zero and lets the user start over. As a general rule, you should let the user back out of any value they have supplied - it is confusing and annoying for users when this isn't possible.

Setting the Tooltips

If the user hovers or slides over a star, the Rating control will display a tooltip. These are numeric by default and reflect the number of stars that the rating represents. If you set the tooltipStrings to an array of strings, then the array values will be used as the tooltip contents. I set the tooltipStrings property explicitly in the script element of the pages/Rating.html file. For convenience, here are the values that I used:

```
...
rating.winControl.tooltipStrings = ["Terrible", "Pretty Bad", "Not So Good",
    "Reasonable", "Good", "Excellent"];
...
```

You can see how one of the tooltip values is presented to the user in Figure 11-4.

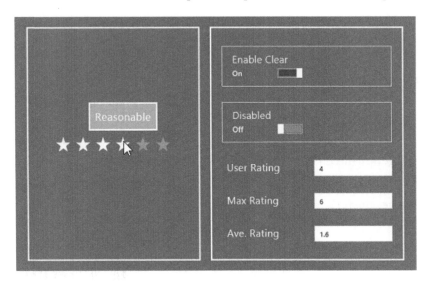

Figure 11-4. The Rating control displaying a tool tip

■ **Tip** If you set an array that contains one more item than the value of the maxRating property, then the last string value will be displayed when the user drags or slides to the left to clear the rating (assuming that the enableClear property is true).

Styling the Rating Control

The Rating control supports a number of styles that you can override to customize the appearance of the control, each of which is described in Table 11-6.

Table 11-6. The CSS classes supported by the Rating control

Class	Description
win-rating	This is the overarching style for the entire Rating control
win-star	This is the overarching style for stars, irrespective of their state
win-disabled	Styles the Rating control when it is disabled
win-empty	Styles empty stars (i.e. when the userRating or averageRating value is less than maxRating)

Class	Description
win-full	Styles full stars (the stars which indicate the rating)
win-user	Styles the stars when the userRating value is displayed
win-average	Styles the stars when the averageRating value is displayed
win-tentative	Styles the stars when the user is making a rating but has yet to release the mouse or remove the finger from the screen

These classes have to be combined into very specific arrangements to style a Rating control. Listing 11-10 shows the CSS from the style element in the Rating.html file, which I used to change the default styling for the Rating control in the example.

Listing 11-10. The CSS from the Rating.htmlfile

```
...
.win-rating .win-star.win-user.win-full {
    color: yellow;
}
.win-rating .win-star.win-average.win-full {
    color:  #000;
}
.win-rating .win-star.win-average.win-full,
.win-rating .win-star.win-tentative.win-full {
    color:  white;
}
...
```

The sequence you must use to apply the styles in the table is:

.win-rating **.win-star.win-[rating value].win-[star state]**

The classes I have marked in bold are applied to the same element, which means that you don't uses spaces to separate them. If you wanted to style the full stars displayed for the userRating value, you would override this sequence:

.win-rating .win-star.win-**user**.win-**full**

You can override styles for multiple sets of stars, but you need to be careful. The safest approach is to list out multiple complete combinations of classes, like this:

```
...
.win-rating .win-star.win-average.win-full,
.win-rating .win-star.win-user.win-full,
.win-rating .win-star.win-tentative.win-full {
    color:  white;
}
...
```

You can omit some classes to cast a wider net with the selector, but you still have to make sure that the selector is more specific that the ones defined by Microsoft, which use the full sequence of classes. The most direct way of doing this is to use the id of element to which the Rating control has been applied, like this:

```
...
#rating .win-star.win-full {
    color:  green;
}
...
```

Handling the Rating Control Events

The Rating control supports three events, which I have described in Table 11-7.

Table 11-7. The events supported by the Rating control

Event	Description
change	Emitted when the rating is changed by the user
cancel	Emitted when the user starts selecting a rating but abandons the interaction before specifying a value
previewchange	Emitted each time a tentative star is displayed

Listing 11-11 shows how I have added to the script element in the /pages/Ratings.html file to handle the change event. I use this event to update the configuration control in the right-hand panel of the layout which affects the userRating property.

Listing 11-11. Handling the Rating change event

```
...
<script>
    WinJS.UI.Pages.define("/pages/Rating.html", {
        ready: function () {
            Templates.createControls(rightPanel, rating, "rating")
            .then(function () {
                rating.winControl.tooltipStrings = ["Terrible", "Pretty Bad",
                    "Not So Good", "Reasonable", "Good", "Excellent"];

                rating.addEventListener("change", function () {
                    userRating.value = rating.winControl.userRating;
                });

            });
        }
    });
</script>
...
```

I use the then method on the Promise object returned by the Template.createControls method to ensure that I don't create the event handler until the configuration elements are created and have been added to the app layout.

Using the Tooltip Control

The Tooltip control pops up a window containing useful information when the mouse or finger is held over an element or when the keyboard focus is gained. This is a simple control, but there is still a lot of flexibility in how you configure and apply a Tooltip. You can see an example of a Tooltip in Figure 11-5. The other controls in the HTML are used to configure different aspects of the Tooltip, as I'll explain in the following sections.

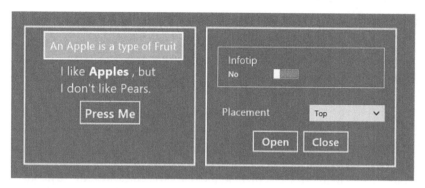

Figure 11-5. A Tooltip control

When to use the Tooltip Control

The Tooltip control is used when you want to provide guidance to the user or some supplementary information, perhaps to help them make an informed choice about selecting a specific option in the app or just some additional information about the content they are looking at.

■ **Tip** The Tooltip is a *transient* control and will disappear automatically (I explain the circumstances in which this happens below). You cannot use a transient control for any kind of interactive content, such as button or Rating control. For that, you need to use the Flyout control, which I introduced in Chapter 7 and revisit in Chapter 12 to describe it in depth.

Demonstrating the Tooltip Control

You can see the definition objects that I added to the controls.js file to demonstrate the Tooltip control in Listing 11-12. These objects will be accessed using the key tooltip.

Listing 11-12. The definition objects for the Tooltip control

```
...
tooltip: [
    { type: "toggle", id: "infotip", title: "Infotip", value: false,
        labelOn: "Yes", labelOff: "No" },
    { type: "select", id: "placement", title: "Placement",
        values: ["top", "bottom", "left", "right"],
        labels: ["Top", "Bottom", "Left", "Right"]},
```

```
    { type: "buttons", labels: ["Open", "Close"] }],
...
```

The definition objects are used in a new HTML file I added to the pages folder of the UIControls project. You can see the contents of this file, called Tooltip.html, in Listing 11-13.

Listing 11-13. The contents of the /pages/Tooltip.html file

```
<!DOCTYPE html>
<html>
<head>
    <style>
        #tooltipContent img { float: left; }
        #blockTooltip button { font-size: 18pt; margin: 10px;}
    </style>
    <title></title>
    <script>
        WinJS.UI.Pages.define("/pages/Tooltip.html", {
            ready: function () {

                Templates.createControls(rightPanel, inlineTooltip, "tooltip");

                $("#rightPanel button").listen("click", function (e) {
                    inlineTooltip.winControl[e.target.innerText.toLowerCase()]();
                });
            }
        });
    </script>
</head>
<body>
    <div id="tooltipContainer" class="flexContainer">
        <div class="controlPanel">
            <div class="textPara">I like
                <span id="inlineTooltip" data-win-control="WinJS.UI.Tooltip"
                    data-win-options="{innerHTML: 'An Apple is a type of Fruit'}">
                    <b>Apples</b>
                </span>, but I don't like Pears.</div>

            <div id="blockTooltip" data-win-control="WinJS.UI.Tooltip"
                data-win-options="{contentElement: tooltipContent, infotip: true}">
                <button>Press Me</button>
            </div>
        </div>

        <div id="rightPanel" class="controlPanel"></div>
    </div>

    <div style="display: none">
        <div id="tooltipContent">
            <img src="/images/apple.png" />
            <span>Apples grow on small, deciduous trees.
```

```
                    Apples have been grown for thousands of years in Asia
                    and Europe, and were brought to North America by European
                    colonists.
                </span>
            </div>
        </div>
    </body>
</html>
```

This file follows the same basic pattern as the previous examples. The file is longer than previous examples because it includes some simple content that I display using the Tooltip controls I demonstrate in this section.

The other difference is that I have added a handler for the click events for the button elements I create in the right-hand panel in the app layout. This handler invokes the method defined by the winControl property that corresponds to the clicked button content, so that clicking the Open button calls the winControl.open method and clicking the Close button calls the winControl.close method. I'll explain both of these methods shortly.

The last step in demonstrating this control is to add the Tooltip.html file to the NavBar, which I do by making the addition to the templates.js file shown in Listing 11-14.

Listing 11-14. Adding the Tooltip.html file to the NavBar

```
...
var navBarCommands = [
    //{ name: "AppTest", icon: "target" },
    { name: "ToggleSwitch", icon: "\u0031" },
    { name: "Rating", icon: "\u0032" },
    { name: "Tooltip", icon: "\u0033" },
];
...
```

■ **Note**   The markup in the Tooltip.html file contains an img element whose src attribute refers to a file called apple.png in the images folder. You can get the image I have used as part of the source code download for this book or, if you prefer, just rename an image you have to hand to apple.png and copy it into the images folder of the Visual Studio project.

Applying and Configuring the Tooltip Control

The basic premise is to wrap the HTML elements that the Tooltip relates to in a div element to which the WinJS.UI.Tooltip control has been applied, as shown in Listing 11-15.

Listing 11-15. Applying a Tooltip control to a block element

```
...
<div id="blockTooltip" data-win-control="WinJS.UI.Tooltip"
    data-win-options="{contentElement: tooltipContent, infotip: true}">
        <button>Press Me</button>
</div>
...
```

In this fragment, taken from the /pages/Tooltip.html file, I have wrapped a button element in a div element to which the Tooltip has been applied. When the user hovers the mouse pointer or holds a finger over the button element, the contents of the element specified by the contentElement property will be displayed. In the example, I have set the contentElement property to tooltipContent, which refers to the element shown in Listing 11-16.

Listing 11-16. The content used for the Tooltip control

```
...
<div style="display: none">
    <div id="tooltipContent">
        <img src="/images/apple.png" />
        <span>Apples grow on small, deciduous trees.
            Apples have been grown for thousands of years in Asia
            and Europe, and were brought to North America by European
            colonists.
        </span>
    </div>
</div>
...
```

The content of this element is standard HTML markup consisting of img and span elements. Notice that I have put the content element inside a div element whose CSS display property is set to none – this prevents the user from seeing the content until it is displayed by the Tooltip control.

■ **Tip**   This is where I have used the /images/apple.png file that I added to the project in the previous section. You can see this image displayed in Figure 11-6.

You can see the result when the mouse pointer hovers over the Press Me button in Figure 11-6.

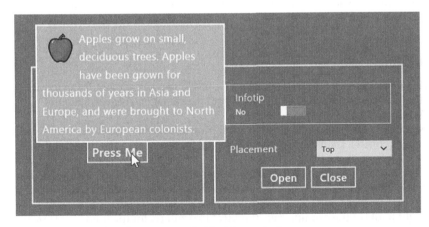

Figure 11-6. Setting the content of a Tooltip control

The contentElement is one of the properties that you can set on a Tooltip control, either through the data-win-options attribute or programmatically, via the winControl property. You can see the complete set of properties in Table 11-8, and I demonstrate them all in the sections that follow.

Table 11-8. The configuration properties for the Tooltip control

Property	Description
contentElement	Specifies an element in the document to use as the `Tooltip` content
innerHTML	Specifies the `Tooltip` content as a string
infotip	Gets or sets whether this `Tooltip` has a lot of information and should be displayed for longer than a regular `Tooltip`.
placement	Specifies where the `Tooltip` appears relative to its target element

Creating an Inline Tooltip & Using the innerHTML Property

You can also apply the `Tooltip` control to a span element, which is useful if you are using content which is being displayed inline and where a div element would disrupt the layout. The other Tooltip I defined in the `Tooltip.html` file has been applied in this way, as shown in Listing 11-17.

Listing 11-17. Applying a Tooltip control to a span element

```
...
<div class="textPara">I like
    <span id="inlineTooltip" data-win-control="WinJS.UI.Tooltip"
        data-win-options="{innerHTML: 'An Apple is a type of Fruit'}">
            <b>Apples</b>
    </span>, but I don't like Pears.
</div>
...
```

The element to which the `Tooltip` will apply is still wrapped around the content it relates to, which is this example is the word Apples. When the mouse pointer hovers over the word Apples in the block of text, the `Tooltip` will be displayed to the user.

As an alternative to using the `contentElement` property, I have set the content of the `Tooltip` control using the `innerHTML` property. This property lets you set the content of the `Tooltip` as a string value and this is the Tooltip that I showed in Figure 11-5.

Setting the Display Duration

The user can trigger the `Tooltip` in a number of ways. If the user touches or presses and holds the mouse button on the element, then the `Tooltip` popup will be displayed until the finger is removed from the display or the mouse button is released.

If the user triggers the `Tooltip` by a keyboard action (such as tabbing between elements) or by hovering the mouse over the target control, then the popup is displayed for 5 seconds, after which it is closed automatically.

You can extend this to 15 seconds by setting the `infotip` property to `true`. This value is intended to be used for `Tooltip`s which contain a lot of information and which the user is unlikely to be able to parse in the shorter period.

The `ToggleSwitch` in the right panel of the example sets the `infotip` property for the inline `Tooltip` in the left panel. By using this switch, you can see the effect of the different timespans.

■ **Tip**   If you need to make all of your Tooltips display for 15 seconds, you may want to rethink the way that you are presenting content to the user. Tooltips are perfect for small snippets of information that guide the user through your app. Consider using a Flyout as a general-purpose popup window, as I describe in Chapter 12.

Setting the Tooltip Placement

The placement property governs where the Tooltip popup appears relative to the target element. The default value is top, meaning that the popup is shown slightly above the element, but you can also specify left, right and bottom. The select element in the right panel in the example sets the placement property on the inline Tooltip in the left panel. You can see the effect of the alternate placements in Figure 11-7.

Figure 11-7. The left, bottom and right Tooltip placements

You don't have to worry about adjusting the placement value to make sure the Tooltip popup fits on the screen. WinJS will automatically adjust the location of a popup if the value specified by the placement property means that the popup won't fit. Table 11-9 shows the series of fallback placements that will be tried for each possible value of the placement property if the popup can't be displayed for the specified value.

■ **Tip**   The order of the right and left placements in the fallback sequence will be reversed for devices which have been configured for left-handed users.

Table 11-9. The fallback placement sequence for the Tooltip contro.

Placement Value	Fallback Sequence
top	bottom, left, right
bottom	top, left, right
left	right, top, bottom
right	left, top, bottom

The exact position of the popup is relative to the position of the mouse or touch event and is subject to an offset which depends on the kind of event that triggered the Tooltip. The offset is 15 pixels for keyboard events (for example, when the user tabs to the target element), 20 pixels for mouse events and 45 pixels for touch events. The larger offsets are intended to allow the user to read the Tooltip content without it being obscured by a cursor, stylus, or finger.

Managing the Tooltip Control Programmatically

You can take direct control when a Tooltip is displayed and hidden by using the open and close methods - although if you use these methods, you should pause for a moment and consider if you are using the Tooltip in a way which is consistent with other Windows apps. (And if you want a general purpose popup, you should use a Flyout, as I describe in Chapter 12).

For quick reference, I have describes these methods in Table 11-10. This may seem redundant, but the WinJS UI controls don't use a consistent method naming scheme and there will come a point when you want to be able to quickly find out if the Tooltip control defines show or open and close or hide.

Table 11-10. The Tooltip methods

Method	Description
open()	Displays the Tooltip control
close()	Hides the Tooltip control

The open method takes an optional argument which is used to simulate different kinds of trigger event and the supported values are touch, mouseover, mousedown and keyboard. If you don't provide an argument, the default value is used. Each value has a slightly different effect, including the offset used to position the popup (as I described in the previous section), the delay before the popup is shown and the period for which the popup is shown before it is closed.

You need to be careful because the touch, mousedown and default arguments will not automatically dismiss the popup. In the case of the touch and mousedown modes, this is because the popup is displayed until the finger is removed from the screen or the mouse button is released. If you use these arguments to the open menu, then you must explicitly dismiss the Tooltip popup using the close method. The Open and Close buttons in the right panel of the example call the open and close methods (the open method is called without arguments so that the popup won't be dismissed until the Close button is used).

■ **Tip** I find calling the open method without an argument to be useful during development because it lets me see how the contents of a Tooltip will be displayed without having to perform a trigger action.

Styling the Tooltip Control

The Tooltip control supports a single CSS class: win-tooltip. You can use this class as the starting point for styling the content you display. There are no other classes because there is no fixed element structure in a Tooltip. Listing 11-18 shows the style I defined for Tooltip controls in the /css/default.css file.

Listing 11-18. Styling the Tooltip control

```
...
.win-tooltip {
    background-color: #8ED09C;
    color: white;
    border: medium solid white;
    font-size: 16pt;
}
...
```

Handling the Tooltip Events

The Tooltip control supports the four events that I have described in Table 11-11. I have listed these for completeness, but I have yet to find a use for these events in a real project because Tooltips are intended to present simple, self-contained content.

Table 11-11. The events supported by the Tooltip control

Event	Description
beforeopen	Triggered before the Tooltip is displayed
opened	Triggered when the Tooltip has been displayed
beforeclose	Triggered before the Tooltip is closed
closed	Triggered when the Tooltip has closed

As with some of the other features of the Tooltip control, I suggest that you stop and consider your app design if you need these events. It might be that you have very specialized needs, but it is more likely that you are about to force the Tooltip control into doing something which breaks the regular rules of Windows app interactions. Consider if the Flyout control, which I describe in Chapter 12, would be a more appropriate choice.

Summary

I have introduced you to the three simplest WinJS UI controls in this chapter - although, as you have seen, there is plenty of detail to consider to get the right effect in your app. In the next chapter, I'll turn my attention to the time and date pickers and the Flyout and Menu controls.

CHAPTER 12

■ ■ ■

Using the Time/Date Pickers & Flyouts

In this chapter, I continue my exploration of the WinJS UI controls, focusing on the TimePicker, DatePicker, Flyout and Menu controls. The TimePicker and DatePicker controls allow the user to specify, as their names suggest, times and dates. These are basic controls with some design problems that make them more difficult to work with (and less useful) than they could be. You have already seen the Flyout control in Chapter 7, where I used it with an AppBar. The Flyout has a broader existence as a general-purpose control and I explain all that you need to know to use it in this context. Table 12-1 provides the summary for this chapter.

Table 121. *Chapter Summary*

Problem	Solution	Listing
Use the TimePicker control	Apply the data-win-control attribute to a div element with a value of WinJS.UI.TimePicker.	1-3
Set the display patterns used by the TimePicker control	Translate numeric lengths into the fragments required for the display templates	4
Style a TimePicker	Define styles for the win-timepicker CSS class	5
Receive a notification when the user selects a time	Listen for the change event	6
Use the DatePicker control	Apply the data-win-control attribute to a div element with a value of WinJS.UI.DatePicker.	7-9
Style a DatePicker	Define styles for the win-datepicker CSS class	10
Receive a notification when the user selects a date	Listen for the change event	11
Use the Flyout control	Apply the data-win-control attribute to a div element with a value of WinJS.UI.Flyout.	12-14
Control the location of the Flyout	Use the alignment and placement properties	-
Control the visibility of the Flyout	Use the show and hide methods	-
Styling the Flyout control	Define styles for the win-flyout CSS class	15

Using the TimePicker Control

The WinJS.UI.TimePicker control allows the user to select a time. There are HTML5 additions to the input element to support time and date input, but these are not supported in Internet Explorer 10 and you must use the TimePicker and DatePicker controls instead (I describe the DatePicker later in this chapter). You can see how the TimePicker control is displayed to the user in Figure 12-1.

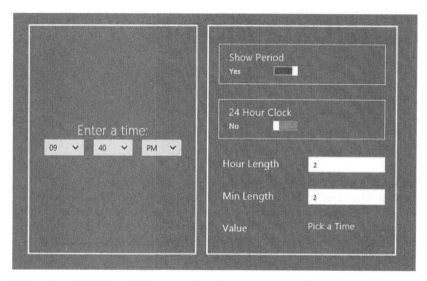

Figure 12-1. The TimePicker control and supporting configuration settings

When to use the TimePicker Control

You should use the TimePicker control when you need the user to specify a time of day. The TImePicker control respects the locale settings of the user's machine and so captures a time using the localized time preferences - although, as you'll see, this isn't entirely successful.

The quality of the TimePicker control isn't as good as I would like. Localized time and date preferences are notoriously difficult to get right and some allowances have to be made, but even so, there unfortunate design choices reflected in the TimePicker which make it a lot less useful that it would be otherwise. My overall impression of this control and its companion, the DatePicker, is that it is a rushed job with little thought to how the controls would be used.

Demonstrating the TimePicker Control

Following the pattern from the previous chapter, I have added a file called TimePicker.html to the pages folder of the Visual Studio project I started in Chapter 10. You can see the contents of the file in Listing 12-1.

Listing 12-1. The contents of the TimePicker.html file

```
<!DOCTYPE html>
<html>
<head>
```

```
    <title></title>
    <script>
        WinJS.UI.Pages.define("/pages/TimePicker.html", {
            ready: function () {

                var proxyObject = WinJS.Binding.as({
                    showPeriod: true,
                    clock: false,
                    hourLength: 2,
                    minuteLength: 2,
                });

                Templates.createControls(rightPanel, picker, "timePicker", proxyObject)
                .then(function () {

                    proxyObject.bind("showPeriod", function (val) {
                        $('.win-timepicker-period').setStyle("display",
                            val ? "block" : "none");
                    });

                    proxyObject.bind("clock", function (val) {
                        picker.winControl.clock = val ? "24HourClock" : "12HourClock";
                    });

                    ["hour", "minute"].forEach(function (item) {
                        proxyObject.bind(item + "Length", function (val) {
                            picker.winControl[item + "Pattern"] = "{" + item +
                                ".integer(" + val + ")}";
                        });
                    });
                });
            }
        });
    </script>
</head>
<body>
    <div id="timePickerContainer" class="flexContainer">
        <div class="controlPanel">

            <h2>Enter a time:</h2>
            <div id="picker" data-win-control="WinJS.UI.TimePicker"
                data-win-options="{minuteIncrement: 10}">
            </div>
        </div>

        <div id="rightPanel" class="controlPanel"></div>
    </div>
</body>
</html>
```

This is the first control for which I have needed the proxy object feature that I added to the example framework in Chapter 10. As you'll see when I explain how the properties defined by the TimePicker control work, I couldn't easily map from the values in the configuration controls that I generate for the right-hand panel in the layout to values I could use with the TimePicker properties.

You can see how I use the proxy object in the definition objects I added to the /js/controls.js file to demonstrate the TimePicker control in Listing 12-2.

Listing 12-2. Adding definition objects to the controls.js file for the TimePicker controls

```
...
timePicker: [
    { type: "toggle", id: "showPeriod", title: "Show Period", value: true,
        useProxy: true, labelOn: "Yes", labelOff: "No" },
    { type: "toggle", id: "clock", title: "24 Hour Clock", value: false,
        useProxy: true, labelOn: "Yes", labelOff: "No" },
    { type: "input", id: "hourLength", title: "Hour Length", value: 2,
        useProxy: true },
    { type: "input", id: "minuteLength", title: "Min Length", value: 2,
        useProxy: true },
    { type: "span", id: "current", value: "Pick a Time", title: "Value" }],
...
```

Finally, to enable the user to navigate to the TimePicker.html file through the NavBar, I made the addition to the templates.js file shown in Listing 12-3.

Listing 12-3. Adding support for navigating to the TimePicker.html file via the NavBar

```
...
var navBarCommands = [
    //{ name: "AppTest", icon: "target" },
    { name: "ToggleSwitch", icon: "\u0031" },
    { name: "Rating", icon: "\u0032" },
    { name: "Tooltip", icon: "\u0033" },
    { name: "TimePicker", icon: "\u0034" },
];
...
```

Applying and Configuring the TimePicker Control

The TimePicker control is applied to div elements by setting the data-win-control attribute to WinJS.UI.TimePicker. The TimePicker control supports a number of configuration properties which I have summarized in Table 12-2 and which I have created configuration controls for. I'll explain each of these properties in detail in the sections that follow.

Table 12-2. The configuration properties for the TimePicker control

Property	Description
clock	Gets or sets whether this is a 12- or 24-hour clock. The supported values are 12HourClock and 24HourClock.
current	Gets or sets the time displayed by the TimePicker control. This defaults to the current system time if unspecified

Property	Description
disabled	Gets or sets whether the control is enabled
hourPattern	Gets or sets the pattern used to display the hour
minutePattern	Gets or sets the pattern used to display the minute
periodPattern	Gets or sets the pattern used to display the AM/PM period
minuteIncrement	Gets or sets the increments by which minute values can be specified

Setting the Clock Type

You can select the kind of time that will be displayed using the clock property. If this property is set to 12HourClock, the TimePicker displays three select elements, allowing the user to select the hours, the minutes and the period (AM or PM). If the clock property is set to 24HourClock, then only two select elements are displayed, but there are 24 items in the hour menu, allowing a 24 hour time to be specified. You can change the clock property in the example using the control labeled 24 Hour Clock and the 12- and 24-hour clock displays are shown in Figure 12-2.

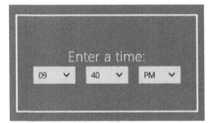

Figure 12-2. Setting the clock type for the TimePicker control

Setting the Minute Increment

The minuteIncrement property specifies the smallest interval that can be selected for the minute value. For example, setting the minuteIncrement property to 10 will allow the user to set the minute to 0, 10, 20, 30, 40 and 50 minutes. A value of 15 would allow 0, 15, 30 and 45 minutes. The problem is that changing the property after the control has been initialized has no effect - you have to decide which interval you want and specify it has a configuration option using the data-win-options attribute.

In the example, I use the data-win-options attribute to set the minuteIncrement property to 10, like this:

```
...
<div id="picker" data-win-control="WinJS.UI.TimePicker"
    data-win-options="{minuteIncrement: 10}">
</div>
...
```

You can see the effect this has in Figure 12-3, where I have clicked on the minute component of the TimePicker control to reveal the available increments.

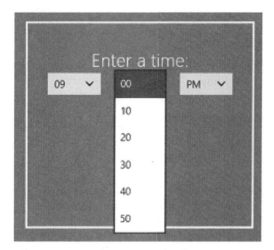

Figure 12-3. Restricting the minute increments on a TimePicker control

Specifying the Display Patterns

The `hourPattern`, `minutePattern` and `periodPattern` properties let you specify how the individual components of the time are displayed. Well, sort of - in fact, they only really let you specify how many characters are used for the time and, even then, you have to work hard for it.

The `Windows.Globalization.DateTimeFormatting` namespace contains the `DateTimeFormatter` object, which the `TimePicker` control uses to format and parse time values. The `DateTimeFormatter` supports a comprehensive template-based system for processing times and dates. Here is an example:

```
{hour.integer}:{minute.integer(2)}:{second.integer(2)} {period.abbreviated}
```

This template has components for the hour, minute, and second. The minutes and seconds are displayed using two characters and the period is shown in an abbreviated form (AM or PM, for example).

The pattern properties in the `TimePicker` control work on fragments of this template. You can't change the order in which the elements appear, but you can change the number of characters used for each element. So, for example, if you want to make sure that the hour is always displayed using on a 12-hour clock, then you would set the `minutePattern` property to `{hour.integer(2)}`. The brace characters (`{` and `}`) are a required part of the value, which means you must be careful when setting values for these properties using the `data-win-options` property - it is very easy to get the sequence of braces and quote characters muddled up.

Given that the sole change you can make with these properties is to set the number of characters, I think it would have been more sensible for the `TimePicker` control to take responsibility for converting integer values into template fragments. As it is, you need to know enough about the underlying working of date/time formatting without getting any benefit in doing so. But, as I said before, the `TimePicker` control is not especially well-thought out or implemented.

I have included two `input` elements in the right panel of the example that lets you change the number of characters used for the hour and minute elements. I update the `hourPattern` and `minutePattern` properties through the proxy object, as shown in Listing 12-4.

Listing 12-4. Converting between integer values and template fragments

```
...
["hour", "minute"].forEach(function (item) {
```

```
    proxyObject.bind(item + "Length", function (val) {
        picker.winControl[item + "Pattern"] = "{" + item + ".integer(" + val + ")}";
    });
});
...
```

You can see the effect of entering 3 in the Hour Length and Min Length input elements in Figure 12-4.

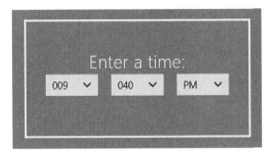

Figure 12-4. Specifying the number of characters used to display the hour and minute time components

Managing the TimePicker Programmatically

The TimePicker control doesn't define any methods. I have included this section only to preserve consistency with the other controls so that you don't think it has been omitted by error.

Styling the TimePicker Control

The TimePicker control supports a number of CSS classes which can be used to style the entire control or one of the individual elements. I have described the set of classes in Table 12-3.

Table 12-3. The TimePicker CSS classes

Class	Description
win-timepicker	Styles the entire TimePicker control
win-timepicker-hour	Styles the hour component
win-timepicker-minute	Styles the minute component
win-timepicker-period	Styles the period component

In the example, I use the Show Period configuration control to change the visibility of the period component through the win-timepicker-period class, as shown in Listing 12-5.

Listing 12-5. Using a CSS class to locate a component of the TimePicker control

```
...
proxyObject.bind("showPeriod", function (val) {
    $('.win-timepicker-period').setStyle("display", val ? "block" : "none");
});
...
```

Changing the state of the ToggeSwitch marked Show Period will change the visibility of the period select element when the clock property is set to 12HourClock.

Responding to the TimePicker Event

The TimePicker emits the change event when the user changes the time displayed by the control. You can see the addition I made to the script element in the TimePicker.html file to handle the change event in Listing 12-6, where I display the time that the user has picked with the TimePicker as the content of the span element in the right-hand panel of the app layout.

Listing 12-6. Handling the change event from the TimePicker control

```
...
<script>
    WinJS.UI.Pages.define("/pages/TimePicker.html", {
        ready: function () {

            var proxyObject = WinJS.Binding.as({
                showPeriod: true,
                clock: false,
                hourLength: 2,
                minuteLength: 2,
            });

            Templates.createControls(rightPanel, picker, "timePicker", proxyObject)
            .then(function () {

                proxyObject.bind("showPeriod", function (val) {
                    $('.win-timepicker-period').setStyle("display", val ? "block" :
                        "none");
                });

                proxyObject.bind("clock", function (val) {
                    picker.winControl.clock = val ? "24HourClock" : "12HourClock";
                });

                ["hour", "minute"].forEach(function (item) {
                    proxyObject.bind(item + "Length", function (val) {
                        picker.winControl[item + "Pattern"] = "{" + item + ".integer("
                            + val + ")}";
                    });
                });

                picker.addEventListener("change", function (e) {
                    current.innerText = picker.winControl.current.toLocaleTimeString();
                });

            });
        }
    });
```

```
</script>
...
```

The `TimePicker.current` property returns a standard JavaScript `Date` object, which allows me to call the `toLocaleTimeString` method to get a value that I can safely display in layout, as shown in Figure 12-5, where I have used the picker to select 9:50 pm.

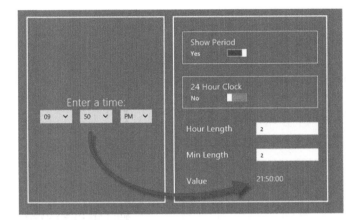

Figure 12-5. *Responding to the change event from a TimePicker control*

Using the DatePicker Control

The `DatePicker` control is the complement to the `TimePicker` and allows the user to select a date. The `DatePicker` shares a lot of similarities with the `TimePicker` control - including, sadly, some of the less useful characteristics such as template fragments.

The `DatePicker` control is very similar in structure and appearance to the `TimePicker` control and presents the user with three `select` elements with which they can pick a date. You can see how the `DatePicker` is displayed, along with the configuration controls I generated to demonstrate different date-related features, in Figure 12-6.

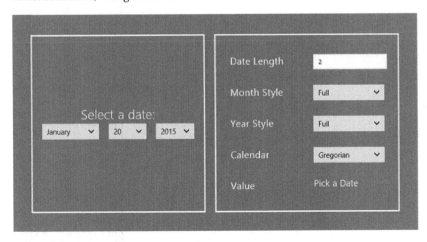

Figure 12-6. *The DatePicker control*

When to use the DatePicker Control

The DatePicker control is suitable for use when you want the user to select a date. The DatePicker control performs much of its date formatting using the device regional settings and, like TimePicker, doesn't provide a mechanism for overriding locales (although there is an option to use different kinds of calendar). This means that you should only use the DatePicker in an app which has been thoroughly tested in each of the regions in which it will be deployed.

Demonstrating the DatePicker Control

I have added a file called DatePicker.html to the pages folder of the Visual Studio project I started in Chapter 10. You can see the contents of the file in Listing 12-7.

Listing 12-7. The contents of the DatePicker.html file

```
<!DOCTYPE html>
<html>
<head>
    <title></title>
    <script>
        WinJS.UI.Pages.define("/pages/DatePicker.html", {
            ready: function () {

                var proxyObject = WinJS.Binding.as({
                    dateLength: 2
                });

                Templates.createControls(rightPanel, picker, "datePicker", proxyObject)
                .then(function () {
                    proxyObject.bind("dateLength", function (val) {
                        picker.winControl.datePattern = "{day.integer(" + val + ")}";
                    });
                });
            }
        });
    </script>
</head>
<body>
    <div id="datePickerContainer" class="flexContainer">
        <div class="controlPanel">

            <h2>Select a date:</h2>
            <div id="picker" data-win-control="WinJS.UI.DatePicker">
            </div>
        </div>

        <div id="rightPanel" class="controlPanel"></div>
    </div>
</body>
</html>
```

This is another control for which I have needed the proxy object feature I added to the example framework in Chapter 10. The DatePicker control uses the same template pattern system as the TimePicker control, which means I need the proxy object to change the format of the date that is displayed (which I'll demonstrate shortly).

You can see how I use the proxy object in the definition objects I added to the /js/controls.js file to demonstrate the DatePicker control in Listing 12-8.

Listing 12-8. Adding definition objects to the control.js file for the DatePicker controls

```
...
datePicker: [
    { type: "input", id: "dateLength", title: "Date Length", value: 2, useProxy: true },
    { type: "select", id: "monthPattern", title: "Month Style", values: ["{month.full}",
        "{month.abbreviated}"], labels: ["Full", "Abbreviated"]},
    { type: "select", id: "yearPattern", title: "Year Style", values: ["{year.full}",
        "{year.abbreviated}"], labels: ["Full", "Abbreviated"]},
    { type: "select", id: "calendar", title: "Calendar", values: ["GregorianCalendar",
        "HebrewCalendar", "ThaiCalendar"], labels: ["Gregorian", "Hebrew", "Thai"]},
    { type: "span", id: "current", value: "Pick a Date", title: "Value"}],
...
```

Finally, to enable the user to navigate to the TimePicker.html file through the NavBar, I made the addition to the templates.js file shown in Listing 12-9.

Listing 12-9. Adding support for navigating to the TimePicker.html file via the NavBar

```
...
var navBarCommands = [
    //{ name: "AppTest", icon: "target" },
    { name: "ToggleSwitch", icon: "\u0031" },
    { name: "Rating", icon: "\u0032" },
    { name: "Tooltip", icon: "\u0033" },
    { name: "TimePicker", icon: "\u0034" },
    { name: "DatePicker", icon: "\u0035" },
];
...
```

Applying and Configuring the DatePicker Control

The DatePicker control is applied to div elements by setting the data-win-control attribute to WinJS.UI. DatePicker. Three drop-down menus are present by default (but can be hidden using CSS classes - see the Styling the DatePicker Control section for details), allowing the user to pick the day, month and year components of the date. The DatePicker control supports the configuration properties listed and described in Table 12-4.

Table 12-4. The configuration properties for the DatePicker control

Property	Description
calendar	Sets the type of calendar displayed by the DatePicker control.
current	Gets or sets the date displayed by the DatePicker. Defaults to today's date.

Property	Description
datePattern	Sets the pattern used to display the date
disabled	Enables and disables the control.
maxYear	Sets the latest year that can be selected. This value is expressed as a year in the Gregorian calendar, even if another calendar has been specified with the calendar property. The default is 100 years from the current year.
minYear	Sets the earliest year that can be selected. This value is expressed as a year in the Gregorian calendar, even if another calendar has been specified with the calendar property. The default is 100 years before the current year.
monthPattern	Sets the pattern used to display the month.
yearPattern	Sets the pattern used to display the year.

Using Different Calendars

The calendar property allows you to specify a calendar for the DatePicker to use. The default value is derived from the device region settings. In the example, I have added a select element to the right-hand panel which allows you to select the GregorianCalendar, HebrewCalendar and ThaiCalendar values, the effect of which can be seen in Figure 12-7.

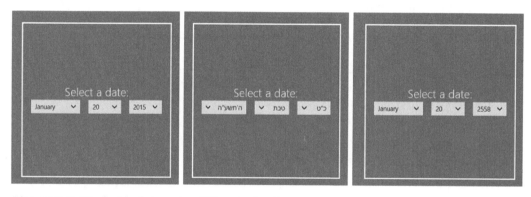

Figure 12-7. *Displaying dates using different calendars*

I added support for these calendar types to demonstrate the cross-section that is available. The full set of supported values for this property is: GregorianCalendar, HijriCalendar, HebrewCalendar, JapaneseCalendar, KoreanCalendar, ThaiCalendar, TaiwanCalendar, UmAlQuraCalendar and JulianCalendar.

Specifying the Display Patterns

The DatePicker control uses template fragments in a similar way to the TimePicker control, exposed through the datePattern, monthPattern and yearPattern properties.

The format for the datePattern is {day.integer(*n*)} where n is the number of characters that should be used to display the day. Notice that although the name of the property is ***date*Pattern**, the fragment is ***day*.integer** (i.e. date versus day). For the month and year components, you can select between full and abbreviated values. Table 12-5 shows the set of supported values for these two properties.

Table 12-5. The supported values for the monthPattern and yearPattern properties

Property	Value	Example
monthPattern	{month.full}	January
monthPattern	{month.abbreviated}	Jan
yearPattern	{year.full}	2013
yearPattern	{year.abbreviated}	13

I added three configuration controls to manage the way that the date is displayed. The Date Length input element lets you change the number of characters used to display the day component, and the Month Style and Year Style select elements let you see what the full and abbreviated displays look like. In Figure 12-8, you can see how the abbreviated month and year settings are displayed.

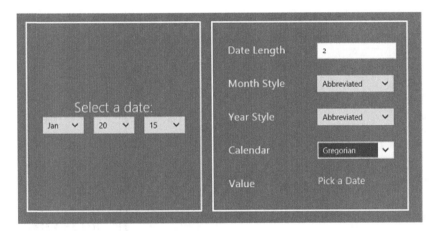

Figure 12-8. Displaying the abbreviated month and year values

Managing the DatePicker Programmatically

The DatePicker control doesn't define any methods. I have included this section only to preserve consistency with the other controls so that you don't think it has been omitted by error.

Styling the DatePicker Control

The DatePicker control supports a number of CSS classes which can be used to style the entire control or one of the individual elements. I have described the set of classes in Table 12-6.

Table 12-6. The DatePicker CSS classes

Class	Description
win-datepicker	Styles the entire DatePicker control
win-datepicker-date	Styles the date component
win-datepicker-month	Styles the month component
win-datepicker-year	Styles the year component

I have not used any of the styles in the example, but I do find them useful for hiding individual components in the control so that the user can specify a less precise date. So, for example, if I wanted the user to pick just a month and year, I would add a style element to the DatePicker.html file as shown in Listing 12-10.

Listing 12-10. Using a CSS class to hide a component of the DatePicker control

```
...
<style>
    .win-datepicker-date {
        display: none;
    }
</style>
...
```

Hiding one of the components causes the control to be resized, as you can see in Figure 12-9.

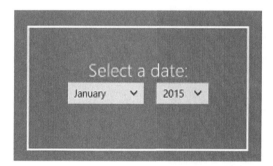

Figure 12-9. Showing a subset of the components in the DatePicker control

Responding to the DatePicker Event

The DatePicker emits the change event when the user picks a new date. You can see the addition I made to the script element in the DatePicker.html file to handle the change event in Listing 12-11, where I use the date that the user has picked with the DatePicker to update the contents of the span element in the right-hand panel of the app layout.

Listing 12-11. Handling the change event from the DatePicker control

```
...
<script>
    WinJS.UI.Pages.define("/pages/DatePicker.html", {
        ready: function () {

            var proxyObject = WinJS.Binding.as({
                dateLength: 2
            });

            Templates.createControls(rightPanel, picker, "datePicker", proxyObject)
                .then(function () {
```

```
                proxyObject.bind("dateLength", function (val) {
                    picker.winControl.datePattern = "{day.integer(" + val + ")}";
                });

                picker.addEventListener("change", function (e) {
                    current.innerText = picker.winControl.current.toLocaleDateString();
                });
            });
        }
    });
</script>
...
```

The DatePicker.current property returns a standard JavaScript Date object, which allows me to call the toLocaleDateString method to get a value that I can display.

Revisiting the Flyout Control

I introduced you to the WinJS.UI.Flyout control in Chapter 7, when I showed you how to use a Flyout to respond to an AppBar command. The Flyout control is a general purpose popup and can be used in any situation, which is why I am returning to this control so that I can show you how it is used away from the AppBar. I use two Flyout controls in the example for this section, one of which you can see in Figure 12-10. The controls in the right panel allow you to configure the visible Flyout control.

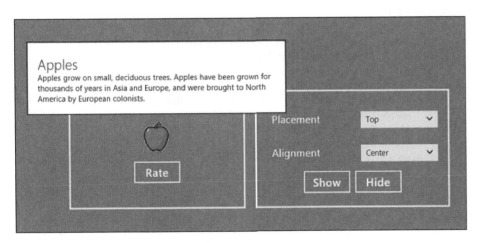

Figure 12-10. Using Flyout controls

When to use the Flyout Control

The Flyout is a general purpose control that can be used in any situation where you want to present content outside of the main layout. There are specialized uses for the Flyout, such as with an AppBar (see Chapter 7) or with a Menu control (described later in this chapter), but otherwise you can do whatever makes sense in the context of your app. For simple information-only content, consider using the WinJS.UI.Tooltip control instead, which I describe in Chapter 11 and which requires less programmatic control.

■ **Tip** Be sure to read the *Using the Flyout for User Interactions* section later in this chapter for guidance about using a Flyout to display elements that require user interaction, such as button elements and Rating controls. There are some characteristics of the Flyout that require special attention in these situations.

Demonstrating the Flyout Control

In order to demonstrate the Flyout control, I added a new file to the pages folder of the Visual Studio project called Flyout.html. You can see the contents of this file in Listing 12-12. This file is slightly larger than some of the others I have added to the project because it contains the Flyout controls and the content that I will display in them.

Listing 12-12. The content of the Flyout.html file

```
<!DOCTYPE html>
<html>
<head>
    <title></title>
    <style>
        #rateButton, #flyoutInteractive button { font-size: 16pt; margin-top: 10px}
    </style>
    <script>
        WinJS.UI.Pages.define("/pages/Flyout.html", {
            ready: function () {

                Templates.createControls(rightPanel, flyout, "flyout").then(function () {
                    $("button").listen("click", function (e) {
                        if (e.target.id == "rateButton") {
                            flyoutInteractive.winControl.show(e.target);
                        } else if (e.target.id == "flyoutInteractiveButton") {
                            flyoutInteractive.winControl.hide();
                        } else if (e.target.innerText == "Show") {
                            flyout.winControl.show(targetImg);
                        } else if (e.target.innerText == "Hide") {
                            flyout.winControl.hide();
                        }
                    });
                });
            }
        });
    </script>
</head>
<body>
    <div id="flyoutContainer" class="flexContainer">
        <div class="controlPanel">
            <img id="targetImg" src="/images/apple.png" />
            <button id="rateButton">Rate</button>
        </div>
        <div id="rightPanel" class="controlPanel"></div>
```

```
    </div>

    <div id="flyout" data-win-control="WinJS.UI.Flyout">
        <h2>Apples</h2>
        <span>
            Apples grow on small, deciduous trees.
            Apples have been grown for thousands of years in Asia
            and Europe, and were brought to North America by European
            colonists.
        </span>
    </div>

    <div id="flyoutInteractive" data-win-control="WinJS.UI.Flyout">
        <h2>How much do you like apples?</h2>
        <div data-win-control="WinJS.UI.Rating"></div>
        <div>
            <button id="flyoutInteractiveButton">Close</button>
        </div>
    </div>
</body>
</html>
```

To create the configuration controls that you can see in the right-hand panel of Figure 12-10, I added the definition objects to the controls.js file that you can see in Listing 12-13.

Listing 12-13. The definition objects for the Flyout control

```
...
flyout: [
    { type: "select", id: "placement", title: "Placement", values: ["top", "bottom",
        "left", "right"], labels: ["Top", "Bottom", "Left", "Right"]},
    { type: "select", id: "alignment", title: "Alignment", values: ["left", "center",
        "right"], labels: ["Left", "Center", "Right"]},
    { type: "buttons", labels: ["Show", "Hide"] }],
...
```

Finally, so that the user can navigate to the Flyout.html file through the NavBar, I made the addition to the templates.js file that you can see in Listing 12-14.

Listing 12-14. Adding the Flyout.html file to the NavBar

```
...
var navBarCommands = [
    //{ name: "AppTest", icon: "target" },
    { name: "ToggleSwitch", icon: "\u0031" },
    { name: "Rating", icon: "\u0032" },
    { name: "Tooltip", icon: "\u0033" },
    { name: "TimePicker", icon: "\u0034" },
    { name: "DatePicker", icon: "\u0035" },
    { name: "Flyout", icon: "\u0036" },
];
...
```

297

Applying and Configuring the Flyout Control

The WinJS.UI.Flyout control is applied to div elements. There is no fixed internal structure to a Flyout and you can create any mix of elements and controls to suit your needs, including content with which the user can interact – a technique I'll show you in more detail shortly.

Displaying a Flyout Control

The Flyout defines the show and hide methods, which you can use to control the visibility of the control. Table 12-7 summarizes these methods for quick reference.

Table 12-7. The Flyout methods

Method	Description
show(anchor)	Displays the Flyout relative to the anchor element
hide()	Hides the Flyout control

The show method has a mandatory argument with which you specify an *anchor element*, which is the near which the Flyout is positioned. The show method supports two optional arguments which allow you to override the values for the placement and alignment properties – I'll explain the purpose and values for these properties in the next section.

The Flyout control supports light-dismiss technique I mentioned in Chapter 12, and will be dismissed automatically when the user clicks or touches the display outside of the Flyout popup. You *can* explicitly dismiss a Flyout by calling the hide method, but this is only of use when you are responding to an interactive control in the Flyout, which I'll demonstrate shortly.

There are two Flyout controls in the example and you can see how the show and hide methods are applied by clicking the Show and Hide buttons in the right-hand panel. Clicking the Show button will present you with a Flyout that displays some static text (this is the Flyout shown in Figure 12-10). When the Show button is clicked, I use the img element in the markup as the anchor element, which is why the Flyout is position just above the image in the figure. You can dismiss the Flyout either by clicking the Hide button or clicking anywhere in the app layout which is outside of the Flyout.

■ **Tip**   The other Flyout in the example is shown when you click the Rate button. I come back to this control later in this section when I discuss using Flyout controls to present the user with interactive content.

Configuring a Flyout Control

As you would expect by now, there are a number of properties defined by the Flyout control which you can use to change its behavior. These properties are summarized by Table 12-8.

Table 12-8. The configuration properties for the Flyout control

Property	Description
anchor	Gets or sets the element to which the Flyout is anchored when it is displayed
placement	Specifies the position of the Flyout relative to the anchor element
alignment	Specifies the alignment of the Flyout when the placement is top or bottom
hidden	Returns true if the Flyout is not visible or is in the process of being hidden

Setting the anchor property isn't useful because the value will be replaced by the mandatory argument required by the show method. You can, however, read the value of this property to see which element a Flyout is anchored to.

You can override the default position of a Flyout by using the placement property. This works in the same way as the Tooltip control and the supported values are top, bottom, left and right. These values are relative to the anchor element you pass to the show method.

If the placement property is top or bottom, you can further refine the position using the alignment property, which accepts values of left, right and center.

The select elements I added to the right panel in the example let you change the placement and alignment properties of the Flyout which is controlled by the Show and Hide buttons. Select the combination of values you require and click the Show button to see how the Flyout is positioned. The Flyout will be repositioned automatically so that it fits on the screen completely - however, this can mean that the anchor element may be obscured by the Flyout.

You can see the left and right values for alignment values for the top value for placement in Figure 12-11.

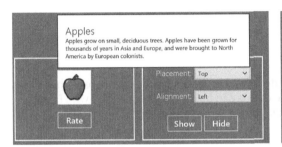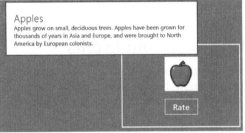

Figure 12-11. The effect of the left and right values for the placement property

Styling the Flyout Control

The Flyout control supports a single CSS class: win-flyout. You can use this class as the starting point for styling the content you display. There are no other classes because there is no fixed structure in a Flyout control. I tend not to use this class, preferring to apply styles directly to the content that I display within the Flyout control. In Listing 12-15, you can see a style element that I added to the Flyout.html file which uses the win-flyout class.

Listing 12-15. Styling the Flyout control

```
...
<style>
    .win-flyout { text-align: center }
</style>
...
```

The effect of this style is to center the text in all Flyout controls. You can see the effect it has in Figure 12-12.

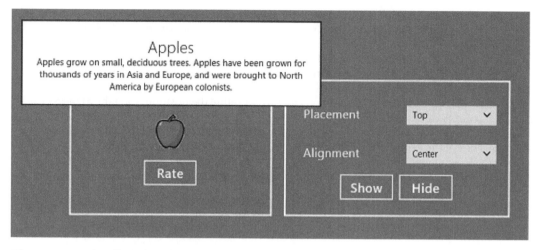

Figure 12-12. The effect of applying a style to the Flyout control

Handling the Flyout Events

The Flyout control supports the four events that I have described in Table 12-9. I have not used these events in the example, but the beforehide and afterhide events can be useful when dealing with Flyout controls that contain interactive content - see the next section for more information.

Table 12-9. The events supported by the Flyout control

Event	Description
beforeshow	Triggered before the Flyout is shown
aftershow	Triggered after the Flyout is shown
beforehide	Triggered before the Flyout is hidden
afterhide	Triggered after the Flyout is hidden

Using the Flyout for User Interactions

The second Flyout in the example app displays controls which require user interaction - you can see how these controls are shown in Figure 12-13. You can use a Flyout to display any content, but there are some special considerations when you gather data from the user.

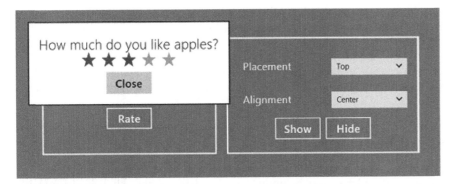

Figure 12-13. A Flyout containing interactive content

In this example, my Flyout contains a Rating control to allow the user to express the extent to which they like apples. The Flyout is shown when the user clicks the Rate button in the left panel of the example app. You must take care to design your Flyout interactions to offer a consistent and smooth user experience. In the sections that follow, I describe the guidelines that I follow and which I recommend you adopt.

Ensure Consistent Showing and Hiding

I am always careful to ensure that the user can hide the Flyout using the same type of interaction that was used to show it. If the Flyout appears as a result of a button click, then I make sure that there is a button in the Flyout content that will hide the popup. This is the approach I have taken in the example for this chapter: the Flyout is shown in response to the Rate button being clicked and clicking the Close button will hide the popup. I don't try to interfere with the light-dismiss feature, which makes the button a complement, not a replacement, to the other ways of hiding a Flyout.

Keep Flyouts Simple

I use Flyouts for performing small and simple user interactions. I don't use Flyouts for complex HTML-style forms where there are lots of data values to gather from the user and dependencies between those values. In such situations, use navigate to a different part of the app and gather the data in a dedicated layout, making it clear to the user that this is an import interaction.

Respond Immediately to Data Values

I update my view model and app state as soon as the user provides me with information in a Flyout. In the case of the example, I would respond to the change event from the Rating control rather than wait until the Flyout is dismissed before I updated the app based on the user's opinion. (I have done neither, since this is an example about Flyout controls, but you get the idea).

Make It Easy to Undo or Redo a Flyout Interaction

I try to make the interactions in Flyouts as frictionless as possible and allow the user to easily change the data they have entered or return to the state where no data has entered at all. For the most part, this means

I try to make it very obvious to the user how a specific Flyout can be shown, and I take advantage of the WinJS control features and data binding to allow the user to change or remove data. In this case of the example, allowing the user to remove data would require me to set the enableClear property of the Rating control to true.

I also avoid prompting the user with "are you sure?" messages when a value is changed or removed. Making it easy to change values and by reflecting new values in the app immediately makes checking the user's intent redundant.

Clearly Signaling Destructive Actions

The counterpart to making it easy to change data values is that I make it very obvious when the user is about to perform a destructive action which cannot be undone, such as irreversibly deleting a file. In these situations, I require the user to give me explicit confirmation using a button displayed in a Flyout and treat a light-dismissal as a cancellation. Even so, I make it easy for the user to group together destructive actions so that I don't prompt the user to confirm that each individual item should be destroyed.

Summary

In this chapter, I have shown you four more WinJS UI controls. These are more complex that the ones I described in the last chapters, but they can be applied more generally and, in the case of the Flyout control, can form a critical part of the structure of your app. In the next chapter, I'll show how to use the Menu control and demonstrate some UI controls which are not part of the WinJS namespace.

CHAPTER 13

■ ■ ■

Using Menus & Dialogs

In this chapter, I show you how to create two kinds of popup UI controls. The first, the WinJS.UI.Menu control, is used to create context menus, which allow the user to perform actions directly on elements in your app layout. The Menu control is flexible and has some useful features, but I find the mechanism by which users activate context menus to be less than obvious, which means that careful thought is required when using this control.

The second control I describe in this chapter is slightly different from the others I describe in this book. The MessageDialog control is part of the Windows namespace and doesn't share the common characteristics I have described for the WinJS UI controls: it isn't applied to HTML elements and it doesn't have a winControl property, for example. The MessageDialog control can be used by any of the Windows app development languages, which makes using it ever so slightly different. However, it provides a user interaction that you can't get using any of the WinJS controls, which can make the effort of mastering it worthwhile. Table 13-1 provides the summary for this chapter.

Table 13-1. Chapter Summary

Problem	Solution	Listing
Use the Menu control	Apply the data-win-control attribute to a div element with a value of WinJS.UI.Menu.	1-3
Display the Menu control	Listen for the contextmenu event (and use the preventDefault method to prevent the NavBar and AppBar from being shown)	4
Create menu items which open new Menus	Configure the MenuCommand property so that the type property is flyout and the flyout property is set to an element to which the Menu command has been applied	5-6
Create a set of mutually exclusive menu items	Use binding converters tailored to each menu item in the mutually exclusive set	7
Style a Menu	Define styles for the win-menu and win-command CSS classes	8-9
Use the MessageDialog control	Create a Windows.UI.Popups. MessageDialog object and call the showAsync method	10-12

Problem	Solution	Listing
Add custom buttons to a MessageDialog	Create UICommand objects and use the append method on the object returned by the MessageDialog.controls property.	13
Determine which button is clicked	Use the then method to on the object returned by the showAsync method. The clicked UICommand will be the argument passed to the function you create.	14
Specify the default commands used when the user dismisses the dialog with the keyboard	Set values for the defaultCommandIndex and cancelCommandIndex properties.	15
Briefly disable user input when the dialog is displayed	Use the acceptUserInputAfterDelay value from the MessageDialogOptions object	16

Using the Menu Control

The Menu control provides a popup context menu which is structured to offer the user one or more commands represented by the MenuCommand control. The relationship between the MenuCommand and Menu controls is similar to that between AppBarCommand and AppBar, which I described in Chapter 7.

The Menu control isn't displayed by default, so the main element in the left panel for this example is an image. If you right-click with the mouse or touch and hold the image, the contextmenu event will be triggered. I handle this event by making the Menu control appear, as shown in Figure 13-1.

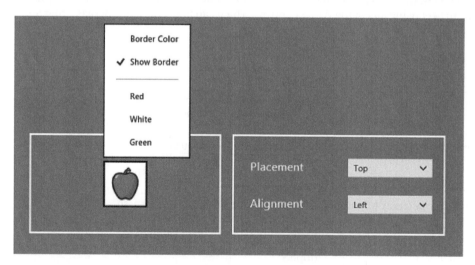

Figure 13-1. Displaying the Menu control

When to use the Menu Control

The main mechanism for providing users with commands is to use the AppBar, which I described in Chapter 7. The Menu control provides a fallback mechanism that you can use when the object on which the user wants to operate doesn't fit into the AppBar model. To be frank, this is a very subjective decision and the rule I follow in my projects is to favor the AppBar whenever I can simply because not all users realize that context menus are available in Windows apps.

Commands should appear only once in your app, meaning that you should not duplicate commands on a Menu that are supported by the AppBar. Microsoft recommends a maximum of 5 commands on a Menu, although limit is not presently enforced by Windows.

Demonstrating the Menu Control

I have added a pages/Menu.html file to the example app to demonstrate the Menu and MenuCommand controls and you can see the contents of the file in Listing 13-1. This is a long listing because there are two Menu controls in this example and many menu commands.

Listing 13-1. The contents of the Menu.html file

```
<!DOCTYPE html>
<html>
<head>
    <title></title>
    <script>
        WinJS.UI.Pages.define("/pages/Menu.html", {
            ready: function () {

                var proxyObject = WinJS.Binding.as({
                    placement: "top",
                    alignment: "left"
                });

                Templates.createControls(rightPanel, menu, "menu", proxyObject);

                ["placement", "alignment"].forEach(function (propName) {
                    proxyObject.bind(propName, function (val) {
                        menu.winControl.placement = proxyObject.placement;
                        menu.winControl.alignment = proxyObject.alignment;
                        borderMenu.winControl.placement = proxyObject.placement;
                        borderMenu.winControl.alignment = proxyObject.alignment;
                    });
                });

                targetImg.addEventListener("contextmenu", function (e) {
                    menu.winControl.show(e.target);
                    e.preventDefault();
                });

                $("#menu, #borderMenu").listen("click", function (e) {
                    if (WinJS.Utilities.hasClass(e.target, "background")) {
                        targetImg.style.backgroundColor =
                            e.target.winControl.label.toLowerCase();
                    } else if (e.target.winControl
                        && e.target.winControl.id == "menuCmdShowBorder") {
```

```
                              var showBorder = e.target.winControl.selected;
                              if (!showBorder) {
                                  targetImg.style.border = "none";
                              }
                              this.winControl.getCommandById("menuCmdBorderColor").disabled =
                                  !showBorder

                      } else if (e.target.hasAttribute("data-color")) {
                          targetImg.style.border = "medium solid "
                              + e.target.getAttribute("data-color");
                      }
                  });
              }
          });
      </script>
  </head>
  <body>
      <div id="menuContainer" class="flexContainer">
          <div class="controlPanel">
              <img id="targetImg" src="/images/apple.png"/>
          </div>

          <div id="rightPanel" class="controlPanel"></div>

          <div id="menu" data-win-control="WinJS.UI.Menu">

              <button data-win-control="WinJS.UI.MenuCommand" class="border" disabled
                  data-win-options="{id: "menuCmdBorderColor", label:"Border Color",
                      type:"flyout", flyout:"borderMenu"}"></button>

              <button data-win-control="WinJS.UI.MenuCommand" class="border"
                  data-win-options="{id: "menuCmdShowBorder",
                      label:"Show Border", type:"toggle"}"></button>

              <hr data-win-control="WinJS.UI.MenuCommand"
                  data-win-options="{type:"separator"}" />

              <button data-win-control="WinJS.UI.MenuCommand" class="background"
                  data-win-options="{id: "menuCmdRed", label:"Red"}"></button>

              <button data-win-control="WinJS.UI.MenuCommand" class="background"
                  data-win-options="{id: "menuCmdWhite", label:"White"}"></button>

              <button data-win-control="WinJS.UI.MenuCommand" class="background"
                  data-win-options="{id: "menuCmdGreen", label:"Green"}"></button>
          </div>

          <div id="borderMenu" data-win-control="WinJS.UI.Menu">
              <button data-win-control="WinJS.UI.MenuCommand" data-color="red"
                  data-win-options="{id: "menuCmdRedBorder", label:"Red Border"}">
              </button>
```

```
            <button data-win-control="WinJS.UI.MenuCommand" data-color="black"
                data-win-options="{id: "menuCmdBlackBorder", label:"Black Border"}">
            </button>
            <button data-win-control="WinJS.UI.MenuCommand" data-color="white"
                data-win-options="{id: "menuCmdWhiteBorder", label:"White Border"}">
            </button>
        </div>
    </div>
</body>
</html>
```

To create the configuration controls in the right panel of Figure 13-1, I made the additions to the /js/ controls.js file shown in Listing 13-2.

Listing 13-2. The definition objects for the Menu control

```
...
menu: [{ type: "select", id: "placement", title: "Placement",
        values: ["top", "bottom", "left", "right"],
        labels: ["Top", "Bottom", "Left", "Right"], useProxy: true},
      { type: "select", id: "alignment", title: "Alignment",
        values: ["left", "center", "right"],
        labels: ["Left", "Center", "Right"], useProxy: true}],
...
```

To allow the user to navigate to the Menu.html file, I make the addition to the templates.js file shown in Listing 13-3. As you will recall from Chapter 7, these entries are used to generate commands on the app's NavBar to support navigation between the pages of content.

Listing 13-3. Adding Menu.html to the NavBar

```
...
var navBarCommands = [
    //{ name: "AppTest", icon: "target" },
    { name: "ToggleSwitch", icon: "\u0031" },
    { name: "Rating", icon: "\u0032" },
    { name: "Tooltip", icon: "\u0033" },
    { name: "TimePicker", icon: "\u0034" },
    { name: "DatePicker", icon: "\u0035" },
    { name: "Flyout", icon: "\u0036" },
    { name: "Menu", icon: "\u0037" },
];
...
```

Applying and Configuring the Menu Control

The WinJS.UI.Menu control is applied to a div element and shares some common traits and features with the AppBar and Flyout controls. Commands are defined in the Menu using the MenuCommand control, which is applied to button and hr elements, just like the AppBarCommand control I described in Chapter 7. The Menu control supports the same set of configuration properties as the Flyout control. Table 13-2 summarizes the properties.

Table 13-2. The configuration properties for the Menu control

Property	Description
anchor	Gets or sets the element to which the Menu is anchored when it is displayed
placement	Specifies the position of the Menu relative to the anchor element
alignment	Specifies the alignment of the Menu when the placement is top or bottom
hidden	Returns true if the Menu is not visible or is in the process of being hidden

The default position for a Menu is immediately above the anchor element (if there is sufficient screen space available). You can use the select elements in the right panel of the example to change the position of the Menu. In Figure 13-2, you can see effect of the left and right values for the placement property.

Figure 13-2. The effect of the left and right values for the Menu placement property

■ **Note** If you are used to the context menus from the Windows desktop, the positioning of the Menu popup can seem a little odd - almost as though the Menu is disconnected from the element that the user is interacting with. I found this sufficiently annoying that I spent some time working out how to move the popup so that it was displayed immediately next to the point at which I had clicked the mouse. Having spent some time with WinJS Menu controls since, I have come to realize that the default position makes a lot of sense because it allows the user to immediately see the effect of the command they select. This is something I'll come back to later in the chapter, but I recommend that you leave the Menu positioning as it is.

Displaying the Menu

Windows triggers the contextmenu event when the user right-clicks with the mouse or touches and hold the screen. Unfortunately, this is the same event which shows the NavBar and AppBar, so you need to make sure to call the preventDefault method on the event passed to your handler function, as shown in Listing 13-4. It is important to handle the contextemenu event only on those elements for which you will show a Menu control and have the app show the NavBar and AppBar for all other elements.

Listing 13-4. Showing the Menu control and preventing the default behavior

```
...
targetImg.addEventListener("contextmenu", function (e) {
    menu.winControl.show(e.target);
```

```
    e.preventDefault();
});
...
```

Defining the Menu Commands

You define the commands that are shown on the Menu using the MenuCommand control. The MenuCommand control supports a subset of the properties defined by the AppBarCommand control, which I have summarized in Table 13-3. I am not going to go into the detail for all of these properties because you can see the effect they have in Chapter 7. There are a couple of techniques that are worth pointing out and I explain these in the sections that follow. Otherwise, you can see how to create items in the Menu control from the listing.

■ **Tip**   You can create a separator in a Menu to group related commands together. To do this, apply the MenuCommand control to an hr element and use the data-win-options attribute to set the type property to separator. You can see an example of a separator in Listing 13-1.

Table 13-3. The properties defined by the MenuCommand control

Property	Description
id	Identifies the command that the menu item relates to
label	Gets or sets the text used for the menu item
type	Gets or sets the command type
hidden	Returns true if the menu item is hidden
disabled	Gets or sets the disabled status of the menu item
element	Return the element to which the MenuCommand control has been applied
selected	Gets or sets the selection status for the menu item
flyout	Sets the flyout that will be displayed when the menu item is selected

Creating Sequences of Menus

You can configure a MenuCommand control to show another menu when it is selected, creating a chain of menus that allows the user to navigate through a complex set of options. You associate menus together using the type and flyout properties. You can see how I did this in the example app in Listing 13-5.

Listing 13-5. Chaining methods together using the flyout property

```
...
<button data-win-control="WinJS.UI.MenuCommand" class="border"
    data-win-options="{id: "menuCmdBorderColor", label:"Border Color",
        type:"flyout", flyout:"borderMenu"}">
</button>
...
```

For this MenuCommand, which has the label Border Color, I have set the type property to flyout and the flyout property to the id of another element to which the Menu control has been applied. You can see the definition of the second Menu in Listing 13-6.

Listing 13-6. Applying a second Menu control

```
...
<div id="borderMenu" data-win-control="WinJS.UI.Menu">
    <button data-win-control="WinJS.UI.MenuCommand" data-color="red"
        data-win-options="{id: "menuCmdRedBorder", label:"Red Border"}">
    </button>
    <button data-win-control="WinJS.UI.MenuCommand" data-color="black"
        data-win-options="{id: "menuCmdBlackBorder", label:"Black Border"}">
    </button>
    <button data-win-control="WinJS.UI.MenuCommand" data-color="white"
        data-win-options="{id: "menuCmdWhiteBorder", label:"White Border"}">
    </button>
</div>
...
```

The result is when you select the Border Color item from the first Menu, the second Menu is displayed. You can see the effect in Figure 13-3. The second Menu replaces the first, rather than appearing alongside it.

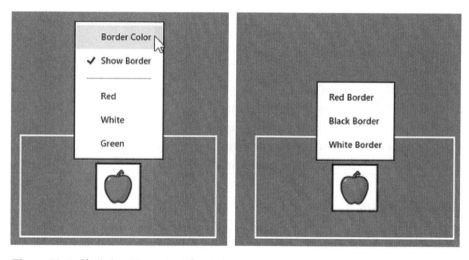

Figure 13-3. Chaining Menus together

■ **Tip** You can use a Flyout control instead of a second Menu if you prefer. This can be useful for providing the user with options which are too complex to handle with a set of menu items. That said, if you need a Flyout then you might want to rethink your strategy and see if there is a simpler way of presenting your commands to the user.

Creating Sets of Mutually-Exclusive Menu Items

I use the MenuCommand most frequently to create sets of mutually-exclusive menu items. I want to create two such sets in the example app: the first is the Red, White and Green items in the main menu and the second set consists of the Red Border, Black Border and White Border items in the smaller, secondary, menu.

The first set corresponds to the background color used for the img element and the second corresponds to the border color. In both cases, I want the MenuCommand which represents the current setting to be selected and for this selection to be kept up to date when one of the other items is clicked. Mutually exclusive menu items are easy to set up, but it is a manual process and there is no specific support in the Menu or MenuCommand controls.

The technique is simple – I need to set the selected property on the MenuCommand controls to true for the item the user has picked and to false for all of the other MenuCommands in the same mutually-exclusive set – and the most effective way to do this is to use the WinJS.Utilities.query method to locate all the elements in a given set. To help me do this, I have made sure that the MenuCommand controls in each set have a shared characteristic that I can easily identify. For the Red, White and Green items in the main menu, I assigned all of the button elements to which the MenuCommand control was applied to the background class, like this:

```
...
<button data-win-control="WinJS.UI.MenuCommand" class="background"
    data-win-options="{id: "menuCmdRed", label:"Red"}"></button>

<button data-win-control="WinJS.UI.MenuCommand" class="background"
    data-win-options="{id: "menuCmdWhite", label:"White"}"></button>

<button data-win-control="WinJS.UI.MenuCommand" class="background"
    data-win-options="{id: "menuCmdGreen", label:"Green"}"></button>
...
```

For the button elements which are used in the other menu, I have added a custom data-* property, as follows:

```
...
<button data-win-control="WinJS.UI.MenuCommand" data-color="red"
    data-win-options="{id: "menuCmdRedBorder", label:"Red Border"}">
</button>
<button data-win-control="WinJS.UI.MenuCommand" data-color="black"
    data-win-options="{id: "menuCmdBlackBorder", label:"Black Border"}">
</button>
<button data-win-control="WinJS.UI.MenuCommand" data-color="white"
    data-win-options="{id: "menuCmdWhiteBorder", label:"White Border"}">
</button>
...
```

You would usually stick to one identifiable characteristic, but I wanted to show you the two approaches that I use most often. Now that I can easily query the document with a CSS selector to locate all of the MenuCommands in a set, I can update the script element in the Menu.html file to set the selected property when the user picks a menu item, as shown in Listing 13-7.

Listing 13-7. Ensuring mutual-exclusion on sets of MenuCommand controls

```
...
$("#menu, #borderMenu").listen("click", function (e) {
```

```
        if (WinJS.Utilities.hasClass(e.target, "background")) {
            targetImg.style.backgroundColor = e.target.winControl.label.toLowerCase();
            WinJS.Utilities.query("button.background").forEach(function (menuButton) {
                menuButton.winControl.selected = (menuButton == e.target);
            });
        } else if (e.target.winControl && e.target.winControl.id == "menuCmdShowBorder") {

            var showBorder = e.target.winControl.selected;
            if (!showBorder) {
                targetImg.style.border = "none";
            }
            this.winControl.getCommandById("menuCmdBorderColor").disabled = !showBorder

        } else if (e.target.hasAttribute("data-color")) {
            targetImg.style.border = "medium solid " + e.target.getAttribute("data-color");
            WinJS.Utilities.query("button[data-color]").forEach(function (menuButton) {
                menuButton.winControl.selected = menuButton == e.target;
            });
        }
    });
    ...
```

You can see the effect of selecting one item and then another on the main menu in Figure 13-4.

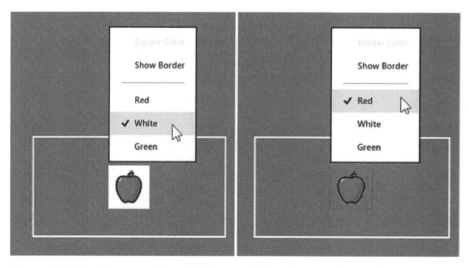

Figure 13-4. Creating mutually exclusive sets of MenuCommand controls

Managing the Menu Programmatically

The methods that the Menu control supports are similar to those defined by the AppBar controls, as shown by Table 13-4, where I have described the methods.

Table 13-4. The Menu methods

Method	Description
show(anchor)	Displays the Menu relative to the anchor element
hide()	Hides the Menu control
getCommandById(id)	Returns the MenuCommand control with the corresponding id value
showCommands([])	Shows the specific commands, which may be expressed as an array of MenuCommand controls or an array of id values.
showOnlyCommands([])	Similar to showCommands except that any command which is not in the array is hidden
hideCommands([])	Hides the specific commands, which may be expressed as an array of MenuCommand controls or an array of id values.

I tend not to use the methods that show and hide menu commands, because they make me feel that my Menu structure is too complex. I also prefer to keep the same set of commands on the Menu and simply disable the ones which are not presently available. This is what I have done in the example. The Border Color command is unselected until you check the Border command, as shown in Figure 13-5. I'd rather make it obvious that the command *does* exist but doesn't apply than present a changing set of commands.

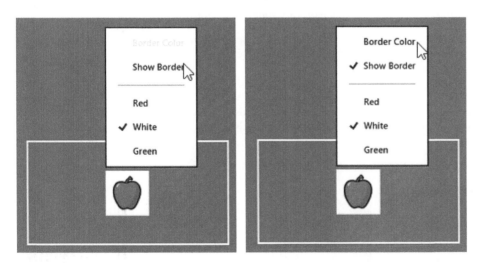

Figure 13-5. Disabling a MenuCommand rather than hiding it

Styling the Menu Control

The Menu control supports two CSS classes for styling, as described in Table 13-5.

Table 5. The Menu CSS classes

Class	Description
win-command	Styles the MenuCommand control
win-menu	Styles the entire Menu control (including the MenuCommands)

To apply styles to `Menu` and `MenuCommand` controls, you need to take a look at the HTML and CSS that Microsoft uses to create the controls and work out a selector that overrides the default defined in the `ui-light.css` and `ui-dark.css` files that are added to a Visual Studio app project by default. In Listing 13-8 you can see how I have applied a style which changes the colors used to display disabled `MenuCommand` controls.

Listing 13-8. Using the win-menu CSS class to (try to) style a MenuCommand control

```
...
<style>
    #menu button.win-command:disabled {
        background-color: lightgray;
        color: gray;
    }
</style>
...
```

I have used the `id` attribute value of one of the `Menu` controls in the example to ensure that the style I have defined is more specific than the one in the `ui-dark.css` file. You can see the style which determines the background color by default in Listing 13-9, (which I determined using the `DOM Explorer` window that I introduced in Chapter 2).

Listing 13-9. The default style for setting the background color of a disabled MenuCommand

```
.win-menu.win-ui-light button:focus, .win-ui-light .win-menu button:focus, .win-menu.win-ui-
light button:active, .win-ui-light .win-menu button:active {
   background-color: rgb(222, 222, 222);
}
```

You can see how the class `.win-ui-light` has been used. This isn't ideal, but working around this additional specificity is simple enough once you know that it exists. You can see the effect of the style I defined in Figure 13-6.

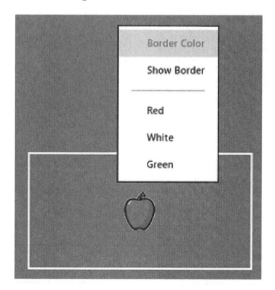

Figure 13-6. Changing the colors of disabled MenuCommand controls

Handling the Menu Events

The main event that is of interest when dealing with the Menu control is the click event, which is triggered by the MenuCommand control when the user clicks it, indicating that a menu item has been selected – you can see how I have handled this event in Listing 13-1 and again in Listing 13-7 to respond.

The Menu control itself supports the four events that I have described in Table 13-6, which are the same four events supported by the Flyout control. I have yet to find a compelling use for these events, which is why I have not included them in the example for the Menu control.

Table 13-6. The events supported by the Menu control

Event	Description
beforeshow	Triggered before the Flyout is shown
aftershow	Triggered after the Flyout is shown
beforehide	Triggered before the Flyout is hidden
afterhide	Triggered after the Flyout is hidden

Using the MessageDialog Control

All of the other UI controls that I describe in this book are in the WinJS.UI namespace and are written in JavaScript. There is one control, however, which is outside of this namespace, but which can be very useful in creating apps which follow the Windows look and feel. This control is the Windows.UI.Popups.MessageDialog control and you use it to present a dialog to the user. You can see an example of the MessageDialog in Figure 13-7.

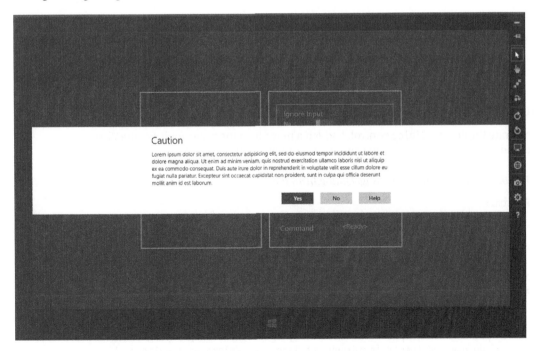

Figure 13-7. The MessageDialog UI Control

■ **Note**   The `Windows.UI.Popups` namespace also contains the `PopupMenu` control. I have not described this control in this book because it has the same functionality as the `WinJS.UI.Menu` control I described in the previous section.

When to use the MessageDialog Control

The `MessageDialog` is useful when you need to bring something of importance to the user's attention or when you need an important decision to be taken. The key word is *important*, because when the `MessageDialog` control is used, the app layout is dimmed and the dialog is displayed across the entire screen. All user interaction is blocked until the user dismisses the dialog (by pressing the `Escape` or `Enter` keys) or by clicking/touching one of the dialog buttons.

I think of the `MessageDialog` as being the UI control of last resort because it interrupts the user's work flow – something which runs counter to the broad design ethos of Windows.

You can add up to three buttons to the dialog window displayed by the `MessageDialog` control, which means that you can't present the user with nuanced choices. This means that not only are you interrupting the user, but you are forcing them to make an explicit and well-defined decision, most often a yes/no choice.

You should use the `MessageDialog` sparingly and reluctantly. In my own app projects, I use the `MessageDialog` only when the user is about to initiate an action which will lead to permanent, irrevocable data loss, such as deleting files or other data. I suggest you use the same restraint – not only because the `MessageDialog` is intrusive, but because if you use it too freely, the user will learn to dismiss the dialog without reading it – increasing the chances that they will ignore the truly important messages when they are shown.

■ **Tip**   You could use a `Flyout` to present a dialog to the user, but it won't automatically dim the rest of the layout and it won't block user interaction the way that the dialog shown by the MessageDialog control does.

Demonstrating the MessageDialog Control

To demonstrate the `MessageDialog` control, I added a new file to the pages folder in the Visual Studio project called `MessageDialog.html`. You can see the contents of this file in Listing 13-10.

Listing 13-10. The contents of the MessageDialog.html file

```
<!DOCTYPE html>
<html>
<head>
<title></title>
<style> #showButton {font-size: 20pt}
</style>
<script>
    var winpop = Windows.UI.Popups;

    var loremipsum = "Lorem ipsum dolor sit amet, consectetur adipisicing elit, "
        + "sed do eiusmod tempor incididunt ut labore et dolore magna aliqua. "
        + "Ut enim ad minim veniam, quis nostrud exercitation ullamco laboris "
```

```
                + "nisi ut aliquip ex ea commodo consequat. Duis aute irure dolor in "
                + "reprehenderit in voluptate velit esse cillum dolore eu fugiat nulla "
                + "pariatur. Excepteur sint occaecat cupidatat non proident, sunt in "
                + " culpa qui officia deserunt mollit anim id est laborum.";

    WinJS.UI.Pages.define("/pages/MessageDialog.html", {
        ready: function () {

            var proxyObject = WinJS.Binding.as({
                delay: false,
                title: true,
                addcommands: true,
            });

            Templates.createControls(rightPanel, showButton, "messagedialog",
                proxyObject).then(function () {

                showButton.addEventListener("click", function (e) {

                    var md = new winpop.MessageDialog(loremipsum);
                    if (proxyObject.title) {
                        md.title = "Caution";
                    }
                    if (proxyObject.delay) {
                        md.options
                            = winpop.MessageDialogOptions.acceptUserInputAfterDelay;
                    }

                    if (proxyObject.addcommands) {
                        ["Yes", "No", "Help"].forEach(function (text) {
                            md.commands.append(new winpop.UICommand(text));
                        });
                        md.defaultCommandIndex = 0;
                        md.cancelCommandIndex = 1;
                    }

                    md.showAsync().then(function (command) {
                        commandSpan.innerText = command.label;
                    });
                });
            });
        }
    });
</script>
</head>
<body>
    <div id="ratingContainer" class="flexContainer">

        <div class="controlPanel">
            <button id="showButton">Show MessageDialog</button>
        </div>
```

```
        <div id="rightPanel" class="controlPanel"></div>
    </div>
</body>
</html>
```

To generate the configuration controls in the right panel of the layout that I'll need to demonstrate the MessageDialog control, I have added the definition objects shown in Listing 13-11 to the /js/controls.js file.

Listing 13-11. The definition objects for the MessageDialog control

```
...
messagedialog: [
    { type: "toggle", id: "delay", title: "Ignore Input", value: false, labelOn: "Yes",
        labelOff: "No", useProxy: true },
    { type: "toggle", id: "title", title: "Title", value: true, labelOn: "Yes",
        labelOff: "No", useProxy: true },
    { type: "toggle", id: "addcommands", title: "Add Commands", value: true,
        labelOn: "Yes", labelOff: "No", useProxy: true },
    { type: "span", id: "commandSpan", value: "<Ready>", title: "Command" }],
...
```

Finally, I made the addition shown in Listing 13-12 to the /js/templates.js file so that the user can navigate to the MessageDialog.html file using the app's NavBar.

Listing 13-12. Enabling navigation to the MessageDialog.html file

```
...
var navBarCommands = [
    //{ name: "AppTest", icon: "target" },
    { name: "ToggleSwitch", icon: "\u0031" },
    { name: "Rating", icon: "\u0032" },
    { name: "Tooltip", icon: "\u0033" },
    { name: "TimePicker", icon: "\u0034" },
    { name: "DatePicker", icon: "\u0035" },
    { name: "Flyout", icon: "\u0036" },
    { name: "Menu", icon: "\u0037" },
    { name: "MessageDialog", icon: "\u0038" },
];
...
```

You can see the layout that these additions create in Figure 13-8. As with the other controls in this part of the book, you can use the controls in the right-hand panel of the layout to configure the MessageDialog control to explore the features that I describe in the sections that follow.

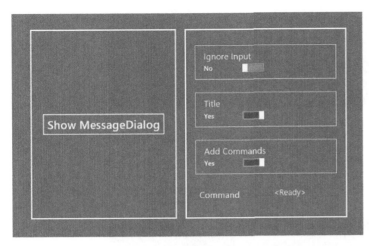

Figure 13-8. *The layout of the MessageDialog.html file*

Using the MessageDialog Control

The MessageDialog control doesn't work in the same way as the WinJS UI controls. The control isn't applied to an HTML element and there isn't a winControl property. Instead, you create a Windows.UI.Popups. MessageDialog object and use the properties it defines to configure the dialog and show it to the user. The MessageDialog control supports the properties and method shown in Table 13-7, which I describe and demonstrate in the sections that follow.

Table 13-7. *The properties and method defined by the MessageDialog control*

Name	Description
cancelCommandIndex defaultCommandIndex	Sets the default commands that are used when the user dismisses the dialog with the keyboard.
commands	Sets the commands that will be displayed on the dialog
content	Sets the text content of the dialog
options	Defines the behavior of the dialog using values from the MessageDialogOptions object.
title	Sets the (optional) title for the dialog
showAsync()	Shows the dialog to the user. Returns an object which defines the same methods as a WinJS.Promise and which is fulfilled when the dialog has been dismissed by the user.

Creating the Basic Dialog

The simplest way to display a dialog is to create a new MessageDialog object and call the showAsync method. The constructor MessageDialog has one mandatory argument, which is a string containing the content that should be displayed in the dialog. There is an optional argument, which is used as the value for the title property.

You can see the most basic dialog using the example app. Set all of the ToggleSwitch controls in the right panel to No and click the Show MessageDialog button. You can see the result in Figure 13-9. (I have edited the images in this section to make it easier to see the detail).

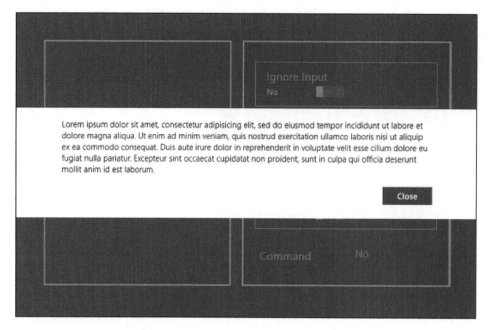

Figure 13-9. A basic dialog created with the MessageDialog control

When you create a basic dialog, the MessageDialog control adds a Close button for you that automatically dismisses the dialog when it is clicked. You can see the effect of adding a title to the dialog in Figure 13-10 – an effect I achieved in the example by setting the Title ToggleSwitch to Yes.

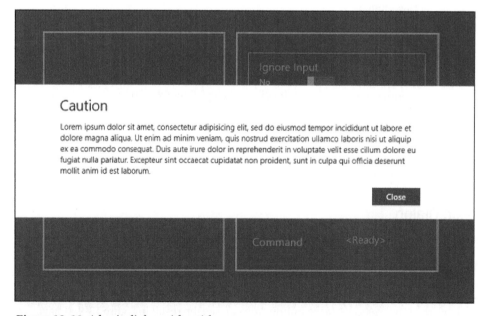

Figure 13-10. A basic dialog with a title

Adding Custom Commands

You can customize the dialog by placing the Close button with up to three custom buttons. These buttons are specified using the Windows.UI.Popups.UICommand object, which defines the properties shown in Table 13-8.

Table 13-8. The properties defined by the UICommand object

Property	Description
id	Gets or sets the identifier for the command
label	Gets or sets the label that will be displayed to the user
invoked	Gets or sets a function that will be invoked when the command is clicked

In the example app, you can add commands to the dialog by setting the ToggleSwitch labeled Add Commands to Yes. I add the commands by creating new UICommand objects and using the append method on the object I get back from the commands property of the MessageDialog object. I have repeated the relevant statements from the example in Listing 13-13.

Listing 13-13. Adding commands to the dialog

```
...
if (proxyObject.addcommands) {
    ["Yes", "No", "Help"].forEach(function (text) {
        md.commands.append(new winpop.UICommand(text));
    });
    md.defaultCommandIndex = 0;
    md.cancelCommandIndex = 1;
}
...
```

The commands are displayed in the order they are added and you can see the effect of adding these command buttons in Figure 13-7.

Determining the Clicked Command

You can determine which button the user clicks to dismiss the dialog using the object that is returned from the showAsync method. The showAsync method doesn't actually return a WinJS.Promise object, but the object that it does return defines the then, cancel and done methods and can generally be used just like a Promise. The reason that you don't get a WinJS.Promise object back is that the MessageDialog control isn't part of the WinJS library and doesn't know anything about how JavaScript works in an app. The reason that the object can be used like a Promise is because of the efforts Microsoft has made to ensure consistency in the API across all of the Windows app development languages and wraps up the asynchronous operation in a way that JavaScript can consume.

When you use the then method on the object returned from the showAsync method, your function is passed the UICommand representing the dialog button that the user clicked. You can see how I use this feature to set the content of the span element in the right panel of the example layout in Listing 13-14, where I have duplicated the relevant code from the example app.

Listing 13-14. Determining which dialog button the user clicked

```
...
md.showAsync().then(function (command) {
    commandSpan.innerText = command.label;
});
...
```

The `Promise`-like object that you get back from the `showAsync` method isn't fulfilled until the user dismisses the dialog.

Setting the Default Commands

You can use the `defaultCommandIndex` and `cancelCommandIndex` to specify the `UICommand` that will be passed to the `then` function when the user hits the `Enter` or `Escape` keys. These properties are set to the index of the `UICommands` objects added using the `commands` property, and you can see how I have set these in the example in Listing 13-15.

Listing 13-15. Specifying the default commands

```
...
if (proxyObject.addcommands) {
    ["Yes", "No", "Help"].forEach(function (text) {
        md.commands.append(new winpop.UICommand(text));
    });
    md.defaultCommandIndex = 0;
    md.cancelCommandIndex = 1;
}
...
```

Your `then` function will be passed the `UICommand` at the index you specified, even though the user hasn't explicitly clicked any of the dialog buttons. In the listing, the index values I have specified mean that using the `Enter` key will be equivalent to clicking the `Yes` button and using the `Escape` key will be equivalent to clicking the `No` button.

■ **Note**   Ensure that you use the default commands feature consistently, so that the `Escape` key always cancels and the `Enter` key always confirms the action or decision you are presenting to the user.

Delaying Responding to User Interaction

The `MessageDialog.options` property lets you configure the behavior of the control using values from the `Windows.UI.Popup.MessageDialogOptions` object, which are described in Table 13-9. For some reason, the `MessageDialogOptions` object only defines values for one specific behavior, which is to disable user interaction for a brief period when the dialog is displayed by the `MessageDialog` object.

Table 13-9. The values defined by the MessageDialogOptions object

Name	Description
none	The default dialog behavior is used
acceptUserInputAfterDelay	User input is ignored for a brief period

You can apply the `acceptUserInputAfterDelay` behavior in the example app by setting the `ToggleSwitch` labeled `Ignore Input` to `true`. When you click the `Show MessageDialog`, the command buttons shown on the dialog will be briefly disabled, preventing the commands from being clicked. After a couple of second, the buttons are enabled, allowing the user to interact with the dialog as usual.

Summary

In the next chapter, I will return to the `WinJS.UI` namespace and describe the `FlipView` control. This is the first, and simplest, of the WinJS data-driven controls, which offer functionality which is underpinned by a collection of data objects. As you'll learn, data-driven controls build on the data binding and template features I introduced in Chapter 8 in order display those data items flexibly to the user.

CHAPTER 14

■ ■ ■

Using the FlipView Control

In this chapter, I am going to describe the FlipView control, which is one of the WinJS *data-driven* UI controls. Data-driven controls get their content from a *data source* and monitor the data source to make sure that they display the latest available data. The FlipView control displays one item at a time from the data source and allows the user to move between them either by clicking on a button or by making a flip touch gesture.

In this chapter, I'll show you how to prepare a data source for a data-driven control and combine it with templates that are used to represent each item to the user. You'll see a how a number of WinJS features come together in a data-driven control, including observable arrays, data binding and templates. I will also show you how some of these features interact to cause a tricky problem. Finally, I'll touch on the animations that the FlipView control uses as it moves from one data item to the next, as a precursor to covering the topic fully in Chapter 18. Table 14-1 provides the summary for this chapter

Table 14-1. Chapter Summary

Problem	Solution	Listing
Use the FlipView control	Apply the data-win-control attribute to a div element with a value of WinJS.UI.FlipView.	1-5
Create a data source	Create a WinJS.Binding.List object and read the dataSource property to get an object that can be used as a data source with data-driven controls	6-7
Define a template for data items	Apply the WinJS.UI.Template control to a div element	7
Avoid the first-image problem	Set the name of the template via data binding or use a function to generate template elements	8-10
Programmatically page through the data items	Use the previous and next methods	11
Change the data displayed by the FlipView control	Manipulate the data source which the FlipView is operating on	12-13
Obtain the number of data items in the data source	Use the count property	13
Respond to changes in the state of the FlipView control	handle the datasourcecountchanged, pageselected or pagevisibilitychanged events	14
Style the FlipView control	Define styles for the CSS classes supported by the FlipView	15
Change the animations used by the FlipView control	Use the setCustomAnimations method	16

Using the FlipView Control

Data-driven WinJS UI controls use templates to render items from the data source. In this chapter, I will use a FlipView to perform a very common task - display one image at a time from a collection of photos. You can see how the FlipView appears in Figure 14-1. As with the other chapters in this part of the book, I created the layout shown in the figure using the framework I created in Chapter 10.

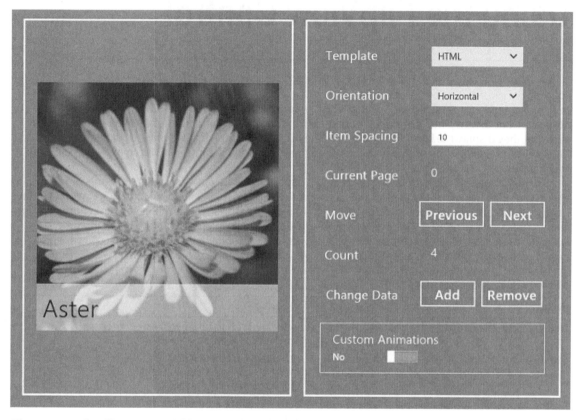

Figure 14-1. The FlipView control being used to display a set of photos

There are three data-driven WinJS UI controls, but I have picked FlipView as the first to describe because it is relatively simple, but sits on top of a lot of useful and important functionality. I can deal with the use of the control relatively quickly and then focus on some of the critical underpinnings which are shared with the more complex controls I describe later.

DATA SOURCES AND INTERFACES

WinJS defines a set of *interfaces* which specify the functionality for a data source. You don't need to worry about these interfaces if you are using the standard data source objects, which are suitable for most projects. However, if you want to create a custom data source, then you need to understand the role these interfaces play.

The first thing to understand is that idea of interfaces doesn't have any meaning in JavaScript. This is one of the areas where you can see the fit between JavaScript and the other Windows app programming languages show through. In a language like C#, defining an interface means listing the abstract functionality that is required for a particular purpose. A programmer implementing an interface is effectively agreeing to implement that functionality in some way. The compiler checks to make sure that all of the facets of the interface are implemented and reports an error if they are not. Interfaces are a useful technique in creating loosely-coupled software systems in strongly-typed languages.

The idea of interfaces relies on assumptions that don't fit in JavaScript, but Microsoft needed to articulate a way in which an expected set of properties and methods can be described and so we have the idea, but not the implementation of interfaces. When I refer to interfaces, I am referring to a list of required members that you must implement in your object if you want it to be suitable for a particular use, such as being used as a data source for a UI control like FlipView.

When to use the FlipView Control

The FlipView control can be used whenever you need to present content one item at a time. In this chapter, I have shown the most common use for this control, which is to allow the user to page through media - some photos of glowers in this case. However, the FlipView control can display *any* content and has a nice template system that gives you control over how each item is presented to the user. You can see examples of using other kinds of data to drive WinJS UI controls in later chapters.

Creating the FlipView Control Example

The data-driven controls are more complex than the others in the WinJS.UI namespace, and so I have taken a slightly different approach to creating the code that demonstrates the FlipView control. I am going to break down the example code so that the HTML, CSS and JavaScript are in separate files and, more importantly, the example won't be complete at the end of this section. I'll complete the example as I explain some core characteristics and features of the data sources and the UI control that use them.

To start, then, I have created a new file in the pages folder of the Visual Studio project called FlipView. html, the contents of which you can see in Listing 14-1. This file contains the markup that creates a basic FlipView control, but it doesn't contain any reference to a data source, which is required to make the FlipView display data.

Listing 14-1. The initial contents of the FlipView.html file

```
<!DOCTYPE html>
<html>
<head>
    <title></title>
    <link href="/css/flipview.css" rel="stylesheet" />
    <script src="/js/pages/flipview.js"></script>
</head>
<body>
    <div id="flipViewContainer" class="flexContainer">
        <div class="controlPanel">
            <div id="flip" data-win-control="WinJS.UI.FlipView"></div>
        </div>

        <div id="rightPanel" class="controlPanel"></div>
```

```
        </div>
    </body>
</html>
```

You can see the element in the listing to which I have applied the FlipView control using the data-win-control. You can also see the link and script elements I have added for the CSS and JavaScript files. The /css/flipview.css file contains some styles that I need to control the layout of the FlipView control and the data that I will use it to display. You can see the contents of the flipview.css file in Listing 14-2.

Listing 14-2. The contents of the /css/flipview.css file

```
#flip { width: 400px; height: 400px }
.flipItem img { height: 400px }
.flipTitle { position: absolute; color: black;
    bottom: 2px; font-size: 30pt; width: 100%;
    padding: 10px; background-color: rgba(255, 255, 255, 0.6)}
.renderDiv { border: thick solid white; height: 200px}
.renderDiv img { height: 200px; width: 200px }
.renderDiv div { text-align: center; font-size: 30pt }
```

You can see the contents of the JavaScript file in Listing 14-3. I wanted to keep the code for the data-driven controls separate from the rest of the JavaScript, so I created the /js/pages folder and then added the flipview.js file there – this is the file you can see in the listing.

Listing 14-3. The contents of the flipview.js file

```
(function() {

    WinJS.UI.Pages.define("/pages/FlipView.html", {
        ready: function () {

            var proxyObject = WinJS.Binding.as({
                itemTemplate: null,
                customAnimations: false
            });

            Templates.createControls(rightPanel, flip, "flipView", proxyObject)
            .then(function () {

            });
        }
    });
})();
```

At the moment, the flipview.js file contains only the proxy object that I'll use to respond to some of the configuration controls and the call to the Templates.createControls method that will create them. I'll be adding addition code as I go through this chapter and explaining the different features of data-driven controls in general and the FlipView control in particular. In Listing 14-4, you can see the definition objects that I added to the controls.js file to create the configuration controls shown in the right-hand panel of Figure 14-1. In keeping with the other chapters in this part of the book, I'll use these controls to demonstrate the key features of the FlipView control.

Listing 14-4 The definition objects added to the controls.js file for the FlipView control

```
...
flipView: [
    { type: "select", id: "itemTemplate", title: "Template",
        values: ["HTML", "Function"], useProxy: true},
    { type: "select", id: "orientation", title: "Orientation",
        values: ["horizontal", "vertical"], labels: ["Horizontal", "Vertical"]},
    { type: "input", id: "itemSpacing", title: "Item Spacing", value: 10 },
    { type: "span", id: "currentPage", value: 0, title: "Current Page" },
    { type: "buttons", title: "Move", labels: ["Previous", "Next"] },
    { type: "span", id: "itemCount", value: 4, title: "Count" },
    { type: "buttons", title: "Change Data", labels: ["Add", "Remove"] },
    { type: "toggle", id: "customAnimations", title: "Custom Animations", value: false,
        useProxy: true, labelOn: "Yes", labelOff: "No" }],
...
```

The last step in setting up the basic structure in this chapter is to enable navigation to the FlipView. html page from the NavBar. You can see how I have done this in Listing 14-5, which shows the addition I made to the /js/templates.js file.

Listing 14-5. Enabling navigation to the FlipView.html page via the NavBar

```
...
var navBarCommands = [
    //{ name: "AppTest", icon: "target" },
    { name: "ToggleSwitch", icon: "\u0031" },
    { name: "Rating", icon: "\u0032" },
    { name: "Tooltip", icon: "\u0033" },
    { name: "TimePicker", icon: "\u0034" },
    { name: "DatePicker", icon: "\u0035" },
    { name: "Flyout", icon: "\u0036" },
    { name: "Menu", icon: "\u0037" },
    { name: "MessageDialog", icon: "\u0038" },
    { name: "FlipView", icon: "pictures" },
];
...
```

The FlipView control is the first of the WinJS data-driven controls that I describe and, as the name suggests, I need some data to work with. In this chapter, I will use the FlipView to display some image files, which is a typical use for this control. You can use any kind of data with the data-driven WinJS controls, including the FlipView, but I want to keep things simple for the moment.

In order to keep the data images separate from the app images, I created a /images/data folder and copied my image files there. The images are photos of flowers and you can see them listed in the Solution Explorer in Figure 14-2. I have included the images in the source code download that accompanies this book (available from Apress.com).

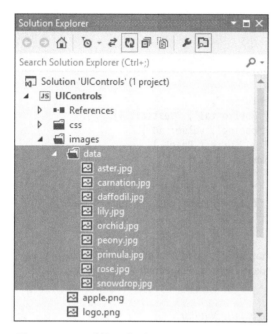

Figure 14-2. Adding the data images to the Visual Studio project

You'll see the layout shown in Figure 14-3 if you run the app at this point. The FlipView control is in the layout but it isn't visible yet – that's because I haven't set up the relationship between the images I want to display and the FlipView control – something that I'll address shortly.

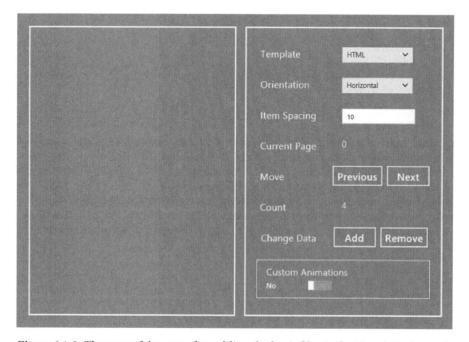

Figure 14-3. The state of the app after adding the basic files to the Visual Studio project

Creating and Using a Data Source

The key step in using a data-driven UI control is to create the data source. The methods are properties implemented by data sources are defined by the WinJS.UI.IListDataSource interface and if you want to create your own data source, you need to define an object that implements all of the methods and properties that IListDataSource defines in order to expose your data.

I am not going to go into detail about the interface because there are a couple of pre-defined data sources that can be used in almost every situation. The WinJS.UI.StorageDataSource can be used to load data from the device file system - I'll come back to files and data more broadly in Part 4 of this book and I demonstrate the StorageDataSource object in Chapter 23.

In this chapter, I am going to use the other pre-defined data source, which is the WinJS.Binding.List object. I showed you in Chapter 8 when I explained how to create observable arrays for data binding and I have been using it in examples since. The List object has a dataSource property which returns an object implements all of the methods and properties needed for a data source. This makes the List perfect for use with data-driven UI controls when you are dealing with in-memory data.

So, to start, I am going to create a List object that contains details of the images I want to display. In Listing 14-6 you can see the additions I have made to the /js/viewmodel.js file.

Listing14- 6. *Defining a List in the /js/viewmodel.js file*

```
(function () {
    "use strict";

    WinJS.Namespace.define("ViewModel", {
        data: {
            images: new WinJS.Binding.List([
                { file: "/images/data/aster.jpg", name: "Aster"},
                { file: "/images/data/carnation.jpg", name: "Carnation"},
                { file: "/images/data/daffodil.jpg", name: "Daffodil"},
                { file: "/images/data/lily.jpg", name: "Lilly"},
            ]),
        }
    });

})();
```

I created a new List object called images and assigned it to the ViewModel.data namespace. Each object in the List has a file property which contains the path of the image file and a name property which contains a name that I will display to the user.

■ **Tip** The List only contains objects for four of the image files – I'll use the other images later in the chapter.

Applying the Data Source

To apply the data source, you need to set two FlipView properties. The itemDataSource property tells the FlipView where to find the data. The itemTemplate property specifies a template that will be used to display the items in the data source – this is the same kind of data binding template that I described in Chapter 8. In Listing 14-7, you can see how I have defined the template and set the values for the FlipView properties in the /pages/FlipView.html file.

Listing 14-7. *Setting the data source and the template*

```
<!DOCTYPE html>
<html>
<head>
    <title></title>
    <link href="/css/flipview.css" rel="stylesheet" />
    <script src="/js/pages/flipview.js"></script>
</head>
<body>
    <div id="ItemTemplate" data-win-control="WinJS.Binding.Template">
        <div class="flipItem">
            <img data-win-bind="src: file" />
            <div class="flipTitle" data-win-bind="innerText: name"></div>
        </div>
    </div>

    <div id="flipViewContainer" class="flexContainer">
        <div class="controlPanel">
            <div id="flip" data-win-control="WinJS.UI.FlipView"
                data-win-options="{itemTemplate: select('#ItemTemplate'),
                    itemDataSource: ViewModel.data.images.dataSource}">
            </div>
        </div>

        <div id="rightPanel" class="controlPanel"></div>
    </div>
</body>
</html>
```

The template that I have defined uses the file property of the data object to set the src attribute of an img element and displays the value of the name property – the styles that I used to layout the elements in the template are in the /css/flipview.css file, which I listed earlier in the chapter.

I have set the options for the UI control using the data-win-options attribute. Notice how I have specified the value for the itemTemplate property:

`itemTemplate: `**`select('#ItemTemplate')`**

The select keyword is used to locate an element in the markup and it takes a CSS selector as an argument which, in this case, is the id attribute value of the element to which I have applied the WinJS. Binding.Template control.

For the itemDataSource property, notice that I have specified the dataSource property of the WinJS. Binding.List object I created in the /js/viewmodel.js file, like this:

`itemDataSource: ViewModel.data.images.`**`dataSource`**

The FlipView control – and indeed, all of the data-driven UI controls – have no special knowledge about the capabilities of the List object and expect to receive an object which defines the set of methods and properties listed in the IListDataSource object. This means that you must remember to use the dataSource property when you are telling a data-driven UI control to use a List object as a data source.

Fixing the First Image Problem

I have set up the template and the data source, but if you run the app at this point you'll see a problem. The first item in the data source isn't displayed properly. However, if you swipe the FlipView control or move the mouse over it and click the arrow that appears, you will see that the second and subsequent items are displayed just fine. You can see the problem in Figure 14-4. This is a problem commonly encountered when using the FlipView control and I tend to think of it as the *first image problem*.

Figure 14-4. *The FlipView first image problem*

The problem is caused by an unfortunate interaction between the WinJS.UI.Pages API, the WinJS. Binding API and the FlipView control itself. When you click on the NavBar command for the FlipView control, the WinJS.UI.Pages.render method is used to load the FlipView.html file.

As part of this process, the render method automatically calls the WinJS.UI.processAll method so that any WinJS UI controls in the imported content are properly created.

The automatic call to the processAll method initializes the FlipView control. As part of this initialization, the FlipView locates the element I specified using the itemTemplate property uses this template to generate the content it needs to display the first item, which includes processing the data bindings to set the src property for the img element.

At this stage, the FlipView has created HTML from the template that looks like this:

```
...
<div class="flipItem">
    <img src="/images/data/aster.jpg" data-win-bind="src: file">
    <div class="flipTitle" data-win-bind="innerText: name">Aster</div>
</div>
...
```

You can see from the code fragment that the data bindings have been processed so that the values from the first data source item are reflected in the HTML elements.

However, you can also see (and I have highlighted them for emphasis) that the original data-win-bind attributes from the template have been copied into the new content.

Those lingering data-win-bind attributes are part of the problem. Although the WinJS.UI.processAll method is called automatically for imported content, the WinJS.Binding.processAll method is not. To make sure my bindings are resolved, I call this method directly in my handler for the WinJS.Navigation event in the default.js file, as follows:

```
...
WinJS.Navigation.addEventListener("navigating", function (e) {
    WinJS.UI.Animation.exitPage(contentTarget.children).then(function () {
        WinJS.Utilities.empty(contentTarget);
        WinJS.UI.Pages.render(e.detail.location, contentTarget)
            .then(function () {
                return WinJS.Binding.processAll(contentTarget, ViewModel.State)
                    .then(function () {
                        return WinJS.UI.Animation.enterPage(contentTarget.children)
                    });
            });
    });
});
...
```

The code in the default.js file performs a very common sequence of actions for this situation: import the content, process the data bindings and perform an animation.

The problem is that when the WinJS.Binding.processAll method runs, it walks through the DOM looking for elements that define the data-win-bind attribute and finds the elements that the FlipView control has created from the template. Even though the data bindings for these elements have already been resolved, the processAll method looks at them again and tries to make sense of them.

The WinJS.Binding.processAll method inserts undefined into any data binding that refers to a data value that it can't resolve. It leaves the content of any element with an innerText binding that it can't resolve empty. This isn't the most helpful behavior, and since the processAll method is trying to apply the ViewModel.State object and the bindings are intended to process data source items, the processAll method overwrites the values in the template elements, as follows:

```
...

<div class="flipItem">
    <img src="undefined" data-win-bind="src: file">
    <div class="flipTitle" data-win-bind="innerText: name"></div>
</div>
...
```

And so, the interaction between various bits of WinJS functionality means that the first data item isn't displayed properly, because the src attribute on the img element is set to undefined and the content of the div element I use for the image name is left empty.

The FlipView control generates the elements it needs to display a data item on demand, which means that the elements for the second and subsequent data items are not generated from the template until you advance to the next item by clicking or swiping, long after the WinJS.Binding.processAll method has finished its work – which is why only the first data item is affected.

Solutions to the First Image Problem

There are two ways that this problem can be solved, both of which have the benefit of not requiring me to change changing the handler for the WinJS.Navigation event. The pattern of functionality that I use to handle navigation is fine in other situations and makes working with data bindings in imported content a breeze. In the sections that follow, I'll show you solutions which resolve the problem.

Specify the Template or Data Source Programmatically

The first solution is to set the itemTemplate property or itemDataSource property on the FlipView control in the content page's ready function. When you change the value of either property, the FlipView control will regenerate its content, on the basis that there has been an important change that needs to be displayed to the user. To demonstrate this solution, I have to add the statement to the /js/pages/flipview.js file shown in Listing 14-8.

Listing 14-8. Setting the value of the itemTemplate property

```
(function() {

    WinJS.UI.Pages.define("/pages/FlipView.html", {
        ready: function () {
            var proxyObject = WinJS.Binding.as({
                itemTemplate: ItemTemplate,
                customAnimations: false
            });

            Templates.createControls(rightPanel, flip, "flipView", proxyObject)
            .then(function () {

                flip.winControl.itemTemplate = ItemTemplate;
            });
        }
    });
})();
```

When you start the app now, you will see that the first item is displayed correctly, as shown in Figure 14-5. This solution works because the code in the ready function is executed after WinJS.Binding. processAll method has been called, meaning that the elements that the FlipView generates from the template are not re-processed for the data-win-bind attribute a second time.

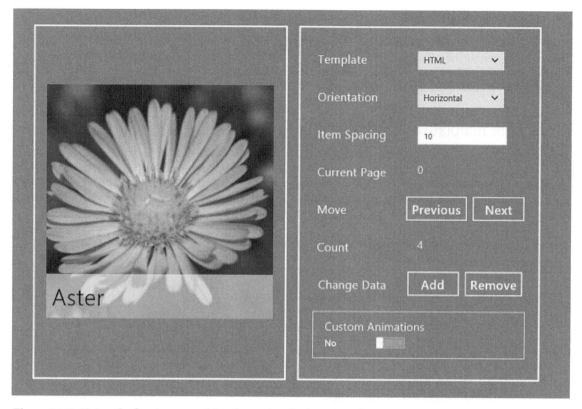

Figure 14-5. Fixing the first image problem by setting the itemTemplate property programmatically

You may notice a slight flicker when you navigate to the FlipView.html page, where the broken image is displayed for a second before being corrected. This is because the itemTemplate property is still being set declaratively and processed when the page is first loaded. To address this, I need to remove the declarative value for the itemTemplate property from the data-win-options attribute of the element to which the FlipView control is applied, as shown in Listing 14-9, leaving just the value for the itemDataSource property.

Listing 14-9. Removing the declarative value for the itemTemplate property

```
...
<div id="flipViewContainer" class="flexContainer">
    <div class="controlPanel">
        <div id="flip" data-win-control="WinJS.UI.FlipView"
            data-win-options="{itemDataSource: ViewModel.data.images.dataSource}">
        </div>
    </div>

    <div id="rightPanel" class="controlPanel"></div>
</div>
...
```

Using a Function as a Template

The alternative solution is to do away with declarative templates and use a function to generate the elements that the FlipView control uses to display each data item. You can see how I have added such a function in the /js/pages/flipview.js file in Listing 14-10.

Listing 14-10. Adding a function to generate display elements

```
(function() {

    function renderItem(itemPromise) {
        return itemPromise.then(function (item) {
            var topElem = document.createElement("div");
            WinJS.Utilities.addClass(topElem, "renderDiv");
            var imgElem = topElem.appendChild(document.createElement("img"));
            imgElem.src = item.data.file;
            var titleElem = topElem.appendChild(document.createElement("div"));
            titleElem.innerText = item.data.name;
            return topElem;
        });
    }

    WinJS.UI.Pages.define("/pages/FlipView.html", {
        ready: function () {

            var proxyObject = WinJS.Binding.as({
                itemTemplate: ItemTemplate,
                customAnimations: false
            });

            Templates.createControls(rightPanel, flip, "flipView", proxyObject)
            .then(function () {

                proxyObject.bind("itemTemplate", function (val) {
                    flip.winControl.itemTemplate =
                        val == "HTML" ? ItemTemplate : renderItem;
                });

            });
        }
    });
})();
```

When you use a function to generate the item templates, the argument you are passed is an IItemPromise object. This is a regular WinJS.Promise but the argument passed to the then function when the Promise is fulfilled is an IItem object. (These double Is are deliberate - the initial I indicates an interface). The IItem object provides access to the data source item and defines the properties I have described in Table 14-2.

Table 14-2. The properties defined by IItem

Property	Description
data	Returns the object from the data source for which a template is required
index	Returns the index of the object in the data source
key	Returns the key that identifies the item in data source. When using a WinJS.Binding.List as the data source, the key is a string representation of the index property.

To create a template, you call the then method on the IItemPromise object, specifying a function that will receive the IItem object when it is ready (this allows for data sources which have to perform some kind of background operation - such as query a database or reading files from the disk - to complete asynchronously). When you get the IItem object, you can query it using the properties in the table to generate the elements that are required to display it to the user.

■ **Tip**   When using a function to generate a template, you must return a single HTMLElement object, although this top-level element can contain as many child elements as you need. This is the same constraint as for declarative HTML templates.

To help demonstrate the different template approaches, I have changed the way that the itemTemplate property is set in the JavaScript file, linking it to the select element in the right-hand panel of the app layout. When you pick the HTML value from the select element, the declarative template from the previous section is used and when you pick the Function value, the renderItem function from the listing is applied. The renderItem function produces a different style of layout for data items in order to make it easier to see which is being used, as illustrated by Figure 14-6.

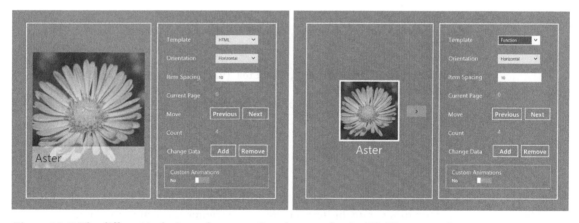

Figure 14-6. The different techniques for generating elements for the FlipView control

Both of these approaches solve the first image problem, and you can choose whichever suits your programming style. I tend to prefer declarative templates for most situations, but generating elements using a function can be more flexible, especially if you want to tailor the content of the elements based on individual data items.

Configuring the FlipView Control

Now that I have got the first image problem and solution out of the way, I can turn to the other configuration properties that the FlipView control supports, which I have summarized in Table 14-3.

Table 14-3. The properties defined by FlipView control

Property	Description
currentPage	Gets or sets the index of the item currently displayed
orientation	Gets or sets the direction in which the user moves between items.
itemSpacing	Gets or sets the spacing between items, expressed in pixels. This property has a visible effect only when the user navigates between items using touch
itemDataSource	Gets or sets the source for items to display
itemTemplate	Gets or sets the template or function that will generate the elements required to display the items in the data source

The itemTemplate and itemDataSource are the most important properties and I have already explained how to use them in explaining how to resolve the first image problem. In the sections that follow, I'll use some of the configuration controls I created in the right-hand panel of the app layout to demonstrate the orientation and itemSpacing properties. I'll demonstrate the currentPage property when I talk about manipulating the FlipView control programmatically, later in the chapter.

Setting the Orientation

The orientation property lets you change the direction in which the user moves backwards and forwards through the items in the data source. The default value is horizontal, meaning that the user swipes to the left and right on a touch screen or clicks on buttons at the left and right edge of the control with the mouse. The other support value is vertical, which requires the user to swipe up and down and which changes the position of the buttons for mouse users so they appear at the top and bottom of the control. I have added a select element to the right panel labeled Orientation, which lets you change the value of the orientation property on the FlipView control in the left panel. In Figure 14-7, you can see the different button positions that are displayed for mouse users for the horizontal and vertical values. I have highlighted the buttons in the figure because they are hard to see with their default styling (I'll show you how to change the button style later in the chapter).

Figure 14-7. The different positions of the buttons for the horizontal and vertical orientation values

Setting the Item Spacing

The itemSpacing property sets the gap shown between items when the user uses touch to flip from one item to the other. You can see two examples of this gap, with the default of 10 pixels and a larger value of 100 pixels, in Figure 14-8.

Figure 14-8. Setting the spacing displayed between items for touch interaction

I have included a configuration control in the example for this property – an input element labeled Item Spacing. The effect of the itemSpacing property may seem small, but setting the item spacing can make a significant difference to the appearance and feel of the FlipView control. In particular, I find that using a larger space when the data source contents are only loosely related creates a more natural feel. Of course, that's a purely subjective feeling and you should do what makes sense for your own apps and preferences.

Managing the FlipView Programmatically

For the most part, the FlipView control provides the user with everything they need to interact with the content that is being displayed. Mouse users are presented with popup buttons when the move the mouse over the FlipView and touch users can making a swiping motion to move from one item to the next. Even so, there are times when you need to take more direct control of how the control operates and for these situations the FlipView defines the methods that I describe in Table 14-4. In the sections that follow, I'll show you how these methods are used.

Table 14-4. The methods defined by FlipView control

Method	Description
count()	Returns a Promise which, when complete, returns the number of items in the data source.
next()	Displays the next item in the data source. Returns true if the FlipView moves to a new item and false if not (typically because the last item was already being displayed).
previous()	Displays the previous item in the data source. Returns true if the FlipView moves to a new item and false otherwise (typically because the first item is already being displayed).
setCustomAnimations(animations)	Changes the animations used by the FlipView. See Chapter 18 for details of WinJS animations.

Moving through the FlipView Items

You can move programmatically through the items in the data source by calling the next and previous methods. I added buttons to the right panel of the example to demonstrate this feature and you can see the code that handles the click events from these buttons in Listing 14-11.

Listing 14-11. Moving through the FlipView items using the next and previous methods

```
...
WinJS.UI.Pages.define("/pages/FlipView.html", {
    ready: function () {

        var proxyObject = WinJS.Binding.as({
            itemTemplate: ItemTemplate,
            customAnimations: false,
        });

        Templates.createControls(rightPanel, flip, "flipView", proxyObject)
        .then(function () {
```

```
        proxyObject.bind("itemTemplate", function (val) {
            flip.winControl.itemTemplate =
                val == "HTML" ? ItemTemplate : renderItem;
        });

        $('#rightPanel button').listen("click", function (e) {
            var buttonText = e.target.innerText.toLowerCase();
            switch (buttonText) {
                case "previous":
                case "next":
                    flip.winControl[buttonText]();
                    currentPage.innerText = flip.winControl.currentPage;
                    break;
            }
        });
    });
    }
});
...
```

These methods will only change the displayed items if there another item in the data source to move to. This means that the next method has no effect when the FlipView is showing the last item in the data source and the previous method has no effect when the first item is showing. After I call the previous or next method, I use the value of the currentPage property to update the value of the corresponding span element in the right-hand panel.

■ **Tip** You can set the value of the currentPage property if you want to navigate directly to a specific element.

Manipulating the Data Source

One of the most useful features of the data-driven UI controls is that they respond automatically when the contents of the data source changes. This allows you to create dynamic and adaptable layouts for your app, which respond immediately to changes in the underlying data. To demonstrate this responsiveness, I added some additional data items to the view model, as shown in Listing 14-12.

Listing14- 12. Additional data items defined in the view model

```
(function () {
    "use strict";

    WinJS.Namespace.define("ViewModel", {
        data: {
            images: new WinJS.Binding.List([
                { file: "/images/data/aster.jpg", name: "Aster"},
                { file: "/images/data/carnation.jpg", name: "Carnation"},
                { file: "/images/data/daffodil.jpg", name: "Daffodil"},
                { file: "/images/data/lily.jpg", name: "Lilly"},
            ]),
```

```
        extraImages: [{ file: "/images/data/orchid.jpg", name: "Orchid"},
            { file: "/images/data/peony.jpg", name: "Peony"},
            { file: "/images/data/primula.jpg", name: "Primula"},
            { file: "/images/data/rose.jpg", name: "Rose"},
            { file: "/images/data/snowdrop.jpg", name: "Snowdrop"}]
    }
});

})();
```

These data items are not part of the data source when the app starts, but I will move items to and from the from the List object when you click the Add and Remove buttons on the right panel of the example. I have added to my click event handler function in the flipview.js file to support these buttons, as shown in Listing 14-13.

Listing 14-13. Adding support for the Add and Remove buttons to the click event handler

```
...
$('#rightPanel button').listen("click", function (e) {
    var data = ViewModel.data.images;
    var extras = ViewModel.data.extraImages;
    var buttonText = e.target.innerText.toLowerCase();
    switch (buttonText) {
        case "add":
        case "remove":
            if (buttonText == "add" && extras.length > 0) {
                data.push(extras.pop());
            } else if (buttonText == "remove" && data.length > 1) {
                extras.push(data.pop());
            }
            setImmediate(function () {
                flip.winControl.count().then(function (countVal) {
                    itemCount.innerText = countVal;
                });
            });
            break;
        case "previous":
        case "next":
            flip.winControl[buttonText]();
            currentPage.innerText = flip.winControl.currentPage;
            break;
    }
});
...
```

You can add new items to the List object by clicking the Add button and take them away them by clicking the Remove button. The best way to see how well the FlipView control responds to changes in the data source is to move to the last data item and click the Remove button. The FlipView will automatically move to the previous item to reflect the change in the data source.

Getting the Number of Items in the Data Source

You will notice that I added some code to the previous listing that calls the count method. As you can see this method requires a little explanation. When you call the count method, you get back a WinJS.Promise object which, when it is fulfilled, will pass the number of items in the data source as the argument to the then method. This is another example of how data sources and the data-driven UI controls are designed to support asynchronous operations, even though the number of items in the List object can be obtained synchronously.

I placed the call to the count method inside a function I passed to the setImmediate function. As I explained in Chapter 9, the setImmediate function defers execution of a function until events and other functions which have been passed to the setImmediate function are processed. The reason I do this is because the data source uses events to signal the FlipView control that the data it contains has changed and that event isn't processed when I call the count method immediately. To ensure that I display the update-to-date value, I defer my call to the count method using setImmediate. I'll show you another approach using events supported by the FlipView UI control later in the next section.

Responding to the FlipView Events

The FlipView defines three events which I have described in Table 14-5.

Table 14-5. The events supported by the FlipViewcontrol

Event	Description
datasourcecountchanged	Triggered when the number of items in the data source changes
pageselected	Triggered when the FlipView flips to a page
pagevisibilitychanged	Triggered when the visible item changes

The datasourcecountchanged event is only triggered when the number of items in the data source changes and not when one item is replaced with another. This means that when you are using a WinJS.Binding.List object as your data source, using the setAt method will cause the FlipView control to display the item you specify, but it won't trigger the datasourcecountchanged event.

The pageselected event is triggered when a new page is displayed. This event is triggered when the user clicks a navigation button, or when the next and previous methods are called or when the currentPage property is used to jump to a particular item. The event isn't triggered while the user slides across the control to select an item, but is triggered when the touch is released.

The pagevisibilitychanged event is triggered every time the FlipView changes the visibility of an item. This is a nice idea, but it isn't executed in a particular useful manner. The Event that is passed to handler functions for pagevisibilitychanged doesn't include details of which item the event relates to, so you just get a succession of pretty much useless notifications.

I can use the datasourcecountchanged event to replace the call I make to the setImmediate function to defer using the count method. You can see the change I have made to the flipview.js file in Listing 14-14.

Listing 14-14. Handling the datasourcecountchanged event

```
...
WinJS.UI.Pages.define("/pages/FlipView.html", {
    ready: function () {

        var proxyObject = WinJS.Binding.as({
```

```
        itemTemplate: ItemTemplate,
        customAnimations: false,
    });

    Templates.createControls(rightPanel, flip, "flipView", proxyObject)
    .then(function () {

        proxyObject.bind("itemTemplate", function (val) {
            flip.winControl.itemTemplate =
                val == "HTML" ? ItemTemplate : renderItem;
        });

        flip.addEventListener("datasourcecountchanged", function () {
            flip.winControl.count().then(function (countVal) {
                itemCount.innerText = countVal;
            });
        });

        $('#rightPanel button').listen("click", function (e) {
            var data = ViewModel.data.images;
            var extras = ViewModel.data.extraImages;
            var buttonText = e.target.innerText.toLowerCase();
            switch (buttonText) {
                case "add":
                case "remove":
                    if (buttonText == "add" && extras.length > 0) {
                        data.push(extras.pop());
                    } else if (buttonText == "remove" && data.length > 1) {
                        extras.push(data.pop());
                    }

                    break;
                case "previous":
                case "next":
                    flip.winControl[buttonText]();
                    currentPage.innerText = flip.winControl.currentPage;
                    break;
            }
        });
    });
    }
});
...
```

I have removed the call to the setImmediate function and replaced it with an event listener which calls the count method and updates the content of the span element in the right panel. The datasourcecountchanged event isn't triggered until after the FlipView has processed the new changed in the data source, which means that I no longer have to worry about deferring the method call.

Styling the FlipView Control

The `FlipView` supports uses six classes that you can use to style different aspects of the control's appearance, as summarized in Table 14-6.

Table 14-6. The FlipView CSS classes

Class	Description
win-flipview	Styles the entire control
win-item	Styles the items in the control
win-navbottom	Styles the lower navigation button in the vertical orientation
win-navleft	Styles the left navigation button in the horizontal orientation
win-navright	Styles the right navigation button in the horizontal orientation
win-navtop	Styles the upper navigation button in the vertical orientation

The `FlipView` doesn't size itself automatically, so you need to put the control into a layout that will allocate sizes automatically, or assign explicit width and height values. You can do this using the win-flipview class, but I tend to use the id for the class to which the control has been applied so that multiple `FlipView` controls on the same page are handled separately (for some reason, my projects rarely require multiple `FlipView` controls of the same size).

I tend not to use the win-item class either, because I prefer to handle the styling for my items via the item template. That's just my preference, of course, and the win-item class can be useful when you are using a function to generate different sets of elements to display items and you want to apply an overarching set of styles.

The classes that I do use often are those which style the navigation buttons which appear when the mouse is moved over the `FlipView` control. These buttons can be difficult to see when a light-colored image is being displayed and in Listing 14-15 you can see a style element I added to the `FlipView.html` file which makes them more obvious by applying a border.

Listing 14-15. Styling the navigation buttons

```
...
<head>
    <title></title>
    <link href="/css/flipview.css" rel="stylesheet" />
    <script src="/js/pages/flipview.js"></script>
    <style>
        #flip .win-navleft, #flip .win-navright {
            border: medium solid black;
        }
    </style>
</head>
...
```

You can see the effect of this style in Figure 14-9. If you test these additions yourself, bear in mind that I have only applied the style to the left and right buttons, which will have no effect if the `FlipView` orientation property is set to vertical.

Figure 14-9. Making the navigation buttons easier to see on a light image

Using Custom Animations

If you look at the controls in the right panel of the layout, you'll notice that I added a `ToggleSwitch` to enable custom animations. Many of the WinJS UI controls use animations in some form, either to show transitions from one state to another or to indicate that content has changed in some way. Often, the animations are so brief that they become almost invisible - but they still catch the eye just enough to send important signals to the user.

I explain the animation system in depth in Chapter 18, but the `FlipView` control provides support for changing the animations it uses and I wanted to explain how to do this as part of this chapter. This means that I am going to explain how to use a feature that I have not properly introduced yet, so you may want to go and read Chapter 18 and then return to this section afterwards.

All you need to know about the animation system for this section is that animations are represented by functions in the `WinJS.UI.Animation` namespace and that two such functions are `fadeIn` and `fadeOut`. Both functions take an element as an argument and their names tell you what kind of animation they perform on that element.

Applying Custom Animations

The `FlipView` control uses animations when the user navigates to a different item. To change the animations that are used in one or more of these situations, you pass an object to the `setCustomAnimations` method which has properties called `next`, `previous` and `jump`. The animations for the next and previous properties are used when the user moves to the next or previous data item and the `jump` property is used when the user navigates further afield.

The value of these properties must be functions which return a WinJS.Promise object that is fulfilled when the animation has finished. The function you define is passed arguments representing the element that is about to be removed and the one that will replace it as the selected item displayed by the FlipView.

In Listing 14-16, you can see the code I added to the flipview.js file to set custom animations for the next property, which I apply when the ToggleSwitch control labeled Custom Animations in the right-hand panel is set to Yes.

Listing 14-16. Using custom animations with a FlipView control

```
...

WinJS.UI.Pages.define("/pages/FlipView.html", {
    ready: function () {

        var proxyObject = WinJS.Binding.as({
            itemTemplate: ItemTemplate,
            customAnimations: false,
        });

        Templates.createControls(rightPanel, flip, "flipView", proxyObject)
        .then(function () {

            proxyObject.bind("itemTemplate", function (val) {
                flip.winControl.itemTemplate =
                    val == "HTML" ? ItemTemplate : renderItem;
            });

            flip.addEventListener("datasourcecountchanged", function () {
                flip.winControl.count().then(function (countVal) {
                    itemCount.innerText = countVal;
                });
            });
        });

        $('#rightPanel button').listen("click", function (e) {
            var data = ViewModel.data.images;
            var extras = ViewModel.data.extraImages;
            var buttonText = e.target.innerText.toLowerCase();
            switch (buttonText) {
                case "add":
                case "remove":
                    if (buttonText == "add" && extras.length > 0) {
                        data.push(extras.pop());
                    } else if (buttonText == "remove" && data.length > 1) {
                        extras.push(data.pop());
                    }

                    break;
                case "previous":
                case "next":
                    flip.winControl[buttonText]();
                    currentPage.innerText = flip.winControl.currentPage;
```

```
                    break;
            }
        });

        proxyObject.bind("customAnimations", function (val) {
            if (val) {
                flip.winControl.setCustomAnimations({
                    next: function (pageout, pagein) {
                        return WinJS.Promise.join([WinJS.UI.Animation.fadeOut(pageout),
                            WinJS.UI.Animation.fadeIn(pagein)]);
                    }
                });
            } else {
                flip.winControl.setCustomAnimations({
                    next: null
                });
            }
        });
    });
}
});
...
```

When the view model property is set to true, I call the setCustomAnimations method and provide the FlipView control with details of the animations I want it to use and when they should be applied. The object that I have passed to the setCustomAnimations method defines just the next property, which tells the FlipView control to use the default animations for the previous and jump scenarios.

I want to perform two animations - I want the fadeOut animation to be performed on the outgoing element and the fadeIn animation to be performed on the incoming element. I need to return a single Promise object that only completes when both of these animations are complete, which is why I have used the Promise.join method, which I described in Chapter 9.

When the ToggleSwitch is set to No, I return to the default animations by passing another object to the setCustomAnimations method which has null values for the properties I want to reset.

You can test out this feature by starting the app and using the control navigation button to advance to the next data item. A very brief animation will create the effect of the new item appearing from the right. When you set the ToggleSwitch to Yes and use the navigation button again, the existing item will fade out and be replaced by the next data item.

■ **Caution**   Think carefully about the animations that you select. Although the animations are quick, a poor selection which is inconsistent with other Windows apps can signal a different kind of interaction than the one that the user is performing. Stick with the default animations when you can and try to correlate the actions the user performs with the animations you select when this isn't possible. This is a topic I return to in Chapter 18 when I explain the WinJS animation features in more detail.

Summary

In this chapter, I have described the first of the WinJS data controls, FlipView. I showed you how to use the WinJS.Binding.List object to create data sources and how to associated templates with the data to configure the way that items are displayed to the user. I also showed you the first-image problem, explained how it arises, and offered different ways of resolving the issue. I finished by showing you how to use custom animations with the FlipView control – information that will have more resonance once you have read Chapter 18, which goes into the WinJS animation system in depth. In the next chapter, I will show you the ListView control, which is the bigger and more complex complement to the FlipView control.

CHAPTER 15

■ ■ ■

Using the ListView Control

In this chapter, I describe the ListView control, which is another of the WinJS data-driven UI controls. There is a common foundation with the FlipView control from the last chapter, but ListView displays multiple items and provides some flexibility in how this is done. In this chapter, I explain the different kinds of template and layout that can be used, describe the differences between invoked and selected items and how you how to handle the various events that the ListView control emits. I also show you how to work with the abstractions that describe a data source so that you can write code that will work with any data source, not just those which are created using the WinJS.Binding.List object. Table 15-1 provides the summary for this chapter.

Table 15-1. Chapter Summary

Problem	Solution	Listing
Use the ListView control	Apply the data-win-control attribute to a div element with a value of WinJS. UI.ListView.	1-6
Set the layout of the ListView	Set the layout property to a WinJS.UI. GridLayout or WinJS.UI.ListLayout object	7
Limit the rows in the grid layout	Set the maxRows property of the GridLayout object	8
Generate groups for data items	Call the createGrouped method to generate the group information and use this as the basis for the groupDataSource property.	9-10
Position the header for groups in the grid	Set the groupHeaderPosition property	11
Use a template for group headers	Ensure that the function passed to the createGrouped method returns an object suitable for data binding and associate a Template with the groupHeaderTemplate property.	12-13
Receive notifications when the user invokes an item	Listen for the iteminvoked event	14-15
Receive notifications when the user selects items	Listen for the selectionchanged event	16

Problem	Solution	Listing
Style the ListView control	Define styles for the win-listview CSS class	17
Ensure that an item is visible	Use the ensureVisible method	18
Work directly with the data source	Use the methods defined by the IListDataSource interface	19-22
Receive notifications when the data source changes	Use the createListBinding method	23

When to use the ListView Control

The ListView is such a flexible control that there are no real constraints on how it can be used. In short, if you want to present the user with multiple items, then the ListView is probably the best of the WinJS UI controls to use. You must, however, make sure that the user can readily find a specific item or group of items. The ListView is excellent for displaying items, including large data sets, but it is easy to get carried away and present the user with an overwhelming array of items to choose from. For large data sets, consider providing the user with tools to search or filter the items or implement a layout based on the semantic zoom control, which I describe in Chapter 16.

Adding the ListView Example

I am going to start by describing the basic features of the ListView control and then build on the example to demonstrate some of the more advanced options and features. Although the ListView control only does one thing (present the user with a list of multiple items), there are a lot of permutations and configuration options. To get started, I have defined a data source in the /js/viewmodel.js file, as shown in Listing 15-1.

Listing 15-1. Additions in the viewmodel.js file for the ListView example

```
(function () {
    "use strict";

    WinJS.Namespace.define("ViewModel", {
        data: {
            images: new WinJS.Binding.List([
                { file: "/images/data/aster.jpg", name: "Aster"},
                { file: "/images/data/carnation.jpg", name: "Carnation"},
                { file: "/images/data/daffodil.jpg", name: "Daffodil"},
                { file: "/images/data/lily.jpg", name: "Lilly"},
            ]),

            extraImages: [{ file: "/images/data/orchid.jpg", name: "Orchid"},
                { file: "/images/data/peony.jpg", name: "Peony"},
                { file: "/images/data/primula.jpg", name: "Primula"},
                { file: "/images/data/rose.jpg", name: "Rose"},
                { file: "/images/data/snowdrop.jpg", name: "Snowdrop" }],
```

```
            letters: new WinJS.Binding.List(),
        },
    });

    var src = ["A", "B", "C", "D", "E", "F", "G", "H", "I", "J", "K", "L", "M", "N", "O",
               "P", "Q", "R", "S", "T", "U", "V", "W", "X", "Y", "Z"];
    src.forEach(function (item, index) {
        ViewModel.data.letters.push({
            letter: item,
            group: index % 3
        });
    });

})();
```

I have created a new WinJS.Binding.List object contains an object for each letter of the alphabet. Each object has a letter property, which returns the letter that the object corresponds to and a group property, which I use to assign the object to one of three numerical groups. I'll use the value of the letter property when I display the items and use the group property when I describe the ListView feature for grouping related items together, later in the chapter.

Defining the ListView HTML

To demonstrate the ListView control, I have added a new file called ListView.html to the pages folder in the Visual Studio project. You can see the contents of this file in Listing 15-2.

Listing 15-2. The initial contents of the ListView.html file

```html
<!DOCTYPE html>
<html>
<head>
    <title></title>
    <link href="/css/listview.css" rel="stylesheet">
    <script src="/js/pages/listview.js"></script>
</head>
<body>
    <div id="ItemTemplate" data-win-control="WinJS.Binding.Template">
        <div class="listItem">
            <div class="listData" data-win-bind="innerText: letter"></div>
            <div class="listTitle" data-win-bind="innerText: group"></div>
        </div>
    </div>

    <div id="listViewContainer" class="flexContainer">
        <div class="controlPanel">
            <div id="list" data-win-control="WinJS.UI.ListView"
                data-win-options="{ itemTemplate: ItemTemplate,
                    itemDataSource: ViewModel.data.letters.dataSource}">
            </div>
        </div>
    </div>
```

```
            <div id="midPanel" class="controlPanel"></div>
            <div id="rightPanel" class="controlPanel"></div>
        </div>
    </body>
</html>
```

The `ListView` control is applied to `div` elements by setting the `data-win-control` attribute to `WinJS.UI.ListView`. When using the `ListView` control, you set the data source and the template used to display data items using the `itemDataSource` and `itemTemplate` properties, just like with the `FlipView` control.

The `ListView` control doesn't suffer from the first-image problem that I described for the `FlipView` in Chapter 14, so you can safely set the `itemDataSource` and `itemTemplate` properties declaratively using the `data-win-options` attribute (although you can also set these values programmatically and use a function to generate your template elements if you prefer – see Chapter 14 for details and examples). In my listing, I am using the `List` of letter-related objects I added to the `viewmodel.js` file as the data source and the `WinJS.Binding.Template` control defined in the `ListView.html` file as the template.

Defining the CSS

I have placed the CSS for this example into a file called `/css/listview.css`, the contents of which you can see in Listing 15-3. There are no new techniques in this CSS and all of the styles are simple and standard.

Listing 15-3. The contents of the listview.css file

```
#list {width:  500px;height: 500px;}
*.listItem {width: 100px;}
*.listData {background-color: black;
    text-align: center; border: solid medium white;font-size: 70pt;}
.listTitle {position: absolute; background-color: rgba(255, 255, 255, 0.6);
    color: black; bottom: 3px;font-size: 20pt; width: 86px;
    padding-left: 10px; padding-top: 20px;font-weight: bold;}
*.invoked {color: red;}
*.invoked .listData {font-weight: bold;}
*.invoked .listTitle {background-color: transparent}
#midPanel, #rightPanel { -ms-flex-pack: start;  }
#list .win-container {background-color: transparent;}
```

Defining the JavaScript

I have placed the JavaScript for this example into a file called `/js/pages/listview.js` and you can see the contents of this file in Listing 15-4.

Listing 15-4. The initial contents of the listview.js file

```
(function () {

    WinJS.UI.Pages.define("/pages/ListView.html", {
        ready: function () {

            var proxyObject = WinJS.Binding.as({
                layout: "Grid",
                groups: false,
```

```
                groupHeaderPosition: "top",
                maxRows: 3,
                ensureVisible: null,
                searchFor: null,
            });

            Templates.createControls(midPanel, list, "listView1", proxyObject);
            Templates.createControls(rightPanel, list, "listView2", proxyObject);
        }
    });
})();
```

You will notice that I make two calls to the `Templates.createControls` method in this listing. When I defined the HTML for this example, I added an extra container element for configuration controls, as follows:

```
...
<div id="midPanel" class="controlPanel"></div>
<div id="rightPanel" class="controlPanel"></div>
...
```

I need too many configuration controls in this chapter for them to fit into one container on the simulator's standard resolution screen, so I have split the elements into two containers and, as a consequence, need to make two calls to the `createControls` method. You can see the two sets of definition controls I added to the `controls.js` file for this example in Listing 15-5.

Listing 15-5. The definition objects for the ListView control

```
...
listView1: [
    { type: "select", id: "layout", title: "Layout", values: ["Grid", "List"],
        useProxy: true },
    { type: "toggle", id: "groups", title: "Groups", useProxy: true, value: false },
    { type: "select", id: "groupHeaderPosition", title: "Group Position",
        values: ["top", "left"], labels: ["Top", "Left"], useProxy: true },
    { type: "input", id: "maxRows", title: "Max Rows", value: 3, useProxy: true },
    { type: "span", id: "invoked", value: "Invoke an Item", title: "Invoked" },
    { type: "span", id: "selected", value: "Select an Item", title: "Selected" }],

listView2: [
    { type: "select", id: "tapBehavior", title: "tapBehavior",
        values: ["directSelect", "toggleSelect", "invokeOnly", "none"] },
    { type: "select", id: "selectionMode", title: "selectionMode",
        values: ["multi", "single", "none"] },
    { type: "input", id: "ensureVisible", title: "EnsureVisible", value: "",
        useProxy: true },
    { type: "input", id: "searchFor", title: "Search For", value: "", useProxy: true },
    { type: "span", id: "itemCount", value: 26, title: "Count" },
    { type: "buttons", labels: ["Add Item", "Delete Item"] }],
...
```

As I mentioned earlier, the `ListView` control is quite flexible and this is reflected in the number of configuration controls that I need to demonstrate the most important features.

Finally, I need to ensure that the user can navigate to the ListView.html file from the NavBar, so I have made the addition to the templates.js file shown in Listing 6.

Listing 15-6. Ensuring that the ListView.html file is reachable from the NavBar

```
...
var navBarCommands = [
    //{ name: "AppTest", icon: "target" },
    { name: "ToggleSwitch", icon: "\u0031" },
    { name: "Rating", icon: "\u0032" },
    { name: "Tooltip", icon: "\u0033" },
    { name: "TimePicker", icon: "\u0034" },
    { name: "DatePicker", icon: "\u0035" },
    { name: "Flyout", icon: "\u0036" },
    { name: "Menu", icon: "\u0037" },
    { name: "MessageDialog", icon: "\u0038" },
    { name: "FlipView", icon: "pictures" },
    { name: "Listview", icon: "list" },
];
...
```

Working with the ListView Control

If you run app at this point and navigate to the ListView.html file via the NavBar, you'll see the layout shown in Figure 15-1. In the left-hand panel is the ListView control, which is displaying the items in the alphabet data source I added to the viewmodel.js file. The other two panels contain the configuration controls that I will use to demonstrate different ListView features.

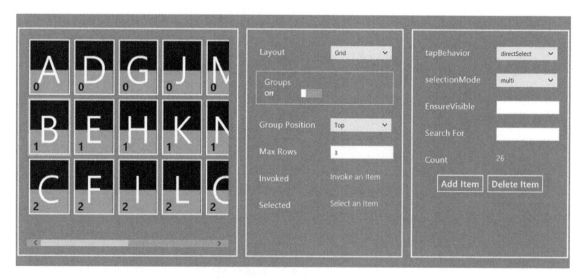

Figure 15-1. The layout of the ListView.html file

In the sections that follow, I'll explain different aspects of the ListView functionality and demonstrate the different ways that the ListView control can be used to display data items.

Selecting the Layout

The ListView can display the data items using two different layouts. By default, the ListView control displays the items from the data source in a grid, which is what you can see in Figure 1. Notice the order in which the data items are displayed. Each column in the grid is filled from top-to-bottom creating a vertical-first layout. Horizontal scrolling is used if there are more items in the data source than can be displayed in the screen space occupied by the ListView control. To make the layout more obvious to the user, a horizontal scrollbar is displayed when the user moves the mouse over the ListView control or swipes left or right with a touch interaction.

The other layout that can be used is a vertical list. You can switch between the grid and the list using the first select element in the right panel of the example, which I have labeled Layout. In Listing 15-7 you can see the code I have added to the /js/pages/listview.js file to link the select element to the ListView control.

Listing 15-7. Switching the layout of the ListView control

```
(function () {

    WinJS.UI.Pages.define("/pages/ListView.html", {
        ready: function () {

            var proxyObject = WinJS.Binding.as({
                layout: "Grid",
                groups: false,
                groupHeaderPosition: "top",
                maxRows: 3,
                ensureVisible: null,
                searchFor: null,
            });

            Templates.createControls(midPanel, list, "listView1", proxyObject);
            Templates.createControls(rightPanel, list, "listView2", proxyObject);

            proxyObject.bind("layout", function (val) {
                list.winControl.layout = val == "Grid" ?
                    new WinJS.UI.GridLayout() : new WinJS.UI.ListLayout();
            });
        }
    });
})();
```

The ListView control defines the layout property and that is what I change in the listing. You set this property to an object – a WinJS.UI.GridLayout object if you want the grid and a WinJS.UI.ListLayout object if you want the vertical list.

You can see the effect of switching to the List layout in Figure 15-2. The layout in the figure looks a little odd because the ListView control is sized to display multiple columns.

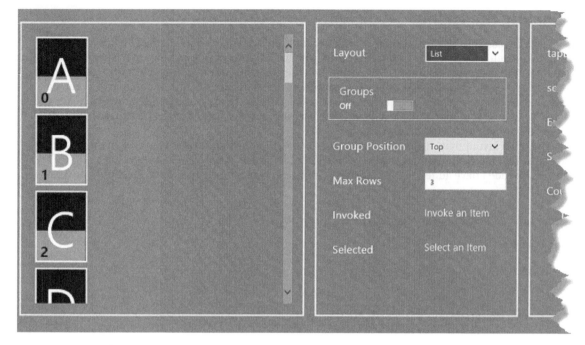

Figure 15-2. *Displaying elements using the list layout*

This is a much more traditional vertical list. I tend not to use the list layout on its own like this, but it can be very useful when creating a semantic zoom layout, which I describe in Chapter 16.

A common mistake is to set the layout property to the name of the object as a string. That won't work – you need to use the new keyword to create a new object and assign that as the value, just as I have done in the listing. If you want to set the layout declaratively, then you must use a special notation in the data binding, like this:

```
...
data-win-options="{layout: {type: WinJS.UI.ListLayout}}"
...
```

This notation tells the ListView control to create a new instance of the ListLayout object. It is an awkward syntax and I tend to avoid it by setting the layout in code.

■ **Note**   You could, in principle, create your own layout object to implement a custom layout policy, but it is hard to tease apart the base functionality defined in the WinJS.UI.Layout object and the assumptions made about the layout capabilities by the ListView control.

Setting the Maximum Numbers of Grid Rows

The GridLayout object defines the maxRows property which puts an upper limit on the number of rows that will be used to layout the items in the data source. Setting a value for the maxRows property will only put a cap on the number of rows - it won't, for example, force the grid to occupy the number of rows that you specify. The main reason that the actual number of rows will differ is that the GridLayout will never use vertical scrolling. So, a new row won't be added unless there is enough vertical space available to completely accommodate the element generated from the template.

To demonstrate this feature, there is an input element in the middle panel of the app layout labeled Max Rows. In Listing 15-8, you can see the code I added to the /js/pages/listview.js file to link the value entered into this control to the maxRows property.

Listing 15-8. Adding support for the maxRows feature to the listview.js file

```
(function () {

    WinJS.UI.Pages.define("/pages/ListView.html", {
        ready: function () {

            var proxyObject = WinJS.Binding.as({
                layout: "Grid",
                groups: false,
                groupHeaderPosition: "top",
                maxRows: 3,
                ensureVisible: null,
                searchFor: null,
            });

            Templates.createControls(midPanel, list, "listView1", proxyObject);
            Templates.createControls(rightPanel, list, "listView2", proxyObject);

            proxyObject.bind("layout", function (val) {
                list.winControl.layout = val == "Grid" ?
                    new WinJS.UI.GridLayout() : new WinJS.UI.ListLayout();
            });

            proxyObject.bind("maxRows", function (val) {
                list.winControl.layout.maxRows = val;
            });
        }
    });
})();
```

This is a feature of the GridLayout object, which you create and set as the value for the ListView control's layout property – it is not a feature defined directly by the ListView itself. This means that the feature only works in the grid layout and that you must ensure that you set the value via the object returned from the layout property. Don't worry if you assign a value to the maxRows property on a ListLayout object – it will have no ill effects, but it won't change the layout. You can see the effect of entering a value of 2 in the Max Rows input element in Figure 3.

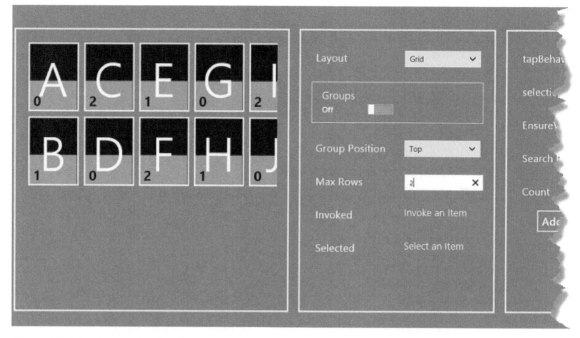

Figure 15-3. Setting a value for the maxRows property

Displaying Groups

The ListView control is able to display the items in groups, where details of the groups are provided via a special kind of data source named, obviously enough, a *group data source*. It was in preparation for this feature that I defined the group property for the objects I added to the data list in the /js/viewmodel.js file when I set up the example app earlier in this chapter.

It is pretty simple to create a group data source when you are using the WinJS.Binding.List object – you just call the createGrouped method. You can see the addition I made to the /js/viewmodel.js file to call this method in Listing 15-9.

Listing 15-9. Creating a grouped data source from a List object

```
(function () {
    "use strict";

    WinJS.Namespace.define("ViewModel", {
        data: {
            images: new WinJS.Binding.List([
                { file: "/images/data/aster.jpg", name: "Aster"},
                { file: "/images/data/carnation.jpg", name: "Carnation"},
                { file: "/images/data/daffodil.jpg", name: "Daffodil"},
                { file: "/images/data/lily.jpg", name: "Lilly"},
            ]),

            extraImages: [{ file: "/images/data/orchid.jpg", name: "Orchid"},
```

```
                { file: "/images/data/peony.jpg", name: "Peony"},
                { file: "/images/data/primula.jpg", name: "Primula"},
                { file: "/images/data/rose.jpg", name: "Rose"},
                { file: "/images/data/snowdrop.jpg", name: "Snowdrop" }],

        letters: new WinJS.Binding.List(),
        groupedLetters: null,
    },
});

var src = ["A", "B", "C", "D", "E", "F", "G", "H", "I", "J", "K", "L", "M", "N", "O",
            "P", "Q", "R", "S", "T", "U", "V", "W", "X", "Y", "Z"];
src.forEach(function (item, index) {
    ViewModel.data.letters.push({
        letter: item,
        group: index % 3
    });
});

ViewModel.data.groupedLetters = ViewModel.data.letters.createGrouped(
    function (item) { return item.group.toString(); },
    function (item) { return "Group " + item.group; },
    function (g1, g2) { return g1 - g2; }
);
})();
```

I have defined a new property in the ViewModel.data namespace called groupedLetters to which I assign the result from the List.createGrouped method. The createGrouped method returns a new List object in which the items are organized by group. The createGrouped method takes three functions, which you use to provide the information about the grouping for each item.

The first function returns the key of the group that an item belongs to. It is called for each item in the data source and you must return a string. In my example, I am able to return the string value of the group property I defined for each data item.

The second function is called once for the first item in each group. The result is the text description you want to assign to the group. I have gone for a simple variation of the numeric value of the group property, so that I return the names Group 1, Group 2, and so on. Note that you are passed a complete data item, so you can generate the group description using any characteristic of the data item you choose.

The third function is used to sort the groups. You are passed the keys for two groups are you are required to return a numeric value. Returning a value of 0 indicates that the groups have equal rank, returning a value less than zero indicates that the first group should be displayed before the second, and returning a value greater than zero indicates that the second group should be displayed before the first. Since my group keys are numeric, I can just return the result of subtracting one from the other to get the effect I want.

Applying the Group Data Source

I am going to switch between the regular data source and the group data source in response to the ToggleSwitch control labeled Groups in the middle panel. You can see the code I have added to the /js/pages/listview.js that responds when the switch position is changed in Listing 10.

Listing 15-10. Adding support for switching between data sources

```
(function () {

    WinJS.UI.Pages.define("/pages/ListView.html", {
        ready: function () {

            var proxyObject = WinJS.Binding.as({
                layout: "Grid",
                groups: false,
                groupHeaderPosition: "top",
                maxRows: 3,
                ensureVisible: null,
                searchFor: null,
            });

            Templates.createControls(midPanel, list, "listView1", proxyObject);
            Templates.createControls(rightPanel, list, "listView2", proxyObject);

            proxyObject.bind("layout", function (val) {
                list.winControl.layout = val == "Grid" ?
                    new WinJS.UI.GridLayout() : new WinJS.UI.ListLayout();
            });

            proxyObject.bind("maxRows", function (val) {
                list.winControl.layout.maxRows = val;
            });

            proxyObject.bind("groups", function (val) {
                if (val) {
                    var groupDataSource = ViewModel.data.groupedLetters;
                    list.winControl.itemDataSource = groupDataSource.dataSource;
                    list.winControl.groupDataSource = groupDataSource.groups.dataSource;
                } else {
                    list.winControl.itemDataSource = ViewModel.data.letters.dataSource;
                    list.winControl.groupDataSource = null;
                }
            });
        }
    });
})();
```

To display grouped data, I must update two properties: itemDataSource and groupDataSource. The itemDataSource property is used to obtain the items that will be displayed and the groupDataSource property is used to get information about the way that the items are grouped together.

The first step is to set the itemDataSource property so that it points at the dataSource property of the *grouped* List object. The second step is to set the groupDataSource to the groups.dataSource property of the *grouped* List object.

■ **Note** This causes a lot of confusion and bears emphasis: you must use the *grouped* data source for *both* the itemDataSource and groupDataSource properties.

The itemDataSource property is set to the List.dataSource property, following the same syntax as for regular data sources. The groupDataSource property is set to the List.groups.dataSource property - notice the addition of groups in the path to the property. With these two properties set, the ListView control will display the data source items in groups and show the headers for each group as shown in Figure 15-4.

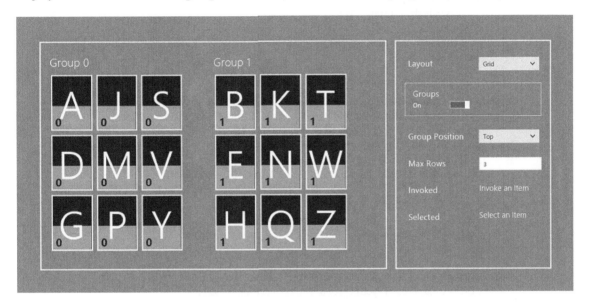

Figure 15-4. Displaying grouped data

To make it easier to see the groups, I temporarily adjusted the layout of the app by entering the following statements into the JavaScript Console window after navigating to the ListView.html page:

```
rightPanel.style.display = "none";
list.style.width = "800px"
```

When you switch back to the regular (ungrouped) data source, you must set the groupDataSource property to null. The app will throw an exception if you do not, because the data source lacks the structure it needs to associate the groups with the individual data items.

Setting the Header Position

As you can see in Figure 15-4, a header is displayed for each group above the set of items. You can change this position through the groupHeaderPosition property, which is defined by the GroupLayout object (rather than by the ListView control itself). The select element in the middle panel can be used to change the position of the group headers and you can see the code I added to the /js/pages/listview.js file to responds when a new select value is picked in Listing 15-11.

363

Listing 15-11. Adding support for changing the group header position

```
(function () {

    WinJS.UI.Pages.define("/pages/ListView.html", {
        ready: function () {

            var proxyObject = WinJS.Binding.as({
                layout: "Grid",
                groups: false,
                groupHeaderPosition: "top",
                maxRows: 3,
                ensureVisible: null,
                searchFor: null,
            });

            Templates.createControls(midPanel, list, "listView1", proxyObject);
            Templates.createControls(rightPanel, list, "listView2", proxyObject);

            proxyObject.bind("layout", function (val) {
                list.winControl.layout = val == "Grid" ?
                    new WinJS.UI.GridLayout() : new WinJS.UI.ListLayout();
            });

            proxyObject.bind("maxRows", function (val) {
                list.winControl.layout.maxRows = val;
            });

            proxyObject.bind("groupHeaderPosition", function (val) {
                list.winControl.layout.groupHeaderPosition = val;
            });

            proxyObject.bind("groups", function (val) {
                // ...code removed for brevity...
            });
        }
    });
})();
```

The supported values for the groupHeaderPosition property are top (the default) and left. You can see how the left value alters the layout in Figure 15-5. Displaying the header at the top of the group can reduce the number of rows in the grid, so left setting is useful when it is more important to have those rows, even though the grid itself will be wider and require more horizontal scrolling.

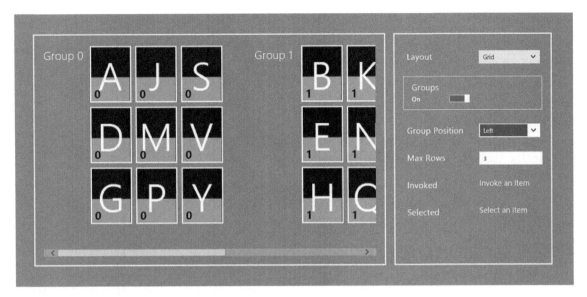

Figure 15-5. Displaying the group header to the left of the group

Using a Group Header Template

The ListView just displays the group header as a string by default, but you can customize the appearance by supplying a custom template. However, requires an adjustment to the data source so that the group key can be used with a WinJS binding template. You can see the changes UI have made to the group data in the /js/viewmodel.js file in Listing 15-12.

Listing 15-12. Changing the group data to support using a header template

```
...
ViewModel.data.groupedLetters = ViewModel.data.letters.createGrouped(
    function (item) { return item.group.toString(); },
    function (item) {
        //return "Group " + item.group;
        return {
            title: "Group " + item.group
        };
    },
    function (g1, g2) { return g1 - g2; }
);
...
```

The problem is that the WinJS data binding system doesn't have a mechanism to allow you to refer to the data object passed to the render method of the Template control. (See Chapter 8 for details of how to use data binding templates). To work around this, I need to change the result of the second function that I passed to the createGrouped method so that it returns an object with a property that I can refer to in the data binding.

In Listing 15-13, you can see the template I have added to the ListView.html file and the way I have used the groupHeaderTemplate property in the data-win-options attribute to associated the template with the ListView control. I have also added a style element which applies to the elements created from the template.

Listing 15-13. Adding and applying a group header template to the ListView.html file

```
<!DOCTYPE html>
<html>
<head>
    <title></title>
    <link href="/css/listview.css" rel="stylesheet">
    <script src="/js/pages/listview.js"></script>
    <style>
        .groupHead {border: thin solid white;background-color: black;
            color: white;padding: 5px;font-weight: bold;}
    </style>
</head>
<body>
    <div id="ItemTemplate" data-win-control="WinJS.Binding.Template">
        <div class="listItem">
            <div class="listData" data-win-bind="innerText: letter"></div>
            <div class="listTitle" data-win-bind="innerText: group"></div>
        </div>
    </div>

    <div id="GroupHeaderTemplate" data-win-control="WinJS.Binding.Template">
        <div class="groupHead" data-win-bind="innerText: title"></div>
    </div>

    <div id="listViewContainer" class="flexContainer">
        <div class="controlPanel">
            <div id="list" data-win-control="WinJS.UI.ListView"
                data-win-options="{ itemTemplate: ItemTemplate,
                    groupHeaderTemplate: GroupHeaderTemplate,
                    itemDataSource: ViewModel.data.letters.dataSource}">
            </div>
        </div>

        <div id="midPanel" class="controlPanel"></div>
        <div id="rightPanel" class="controlPanel"></div>
    </div>
</body>
</html>
```

There is nothing special about the template - it follows all of the conventions I showed you in Chapter 8 and used for the item templates for the ListView and FlipView controls. You can see the result in Figure 15-6, where I have shown the group header, generated from the template, in both positions.

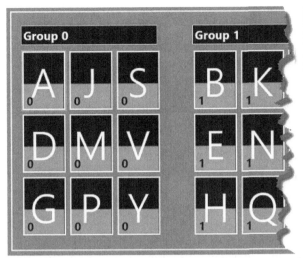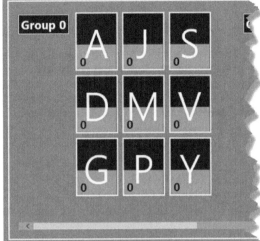

Figure 6. Displaying a group header using a template

Handling the ListView Events

The ListView control defines the four events I have described in Table 15-2. For the most part, these events relate to user interaction, which I explain in the following sections.

Table 15-2. The events supported by the ListView control

Event	Description
contentanimating	Triggered when the ListView is animating a change in the content – see Chapter 18 for details of animations in Windows apps.
iteminvoked	Triggered when the user selects a single item
selectionchanged	Triggered when the user changes the set of selected items
selectionchanging	Triggered during the selection interaction as the user adds or excludes items from the selection

Dealing with Invoked Items

The iteminvoked event is triggered when the user selects an item by tapping it or clicking it with the mouse. The object passed to the event handler function is an IItemPromise, which is a regular Promise that returns an IItem object when it is fulfilled (and which I described in Chapter 9). In Listing 15-14, you can see how I have used the IItemPromise to update the span element labeled Invoked in the middle panel.

Listing 15-14. Handling the iteminvoked event

```
...
list.addEventListener("iteminvoked", function (e) {
    e.detail.itemPromise.then(function (item) {
        invoked.innerText = item.data.letter;
        $('.invoked').removeClass("invoked");
        WinJS.Utilities.addClass(e.target, "invoked");
```

```
        });
    });
    ...
```

There is no visual cue to show which item has been invoked and so, if you want to make it clear to the user, you will have to handle this yourself. In the example, I apply the invoked class to the element representing the item which has been invoked (and, since only one item can be invoked at once, make sure that no other elements belong to the class). The invoked class corresponds to the styles in the /css/ listview.css file I showed you at the start of the chapter. I have repeated the styles in in Listing 15-15.

Listing 15-15. Defining styles for invoked items

```
...
*.invoked {color: red;}
*.invoked .listData { font-weight: bold;}
*.invoked .listTitle {background-color: transparent;}
...
```

You can see the result in Figure 15-7 which shows the same item in its normal and invoked states. You don't have to indicate invoked items, however, especially if it conflicts with the selection of items, which I describe in the following section.

Figure 15-7. Marking an invoked item for the user

Setting the Tap Behavior

You can change the way that the ListView responds to the user tapping an item by changing the value of the tapBehavior property. This property can be set to one of the values in the WinJS.UI.TapBehavior enumeration, which I have described in Table 15-3.

Table 15-3. The values defined by the TapBehavior enumeration

Value	Description
directSelect	The item is invoked and selected
toggleSelect	The item is invoked and selected if it was not already selected. If it was already selected, then the item is deselected.
invokeOnly	The item is invoked but not selected
none	The item is not invoked and not selected

These values define the relationship between invoking and selecting items. If you just want to have the user invoke items, then the value you should use is invokeOnly. If you want the user to be able to select, but not invoke items, then you should use the none value. The other values allow an item to be invoked and selected at the same time. I explain item selection in the next section.

You can change the value of the tapBehavior property by picking a value from the select element in the right-hand panel of the app layout labeled, obviously enough, tapBehavior.

Handling Item Selection

Users can select items as well as invoke them. This can lead to some complex interactions, and so it is important to configure the ListView so that you get just the effect you are looking for. You do this by using the tapBehaviour property I mentioned in the previous section and the selectionMode property, which is set using values from the WinJS.UI.SelectionMode enumeration. I have described the values in this enumeration in Table 15-4.

■ **Tip**   You can change the value of the selectionMode property by picking a value from the select element in the right-hand panel of the app layout labeled selectionMode.

Table 15-4. The values defined by the SelectionMode enumeration

Value	Description
none	The user cannot select items
single	The user can only select one item. Selecting a new item deselects the previously selected item
multi	The user can select multiple items. Selecting a new item adds it to the selection

You can receive notification when the selection has changed by listening for the selectionchanged event. When the selectionMode is set to multi, you can receive updates as the user adds items to the selection by listening for the selectionchanging event. You can see how I have defined a handler for selectionchanged in Listing 15-16.

Listing 15-16. Handling the selectionchanged event

```
...
list.addEventListener("iteminvoked", function (e) {
    e.detail.itemPromise.then(function (item) {
        invoked.innerText = item.data.letter;
        $('.invoked').removeClass("invoked");
```

```
        WinJS.Utilities.addClass(e.target, "invoked");
    });
});

list.addEventListener("selectionchanged", function (e) {
    this.winControl.selection.getItems().then(function (items) {
        var selectionString = "";
        items.forEach(function (item) {
            selectionString += item.data.letter + ", ";
        });
        selected.innerText = selectionString.slice(0, -2);
    });
});
...
```

The set of items that the user has selected is available through the selected property, which returns an ISelection object. This object defines some useful methods for working with the selected items, which I have described in Table 15-5.

Table 15-5. *The methods defined by the ISelection interface*

Method	Description
add([])	Adds items to the selection, specified as an array of index values. This method returns a Promise which is fulfilled when the selection has been changed.
clear()	Clear the selection. This method returns a Promise that is fulfilled when the selection has been cleared
count()	Returns the number of items in the selection
getIndices()	Returns an array of the index values of the selection items
getItems()	Returns an array of IItem objects that represent the selected items
getRanges()	Returns an array of ISelection objects that represent each contiguous range of selected items in the overall selection
isEverything()	Returns true if the selected items represent the complete set of items in the data source
remove([])	Removes items from the selection, expressed by an array of index values. This method returns a Promise object which is fulfilled when the selection has been changed.
set([])	Replaces the existing selection with the set of items that correspond to the index values specified by the argument array. This method returns a Promise object which is fulfilled when the selection has been changed.
selectAll()	Selects all of the items.

In the listing, I use the getItems method to get the set of selected items in order to build a value I can set in the view model to display the selection in the right panel of the example. The getItems method returns an array of IItem objects, each of which corresponds to a selected item. As you will recall from Chapter 14, the IItem makes its content available via a Promise, which is why I have to use the then method to get the details of each item (see Chapter 9 for more details of Promise objects). The ListView adds emphasis to selected items so that the user can see the overall selection, as shown in Figure 15-8. Notice that the item for the letter D is selected *and* invoked.

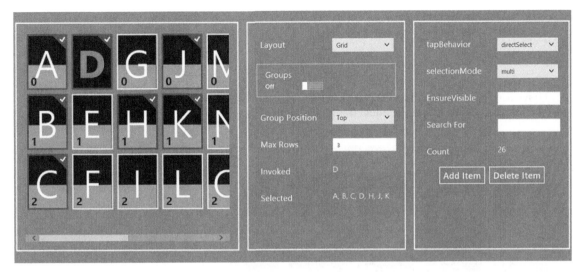

Figure 15-8. The emphasis added to selected items by the ListView control

Styling the ListView Control

The ListView supports a number of classes that you can use to style different aspects of the control's appearance, as summarized in Table 15-6.

Table 15-6. The ListView CSS classes

Class	Description
win-listview	Styles the entire ListView control
win-groupheader	Styles the group header elements in a ListView
win-item	Styles the individual items
win-progress	Styles the progress indicator displayed when data is loading
win-selectionbackground	Styles the backgrounds of selected elements
win-selectioncheckmark	Styles the checkmark applies to selected elements
win-viewport	Styles the ListView viewport area

Not all of these CSS classes are unique to the ListView control – you will notice that the win-item class, for example, is shared with the FlipView control I described in Chapter 14. When applying these styles, you will need to make sure that you narrow the focus to just the elements to which the ListView control has been applied. In Listing 15-17 you can see the addition I made to the style element in the ListView.html file to demonstrate these styles.

Listing 15-17. Styling the ListView selection using CSS

```
...
<style>
    .groupHead {border: thin solid white;background-color: black;
        color: white;padding: 5px;font-weight: bold;}
```

```
    .win-selectioncheckmark {
        color: red; font-size: 20pt;
    }
</style>
...
```

I have used the win-selectioncheckmark class to change the size and color of the check displayed on selected items and you can see the effect this has in Figure 15-9.

Figure 15-9. Using CSS to style the ListView control

Managing the ListView Control Programmatically

You can control the behavior of the ListView using a number of different methods and properties. I have already described some of these, such as the add, remove and set methods available through the selection property, as well as the itemTemplate and groupHeaderTemplate properties to control how data items are displayed. Table 15-7 shows some additional methods and properties that are useful when driving the behavior of a ListView control from code.

Table 15-7. Useful methods and properties for managing the ListView

Method/Property	Description
currentItem	Gets or sets the item which receives the keyboard focus
indexOfFirstVisible	Gets or sets the index of the first visible item
indexOfLastVisble	Gets or sets the index of the last visible item
elementFromIndex(index)	Returns the DOM element that is used to display the data item at the specified index
ensureVisible(index)	Ensures that the item at the specified index is visible to the user
indexOfElement(elem)	Returns the index of the specified DOM element

I tend not to use the indexOfElement and elementFromIndex methods because I prefer to let the ListView control deal with the appearance and layout of its contents. The other methods, however, can be very useful, especially when you are driving the ListView from external UI controls. As an example, I included an input element in the right panel of the example which is labeled Ensure Visible. Listing 15-18 shows the code I have added to the /js/pages/listview.js file to call the ensureVisible method when the content of the input element is changed.

Listing 15-18. *Calling the ensureVisible method*

```
...
proxyObject.bind("ensureVisible", function (val) {
    list.winControl.ensureVisible(val == null ? 0 : val);
});
...
```

If you set the value in the input element to 26, for example, you will see the ListView scroll its content so that the letter Z is visible.

Searching for Elements

Users don't typically think about data items by their index, so as a related example I defined another input element in the right-hand panel labeled Search For. In Listing 15-19, you can see the code I have added to the /js/pages/listview.js file that responds when a value is entered into the input element by locating the corresponding item and selecting it. This is a simple technique, but is one that is needed so often that I wanted to include it in this chapter for your future reference.

Listing 15-19. *Locating and selecting an item by its content*

```
...
proxyObject.bind("searchFor", function (val) {
    if (val != null) {
        var index = -1;
        ViewModel.data.letters.forEach(function (item) {
            if (item.letter == val.toUpperCase()) {
                index = ViewModel.data.letters.indexOf(item);
            }
        });
        if (index > -1) {
            list.winControl.ensureVisible(index);
            list.winControl.selection.set([index]);
        }
    }
});
...
```

The first part of the code locates the index of the item in the data source that matches the letter entered by the user in the input element. If there is a match, I use the index to set the ListView selection and ensure that the selected item is visible. In Figure 15-10, you can see what happens when you enter the letter J into the Search For input element.

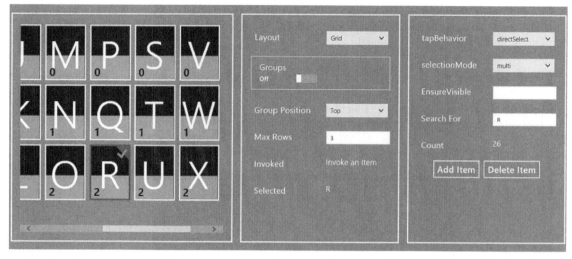

Figure 15-10. Searching for the letter J

Working with the Data Source

In my example, the data source for the ListView control is a WinJS.Binding.List object. This is a convenient arrangement because it means that I can alter the data displayed by the ListView by manipulating the contents of the List.

While this is convenient, it isn't that realistic. You may not be able to modify the data through such a helpful side-channel or even know what kind of data source you are dealing with. In these situations, you need to rely on the functionality defined by the IListDataSource interface. This interface defines the methods that all data sources must implement and you can rely on these methods being defined by the object returned by the ListView.itemDataSource property. I have described the methods defined by IListDataSource in Table 15-8.

Table 15-8. Methods defined by the IListDataSource interface

Method	Description
beginEdits()	Instructs the data source to suppress events while data items are modified.
change(key, newItem)	Replaces the item at the specified key with newItem. This method returns a Promise which is fulfilled when the change is complete.
endEdits()	Instructs the data source to resume emitting events when the data source changes
getCount()	Returns a Promise which passes the number of items in the data source as the result (which can be received using the then method)
insertAfter(newKey, newItem, existingKey)	Inserts newItem into the data source using the specified key. The new item will be inserted after the item which has the key existingKey. This method returns a Promise which is fulfilled when the insertion is complete.
insertBefore(newKey, newItem, existingKey)	As for insertAfter, except that the new item is inserted before the item which has the existingKey key.

Method	Description
insertAtStart(key, item)	Inserts the specified item at the first position in the data source, using the specified key. This method returns a Promise which is fulfilled when the insertion is complete.
insertAtEnd(key, item)	As for insertAtStart, except that the item is appended to the data source.
itemFromKey(key)	Returns a Promise whose result is the item with the specified key. You can access the item by using the then method.
itemFromIndex(index)	Returns a Promise whose result is the item at the specified index. You can access the item by using the then method.
moveAfter(key, prevKey)	Moves the item with the specified key so that it follows the item whose key is prevKey. This method returns a Promise which is fulfilled when the move has been completed.
moveBefore(key, beforeKey)	As for moveAfter, except that the item is placed before the item whose key is beforeKey.
moveToEnd(key)	Moves the item with the specified key to the last position in the data source. This item returns a Promise which is fulfilled when the move has been completed.
moveToStart(key)	As for moveToEnd, except that the specified item is moved to the first position in the data source.
remove(key)	Removes the item with the specified key from the data source. This method returns a Promise which is fulfilled when the removal has been completed.
createListBinding(handler)	Establishes the handler object to receive notifications when there are changes to the data source.

I have defined two button elements in the right-hand panel of the example, labeled Add Item and Delete Item. You can see the code I added to the /js/pages/listview.js file to handle the click event from these buttons in Listing 15-20. In this code, I use methods from the IListDataSource interface to edit the contents of the data source.

Listing 15-20. Editing the contents of a data source using the IListDataSource methods

```
...
$(".buttonContainer button").listen("click", function (e) {
    var ds = list.winControl.itemDataSource;
    ds.beginEdits();
    var promise;
    if (this.innerText == "Add Item") {
        promise = ds.insertAtEnd(null, { letter: "A", group: 4 });
    } else {
        promise = ds.remove("1");
    }
    promise.then(function () {
        ds.endEdits();
    });
});
...
```

If you click the Add Item button, a new data item is added to the data source and displayed by the ListView control – this item always has the letter A and belongs to group 4. If you click the Delete Item button, the element at index 1 is removed.

Dealing with Keys

If you look through the methods in the table, you will notice that keys place an important part in identifying items in the data source. I have not had to worry about keys so far because they are assigned automatically by the List object, but they come to the surface when you work directly with the data source.

The WinJS.Binding.List object follows a simple system for generating keys, based on order in which items are added to the list. The first item is assigned a key of 1, the second 2, and so on. Keys are expressed as string values, so if you want to locate a key by its index, you have to use "1" and not the numeric value. You can see how I have used the key value in response to the Delete Item button being clicked:

```
...
promise = ds.remove("1");
...
```

This method call removes the item which was added to the List first. However, keys are not changed when the contents of the data source are altered, so clicking the button a second time will generate an error because there is no item with the specified key in the data source.

This is a very common error to make when working with List objects as data sources because it is easy to assume the key refers to the index of the element, rather than the order in which it was added. To delete the first item, I need to take a different approach, as shown in Listing 15-21, which obtains an item by position, then gets the key and uses it to request the removal.

Listing 15-21. Removing an item based on its position in the data source

```
...
$(".buttonContainer button").listen("click", function (e) {
    var ds = list.winControl.itemDataSource;
    ds.beginEdits();
    var promise;
    if (this.innerText == "Add Item") {
        promise = ds.insertAtEnd(null, { letter: "A", group: 4 });
    } else {
        //promise = ds.remove("1");
        promise = ds.itemFromIndex(0).then(function (item) {
            return ds.remove(item.key);
        });
    }
    promise.then(function () {
        ds.endEdits();
    });
});
...
```

The result from the Promise returned by the itemFromIndex method is an IItem object, which I introduced in Chapter 14. This object helpfully includes the key, which I can pass to the remove method. Notice that almost all of the methods defined by the IListDataSource interface return a Promise. You need to be use the `Promise.then` method to chain together actions that operate on the contents of a data source – see Chapter 9 for full details of the `Promise` object and how to use the `then` method.

Adding Items without Keys

Clicking on the `Add Item` button adds a new item to the data source. I don't want to have to worry about generating unique keys for my data objects, so I set the first argument to the `insertAtEnd` method to `null`, like this:

```
...
promise = ds.insertAtEnd(null, { letter: "A", group: 4 });
...
```

This tells the data source implementation object (which is the `List` in my example) that it should generate a key using its standard algorithm.

Suppressing Update Events

Data sources will emit events each time an item is changed and this causes the `ListView` to update its layout so that it stays in sync with the data. This is great functionality, but it means that you need to explicitly disable these events if you are making multiple edits – if you don't then the `ListView` will update itself after each change, which is a resource intensive operation and may result in the user being presented with an inconsistent or confusing view of the data items.

You disable the events using the `beginEdits` method. I have done this in the example, even though I am only editing one item (I find it good practice to always call `beginEdits` so that I don't have problems if I update my editing code later). Once you have called this method, you are free to make sweeping changes to the data source without having to worry about unwanted `ListView` updates.

You must make sure to call the `endEdits` method when you finish the edits. The data source won't send any events and the `ListView` won't be updated if you forget. You need to ensure that all of the editing operations have been completed before calling `endEdits`, and this means keeping track of the `Promise` objects that the `IListDataSource` methods return and using the `then` method to chain the method call at the right time. You can see how I have done this in Listing 15-22.

Listing 15-22. Using the then method to ensure that the endEdits method has the right effect

```
...
$(".buttonContainer button").listen("click", function (e) {
    var ds = list.winControl.itemDataSource;
    ds.beginEdits();
    var promise;
    if (this.innerText == "Add Item") {
        promise = ds.insertAtEnd(null, { letter: "A", group: 4 });
    } else {
        //promise = ds.remove("1");
        promise = ds.itemFromIndex(0).then(function (item) {
            return ds.remove(item.key);
        });
    }
    promise.then(function () {
        ds.endEdits();
    });
```

```
});
...
```

If you call the endEdits method before the edit operations have finished, then you will see per-change updates in the ListView for the last few edits you have made, which defeats the point of calling beginEdits in the first place.

Listening for Changes in the Data Source

You can receive notifications of changes in the data source by using the createListBinding method. The argument to this method is an object that implements methods defined by the IListNotificationHandler interface, which I have described in Table 15-9.

Table 15-9. Methods defined by the IListNotificationHandler interface

Method	Description
changed(newItem, oldItem)	Indicates that newItem has replaced oldItem in the data source
countChanged(newCount, oldCount)	Indicates that the number of items in the data source has changed from oldCount to newCount items.
indexChanged(key, newIndex, oldIndex)	Indicates that the item with the key has moved from oldIndex to newIndex.
inserted(promise, prevKey, nextKey)	Indicates than an item has been inserted between the items whose keys are prevKey and nextKey. The promise argument is a Promise object that returns an IItem when it is fulfilled.
moved(promise, prevKey, nextKey)	Indicates that an item was moved so that it is now between the items whose keys are prevKey and nextKey. The promise argument is a Promise object that returns an IItem when it is fulfilled.
removed(key)	Indicates that the item with the specified key was removed.

The way that you listen for events is slightly odd and the best way to explain is with an example. Listing 15-23 shows the handler that I defined in the example.

Listing 15-23. Using a notification handler with a data source

```
...
var handler = {
    countChanged: function (newCount, oldCount) {
        itemCount.innerText = newCount;
    }
};
list.winControl.itemDataSource.createListBinding(handler);
...
```

The first step is to create an object which defines methods that match those in the table. You can see in the listing that I defined a method called countChanged which has two arguments – this matches the countChanged method defined by the IListNotificationHandler interface.

Once you have implemented the methods you are interested in, you pass the handler object to the createListBinding method. From this point, the handler methods will be invoked when there are changed in the data source. In my example, my countChanged method will be executed when the number of items in the data source changes. You can cause this to happen by clicking the Add Item or Delete Item buttons and see the result displayed next to the Count label in the right panel of the example.

Summary

In this chapter, I have shown you the ListView control, which is a rich and complex UI control. The layout and template system allows you to control how your items are laid out and I explained the difference between invoking and selecting items and the events that relate to each of them. I finished this chapter by showing you how to work with the data source, rather than manipulating the implementation object directly. This allows you to create code that will work with any data source and not just those based on the WinJS.Binding.List object. In the next chapter, I will show you how to use semantic zoom, which is combines different WinJS UI controls to create a key Windows interaction.

CHAPTER 16

■ ■ ■

Using Semantic Zoom

In this chapter, I describe the last of the WinJS UI controls, which is called SemanticZoom. This control represents one of the key user interactions in Windows and allows the user to zoom between two levels of detail in a data set. The control itself is relatively simple and relies on a pair of ListView controls to do all the hard work (I described in ListView control in Chapter 15). In this chapter, I show you how to use the SemanticZoom and demonstrate an alternative approach which shows two levels of detail simultaneously. Table 16-1 provides the summary for this chapter.

Table 16-1. Chapter Summary

Problem	Solution	Listing
Set the foundation for using SemanticZoom control	Define two ListView controls and configure them so that they display just the groups and the groups and data.	1-8
Apply the SemanticZoom control	Set the data-win-control attribute to WinJS.UI. SemanticZoom on the div element which is the parent to the two ListView controls	9
Receive notifications when the user zooms between the two views	Listen for the zoomchanged event	10
Simultaneously display two levels of detail for a data source	Use two ListView controls without employing a SemanticZoom control	11-14
Keep the ListView controls in the alternative approach in sync	Listen for the iteminvoked and scroll events and ensure that the appropriate elements in the other ListView are visible.	15-19

When to use the SemanticZoom Control

The SemanticZoom control should only be used when data can be meaningfully grouped into categories, because this is the basis on which navigation and context are provided. I say *meaningfully* grouped because it is important to represent the data in a way that makes sense to the user and the task they are performing with the data. It is easy to apply groups to data just to make using a SemanticZoom feasible, but the result is a little bewildering to the user who has to work with data that is organized in a nonsensical way. You may wish to read this entire chapter before using the SemanticZoom control: aside from details of how to use the SemanticZoom, I also demonstrate an alternative approach which is useful for data sets where the way in which the data has been grouped is less immediately obvious to the user.

Adding the SemanticZoom Example

The SemanticZoom control is relatively simple because it builds on the functionality of the ListView control. The SemanticZoom control is easiest to demonstrate with a larger data set, so I have started by making some additions to the /js/viewmodel.js file, as shown in Listing 16-1.

Listing 16-1. Adding data to the viewmodel.js file

```
(function () {
    "use strict";

    WinJS.Namespace.define("ViewModel", {
        data: {
            images: new WinJS.Binding.List([
                { file: "/images/data/aster.jpg", name: "Aster"},
                { file: "/images/data/carnation.jpg", name: "Carnation"},
                { file: "/images/data/daffodil.jpg", name: "Daffodil"},
                { file: "/images/data/lily.jpg", name: "Lilly"},
            ]),

            extraImages: [{ file: "/images/data/orchid.jpg", name: "Orchid"},
                { file: "/images/data/peony.jpg", name: "Peony"},
                { file: "/images/data/primula.jpg", name: "Primula"},
                { file: "/images/data/rose.jpg", name: "Rose"},
                { file: "/images/data/snowdrop.jpg", name: "Snowdrop" }],

            letters: new WinJS.Binding.List(),
            groupedLetters: null,
            names: new WinJS.Binding.List(),
            groupedNames: null,
        },
    });

    // ...code for previous chapters removed for brevity...

    var namesSrcData = ['Aaliyah', 'Aaron', 'Abigail', 'Abraham', 'Adam', 'Addison',
    'Adrian', 'Adriana', 'Aidan', 'Aiden', 'Alex', 'Alexa', 'Alexander', 'Alexandra',
    'Alexis', 'Allison', 'Alyssa', 'Amelia', 'Andrew', 'Angel', 'Angelina',
    'Anna', 'Anthony', 'Ariana', 'Arianna', 'Ashley', 'Aubrey', 'Austin', 'Ava',
    'Avery', 'Ayden', 'Bella', 'Benjamin', 'Blake', 'Brandon', 'Brayden', 'Brian',
    'Brianna', 'Brooke', 'Bryan', 'Caleb', 'Cameron', 'Camila', 'Carter', 'Charles',
    'Charlotte', 'Chase', 'Chaya', 'Chloe', 'Christian', 'Christopher', 'Claire',
    'Connor', 'Daniel', 'David', 'Dominic', 'Dylan', 'Eli', 'Elijah', 'Elizabeth',
    'Ella', 'Emily', 'Emma', 'Eric', 'Esther', 'Ethan', 'Eva', 'Evan', 'Evelyn',
    'Faith', 'Gabriel', 'Gabriella', 'Gabrielle', 'Gavin', 'Genesis', 'Gianna',
    'Giovanni', 'Grace', 'Hailey', 'Hannah', 'Henry', 'Hunter', 'Ian', 'Isaac',
    'Isabella', 'Isaiah', 'Jack', 'Jackson', 'Jacob', 'Jacqui', 'Jaden', 'Jake',
    'James', 'Jasmine', 'Jason', 'Jayden', 'Jeremiah', 'Jeremy', 'Jessica', 'Joel',
    'John', 'Jonathan', 'Jordan', 'Jose', 'Joseph', 'Joshua', 'Josiah', 'Julia',
    'Julian', 'Juliana', 'Julianna', 'Justin', 'Kaitlyn', 'Katherine', 'Kayla',
    'Kaylee', 'Kevin', 'Khloe', 'Kimberly', 'Kyle', 'Kylie', 'Landon', 'Lauren',
```

```
'Layla', 'Leah', 'Leo', 'Liam', 'Lillian', 'Lily', 'Logan', 'London', 'Lucas',
'Luis', 'Luke', 'Mackenzie', 'Madeline', 'Madelyn', 'Madison', 'Makayla', 'Maria',
'Mason', 'Matthew', 'Max', 'Maya', 'Melanie', 'Mia', 'Michelle', 'Miriam', 'Molly',
'Morgan', 'Moshe', 'Naomi', 'Natalia', 'Natalie', 'Nathan', 'Nathaniel', 'Nevaeh',
'Nicholas', 'Nicole', 'Noah', 'Oliver', 'Olivia', 'Owen', 'Paige', 'Patrick',
'Peyton', 'Rachel', 'Rebecca', 'Richard', 'Riley', 'Robert', 'Ryan', 'Samantha',
'Samuel', 'Sara', 'Sarah', 'Savannah', 'Scarlett', 'Sean', 'Sebastian', 'Serenity',
'Sofia', 'Sophia', 'Sophie', 'Stella', 'Steven', 'Sydney', 'Taylor', 'Thomas',
'Tristan', 'Tyler', 'Valentina', 'Victoria', 'Vincent', 'William', 'Wyatt',
'Xavier', 'Zachary', 'Zoe', 'Zoey'];

namesSrcData.forEach(function (item, index) {
    ViewModel.data.names.push({name: item, firstLetter: item[0]
    });
});

ViewModel.data.groupedNames = ViewModel.data.names.createGrouped(
    function (item) { return item.firstLetter; },
    function (item) { return item; },
    function (g1, g2) { return g1 < g2 ? -1 : g1 > g2 ? 1 : 0; }
);
})();
```

The data that I will be working with is a list of names. These are the most popular names for babies in the state of New York in 2011.

I begin by processing the list of names in order to populate the WinJS.Binding.List object I assigned to the names property in the ViewModel.data namespace. For each name, I create an object which has a name property and a firstLetter property. I assign the complete name to the name property and, as the name might suggest, the first character of the name to the firstLetter property (this will make it a little easier for me to organize the data into groups later). So, for the name Sophie, for example, I create an object in the ViewModel.data.names List like this:

```
...
{
    name: "Sophie",
    firstLetter: "S"
}
...
```

I use the data objects in the ViewModel.data.names List to create grouped data, using the same technique that I showed you in Chapter 15. As you'll see, groups play an important part when using the SemanticZoom control. In this case, I have grouped the items by their first letter, so that all of the names that begin with A are in the same group, as are all the names that begin with B and so on. The grouped data is available through the ViewModel.data.groupedNames property.

Defining the HTML File

To demonstrate the SemanticZoom control I have created a new file called SemanticZoom.html in the pages folder of the Visual Studio project. You can see the contents of this file in Listing 16-2.

Listing 16-2. The initial contents of the SemanticZoom.html file

```html
<!DOCTYPE html>
<html>
<head>
    <title></title>
    <link href="/css/listview.css" rel="stylesheet">
    <link href="/css/semanticzoom.css" rel="stylesheet">
    <script>
        WinJS.UI.Pages.define("/pages/SemanticZoom.html", {
            ready: function () {
                Templates.createControls(rightPanel, semanticZoomer, "semanticZoom");
            }
        });
    </script>
</head>
<body>
    <div id="zoomedInItemTemplate" data-win-control="WinJS.Binding.Template">
        <div class="zoomedInListItem">
            <div class="zoomedInListData" data-win-bind="innerText: name"></div>
        </div>
    </div>

    <div id="zoomedOutItemTemplate" data-win-control="WinJS.Binding.Template">
        <div class="listItem">
            <div class="listData" data-win-bind="innerText: firstLetter"></div>
        </div>
    </div>

    <div id="groupHeaderTemplate" data-win-control="WinJS.Binding.Template">
        <div>Letter: <span data-win-bind="innerText: firstLetter"></span></div>
    </div>

    <div id="semanticZoomContainer" class="flexContainer">
        <div class="controlPanel">
            <div id="semanticZoomer">
            </div>
        </div>

        <div id="rightPanel" class="controlPanel"></div>
    </div>
</body>
</html>
```

This file contains the standard two-panel layout that I have used for most of the examples in this part of the book and three templates that I will use to demonstrate the features of the SemanticZoom control. The one thing is doesn't contain is any reference to the SemanticZoom control itself – that's because it is easier for me to explain how this control works by showing you the underlying building blocks and then add the control later.

The JavaScript for this example consists of just a call to the Templates.createControl method, so I have included it in script element within the HTML file.

Defining the CSS

There are two link elements in the SemanticZoom.html file. The first is to the /css/listview.css file that I created in Chapter 15 and which contains the styles I defined for the templates I used to display the data – I use these styles again in this chapter for the same purpose. The second link element refers to a new file I added to the Visual Studio project called /css/semanticzoom.css, and it contains some additional styles I use for the SemanticZoom control. You can see the contents of the semanticzoom.css file in Listing 16-3. There are no new techniques in this file – I just set the size of the element to which I will be applying the SemanticZoom control and define some basic styles for one of the underlying controls that SemanticZoom relies on (which I'll explain shortly).

Listing 16-3. The contents of the semanticzoom.css file

```
#semanticZoomer {
    width: 500px; height: 500px;
}


*.zoomedInListItem {
    width: 150px;
}


*.zoomedInListData { background-color: black; text-align: center;
    border: solid medium white; font-size: 20pt; padding: 10px;
}
```

Completing the Example

You can see the definitions objects that I added to the /js/controls.js file in Listing 16-4. The SemanticZoom control is relatively simple, and you can see the reflected in the small number of configuration controls I have defined.

Listing 16-4. The definition objects for the controls.js file

```
...
semanticZoom: [
    { type: "toggle", id: "enableButton", title: "EnableButton", value: true },
    { type: "toggle", id: "locked", title: "Locked", value: false },
    { type: "toggle", id: "zoomedOut", title: "Zoomed Out", value: false },
    { type: "input", id: "zoomFactor", title: "Zoom Factor", value: 0.65 },
],
...
```

The last step is to ensure that the user can navigate to the SemanticZoom.html file, which I do by making the addition shown in Listing 16-5 to the /js/templates.js file.

Listing 16-5. Adding support for navigating to the SemanticZoom.html file

```
var navBarCommands = [
    //{ name: "AppTest", icon: "target" },
    { name: "ToggleSwitch", icon: "\u0031" },
    { name: "Rating", icon: "\u0032" },
    { name: "Tooltip", icon: "\u0033" },
```

```
    { name: "TimePicker", icon: "\u0034" },
    { name: "DatePicker", icon: "\u0035" },
    { name: "Flyout", icon: "\u0036" },
    { name: "Menu", icon: "\u0037" },
    { name: "MessageDialog", icon: "\u0038" },
    { name: "FlipView", icon: "pictures" },
    { name: "Listview", icon: "list" },
    { name: "SemanticZoom", icon: "zoom" },
];
```

If you run the example app at this point and navigate to the SemanticZoom.html page you will see the app layout shown in Figure 16-1. The panel structure and the configuration controls are in place, but there are no controls in the left-hand panel. In the sections that follow, I'll show you how to apply the SemanticZoom control.

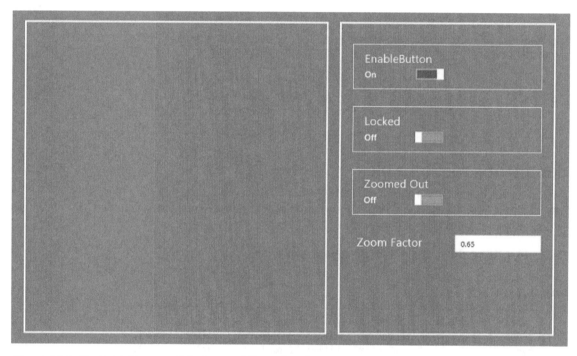

Figure 16-1. The initial layout of the SemanticZoom.html page

Understanding the SemanticZoom Control

The SemanticZoom control presents the user with a choice of two views of the same data – a *zoomed-in* view, which shows individual data items arranged in groups, and a *zoomed-out* view which just shows the groups but no data items. The user can use the zoomed-out view to navigate their way around large and complex sets of data and then dive into the detail of a particular group.

The best way to show you how to apply the SemanticZoom is to start by focusing on how the two views are created, which relies on two instances of the WinJS.UI.ListView control, which I described in Chapter

15. In the sections that follow, I'll show you how to create the underlying `ListView` controls and then how to apply the `SemanticZoom` control to coordinate and their behavior and appearance.

Creating the Zoomed In ListView Control

The `SemanticZoom` control relies on two `ListView` controls to represent the zoomed in and zoomed out views of the data. You can see how I have defined the zoomed in view in Listing 16-6, which I have added to the `SemanticZoom.html` file.

Listing 16-6. Defining the zoomed in ListView control

```
...
<div id="semanticZoomer">
    <div id="zoomedInList" data-win-control="WinJS.UI.ListView"
        data-win-options="{itemTemplate: zoomedInItemTemplate,
            itemDataSource: ViewModel.data.groupedNames.dataSource,
            groupDataSource: ViewModel.data.groupedNames.groups.dataSource,
            groupHeaderTemplate: groupHeaderTemplate}">
    </div>
</div>
...
```

To create the zoomed-in view, set the `itemDataSource` to the `dataSource` of the grouped data source and the `groupDataSource` property to the `groups.dataSource` object. This sets up the `ListView` so that the data items are displayed in groups and are shown with a group header. (This is the same technique I used when I described the `ListView` control in Chapter 15.)

You set up the `itemTemplate` and `groupHeaderTemplate` with regular templates to display the items and the group headers. These are the templates that I defined in the `SemanticZoom.html` file and I have listed them again in Listing 16-7.

Listing 16-7. The item and display templates for the zoomed in ListView control

```
...
<div id="zoomedInItemTemplate" data-win-control="WinJS.Binding.Template">
    <div class="zoomedInListItem">
        <div class="zoomedInListData" data-win-bind="innerText: name"></div>
    </div>
</div>
...
<div id="groupHeaderTemplate" data-win-control="WinJS.Binding.Template">
    <div>Letter: <span data-win-bind="innerText: firstLetter"></span></div>
</div>
...
```

If you run the example and navigate to the `SemanticZoom.html` file at this point, you will be able to see the effect of adding and configuring the `ListView` control, as shown in Figure 16-2. I still don't have the `SemanticZoom` control yet, but one of the two views of the data are in place.

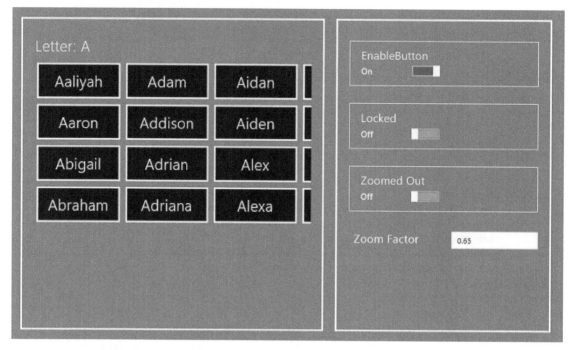

Figure 16-2. Adding the zoomed-in view to the SemanticZoom.html file

Creating the Zoomed Out ListView Control

The next step is to add the ListView control that will display the zoomed-out view, displaying the list of groups to the user without showing any of the data item in those groups. You can see the addition I have made to the SemanticZoom.html file to add the ListView control in Listing 16-8.

Listing 16-8. Adding the ListView control for the zoomed-out view

```
...
<div id="semanticZoomer">
    <div id="zoomedInList" data-win-control="WinJS.UI.ListView"
        data-win-options="{itemTemplate: zoomedInItemTemplate,
            itemDataSource: ViewModel.data.groupedNames.dataSource,
            groupDataSource: ViewModel.data.groupedNames.groups.dataSource,
            groupHeaderTemplate: groupHeaderTemplate}">
    </div>
    <div id="zoomedOutList" data-win-control="WinJS.UI.ListView"
        data-win-options="{itemTemplate: zoomedOutItemTemplate,
            itemDataSource: ViewModel.data.groupedNames.groups.dataSource}">
    </div>
</div>
...
```

This ListView will only display the groups, which means that I have to use the *group data source* as the value for the itemDataSource property. This is a neat trick because it allows the ListView control to display the zoomed-out data without it needing to understand the structure of the data it is working with – it is the SemanticZoom control, which I'll add to the example shortly, which provides the context and correlates the two views of the data.

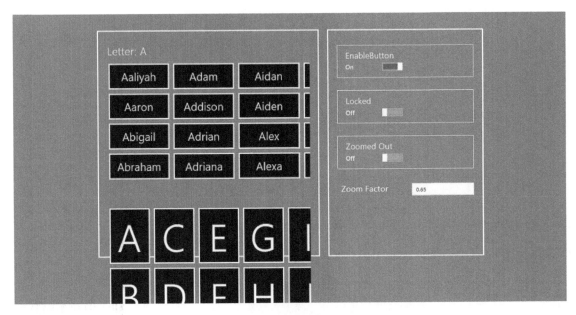

Figure 16-3. Both ListView controls displayed in the app layout

If you run the example at this point, you will be able to see both ListView controls in the app layout, as shown in Figure 16-3.

Depending on your device resolution, there may not be enough space in the layout to display both ListView controls, so one of them may flow over the bottom of the screen. Even so, this is an opportunity to make sure that they have been configured properly before the SemanticZoom control is applied and starts managing the visibility of the controls.

Applying the SemanticZoom Control

The SemanticZoom control is applied to a div element by setting the data-win-control attribute to WinJS. UI.SemanticZoom, where the div element contains the ListView controls that display the two views of the data.

When you have the ListView controls set up and displaying the data in the way you want, you can add the SemanticZoom control. You can see how I have done this in the SemanticZoom.html file in Listing 16-9.

■ **Note** The order in which the ListView controls are declared inside of the SemanticZoom div element is important – the zoomed-in view must appear before the zoomed-out view.

Listing 16-9. Applying the SemanticZoom control

```
...
<div class="controlPanel">
    <div id="semanticZoomer" data-win-control="WinJS.UI.SemanticZoom">
        <div id="zoomedInList" data-win-control="WinJS.UI.ListView"
            data-win-options="{itemTemplate: zoomedInItemTemplate,
                itemDataSource: ViewModel.data.groupedNames.dataSource,
                groupDataSource: ViewModel.data.groupedNames.groups.dataSource,
                groupHeaderTemplate: groupHeaderTemplate}">
        </div>
        <div id="zoomedOutList" data-win-control="WinJS.UI.ListView"
            data-win-options="{itemTemplate: zoomedOutItemTemplate,
                itemDataSource: ViewModel.data.groupedNames.groups.dataSource}">
        </div>
    </div>
</div>
...
```

The result of applying the SemanticZoom control is that only one of the ListView elements and, initially, this is the zoomed in view. If you move your mouse over the SemanticZoom control, you will see a small button appear above the scrollbar. In Figure 16-4, you can see the zoomed-in view and I have highlighted the button to make it easier to see (it isn't that obvious until you know it is there).

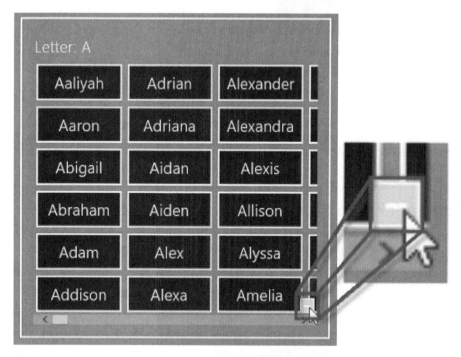

Figure 16-4. The zoomed-in view and the zoom out button.

Clicking the button will cause the SemanticZoom control to animate the transition to the zoomed-out view, allowing the user to navigate through the data at the group level, as shown in Figure 16-5.

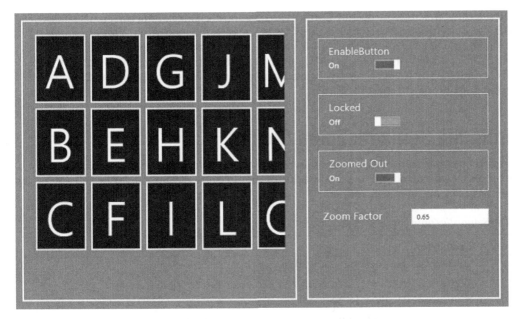

Figure 16-5. The zoomed-out view shown by the SemanticZoom control

If you click on a group, then the SemanticZoom control will animate the transition back to the zoomed-in view, displaying the items in the group you have selected.

Navigating between the SemanticZoom views

I showed you the zoom-out button because it is hard to notice without a hint, but there are several different ways in which you can navigate between the two views shown in by the SemanticZoom control. If you have a mouse with a scroll wheel, you can hold down the Control key and move the mouse wheel up to zoom in and down to zoom out. If you prefer to use the keyboard then you can use Control and the plus key (+) to zoom in and Control and the minus key (-) to zoom out.

If you are a touch user, then you can zoom in and out using the pinch/zoom touch gesture. I return to the topic of touch gestures in detail in Chapter 17, but the Visual Studio simulator will allow you to perform pinch/zoom gestures if you select the button I have highlighted in Figure 16-6.

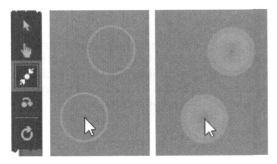

Figure 16-6. The pinch gesture simulation button and display

When you select the pinch/zoom gesture button, you cursor will change to the two empty circles shown in the figure, each of which represents a finger. Press and hold the mouse buttons to simulate touching the screen with the fingers – the cursor will change so that the circles become filled, as shown in the final frame of the figure. Use the mouse scroll wheel to move the simulated fingers closer together or further apart, creating the pinch/zoom gesture. Bring the fingers together to make the SemanticZoom control zoom out and move them apart to zoom in.

Configuring the SemanticZoom Control

The SemanticZoom control supports the configuration properties that I have described in Table 16-2. This is a small set of properties compared with other WinJS UI controls because the complexity in a SemanticZoom is delegated to the ListView controls it relies on.

Table 16-2. *The SemanticZoom configuration properties*

Event	Description
enableButton	When true, the SemanticZoom displays a button for zooming out
locked	When true, the SemanticZoom will not allow the user to zoom in or out
zoomedOut	Gets or sets whether the SemanticZoom is zoomed out
zoomFactor	Sets the relative scale of the zoomed out view, which affects the transition animation

I have defined configuration controls in the right panel of the example to demonstrate all four of the SemanticZoom properties. The locked and zoomedOut properties are self-evident, but I explain the other two properties in the sections that follow.

Enabling and Disabling the Zoom Out Button

The enableButton property controls the visibility of the zoom out button I showed you in Figure 16-4. I have included a ToggleSwitch in the right panel of the example that changed the enableButton property on the SemanticZoom control.

The default for this property is true, meaning that the SemanticZoom control will display the button. Setting the property to false will prevent the button from being displayed, but the user will still be able to navigate between the views using the other techniques I described in the previous section. If you want to prevent the user from switching between views, then set the locked property to true instead.

Setting the Zoom Factor

As you will have noticed, the SemanticZoom control switches between views using an animation and the zoomFactor property determines how dramatic that animation is. The value can be between 0.2 and 0.85 and the default is 0.6. I can't demonstrate an animation on the printed page, but smaller values result in a more dramatic zoom effect. I prefer a more subtle animation, which means that if I change the default, it is usually to a value of 0.8, which creates an effect that clearly indicates a transition without being too striking.

Handling the SemanticZoom Control Event

The SemanticZoom control defines one event, which is emitted when the control switches between zoom levels. I have described this event in Table 16-3.

Table 16-3. The event supported by the SemanticZoom control

Event	Description
zoomchanged	Triggered when the user zooms in or out

You can see how I have handled this event in Listing 16-10. When the event is triggered, I update a property in the view model, which has the effect of keeping the ToggleSwitch configuration control labeled Zoomed Out in step with the state of the SemanticZoom.

Listing 16-10. Handling the SemanticZoom event

```
...
<script>
    WinJS.UI.Pages.define("/pages/SemanticZoom.html", {
        ready: function () {
            Templates.createControls(rightPanel, semanticZoomer, "semanticZoom");

            semanticZoomer.addEventListener("zoomchanged", function (e) {
                zoomedOut.winControl.checked = e.detail;
            });
        }
    });
</script>...
```

The detail property of the Event object passed to the handler function is set to true when the SemanticZoom is zoomedOut and false when it is zoomed in.

■ **Tip** You respond to user interaction with the zoomed in ListView by handling events from that control directly. See Chapter 15 for details of the events that the ListView uses to send notifications when items are invoked or selected.

Styling the SemanticZoom Control

Most of the styling for a SemanticZoom is done through the templates used by the underlying ListView controls (which I described in Chapter 15). There are two classes, however, that can be used to style this control directly, as described in Table 16-4.

Table 16-4. The SemanticZoom CSS classes

Class	Description
win-semanticzoom	Styles the entire SemanticZoom control
win-semanticzoomactive	Styles the active view displayed by the SemanticZoom control

I don't use these styles in my projects. If I want to apply general styling, then I target the parent element which contains the SemanticZoom control (this is the div element with the id of semanticZoomContainer in my example and I generally have an equivalent container element in all of my content). If I want to style a more specific part of the layout, then I target the ListView controls or, often, rely on the item and group header templates to get the effect I want.

An Alternative to the SemanticZoom Control

To my mind, the interaction presented by the SemanticZoom control has a flaw, which is that the overall context presented by the zoomed out view is lost when the zoomed in view is displayed. This isn't a problem when the context can be inferred from the data, which is the case for my name data. You can see what I mean in Figure 16-7.

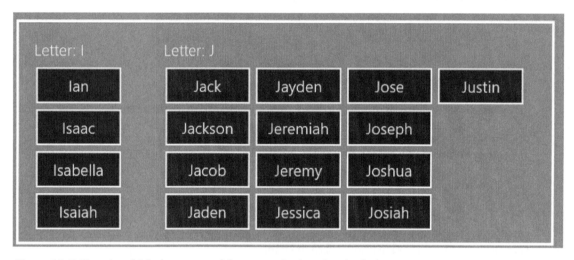

Figure 16-7. Data in which the nature of the groups is abundantly obvious

I only have to show you one or two groups for it to become obvious that the data is grouped alphabetically and that, given the groups that are shown, that the SemanticZoom is showing data that is close to 50% through the data source. In these situations, the SemanticZoom control is perfect because everything the user needs to know is shown, or can be readily inferred, from the layout.

■ **Note**   The following sections show how to connect the two ListView controls together. However, it can be hard going to wade through all the references to the zoomed in and zoomed out views. My advice is to follow these sections in Visual Studio so that you can see the effect of each change – it will give context to the descriptive text.

There are times when this approach doesn't work and you want to display both views at once so that the overall context and the detail are both visible at the same time. I find myself with this problem reasonably frequently and I solve it by replacing the SemanticZoom control with two ListView controls and some event handler code.

Creating the List Context Example

To demonstrate arrangement of the two ListView controls, I have added a new file to the pages directory of the example project called ListContext.html, the contents of which are shown in Listing 16-11.

Listing 16-11. The contents of the ListContext.html file

```html
<!DOCTYPE html>
<html>
<head>
    <title></title>
    <link href="/css/semanticzoom.css" rel="stylesheet">
    <link href="/css/listcontext.css" rel="stylesheet">
    <script src="/js/pages/listcontext.js"></script>
</head>
<body>
    <div id="contextZoomedInItemTemplate" data-win-control="WinJS.Binding.Template">
        <div class="zoomedInListItem">
            <div class="zoomedInListData" data-win-bind="innerText: name"></div>
        </div>
    </div>

    <div id="contextZoomedOutItemTemplate" data-win-control="WinJS.Binding.Template">
        <div class="contextListItem">
            <div class="contextListData" data-win-bind="innerText: firstLetter"></div>
        </div>
    </div>

    <div id="contextGroupHeaderTemplate" data-win-control="WinJS.Binding.Template">
        <div>Letter: <span data-win-bind="innerText: firstLetter"></span></div>
    </div>

    <div id="contextContainer">
        <div id="zoomedOut" data-win-control="WinJS.UI.ListView"
            data-win-options="{
                itemDataSource: ViewModel.data.groupedNames.groups.dataSource,
                itemTemplate: contextZoomedOutItemTemplate,
                layout: {type: WinJS.UI.ListLayout}}">
        </div>

        <div id="zoomedIn" data-win-control="WinJS.UI.ListView"
            data-win-options="{
                itemDataSource: ViewModel.data.groupedNames.dataSource,
                groupDataSource: ViewModel.data.groupedNames.groups.dataSource,
                itemTemplate: contextZoomedInItemTemplate,
                groupHeaderTemplate: contextGroupHeaderTemplate}">
        </div>
    </div>
</body>
</html>
```

This file contains two ListView elements which use the same data source that I defined for the SemanticZoom control. Like the SemanticZoom example, I have used one ListView to display the data items in groups (to create the zoomed-in view) and one ListView to display just the groups themselves (to create the zoomed-out view).

Defining the CSS

I have reused the semanticzoom.css file in this example so that don't have to refine the styles I use in the template. I also added the /css/listcontext.css file to out the ListView objects and define some additional styles I'll use later in the chapter. You can see the contents of the listcontext.css file in Listing 16-12. There are no new techniques in this file and all of the styles are simple and use standard CSS.

Listing 16-12. The content of the listcontext.css file

```css
#contextContainer { height: 100%; display: -ms-flexbox;
    -ms-flex-direction: row; -ms-flex-align: center; -ms-flex-pack: center;
}

#contextContainer div[data-win-control="WinJS.UI.ListView"] {
    border: thick solid white; height: 650px; padding: 20px; margin: 10px;
}

#zoomedOut { width: 200px;}
#zoomedIn { width: 900px; padding: 20px;}
#zoomedIn .win-groupheader {display: none;}

*.contextListItem {width: 170px;}
*.contextListData { background-color: black; text-align: center;
    border: solid medium white; font-size: 20pt;}

*.highlighted { color: #4cff00; font-weight: bold;}
*.notHighlighted { color: white; font-weight: normal;
    -ms-transition-delay: 100ms; -ms-transition-duration: 500ms;}
```

Defining the JavaScript Code

The JavaScript code for this example is in the /js/pages/listcontext.js file. To start with, this file contains just an empty self-executing function, but I'll add code as I work through the example. You can see the initial content for this file in Listing 16-13.

Listing 16-13. The initial content of the listcontext.js file

```javascript
(function () {

WinJS.UI.Pages.define("/pages/ListContext.html", {
    ready: function () {
        // ...code will go here...
    }
});

})();
```

There are no definition objects for this example because I don't need to demonstrate any specific UI control features. This means that the only additional step I need to take is to ensure that the user can navigate to the ListContext.html file through the NavBar, which I have done with the addition to the /js/ templates.js file shown in Listing 16-14.

Listing 16-14. Enabling navigation to the ListContext.html file via the NavBar

```
...
var navBarCommands = [
    //{ name: "AppTest", icon: "target" },
    { name: "ToggleSwitch", icon: "\u0031" },
    { name: "Rating", icon: "\u0032" },
    { name: "Tooltip", icon: "\u0033" },
    { name: "TimePicker", icon: "\u0034" },
    { name: "DatePicker", icon: "\u0035" },
    { name: "Flyout", icon: "\u0036" },
    { name: "Menu", icon: "\u0037" },
    { name: "MessageDialog", icon: "\u0038" },
    { name: "FlipView", icon: "pictures" },
    { name: "Listview", icon: "list" },
    { name: "SemanticZoom", icon: "zoom" },
    { name: "ListContext", icon: "list" },
];
...
```

If you run the example and navigate to the ListContext.html file, you will see the layout shown in Figure 16-8. The two ListView controls are in place and populated with data, but they are not yet linked together, so there is no interaction between them when you invoke individual items.

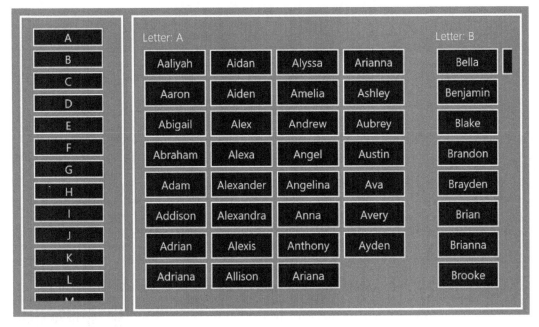

Figure 16-8. The layout of the ListContext.html file

Adding the Event Handler Code for the List Context Example

The building blocks for this example are in place – what remains is purely JavaScript to create the relationship between the two ListView controls, emulating the basic behavior of the SemanticZoom control but ensuring that the user can see the both the context of the groups and the fine detail of individual elements. In the sections that follow, I add the required code to the /js/pages/listcontext.js file and explain how each addition builds a key part of the interactions between the ListView controls.

Selecting Groups from the Zoomed Out ListView Control

The first thing I want to do is respond to an item being invoked in the zoomed out-view by displaying the corresponding group in the zoomed in view. You can see how I have done this in Listing 16-15, where I have added a function to handle the iteminvoked event in the ListContext.js file.

Listing 16-15. Handling invoked items in the zoomed out view

```
(function () {

WinJS.UI.Pages.define("/pages/ListContext.html", {
    ready: function () {

        zoomedOut.addEventListener("iteminvoked", function (e) {
            e.detail.itemPromise.then(function (item) {
                var invokedGroup = item.key;
                zoomedIn.winControl.groupDataSource.itemFromKey(invokedGroup)
                .then(function (item) {
                    var index = item.firstItemIndexHint;
                    zoomedIn.winControl.indexOfFirstVisible = index;
                });
            });
        });
    }
});

})();
```

As you will recall from Chapter 15, the iteminvoked event is triggered when the user clicks on an item. The detail property of the Event object passed to the handler function is a Promise object which returns the item when it is fulfilled. I use the then method to get the item and get the key of the invoked item using the key property.

The key property tells me which group the user has invoked. To display this group in the zoomed-in view, I use the itemFromKey method on the grouped data source. This gives me another Promise which returns an item when it fulfilled. The difference is that the item returned from a grouped data source contains a firstItemIndexHint property that returns the index of the first item in the group. I ensure that the group that the user invoked in the zoomed-out view is displayed in the zoomed-in view by setting the value of the indexOfFirstVisible property, which causes the ListView to jump to the correct position in the data.

The result of this addition is that invoking an item in the zoomed-out ListView will cause the corresponding group to be displayed to the user in the zoomed-in ListView. You can see the effect of invoking the J group in the zoomed-out view in Figure 16-9.

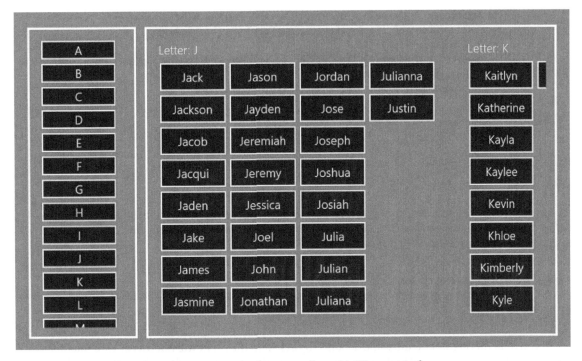

Figure 16-9. The effect of invoking a group in the zoomed-out ListView control

Responding to Scrolling in the Zoomed-In ListView Control

I now want to set up the complementary relationship, so that scrolling the content in the zoomed-in ListView is reflected in the zoomed-out view. I do this by adding a handler function for the scroll event on the zoomed-in ListView control in the ListContext.js file, as shown in Listing 16-16

Listing 16-16. Adding a scroll event handler for the zoomed-in ListView control

```
(function () {

WinJS.UI.Pages.define("/pages/ListContext.html", {
    ready: function () {

        zoomedOut.addEventListener("iteminvoked", function (e) {
            e.detail.itemPromise.then(function (item) {
                var invokedGroup = item.key;
                zoomedIn.winControl.groupDataSource.itemFromKey(invokedGroup)
                .then(function (item) {
                    var index = item.firstItemIndexHint;
                    zoomedIn.winControl.indexOfFirstVisible = index;
                });
            });
        });

        zoomedIn.addEventListener("scroll", function (e) {
```

```
                var firstIndex = zoomedIn.winControl.indexOfFirstVisible;
                zoomedIn.winControl.itemDataSource.itemFromIndex(firstIndex)
                .then(function (item) {
                    zoomedOut.winControl.itemDataSource.itemFromKey(item.groupKey)
                    .then(function (item) {
                        zoomedOut.winControl.ensureVisible(item.index);
                    });
                });
            }, true);
        }
    });

})();
```

To receive the scroll event from a ListView control you have to set the optional third argument to the addEventListener method to true, so that the event bubbles up from the element contained in the ListView that generates the event (known as the viewport):

```
...
zoomedIn.addEventListener("scroll", function (e) {
        //...function statements go here...
}, true);
...
```

If you omit this argument, the value defaults to false and the event will not trigger your handler function. In my code, I respond to the scroll event by reading the value of the indexOfFirstVisible property to Figure 16-out which element is left-most in the zoomed in ListView.

I use this index of this element to obtain the data item itself by calling the itemFromIndex method on the data source – this is another method that returns a data item when a Promise is fulfilled.

Once I have the item, I use the groupKey property (which is defined on items which are in grouped data sources) to identify the left-most group and make sure that the corresponding item is visible in the zoomed-out ListView. The result is that both ListView items are now in sync. If you invoke an item in the zoomed out view, the corresponding group will be shown in the zoomed in view. Equally, as you scroll the zoomed in view, the item representing the currently displayed group is always visible.

Dealing with the Last Item

I don't quite have the effect I want yet. The code that I have written ensures that the zoomed out item that corresponds to the first group in the zoomed in ListView is visible, but it doesn't handle the last few groups in the data source very well. You can see the issue in Figure 16-10, which shows the effect when I scroll the zoomed-in ListView to show the final groups of elements.

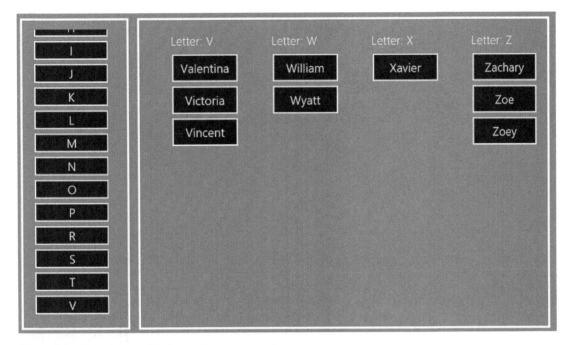

Figure 16-10. *An issue with the last few groups of content*

As the Figure 16-shows, the zoomed-out `ListView` doesn't show items that correspond to the last few groups in the zoomed-in view. To remedy this, I need to make an addition to the event handler code to specifically check for the last groups in the display, as shown in Listing 16-17.

Listing 16-17. *Ensuring that the last groups are handled correctly*

```
(function () {

WinJS.UI.Pages.define("/pages/ListContext.html", {
    ready: function () {

        zoomedOut.addEventListener("iteminvoked", function (e) {
            e.detail.itemPromise.then(function (item) {
                var invokedGroup = item.key;
                zoomedIn.winControl.groupDataSource.itemFromKey(invokedGroup)
                .then(function (item) {
                    var index = item.firstItemIndexHint;
                    zoomedIn.winControl.indexOfFirstVisible = index;
                });
            });
        });

        zoomedIn.addEventListener("scroll", function (e) {

            var firstIndex = zoomedIn.winControl.indexOfFirstVisible;
            var lastIndex = zoomedIn.winControl.indexOfLastVisible;
```

```
            zoomedIn.winControl.itemDataSource.getCount().then(function (count) {
                var targetIndex = lastIndex == count - 1 ? lastIndex : firstIndex;

                zoomedIn.winControl.itemDataSource.itemFromIndex(targetIndex)
                .then(function (item) {
                    zoomedOut.winControl.itemDataSource.itemFromKey(item.groupKey)
                    .then(function (item) {
                        zoomedOut.winControl.ensureVisible(item.index);
                    });
                });
            });
        }, true);
    }
});

})();
```

The difference from the last example is that I check to see if the last item in the data source is visible by using the ListView control's count method and the indexOfLastVisible property, both of which I described in Chapter 15. If the last data item is visible, then I ensure that the zoomed-out view shows the last set of groups. You can see the result of this change in Figure 16-11, in which you can see that scrolling the zoomed-in view to the end of the data set causes the zoomed-out control to display the last few groups.

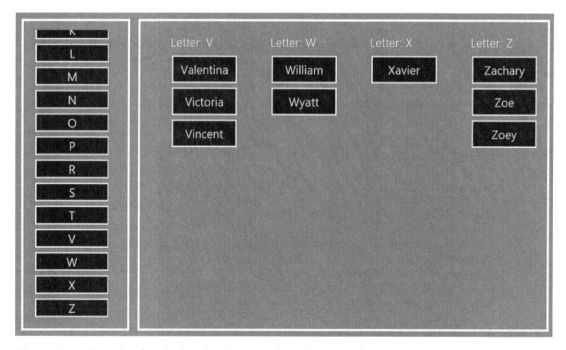

Figure 16-11. Ensuring that the last data items are handled correctly

Emphasizing Transitions in the Zoomed Out Control

It isn't very obvious to the user that the zoomed-out view is kept up-to-date as the zoomed-in view is scrolled. The user's attention will be on the ListView that is being scrolled and they won't always notice subtle changes elsewhere.

To help draw the user's attention and emphasize the bi-directional relationship between the two ListView controls, I am going to add a brief color highlight to the zoomed out ListView when the group shown in the zoomed-in view changes.

To do this, I will be using two styles from the /css/listContext.css file that I added when I created the example earlier in the chapter and which I have shown again in Listing 16-18. These styles use CSS3 transitions which cause the values defined in a style to be applied gradually.

Listing 16-18. Styles for highlighted transitions in the zoomed out view

```
...
*.highlighted {
    color: #4cff00;
    font-weight: bold;
}

*.notHighlighted {
    color: white;
    font-weight: normal;
    -ms-transition-delay: 100ms;
    -ms-transition-duration: 500ms;
}
...
```

Elements to which the highlighted class is applied will have green and bold text. The notHighlighted class reverses these changes, but does so after a 100 millisecond delay and over a direction of 500 milliseconds. To apply these styles, I have made the changes to the /js/pages/listcontext.js file shown in Listing 16-19.

Listing 16-19. Applying CSS styles to emphasize an item in a ListView control

```
...
zoomedIn.addEventListener("scroll", function (e) {

    var firstIndex = zoomedIn.winControl.indexOfFirstVisible;
    var lastIndex = zoomedIn.winControl.indexOfLastVisible;

    zoomedIn.winControl.itemDataSource.getCount().then(function (count) {
        var targetIndex = lastIndex == count - 1 ? lastIndex : firstIndex;

        var promises = {
            hightlightItem: zoomedIn.winControl.itemDataSource.itemFromIndex(firstIndex),
            visibleItem: zoomedIn.winControl.itemDataSource.itemFromIndex(targetIndex)
        };

        WinJS.Promise.join(promises).then(function (results) {
            zoomedOut.winControl.itemDataSource.itemFromKey(results.visibleItem.groupKey)
            .then(function (item) {
```

```
                    zoomedOut.winControl.ensureVisible(item.index);
            });


        zoomedOut.winControl.itemDataSource.itemFromKey(results.hightlightItem.groupKey)
            .then(function (item) {
                var elem = zoomedOut.winControl.elementFromIndex(item.index);
                $('*.highlighted').removeClass("highlighted")
                    .removeClass("notHighlighted");
                WinJS.Utilities.addClass(elem, "highlighted");
                WinJS.Utilities.addClass(elem, "notHighlighted");
            });

        });
    });
}, true);
...
```

I use a feature of the WinJS.Promise.join method which lets you pass an object with properties whose values are Promise objects. The results that the Promise returned by the join methods yields contains the same property names but the value of each is the result yielded by the corresponding Promise you passed in the object – this is a nice alternative to working with array indices.

Otherwise, the code for this addition is simple and I apply the CSS classes to highlight items in the zoomed-out view when the groups displayed by the zoomed-in view change. The effect is so quick that I can't easily show you in a screenshot, but if you start the example app and scroll through the zoomed in content, you will see the flash of emphasis appear in the zoomed out view.

Summary

In this chapter, I showed you the SemanticZoom control, which plays an important role in the overall Windows user experience by tying together two ListView controls and allowing the user to zoom from one to the other to see the same data at two different levels of detail.

I also showed you an alternative approach where the overall context and the detailed view are shown simultaneously. You should use the standard SemanticZoom control when the data you are working with make sense without the broader context being present – to my mind, this means data where the way that groups have been applied and the relative position into the content are self-evident. For other data sets, you should consider using an approach that ensures that the broad context and the fine details are shown side-by-side. In the next chapter, I describe the way that Windows apps can deal with input events and touch gestures.

CHAPTER 17

■ ■ ■

Using Pointers & Gestures

So far in this book, I have relied on the standard DOM events, such as click and moveover to respond to user input. This is a workable approach for simple interactions, but different techniques are required to get the most from Windows apps, especially to support touch gestures, which make it easy for users to express complex commands. In this chapter, I show you how to determine which input technologies are supported on a Windows 8 device, explain how Windows uses a generalized system of *pointers* to represent these inputs and how to recognize touch gestures. Table 17-1 provides the summary for this chapter.

Table 17-1. Chapter Summary

Problem	Solution	Listing
Determine the input capabilities of the current device	Use the objects in the Windows.Devices.Input namespace	1-4
Determine is a keyboard is present	Use the KeyboardCapabilities object	5
Determine the presence and capabilities of the mouse	Use the MouseCapabilities object	6
Determine the presence and capabilities of a touch screen or digitizer	Use the TouchCapabilities object	7
Receive details of touch interactions	Listen for the MSPointer events	8-11
Detect simple gestures	Use the MSGesture object and listen for the MSGestureTap and MSGestureHold events	12-13, 15
Start recognizing a gesture	Pass the value of the pointerId property from a MSPointerDown event to an MSGesture object	14
Detect manipulation gestures	Listen for the MSGestureStart, MSGestureEnd and MSGestureChange events	16-17
Determine the motion the user has made during a manipulation gesture	Read the values of the rotation, scale, translationX and translationY properties from the MSGesture events	18-19
Zoom the content of an element rather than the element itself	Use the content zoom feature by applying the CSS -ms-content-zooming property	20-21
Limit the range that the user can scale content to	Use the -ms-content-zoom-limit-min and -ms-content-zoom-limit-max properties	22
Receive notifications when content is zoomed or set the zoom level programmatically	Listen for the MSContentZoom event and use the msContentZoomFactor property	23

Creating the Example Project

I have created a project called AppInput to demonstrate the different events and gestures that Windows apps can support. I'll be showing each major feature in its own content page, so I have created the familiar app structure of a master content page with a NavBar, which will allow the user to navigate around the app. In Listing 17-1, you can see the contents of the default.html file, which will act as the master page for the example app.

Listing 17-1. The contents of the default.html file

```html
<!DOCTYPE html>
<html>
<head>
    <meta charset="utf-8">
    <title>AppInput</title>
    <link href="//Microsoft.WinJS.1.0/css/ui-dark.css" rel="stylesheet" />
    <script src="//Microsoft.WinJS.1.0/js/base.js"></script>
    <script src="//Microsoft.WinJS.1.0/js/ui.js"></script>
    <link href="/css/default.css" rel="stylesheet">
    <script src="/js/default.js"></script>
</head>
<body>
    <div id="contentTarget">
        <h1>Select a page from the NavBar</h1>
    </div>
    <div id="navbar" data-win-control="WinJS.UI.AppBar"
            data-win-options="{placement:'top'}">
        <button data-win-control="WinJS.UI.AppBarCommand"
            data-win-options="{id:'DeviceCapabilities', label:'Capabilities',
                icon:'\u0031', section:'selection'}">
        </button>
        <button data-win-control="WinJS.UI.AppBarCommand"
            data-win-options="{id:'PointerEvents', label:'Pointer Events',
                icon:'\u0032', section:'selection'}">
        </button>
        <button data-win-control="WinJS.UI.AppBarCommand"
            data-win-options="{id:'Gestures', label:'Gestures',
                icon:'\u0033', section:'selection'}">
        </button>
        <button data-win-control="WinJS.UI.AppBarCommand"
            data-win-options="{id:'Manipulations', label:'Manipulations',
                icon:'\u0034', section:'selection'}">
        </button>
        <button data-win-control="WinJS.UI.AppBarCommand"
            data-win-options="{id:'CSSGestures', label:'CSS Gestures',
                icon:'\u0035', section:'selection'}">
        </button>
    </div>
</body>
</html>
```

This file contains an initial message to the user and NavBar commands which allow the user to navigate to the five content pages that I'll be adding in this chapter. This is a much simpler app structure than I used for the UI controls and I won't need to generate elements from definition objects, for example.

Defining the CSS

The CSS for all of the content pages can be found in the /css/default.css file, the content of which you can see in Listing 17-2. There are no new techniques in this file and I have included it only so you can see every aspect of the example app.

Listing 17-2. The contents of the /css/default.css file

```
body { background-color: #5A8463; display: -ms-flexbox;
    -ms-flex-direction: column; -ms-flex-align: center; -ms-flex-pack: center;}

.container { display: -ms-flexbox; -ms-flex-direction: row;
    -ms-flex-align: stretch; -ms-flex-pack: center; }

.panel { border: medium white solid; margin: 10px; padding: 20px;
    display: -ms-flexbox; -ms-flex-direction: column; -ms-flex-align: stretch;
    -ms-flex-pack: center; text-align: center;}

.sectionHeader { font-size: 30pt; text-align: center; padding-bottom: 10px;}

.coloredRect { background-color: black; color: white; width: 300px; height: 300px;
    margin: 20px; font-size: 40pt; display: -ms-flexbox;
    -ms-flex-direction: column; -ms-flex-align: stretch; -ms-flex-pack: center; }

#eventList { width: 500px; height: 500px;}

.eventDisplay { background-color: #5A8463;}
.pointerDetail, .eventDetail, .primaryDetail {
    display: inline-block; width: 250px; font-size: 20pt; text-align: left;}
.pointerDetail {width: 100px;}
.primaryDetail {width: 75px;}

input.cinput {width: 75px;display: inline-block;margin-left: 20px;font-size: 18pt;}
.imageRect {width: 600px;height: 80vh;}

#capabilitiesContainer div.panel {-ms-flex-pack: start;}
.capabilityTitle {text-align: right; width: 250px; }
span.capabilityResult { text-align: left; font-weight: bold; width: 80px; }
div.capability {font-size: 20pt;width: 350px;}
div.capability > * {display: inline-block;padding-bottom: 10px;}
```

Defining the JavaScript

The /js/default.js file contains the navigation code for the app, using the same pattern that you will now be familiar with. This is a slightly simplified version because the only data bindings that I use in this app are in templates, so I don't have to call the WinJS.Binding.processAll method when I load new content pages. As with my other example pages, the navigation code loads content files from the pages folder of the Visual Studio project. You can see the content of the default.js file in Listing 17-3.

Listing 17-3. The content of the /js/default.js file

```
(function () {
    "use strict";

    var app = WinJS.Application;

    WinJS.Navigation.addEventListener("navigating", function (e) {

        WinJS.UI.Animation.exitPage(contentTarget.children).then(function () {
            WinJS.Utilities.empty(contentTarget);
            WinJS.UI.Pages.render(e.detail.location, contentTarget)
            .then(function () {
                return WinJS.UI.Animation.enterPage(contentTarget.children)
            });
        });
    });

    app.onactivated = function (eventObject) {
        WinJS.UI.processAll().then(function () {
            navbar.addEventListener("click", function (e) {
                var navTarget = "pages/" + e.target.winControl.id + ".html";
                WinJS.Navigation.navigate(navTarget);
            });
        })
    };

    app.start();
})();
```

Figure 17-1 shows the basic layout of the app that you will see if you run the app at this point and bring up the NavBar. In the sections that follow, I'll add content pages to the app to demonstrate the different ways in which apps can support pointers and gestures.

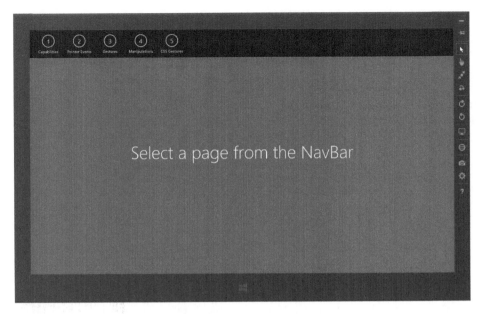

Figure 17-1. *The initial layout of the app*

Determining the Input Capabilities of the Device

The starting point for this chapter is the technique for figuring out what forms of input the user's device supports. You can get this information by using the objects in the `Windows.Devices.Input` namespace, which provides information about the device's support for keyboard, mouse and touch interactions.

Determining what input capabilities are available is useful for tailoring the user experience presented by your app. For example, you may not want to show settings that allow the user to configure keyboard shortcuts if there is no keyboard. (As an aside, I show you how to manage app settings and present them to the user in Chapter 20).

To demonstrate how you determine the device input capabilities, I have added a new file called `DeviceCapabilities.html` to the pages folder of the example Visual Studio project. You can see the content of this file in Listing 17-4.

Listing 17-4. *The contents of the DeviceCapabilities.html file*

```
<!DOCTYPE html>
<html>
<head>
    <title></title>
    <script>
        var input = Windows.Devices.Input;

        WinJS.UI.Pages.define("/pages/DeviceCapabilities.html", {
            ready: function () {
                var kbd = new input.KeyboardCapabilities();
                generateCapabilityPanel("Keyboard", [{
                    name: "Keyboard Present", value: kbd.keyboardPresent == 1
```

```
                }]);
            }
        });

        function generateCapabilityPanel(name, capabilities) {
            panelTemplate.winControl.render({section: name}).then(function (panelElem) {
                WinJS.Utilities.addClass(panelElem, "panel");
                capabilities.forEach(function (capability) {
                    capabilityTemplate.winControl.render(capability)
                    .then(function (capabilityTemplate) {
                        WinJS.Utilities.addClass(capabilityTemplate, "capability");
                        panelElem.appendChild(capabilityTemplate);
                    });
                });
                capabilitiesContainer.appendChild(panelElem);
            });
        }
    </script>
</head>
<body>
    <div id="panelTemplate" data-win-control="WinJS.Binding.Template">
        <h1 class="sectionHeader" data-win-bind="innerText: section"></h1>
    </div>

    <div id="capabilityTemplate" data-win-control="WinJS.Binding.Template">
        <h2 class="capabilityTitle" data-win-bind="innerText: name"></h2>:
        <span class="capabilityResult" data-win-bind="innerText: value"></span>
    </div>

    <div id="capabilitiesContainer" class="container"></div>
</body>
</html>
```

I have used the WinJS.Binding.Template feature to generate a layout which displays the capabilities of the device. The generateCapabilityPanel function accepts a title and a set of capabilities and generates elements in the DOM to show them. I have taken this approach so that I don't have to list reams of HTML markup and because I want to show this form of template binding.

When I call the Template.render method, I receive a Promise object which is fulfilled when new elements have been generated from the template. The object passed to the then function is the top-level element that has been created (this is because I omitted the second argument to the render method which specifies the container element into which the template elements are to be inserted – if I had specified an element, then this container element would be passed to the then function).

I use this approach because the Template control strips out the value of the class attribute when it creates elements from a template. To work around this, I use the WinJS.Utilities.addClass method and inset the template elements into the document using the DOM appendChild method. None of this is directly related to device capabilities, but I couldn't resist showing another approach to using WinJS templates.

Determining the Keyboard Capabilities

You can get information about the keyboard capabilities of the user's device by creating a new `Windows.Devices.Input.KeyboardCapabilities` object. This object defines only one property, which indicates if there is a keyboard present on the device. I have summarized this property in Table 17-2 so that you can find it easily when you return to this chapter later and don't want to read the text to find the property name.

Table 17-2. The property defined by the KeyboardCapabilities object

Property	Description
keyboardPresent	Returns 1 if the device has a hardware keyboard and 0 if not.

You can see how I created the `KeyboardCapabilities` object and read the value of the property in Listing 17-5. Notice that this property returns 1 rather than `true`, and so to get a `true`/`false` value I have to compare the property value to the numeric literal value 1.

Listing 17-5. Detecting the presence of the hardware keyboard

```
...
var kbd = new input.KeyboardCapabilities();
generateCapabilityPanel("Keyboard", [{
    name: "Keyboard Present", value: kbd.keyboardPresent == 1
}]);
...
```

The keyboardPresent property relates to the *hardware* keyboard. Devices which don't have a hardware keyboard still support text input through a software keyboard, which is displayed automatically when the focus is gained by a suitable HTML element (such as `input` or `textarea` elements).

If you run the app at this point and navigate using the Capabilities NavBar command, you will see the content shown in Figure 17-2. The Figure 17-shows the app running on my development PC which, as you might expect, has a keyboard attached.

Figure 17-2. Determining if the device has a keyboard

Determining the Mouse Capabilities

You can get information about the mouse through the `Windows.Devices.Input.MouseCapabilities` object, which defines the properties shown in Table 17-3.

Table 17-3. The properties defined by the MouseCapabilities object

Property	Description
mousePresent	Returns 1 if the device has a mouse and 0 if not.
numberOfButtons	Returns the number of buttons that the mouse has
swapButtons	Returns 1 if the user has swapped the left and right mouse buttons and 0 otherwise.
verticalWheelPresent	Returns 1 if the mouse has a vertical scroll wheel and 0 otherwise
horizontalWheelPresent	Returns 1 if the mouse has a horizontal scroll wheel and 0 otherwise

Be careful not to assume that the user is left-handed just because the SwapButtons property returns 1. If you have an interface that would benefit from left- and right-handed configurations, then take the SwapButtons value as a hint, but ask the user to explicitly confirm they want an alternative configuration. In Listing 17-6, you can see how I determine and display the values of the properties defined by the MouseCapabilities object in the example app in the script element of the DeviceCapabilities.html file.

Listing 17-6. Determining the presence and capabilities of the mouse

```
...
<script>
    var input = Windows.Devices.Input;

    WinJS.UI.Pages.define("/pages/DeviceCapabilities.html", {
        ready: function () {
            var kbd = new input.KeyboardCapabilities();
            generateCapabilityPanel("Keyboard", [{
                name: "Keyboard Present", value: kbd.keyboardPresent == 1
            }]);

            var mouse = new input.MouseCapabilities();
            generateCapabilityPanel("Mouse", [
                { name: "Mouse Present", value: mouse.mousePresent == 1},
                { name: "Buttons", value: mouse.numberOfButtons },
                { name: "Buttons Swapped", value: mouse.swapButtons == 1},
                { name: "Horizontal Wheel", value: mouse.horizontalWheelPresent == 1},
                { name: "Vertical Wheel", value: mouse.verticalWheelPresent == 1}
            ]);
        }
    });

    function generateCapabilityPanel(name, capabilities) {
        panelTemplate.winControl.render({section: name}).then(function (panelElem) {
            WinJS.Utilities.addClass(panelElem, "panel");
            capabilities.forEach(function (capability) {
                capabilityTemplate.winControl.render(capability)
                .then(function (capabilityTemplate) {
                    WinJS.Utilities.addClass(capabilityTemplate, "capability");
                    panelElem.appendChild(capabilityTemplate);
                });
            });
        });
```

```
            capabilitiesContainer.appendChild(panelElem);
        });
    }
</script>
...
```

I advise caution when it comes to making assumptions about the mouse. Although most users use the mouse in a standard way, a surprising number of users reconfigure the way that there mouse operates so that buttons are remapped or macros are executed in certain situations. The quality of the software that reconfigures mouse devices is incredibly variable and the good ones work nicely by remapping the hardware capabilities through the operating system. The badly written code (and there is a lot of it around) uses all sorts of nasty hacks and the input you get from the user won't always correspond to the capabilities reported by Windows. My advice is not to assume that the user will be able to use the vertical scroll wheel, for example, when the verticalWheelPresent property returns 1 – it might well be remapped to some other function entirely and so you should remain flexible about how the navigates around the content in your app. In Figure 17-3, you can see the results of running the app and selecting the Capabilities NavBar command on my development PC.

■ **Tip** The Visual Studio simulator will always report a 2 button mouse without scroll wheels, irrespective of the hardware attached to the PC running the simulator.

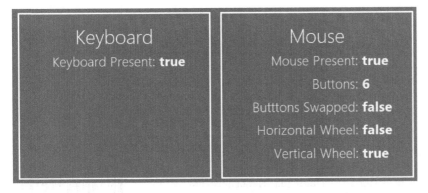

Figure 17-3. Determining the mouse capabilities of the current device

Determining Touch Capabilities

The final category of input is touch, which includes a wide range of device types including touch screen and digitizer tablets. You can see if the device has touch support by using the Windows.Devices.Input. TouchCapabilities object, which defines the properties shown in Table 17-4.

Table 17-4. The properties defined by the TouchCapabilities object

Property	Description
touchPresent	Returns 1 if the device is touch-capable and 0 otherwise.
contacts	Returns the lowest number of simultaneous touch points supported by all touch surfaces

If the device has multiple touch surfaces, then the contacts property returns the number of contact points supported by the least capable one. You can see how I have used the TouchCapabilities object in Listing 17-7, which shows the additions I have made to the script element of the DeviceCapabilities.html file.

■ **Caution**   I find that the TouchPresent property often returns 1 when the device it is describing has more touch points.

Listing 17-7. Using the TouchCapabilities object

```
...
<script>
    var input = Windows.Devices.Input;

    WinJS.UI.Pages.define("/pages/DeviceCapabilities.html", {
        ready: function () {
            var kbd = new input.KeyboardCapabilities();
            generateCapabilityPanel("Keyboard", [{
                name: "Keyboard Present", value: kbd.keyboardPresent == 1
            }]);

            var mouse = new input.MouseCapabilities();
            generateCapabilityPanel("Mouse", [
                { name: "Mouse Present", value: mouse.mousePresent == 1},
                { name: "Buttons", value: mouse.numberOfButtons },
                { name: "Butttons Swapped", value: mouse.swapButtons == 1},
                { name: "Horizontal Wheel", value: mouse.horizontalWheelPresent == 1},
                { name: "Vertical Wheel", value: mouse.verticalWheelPresent == 1}
            ]);

            var touch = new input.TouchCapabilities();
            generateCapabilityPanel("Touch", [
                { name: "Touch Present", value: touch.touchPresent == 1},
                { name: "Contacts", value: touch.contacts }
            ]);
        }
    });

    function generateCapabilityPanel(name, capabilities) {
        panelTemplate.winControl.render({section: name}).then(function (panelElem) {
            WinJS.Utilities.addClass(panelElem, "panel");
            capabilities.forEach(function (capability) {
                capabilityTemplate.winControl.render(capability)
                .then(function (capabilityTemplate) {
                    WinJS.Utilities.addClass(capabilityTemplate, "capability");
                    panelElem.appendChild(capabilityTemplate);
                });
            });
        });
```

```
        capabilitiesContainer.appendChild(panelElem);
    });
    }
</script>
...
```

You can see the results generated by this code in Figure 17-4. I have run the example app on my development PC, to which I attached a cheap digitizer tablet.

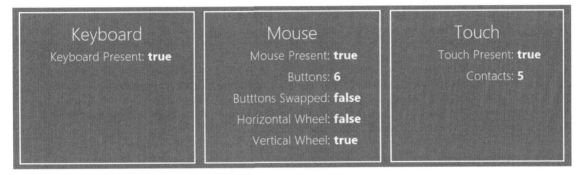

Figure 17-4. Displaying details of the device touch capabilities

Handling Pointer Events

You can quite happily use standard DOM events like click and mouseover in a Windows app. Internet Explorer 10, which is responsible for running JavaScript Windows apps will generate these events irrespective of the input device used to generate them. This means that, for example, a button element will trigger a click event when it is clicked, irrespective of whether the user performed the interaction with a mouse, a finger on a touch screen or a pen on a digitizer. These events are generated by IE10 to provide compatibility with web apps and you can use them quite safely in your app code, as I have been doing in the example apps throughout this book.

However, if you want to work with Windows touch gestures, then you need to use the MSPointer events. These are events which correspond to the standard DOM events that you will know from web app development, but they have additional properties that give details about the type of input that was used. In Table 17-5 I have listed the MSPointer events and described the circumstances under which they are triggered. There is no event called MSPointer – the name refers to the fact that the event names *start* with MSPointer – MSPointerDown, MSPointerUp, etc.

■ **Tip** The MSPointer events are generated alongside the DOM compatibility events. You can listen to a mix of events like MSPointerMove and mousemove without any problems, although there can sometimes be a small delay between the MSPointer event and the standard DOM event being triggered.

Table 17-5. The MSPointer events

Event	Description
MSPointerDown	Triggered when a pointer touches an element on the screen
MSPointerUp	Triggered when a pointer is released from an element on the screen
MSPointerOut	Triggered when a pointer is moved from inside the boundary of an element
MSPointerOver	Triggered when a pointer is moved into the boundary of a screen element
MSPointerMove	Triggered when a pointer is moved
MSPointerHover	Triggered when a pointer is over an element but contact is not made
MSPointerCancel	Triggered when a pointer interaction is canceled

The descriptions for these events are necessarily vague because they deal with a wide range of types of interaction. A pointer can *touch* an element when the user clicks the mouse, when a finger or stylus touches the screen, or some other interaction using a less common device entirely. To demonstrate how these events work, I have added a file to the pages folder of the example Visual Studio project called PointerEvents.html, which you can see in Listing 17-8.

Listing 17-8. The contents of the PointerEvents.html file

```
<!DOCTYPE html>
<html>
<head>
    <title></title>
    <script>
        var input = Windows.Devices.Input;
        var eventList = new WinJS.Binding.List();

        var pointerTypeConverter = WinJS.Binding.converter(function (typeCode) {
            switch (typeCode) {
                case MSPointerEvent.MSPOINTER_TYPE_MOUSE:
                    return "Mouse";
                case MSPointerEvent.MSPOINTER_TYPE_PEN:
                    return "Pen";
                case MSPointerEvent.MSPOINTER_TYPE_TOUCH:
                    return "Touch";
                default:
                    return "Unknown";
            }
        });

        WinJS.UI.Pages.define("/pages/PointerEvents.html", {
            ready: function () {
                var eventTypes = [
                    "MSPointerUp", "MSPointerDown","MSPointerOut",
                    "MSPointerOver","MSPointerCancel","MSPointerHover",
                    /*"MSPointerMove" */
                    "MSGotPointerCapture", "MSLostPointerCapture"];

                eventTypes.forEach(function (eventType) {
```

```
                    targetElem.addEventListener(eventType, function (e) {
                        eventList.unshift(e);
                    }), true;
                });
            }
        });
    </script>
</head>
<body>
    <div id="eventDisplayTemplate" data-win-control="WinJS.Binding.Template">
        <div class="eventDisplay">
            <div class="pointerDetail" data-win-bind="innerText: pointerType
                pointerTypeConverter"></div>
            <div class="eventDetail" data-win-bind="innerText: type"></div>
            <div class="primaryDetail" data-win-bind="innerText: isPrimary"></div>
        </div>
    </div>
    <div id="pointerEventsContainer" class="container">
        <div class="panel">
            <div id="targetElem" class="coloredRect">
                Basic Pointer Events
            </div>
        </div>
        <div id="eventListContainer" class="panel">
            <div id="eventList" data-win-control="WinJS.UI.ListView"
                data-win-options="{itemTemplate: eventDisplayTemplate,
                    layout: {type: WinJS.UI.ListLayout},
                    itemDataSource: eventList.dataSource}">
            </div>
        </div>
    </div>
</body>
</html>
```

This layout of this page consists of a simple colored block which you can interact with in order to generate events. I handle the events by adding them to a WinJS.Binding.List object which is the data source for a ListView control (you can learn about the List object in Chapter 8 and the ListView UI control in Chapter 15). You can see the result in Figure 17-5, which shows the content after a simple interaction.

Figure 17-5. Responding to MSPointer events

You register your interest in the pointer events just like you do regular DOM events – but you must take care to use the right capitalization. The event name is, for example, MSPointerDown and not mspointerdown, MsPointerDown or any other permutation. You can see how I have set up my handler functions in Listing 17-9. I have commented out the MSPointerMove event because any interaction will generate dozens of them and make it hard to spot other event types.

Listing 17-9. Registering a function to handle the MSPointer events

```
...
var eventTypes = [
    "MSPointerUp", "MSPointerDown","MSPointerOut",
    "MSPointerOver","MSPointerCancel","MSPointerHover",
    /*"MSPointerMove" */
    "MSGotPointerCapture", "MSLostPointerCapture"];

eventTypes.forEach(function (eventType) {
    targetElem.addEventListener(eventType, function (e) {
        eventList.unshift(e);
    }), true;
});
...
```

The MSPointer events are not direct equivalents of the ones you known from the HTML DOM, but for the most part they are pretty similar and are triggered in a way that is consistent with mouse-only interaction. So, for example, the MSPointerDown and MSPointerUp events are triggered when the user touches an element on the screen and this is true whether the user has a mouse or a touch screen.

There are two events that are troublesome. The MSPointerHover event is meant to be triggered when a point moves over an element without touching the screen. This sounds sensible, but I can't trigger this event on real hardware – although it is easy to trigger it in the app simulator (just select the Basic Touch Mode button on the right edge of the simulator window and move the mouse pointer over the element).

I can't get the MSPointerCancel event to trigger, either. This event is triggered when a device aborts an interaction and the example that Microsoft gives is when the number of simultaneous touch points exceeds the ability of a touch screen or digitizer to process them. I have tested the code in Listing 17-8 on all of the hardware I can find, and have not been able to get this event to trigger.

Getting Pointer Information

The handler function for an MSPointer event is passed an MSPointerEvent object, which implements all of the methods and properties of a regular DOM Event, but with some additions. Many of the additions are used by the system to work out how multiple events form a gesture, but there are some properties that can be useful more generally and I have described these in Table 17-6.

Table 17-6. The additional members defined by the MSPointerEvent object

Name	Description
hwTimestamp	Returns the time at which the event was created (expressed in milliseconds)
isPrimary	Returns true if this event is from the primary pointer on a multi-touch device
pointerId	Uniquely identifies the pointer. This property is used for recognizing gestures, as described below.
pointerType	Returns the type of pointer
pressure	Returns the pressure applied to the point on a scale from 0 to 255.

You can see how I have displayed some of these properties through my ListView template, as shown in Listing 17-10.

Listing 17-10. Displaying selected MSPointerEvent values in the ListView template

```
...
<div id="eventDisplayTemplate" data-win-control="WinJS.Binding.Template">
    <div class="eventDisplay">
        <div class="pointerDetail" data-win-bind="innerText: pointerType
            pointerTypeConverter"></div>
        <div class="eventDetail" data-win-bind="innerText: type"></div>
        <div class="primaryDetail" data-win-bind="innerText: isPrimary"></div>
    </div>
</div>
...
```

You can generate different types of event in the simulator by selecting different input modes. The buttons on the right side of the emulator window allow you to move between mouse and touch input.

The type of pointer that has caused an MSPointer event to be triggered is available through the pointerType property. This property returns a numeric value which you can compare against an enumeration of such values defined by the MSPointerEvent object. In the example, I used a binding converter to translate the numeric values into meaningful text, as shown in Listing 17-11.

Listing 17-11. Determining the type of an MSPointer event

```
...
var pointerTypeConverter = WinJS.Binding.converter(function (typeCode) {
    switch (typeCode) {
        case MSPointerEvent.MSPOINTER_TYPE_MOUSE:
            return "Mouse";
```

```
        case MSPointerEvent.MSPOINTER_TYPE_PEN:
            return "Pen";
        case MSPointerEvent.MSPOINTER_TYPE_TOUCH:
            return "Touch";
        default:
            return "Unknown";
    }
});
...
```

The values MSPOINTER_TYPE_MOUSE, MSPOINTER_TYPE_PEN and MSPOINTER_TYPE_TOUCH correspond to the values that the pointerType property returns.

■ **Tip**   Events from digitizer tablets are often reported being MSPOINTER_TYPE_MOUSE events instead of as MSPOINTER_TYPE_PEN events. It depends on how the digitizer hardware is recognized – many of the input devices I have tried this code on appear as mice to the system, presumably for broader compatibility.

The third field that I display in my template indicates whether an event has been generated by the primary point on an input device. This relates to multi-touch devices where the first point of contact (typically, the first finger that touches the screen) is considered to be the primary point. Events which are triggered in response to movements or contacts by other fingers will return false for the isPrimary property.

Handling Gestures

Gestures are a sequences of events received in a particular order. So, for example, a tap gesture is made up of an MSPointerDown event followed, at some point, by an MSPointerUp event. I say *at some point* because gesture interactions are complex – the user's finger may move between the moments when the pointer is pressed and then released, the pointer may move outside of the element whose events you are listening to, and so on. Microsoft has included some useful tools that make it easier to deal with gestures without having to deal with the individual events that they derived from and in the sections that follow, I'll show you how to receive notifications when the user performs a gesture and some different ways in which you can respond to gestures in your app.

Dealing with gestures can be quite complex, so I am going to start with the simplest of the gestures and build up to the more complex ones. To demonstrate the basics I have added a file called Gestures.html to the pages directory of the Visual Studio project, which you can see in Listing 17-12.

Listing 17-12. The contents of the Gestures.html file

```
<!DOCTYPE html>
<html>
<head>
    <title></title>
    <script>
        var input = Windows.Devices.Input;
        var eventList = new WinJS.Binding.List();

        var holdConverter = WinJS.Binding.converter(function (detail) {
            if (detail == MSGestureEvent.MSGESTURE_FLAG_BEGIN) {
```

```
                    return "Start";
            } else if (detail == MSGestureEvent.MSGESTURE_FLAG_END) {
                    return "End";
            } else if (detail == MSGestureEvent.MSGESTURE_FLAG_CANCEL) {
                    return "Cancel";
            } else {
                    return "";
            }
        });

        WinJS.UI.Pages.define("/pages/Gestures.html", {
            ready: function () {

                var eventTypes = ["MSPointerDown", "MSGestureTap", "MSGestureHold"];

                var ges = new MSGesture();
                ges.target = targetElem;

                eventTypes.forEach(function (eventType) {
                    targetElem.addEventListener(eventType, function (e) {
                        if (e.type == "MSPointerDown") {
                            ges.addPointer(e.pointerId);
                        } else {
                            eventList.unshift(e);
                        }
                    }, false);
                });
            }
        });
    </script>
</head>
<body>
    <div id="eventDisplayTemplate" data-win-control="WinJS.Binding.Template">
        <div class="eventDisplay">
            <div class="eventDetail" data-win-bind="innerText: type"></div>
            <div class="primaryDetail"
                data-win-bind="innerText: detail holdConverter"></div>
        </div>
    </div>
    <div id="pointerEventsContainer" class="container">
        <div id="sourceElements" class="panel">
            <div id="targetElem" class="coloredRect">
                Gestures
            </div>
        </div>
        <div id="eventListContainer" class="panel">
            <div id="eventList" data-win-control="WinJS.UI.ListView"
                data-win-options="{
                    itemTemplate: eventDisplayTemplate,
                    layout: {type: WinJS.UI.ListLayout},
                    itemDataSource: eventList.dataSource,
```

421

```
                }">
            </div>
        </div>
    </div>
</body>
</html>
```

This content follows the same pattern that I used for the pointer events. There is a colored rectangle whose events I listen to – but there are some key differences in this example.

The most basic gestures are tap and hold, which are represented by the MSGestureTap and MSGestureHold events. To receive these events from an element, I have to create an MSGesture object and tell it which element I want it to operate on, as shown in Listing 17-13.

Listing 17-13. Creating the MSGesture object

```
...
var ges = new MSGesture();
ges.target = targetElem;
...
```

The MSGesture object is built in to Internet Explorer 10, and so you don't need to use a namespace to refer to it. You set the element you want to receive gesture events from using the target property – in the example I specified the div element that is my colored rectangle.

■ **Tip**   The MSGesture object only deals with a single element. If you want to receive gesture events for multiple elements, then you need to create MSGesture objects for each of them.

The MSGesture object relieves you of the responsibility of tracking individual MSPointer events, but you need to tell it that a new gesture may be starting by passing on details from MSPointerDown events via the addPointer method, which takes the value returned by the pointerId property of the MSPointerEvent object, as shown in Listing 17-14.

Listing 17-14. Initiating a gesture

```
...
ges.addPointer(e.pointerId);
...
```

You don't have to do anything else at this point – the MSGesture object will track the events from the element and generate events when gestures occur. Handler functions for gesture events are passed an MSGestureEvent object, which contains information about the gesture. There is no additional detail for the tap gesture, but the hold gesture can cause multiple MSGestureHold events to be triggered. You can determine the significance of these events by reading the detail property and comparing it with values enumerated by the MSGestureEvent object, as described in Table 17-7.

Table 17-7. The status values defined by the MSGestureEvent object

Name	Description
MSGESTURE_FLAG_BEGIN	This event represents the start of the gesture
MSGESTURE_FLAG_END	This event represents the end of the gesture
MSGESTURE_FLAG_CANCEL	This event indicates that the gesture was canceled before it was completed

In the example, I use a `ListView` with a very simple item template to respond to the basic gestures and details of the events as a list. I have defined a binding converter so that I can read the `detail` values and display a meaningful string, as shown in Listing 17-15.

Listing 17-15. Determining the significance of a gesture event by reading the detail property

```
...
var holdConverter = WinJS.Binding.converter(function (detail) {
    if (detail == MSGestureEvent.MSGESTURE_FLAG_BEGIN) {
        return "Start";
    } else if (detail == MSGestureEvent.MSGESTURE_FLAG_END) {
        return "End";
    } else if (detail == MSGestureEvent.MSGESTURE_FLAG_CANCEL) {
        return "Cancel";
    } else {
        return "";
    }
});
...
```

You can see how these values are displayed, along with the type of the gesture event in Figure 17-6.

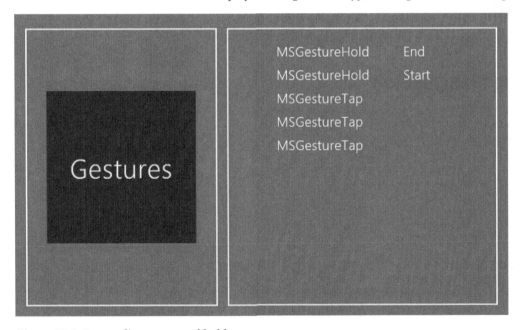

Figure 17-6. Responding to top and hold gestures

Performing Basic Gestures

To test this example, you need to know how to perform the gestures. As I introduce each gesture, I'll show you how to create it with the mouse, on a touch screen and using a mouse to simulate touch in the Visual Studio simulator.

To perform the tap gesture with the mouse, simply click the mouse button on the element and immediately release – for mouse uses, performing the tap gesture is just the same as generating the click event and the MSGestureTap event is triggered. To perform the hold gesture, click the mouse button and hold it – after a few seconds the MSGestureHold event will be triggered.

On a touch screen, you press and immediately release the element with one finger to perform the tap gesture and press and hold (i.e., don't remove your finger from the screen) to perform the hold gesture.

In the simulator, select the Basic Touch Mode using the buttons on the right edge of the simulator window, as shown in Figure 17-7. The cursor changes to represent a finger (presented as a large circle with crosshairs). Your cursor is now a finger - pressing the mouse button simulates touching the screen with a finger and releasing the button simulates removing the finger. If you want to return to regular mouse interactions in the simulator, then select Mouse Mode, which is immediately above the Basic Touch Mode button.

Figure 17-7. Selecting Basic Touch Mode in the Visual Studio simulator

Handling Manipulations

Manipulations are more complex gestures that allow the user to scale, rotate and translate and swipe elements. To demonstrate the manipulation gestures, I have added a file to the Visual Studio project called Manipulations.html. You can see the content of this file in Listing 17-16.

Listing 17-16. The contents of the Manipulations.html file

```
<!DOCTYPE html>
<html>
<head>
    <title></title>
    <script>
        WinJS.UI.Pages.define("/pages/Manipulations.html", {
            ready: function () {
                var eventTypes = ["MSPointerDown", "MSGestureStart",
                    "MSGestureEnd", "MSGestureChange"];

                function handleGestureEvent(e) {
                    if (e.type == "MSPointerDown") {
                        gestures[e.target.id].addPointer(e.pointerId);
                    } else {
                        e.target.style.transform = filterGesture(e);
                    }
                }
```

```
            function filterGesture(e) {
                var matrix = new MSCSSMatrix(e.target.style.transform);
                switch (e.target.id) {
                    case "rotate":
                        return matrix.rotate(e.rotation * 180 / Math.PI);
                        break;
                    case "scale":
                        return matrix.scale(e.scale);
                        break;
                    case "pan":
                        return matrix.translate(e.translationX, e.translationY)
                        break;
                };
            }

            var ids = ["rotate", "scale", "pan"];
            var elems = [];
            var gestures = [];

            ids.forEach(function (id) {
                elems[id] = document.getElementById(id);
                gestures[id] = new MSGesture();
                gestures[id].target = elems[id];
                eventTypes.forEach(function (eventType) {
                    elems[id].addEventListener(eventType, handleGestureEvent);
                });
            });
        }
    });
    </script>
</head>
<body>
    <div id="pointerEventsContainer" class="container">
        <div class="panel">
            <div id="rotate" class="coloredRect">Rotate</div>
        </div>
        <div class="panel">
            <div id="scale" class="coloredRect">Scale</div>
        </div>
        <div class="panel">
            <div id="pan" class="coloredRect">Pan</div>
        </div>
    </div>
</body>
</html>
```

For this example, I have created three target elements, each of which I have labeled with the manipulation I will apply to it in the sections that follow. You can see the initial layout in Figure 17-8.

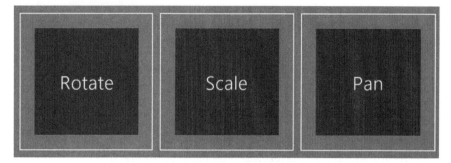

Figure 17-8. Elements to which manipulation gestures can be applied

Performing Manipulation Gestures

The manipulation gestures demonstrated by this example are *rotate, scale* and *pan* and I'll show you how to perform each gesture before digging into the example code. You will need to perform each gesture on the corresponding element in the example.

■ **Note**   You can make the pan motion using touch or the mouse, but the rotate and scale gestures are touch-only.

Rotating an Element

To rotate an element, touch the screen with two fingers and move them in a circular motion around a central point. To perform this gesture in the simulator, select the Rotation Touch Mode button from the right edge of the simulator window. The cursor will change to two circles representing the two fingers of the gesture. Position the cursor over the element and hold down the mouse button. Roll the vertical mouse wheel up to perform an anti-clockwise rotation and roll it wheel down performs a clockwise rotation. Release the mouse button to complete the gesture. You can see the Rotation Touch Mode button, the simulation cursor and the effect in Figure 17-9.

■ **Tip**   Roll the mouse wheel without pressing the mouse button to change the initial position of the simulated fingers.

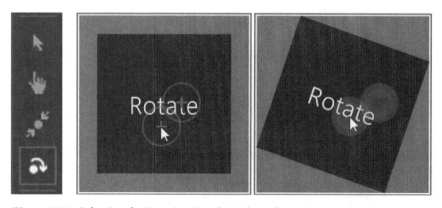

Figure 17-9. Selecting the Rotation Touch Mode and rotating an element

Scaling an Element

To scale an element (which is also known as the *pinch/zoom gesture)* place two fingers on the display and move them apart to scale the element up. Moving your fingers together scales the element down. To simulate this gesture in the simulator, select the `Pinch/Zoom Touch Mode` button. The cursor will change to represent two fingers. Hold the mouse button over the element to begin the gesture and adjust the contact points using the mouse wheel – rolling the wheel up moves the contact points apart and rolling the wheel down moves them together. Release the mouse button to complete the gesture. You can see the `Pinch/Zoom Touch Mode` button, the simulation cursor and the effect of the scale gesture in Figure 17-10.

■ **Tip**   Both contact points need to be within the element to initiate the gesture. Use the mouse wheel without pressing the button to adjust the distance between the contact points so they fit.

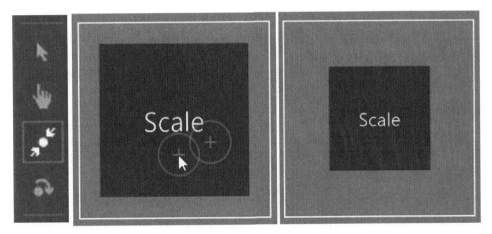

Figure 17-10. Selecting the Pinch/Zoom Touch Mode and scaling an element

Panning an Element

The pan gesture is the only manipulation that can be performed using a mouse: simply hold the mouse button down over the element and move the mouse – the element will follow the mouse pointer. The gesture works in much the same way for touch – touch the element and move your finger to move the element around the screen. To simulate the touch gesture, select the `Basic Touch Mode` and press the mouse button to simulate holding a finger to the screen.

Handling the Manipulation Gesture Events

When working with gestures, you need to create an `MSGesture` object for each element you want to transform and use the `target` element to associate the element it applies to. In Listing 17-17, you can see how I did this in the example, using the `forEach` method on arrays so that I set up all of the elements in the same way and express interest in the same set of events.

Listing 17-17. Setting up the MSGesture objects and listening for the manipulation gesture events

```
...
var eventTypes = ["MSPointerDown", "MSGestureStart", "MSGestureEnd", "MSGestureChange"];
...
var ids = ["rotate", "scale", "pan"];
var elems = [];
var gestures = [];

ids.forEach(function (id) {
    elems[id] = document.getElementById(id);
    gestures[id] = new MSGesture();
    gestures[id].target = elems[id];
    eventTypes.forEach(function (eventType) {
        elems[id].addEventListener(eventType, handleGestureEvent);
    });
});
...
```

Manipulation gestures have their own set of events, which I describe in Table 17-8. The MSGestureStart event is triggered when the user starts to perform a manipulation gesture and the MSGestureEnd event is triggered when the gesture is finished. As the user moves the pointer or pointers, updates about the gestures are sent using the MSGestureChange event.

Table 17-8. The manipulation gesture events

Event	Description
MSGestureStart	Triggered when a manipulation is started
MSGestureEnd	Triggered when a manipulation has finished
MSGestureChange	Triggered when the state of a manipulation changes

The system doesn't differentiate between the different gestures. The handler function for these events is passed an MSGestureEvent object which contains additional properties that contains details about the degree of rotation, scale and panning that the user has made. It is up to you to decide which aspects of those movements you want to respond to. I have summarized these properties in Table 17-9.

Table 17-9. The manipulation-related MSGestureEvent properties

Name	Description
rotation	Returns the rotation of the manipulation, expressed in radians
scale	Returns the scale factor for the manipulation
translationX	Returns the translation along the X-axis
translationY	Returns the translation along the Y-axis
velocityX	Returns the velocity of movement along the X-axis
velocityY	Returns the velocity of movement along the Y-axis

The benefit of this approach is that the user can perform multiple gestures simultaneously. You can choose which property values to read and ignore the ones that represent gestures you are not interested in. This is the approach I have taken in the example, where I only want to support one gesture for each of the elements in the layout.

Responding to Manipulations Using CSS3 Transformations

You can respond to the manipulation gestures in any way that makes sense in your app, but if you want to allow the user to directly manipulate element in the layout then the easiest approach is to use CSS3 transformations, which are supported in Internet Explorer 10. You can see how I have done this in the example using the filterGesture function in Listing 17-18.

Listing 17-18. Processing the details of manipulation gesture events

```
...
function filterGesture(e) {
    var matrix = new MSCSSMatrix(e.target.style.transform);
    switch (e.target.id) {
        case "rotate":
            return matrix.rotate(e.rotation * 180 / Math.PI);
            break;
        case "scale":
            return matrix.scale(e.scale);
            break;
        case "pan":
            return matrix.translate(e.translationX, e.translationY)
            break;
    };
}
...
```

Every DOM object that represents an element in the layout has a style.transform property, which you can use as the constructor argument for the MSCSSMatrix object. Each MSGestureEvent object passed to the event handler function contains the amount of change for each manipulation since the last event and the MSCSSMatrix object make it easy to apply these changes through the rotate, scale and translate methods.

■ **Tip** The CSSMatrix object and the element style.transform properties are part of the CSS3 transition and transform features, which I return to in more detail in Chapter 18.

The only inconvenience is that the MSGestureEvent.rotation value is expressed in radians, whereas the CSS3 transformation works in degrees – you can see how I have converted from one to the other in the listing. You must remember to set the result of the rotate, scale or translate methods to the transform property of the element the user is manipulating, as shown in Listing 17-19.

Listing 17-19. Applying the updated transformation to the manipulated element

```
function handleGestureEvent(e) {
    if (e.type == "MSPointerDown") {
        gestures[e.target.id].addPointer(e.pointerId);
    } else {
        e.target.style.transform = filterGesture(e);
    }
}
```

You can see the result of manipulating all three elements in Figure 17-11.

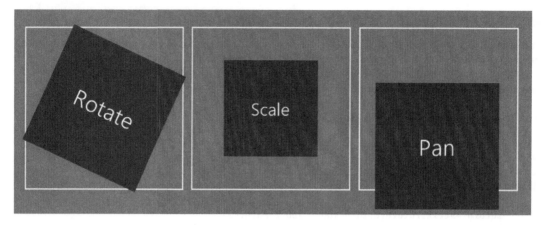

Figure 17-11. Manipulating the elements in the example

Using Content Zoom

Content zoom allows you to scale the content of an element, rather than the element itself. You can see in Figure 17-8 that I scaled one of the elements up so that it overflowed its initial bounds – this is a neat trick, but sometimes you just want to let the user zoom the content in situ, and that is what content zoom allows. To demonstrate this feature, I have added a new file called CSSGestures.html to the pages folder of the example Visual Studio project. You can see the contents of this file in Listing 17-20.

Listing 17-20. The contents of the CSSGestures.html file

```
<!DOCTYPE html>
<html>
<head>
    <title></title>
    <style>
        #contentZoom {
            overflow: scroll;
            -ms-content-zooming: zoom;
            -ms-content-zoom-limit-min: 50%;
            -ms-content-zoom-limit-max: 200%;
            -ms-overflow-style: -ms-autohiding-scrollbar;
            -ms-content-zoom-snap-points: snapList(50%, 75%, 100%, 200%);
            -ms-content-zoom-snap-type: mandatory;
        }
    </style>
</head>
<body>
    <div id="contentZoomContainer" class="container">
        <div id="contentZoom" class="panel">
            <img class="imageRect" src="/images/aster.jpg">
        </div>
    </div>
</body>
</html>
```

The content zoom feature is configured using CSS and there is no `script` block in this example. I rely on an image file called `aster.jpg` which I have added to the `images` directory of the Visual Studio project – you can use any image for this example and the one I used is included in the source code download for this chapter, available from `Apress.com` (and is one of the images I used to demonstrate the `WinJS.UI.FlipView` control in Chapter 14).

The content for this section of the chapter is very simple. The image is shown in a reasonably large format. The user can touch the screen and make the pinch zoom gesture to scale the image. You can see the original state of the layout and the zoomed in content in Figure 17-12. The key difference between this gesture and the standard scale gesture is that the image has been zoomed within the bounds of its container, but the container stays the same size.

Figure 17-12. Using the content zoom gesture

The CSS properties that control the content zoom gesture are described in Table 17-10 and in the sections that follow, I show you how to use each of them and explain the range of supported values.

Table 17-10. The content zoom CSS properties

Name	Description
`-ms-content-zooming`	Setting this property to zoom enables the content zoom feature. The default value is none, which disables content zooming.
`-ms-content-zoom-limit-min`	Sets the smallest size that the content can be scaled to, expressed as a percentage of the original
`-ms-content-zoom-limit-max`	Sets the largest size that the content can be scaled to, expressed as a percentage of the original
`-ms-overflow-style`	Sets the appearance of the scaled content
`-ms-content-zoom-snap-points`	Applies fixed scaling points which the content will snap to
`-ms-content-zoom-snap-type`	Configures the behavior of fixed scaling points

Enabling the Content Zoom Feature

Two properties are required to enable the content zoom gesture. First, you have to set the CSS overflow property to scroll. This property isn't specific to content zooming, but it is required to enable the feature. The second property is -ms-content-zooming, which must be set to zoom. Combining these properties enables the content zoom feature on an element.

You must apply these properties to an element that has content, as in Listing 17-21. You can see that the content is an img element, which is contained in a div. It is the div element to which the content zoom gesture is applied.

Listing 17-21. Applying the content zoom feature to an element which has content

```
<!DOCTYPE html>
<html>
<head>
    <title></title>
    <style>
        #contentZoom {
            overflow: scroll;
            -ms-content-zooming: zoom;
            /* ...other properties removed for brevity... */
        }
    </style>
</head>
<body>
    <div id="contentZoomContainer">
        <div id="contentZoom" class="panel">
            <img class="imageRect" src="/images/aster.jpg">
        </div>
    </div>
</body>
</html>
```

Applying Scaling Limits

You can limit the amount the content can be scaled by using the -ms-content-zoom-limit-min and ms-content-zoom-limit-max properties. These are expressed as percentage of the original size. The user can scale the content beyond these limits while performing the pinch/zoom gesture, but it will snap back to the limit when the gesture ends. In the example, I set a minimum scale of 50% and a maximum scale of 200%, as shown in Listing 17-22. Don't forget the % sign when setting these properties.

Listing 17-22. Applying scaling limits

```
...
-ms-content-zoom-limit-min: 50%;
-ms-content-zoom-limit-max: 200%;
...
```

■ **Tip** The -ms-content-zoom-limit convenience property allows you to specify the min and max values in a single statement.

Setting the Zoomed Content Style

The `-ms-overflow-style` property allows you to configure the way that the content is presented when it has been scaled. The supported values for this property are shown in Table 17-11.

Table 17-11. The values for the -ms-overflow-style property

Value	Description
none	The content won't be shown with scrollbars, even when it is scaled up (although the user can still pan around the content)
scrollbar	Scrollbars are always displayed
-ms-autohiding-scrollbar	Scrollbars are displayed when the user is interacting with the content and are otherwise hidden

I tend to prefer the `-ms-autohiding-scrollbar` value which ensures that the user realizes that they can pan around the content of the element, but uses scrollbars which are overlaid on top of the content and which are only displayed when the user is interacting with the content. By contrast, the scrollbars applied by the `scrollbar` value adds to the size of the element and are always displayed. You can see the difference in Figure 17-13. The image on the left of the figure shows the effect of the `-ms-autohiding-scrollbar` value and the one of the right shows the `scrollbar` value.

Figure 17-13. The different styles of scrollbars available when using the content zoom feature

Limiting the Range of Zoom Levels

You can limit the range of zoom levels by applying the `-ms-content-zoom-snap-points` property. The user can zoom to any level while performing the pinch/zooms gestures, but the content will snap to the nearest zoom level specified by this property. There are two ways to specify snap points, as described in Table 17-12.

Table 17-12. The values for the -ms-content-zoom-snap-points property

Value	Description
snapList(size, size, size)	Explicitly specifies a list of zoom levels, each of which is expressed as a percentage of the original (10%, 20%, 50%)
snapInterval(start, step)	Generates a set of snap points beginning at the first value and stepping up by the amount specified amount. The snap points are applied in both directions, so a property value of snapInterval(50%, 10%) generates snap points both 40% and 60% (and continues to generate points until the limits set by the -ms-content-zoom-limit-min and -ms-content-zoom-limit-max properties are reached)

Working with Content Zoom Programmatically

Although CSS is used to set up content zoom, there are some programmatic features. When the user changes the scale of the content, the MSContentZoom event is triggered and you can get or set the zoom factor using the msContentZoomFactor property. Listing 17-23 shows some additions to the CSSGestures. html file to demonstrate the use of the event and property.

Listing 17-23. Programmatic content zoom features

```
<!DOCTYPE html>
<html>
<head>
    <title></title>
    <style>
        #contentZoom {
            overflow: scroll;
            -ms-content-zooming: zoom;
            -ms-content-zoom-limit-min: 50%;
            -ms-content-zoom-limit-max: 200%;
            -ms-overflow-style: -ms-autohiding-scrollbar;
            -ms-content-zoom-snap-points: snapList(50%, 75%, 100%, 200%);
            -ms-content-zoom-snap-type: mandatory;
        }
    </style>
    <script>
        WinJS.UI.Pages.define("/pages/CSSGestures.html", {
            ready: function () {
                zoomFactor.value = contentZoom.msContentZoomFactor.toFixed(2);

                contentZoom.addEventListener("MSContentZoom", function (e) {
                    zoomFactor.value = contentZoom.msContentZoomFactor.toFixed(2);
                });

                zoomFactor.addEventListener("change", function (e) {
                    contentZoom.msContentZoomFactor = zoomFactor.value;
                });
            }
        });
```

```
        </script>
    </head>
    <body>
        <div id="contentZoomContainer" class="container">
            <div id="contentZoom" class="panel">
                <img class="imageRect" src="/images/aster.jpg">
            </div>

            <div id="zoomDetail" class="panel">
                <div>
                    <h2 class="sectionHeader">Zoom Factor:</h2>
                    <input id="zoomFactor" class="cinput"/>
                </div>
            </div>
        </div>
    </body>
</html>
```

I have added an input element to the layout which is updated when the MSContentZoom event is triggered. When the value of the input element is changed, I handle the change event by updating the msContentZoomFactor property. You can see the revised layout in Figure 17-14.

■ **Note**   The msContentZoomFactor is defined directly on HTMLElement objects, rather than by WinJS. This means that you don't need to use winControl to access the property – you can just get or set the value directly from the object returned from the document.getElementById method.

Figure 17-14. Working with the content zoom feature in JavaScript

Summary

In this chapter, I showed you how to determine which forms of input are available on a device and how to respond to user interactions using the MSPointer events. These offer an important enhancement over the regular DOM events because they contain details of the input mechanism and can be used to recognize gestures. I showed you the gesture system works and demonstrated both simple gestures and manipulations. I finished the chapter by demonstrating how the content zoom feature can be used to create an alternative effect. This feature relies on CSS – a theme I will return to in the next chapter, where I describe the WinJS animation system.

CHAPTER 18

■ ■ ■

Using Animations & Utilities

In this section, I show you how to use the WinJS animation features. The consistency in color and typography that Windows apps typically have can make it difficult for the user to realize that content has been updated or replaced and it can be useful to highlight the change with a short animation. I touched on some of the basic animation features in earlier chapters, but now I return to the topic in depth. I start by showing you how to directly use the CSS features which WinJS relies on and then explain how these are packaged up by the WinJS animation convenience methods. WinJS contains some prepackaged animations for common layout update scenarios, and I show you how to use these – including how to prepare your elements for animation and how to tidy up afterwards.

In the second part of this chapter, I describe some of the useful methods in the WinJS.Utilities namespace. I have been using these methods throughout the book and I have described what they do when I first employed them. In this chapter, I give a more complete guide to their use and demonstrate some additional features, including working out the size and position of elements in the layout and creating a flexible logging system that you can use even when the app isn't attached to a debugger. Table 18-1 provides the summary for this chapter.

Table 18-1. Chapter Summary

Problem	Solution	Listing
Gradually change the value of a CSS property	Use the transition-* CSS properties to create a CSS transition	4-6
Change the position, scale or angle of an HTML element	Use the CSS transform property	7-8
Apply a transition or transform via WinJS	Use the executeAnimation or executeTransform methods	9-11
Use the standard Windows app animations	Use the methods in the WinJS.UI.Animation namespace	12
Prepare for the enterContent and exitContent animations	Ensure that the incoming element isn't visible by setting the display property to none.	13
Prepare for the fadeIn and fadeOut animations	Ensure that the incoming element opacity property is 0 and that both elements are in the same place.	14
Prepare for the crossFade animation	Ensure that the incoming element opacity property is 0 and that both elements are in the same place.	15

Problem	Solution	Listing
Determine the size and position of elements	Use the methods in the `WinJS.Utilities` namespace	16
Write a log message	Use the `WinJS.log` method	17
Define a log filter	Use the `WinJS.Utilities.startLog` method	18
Create a custom log action	Set the `action` property of the object passed to the `startLog` method to a function.	19

Working with Animations

For reasons that I don't fully understand, some programmers go a little crazy when it comes to animations in apps. It isn't just Windows apps – you can see the results of this madness in web apps, desktop apps and, well, anywhere. You can quickly alienate your users, especially if the animations prevent the user from continuing with the current task. Excessive animations are a form of cruelty in line-of-business apps where a user will be performing the same task repeatedly, day after day. What looked like a cool and exciting animation during development will wear down your users when they see it a hundred times a day. I follow a simple set of rules when it comes to animations in Windows apps and I suggest you do the same:

1. Only use animations to draw the user's attention to a change or a result that they might otherwise miss.

2. Keep animations short and make sure they don't prevent the user from working.

3. Use the standard animations where they exist and create subtle effects when they don't.

These three rules will stop your app looking like a Vegas slot machine and make using your app a more pleasant experience.

Creating the Example Project

To demonstrate the different animation and techniques available, I have created an example project called `Animations`. This follows the pattern I have used in earlier chapters and uses the single-page model to import content for each example in the chapter and supports navigation via the NavBar. You can see the contents of the `default.html` file for this project in Listing 18-1 and it contains the NavBar commands for the three content pages that I'll be adding in this chapter.

Listing 18-1. The content of the default.html file from the Animations project

```
<!DOCTYPE html>
<html>
<head>
    <meta charset="utf-8">
    <title>Animations</title>
    <link href="//Microsoft.WinJS.1.0/css/ui-dark.css" rel="stylesheet" />
    <script src="//Microsoft.WinJS.1.0/js/base.js"></script>
    <script src="//Microsoft.WinJS.1.0/js/ui.js"></script>
    <link href="/css/default.css" rel="stylesheet">
    <script src="/js/default.js"></script>
```

```
</head>
<body class="column">
    <div id="contentTarget">
        <h1 class="message">Select a page from the NavBar</h1>
    </div>
    <div id="navbar" data-win-control="WinJS.UI.AppBar"
        data-win-options="{placement:'top'}">

        <button data-win-control="WinJS.UI.AppBarCommand"
            data-win-options="{id:'CSSTransitions', label:'CSS Transitions',
                icon:'\u0031', section:'selection'}">
        </button>

        <button data-win-control="WinJS.UI.AppBarCommand"
            data-win-options="{id:'CoreFunctions', label:'Core',
                icon:'\u0032', section:'selection'}">
        </button>

        <button data-win-control="WinJS.UI.AppBarCommand"
            data-win-options="{id:'ContentAnimations', label:'Content Animations',
                icon:'\u0033', section:'selection'}">
        </button>

    </div>
</body>
</html>
```

To layout the elements in this example, I have defined the styles in Listing 18-2, which shows the content of the /css/default.css file. This is all standard CSS and there are no app-specific techniques in this file.

Listing 18-2. The contents of the /css/default.css file

```
body {background-color: #5A8463;}
.column { display: -ms-flexbox; -ms-flex-direction: column;
    -ms-flex-align: center; -ms-flex-pack: center;}
div.panel { border: medium white solid; margin: 10px; padding: 20px;}
.outerContainer { display: -ms-flexbox; -ms-flex-direction: row;
    -ms-flex-align: stretch; -ms-flex-pack: center;}
.coloredRect { background-color: black; color: white; width: 300px;
    height: 300px; margin: 20px; font-size: 40pt;text-align: center; }
.coloredRectSmall { width: 200px; height: 200px;}
.buttonPanel button { width: 200px; font-size: 20pt; margin: 20px; height: 85px;}
```

The navigation between the content pages is handled by the /js/default/js file, the contents of which you can see in Listing 18-3. This is the same basic navigation code that I used in the previous chapter.

Listing 18-3. The contents of the default.js file

```
(function () {
    "use strict";
```

```
    var app = WinJS.Application;
    window.$ = WinJS.Utilities.query;

    WinJS.Navigation.addEventListener("navigating", function (e) {
        var elem = document.getElementById("contentTarget");

        WinJS.UI.Animation.exitPage(elem.children).then(function () {
            WinJS.Utilities.empty(elem);
            WinJS.UI.Pages.render(e.detail.location, elem)
                .then(function () {
                    return WinJS.UI.Animation.enterPage(elem.children)
                });
        });
    });

    app.onactivated = function (eventObject) {
        WinJS.UI.processAll().then(function () {
            document.getElementById("navbar").addEventListener("click",
                function (e) {
                    var navTarget = "pages/" + e.target.winControl.id + ".html";
                    WinJS.Navigation.navigate(navTarget);
                });
        })
    };

    app.start();
})();
```

Working Directly with Elements

CSS3 defines support for *transitions* and *transforms* to animate elements in HTML markup. Transitions allow you to change the value of CSS properties and transforms allow you to translate, scale and rotate elements.

■ **Tip** I am focused on the CSS3 features that relate directly to WinJS animations in this section. For more complete coverage of CSS3, see my other book *The Definitive Guide to HTML5*, which is also published by Apress.

Transitions and transforms are the underlying mechanism used by WinJS animations. By understanding how the CSS3 features work, you will have a better appreciation of the WinJS features and be able to create your own effects if needed. To demonstrate working directly with these CSS features, I have added a file to the pages folder of the example Visual Studio project. This file is called CSSTransitions. html and is shown in Listing 18-4.

Listing 18-4. Working with CSS transitions and transformations

```
<!DOCTYPE html>
<html>
<head>
```

```
    <title></title>
    <style>
        .colorTransition {
            color: black;
            background-color: white;
            font-size: 50pt;
            transition-delay: 500ms;
            transition-duration: 1000ms;
        }
    </style>
    <script>
        var transforms = ["", "translateX(100px) rotate(45deg)",
            "translateY(50px) scale(1.2)"];
        var durations = ["500ms", "1000ms", "250ms"];
        var colors = ["black", "red", "yellow"];

        WinJS.UI.Pages.define("/pages/CSSTransitions.html", {
            ready: function () {
                $("div.coloredRect").listen("click", function (e) {
                    switch (e.target.id) {
                        case "transitionTarget":
                            WinJS.Utilities.toggleClass(e.target, "colorTransition");
                            break;
                        case "transformTarget":
                            var curr = e.target.style.transform;
                            var index = (transforms.indexOf(curr) + 1) % 3;
                            e.target.style.transitionDuration = durations[index];
                            e.target.style.transform = transforms[index];
                            e.target.style.backgroundColor = colors[index];
                            break;
                    }
                });
            }
        });
    </script>
</head>
<body>
    <div class="outerContainer">
        <div class="panel">
            <div id="transitionTarget" class="coloredRect column">Transition</div>
        </div>
        <div class="panel">
            <div id="transformTarget" class="coloredRect column">Transform</div>
        </div>
    </div>
</body>
</html>
```

This example has two clearly labeled elements in the layout, which I will use to demonstrate transitions and transforms. You can see the initial layout in Figure 18-1 and I explain the functionality in the sections that follow.

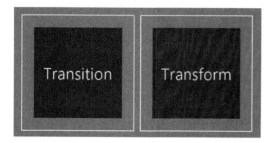

Figure 18-1. The initial layout of the transition and transforms example

Applying Transitions

When you apply a transition, you tell the browser that you want the value of one or more properties to be altered gradually over a period of time. You apply transitions to colors and any property which has a numeric value.

■ **Tip** There are two ways to apply transitions and transforms: via a CSS class or directly to an element using JavaScript. I have used the class-based approach for transitions and show you the code-based approach for transforms later in the chapter.

There are several CSS properties that you use to define the character of a transition and I have described these in Table 18-2.

Table 18-2. The CSS transition properties

Property	Description
transition-delay	Specifies a period of time before the transition is started
transition-duration	Specifies the duration of the transition
transition-property	Specifies which properties are part of the transition. If omitted, any property which is changed is transitioned.
transition-timing-function	Specifies the function used to calculate intermediate values. The default function is ease and other values are linear, ease-in, ease-out and ease-in-out.

In the example, I have defined a CSS class which contains my transition. I have omitted transition-property, which means that any property whose value is changed is subject to the transition-direction and transition-delay properties, as shown in Listing 18-5.

Listing 18-5. Using the CSS transition properties

```
...
<style>
    .colorTransition {
        color: black;
        background-color: white;
```

```
            font-size: 50pt;
            transition-delay: 500ms;
            transition-duration: 1000ms;
    }
</style>
...
```

When this class is applied to an element, new values for the `color`, `background-color` and `font-size` properties will be applied after a 500 millisecond delay and over a period of 1 second. I apply this class to the target element in response to the `click` event, as shown in Listing 18-6.

Listing 18-6. Applying the transition class in response to the click event

```
...
WinJS.Utilities.toggleClass(e.target, "colorTransition");
...
```

The `WinJS.Utilities.toggleClass` method adds the `colorTransition` class if it isn't present on the specified element and removes it if it is. This means that the element will move between its normal and transitioned state with each `click`. You can see the effect in Figure 18-2, which shows the gradual progression from the original state as the transition is applied. These are just snapshots and you will see how smooth the full effect is if you experiment with the example app.

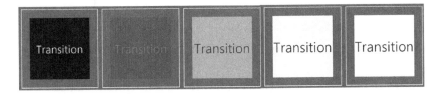

Figure 18-2. The transition of an HTML element

The figure shows the gradual transition that comes from applying the transition. Notice that the values for all of the properties in the `colorTransition` class are modified simultaneously.

If you click the element again it snaps back to its original state immediately. This is because the `transition-delay` and `transition-duration` properties are part of the `colorTransition` class and when the class is removed, the instruction to apply changes gradually is removed as well. You can ensure that all property changes are performed gradually by setting the `transition-duration` property outside of the `colorTransition` class.

Applying Transforms

I used a transform in Chapter 17 when I modified elements in response to gestures. In this section I'll show you a different approach to achieving the same result and demonstrate how transforms and transitions can work together. Transforms are controlled through the `transform` property, which I have summarized in Table 18-3 so you can easily find the reference in the future.

Table 18-3. The CSS transform property

Property	Description
transform	Applies a transform to elements

The value for the transform property can be quite complex, depending on the nature of the changes that you want to make. I have listed the different transform values that are available in Table 18-4.

Table 18-4. The types of value for the CSS transform property

Value	Description
translateX(<length or %>) translateY(<length or %>) translate(<length or %>)	Move an element along the X, Y or both axes.
scaleX(<scale factor>) scaleY(<scale factor>) scale(<scale factor>)	Scale an element along the X, Y or both axes
rotate(<angle>)	Rotate an element
skewX(<angle>) skewY(<angle>) skew(<angle>)	Skew an element along the X, Y, or both axes

You specify a transform by concatenating one or more of these individual transformations as the value for the transform property (which is what the CSSMatrix object I used in Chapter 17 helps to do). For the example, I defined three different transform values, as shown in Listing 18-7.

Listing 18-7. Defining transform values

```
...
var transforms = ["", "translateX(100px) rotate(45deg)", "translateY(50px) scale(1.2)"];
...
```

There are three transform values in this array. The first is the empty string, which means that no transform is applied. The second moves the element 100 pixels along the X axis and rotates it 45 degrees. Rotations are expressed using the CSS degree unit (i.e., 90deg is 90 degrees) and positive values represent clockwise rotations. The final transform moves the element 50 pixels along the Y axis and increases the size of the element by 20%.

These are *absolute transforms*, meaning when you apply one of these values, any previous transform is undone. If you want to apply transforms cumulatively, then you can use the CSSMatix object, which I touched on in Chapter 17.

In the example, I rotate through these transforms in sequence each time the element is clicked. Transforms and transitions can be combined and to demonstrate this I also apply a range of values for the transitionDuration and backgroundColor properties. I applied the value using DOM properties, as shown in Listing 18-8.

Listing 18-8. Applying a transform using the DOM

```
...
var curr = e.target.style.transform;
var index = (transforms.indexOf(curr) + 1) % 3;
e.target.style.transitionDuration = durations[index];
e.target.style.transform = transforms[index];
e.target.style.backgroundColor = colors[index];
...
```

I have highlighted the statement which assigns a new value to the transitionDuration property. When using transforms and transitions via the DOM, it is important to set this value before applying changes to other properties – if you don't take this precaution, then the changes will be applied immediately, without any gradual effect. You can see how the one set of transform and transition are applied to the element Figure 18-3, although you should experiment with the example app to get a feel for how smooth and graceful the real effect is.

Figure 18-3. Applying a transform and a transition via the DOM

Using the Core WinJS Animation Methods

The `WinJS.UI` namespace contains a set of methods to make it easier to apply transitions and transforms in a Windows app. These are wrapper functions that control the overall state of WinJS animations and provide a convenient wrapper around the CSS functionality that I described in the previous section. Table 18-5 summarizes the core animation methods.

Table 18-5. The core WinJS.UI methods

Name	Description
`WinJS.UI.enableAnimations()`	Enables WinJS animations
`WinJS.UI.disableAnimations()`	Disable WinJS animations
`WinJS.UI.isAnimationEnabled()`	Returns **true** if animations will be performed.
`WinJS.UI.executeAnimation(elems, object)`	Performs an animation on an element and restores the element to its original state
`WinJS.UI.executeTransition(elems, object)`	Performs a transition on an element and leave the element in its transitioned state

The first three methods allow you to control all of the animations in the app. It is a good idea to expose this functionality to the user as a setting so that they can disable animations – I show you how to show the user settings in Chapter 20.

■ **Tip** There is a mismatch in terminology here. You can perform CSS transitions and transforms with both the `executeAnimation` and `executeTransition` methods. The difference is the state that the elements are left in when the operation has completed. With the `executeAnimation` method, the elements are returned to their original state, whereas the `executeTransition` leaves the elements in the modified state, much like the previous example. Microsoft are not trying to be difficult with these names – the `executeAnimation` method supports a feature called *key frames*, which perform more complex effects, known as animations - which is where the method name comes from. I don't describe key frames in this chapter because they don't fit well with the broader Windows UX theme, but you can get more details at `http://www.w3.org/TR/css3-transforms`.

The executeAnimation and executeTransition methods apply CSS transforms and transitions to elements. These convenience methods are easier to use than working with CSS classes or style properties directly. To demonstrate these methods, I have added a new page to the example project called CoreFunctions.html, which reproduces the earlier content using the executeAnimation and executeTransition methods. You can see the content of this new file in Listing 18-9.

Listing 18-9. Using the executeAnimation and executeTransition methods

```
<!DOCTYPE html>
<html>
<head>
    <title></title>
    <link href="/css/cssTransitions.css" rel="stylesheet">
    <script>
        var transforms = ["", "translateX(100px) rotate(45deg)",
            "translateY(50px) scale(1.2)"];
        var durations = [500, 1000, 250];
        var colors = ["black", "red", "yellow"];

        WinJS.UI.Pages.define("/pages/CoreFunctions.html", {
            ready: function () {
                $("div.coloredRect").listen("click", function (e) {
                    switch (e.target.id) {
                        case "transitionTarget":
                            WinJS.UI.executeAnimation(e.target, [{
                                property: "background-color", to: "white",
                                duration: 5000, delay: 0,
                                timing: "ease"
                            }, {
                                property: "color", to: "black",
                                duration: 5000, delay: 0, timing: "ease"
                            }]) .then(function () {
                                return WinJS.UI.executeAnimation(e.target, {
                                    property: "font-size", to: "50pt",
                                    duration: 5000, delay: 0, timing: "ease"
                                });
                            });
                            break;
                        case "transformTarget":
                            var curr = e.target.style.transform;
                            var index = (transforms.indexOf(curr) + 1) % 3;

                            WinJS.UI.executeTransition(e.target, [
                                { property: "transform",
                                    to: transforms[index], duration: durations[index],
                                    delay: 0, timing: "ease"
                                }, { property: "background-color",
                                    to: colors[index], duration: durations[index],
                                    delay: 0, timing: "ease"}
                            ]);
                            break;
```

```
                }
            });
        }
    });
    </script>
</head>
<body>
    <div class="outerContainer">
        <div class="panel">
            <div id="transitionTarget" class="coloredRect column">Transition</div>
        </div>
        <div class="panel">
            <div id="transformTarget" class="coloredRect column">Transform</div>
        </div>
    </div>
</body>
</html>
```

The first argument for both methods is the set of elements that you want to operate on. This can be a single element (which is what I used in the example) or an array of elements, which causes the same effect to be applied to all of the elements in the array. The second argument is an object whose properties contain details of the transition or transform you want to apply. I have described the supported property names in Table 18-6.

Table 18-6. The supported properties for the second argument object

Property	Description
property	The CSS property that will be affected. Use transform if you want to apply a CSS transform.
delay	The delay, in milliseconds, before the effect begins
duration	The duration of the effect.
timing	The timing function for the effect
to	The final value for the property

Using the executeAnimation Method

If you want to operate on multiple properties at once, then you pass an array of objects containing the properties in the table as the second argument to the executeAnimation or executeTransition methods. These methods both return WinJS.Promise objects which you can use to chain effects together. As Listing 18-10 shows, I used both techniques in the example and you can learn more about the Promise object in Chapter 9.

■ **Tip**   When specifying the property value, use CSS, and not DOM, property names. So, for example, use background-color and not backgroundColor. The effect won't be applied correctly if you use the DOM property name.

Listing 18-10. Preforming multiple simultaneous effects and chaining effects

```
...
WinJS.UI.executeAnimation(e.target, [{
    property: "background-color", to: "white", duration: 500, delay: 0, timing: "ease"
}, {
    property: "color", to: "black", duration: 500, delay: 0, timing: "ease"
}]) .then(function () {
    return WinJS.UI.executeAnimation(e.target, {
        property: "font-size", to: "50pt", duration: 500, delay: 0, timing: "ease"
    });
});
...
```

This is the fragment that handles the left element – the one marked Transition. I start by using the executeAnimation method to transition the background-color and color property – I do this by passing an array of two objects as the second argument to the method. I use the then method on the Promise that I get back to chain a second call to the executeAnimation method – this time to transition the font-size property. The result is that the background-color and color properties are transitioned together and, when both transitions have finished, the font-size property is transitioned.

The difference between the executeAnimation and executeTransition methods is that at the end of an animation, the element returns to its original state. The best way to see this is by using the example app and clicking on the Transition element, but I have tried to capture the effect in Figure 18-4. There is no gradual return to the initial state – the element just snaps back to where it was before the executeAnimation method was called.

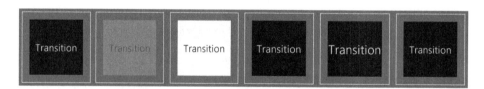

Figure 18-4. Using the executeAnimation method

The state of the element is reset at the end of each call to executeAnimation and you can see the effect this has in the figure. The values for the background-color and color properties are reset before the font-size property is transitioned.

Using the executeTransition Method

The executeTransition method works just like the executeAnimation method, except that the element or elements that are operated on are left in their transitioned state. You can see how I used the executeTransition method in the example in Listing 18-11.

Listing 18-11. Using the executeTransition method

```
...
var curr = e.target.style.transform;
var index = (transforms.indexOf(curr) + 1) % 3;
```

```
WinJS.UI.executeTransition(e.target, [
    { property: "transform", to: transforms[index], duration: durations[index],
          delay: 0, timing: "ease"
    }, { property: "background-color", to: colors[index],
          duration: durations[index], delay: 0, timing: "ease"}
]);
...
```

Using this method is just like using the executeAnimation method and you can see from the listing that I pass an array of objects to the method so that the transform and background properties are transitioned. Using the transform property has the same effect when working directly with the CSS properties and allows transforms to be applied to elements.

In fact, the executeTransform method is just a wrapper around the CSS functionality I showed you earlier and this is illustrated by the statement I have highlighted in the listing. I can read the value of the transform property from the element to figure out where in my loop I am.

Using the WinJS Animations

The WinJS.UI.Animation namespace contains a set of methods that perform predefined animations on app content. These are the standard Windows animations and you should use them whenever you are performing the activity to which they relate in your app – for example, showing a new page of content. There are two benefits in using these methods. First, they are very simple to use and much more terse than using the executeTransition method or working directly with the CSS. The second reason is that you app will be consistent with other Windows apps, and benefit from the user's prior experience as to the significance of these animations. Table 18-7 describes the WinJS content animations.

■ **Tip**   There are other methods in the WinJS.UI.Animation namespace, but they are used by the system to apply animations in UI controls and are not for general use.

Table 18-7. The WinJS.UI.Animation content animation methods

Method	Description
enterContent(elems)	Animates the specified elements so that they slide in from the right
exitContent(elems)	Animates the specified elements so that they slide out to the left
enterPage(elems)	Animates page-level elements so that they slide in from the right
exitPage(elems)	Animates page-level elements so that they slide out to the left
fadeIn(elems)	Fades in the specified elements
fadeOut(elems)	Fades out the specified elements
crossFade(in, out)	Fades in the first set of elements while fading out the second set of elements

These are standardized animations and they are typically used in pairs. As an example, you can see how I have used the enterPage and exitPage animation methods in the default.js in Listing 18-12. I call these methods in response to the navigating event (which I described in Chapter 7) in order to draw the user's attention to the change in content.

Listing 18-12. Using the enterPage and exitPage methods in the default.js file

```
...
WinJS.Navigation.addEventListener("navigating", function (e) {
    var elem = document.getElementById("contentTarget");

    WinJS.UI.Animation.exitPage(elem.children).then(function () {
        WinJS.Utilities.empty(elem);
        WinJS.UI.Pages.render(e.detail.location, elem)
            .then(function () {
                WinJS.UI.Animation.enterPage(elem.children)
            });
    });
});
...
```

All of the methods in the table return a `WinJS.Promise` object which is fulfilled when the animation is complete. I show you how to use the other animations in the sections that follow.

Using the Content Enter and Exit Animations

To demonstrate the content animations I have added a new HTML page called `ContentAnimations.html`. I'll build up this content for each of the animations, starting with the `enterContent` and `exitContent` methods. You can see the initial version of the `ContentAnimations.html` file in Listing 18-13.

Listing 18-13. Using the contentEnter and contentExit animations

```
<!DOCTYPE html>
<html>
<head>
    <title></title>
    <script>
        WinJS.UI.Pages.define("/pages/ContentAnimations.html", {
            ready: function () {

                content2.style.display = "none";

                $('button').listen("click", function (e) {
                    switch (e.target.id) {
                        case "content":
                            var visible = content1.style.display
                                == "none" ? content2 : content1;
                            var hidden = visible == content1 ? content2 : content1;

                            WinJS.UI.Animation.exitContent(visible).then(function () {
                                visible.style.display = "none";
                                hidden.style.display = "";
                                WinJS.UI.Animation.enterContent(hidden);
                            });
                            break;
                    }
```

```
                });
            }
        });
    </script>
</head>
<body>
    <div class="outerContainer">
        <div class="panel">
            <div id="content1" class="coloredRect coloredRectSmall column">One</div>
            <div id="content2"class="coloredRect coloredRectSmall column">Two</div>
            <div class="buttonPanel column">
                <button id="content">Enter/Exit Content</button>
            </div>
        </div>
    </div>
</body>
</html>
```

Although the animation methods come in pairs, you are still responsible for coordinating the calls to these methods and for preparing the elements that will be animated. The element which will be animated using the exitContent method just needs to be visible on the page. The element that is going to be introduced by the enterContent method needs to be added to the DOM but be invisible, which is achieved by setting the display property to none, like this:

```
...
content2.style.display = "none";
...
```

To coordinate the animation sequence so that the transition from one element to the other is smooth, you follow this sequence:

1. Call the exitContent method, passing in the outgoing element as the argument

2. Use the then method on the WinJS.Promise that exitContent returns to:

   a. Set the display property to none on the outgoing element

   b. Clear the display property on the incoming element

   c. Call the enterContent method, passing in the incoming method as the argument

These methods translate the elements while changing the value of the opacity property. This is done very quickly – the exitContent animation takes 80 milliseconds and the enterContent animation takes 370 milliseconds.

_____

■ **Tip**   You can see details of how each animation is set up by searching for the method name in the ui.js file in the References section of the Visual Studio project.

_____

Clicking the button element in the example triggers the animation. I work out which element is visible (and therefore outgoing) and which is hidden (and therefore incoming) for each click event – this allows the example to alternate between elements.

Using the Fade In and Out Animations

The fadeIn and fadeOut methods operate on the opacity property of the animated elements. This means that the outgoing element needs to have an opacity value of 1 and the incoming element a value of 0 before the animation begins. If you want one element to replace another, then you need to ensure that they occupy the same space in the layout – one way of doing this is to use the grid layout and assign both elements to the same grid cell. You can see how I have applied this technique, and call the animation methods, in Listing 18-14 which builds on the previous example.

Listing 18-14. Using the fadeIn and fadeOut methods

```
<!DOCTYPE html>
<html>
<head>
    <title></title>
    <script>
        WinJS.UI.Pages.define("/pages/ContentAnimations.html", {
            ready: function () {

                content2.style.display = "none";
                fade2.style.opacity = 0;

                $('button').listen("click", function (e) {
                    switch (e.target.id) {
                        case "content":
                            var visible = content1.style.display
                                == "none" ? content2 : content1;
                            var hidden = visible == content1 ? content2 : content1;

                            WinJS.UI.Animation.exitContent(visible).then(function () {
                                visible.style.display = "none";
                                hidden.style.display = "";
                                WinJS.UI.Animation.enterContent(hidden);
                            });
                            break;
                        case "fade":
                            var visible = fade1.style.opacity  == "0" ? fade2 : fade1;
                            var hidden = visible == fade1? fade2: fade1;

                            WinJS.UI.Animation.fadeOut(visible).then(function () {
                                WinJS.UI.Animation.fadeIn(hidden);
                            });
                            break;
                    }
                });
            }
```

```
        });
    </script>
</head>
<body>
    <div class="outerContainer">
        <div class="panel">
            <div id="content1" class="coloredRect coloredRectSmall column">One</div>
            <div id="content2"class="coloredRect coloredRectSmall column">Two</div>
            <div class="buttonPanel column">
                <button id="content">Enter/Exit Content</button>
            </div>
        </div>

        <div class="panel">
            <div style="display: -ms-grid">
                <div id="fade1" class="coloredRect coloredRectSmall column">One</div>
                <div id="fade2" class="coloredRect coloredRectSmall column">Two</div>
            </div>
            <div class="buttonPanel column">
                <button id="fade">Fade In/Out</button>
            </div>
        </div>
    </div>
</body>
</html>
```

You can easily position elements in the same place by setting the display property to –ms-grid. If you don't set any values for the rows or columns and don't assign any of the elements to cells, then the result is a 1 x 1 grid with all of the content elements in the same cell. In the example, I have set up this arrangement by applying the style attribute to the container element. I don't usually apply CSS directly to elements, but I have made an exception because this is such a simple example.

The fadeIn and fadeOut don't transform the position of the elements (so there is no need to explicitly change the display properties between animations). You can see the layout of the example in Figure 18-5.

Using the Cross Fade Animation

The crossFade method transitions the opacity property of a pair of elements so that one becomes transparent while the other becomes opaque. The preparation required for the crossFade method is just the same as for the fadeIn and fadeOut methods, in that you need to set the opacity to 1 for the outgoing element and to 0 for the incoming element. The difference is that both animations are started simultaneously. You can see how I have added support for the crossFade method in Listing 18-15.

Listing 18-15. Using the crossFade method

```
<!DOCTYPE html>
<html>
<head>
    <title></title>
    <script>
        WinJS.UI.Pages.define("/pages/ContentAnimations.html", {
            ready: function () {
```

```
                            content2.style.display = "none";
                            fade2.style.opacity = 0;
                            crossfade2.style.opacity = 0;

                            $('button').listen("click", function (e) {
                                switch (e.target.id) {
                                    case "content":
                                        var visible = content1.style.display
                                            == "none" ? content2 : content1;
                                        var hidden = visible == content1 ? content2 : content1;

                                        WinJS.UI.Animation.exitContent(visible).then(function () {
                                            visible.style.display = "none";
                                            hidden.style.display = "";
                                            WinJS.UI.Animation.enterContent(hidden);
                                        });
                                        break;
                                    case "fade":
                                        var visible = fade1.style.opacity  == "0" ? fade2 : fade1;
                                        var hidden = visible == fade1? fade2: fade1;

                                        WinJS.UI.Animation.fadeOut(visible).then(function () {
                                            WinJS.UI.Animation.fadeIn(hidden);
                                        });
                                        break;
                                    case "crossfade":
                                        var visible = crossfade1.style.opacity
                                            == "0" ? crossfade2 : crossfade1;
                                        var hidden = visible == crossfade1 ? crossfade2 : crossfade1;

                                        WinJS.UI.Animation.crossFade(hidden, visible);
                                        break;
                                }
                            });
                        }
                    });
                </script>
            </head>
            <body>
                <div class="outerContainer">
                    <div class="panel">
                        <div id="content1" class="coloredRect coloredRectSmall column">One</div>
                        <div id="content2"class="coloredRect coloredRectSmall column">Two</div>
                        <div class="buttonPanel column">
                            <button id="content">Enter/Exit Content</button>
                        </div>
                    </div>

                    <div class="panel">
                        <div style="display: -ms-grid">
                            <div id="fade1" class="coloredRect coloredRectSmall column">One</div>
```

```
                <div id="fade2" class="coloredRect coloredRectSmall column">Two</div>
            </div>
            <div class="buttonPanel column">
                <button id="fade">Fade In/Out</button>
            </div>
        </div>

        <div class="panel">
            <div style="display: -ms-grid">
                <div id="crossfade1"
                    class="coloredRect coloredRectSmall column">One</div>
                <div id="crossfade2"
                    class="coloredRect coloredRectSmall column">Two</div>
            </div>
            <div class="buttonPanel column">
                <button id="crossfade">Cross Fade</button>
            </div>
        </div>
    </div>
</body>
</html>
```

The cross fade animation is very fast. The fade in and fade out animations both last for 167 milliseconds, so the transition is immediate. I find the effect a little *too* quick and tend to chain the fadeOut and fadeIn methods together. You can see the layout of the elements and the buttons that trigger the animations in Figure 18-5. I recommend that you spend some time experimenting with all three to get a feel for how the user will see the transitions from one element to another.

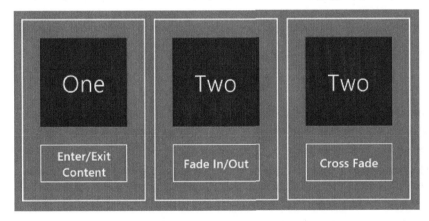

Figure 18-5. Using the enterContent and exitContent animations

Using the WinJS Utilities

I have been using the features of the WinJS.Utilities namespace throughout the examples in this part of the book. In this section, I'll describe the most useful of these features, many of will be familiar if you have used a DOM manipulation library such as jQuery.

Querying the DOM

In many of the examples in this book, I have aliased the $ symbol so that it refers to the WinJS.Utilities. query method. This is a jQuery-like method that searches the DOM for elements that match a CSS selector string. The results are returned from the query method as a QueryCollection object – this object defines the methods described in Table 18-8.

Table 18-8. The methods defined by the QueryCollection object

Method	Description
addClass(name)	Adds the specified class to all of the elements in the collection
removeClass(name)	Removes the specified class from all of the elements in the collection
toggleClass(name)	Adds the specified class to those elements that don't have it and removes it from those that do.
hasClass(name)	Returns true if the first element in the collection has the specified class
foreach(function)	Calls the function for each element in the collection, passing in the element as the function argument
listen(event, callback)	Registers the callback function to handle the specified event for all of the elements in the collection
query(selector)	Queries the elements in the collection. The result is another QueryCollection that contains the matching elements
setAttribute(name, val)	Sets an attribute to the specified value for all the elements in the collection
setStyle(property, val)	Sets a CSS property to the specified value for all the elements in the collection

I have used almost all of these methods in the examples so far in this book and I use them throughout the chapters that follow. I am not going to give any specific examples in this chapter because these methods are self-evident and because most web programmers have at least a passing familiarity with jQuery or a similar library.

■ **Tip**   If you are doing web development and not using something like jQuery, then you are missing out. For more details, see my book Pro jQuery, which is also published by Apress. Your web development will be transformed.

You can use jQuery in Windows app projects. For the most part, though, I have tended to stick to the WinJS.Utilities methods. They do most of the basic functions that jQuery supports and I have found them fast and reliable.

Determining the Size and Position of Elements

In addition to DOM queries, the WinJS.Utilities namespace contains methods which help determine the size and position of elements in the app layout. These methods are described in Table 18-9. These methods operate on single elements, which can be obtained using DOM methods such as getElementById or from QueryCollection objects.

Table 18-9. The utility methods for determining element sizes

Method	Description
getContentHeight(elem)	Returns the height of an element without borders and padding
getContentWidth(elem)	Returns the width of an element without borders and padding
getTotalHeight(elem)	Returns the height of an element, including borders and padding
getTotalWidth(elem)	Returns the width of an element, including borders and padding
getPosition(elem)	Returns an object whose properties describe the top and left positions of the element, along with the element's width and height
getRelativeLeft(elem, parent)	Gets the left coordinate relative to the parent element
getRelativeTop(elem, parent)	Gets the top coordinate relative to the parent element

To demonstrate these methods, I have created a new Visual Studio project called SizeAndPosition. The entire project is contained in the default.html file, which is shown in Listing 18-16, and I have removed the other files that Visual Studio adds to a new project by default.

Listing 18-16. The default.html file from the SizeAndPosition project

```
<!DOCTYPE html>
<html>
<head>
    <meta charset="utf-8" />
    <title>SizeAndPosition</title>
    <link href="//Microsoft.WinJS.1.0/css/ui-dark.css" rel="stylesheet" />
    <script src="//Microsoft.WinJS.1.0/js/base.js"></script>
    <script src="//Microsoft.WinJS.1.0/js/ui.js"></script>
    <style>
        body {
            background-color: #5A8463;
        }
        #container {
            margin: 20px;
             display: -ms-grid;
             -ms-grid-columns: 0.1fr 0.25fr 1fr 0.55fr;
             -ms-grid-rows: 0.2fr 0.5fr 1fr 0.1fr;
        }
        #content {
            -ms-grid-row: 2;
            -ms-grid-row-span: 2;
            -ms-grid-column: 3;
            font-size: 30pt; padding: 20px; margin: 20px;
            border: thick solid white; text-align: center;
        }
    </style>
    <script>
        WinJS.Application.onactivated = function () {

            var elem = document.getElementById("content");
```

```
                console.log("Content Height: " + WinJS.Utilities.getContentHeight(elem));
                console.log("Content Width: " + WinJS.Utilities.getContentWidth(elem));
                console.log("Total Width: " + WinJS.Utilities.getTotalWidth(elem));
                console.log("Total Height: " + WinJS.Utilities.getTotalHeight(elem));

                var position = WinJS.Utilities.getPosition(elem);
                console.log("Position Top: " + position.top);
                console.log("Position Left: " + position.left);
                console.log("Position Width: " + position.width);
                console.log("Position Height: " + position.height);

                var parent = document.getElementById("container");
                console.log("Rel Left: " + WinJS.Utilities.getRelativeLeft(elem, parent));
                console.log("Rel Top: " + WinJS.Utilities.getRelativeTop(elem, parent));
            };
        WinJS.Application.start();
    </script>
</head>
<body>
    <div id="container">
        <div id="content">Here is some content</div>
    </div>
</body>
</html>
```

I have put everything together in this example so you can see how the CSS affects the layout of the elements and how this layout affects the WinJS.Utilities methods. I have defined a simple layout that contains nested div elements. The outer element is set up with a grid layout where the available space has been allocated in varying amounts to the rows and columns. The fractional allocation of space into the grid and the use of padding and margin make it difficult to work out the position of the inner element from the markup. In the script element, I have used the methods from Table 18-9 to get details of the position and write them to the JavaScript console window. You can see how the layout appears in Figure 18-6.

Figure 18-6. Creating a layout to demonstrate the WinJS.Utilties methods

Running this example app produces the output below. Your results will differ depending on the device or simulator configuration you are using. This output will be displayed in the Visual Studio JavaScript Console window.

```
Content Height: 55
Content Width: 608
Total Width: 698
Total Height: 145
```

```
Position Top: 59
Position Left: 284
Position Width: 658
Position Height: 105
Rel Left: 264
Rel Top: 39
```

Logging Messages

The WinJS.Utilities namespace contains three methods that can be used to log messages from your app. This may not seem that useful at first – but there is a neat trick that makes these methods more interesting than they appear at first. These methods are used to set up logging through the WinJS.log method. Table 18-10 summarizes the methods, which I explain in the sections that follow.

■ **Tip** Note that the log method is in the WinJS namespace, but the other methods are in WinJS.Utilities.

Table 18-10. The utility methods for logging

Method	Description
WinJS.Utilities.startlog(options)	Set up a logging policy
WinJS.Utilities.stopLog()	Stop logging
WinJS.Utilities.formatLog(message, tag, type)	Format a log message
WinJS.log(message, tags, type)	Create a new log message

Writing Log Messages

The method you use most in this situation is WinJS.log, which takes three arguments: a *message* to write to the log, a string one or more *tags* (separated by spaces) which categorize the message and a message type, such as info, error, or warn. You can use any string for the tags and the type – whatever makes sense for your app.

The WinJS.log method won't always be defined (for reasons I'll explain shortly), so you need to make sure that it exists before writing log messages. You can see how I have done this in Listing 18-17, where I have revised the default.html file from the SizeAndPosition project to use the WinJS.log method.

Listing 18-17. Applying the WinJS.log method to the SizeAndPosition example

```
<!DOCTYPE html>
<html>
<head>
    <meta charset="utf-8" />
    <title>SizeAndPosition</title>
    <link href="//Microsoft.WinJS.1.0/css/ui-dark.css" rel="stylesheet" />
    <script src="//Microsoft.WinJS.1.0/js/base.js"></script>
    <script src="//Microsoft.WinJS.1.0/js/ui.js"></script>
    <style>
        body { background-color: #5A8463; }
        #container { margin: 20px; display: -ms-grid;
```

```
                    -ms-grid-columns: 0.1fr 0.25fr 1fr 0.55fr;
                    -ms-grid-rows: 0.2fr 0.5fr 1fr 0.1fr;}
            #content {
                -ms-grid-row: 2; -ms-grid-row-span: 2; -ms-grid-column: 3;
                font-size: 30pt; padding: 20px; margin: 20px;
                border: thick solid white; text-align: center;}
        </style>
        <script>

            function logSizeAndPos(msg) {
                if (WinJS.log) {
                    WinJS.log(msg, "winjs app info", "info");
                }
            }

            WinJS.Application.onactivated = function () {

                var elem = document.getElementById("content");

                logSizeAndPos("Content Height: " + WinJS.Utilities.getContentHeight(elem));
                logSizeAndPos("Content Width: " + WinJS.Utilities.getContentWidth(elem));
                logSizeAndPos("Total Width: " + WinJS.Utilities.getTotalWidth(elem));
                logSizeAndPos("Total Height: " + WinJS.Utilities.getTotalHeight(elem));

                var position = WinJS.Utilities.getPosition(elem);
                logSizeAndPos("Position Top: " + position.top);
                logSizeAndPos("Position Left: " + position.left);
                logSizeAndPos("Position Width: " + position.width);
                logSizeAndPos("Position Height: " + position.height);

                var parent = document.getElementById("container");
                logSizeAndPos("Rel Left: " + WinJS.Utilities.getRelativeLeft(elem, parent));
                logSizeAndPos("Rel Top: " + WinJS.Utilities.getRelativeTop(elem, parent));
            };
            WinJS.Application.start();
        </script>
    </head>
    <body>
        <div id="container">
            <div id="content">Here is some content</div>
        </div>
    </body>
</html>
```

I find the easiest way to use the WinJS.log method is through a function defined in the app code, which is what I have done in the example with the logSizeAndPos function. Any message passed to this function is written to the log using the tags winjs, app, info and given the type info. You won't see any output from the app if you run it at this state, because, by default, the WinJS.log method hasn't been defined. I explain how to set things up in the next section.

Starting the Log

There is no WinJS.log method defined until the WinJS.Utilities.startLog method is called. This tells the system which kinds of logging messages you are interested in, allowing you to filter what gets logged out. The argument to the startLog method is an object whose properties have special meaning – I have listed the recognized property names in Table 18-11.

Table 18-11. The property names recognized by the startLog method

Property	Description
type	The type of log messages that will be captured
tags	The tags that will be captured, separated by space characters
excludeTags	One or more tags, separated by spaces, which will cause a message to be ignored
action	A function for processing the message. The default is to log to the JavaScript console.

In essence, the startLog method sets up a filter that captures certain log messages and, by default, writes them to the JavaScript console. Listing 18-18 shows the addition of a call to startLog added to the script block of the SizeAndPosition project.

Listing 18-18. Starting the log

```
...
<script>

    function logSizeAndPos(msg) {
        if (WinJS.log) {
            WinJS.log(msg, "winjs app info", "info");
        }
    }

    WinJS.Utilities.startLog({ type: "info", tags: "app bugs info" });

    WinJS.Application.onactivated = function () {

        var elem = document.getElementById("content");

        logSizeAndPos("Content Height: " + WinJS.Utilities.getContentHeight(elem));
        logSizeAndPos("Content Width: " + WinJS.Utilities.getContentWidth(elem));
        logSizeAndPos("Total Width: " + WinJS.Utilities.getTotalWidth(elem));
        logSizeAndPos("Total Height: " + WinJS.Utilities.getTotalHeight(elem));

        //...other statements removed for brevity...
    };
</script>
...
```

In this Listing 18-I have called the startLog method, specifying that I am interested in messages whose type is info and whose tags are app, bugs or info. A log message only has to have one of the tags you specify to the startLog method to be captured and processed. The call to startLog sets up the filter and, in

461

doing so, creates the WinJS.log method. If you run the app now, you'll see output in the JavaScript Console window. Here is an example line of the output:

```
winjs:app:info: Position Top: 59
```

The Windows app logging system has formatted the output so that the tags are included. If you don't see the message, check the buttons at the top of the JavaScript Console window. These buttons can be used to filter the kinds of messages displayed in the console and you may find that one or more of them are not pressed. You can see the buttons in Figure 18-7.

Figure 18-7. Ensuring that the log messages are displayed

Creating a Custom Logging Action

The problem with the JavaScript console is that it isn't available when the app is deployed and running outside a debugger. This is where the action property of the object passed to the startLog method comes in useful – it allows you to create a custom logging approach that is integrated with the rest of your app and which can work outside the debugger. The action property is set to a function which is passed the log message, tags and type, as shown in Listing 18-19, where I have added a custom log action to the script block of the SizeAndPosition example.

Listing 18-19. Adding a custom log action

```html
<!DOCTYPE html>
<html>
<head>
    <meta charset="utf-8" />
    <title>SizeAndPosition</title>
    <link href="//Microsoft.WinJS.1.0/css/ui-dark.css" rel="stylesheet" />
    <script src="//Microsoft.WinJS.1.0/js/base.js"></script>
    <script src="//Microsoft.WinJS.1.0/js/ui.js"></script>
    <style>
        body { background-color: #5A8463; }
        #container { margin: 20px; display: -ms-grid;
            -ms-grid-columns: 0.1fr 0.25fr 1fr 0.55fr;
            -ms-grid-rows: 0.2fr 0.5fr 1fr 0.1fr;}
        #content {
            -ms-grid-row: 2; -ms-grid-row-span: 2; -ms-grid-column: 3;
            font-size: 30pt; padding: 20px; margin: 20px;
            border: thick solid white; text-align: center;}
        #logMessages {
            font-size: 30pt; text-align: center;
        }
    </style>
    <script>
```

```
    function logSizeAndPos(msg) {
        if (WinJS.log) {
            WinJS.log(msg, "winjs app info", "info");
        }
    }

    WinJS.Utilities.startLog({ type: "info", tags: "app bugs info" });

    WinJS.Utilities.startLog({
        type: "info", tags: "app",
        action: function (msg, tags, type) {
            if (msg.indexOf("Position") == 0) {
                var fMsg = WinJS.Utilities.formatLog(msg, tags, type);
                var newElem = document.createElement("div");
                newElem.innerText = fMsg;
                logMessages.appendChild(newElem);
            }
        }
    });

    WinJS.Application.onactivated = function () {

        var elem = document.getElementById("content");

        logSizeAndPos("Content Height: " + WinJS.Utilities.getContentHeight(elem));
        logSizeAndPos("Content Width: " + WinJS.Utilities.getContentWidth(elem));
        logSizeAndPos("Total Width: " + WinJS.Utilities.getTotalWidth(elem));
        logSizeAndPos("Total Height: " + WinJS.Utilities.getTotalHeight(elem));

        var position = WinJS.Utilities.getPosition(elem);
        logSizeAndPos("Position Top: " + position.top);
        logSizeAndPos("Position Left: " + position.left);
        logSizeAndPos("Position Width: " + position.width);
        logSizeAndPos("Position Height: " + position.height);

        var parent = document.getElementById("container");
        logSizeAndPos("Rel Left: " + WinJS.Utilities.getRelativeLeft(elem, parent));
        logSizeAndPos("Rel Top: " + WinJS.Utilities.getRelativeTop(elem, parent));
    };
    WinJS.Application.start();
    </script>
</head>
<body>
    <div id="container">
        <div id="content">Here is some content</div>
    </div>
    <div id="logMessages"></div>
</body>
</html>
```

In this example, I have used `startLog` to create an action which captures those messages which have the type `info`, the tag app and whose message starts with the work `Position`. For each matching message I create a new `div` element and add it as a child to a new container element I added to the layout. This isn't an especially useful way of displaying the log messages, but it does demonstrate that you can do pretty much anything with the logging information that you need – this might include displaying it to the user, saving it to a file or uploading it to a server.

You can create strings that are formatted in the same way as those written to the JavaScript console by calling the `formatLog` method – this is the same method used by the default actions and produces strings which contain the message and details of the tags. Of course, you can ignore this method entirely and generate any message format that makes sense for your apps. You can see the result of these additions in Figure 18-8, which shows the log messages displayed as part of the layout. (The layout elements are not aligned properly because of the odd grid layout I used for the original example.)

■ **Tip** Notice that I left the original call to `startLog` in the example. The WinJS logging system supports multiple filters and actions, which means that the messages are still being written to the JavaScript console, which can be useful during development and testing.

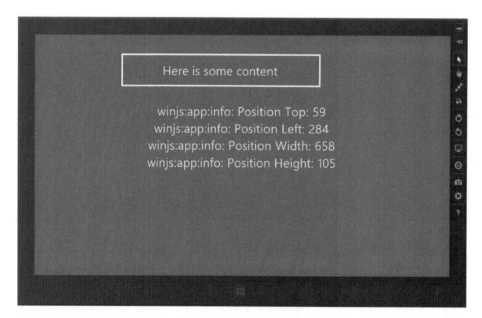

Figure 18-8. Displaying selected log messages in the app layout

Summary

In this chapter, I have wrapped up my coverage of the WinJS UI features by describing the animation features. I showed you how to work directly with the CSS3 features to transition properties and transform elements. I moved on to the WinJS convenience features which can make it easier to work with the CSS features and which contain predefined effects for common situations you want to signal to the user, such as new content arriving in the app layout. As always with effects, WinJS animations should be short, simple and used sparingly.

I finished this chapter by detailing the most useful methods in the `WinJS.Utilities` namespace. I showed you how to query elements, manipulate the DOM, get the size and position of elements in the app layout and how to create a flexible log system that you can use throughout the app lifecycle. I explained the purpose of many of these methods when I used them in earlier chapters and have included them here so that you can refer to them quickly in the future. In the next part of this book, I'll show you how to integrate your app into Windows and, by doing so, improve the experience your app offers to users.

PART 4

Platform Integration

In this part of the book, I show you how to integrate your app into the Windows 8 platform, which lets you provide users with a smoother user experience that can take advantage of features from the operating system and from other Windows 8 apps.

CHAPTER 19

■ ■ ■

Understanding the App Lifecycle

The first area of integration that I will look at is the Metro app lifecycle. So far in this book, I have been glossing over the way that apps are started and managed and I have been relying on one part of the code that Visual Studio adds to the default.js file when creating a new projects and deleting other parts for brevity.

In this chapter, I'll explain the different stages in the life of a Metro app, explain how and why they occur and show you how to understand when your app moves from one stage to another. Along the way, I'll explain why the code that Visual Studio adds isn't all that useful, show you how to fix it and show you to make sure that your app fits into the overall Metro and Windows 8 lifecycle model. Table 19-1 provides the summary for this chapter.

Table 19-1. Chapter Summary

Problem	Solution	Listing
Respond to changes in the app lifecycle	Handle the activated and checkpoint events emitted by the WinJS.Application object.	1-5
Determine the action required when the app receives an activated event	Read the value of the kind and previousExecutionState properties.	6-7
Ensure that WinJS.Application passes on all lifecycle events to the app.	Listen for the resuming event emitted by the WebUIApplication object and respond by creating a synthetic event using the WinJS.Application.queueEvent method.	8
Ensure that the splash screen is visible until the app has finished initializing	Use the setPromise method in the onactivated handler function	9-16
Receive a notification when the splash screen is dismissed	Listen for the dismissed event emitted by the object returned by the IActivatedEventArgs.splashScreen property.	17
Respond to app termination	Persist the state of the app when it is suspended and restore the state if the app is terminated and then launched	18-19
Stopping background work when the app is suspended	Either cancel the Promise handling the background work or single to the Promise that it should fulfill itself and pass it to the setPromise method.	20-26

Understanding the App Lifecycle

Windows 8 aggressively manages Metro apps to keep device memory free. This is done to make sure that the available memory is used to maximum advantage and to reduce the drain on the battery. As part of this strategy, Metro apps have a well-defined lifecycle. All but the simplest apps need to be aware when Windows 8 moves an app from one stage in the lifecycle to another, which is done by listening for some specific system events. I'll describe the events and show you how to handle them shortly, but in this section I am going to describe the lifecycle so that you understand the context that your Metro apps operate in.

Activated

An app is *activated* when it is launched - typically when the user clicks on the app's icon on the start screen. This is the basic initialization of a Metro app and, just like when any kind of app is started, you need to create your layout, load your data, set up event listeners and so on. In short, an activated app goes from not running to running and is responsible for bootstrapping its state to offer services to the user.

■ **Note**   Not all activations are to launch an app – as I'll explain later in this chapter, Windows will also activate your app so it can perform other tasks, including those defined by *contracts*. Contracts are a major theme in this part of the book and you'll start to see how they work in Chapter 24.

Suspended

An app is *suspended* by Windows 8 when it isn't being used, most often because the user has switch to use another app. This is where the aggressive part of the app management comes in: an app is suspended just a few seconds after the user perform the switch to another app. In short, as soon as your app is no longer visible to the user, you can expect it to be suspended.

A suspended app is frozen. The state of the app is preserved, but the app code won't be executed. The user isn't made aware that an app has been suspended and the app's thumbnail is still present in the list of running apps so that it can be selected again.

Resumed

A suspended app is *resumed* when the user selects a suspended app and displays it again. Windows preserves the layout and state of the application, so you don't need to load your data and configure HTML elements when your app is resumed.

Terminated

A suspended Metro app will be terminated if Windows needs to free up memory. A suspended app does not receive any kind of notification when it is terminated and the state of the app and any unsaved data is discarded. The snapshot of the app layout is removed from the list of running apps displayed to the user and replaced with a splash screen as a placeholder. The app returns to the activated state if the user starts the app again.

■ **Note**   Windows does not provide Metro app developers with a well-defined policy about when apps will be terminated. This is an action of last resort, but Windows is free to terminate apps whenever it needs to and you cannot make assumptions about the likelihood of your app being terminated based on the available system resources.

Working with WinJS.Application

Now that you understand the different stages of the lifecycle, I will show you how to deal with them in the app JavaScript code. The key object this section is `WinJS.Application`, which provides access to the lifecycle events and some related features for JavaScript Metro app.

■ **Tip**   `WinJS.Application` is a just a wrapper around the functionality in the `Windows.UI.WebUI.WebUIApplication` object. The value in using `WinJS.Application` is that presents the lifecycle features in a way that is more consistent with JavaScript and web app development in general. You can use the `WebUIApplication` class directly, but there are some useful `WinJS.Application` features that I find make it worth using.

I'll start with the events that `WinJS.Application` supports, which I have described in Table 19-2. For dealing with the app lifecycle, the important events are `activated` and `checkpoint`. In fact, I rarely use the other events.

Table 19-2. The WinJS.Application events

Name	Description
activated	Triggered when the app is activated
checkpoint	Triggered when the app is about to be suspended
loaded	Triggered when the DOM content has been loaded
ready	Triggered when the app is ready
settings	Triggered when the app settings are changed – I describe settings in Chapter 20.
unloaded	Triggered when the app is about to be unloaded
error	Triggered when an unhandled error is encountered

When you create a new Metro project, Visual Studio adds some code to the js/default.js file that provides some basic lifecycle event handling using the `WinJS.Application` object. For this chapter, I have created a new Visual Studio Metro app project called `EventCalc` and you can see the default.js file that Visual Studio creates in Listing 19-1. (I have edited the comments in this listing and highlighted the parts that relate to the `WinJS.Application` object.)

Listing 19-1. The code added to the default.js file by Visual Studio

```
// For an introduction to the Blank template, see the following documentation:
// http://go.microsoft.com/fwlink/?LinkId=232509
```

```
(function () {
    "use strict";

    WinJS.Binding.optimizeBindingReferences = true;

    var app = WinJS.Application;
    var activation = Windows.ApplicationModel.Activation;

    app.onactivated = function (args) {
        if (args.detail.kind === activation.ActivationKind.launch) {
            if (args.detail.previousExecutionState !==
                activation.ApplicationExecutionState.terminated) {
                // app has been launched
            } else {
                // app has been resumed
            }
            args.setPromise(WinJS.UI.processAll());
        }
    };

    app.oncheckpoint = function (args) {
        // app is about to be suspended
    };

    app.start();
})();
```

You can use the addEventListener method to setup your event listener functions, but Microsoft have used the on* properties for the code that Visual Studio generates and that I'll follow this convention in this chapter.

■ **Tip** Notice that the last statement in the listing is a call to the WinJS.Application.start method. The WinJS.Application object queues up events until the start method is called, at which point the events are passed to your code. Calling the stop method causes WinJS.Application to start queuing events again. A common problem is to forget to call start, creating an app which doesn't do anything when it is activated.

There are a couple of problems in this listing. First, the code that Visual Studio adds to a new project isn't very helpful. Second, the WinJS.Application object doesn't forward all of the events that the WebUIApplication object sends. You'll hit a brick wall sooner or later if you use the code in the /js/default.js file to build a complex app without fixing both problems. I'll explain both problems and demonstrate solutions to them after I build out the EventCalc example app.

Building the Example App

The example app is a very simple calculator which allows you to add two numbers together. This app also displays details of the lifecycle events that it receives. You can see the layout of the app without any content in Figure 19-1.

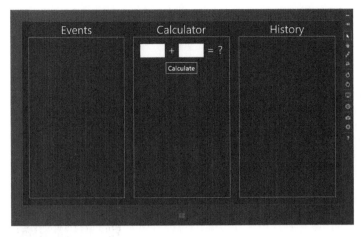

Figure 19-1. The EventCalc app

Defining the View Model

This is a basic simple app, but it will help me to demonstrate the app lifecycle if I add a simple view model. Listing 19-2 shows the content of the viewmodel.js file, which I added to the js folder of the Visual Studio project.

Listing 19-2. The view model for the EventCalc app

```
(function () {

    WinJS.Namespace.define("ViewModel", WinJS.Binding.as({
        State: {
            firstNumber: null,
            secondNumber: null,
            result: null,
            history: new WinJS.Binding.List(),
            eventLog: new WinJS.Binding.List()
        }
    }));

    WinJS.Namespace.define("ViewModel.Converters", {
        calcNumber: WinJS.Binding.converter(function (val) {
            return val == null ? "" : val;
        }),
        calcResult: WinJS.Binding.converter(function (val) {
            return val == null ? "?" : val;
        }),
    });
})();
```

The ViewModel.State object defines properties for the two values that are being added together and the result of the calculation. I have also used two WinJS.Binding.List objects to record calculations and to keep details of the lifecycle events that the app receives. In addition to the state data, I have defined a pair of simple binding converters that will prevent `null` being displayed in the layout when there are no values assigned to the view model properties.

Defining the Markup

My example app contains only one set of content, so I have defined the markup in the `default.html` file, rather than using the single-page content model and the navigation API. You can see the contents of `default.html` in Listing 19-3. I don't use any new techniques in this file. The layout is split into three sections. The first and last section contain `ListView` controls which use the view model List objects as data sources and the middle section contains basic HTML elements to capture the inputs for the calculation from the user and display the results.

Listing 19-3. The contents of the default.html file

```html
<!DOCTYPE html>
<html>
<head>
    <meta charset="utf-8" />
    <title>EventCalc</title>

    <!-- WinJS references -->
    <link href="//Microsoft.WinJS.1.0/css/ui-dark.css" rel="stylesheet" />
    <script src="//Microsoft.WinJS.1.0/js/base.js"></script>
    <script src="//Microsoft.WinJS.1.0/js/ui.js"></script>

    <!-- EventCalc references -->
    <link href="/css/default.css" rel="stylesheet" />
    <script src="/js/viewmodel.js"></script>
    <script src="/js/default.js"></script>
</head>
<body>
    <div id="template" data-win-control="WinJS.Binding.Template">
        <div class="message" data-win-bind="innerText: message"></div>
    </div>

    <div id="eventContainer" class="container">
        <span>Events</span>
        <div id="eventList" data-win-control="WinJS.UI.ListView"
            data-win-options="{
                itemTemplate: template,
                itemDataSource: ViewModel.State.eventLog.dataSource,
                layout: {type: WinJS.UI.ListLayout},
            }">
        </div>
    </div>

    <div id="calcContainer" class="container">
        <span>Calculator</span>
        <div id="calcElems">
            <input id="firstInput" data-win-bind="innerText: firstNumber
```

```
                ViewModel.Converters.calcNumber" />
            <span class="calcSymbol">+</span>
            <input id="secondInput" data-win-bind="innerText: secondNumber
                ViewModel.Converters.calcNumber" />
            <span class="calcSymbol">=</span>
            <span id="result" data-win-bind="innerText: result
                ViewModel.Converters.calcResult"></span>
            <button id="calcButton">Calculate</button>
        </div>
    </div>

    <div id="historyContainer" class="container">
        <span>History</span>
        <div id="historyList" data-win-control="WinJS.UI.ListView"
            data-win-options="{
                itemTemplate: template,
                itemDataSource: ViewModel.State.history.dataSource,
                layout: {type: WinJS.UI.ListLayout},
            }">
        </div>
    </div>
</body>
</html>
```

Defining the CSS

To manage the layout of the HTML elements, I have defined the styles shown in Listing 19-4 in the /css/
default.css file. These styles rely on standard CSS properties and there are no Metro-specific features
used.

Listing 19-4. The contents of the /css/default.css file

```
body {display: -ms-flexbox;-ms-flex-direction: row;
    -ms-flex-align: stretch;-ms-flex-pack: center;}
div.container {width: 30%; display: inline-block;margin: 0 20px;
    text-align: center;font-size: 35pt;}

#eventList, #historyList, #calcElems {
    border: thin solid white;height: 85%;padding-top: 20px;
}

#calcButton {font-size: 20pt; margin: 20px;}
#calcContainer input {font-size: 25pt;width: 100px;}

*.calcSymbol, #result {font-size: 35pt;}
.message {font-size: 20pt;margin: 5px;text-align: left;}
```

Defining the JavaScript

All of the interesting parts of this app happen in the JavaScript code. Listing 19-5 builds on the code added to the default.js file by Visual Studio, so that details of the lifecycle events are displayed in one of the ListView controls and calculations can be performed.

Listing 19-5. Building on the default.js file created by Visual Studio

```javascript
(function () {
    "use strict";

    var app = WinJS.Application;
    var activation = Windows.ApplicationModel.Activation;
    WinJS.strictProcessing();

    function writeEventMessage(msg) {
        ViewModel.State.eventLog.push({ message: msg });
    };

    app.onactivated = function (args) {
        if (args.detail.kind === activation.ActivationKind.launch) {
            if (args.detail.previousExecutionState !==
                activation.ApplicationExecutionState.terminated) {
                // app has been launched
                writeEventMessage("Launched");
                performInitialization();
            } else {
                // app has been resumed
                writeEventMessage("Resumed");
            }

            args.setPromise(WinJS.UI.processAll().then(function () {
                return WinJS.Binding.processAll(calcElems, ViewModel.State);
            }));
        }
    };

    app.oncheckpoint = function (args) {
        // app is about to be suspended
        writeEventMessage("Suspended");
    };

    function performInitialization() {
        calcButton.addEventListener("click",
            function (e) {
                var first = ViewModel.State.firstNumber = Number(firstInput.value);
                var second = ViewModel.State.secondNumber = Number(secondInput.value);
                var result = ViewModel.State.result = first + second;
            });

        ViewModel.State.bind("result", function (val) {
```

```
        if (val != null) {
            ViewModel.State.history.push({
                message: ViewModel.State.firstNumber + " + "
                    + ViewModel.State.secondNumber + " = "
                    + val
            });
        }
    });
};

    app.start();
})();
```

The `writeEventMessage` function adds an item to the view model reporting receipt of a lifecycle event, formatting the message so that it works with the template that I defined in the `default.html` file.

The `performInitialization` function contains the code that I want executed when the application is launched – for this app, this means setting up a handler for the `click` event emitted by the `button` element and setting up a programmatic data binding to generate the calculation history when the view model result property changes.

■ **Tip**   Notice that in the `onactivated` handler, I call the `setPromise` method on the argument object that was passed to the function. I explain this method in the Dealing with the Splash Screen section later in the chapter.

Triggering Lifecycle Changes

The simplest way to move an app from one part of the lifecycle to another is to use Visual Studio. If you look at the toolbar, you will see a menu item that is labeled Suspend. If you click on the small arrow to the right of the label, you will see that the menu also contains selections for Resume and Suspend and Shutdown, as shown in Figure 19-2. (You may have to select Debug Locations from the Visual Studio View – Toolbars menu to see the toolbar.)

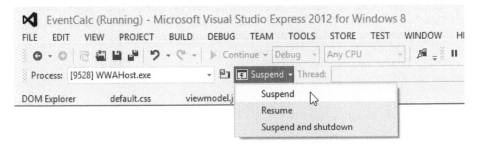

Figure 19-2. Using Visual Studio to control the app lifecycle

The menu items force the app to move from one lifecycle stage to another. They are useful because they allow you to test your code with the debugger attached. I use this feature a lot during the early stages of app development.

However, Visual Studio is only able to *simulate* the lifecycle events, which can mean that there are subtle differences when the debugger is running and when the debugger isn't being used. This means that you should take the time to test the way that your app behaves by generating the events directly from the operating system, without relying on the Visual Studio debugger.

The problem is that when the debugger isn't being used, one effect is that there is no JavaScript Console window available to display debugging messages, making it harder to figure out what's going on. It is for this reason that I have added a ListView control to the example app so that I can record the arrival of lifecycle events in the layout of the app itself – a technique that I often use for final testing of apps.

Generating the Lifecycle Events in Windows 8

Generating the lifecycle events is actually pretty simple, as long as you take your time and wait to see the indications that Windows 8 displays to indicate lifecycle changes. In the sections that follow, I show you how to generate each of the activated, resuming, and suspending events, without using Visual Studio. As I have said, this is the only realistic way to test what your users will see.

Launching the App

The simplest way to trigger the activated event is to launch the app, although it is important that you don't do this with the Visual Studio debugger. You can either select the app's tile from the Start screen or by selecting Start Without Debugging from the Visual Studio Debug menu.

■ **Tip**   The example app's tile won't be added to the Start screen until it has been started from Visual Studio at least once. After that point, you should see the app's tile listed on the far right of the screen. Sometimes the tile won't be visible, especially if you have been switching between the simulator and the local machine to run the app – in this case, I find that searching for the app by typing the first few letters of the app's name and selecting it from the list of results is enough to make the file appear properly.

You will see the default splash screen when you launch the EventCalc app (because I have not changed the manifest settings for the color or icon used) and then see the app layout shown in Figure 19-3. Notice that the activated event has been recorded in the left-hand ListView control. I have recorded this event with the message Launched, to indicate that the event that was received was a request to launch the app – something that I'll come back to and explain in more detail later in this chapter.

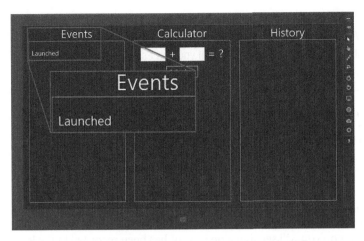

Figure 19-3. Launching the example app without the debugger

Suspending the App

The easiest way to cause Windows to suspend the app is to press Win+D to switch to the desktop. You can track the process of the app lifecycle by launching the Task Manager, switching to the Details tab and finding the WWAHost.exe process (which is the name of the executable which is used to run JavaScript Metro apps – as a consequence, there will be one for each Metro app you have launched). You may have to click on the More Details button in the Task manager to see the Details tab.

■ **Note** You need to start the Task Manager on the local machine, even if the example app is running in the simulator. The Task Manager is prevented from running within the simulator, but the WWAHost.exe process will still be visible in the Task Manager of the local machine.

After a few seconds, Windows will suspend the app and the process status will change to Suspended in the Task Manager. You can see how a suspended app is shown in the Task Manager in Figure 19-4.

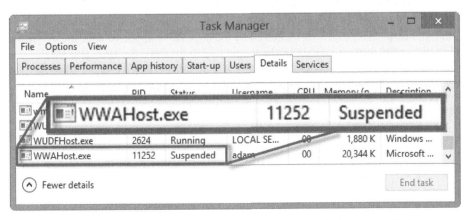

Figure 19-4. Using the Task Manager to observe a Metro app being suspended

■ **Note**   Apps which are connected to the Visual Studio debugger will never be shown as Suspended in the Task Manager because they are kept alive so that debugger can control the app. If you don't see the Suspended message, it is typically because the app was started with the debugger.

I need to use the Task Manager to check the state of the app because I can no longer see the app layout and, since I am not using the debugger, I can't read any debugging messages. You'll see the evidence that the suspending event was received when I resume the app in the next section.

Resuming the App

You can resume the app by bringing it back to the foreground – the easiest way to do this is to move the mouse into the top-left corner (or swipe from the left edge on a touch screen) and click on the thumbnail image. The app will return to fill the screen and you will see that a new event has been recorded in the left-hand ListView control in the app layout, as shown in Figure 19-5.

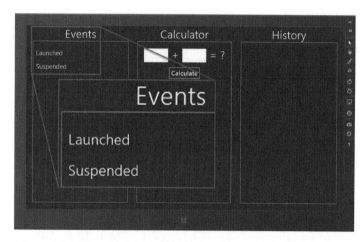

Figure 19-5. The app has received the suspending and resuming events

The figure shows that the suspending event was received by the app. This happened after the app has hidden from the user but before the process was shown as suspended in the Task Manager. This small interval is something I'll return to later in the chapter because it is presents the app an opportunity to prepare itself to be suspended, something that can be invaluable for certain kinds of app.

What the figure *doesn't* show is the receipt of the resuming event. This is one of the problems in the code added to the project by Visual Studio. I'll show you how to ensure that your app gets this event shortly.

Terminating the App

You can terminate the execution of the app by typing Alt+F4. The app is terminated abruptly and no warning event is sent. Exiting the app in this way allows you to ensure that your app recovers properly when it is next launched and to check that any remote services that it consumes (web services, databases, etc.) are able to recover resources correctly.

This is one of the two ways in which your app can be terminated. The other occurs when the app is suspended and Windows needs to free up some resources. In both causes, your app will be terminated without receiving any notification events. Later in this chapter, I'll show you how to prepare for termination when your app is suspended and I show you how to tell how your app was terminated when it is next launched.

You can simulate the circumstances of Windows terminating the app by using the Suspend and Shutdown item from the Visual Studio toolbar menu (the same one that contains the Suspend and Resume items).

Getting the Activation Type and Previous App State

Before I can fix the code in the default.js file so that I get all of the lifecycle events, I need to do some preparatory work so that I can figure out what I am being asked to do when an event arrives. For this, I need to dig into the detail of the events to discover the activation type and the state that my app was in before the event was dispatched.

When an app is sent the activated event, the event object that is passed to the onactivated function has a detail property which returns a Windows.ApplicationModel.Activation.IActivatedEventArgs object.

The IActivatedEventArgs object defines the three properties I have described in Table 19-3, and these properties provide you with all of the information you need to work out what Windows is asking your app to do. I describe two of these properties in the sections that follow and return to the third later in the chapter.

Table 19-3. Properties defined by IActivatedEventArgs

Name	Description
kind	Returns the reason that the app has been activated
previousExecutionState	Returns the state of the app before it was executed
splashScreen	Returns an object that provides information about the splash screen. See the Dealing with the Splash Screen section later in the chapter for details.

Determining the Kind of Activation

An app can be activated for a range of different purposes, such as sharing data between apps, receiving data from a device, and handling a search query. These activation purposes are defined by Windows *contracts*, which allow you to integrate your app into Windows and which I return to later in the chapter – you'll be able to see examples of how I implement contracts in later chapters. For this chapter, I care about *launch* activations, which occur when the user has started the app or the app has been resumed after being suspended.

You can determine what kind of activation you are dealing with by reading the kind property from the activated event. The kind property returns one of the values defined by the Windows.ApplicationModel.Activation.ActivationKind enumeration. The only value I look for in this chapter in launch, which tells me that the app has been started or resumed. You can see how I check for this in in the onactivated function in Listing 19-6.

Listing 19-6. Checking for the launch activation kind

```
...
app.onactivated = function (args) {
```

```
    if (args.detail.kind === activation.ActivationKind.launch) {
        // the app has been launched
        writeEventMessage("Launched");
    }
};
...
```

Determining the Previous App State

When dealing with a launch activation request, you need to know what state the app was in before it was activated, which you can determine by reading the previousExecutionState property. This property returns one of the values defined by the Windows.ApplicationModel.Activation. ApplicationExecutionState enumeration, which I have listed in Table 19-4.

Table 19-4. Values defined by the ApplicationExecutionState enumeration

Value	Description
notRunning	The app was not running
running	The app was running
suspended	The app was suspended
terminated	The app was terminated after it was suspended
closedByUser	The app was closed by the user (using Alt+F4, for example)

If the previous state of your app was notRunning or closedByUser, then you are dealing with a *fresh start* launch. You need to initialize your app (set up UI controls, event listeners, etc.) and prepare the app for its first user interaction.

If the previous state is suspended, then the app will already be initialized and state of the app will be just as it was when the app was suspended. The terminated state is an odd combination of both situations. Apps are terminated by the system, rather than the user, and so the idea is that if the user launches the app again, they should be able to continue as they were before suspension and termination occurred. However, the state of the app is lost when it is terminated. To achieve the right behavior, you need to store the state of the app when it is suspended, in the event that termination occurs. I'll explain how to do this later in this chapter.

The running state is usually encountered when Windows wants your app to fulfill its contract obligations and the app is already running because the user launched it previously. You will also encounter this state when you use the Visual Studio Refresh button to reload the content of your app – although, of course, this is not a situation your app will encounter when deployed to users. How you respond to the running state will depend on your app and the contracts it supports, but in this chapter I will treat the running state in the same was as notRunning, just to make sure that the app behaves properly with the Visual Studio Refresh button. This may not make sense for all apps, but since my user – i.e., you – is likely to be running the app in Visual Studio, this is the most sensible thing to do.

Responding to Different Launch Types

Now that you understand how Windows provides details in the activated event, I can add some code to my /js/default.js file to respond to different situations. You can see the additions I have made in Listing 19-7.

Listing 19-7. Differentiating between activation types and previous execution states

```
...
app.onactivated = function (args) {
    if (args.detail.kind === activation.ActivationKind.launch) {
        switch (args.detail.previousExecutionState) {
            case activation.ApplicationExecutionState.suspended:
                writeEventMessage("Resumed from Suspended");
                break;
            case activation.ApplicationExecutionState.terminated:
                writeEventMessage("Launch from Terminated");
                performInitialization();
                break;
            case activation.ApplicationExecutionState.notRunning:
            case activation.ApplicationExecutionState.closedByUser:
            case activation.ApplicationExecutionState.running:
                writeEventMessage("Fresh Launch");
                performInitialization();
                break;
        }

        args.setPromise(WinJS.UI.processAll().then(function () {
            return WinJS.Binding.processAll(calcElems, ViewModel.State);
        }));
    }
};
...
```

When I receive a launch activation event, I use a switch statement to check for all of the ApplicationExecutionState values. I treat the notRunning, closedByUser and running values the same, and call the performInitialization function to set up my event listener and data binding. I have changed the messages passed to the writeEventMessage function to make the significance of the event I receive clearer.

I also call the performInitialization function when the previous state is terminated. I'll add some extra code later in this chapter to differentiate the way that I handle this state from notRunning, running and closedByUser. For all of these previous states, I need to initialize my app to make sure that my event handlers and data binding are set up.

I don't do anything at all for the suspended value yet, other than to call the writeEventMessage function to record receipt of the event. I don't need to initialize my app because the system is resuming execution and my event handlers and data binding will already exist. I'll add some code to this section when I come to background activities, but for the moment, doing nothing is what sets the response to the suspended state apart.

■ **Tip** You will notice that I call the WinJS.UI.processAll and WinJS.Binding.processAll methods irrespective of what kind of activation I am handling. I'll come back to this code later in the chapter.

You can see two of the three activated event messages I display in Figure 19-6. You can recreate these events yourself very easily using Visual Studio. First, start the app using the Start Debugging item from the Debug menu – this will produce the Fresh Launch message shown in the left-hand side of the figure.

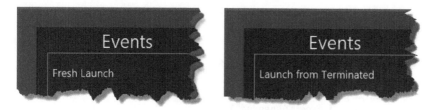

Figure 19-6. Displaying details of launch activation events

Now select the Suspend and Shutdown item from the toolbar menu, which terminates the app. Start the app again and the previous execution state of the activated event will be set to terminated, resulting in the message shown in the right-hand side of the figure.

Capturing the Resuming Event

The code in my default.js file is at the point where I can differentiate between different kinds of activation events and respond based on the previous state of the app – but I still don't get an event when the app is resumed. To remedy this, I have made the addition shown in Listing 19-8 to the default.js file.

Listing 19-8. Capturing the resuming event

```
(function () {
    "use strict";

    var app = WinJS.Application;
    var activation = Windows.ApplicationModel.Activation;
    WinJS.strictProcessing();

    function writeEventMessage(msg) {
        ViewModel.State.eventLog.push({ message: msg });
    };

    app.onactivated = function (args) {
        // ...code removed for brevity...
    };


    app.oncheckpoint = function (args) {
        // app is about to be suspended
        writeEventMessage("Suspended");
    };

    function performInitialization() {
        // ...code removed for brevity...
    };

    Windows.UI.WebUI.WebUIApplication.addEventListener("resuming", function (e) {
        WinJS.Application.queueEvent({
            type: "activated",
```

```
        detail: {
            kind: activation.ActivationKind.launch,
            previousExecutionState: activation.ApplicationExecutionState.suspended
        }
    });
});

app.start();
})();
```

As I mentioned before, the WinJS.Application object is a wrapper around the functionality provided by the Windows.UI.WebUI.WebUIApplication object. For reasons that I don't understand, the WinJS. Application class doesn't forward the resuming event to the app when it is sent by the WebUIApplication object, and my addition to the default.js file fixes this omission: I listen for the resuming event issued by the WebUIApplication object and feed it into the event queue that WinJS.Application maintains by calling the queueEvent object.

The object that I pass into the queueEvent method conforms to the pattern for the activated events that *are* passed on – the type property is set to activated and the detail property has kind and previousExecutionState properties that return the expected values.

This isn't ideal, but it is important if you want to be able to respond to the full set of lifecycle changes. Figure 19-7 demonstrates that the fix works and you can replicate this result by starting the example app and then selecting the Suspend and then the Resume items from the Visual Studio toolbar menu.

Figure 19-7. Illustrating the effect of capturing the resuming event

Responding to Lifecycle Changes

The way that an app responds to changes from one lifecycle change to another will vary, of course, but there are core behaviors that you need to consider whatever facilities your app offers. In the sections that follow, I describe some key techniques that you can use when responding to lifecycle events that will make your app fit into the lifecycle model.

Dealing with the Splash Screen

You may have noticed that I have been using the setPromise method in the onactivated handler function in this chapter, as shown in Listing 19-9. This is a useful WinJS.Application feature that prevents the splash screen from disappearing before an app is initialized.

Listing 19-9. Using the setPromise method to retain the splash screen

```
...
app.onactivated = function (args) {
    if (args.detail.kind === activation.ActivationKind.launch) {
        switch (args.detail.previousExecutionState) {
            case activation.ApplicationExecutionState.suspended:
                writeEventMessage("Resumed from Suspended");
                break;
            case activation.ApplicationExecutionState.terminated:
                writeEventMessage("Launch from Terminated");
                performInitialization();
                break;
            case activation.ApplicationExecutionState.notRunning:
            case activation.ApplicationExecutionState.closedByUser:
            case activation.ApplicationExecutionState.running:
                writeEventMessage("Fresh Launch");
                performInitialization();
                break;
        }

        args.setPromise(WinJS.UI.processAll().then(function () {
            return WinJS.Binding.processAll(calcElems, ViewModel.State);
        }));
    }
};
...
```

The splash screen will be displayed until the Promise passed to the args.setPromise method is fulfilled. In this listing, I use a chain of Promise objects which call the WinJS.UI.processAll and then the WinJS.Binding.processAll methods. Only when both of these methods have completed will the splash screen be replaced by the app layout.

■ **Tip**   I described the WinJS.UI.processAll method in Chapter 10 and the WinJS.Binding.processAll method in Chapter 8.

At the moment, there isn't anything in the example app that will delay the removal of the splash screen – so, in order to demonstrate this feature, I'll add some new functionality in the sections that follow.

Adding to the Example App

My example app is deliberately simple, but there can be a significant amount of initial setup required in a real app. To simulate this, I have changed the example app so that it calculates the result of adding the first 5,000 integer values together when the app first starts and then uses this data to produce results for calculations when they are performed by the user. Forget, if you will, that there is no good reason for doing this, other than it makes for a useful demonstration. To start, I have added a new value to the view model to contain the cached results, as shown in Listing 19-10.

Listing 19-10. Adding a view model property for the cached data

```
...
WinJS.Namespace.define("ViewModel", WinJS.Binding.as({
    State: {
        firstNumber: null,
        secondNumber: null,
        result: null,
        history: new WinJS.Binding.List(),
        eventLog: new WinJS.Binding.List(),
        cachedResult: null
    }
}));
```

To generate the cached results, I have added a new file to the project called tasks.js, which contains a custom WinJS.Promise implementation. You can see the contents of the tasks.js file in Listing 19-11, which shows the implementation of the doWork function. (I explained how Promise objects work and how to implement your own in Chapter 9).

Listing 19-11 Implementing a custom Promise in the tasks.js file

```
(function () {
    WinJS.Namespace.define("Utils", {
        doWork: function (count) {
            var canceled = false;

            return new WinJS.Promise(function (fDone, fError, fProgress) {
                var blockSize = 500;

                var results = {};

                (function calcBlock(start) {
                    for (var first = start; first < start + blockSize; first++) {
                        results[first] = {};
                        for (var second = start; second < start + blockSize; second++) {
                            results[first][second] = first + second;
                        }
                    }
                    if (!canceled && start + blockSize < count) {
                        fProgress(start);
                        setImmediate(function () {
                            calcBlock(start + blockSize);
                        });
                    } else {
                        fDone(results);
                    }
                })(1);

            }, function () {
                canceled = true;
            });
        }
```

```
    });
})();
```

Custom Promise code can be hard to read, but the code in the listing adds together pairs of numbers in blocks of 500 at a time before calling the setImmediate function to avoid locking up the JavaScript runtime. I defined the calcBlock function as a self-executing function and invoke it as soon as it is defined with an argument of 1 to calculate the first set of results.

The data structure that this code creates is an object which has properties for each numeric value and the value of each property is another object whose properties correspond to the second numeric value and whose values are the sum, like this:

```
results = {
    1 = {
        1: 2,
        2: 3,
        3: 4,
    }
}
```

The completed set of results is passed to the Promise completion function, which means that it can be accessed using the then method of the Promise object that the doWork function returns. I have added the tasks.js file to the head section of the default.html file, as shown in Listing 19-12.

Listing 19-12. Adding the tasks.js file to the default.html head section

```
...
<head>
    <meta charset="utf-8" />
    <title>EventCalc</title>

    <!-- WinJS references -->
    <link href="//Microsoft.WinJS.1.0/css/ui-dark.css" rel="stylesheet" />
    <script src="//Microsoft.WinJS.1.0/js/base.js"></script>
    <script src="//Microsoft.WinJS.1.0/js/ui.js"></script>

    <!-- EventCalc references -->
    <link href="/css/default.css" rel="stylesheet" />
    <script src="/js/viewmodel.js"></script>
    <script src="/js/tasks.js"></script>
    <script src="/js/default.js"></script>
</head>
...
```

Generating the Cached Results

To see the problem that the setPromise object solves, it helps to see what happens when you *don't* use the method. To this end, I have called the doWork method within the onactivated handler, but without using the setPromise object. You can see the addition to the default.js file in Listing 19-13.

Listing 19-13. Generating the cached results without using the setPromise object

```
...
app.onactivated = function (args) {
    if (args.detail.kind === activation.ActivationKind.launch) {
        switch (args.detail.previousExecutionState) {
            case activation.ApplicationExecutionState.suspended:
                writeEventMessage("Resumed from Suspended");
                break;
            case activation.ApplicationExecutionState.terminated:
                writeEventMessage("Launch from Terminated");
                performInitialization();
                break;
            case activation.ApplicationExecutionState.notRunning:
            case activation.ApplicationExecutionState.closedByUser:
            case activation.ApplicationExecutionState.running:
                writeEventMessage("Fresh Launch");
                performInitialization();
                break;
        }

        Utils.doWork(5000).then(function (data) {
            ViewModel.State.cachedResult = data;
        });

        args.setPromise(WinJS.UI.processAll().then(function () {
            return WinJS.Binding.processAll(calcElems, ViewModel.State);
        }));
    }
};
...
```

The view model property is only assigned the cached results when all of the values have been calculated. The risk is that the user will be presented with the layout of app before all of the data is available.

■ **Tip** The argument passed to the doWork function specifies how many values are calculated and you may need to change this value so that you get something which occupies your device for long enough for you to try and perform a calculation. I find that a task that takes about 5–10 seconds is about right.

You can see the potential problem in the performInitialization function, which I have modified in Listing 19-14 to use the cached results.

Listing 19-14. Using the cached data in the performInitialization function

```
...
function performInitialization() {
    calcButton.addEventListener("click", function (e) {
        var first = ViewModel.State.firstNumber = Number(firstInput.value);
        var second = ViewModel.State.secondNumber = Number(secondInput.value);
```

```
        if (first < 5000 && second < 5000) {
            ViewModel.State.result = ViewModel.State.cachedResult[first][second];
        } else {
            ViewModel.State.result = first + second;
        }
    });

    ViewModel.State.bind("result", function (val) {
        if (val != null) {
            ViewModel.State.history.push({
                message: ViewModel.State.firstNumber + " + "
                    + ViewModel.State.secondNumber + " = "
                    + val
            });
        }
    });
};
...
```

If the user tries to perform a calculation before the cached data is ready, the attempt to read the result from the view model will generate an exception, like the one that Figure 19-8. The error message in the figure was displayed after trying to perform the calculation 1 + 1 before the cached data was ready. The code in the click event handler, shown in Listing 19-14 attempts to access a variable whose name is 1, but it doesn't yet exist.

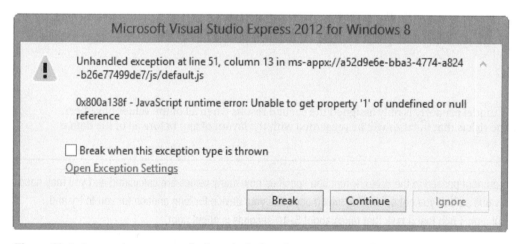

Figure 19-8. Attempting to use cached results before they are generated

Maintaining the Splash Screen

The alternative approach is to use the setPromise method which will ensure that the splash screen is displayed until the Promise it is passed is fulfilled. You can see how I have done this for the example app in Listing 19-15.

Listing 19-15. Using the setPromise method to keep the splash screen displayed

```
...
app.onactivated = function (args) {
    if (args.detail.kind === activation.ActivationKind.launch) {
        switch (args.detail.previousExecutionState) {
            case activation.ApplicationExecutionState.suspended:
                writeEventMessage("Resumed from Suspended");
                break;
            case activation.ApplicationExecutionState.terminated:
                writeEventMessage("Launch from Terminated");
                performInitialization();
                break;
            case activation.ApplicationExecutionState.notRunning:
            case activation.ApplicationExecutionState.closedByUser:
            case activation.ApplicationExecutionState.running:
                writeEventMessage("Fresh Launch");
                performInitialization();
                break;
        }

        var cachedPromise = Utils.doWork(5000).then(function (data) {
            ViewModel.State.cachedResult = data;
        });

        var processPromise = WinJS.UI.processAll().then(function () {
            return WinJS.Binding.processAll(calcElems, ViewModel.State);
        });

        args.setPromise(WinJS.Promise.join([cachedPromise, processPromise]));
    }
};
...
```

There is no reason why the WinJS.UI.processAll and WinJS.Binding.processAll methods can't operate on the markup while the doWork function is generated the cached results, so I have used the WinJS. Promise.join method to create a Promise that lets the two activities be interleaved – it is this combined Promise that I have passed to the setPromise method, which ensures that the splash screen will be displayed until both doWork and the two processAll calls have finished their work.

Of course, I don't quite have the right behavior yet – my results are calculated whenever my app is launched, even if it is being resumed from the suspended state. I need to be more selective about when I perform my initialization and the easiest way to do this is to start to generate the cached results in the performInitialization function, which is called when the app hasn't been resumed from the suspended state. You can see how I have done this in Listing 19-16, which shows further changes to the default.js file.

Listing 19-16. Ensuring that the cached results are not generated when the app is resumed

```
(function () {
    "use strict";

    var app = WinJS.Application;
```

```
    var activation = Windows.ApplicationModel.Activation;
    WinJS.strictProcessing();

    function writeEventMessage(msg) {
        ViewModel.State.eventLog.push({ message: msg });
    };

    app.onactivated = function (args) {
        var promises = [];

        if (args.detail.kind === activation.ActivationKind.launch) {
            switch (args.detail.previousExecutionState) {
                case activation.ApplicationExecutionState.suspended:
                    writeEventMessage("Resumed from Suspended");
                    break;
                case activation.ApplicationExecutionState.terminated:
                    writeEventMessage("Launch from Terminated");
                    promises.push(performInitialization());
                    break;
                case activation.ApplicationExecutionState.notRunning:
                case activation.ApplicationExecutionState.closedByUser:
                case activation.ApplicationExecutionState.running:
                    writeEventMessage("Fresh Launch");
                    promises.push(performInitialization());
                    break;
            }

            promises.push(WinJS.UI.processAll().then(function () {
                return WinJS.Binding.processAll(calcElems, ViewModel.State);
            }));

            args.setPromise(WinJS.Promise.join(promises));
        }
    };

    app.oncheckpoint = function (args) {
        // app is about to be suspended
        writeEventMessage("Suspended");
    };

    function performInitialization() {
        calcButton.addEventListener("click", function (e) {
            var first = ViewModel.State.firstNumber = Number(firstInput.value);
            var second = ViewModel.State.secondNumber = Number(secondInput.value);
            if (first < 5000 && second < 5000) {
                ViewModel.State.result = ViewModel.State.cachedResult[first][second];
            } else {
                ViewModel.State.result = first + second;
            }
        });
```

```
        ViewModel.State.bind("result", function (val) {
            if (val != null) {
                ViewModel.State.history.push({
                    message: ViewModel.State.firstNumber + " + "
                        + ViewModel.State.secondNumber + " = "
                        + val
                });
            }
        });

        return Utils.doWork(5000).then(function (data) {
            ViewModel.State.cachedResult = data;
        });
    };

    Windows.UI.WebUI.WebUIApplication.addEventListener("resuming", function (e) {
        WinJS.Application.queueEvent({
            type: "activated",
            detail: {
                kind: activation.ActivationKind.launch,
                previousExecutionState: activation.ApplicationExecutionState.suspended
            }
        });
    });

    app.start();
})();
```

Learning When the Splash Screen is dismissed

Keeping the splash screen visible is acceptable if your initialization takes a few seconds. Beyond that point, it looks like your app has hung during launch and has become non-responsive. If you have a lot of initialization to perform, then you should avoid using the setPromise object and show the user some kind of progress display instead. To do this, you need to know when the splash screen is dismissed and replaced with the layout of your app.

The splashScreen property of the IActivatedEventArgs object emits a dismissed event when the splash screen is replaced with the app layout. You can get this value through the detail.splashScreen property of the Event object passed to the onactivated handler function, as shown in Listing 19-17.

Listing 19-17. Receiving notification that the splash screen has been dismissed

```
...
app.onactivated = function (args) {
    var promises = [];

    if (args.detail.kind === activation.ActivationKind.launch) {
        switch (args.detail.previousExecutionState) {
            case activation.ApplicationExecutionState.suspended:
                writeEventMessage("Resumed from Suspended");
                break;
```

```
            case activation.ApplicationExecutionState.terminated:
                writeEventMessage("Launch from Terminated");
                promises.push(performInitialization());
                break;
            case activation.ApplicationExecutionState.notRunning:
            case activation.ApplicationExecutionState.closedByUser:
            case activation.ApplicationExecutionState.running:
                writeEventMessage("Fresh Launch");
                promises.push(performInitialization());
                break;
        }

        if (args.detail.splashScreen) {
            args.detail.splashScreen.addEventListener("dismissed", function (e) {
                writeEventMessage("Splash Screen Dismissed");
            });
        }

        promises.push(WinJS.UI.processAll().then(function () {
            return WinJS.Binding.processAll(calcElems, ViewModel.State);
        }));

        args.setPromise(WinJS.Promise.join(promises));
    }
};
...
```

There is no splash screen when the app is resumed – not just because Metro doesn't use one, but also because I am feeding the resuming event to WinJS.Application and don't define a splashScreen property. This means that you need to check to see if the splashScreen property exists.

If you start the app, you will see that a notification message is displayed in the left-hand ListView control reporting that the splash screen has been dismissed, as shown in Figure 19-9. If you still have app initialization to perform, then this will be your cue to display some interim message or content to the user.

Figure 19-9. Displaying a message when the splash screen is dismissed

Dealing with App Termination

Dealing with an app that has been launched after it has been terminated requires some work. An app isn't warned that it is about to be terminated – the system suspends the app and then later, if resources are tight, terminates the app process to free up memory. Windows can't tell the app that it is about to be terminated without bringing it out of suspension, which would require some of the resource that Windows is trying to reclaim.

Dealing with app termination requires some careful work on behalf of the app because Microsoft wants to hide termination from the user. This is a sensible idea and when an app follows this model, it creates a better overall Metro experience for the user, who doesn't care that limited device resources have caused app termination. The user didn't kill the app and when they select the splash screen placeholder from the list of "running" apps, they will have an expectation that the app will let them carry on from where they left off.

To make this work, you need to store the state of your app when it is suspended. This is like taking out app termination insurance – you hope that your app will just be resumed and you won't have to restore the state, but you need to take the precaution just in case your app is terminated.

The `WinJS.Application` object helps you store your app state through its `sessionState` property. You store state by assigning an object to this property and the object is persistently stored as JSON data. The JSON parser that is used is pretty simplistic and won't deal with complex objects, including observable objects, which means that you will generally need to create a new object that represents the state of your app – and, of course, be prepared to use that object to restore that state if your app is terminated and then activated.

To demonstrate this technique, I have added two new functions to the `viewmodel.js` file to persist and restore the app state data, as illustrated by Listing 19-18.

■ **Note** The `sessionState` property should only be used to store app state, like values the user has entered into UI controls, the point to which the user has navigated in the app and other data required to restore the app to its previous state. User data and settings should *not* be stored using the `sessionState` property. I'll show you how to handle settings in Chapter 20 and how to work with the file system in Chapters 22–24.

Listing 19-18. Functions to create and restore from a state object

```
(function () {

    WinJS.Namespace.define("ViewModel", WinJS.Binding.as({
        State: {
            firstNumber: null,
            secondNumber: null,
            result: null,
            history: new WinJS.Binding.List(),
            eventLog: new WinJS.Binding.List(),
            cachedResult: null
        }
    }));

    WinJS.Namespace.define("ViewModel.Converters", {
        calcNumber: WinJS.Binding.converter(function (val) {
            return val == null ? "" : val;
        }),
        calcResult: WinJS.Binding.converter(function (val) {
            return val == null ? "?" : val;
        }),
    });
```

```
WinJS.Namespace.define("ViewModel.State", {
    getData: function () {
        var data = {
            firstNumber: ViewModel.State.firstNumber,
            secondNumber: ViewModel.State.secondNumber,
            history: [],
            events: []
        };
        ViewModel.State.history.forEach(function (item) {
            data.history.push(item);
        });
        ViewModel.State.eventLog.forEach(function (item) {
            data.events.push(item);
        });
        return data;
    },
    setData: function (data) {
        data.history.forEach(function (item) {
            ViewModel.State.history.push(item);
        });
        data.events.forEach(function (item) {
            ViewModel.State.eventLog.push(item);
        });
        ViewModel.State.firstNumber = data.firstNumber;
        ViewModel.State.secondNumber = data.secondNumber;
    }
});

})();
```

Notice that I am selective about the data I include. I don't, for example, include the result property. If I did, and restored that value when the app was launched again, then setting the property would trigger the data binding I defined in default.js and create a new (and unexpected) entry in the history. The downside of not setting this value is that the last result given to the user won't be displayed in the middle column.

This is pretty typical of dealing with app state data – you can get usually get pretty close to returning to the state that the app was in before it was suspended, but there are always a few things that are difficult to restore. It is a matter of judgment as to how far you go in dealing with these issues.

■ **Tip** I also omit the cached calculation data from the app state in this example. Deciding to include relatively large amount of data in the app state is another judgment call. If the data is something that I can quickly reproduce, as in this case, then I tend to omit it from the state on the basis that I expect termination to be a relatively rare occurrence and I'd rather incur the penalty of reproducing the data than the penalty of storing the data, which persist on the device indefinitely and may cause other problems for the user. There is no simple answer to this one, and you'll have to look at the data you are working with and figure out what will give the best experience to the user. You'll be in a position to make an informed decision about how to store larger amount of data after you have read Chapter 20, in which I describe other ways of storing app data.

To save and restore the app state, I call the view model methods from the default.js file, in response to the appropriate lifecycle events, as shown in Listing 19-19.

Listing 19-19. Storing and restoring state data

```
...
app.onactivated = function (args) {
    var promises = [];

    if (args.detail.kind === activation.ActivationKind.launch) {
        switch (args.detail.previousExecutionState) {
            case activation.ApplicationExecutionState.suspended:
                writeEventMessage("Resumed from Suspended");
                break;
            case activation.ApplicationExecutionState.terminated:
                ViewModel.State.setData(app.sessionState);
                writeEventMessage("Launch from Terminated");
                promises.push(performInitialization());
                break;
            case activation.ApplicationExecutionState.notRunning:
            case activation.ApplicationExecutionState.closedByUser:
            case activation.ApplicationExecutionState.running:
                writeEventMessage("Fresh Launch");
                promises.push(performInitialization());
                break;
        }

        if (args.detail.splashScreen) {
            args.detail.splashScreen.addEventListener("dismissed", function (e) {
                writeEventMessage("Splash Screen Dismissed");
            });
        }

        promises.push(WinJS.UI.processAll().then(function () {
            return WinJS.Binding.processAll(calcElems, ViewModel.State);
        }));

        args.setPromise(WinJS.Promise.join(promises));
    }
};

app.oncheckpoint = function (args) {
    // app is about to be suspended
    app.sessionState = ViewModel.State.getData();
    writeEventMessage("Suspended");
};
...
```

The oncheckpoint handler function is called just before the app is suspended, which is my cue to store my app state by assigning the result of the getData method to the sessionState property. I restore the state data by reading the value of the sessionState property if my app is launched and the previous execution state is terminated.

The effect of these changes is that the user gets an (almost) seamless experience when the app is terminated. You can see how the state is restored in Figure 19-10, along with the lifecycle event notifications that show the app was launched having been previously terminated.

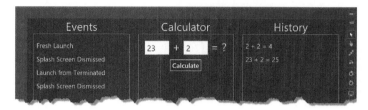

***Figure 19-10.** The effect of preserving and restoring app state*

Dealing with App Suspension

In addition to storing the state of your app, you can use the oncheckpoint handler function to release resources your app is using and to bring any background tasks your app is performing under control.

In terms of resources, you might need to close connections to servers or safely close files, for example. You don't know how long your app is going to be suspended for, or if it will be terminated while it is suspended, so it make sense to use the oncheckpoint handler to get your app to a safe state. If you are using remote servers, it is a good idea to try and close the connections so that they are available for use by other users – most servers will figure out that your app has gone away eventually, but it can take a while and there are still some enterprise servers which have hard limits on the number of concurrent connections, even if those connections are not actively handling requests.

In terms of background tasks, if you have work which has been deferred using the setImmediate, setInterval, or setTimeout methods when the app is suspended, then this work will be performed when the app is resumed again – this isn't always helpful, especially if the state is likely to change when the app is resumed, making dealing with the results of the function whose execution has been deferred more a hindrance.

In this section, I'll show you how to prepare your app before it is suspended. I'll do this using a simple background task, because it means you won't have to set up a server to follow the example. The background task will work out how many seconds have passed since the app was last activated – this is not a useful thing to do in the real world, but it is a helpful example because it allows me to show you what happens when the context for a background activity becomes stale. Listing 19-20 shows the changes I have made to the tasks.js file to define the new activity.

***Listing 19-20.** Defining a background activity for the example app*

```
(function () {
    WinJS.Namespace.define("Utils", {
        doWork: function (count) {
            // ...statements removed for brevity...
        },

        doBackgroundWork: function () {
            var interval = 1000;
            var canceled = false;
            var timeoutid;
```

```
        return new WinJS.Promise(function (fDone, fError, fProgress) {
            var startTime = Date.now();
            (function getElapsedTime() {
                var elapsed = Date.now() - startTime;
                fProgress(elapsed / 1000);
                if (!canceled) {
                    timeoutid = setTimeout(getElapsedTime, interval);
                } else {
                    fDone();
                }
            })();
        }, function () {
            canceled = true;
            if (timeoutid) {
                clearTimeout(timeoutid);
            }
        });
    }
});
})();
```

When the doBackgroundWork function is called, I create a new Promise, which snapshots the current time and then generates progress messages to indicate how many seconds have passed since the task started. I have set the interval for updates to one second so that I don't have to wait too long for updates when testing the lifecycle events.

I have also added code to the default.js file to start the background work and to display the results. You can see the changes in Listing 19-21.

Listing 19-21. Starting the background work and displaying the progress information

```
...
function performInitialization() {
    calcButton.addEventListener("click", function (e) {
        var first = ViewModel.State.firstNumber = Number(firstInput.value);
        var second = ViewModel.State.secondNumber = Number(secondInput.value);
        if (first < 5000 && second < 5000) {
            ViewModel.State.result = ViewModel.State.cachedResult[first][second];
        } else {
            ViewModel.State.result = first + second;
        }
    });

    ViewModel.State.bind("result", function (val) {
        if (val != null) {
            ViewModel.State.history.push({
                message: ViewModel.State.firstNumber + " + "
                    + ViewModel.State.secondNumber + " = "
                    + val
            });
        }
    });
```

```
        startBackgroundWork();

        return Utils.doWork(5000).then(function (data) {
            ViewModel.State.cachedResult = data;
        });
    };

    var backgroundPromise;

    function startBackgroundWork() {
        backgroundPromise = Utils.doBackgroundWork();
        var updatedExistingEntry = false;
        backgroundPromise.then(function () { }, function () { }, function (progress) {
            var newItem = {
                message: "Activated: " + Number(progress).toFixed(0) + " seconds ago"
            };
            ViewModel.State.eventLog.forEach(function (item, index) {
                if (item.message.indexOf("Activated:") == 0) {
                    updatedExistingEntry = true;
                    ViewModel.State.eventLog.setAt(index, newItem);
                }
            });
            if (!updatedExistingEntry) {
                ViewModel.State.eventLog.push(newItem);
            }
        });
    }
...
```

The startBackgroundWork function calls doBackgroundWork and uses the then method to receive progress updates, each of which contains the number of seconds since activation. I write this information to the event log in the view model, but since I don't want to litter the log with messages each and every second, I create a single object in the log and replace it each time I receive a progress update.

In the doBackgroundWork function, I have used the time that the background task is started to represent the moment when the app was activated. To make this a sensible estimation, I call the startBackgroundWork function from the performInitialization function, which is called when the app is launched and was not in the suspended state previously. You can see the result of these changes in Figure 19-11, which shows an instance of the app that has been running for a little while.

Figure 19-11. Showing the elapsed time since the app was activated

To see the stale context problem, start the app and let it run for a while. Then suspend and resume the app. No background work will be done while the app is suspended, but it will start again as soon as the app is resumed. The app, quite literally, continues where it left off and that means that the progress updates generated by the background task are based on the time when the task was first started and not when the app was most recently activated.

This problem in the example is trivial, but similar issues often arise in the real world. The execution of the oncheckpoint function is an opportunity to stop background tasks that rely on data that will be stale when the app is launched again. There are two approaches to stopping background work – *cancel-and-forget* and *stop-and-wait*. I explain both in the sections that follow.

Using the Cancel-and-Forget Technique

This is the simplest technique – you just call the cancel method of Promise that is performing the background work. You can see how I have done this in the oncheckpoint function in Listing 19-22 – quick, simple and easy.

Listing 19-22. Canceling the Promise in the oncheckpoint handler function

```
...
app.oncheckpoint = function (args) {
    // app is about to be suspended
    app.sessionState = ViewModel.State.getData();
    backgroundPromise.cancel();
    writeEventMessage("Suspended");
};
...
```

You can then start the work again when the app is resumed from the suspended state, as shown in Listing 19-23.

Listing 19-23. Starting background work when the app is resumed

```
...
switch (args.detail.previousExecutionState) {
    case activation.ApplicationExecutionState.suspended:
        startBackgroundWork();
        writeEventMessage("Resumed from Suspended");
        break;
    case activation.ApplicationExecutionState.terminated:
        ViewModel.State.setData(app.sessionState);
        writeEventMessage("Launch from Terminated");
        promises.push(performInitialization());
        break;
    case activation.ApplicationExecutionState.notRunning:
    case activation.ApplicationExecutionState.closedByUser:
    case activation.ApplicationExecutionState.running:
        writeEventMessage("Fresh Launch");
        promises.push(performInitialization());
        break;
}
...
```

The drawback with this approach is that the app may be suspended before the Promise has checked to see if it is cancelled or during a period where work is being performed. This can means that there will be one or more stale updates made when the app is resumed. You can easily remedy this by adding an additional check in your Promise code, as illustrated by Listing 19-24, which shows the changes I have made to the tasks.js file.

Listing 19-24. Performing an additional check to avoid stale updates when the app is resumed

```
...
doBackgroundWork: function () {
    var interval = 1000;
    var canceled = false;
    var timeoutid;

    return new WinJS.Promise(function (fDone, fError, fProgress) {
        var startTime = Date.now();
        (function getElapsedTime() {
            var elapsed = Date.now() - startTime;
            if (!canceled) {
                fProgress(elapsed / 1000);
                timeoutid = setTimeout(getElapsedTime, interval);
            } else {
                fDone();
            }
        })();
    }, function () {
        canceled = true;
        if (timeoutid) {
            clearTimeout(timeoutid);
        }
    });
}
...
```

I have moved the call to the progress update function so that it is only called if the Promise has not been canceled. This reduces the likelihood of a stale update being displayed to the user because even if a unit of work is being processed at the moment the app is suspended, the result of that work won't be displayed when the app is resumed.

Using the Stop-and-Wait Technique

The change I made to the way that the progress function is called in the custom Promise reduces the chances of a stale update being made, but doesn't eliminate it entirely – a call to the progress handler could be happening when the app is suspended and it will complete when the app is resumed. This means that the cancel-and-forget technique should only be used when a single stale update doesn't cause serious problems.

If you need to be sure that no stale data is used, then you need the *stop-and-wait* technique. The oncheckpoint handler function is passed an object that supports the setPromise method. If you pass the Promise doing the background work to this method, the suspension of the app will be deferred for up to 5 seconds to allow the Promise to be fulfilled.

You can't cancel a Promise in this situation. A call to the Promise.cancel method returns immediately and puts the Promise into an error condition while the background work that the Promise was performing will continue until the cancellation status is next checked - which defeats the goal.

Instead, you must signal to the Promise that it should terminate, but do so in a way that leaves the Promise in the regular completed condition. I have made some further changes to the tasks,js file to demonstrate this technique, which you can see in Listing 19-25.

Listing 19-25. Modifying the background Promise for early completion

```
...
doBackgroundWork: function () {
    var interval = 1000;
    var canceled = false;
    var timeoutid;

    var p = new WinJS.Promise(function (fDone, fError, fProgress) {
        var startTime = Date.now();
        function getElapsedTime() {
            var elapsed = Date.now() - startTime;
            if (!canceled && !p.stop) {
                fProgress(elapsed / 1000);
                timeoutid = setTimeout(getElapsedTime, interval);
            } else {
                fDone();
            }
        };
        setImmediate(getElapsedTime);
    }, function () {
        canceled = true;
        if (timeoutid) {
            clearTimeout(timeoutid);
        }
    });

    p.stop = false;
    return p;
}
...
```

I defined an additional property on the Promise object returned by the doBackgroundWork function and refer to it within the custom Promise code. This allows me to have a per-Promise flag that signals that the background work should stop and the Promise should indicate that it is fulfilled.

In order to do this, I have changed the way that the getElapsedTime function is initially executed, switching from a self-executing function to a call to the setImmediate method. Deferring the execution of the getElapsedTime function means that the code that creates the stop property on the Promise object is executed before the initial call to getElapsedTime, meaning that I can check the value of the stop property within the function, safe in the knowledge that it will have been defined by then.

You can see how I use the stop property in Listing 19-26, which shows the revisions I have made to the oncheckpoint function in the default.js file.

Listing 19-26. Deferring suspension of the app using the setPromise method

```
...
app.oncheckpoint = function (args) {
    // app is about to be suspended
    app.sessionState = ViewModel.State.getData();
    backgroundPromise.stop = true;
    args.setPromise(backgroundPromise);
    writeEventMessage("Suspended");
};
...
```

The `setPromise` method available on the `args` object in the `oncheckpoint` function plays a different role from the method of the same name in the `onactivated` function: when you pass a `Promise` to the method, it gives your app a moment's grace before it is suspended, waiting for the Promise to be fulfilled.

There are a couple of important points to remember when using this technique. First, using the `setPromise` method will only defer suspension of your app for 5 seconds. After that time, the app will be suspended anyway and you run the risk of having state updates when the app resumes – this means that you need to make sure your background work is performed in short blocks and that you check for the `stop` flag often enough that there is no chance of passing the 5 second deadline. The second point is that you don't cancel the `Promise` with this technique – it will only work if you can arrange things so that the `Promise` is fulfilled without entering the error state – otherwise, your app will be suspended after the `Promise`. `cancel` method is called but before the work the `Promise` is doing is halted.

Summary

In this chapter, I explained the different lifecycle stages for a Metro app and showed you how these are signaled by Windows. I showed you how to address the problems with the `WinJS.Application` object and the code that Visual Studio adds to new projects so that your app gets the full range of lifecycle notifications and can respond appropriately. I demonstrated the different actions that are required when an app is launched based on its previous state and showed you how to ensure that the splash screen is displayed when your app is initializing and how to store and restore state data so that you can respond correctly when your app is launched after it has been terminated by Windows.

The theme of the app lifecycle continues throughout this part of the book. I'll show you different kinds of activation events used to support contracts, which are a key feature of the Windows platform. To get started, I show you how to work with user settings and application data in the next chapter.

CHAPTER 20

■ ■ ■

Working with Settings & App Data

In this chapter, I show you how to present the user with application settings and how to make them persistent. Almost every app will have some features that the user can customize, and presenting the options to the user in a way which is consistent with other apps is an important way of ensuring that your users are able to build on their previous Windows experience when working with your app.

There are special provisions for apps that make working with settings simple and relatively easy. I'll show you different techniques for presenting settings and the Windows features for storing settings (and other data) persistently. Table 20-1 provides the summary for this chapter.

Table 20-1. Chapter Summary

Problem	Solution	Listing
Create a settings flyout	Apply the `WinJS.UI.SettingsFlyout` control to a `div` element. Specify the size you require with the `width` property.	4-5
Add settings flyouts to the settings pane	Handle to the `settings` event emitted by the `WinJS.Application` object and set the `detail.applicationcommands` property to an object which contains details of the flyouts.	6
Read and write persistent name/value pairs which are local to the current device	Use the local settings container	7-9
Read and write name/value pairs which are available wherever the user logs in with a Microsoft account	Use the roaming settings container	10
Specify a roaming data value which is replicated as soon as possible	Use the `HighPriority` property	11
Replicate related properties as a single unit	Use the `ApplicationDataCompositeValue` object	12
Store app data in files	Use the `ApplicationData.current.localFolder` property.	13-18
Read data from the app package	Use the `ms-appx` URL scheme	19-21

Preparing the Example App

I am going to build on the EventCalc example that I used to explain the lifecycle events in Chapter 19. In that chapter, one of the features that I showed you was how to store session state when the app is about to be suspended. I mentioned at the time that you should not store user settings as session data, so it is only fitting that I build on the same example app to tell you the rest of the story. As a reminder, you can see how the EventCalc appears in Figure 20-1.

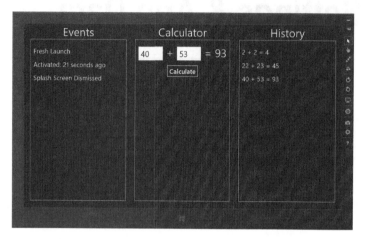

Figure 20-1. The EventCalc app

Preparing the Example App

To prepare the app to demonstrate settings, I have added a new file to the project called /js/settings.js, which you can see in Listing 20-1. This file defines a namespace called ViewModel.Settings, which is where I will store user preferences.

Listing 20-1. The contents of the settings.js file

```
(function () {
    WinJS.Namespace.define("ViewModel", {
        Settings: WinJS.Binding.as({
            backgroundColor: "#1D1D1D",
            textColor: "#FFFFFF",
            showHistory: true
        })
    });

    WinJS.Namespace.define("ViewModel.Converters", {
        display: WinJS.Binding.converter(function (val) {
            return val ? "block" : "none";
        }),
    });

})();
```

The properties in the ViewModel.Settings namespace will control the background and foreground colors for the app layout and the visibility of the panel which shows the calculation history. I have modified the default.html file to bring the settings.js file into scope and added some new data bindings so that the ViewModel.Settings properties are applied to the appropriate elements, as shown in Listing 20-2.

Listing 20-2. Adding bindings for the settings to the default.html file

```html
<!DOCTYPE html>
<html>
<head>
    <meta charset="utf-8" />
    <title>EventCalc</title>

    <!-- WinJS references -->
    <link href="//Microsoft.WinJS.1.0/css/ui-dark.css" rel="stylesheet" />
    <script src="//Microsoft.WinJS.1.0/js/base.js"></script>
    <script src="//Microsoft.WinJS.1.0/js/ui.js"></script>

    <!-- EventCalc references -->
    <link href="/css/default.css" rel="stylesheet" />
    <script src="/js/viewmodel.js"></script>
    <script src="/js/tasks.js"></script>
    <script src="/js/settings.js"></script>
    <script src="/js/default.js"></script>
</head>
<body data-win-bind="style.backgroundColor: backgroundColor; style.color: textColor">
    <div id="template" data-win-control="WinJS.Binding.Template">
        <div class="message" data-win-bind="innerText: message"></div>
    </div>

    <div id="eventContainer" class="container">
        <span>Events</span>
        <div id="eventList" data-win-control="WinJS.UI.ListView"
            data-win-options="{itemTemplate: template,
                itemDataSource: ViewModel.State.eventLog.dataSource,
                layout: {type: WinJS.UI.ListLayout}}">
        </div>
    </div>

    <div id="calcContainer" class="container">
        <span>Calculator</span>
        <div id="calcElems">
            <input id="firstInput" data-win-bind="innerText: firstNumber
                ViewModel.Converters.calcNumber" />
            <span class="calcSymbol">+</span>
            <input id="secondInput" data-win-bind="innerText: secondNumber
                ViewModel.Converters.calcNumber" />
            <span class="calcSymbol">=</span>
            <span id="result" data-win-bind="innerText: result
                ViewModel.Converters.calcResult"></span>
```

```
            <button id="calcButton">Calculate</button>
        </div>
    </div>

    <div id="historyContainer" class="container"
            data-win-bind="style.display: showHistory ViewModel.Converters.display">
        <span>History</span>
        <div id="historyList" data-win-control="WinJS.UI.ListView"
            data-win-options="{itemTemplate: template,
                itemDataSource: ViewModel.State.history.dataSource,
                layout: {type: WinJS.UI.ListLayout}}">
        </div>
    </div>
</body>
</html>
```

The final change I have to make is to add an additional call to the `WinJS.Binding.processAll` method so that the data bindings in the markup are activated. You can see the additional statements I added to the `/js/default.js` file in Listing 20-3.

Listing 20-3. Activating the settings data bindings

```
...
app.onactivated = function (args) {
    var promises = [];

    if (args.detail.kind === activation.ActivationKind.launch) {
        switch (args.detail.previousExecutionState) {
            case activation.ApplicationExecutionState.suspended:
                startBackgroundWork();
                writeEventMessage("Resumed from Suspended");
                break;
            case activation.ApplicationExecutionState.terminated:
                ViewModel.State.setData(app.sessionState);
                writeEventMessage("Launch from Terminated");
                promises.push(performInitialization());
                break;
            case activation.ApplicationExecutionState.notRunning:
            case activation.ApplicationExecutionState.closedByUser:
            case activation.ApplicationExecutionState.running:
                writeEventMessage("Fresh Launch");
                promises.push(performInitialization());
                break;
        }

        if (args.detail.splashScreen) {
            args.detail.splashScreen.addEventListener("dismissed", function (e) {
                writeEventMessage("Splash Screen Dismissed");
            });
        }
```

```
        promises.push(WinJS.UI.processAll().then(function() {
            return WinJS.Binding.processAll(document.body, ViewModel.Settings);
        }).then(function () {
            return WinJS.Binding.processAll(calcElems, ViewModel.State);
        }));

        args.setPromise(WinJS.Promise.join(promises));
    }
};
...
```

The result of these changes and additions is a set of observable properties, defined in the ViewModel. Settings namespace. When these properties change, data bindings in the markup in the default.html file update CSS values for key elements. You can test these properties by starting the app with the debugger (by selecting Start Debugging from the Visual Studio Debug menu) and entering the following statements into the JavaScript Console window:

```
ViewModel.Settings.showHistory = false
ViewModel.Settings.backgroundColor = "#317f42"
```

Changing the value of the settings triggers an update of the data bindings, changing the background color and hiding the calculation history, as shown in Figure 20-2.

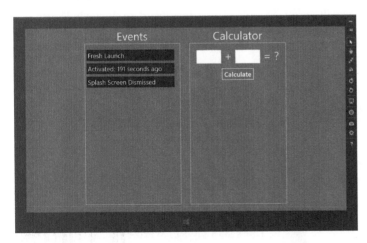

Figure 20-2. Changing the value of the setting properties

In the sections that follow, I'll show you the mechanisms for presenting these settings properties to the user and persistently storing the values that the user selects.

Presenting Settings to the User

Windows provides a standard mechanism for dealing with settings, which is triggered via the Settings Charm (which you can open via the Charm Bar or by using the Win+I shortcut).

Settings are presented via the *settings pane* and, as Figure 20-3 shows, the default settings pane shows some basic details about the app and contains a `Permissions` link, which shows the user which capabilities the app has declared in its manifest. The bottom of the settings pane has a standard set of buttons to configure system-wide settings.

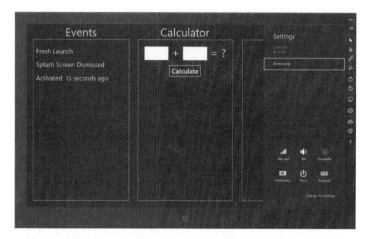

Figure 20-3. *The default settings pane*

If you click on the `Permissions` link, you will see an example of a *settings flyout*, as shown in Figure 20-4. This is how settings are handled – they are grouped together into categories which are shown as links on the settings pane and clicking on a link shows a settings flyout that contains more detail and, typically, controls to let the user change app settings.

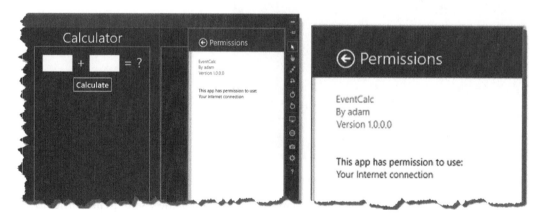

Figure 20-4. *The Permissions flyout*

■ **Tip**   You can change the details shown in the `Permissions` flyout by changing the values in the `Packaging` section of the app manifest.

As the figure shows, settings flyouts have a title area which contains a back button – clicking this button brings back the settings pane. The settings pane and the settings flyouts are all light-touch dismiss, meaning that the user can dismiss them by clicking or touching elsewhere on the screen, just as with the popup UI controls that I described in the previous part of the book.

In this section I am going add additional links to the settings pane to allow the user to view and change the settings that I defined in the /js/settings.js file. I am going to add two new links to the pane: the Colors link will open a pane that will let the user set the backgroundColor and textColor settings properties and the History link will open a pane that will let the user set the showHistory setting property. In doing this, I will demonstrate how your app can integrate itself into the standard settings system and how you can create settings flyouts which look and behave the same as the default Permissions flyout shown in Figure 20-4.

■ **Note**   Supporting settings through the settings charm is an example of a *contract*. A contract is a well-defined set of interactions, events and data objects which allow an app to particulate in a standard Windows feature. Settings is just one of the contracts I explain in this book – you'll see a more complex example in Chapter 21 when I show you how to integrate your app into the Windows search feature.

Defining the Flyout HTML

The first thing I need to do is create an HTML file for each settings pane. To get started, I have created a file called colorsSettings.html, the contents of which you can see in Listing 20-4. This is a relatively simple file, so I have put the CSS and JavaScript in the same file as the HTML markup.

Listing 20-4. The contents of the colorsSettings.html file

```
<!DOCTYPE HTML>
<html>
<head>
    <title></title>
    <style>
        #colorsDiv #backbutton { color: white; border-color: white;}
        #colorsDiv div.win-header { color: white; background-color: #004d60;}
    </style>
    <script>
        WinJS.UI.Pages.define("colorsSettings.html", {
            ready: function () {
                WinJS.Utilities.query("#colorsDiv input").listen("change", function (e) {
                    ViewModel.Settings.backgroundColor = backgroundColorInput.value;
                    ViewModel.Settings.textColor = textColorInput.value;
                });
                backbutton.addEventListener("click", function () {
                    WinJS.UI.SettingsFlyout.show();
                });
                WinJS.Binding.processAll(colorsDiv, ViewModel.Settings);
            }
        });
    </script>
</head>
```

```
<body>
    <div id="colorsDiv" data-win-control="WinJS.UI.SettingsFlyout"
            data-win-options="{width:'narrow'}">
        <div class="win-header">
            <button id="backbutton" class="win-backbutton"></button>
            <div class="win-label">Colors</div>
        </div>
        <div class="win-content">
            <div>
                <h2>Background Color</h2>
                <input id="backgroundColorInput" data-win-bind="value:backgroundColor" />
            </div>
            <div>
                <h2>Text Color</h2>
                <input id="textColorInput" data-win-bind="value:textColor" />
            </div>
        </div>
    </div>
</body>
</html>
```

At the heart of this HTML is a WinJS UI control called SettingsFlyout. This control is applied to div elements and is only used to present settings to the user. The width option is the only configuration option defined by SettingsFlyout and it allows you to request a standard flyout (using the narrow value) or one that has extra space for controls (using the wide value).

The contents of settings flyout files usually require some JavaScript to process user input, and you can see that I have used the WinJS.UI.Pages.define method (which I described in Chapter 7) to ensure that the elements in the document are loaded before I set up my event handlers and apply the data bindings.

■ **Tip**   I recommend that you use the HTML in the listing as a template when you create settings flyouts. It contains everything you need – the header including the title and the back button, and an area for your settings content.

For this setting flyout, I have defined two input elements which are data bound to the ViewModel. Settings properties and which update those properties when the change event is triggered. For the other setting flyout, I have created a very similar file, called historySettings.html, the content of which you can see in Listing 20-5.

Listing 20-5. The contents of the historySettings.html file

```
<!DOCTYPE HTML>
<html>
<head>
    <title></title>
    <style>
        #historyDiv #backbutton { color: white; border-color: white;}
        #historyDiv div.win-header { color: white; background-color: #004d60;}
    </style>
    <script>
        WinJS.UI.Pages.define("historySettings.html", {
            ready: function () {
```

```
                showToggle.addEventListener("change", function () {
                    ViewModel.Settings.showHistory = showToggle.winControl.checked;
                });
                backbutton.addEventListener("click", function () {
                    WinJS.UI.SettingsFlyout.show();
                });
                WinJS.Binding.processAll(historyDiv, ViewModel.Settings);
            }
        });
    </script>
</head>
<body>
    <div id="historyDiv" data-win-control="WinJS.UI.SettingsFlyout"
            data-win-options="{width:'wide'}">
        <div class="win-header">
            <button id="backbutton" class="win-backbutton"></button>
            <div class="win-label">History</div>
        </div>
        <div class="win-content">
            <div id="showToggle" data-win-control="WinJS.UI.ToggleSwitch"
                data-win-options="{title: 'Show Calculation History'}"
                data-win-bind="winControl.checked: showHistory">
            </div>
        </div>
    </div>
</body>
</html>
```

For this flyout, I have selected the `wide` value for the `width` configuration option. The `ToggleSwitch` control (which I described in Chapter 11) allows the user to toggle the visibility of the calculation history. When the toggle value changes, the corresponding property in the `ViewModel.Settings` namespace is updated.

■ **Note** My settings flyouts are a little sparse and in a real project I could readily show all three options on a single flyout. I have done this so I can demonstrate adding multiple categories, but in a real project I recommend that you consolidate settings and use standard HTML elements in the flyout to create sections if you need to group settings together. The approach I have taken in this chapter is useful for an example, but makes the user work harder to configure the app.

Responding to the settings Event

Having defined the flyout HTML files, the next step is to register them with the settings pane. I do this in response to the `settings` event emitted by the `WinJS.Application` object, which is triggered when the user activates the Settings Charm.

You can see how I respond to this event in Listing 20-6. To keep the settings code separate from the rest of the app, I respond to this event in the `settings.js` file, but in a real project, I would do this in the `default.js` file, where I handle the other events that `WinJS.Application` emits.

Listing 20-6. Handling the settings event

```
(function () {
    WinJS.Namespace.define("ViewModel", {
        Settings: WinJS.Binding.as({
            backgroundColor: "#1D1D1D",
            textColor: "#FFFFFF",
            showHistory: true
        })
    });

    WinJS.Namespace.define("ViewModel.Converters", {
        display: WinJS.Binding.converter(function (val) {
            return val ? "block" : "none";
        }),
    });

    WinJS.Application.onsettings = function (e) {
        e.detail.applicationcommands = {
            "colorsDiv": { href: "colorsSettings.html", title: "Colors" },
            "historyDiv": { href: "historySettings.html", title: "History" }
        };
        WinJS.UI.SettingsFlyout.populateSettings(e);
    };
})();
```

I have handled the settings event by assigning a handler function to the WinJS.Application. onsettings property. My function will be invoked when the user activates the Settings Charm, presenting me with the opportunity to add additional categories of settings to the settings pane.

This is a two-step process. First, I assign an object to the detail.applicationcommand property of the object passed to the handler function. The names of the properties my object defines correspond to the div elements in my HTML files to which the WinJS.UI.SettingsFlyout control has been applied.

I assign each of these div name properties an object with href and title properties. The href property must be set to the name of the flyout file you want to display and the title property is set to the text you want contained in the settings pane link. Each div name must be unique and if the div element name or the href value is incorrect, your link will be silently omitted from the settings pane.

The second step is to call the WinJS.UI.SettingsFlyout.populateSettings method, passing in the object that was passed to the handler function (and whose detail.applicationcommands property has been assigned details of the links and flyouts I want). This second step loads the content of the flyout HTML files and processes them. The result of these additions is that when the user activates the Settings Charm, the settings pane contains some new links, as shown in Figure 20-5.

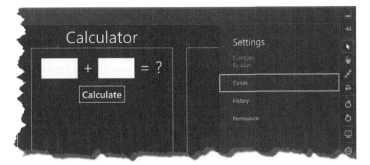

Figure 20-5. *Adding custom links to the settings pane*

If you click on or touch these links, then the appropriate settings pane will be shown. Figure 20-6 shows both of the panes I created, demonstrating the difference between the narrow and wide values for the width settings.

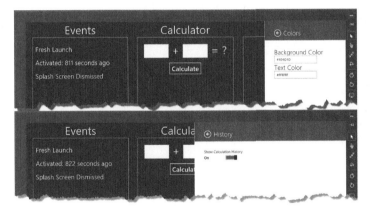

Figure 20-6. *The custom settings flyouts shown when the links are clicked*

I haven't done much to make the settings flyouts appealing because my emphasis in this chapter is the Windows settings mechanism. But in a real project, I wouldn't use the wide setting if I just have a ToggleSwitch to show and I would never expect the user to select colors by entering hex codes or CSS color names. These are no-brainers, and you should put some thought in to how you group and arrange the content of flyouts to make the process of configuring the app as simple and painless as possible.

Making Settings Persistent

I have wired up the controls and elements in the settings flyouts so that the view model is updated as soon as they are changed. You can experiment with the effects of changing the settings and see an immediate effect – but the next time that the app is launched, the default values I defined in the settings.js file will be used and your changes will be lost.

This brings me neatly to the topic of *application data*, or *app data*, which is the data that your app requires to function but which you don't want to give the user direct access to – such as settings. When the user interacts with app data, it is through some form of mediation, as with settings flyouts. In the sections that follow, I'll show you how to store and retrieve app data settings.

■ **Tip** The alternative to app data is *user data*, which the user can work with directly – I'll explain how apps can operate on user data in Chapters 22–24, when I describe the Windows support for working with files.

Storing Settings

The Windows features for working with app data are excellent and settings are the easiest kind of app data to work with. Listing 20-7 shows the additions I have made to the settings.js file to store settings data persistently.

Listing 20-7. Additions to the settings.js file to store settings data persistently

```
(function () {
    WinJS.Namespace.define("ViewModel", {
        Settings: WinJS.Binding.as({
            backgroundColor: "#1D1D1D",
            textColor: "#FFFFFF",
            showHistory: true
        })
    });

    WinJS.Namespace.define("ViewModel.Converters", {
        display: WinJS.Binding.converter(function (val) {
            return val ? "block" : "none";
        }),
    });

    WinJS.Application.onsettings = function (e) {
        e.detail.applicationcommands = {
            "colorsDiv": { href: "colorsSettings.html", title: "Colors" },
            "historyDiv": { href: "historySettings.html", title: "History" }
        };
        WinJS.UI.SettingsFlyout.populateSettings(e);
    };

    var storage = Windows.Storage;
    var settingNames = ["backgroundColor", "textColor", "showHistory"];

    settingNames.forEach(function (setting) {
        ViewModel.Settings.bind(setting, function (newVal, oldVal) {
            if (oldVal != null) {
                storage.ApplicationData.current.localSettings.values[setting] = newVal;
            }
        });
    });
})();
```

■ **Note**   Unless otherwise noted, all of the new objects I refer to in this section are part of the `Windows.Storage` namespace.

At the heart of this technique is the `ApplicationDataContainer` object, in which data is stored as key/value pairs. There are two built-in containers – the first allows you to store data so that it is local to the device on which the app is running and the other stores roaming data which is automatically copied to any device that the user logs in to.

I'll come back to the roaming data container later, but I have started with the simplest option for this example by using the local container. To obtain the local container object, I read the `ApplicationData.current.localSettings` property, like this:

```
...
storage.ApplicationData.current.localSettings.values[setting] = newVal;
...
```

The `ApplicationData.current` property returns an `ApplicationData` object which can be used to store data. Data in a container is stored persistently, which means that you don't have to worry about explicitly instructing Windows to save your app data – your data is stored as soon as you set the value in the storage container.

The `ApplicationData` defines a number of useful properties, which I have summarized in Table 20-2 and which I describe in the sections that follow.

Table 20-2. Properties of the ApplicationData object

Name	Description
current	Returns the `ApplicationData` object for the current app
localSettings	Returns an `ApplicationDataContainer` object for local data
roamingSettings	Returns an `ApplicationDataContainer` object for roaming data
localFolder	Returns a folder for storing local app data
roamingFolder	Returns a folder for storing roaming app data
roamingStorageQuota	Returns the maximum amount of data (in KB) of roaming data
version	Returns the current version of the data in the app data store

Once you have obtained the container you want to work with, you can store key/value pairs through the values property, which returns an `ApplicationDataContainerSettings` object. In the example I have used this object like an array, and assigned a value as follows:

```
...
storage.ApplicationData.current.localSettings.values[setting] = newVal;
...
```

You can use array notation to assign and read values, but an `ApplicationDataContainerSettings` object doesn't implement all of the behaviors of a real array, and you may need to use the methods and property that I have described in Table 20-3 instead.

Table 20-3. The methods and property of the ApplicationDataContainerSettings object

Name	Description
clear()	Removes all of the settings in the container
insert(key, value)	Inserts the key/value pair into the container
lookup(key)	Returns the value associated with the key, if it is present in the container
remove(key)	Removes the value associated with the key if it is present in the container
size	Returns the number of key/value pairs in the container

Now that you understand the objects involved, you can see how I persistently store the settings values in the example. I use WinJS programmatic data bindings (as described in Chapter 8) to monitor the ViewModel.Settings properties and store new values when the settings change, which I have emphasized in Listing 20-8.

Listing 20-8. Binding to view model changes to persist user choices

```
...
var storage = Windows.Storage;
var settingNames = ["backgroundColor", "textColor", "showHistory"];

settingNames.forEach(function (setting) {
    ViewModel.Settings.bind(setting, function (newVal, oldVal) {
        if (oldVal != null) {
            storage.ApplicationData.current.localSettings.values[setting] = newVal;
        }
    });
});
...
```

■ **Tip** I ignore any update where the old value for the observable property is null. This is because programmatic data bindings are sent an update when they are first created, providing the initial value and null for the old value. I only want to store values when they change, hence the check for null.

Restoring Settings

Being able to store settings as app data isn't much use if you can't also read them back when you need to. In Listing 20-9, you can see the additions I have made to the /js/settings.js file to restore any saved settings when the app is first loaded.

■ **Note** I define the function to restore the settings and call that function in the settings.js file, but in a real project I would call the function from the default.js file in response to the application being launched. I have put everything together in this project so that I don't have to list out pages of code to show simple changes.

Listing 20-9. Loading app data settings

```
(function () {
    WinJS.Namespace.define("ViewModel", {
        Settings: WinJS.Binding.as({
            backgroundColor: "#1D1D1D",
            textColor: "#FFFFFF",
            showHistory: true
        })
    });

    WinJS.Namespace.define("ViewModel.Converters", {
        display: WinJS.Binding.converter(function (val) {
            return val ? "block" : "none";
        }),
    });

    WinJS.Application.onsettings = function (e) {
        e.detail.applicationcommands = {
            "colorsDiv": { href: "colorsSettings.html", title: "Colors" },
            "historyDiv": { href: "historySettings.html", title: "History" }
        };
        WinJS.UI.SettingsFlyout.populateSettings(e);
    };

    var storage = Windows.Storage;
    var settingNames = ["backgroundColor", "textColor", "showHistory"];
    var loadingSettings = false;

    settingNames.forEach(function (setting) {
        ViewModel.Settings.bind(setting, function (newVal, oldVal) {
            if (!loadingSettings && oldVal != null) {
                storage.ApplicationData.current.localSettings.values[setting] = newVal;
            }
        });
    });

    function loadSettings() {
        loadingSettings = true;
        var container = storage.ApplicationData.current.localSettings;
        settingNames.forEach(function (setting) {
            value = container.values[setting];
            if (value != null) {
                ViewModel.Settings[setting] = value;
            }
        });
        setImmediate(function () {
            loadingSettings = false;
        })
    };
```

```
    loadSettings();
```

```
})();
```

I get the local settings container by reading the `ApplicationData.current.localSettings` property. I then use the array notation to check to see if there is a stored value for each of the settings that I am interested in. If there is, then I use that value to update the corresponding `ViewModel.Settings` property value, which has the effect of triggering the data bindings I defined, returning the app to its previous configuration.

To avoid storing the same values that I am loading, I have defined the `loadSettings` variable, which I set to `true` before I read the stored settings. I check the value of this variable when I get a data binding notification and discard the update if loading is in progress.

■ **Tip** Notice that I set the `loadingSettings` variable to `false` inside a function I pass to the `setImmediate` method. I do this to ensure that all of the data binding events are processed before I start storing values again. I explain the `setImmediate` method in Chapter 9.

The result of these additions is that changes to the settings shown on the settings flyout are now persistent. To test this, start the app, activate the Settings Charm, select the `History` link and change the `ToggleSwitch` control to the `Off` position.

The calculation history will be immediately hidden. Now restart the app, either by restarting the debugger or using `Alt+F4` and launching the app again. You will see that the calculation history isn't shown when the app starts.

Using Roaming Settings

In the previous example, I used local app storage for my settings. This means that the data is stored on the current device only – if the user runs the app on another device, then the default settings will be used. In this way, the user can end up with the same app running on two devices where each instance has an entirely different configuration.

If you want the same settings to be applied wherever the user logs in, then you need to use *roaming settings*. This is one of the most promising features of Windows apps, where app and user data is replicated seamlessly for users who associate their Windows account with a Microsoft account.

As a Windows app programmer, you don't have to worry about the details of the account sign in process, the Microsoft account that is being used, or details of how the data is replicated. Instead, you just store your settings in the roaming container, rather than the local one. You can see the changes I have made to the `/js/settings.js` file to use roaming settings in Listing 20-10.

Listing 20-10. Using the roaming settings container

```
(function () {
    WinJS.Namespace.define("ViewModel", {
        Settings: WinJS.Binding.as({
            backgroundColor: "#1D1D1D",
            textColor: "#FFFFFF",
            showHistory: true
        })
    });
```

```
WinJS.Namespace.define("ViewModel.Converters", {
    display: WinJS.Binding.converter(function (val) {
        return val ? "block" : "none";
    }),
});

WinJS.Application.onsettings = function (e) {
    e.detail.applicationcommands = {
        "colorsDiv": { href: "colorsSettings.html", title: "Colors" },
        "historyDiv": { href: "historySettings.html", title: "History" }
    };
    WinJS.UI.SettingsFlyout.populateSettings(e);
};

var storage = Windows.Storage;
var settingNames = ["backgroundColor", "textColor", "showHistory"];
var loadingSettings = false;

settingNames.forEach(function (setting) {
    ViewModel.Settings.bind(setting, function (newVal, oldVal) {
        if (!loadingSettings && oldVal != null) {
            storage.ApplicationData.current.roamingSettings.values[setting] = newVal;
        }
    });
});

function loadSettings() {
    loadingSettings = true;
    var container = storage.ApplicationData.current.roamingSettings;
    settingNames.forEach(function (setting) {
        value = container.values[setting];
        if (value != null) {
            ViewModel.Settings[setting] = value;
        }
    });
    setImmediate(function () {
        loadingSettings = false;
    })
};
loadSettings();

storage.ApplicationData.current.addEventListener("datachanged", function (e) {
    loadSettings();
});
```

```
})();
```

To switch to roaming, rather than local storage, I simply use the `ApplicationData.current.`
`roamingSettings` property. The approach for storing and retrieving individual settings is the same.

When using roaming settings, Windows will replicate your app data wherever the user logs in, meaning that you can create a consistent experience across multiple devices.

■ **Note**   There are no errors to deal with if the user doesn't have a Microsoft account associated with their Windows login – in this situation, the data just won't be replicated.

The `ApplicationData` object triggers the `datachanged` event if the roaming settings are modified when the app is running. This gives you the opportunity to update your app state to reflect the new data, ensuring that changes that the user has made elsewhere are applied as quickly as possible.

■ **Tip**   In the example, I simply call the `loadSettings` function to apply the update when the `datachanged` event is received, but you may want to ask the user if they want to apply the revised settings before making changes in a real app.

To test the support for roaming data in the example app, you will need to have two Windows 8 devices or virtual machines and log into them using the same Microsoft account. The account will have to have explicitly trusted both devices before replication of app data will be performed (to trust a device, open the Settings Charm, select `Change PC Settings Users` and click the `Trust this PC` link). Run the app on both devices and then make a change to the app settings on one of the devices. You will see the same change applied to the other device after a few minutes.

Understanding How Roaming Data Works

The roaming data feature is simple to use, but there are some important limitations. First, the data is replicated on a *best-efforts* basis. Roaming data is intended to allow your app to provide a consistent experience across devices, but there are no performance guarantees. Your data will be replicated when it suits Windows and you have no control over the replication process (with one exception that I describe in the next section). Windows may choose to defer replication of your data indefinitely, especially if power or resources are low. Windows doesn't promise to perform replication before the device is shutdown or put to sleep, which means that a significant period of time can pass between when a new setting value is stored and when it is replicated to other devices.

Second, roaming data is a low-volume, low-frequency service. Windows will stop replicating your data for a while if you make frequent updates to the roaming container. This means that you should not use roaming data to keep multiple instances of an app in lockstep – after the first few updates Windows will start deferring updates for your app.

Third, there is a limit to the amount of data that Windows will replicate. You can determine what the quota is by reading the `ApplicationData.current.roamingStorageQuota` property, but it is set to 100KB in the initial release of Windows 8. This may seem like a lot but, as I explain later in the chapter, you can also use roaming storage to replicate files, so the quota can be exhausted quickly. There is no warning when you are over the roaming quota and Windows will just (silently) stop replicating data for your app. And, since there is no reliable way to figure out how much data your app has stored, you need to be very conservative when you plan out which data will be roamed and which will be stored locally.

Finally, the roaming feature is intended to give the user a consistent experience as they move from device to device and not when running the same app simultaneously. There is no conflict resolution for roaming settings which are changed on different devices – Windows just discards any but the most recently made changes.

When you consider these points, you can understand that roaming data should be used carefully. You should send as little data as possible, store updates only when essential, and think carefully about opportunities for sending references to data instead of the data itself (such as replicating a URL rather than the contents of a web page). That's not to say that you shouldn't use roaming – it is an excellent feature and it can transform the experience of a user who installs your app on multiple devices – but do so thoughtfully and sparingly.

Using the High Priority Setting

The roaming settings container treats one setting differently. If you assign a value to the HighPriority setting, Windows will make more of an effort to replicate the setting quickly. There is still no performance guarantee and the quota and frequent-update throttling still applies, but you can use this special setting to try to ensure that the most critical information is available on other devices as quickly as possible.

The HighPriority setting is intended to allow you create a smooth user experience, and you should use this setting to replicate the key parts of your app state so that the user can continue their workflow seamlessly when they move to a new device. What this means will depend on the nature of your app, but an example that Microsoft gives is replicating a part-composed email from one device to the other, allowing the user to start writing the message on a PC at home, for example, and then continue using a tablet on the train as they commute to work.

To demonstrate the use of the HighPriority setting, I have given priority to the showHistory setting. When this setting changes, I assign the new value to HighPriority so that it is replicated as quickly as possible. You can see the changes I made to the settings.js file in Listing 20-11.

Listing 20-11. Using the HighPriority setting

```
(function () {
    WinJS.Namespace.define("ViewModel", {
        Settings: WinJS.Binding.as({
            backgroundColor: "#1D1D1D",
            textColor: "#FFFFFF",
            showHistory: true
        })
    });

    // ...statements removed for brevity...

    var storage = Windows.Storage;
    var settingNames = ["backgroundColor", "textColor", "showHistory"];
    var loadingSettings = false;

    settingNames.forEach(function (setting) {
        ViewModel.Settings.bind(setting, function (newVal, oldVal) {
            if (!loadingSettings && oldVal != null) {
                if (setting == "showHistory") {
                    setting = "HighPriority";
                }
                storage.ApplicationData.current.roamingSettings.values[setting] = newVal;
            }
        });
    });

    function loadSettings() {
        loadingSettings = true;
```

```
        var container = storage.ApplicationData.current.roamingSettings;
        settingNames.forEach(function (setting) {
            value = container.values[setting == "showHistory" ?
                "HighPriority" : setting];
            if (value != null) {
                ViewModel.Settings[setting] = value;
            }
        });
        setImmediate(function () {
            loadingSettings = false;
        })
    };
    loadSettings();

    storage.ApplicationData.current.addEventListener("datachanged", function (e) {
        loadSettings();
    });
```

```
})();
```

The approach I have taken here is to intercept updates for the showHistory setting and store the new value in the container using the HighPriority key. It is the key name that triggers the expedited behavior and no explicit action is required to trigger the replication.

■ **Note**   Although there are no performance guarantees when using replication, my experience has been that regular settings are replicated every 5 minutes or so, whereas the HighPriority setting is replicated within a few seconds. At peak times, replication of regular settings often slows down to once every 10 minutes or so.

Ensuring Data Consistency

Some app settings can't be safely replicated on their own. Consider the following scenario for the example app:

1. One their main PC, the user sets their backgroundColor to white and the textColor settings to green. The user is just about to leave the house and they shut down the PC before Windows replicates the changes. This means that the settings are stored locally and affect the app when it runs on the PC, but have not been replicated to affect other devices.

2. The user gets on a train and launches the same app on another device. They change the backgroundColor to green, but don't leave the textColor property set to its default value (white). Windows replicates the new backgroundColor value.

3. The user returns home and launches the app on the PC again. Windows doesn't replicate the setting values made in step 1 because they have been superseded by the value changed in step 2.

4. The app applies the new value for the backgroundColor setting, presenting the user with green text on a green background and rendering the app unusable.

There are several lessons to take from this scenario. First, it can be important to explicitly ask the user if they want to apply updated settings – for my example app, I just apply the update, and in the scenario I have laid in this section, the user would have no understanding that a series of settings changes they made hours ago have been combined to render the app useless. Equally, you should take the time to ensure that there is a simple way to reset the app to the default settings or prevent combinations of settings being selected that would render the app unusable.

The most important lesson however, is that some settings need to be replicated in groups, especially when those settings can be combined in dangerous ways. You can do this by using an ApplicationDataCompositeValue object, which allows you to combine several settings into a single object and ensure that they are replicated as a single, atomic unit. You can see how I have used this object in Listing 20-12 to ensure that the scenario I described at the start of this section doesn't arise.

Listing 20-12. Using the ApplicationDataCompositeValue object to replicate multiple values

```
(function () {
    WinJS.Namespace.define("ViewModel", {
        Settings: WinJS.Binding.as({
            backgroundColor: "#1D1D1D",
            textColor: "#FFFFFF",
            showHistory: true
        })
    });

    // ...statements removed for brevity...

    var storage = Windows.Storage;
    var settingNames = ["backgroundColor", "textColor", "showHistory"];
    var loadingSettings = false;

    settingNames.forEach(function (setting) {
        ViewModel.Settings.bind(setting, function (newVal, oldVal) {
            if (!loadingSettings && oldVal != null) {
                var container = storage.ApplicationData.current.roamingSettings;
                if (setting == "showHistory") {
                    container.values["HighPriority"] = newVal;
                } else if (setting == "backgroundColor" || setting == "textColor") {
                    var comp = new storage.ApplicationDataCompositeValue();
                    comp["backgroundColor"] = ViewModel.Settings.backgroundColor;
                    comp["textColor"] = ViewModel.Settings.textColor;
                    container.values["colors"] = comp;
                }
            }
        });
    });

    function loadSettings() {
        loadingSettings = true;
        var container = storage.ApplicationData.current.roamingSettings;
        ["HighPriority", "colors"].forEach(function (setting) {
            value = container.values[setting];
            if (value != null) {
```

```
                    if (setting == "HighPriority") {
                        ViewModel.Settings.showHistory = value;
                    } else {
                        ViewModel.Settings.backgroundColor = value["backgroundColor"];
                        ViewModel.Settings.textColor = value["textColor"];
                    }
                }
            });
            setImmediate(function () {
                loadingSettings = false;
            })
        };
        loadSettings();

        storage.ApplicationData.current.addEventListener("datachanged", function (e) {
            loadSettings();
        });
})();
```

The `ApplicationDataCompositeValue` object is like a container in its own right, and you assign multiple settings to it using the array notation style. You can then add the combined set of properties as a single setting and rely on them being replicated together. I added two properties to the `ApplicationDataCompositeValue` object in the listing, but you can add as many as you need for your app (subject to the quota and volume limits that Windows applies to roaming data).

■ **Tip**   You can use an `ApplicationDataCompositeValue` object as the value for the `HighPriority` setting. This allows you to give preference to a set of related properties to preserve your app state between devices.

With this change, there is no direct link between the properties in the `ViewModel.Settings` namespace and the names of the settings in the app data container. I replicate the value of the `showHistory` property using the special `HighPriority` setting and the `backgroundColor` and `textColor` properties are replicated as a single setting called `colors`. This is a perfectly reasonable approach, but you need to make sure that you map your settings and properties correctly and test thoroughly. Be warned, testing is a painful process because there is no way to force replication – this means that you have to make a change on one device and then wait several minutes to see it reflected on other devices (unless you are using the `HighPriority` setting, of course).

Using App Data Files

Not all data can be useful represented using key/value pairs. Fortunately, settings are not the only app data that apps can use – you can also store the data you need using files. To demonstrate this feature, I have added a new file to the js project folder called `appDataFiles.js` the contents of which you can see in Listing 20-13.

Listing 20-13. The contents of the appDataFiles.js

```
(function () {
```

```
var storage = Windows.Storage;
var historyFileName = "calcHistory.json";
var folder = storage.ApplicationData.current.localFolder;

ViewModel.State.history.addEventListener("iteminserted", function (e) {
    folder.createFileAsync(historyFileName,
            storage.CreationCollisionOption.openIfExists)
    .then(function (file) {
        var stringData = JSON.stringify(e.detail.value);
        storage.FileIO.appendLinesAsync(file, [stringData]);
    });
});
})();
```

This code uses data binding to observe the `ViewModel.State.history` object, which is a `WinJS.Binding.List` object. A new item is added to the `List` each time the user performs a calculation and the code in the `appDataFiles.js` file creates a persistent record of the user's actions. Later in the chapter, I'll extend the example and use the file to populate the history when the app is launched. First, however, I am going to take about the code in the example and explain how all of the objects fit together. Working with files in a Windows app is pretty straightforward when you understand the basic techniques, but it is unlike any other approach I have seen for dealing with the file system. In the sections that follow, I'll show you each step and explain the options in detail.

■ **Note**   Unless I explicitly state otherwise, all of the new objects I refer to in this section are part of the `Windows.Storage` namespace.

In Listing 20-14, you can see the script element I added to the head section of the `default.html` file to bring the code in the `appDataFiles.js` file into the example app.

Listing 20-14. Adding a script element to default.html for the appDataFiles.js file

```
...
<head>
    <meta charset="utf-8" />
    <title>EventCalc</title>

    <!-- WinJS references -->
    <link href="//Microsoft.WinJS.1.0/css/ui-dark.css" rel="stylesheet" />
    <script src="//Microsoft.WinJS.1.0/js/base.js"></script>
    <script src="//Microsoft.WinJS.1.0/js/ui.js"></script>

    <!-- EventCalc references -->
    <link href="/css/default.css" rel="stylesheet" />
    <script src="/js/viewmodel.js"></script>
    <script src="/js/tasks.js"></script>
    <script src="/js/settings.js"></script>
    <script src="/js/appDataFiles.js"></script>
    <script src="/js/default.js"></script>
</head>
...
```

Obtaining the Folder and File Objects

The starting point is the `StorageFolder` object returned by the `ApplicationData.current.localFolder` property. There are a lot of options when using the `StorageFolder` object and I am only going to focus on the basics in this chapter. I'll show you more of the features available in Chapters 22–24, when I describe how to work with user, as opposed to app, data.

■ **Note**   As with settings, the app data support for files can be local or roaming and I have chosen the local option. The API is the same in both instances and the difference is that roaming files are replicated. If you want to use roaming app data files, then you should use the `StorageFolder` returned by the `ApplicationData.current.roamingFolder` property. Be careful not to exceed the roaming data quote, or you files will not be replicated.

Table 20-4 summarizes the basic methods that you can use to open, create or delete files using the `StorageFolder` object. (I describe other `StorageFolder` methods in Chapter 22, but these are the ones that you'll use most often for app data files.)

Table 20-4. The basic methods defined by the Windows.Storage.StorageFolder object

Name	Description
`createFileAsync(name)` `createFileAsync(name, option)`	Creates a new file in the folder using the specified name in the folder using the specified option for dealing with collisions. The result of this method is a `Promise` which yields a `StorageFile` when fulfilled.
`getFileAsync(name)`	Returns the file in the folder with the specified name. The result of this method is a `Promise` which yields a `StorageFile` when fulfilled.
`getFilesAsync(name)`	Returns all of the files in the folder. The result of this method is a `Promise` which yields an array of `StorageFile` objects when fulfilled.

Almost every file-related operation in a Windows app is performed asynchronously, which is why all of the methods in the table return a `Promise` object. When fulfilled, these `Promise` objects will pass one or more `StorageFile` objects to the then method, representing the specified files. You can see how I have used the `createFileAsync` method in Listing 20-15 to get a `StorageFile` object.

■ **Tip**   The remainder of this chapter relies heavily on the `WinJS.Promise` object. If you have not read Chapter 9, then you should do so now and return here when you have finished. There is no getting around the asynchronous nature of the `Windows.Storage` namespace objects. One of Microsoft's main goals in introducing asynchronous supports for Windows apps was to prevent apps from hanging while they perform file operations. You must use Promises when dealing with files, even though it may feel a little counter-intuitive at first.

Listing 20-15. Obtaining the StorageFolder and StorageFile objects

```
...
folder.createFileAsync(historyFileName, storage.CreationCollisionOption.openIfExists)
    .then(function (file) {
        // statements to operate on the StorageFile go here
});
...
```

■ **Caution** Any errors that arise in asynchronous file operations are passed to the error function of the then method. I have not defined error handlers in this section because I want to show you how to work with files, rather than handle errors, but you should be careful to handle errors in a real project. See Chapter 9 for details of how errors are reported when Promises are used.

The optional argument to the createFileAsync method is a value from the CreationCollisionOption object, which enumerates values that determine what action Windows will take if you try to create a file that already exists. Table 20-5 describes the available values.

Table 20-5. The values defined by the CreationCollisionOption enumeration

Value	Description
generateUniqueName	Appends a number to the name you have specified for the file to avoid collision with any existing files.
replaceExisting	Replaces any existing file with a new, empty, file
failIfExists	Returns an error if a file with the name you have specified already exists
openIfExists	Opens any existing file

I used the openIfExists value, which means that the example app will create a new file if there isn't one there and reuse the existing file if there is.

Writing to the File

The StorageFile object supports all of the operations you would expect for a file – you can rename or delete the file it represents, open streams that let you read or write data and so on.

I won't be doing any of those things directly, because the FileIO object defines a set of extremely convenient methods that make performing basic read and write options simple (and much easier than working directly with the StorageFile object methods). Table 20-6 describes the convenience methods that FileIO defines.

Table 20-6. The methods defined by the Windows.Storage.FileIO object

Name	Description
appendLinesAsync(file, string[])	Appends the array of strings, one per line, to the file
appendTextAsync(file, string)	Append the string to the file
readBufferAsync(file)	Returns the content of the file as bytes
readLinesAsync(file)	Returns the content of the file as a string array
readTextAsync(file)	Returns the content of the file as a single string
writeBufferAsync(file, buffer)	Writes a data buffer to the file
writeBytesAsync(file, bytes)	Writes a byte array to the file
writeLinesAsync(file, string[])	Writes an array of strings to the file
writeTextAsync(file, string)	Writes a string to the file

■ **Tip**   The methods that read and write buffers are not especially useful on their own. They are intended for use with objects from the `Windows.Storage.Streams` namespace, which allow you to perform operations in a more traditional way (i.e., calls to read a byte or a string of data). The convenience methods in `FileIO` are sufficient for most situations and I encourage you to see if they can be used to meet your needs first.

I find that the most useful method is appendLinesAsync, because I can use it to write JSON data to the file without having to worry about line terminators. You can see that this is the method I use to write details of the calculation in Listing 20-16, even though I only have one item to write at a time.

Listing 20-16. Writing the JSON data to the file using the FileIO object

```
...
ViewModel.State.history.addEventListener("iteminserted", function (e) {
    folder.createFileAsync(historyFileName,
            storage.CreationCollisionOption.openIfExists)
    .then(function (file) {
        var stringData = JSON.stringify(e.detail.value);
        storage.FileIO.appendLinesAsync(file, [stringData]);
    });
});
...
```

Notice that I don't have to explicitly open the file I am working with, move a write cursor to the end of the file or close the file when I am finished. These mundane (and error-prone) tasks are taken care of for me by the `FileIO` object.

The result is that I append a string to my file every time the user performs a calculation. This is a real, regular file and you can find the file on the Windows file system by entering `Windows.Storage.ApplicationData.current.localFolder.path` into the Visual Studio JavaScript Console window. For my system, the value of this property is:

```
"C:\Users\adam\AppData\Local\Packages\a52d9e6e-bba3-4774-a824b26e77499de7_6fxp0bkxjs8ye
\LocalState"
```

The path will be different on your system, of course. If you use the app to perform some calculations and then open the folder, you will see the `calcHistory.json` file, which will contain a simple JSON description of each calculation, similar to the ones shown in Listing 20-17.

Listing 20-17. Content from the calcHistory.json file

```
{"message":"1 + 2 = 3"}
{"message":"1 + 3 = 4"}
{"message":"1 + 4 = 5"}
```

The message property exists because I use a single WinJS template in the `default.html` file to display event messages and the calculation history. I just convert the object to JSON and write it to the file for simplicity in this example, but you can reformat the object or express the data in an entirely different way if need be.

Reading from the File

The code required to read the calculation history from the file will be simple to understand now that you have seen the objects involved in writing data to the file. Listing 20-18 shows the additions I have made to the appDataFiles.js file to read the history in when the app starts. (I have inserted the code that adds the data to the view model before the code that saves new data so that I don't respond to changes until the initial data has been loaded.)

Listing 20-18. Reading the calculation history in from the app data file

```
(function () {

    var storage = Windows.Storage;
    var historyFileName = "calcHistory.json";
    var folder = storage.ApplicationData.current.localFolder;

    function readHistory() {
        folder.getFileAsync(historyFileName)
        .then(function (file) {
            var fileData = storage.FileIO.readLinesAsync(file)
            .then(function (lines) {
                lines.forEach(function (line) {
                    ViewModel.State.history.push(JSON.parse(line));
                });
            })
        });
    }

    readHistory();

    ViewModel.State.history.addEventListener("iteminserted", function (e) {
        folder.createFileAsync(historyFileName,
                storage.CreationCollisionOption.openIfExists)
        .then(function (file) {
            var stringData = JSON.stringify(e.detail.value);
            storage.FileIO.appendLinesAsync(file, [stringData]);
        });
    });

})();
```

I use the FileIO.readLinesAsync method to get the contents of the file as an array of strings. This positions me nicely to parse each JSON string into a JavaScript object and push it into the ViewModel. State.history object, which causes each item to be displayed to the user.

■ **Note** If you didn't run this app before adding the readHistory function, then Visual Studio will complain of an exception. This is because the readHistory function is called when the app first starts and the file doesn't exist. The readHistory function copes with missing files and you can click the Continue button to ignore this file once or uncheck the checkbox to prevent Visual Studio reporting the same exception in the future.

Loading Files from the App Package

You don't have to generate settings and files from scratch – you can also include data files in your app package and process them other app data files. This is useful when identical data will be required for all users and there is little or no customization involved.

The EventCalc app that I have been using as the example in this chapter generates a set of calculations which is stores in a cache. I added this feature in Chapter 19 when I was demonstrating how to perform tasks within the scope of the app lifecycle. In this chapter, I am going to update the app so that it loads the pre-calculated results from a data file which is included in the app deployment to the user's device. To begin with, I have created a data folder in the project and added a new file called calcData.json. Each line in this file contains a JSON representation of a calculation and you can see a sample of this data in Listing 20-19. In Chapter 19, I wanted a task which took a while to perform, so I generated the sums of the first 5000 integers. For this chapter, I want a manageable file size, so the data file contains only the results of adding the first 100 integer values.

Listing 20-19. A sample of the JSON data in the calcData.json file

```
...
{"first":3,"second":50,"result":53}
{"first":3,"second":51,"result":54}
{"first":3,"second":52,"result":55}
{"first":3,"second":53,"result":56}
{"first":3,"second":54,"result":57}
{"first":3,"second":55,"result":58}
{"first":3,"second":56,"result":59}
{"first":3,"second":57,"result":60}
...
```

This file is too long for me to list out fully in this chapter, so there are two ways that you can get the contents of this file if you want to follow along with the example. The first is to download the source code that accompanies this book, which contains all of the files for all of the examples in every chapter. The second approach is to generate the data yourself, instructions for which you will find in the Generating the Sample Data sidebar.

GENERATING THE SAMPLE DATA

If you don't want to download the calcData.json file from apress.com, then you can easily generate it yourself. Create a new Windows app project in Visual Studio and replace the contents of the default.html file with the following:

```
<!DOCTYPE html>
<html>
<head>
    <meta charset="utf-8" />
    <title>DataGen</title>
    <link href="//Microsoft.WinJS.1.0/css/ui-dark.css" rel="stylesheet" />
    <script src="//Microsoft.WinJS.1.0/js/base.js"></script>
    <script src="//Microsoft.WinJS.1.0/js/ui.js"></script>
    <style>
        body {display: -ms-flexbox; -ms-flex-align: center;-ms-flex-pack: center;}
```

```
            button {font-size: 25pt;}
        </style>
        <script>
            WinJS.Application.onactivated = function (args) {
                gen.addEventListener("click", function (e) {
                    var picker = Windows.Storage.Pickers.FileSavePicker();
                    picker.defaultFileExtension = ".json";
                    picker.suggestedFileName = "calcData";
                    picker.fileTypeChoices.insert("JSON", [".json"]);
                    picker.pickSaveFileAsync().then(function (saveFile) {
                        if (saveFile) {
                            var dataObjects = [];
                            for (var first = 1; first <= 100; first++) {
                                for (var second = 1; second <= 100; second++) {
                                    dataObjects.push(JSON.stringify({
                                        first: first,
                                        second: second,result: first + second
                                    }));
                                }
                            }
                            Windows.Storage.FileIO.writeLinesAsync(saveFile,
                                dataObjects);
                        }
                    });
                });
            }
            WinJS.Application.start();
        </script>
    </head>
    <body>
        <button id="gen">Generate</button>
    </body>
</html>
```

This listing defines a simple app where the HTML, CSS and JavaScript are all defined in the same file. The layout for the app contains a single Generate button which, when clicked, will prompt you to save the calcData.json file on your system, which you can then copy into the data folder of your Visual Studio project. The results will be generated and saved to the file. This app uses features that I don't describe until later in this chapter, so treat this as a black box for the purposes of creating the data required for the example.

To disable the caching background task and reduce the number of cached results that are expected, I have updated the performInitialization function in the default.js file, as shown in Listing 20-20. The changes reduce the scope of the pre-calculated data and stop generating the results each time the app is launched.

Listing 20-20. Changes to the default.js file to prepare for loading the calculation results

```
...
function performInitialization() {
    calcButton.addEventListener("click", function (e) {
```

533

```
            var first = ViewModel.State.firstNumber = Number(firstInput.value);
            var second = ViewModel.State.secondNumber = Number(secondInput.value);
            if (first < 100 && second < 100) {
                ViewModel.State.result = ViewModel.State.cachedResult[first][second];
            } else {
                ViewModel.State.result = first + second;
            }
        });

        ViewModel.State.bind("result", function (val) {
            if (val != null) {
                ViewModel.State.history.push({
                    message: ViewModel.State.firstNumber + " + "
                        + ViewModel.State.secondNumber + " = "
                        + val
                });
            }
        });

        startBackgroundWork();

        //return Utils.doWork(5000).then(function (data) {
        //    ViewModel.State.cachedResult = data;
        //});
    };
...
```

The key part of this example is shown in Listing 20-21, which details the additions I have made to the appDataFiles.js file. I have added a self-executing function that opens the data/calcData.json file, parses the contents and assigns the results as the cached data.

Listing 20-21. Additions to the appDataFiles.json file to load pre-calculated data

```
(function () {

    var storage = Windows.Storage;
    var historyFileName = "calcHistory.json";
    var folder = storage.ApplicationData.current.localFolder;

    ViewModel.State.history.addEventListener("iteminserted", function (e) {
        folder.createFileAsync(historyFileName,
                storage.CreationCollisionOption.openIfExists)
        .then(function (file) {
            var stringData = JSON.stringify(e.detail.value);
            storage.FileIO.appendLinesAsync(file, [stringData]);
        });
    });

    function readHistory() {
        folder.getFileAsync(historyFileName)
        .then(function (file) {
```

```
            var fileData = storage.FileIO.readLinesAsync(file)
            .then(function (lines) {
                lines.forEach(function (line) {
                    ViewModel.State.history.push(JSON.parse(line));
                });
            })
        });
    }

    readHistory();

    (function () {
        storage.StorageFile.getFileFromApplicationUriAsync(
            Windows.Foundation.Uri("ms-appx:///data/calcData.json"))
        .then(function (file) {
            var cachedData = {};
            storage.FileIO.readLinesAsync(file).then(function (lines) {
                lines.forEach(function (line) {
                    var calcResult = JSON.parse(line);
                    if (cachedData[calcResult.first] == null) {
                        cachedData[calcResult.first] = {};
                    }
                    cachedData[calcResult.first][calcResult.second] = calcResult.result;
                });
            });
            ViewModel.State.cachedResult = cachedData;
        });
    })();
})();
```

This is similar to the way that I read the history file in the previous section, but the key difference is the way that I get the StorageFile object that corresponds to the calcData.json file. I can't use the ApplicationData object in this case, because files in the application package are handled differently.

The first step is to create a Windows.Foundation.Url object. The Windows.Foundation namespace contains objects that, for the most part, are artifacts required by the .NET programming language and which have little bearing on JavaScript. The Uri object takes a URI string and prepares it in a way that can be used with the Windows.Storage objects. It doesn't do anything else that's useful for JavaScript programmers.

The format of the URI is important. The protocol component must be set to ms-appx, you must use three / characters and then include the path to the file you want to load. For the data/calcData.json file, this means that the string I need to use is:

```
ms-appx:///data/calcData.json
```

Once you have a Windows.Foundation.Uri object, you can use it as an argument to the StorageFile. getFileFromApplicationUriAsync method, which returns a StorageFile that represents the file in the app package. From this point on, you can use the FileIO object to read the contents of the file as you would for regular app data files. (Don't try to write to these files - they are read only.) The result of these changes is that I am able to deploy data as part of my application distribution and load it when the app is launched – for my example app, this means that I don't have to rely on the potentially limited capabilities of the user's device to generate the cached data.

Summary

In this chapter, I showed you how to implement the settings contract in order to integrate your app into the standard Windows model for presenting settings to the user. Contracts are a powerful technique for ensuring that your app presents a consistent set of interactions to the user and, as you'll see in later chapters, some contacts can be quite complex.

There is no point presenting the user with settings if you can't persistently store the values they select. To this end, I explained how the app data system works, allowing you to store key/value pairs and data files. Windows apps can store settings and files so that they are local to the current device, or so that they roam and follow the user wherever they log on. The roaming features are easy to use, but there are some constraints on their use and I showed you some advanced features to help you get specific kinds of roaming behavior.

I finished this chapter by showing you how to load data distributed to the user as part of the app package. This is useful when all users will need the same data and avoids the need to generate or download data when the app is launched.

In the next chapter, I'll show you how to use the Windows search feature to allow the user to search your app data.

CHAPTER 21

■ ■ ■

The Search Contract

Windows defines a series of *contracts*, which Windows apps can implement to integrate with key platform-wide services. These contracts set out a model for interaction between the app and the operating system for a particular feature. In this chapter, I introduce you to the *search contract*, which allows an app to participate seamlessly in the Windows search mechanism, allowing the user to find data in your app in exactly the same way that he locates files and apps in the operating system.

This chapter isn't about adding a search capability to your app. It is about taking an app that *already* has the ability to handle searches and using the contract to expose that ability to the user. You can provide any kind of search capability that makes sense for your app and your app data and, as you'll see, make it easy for the user to access and use it. I'll start this chapter by building a simple app that is able to search its app data and then I'll use that app to demonstrate how to implement the search contract.

Table 21-1. Chapter Summary

Problem	Solution	Listing
Prepare to implement the search contract	Add a search capability to your app	21-1–21-4
Implement the search contract	Declare the implementation in the app manifest and handle search activation events	21-5
Explicitly show the search pane	Call the show method on a SearchPane object obtained from SearchPane.getForCurrentView	21-6–21-7
Offer query suggestions to the user	Handle the suggestionsrequested event and use the SearchSuggestionCollection.appendQuerySuggestion method	21-8–21-10
Break the suggestions into sections	Use the SearchSuggestionCollection.appendSearchSeparator method	21-11
Offer result suggestions to the user	Use the SearchSuggestionCollection.appendResultSuggestion method and listen for the resultsuggestionchosen event	21-12–21-13
Disable search history	Set the SearchPane.searchHistoryEnabled property to false	21-14
Generate suggestions using an asynchronous method	Use the getDeferral method to get a SearchPaneSuggestionsRequestDeferral object and call the complete method on it when the suggestions are ready	21-15–21-16

Creating the Example App

In Chapter 16, I used a list of popular names to help demonstrate the SemanticZoom UI control. I am going to use the same data in this chapter as the basis for demonstrating the different ways in which you can support the search contract. My example app for this chapter is called SearchContract and you can see the contents of the default.html file in Listing 21-1.

Listing 21-1. The contents of the default.html file from the SearchContract app

```html
<!DOCTYPE html>
<html>
<head>
    <meta charset="utf-8" />
    <title>SearchContract</title>

    <!-- WinJS references -->
    <link href="//Microsoft.WinJS.1.0/css/ui-dark.css" rel="stylesheet" />
    <script src="//Microsoft.WinJS.1.0/js/base.js"></script>
    <script src="//Microsoft.WinJS.1.0/js/ui.js"></script>

    <!-- SearchContract references -->
    <link href="/css/default.css" rel="stylesheet" />
    <script src="/js/viewmodel.js"></script>
    <script src="/js/default.js"></script>
</head>
<body>
    <div id="NameItemTemplate" data-win-control="WinJS.Binding.Template">
        <div class="ListItem">
            <div class="ListData" data-win-bind="innerText: name"></div>
        </div>
    </div>

    <div id="MessageTemplate" data-win-control="WinJS.Binding.Template">
        <div class="message" data-win-bind="innerText: message"></div>
    </div>

    <div id="nameContainer" class="listContainer">
        <div id="nameList" data-win-control="WinJS.UI.ListView"
            data-win-options="{itemTemplate: NameItemTemplate,
                itemDataSource: ViewModel.filteredNames.dataSource}">
        </div>
    </div>

    <div id="messageContainer" class="listContainer">
        <div id="messageList" data-win-control="WinJS.UI.ListView"
            data-win-options="{itemTemplate: MessageTemplate,
                itemDataSource: ViewModel.messages.dataSource,
                layout: {type: WinJS.UI.ListLayout}}">
        </div>
    </div>
```

```
</body>
</html>
```

The key parts of the layout for this app are the two ListView controls. The first ListView will display the set of names and I'll use the second ListView control to display a series of messages, similar to the approach I took in Chapter 19 when I showed you app life-cycle events in the UI. The markup also contains a couple of templates that I'll use for the ListView content items and a script element that imports the viewmodel.js file, which I'll create shortly.

To create the layout for this app, I defined a number of styles in the /css/default.css file, as shown in Listing 21-2. These styles are built using regular CSS properties and don't rely on any Windows-specific functionality.

Listing 21-2. The contents of the /css/default.css file

```
body { background-color: #5A8463; display: -ms-flexbox;
    -ms-flex-direction: row; -ms-flex-align: center; -ms-flex-pack: center;}
.listContainer {height: 80%; margin: 10px; border: medium solid white; padding: 10px;}

#nameContainer { width: 50%;}
#messageContainer {width: 25%;}
#nameList, #messageList {height: 100%; margin-bottom: 10px;}

*.ListData, .message { background-color: black; text-align: center;
    border: solid medium white; font-size: 20pt; padding: 10px; width: 140px;}

.message { width: 95%; font-size: 18pt; padding: 5px;}
#buttonContainer > button {font-size: 20pt; margin: 10px;}
```

Defining the View Model

To define the data and prepare it so that it can be used with the ListView control, I have added a file called js/viewmodel.js, the contents of which you can see in Listing 21-3.

Listing 21-3. The initial contents of the viewmodel.js file

```
(function () {

    var rawData = ['Aaliyah', 'Aaron', 'Abigail', 'Abraham', 'Adam', 'Addison', 'Adrian',
        'Adriana', 'Aidan', 'Aiden', 'Alex', 'Alexa', 'Alexander', 'Alexandra', 'Alexis',
        'Allison', 'Alyssa', 'Amelia', 'Andrew', 'Angel', 'Angelina', 'Anna', 'Anthony',
        'Ariana', 'Arianna', 'Ashley', 'Aubrey', 'Austin', 'Ava', 'Avery', 'Ayden',
        'Bella', 'Benjamin', 'Blake', 'Brandon', 'Brayden', 'Brian', 'Brianna', 'Brooke',
        'Bryan', 'Caleb', 'Cameron', 'Camila', 'Carter', 'Charles', 'Charlotte', 'Chase',
        'Chaya', 'Chloe', 'Christian', 'Christopher', 'sClaire', 'Connor', 'Daniel',
        'David', 'Dominic', 'Dylan', 'Eli', 'Elijah', 'Elizabeth', 'Ella', 'Emily',
        'Emma', 'Eric', 'Esther', 'Ethan', 'Eva', 'Evan', 'Evelyn', 'Faith', 'Gabriel',
        'Gabriella', 'Gabrielle', 'Gavin', 'Genesis', 'Gianna', 'Giovanni', 'Grace',
        'Hailey', 'Hannah', 'Henry', 'Hunter', 'Ian', 'Isaac', 'Isabella', 'Isaiah',
        'Jack', 'Jackson', 'Jacob', 'Jacqui', 'Jaden', 'Jake', 'James', 'Jasmine',
        'Jason', 'Jayden', 'Jeremiah', 'Jeremy', 'Jessica', 'Joel', 'John', 'Jonathan',
```

```
        'Jordan', 'Jose', 'Joseph', 'Joshua', 'Josiah', 'Julia', 'Julian', 'Juliana',
        'Julianna', 'Justin', 'Kaitlyn', 'Katherine', 'Kayla', 'Kaylee', 'Kevin',
        'Khloe', 'Kimberly', 'Kyle', 'Kylie', 'Landon', 'Lauren', 'Layla', 'Leah', 'Leo',
        'Liam', 'Lillian', 'Lily', 'Logan', 'London', 'Lucas', 'Luis', 'Luke',
        'Mackenzie', 'Madeline', 'Madelyn', 'Madison', 'Makayla', 'Maria', 'Mason',
        'Matthew', 'Max', 'Maya', 'Melanie', 'Mia', 'Michelle', 'Miriam', 'Molly',
        'Morgan', 'Moshe', 'Naomi', 'Natalia', 'Natalie', 'Nathan', 'Nathaniel',
        'Nevaeh', 'Nicholas', 'Nicole', 'Noah', 'Oliver', 'Olivia', 'Owen', 'Paige',
        'Patrick', 'Peyton', 'Rachel', 'Rebecca', 'Richard', 'Riley', 'Robert', 'Ryan',
        'Samantha', 'Samuel', 'Sara', 'Sarah', 'Savannah', 'Scarlett', 'Sean',
        'Sebastian', 'Serenity', 'Sofia', 'Sophia', 'Sophie', 'Stella', 'Steven',
        'Sydney', 'Taylor', 'Thomas', 'Tristan', 'Tyler', 'Valentina', 'Victoria',
        'Vincent', 'William', 'Wyatt', 'Xavier', 'Zachary', 'Zoe', 'Zoey'];

    WinJS.Namespace.define("ViewModel", {
        allNames: [],
        filteredNames: new WinJS.Binding.List(),
        messages: new WinJS.Binding.List(),
        writeMessage: function (msg) {
            ViewModel.messages.push({ message: msg });
        },
        searchTerm: ""
    });

    rawData.forEach(function (item, index) {
        var item = { name: item, firstLetter: item[0] };
        ViewModel.allNames.push(item);
    });

    ViewModel.search = function (term) {
        ViewModel.writeMessage("Searched for: " + (term == "" ? "empty string" : term));
        term = term.toLowerCase();
        ViewModel.filteredNames.length = 0;
        ViewModel.allNames.forEach(function (item) {
            if (item.name.toLowerCase().indexOf(term) > -1) {
                ViewModel.filteredNames.push(item)
            }
        });
        ViewModel.searchTerm = term;
    };
})();
```

The rawData array contains the list of names as a set of strings. These are not much use to me as they are, so I process the values to create two sets of objects I can use with data binding templates. The first set, ViewModel.allNames, contains a complete set of objects—this will be my reference data, against which I'll perform searches. The second set of objects is ViewModel.filteredNames, which I use as the data source for the left-hand ListView control in the layout. I'll use the data source to display the results of some kinds of search as I go through the chapter.

I also use the viewmodel.js file to define the ViewModel.search function, which performs a simple search by checking each name in turn—this is an inefficient search technique, but it is sufficient for my example app.

Defining the JavaScript Code

All that remains now is to implement the default.js file. I have used just the minimum life-cycle event handling code and I won't worry about the effects of app suspension or termination in this chapter. You can see the contents of the default.js file following my changes in Listing 21-4.

Listing 21-4. The initial default.js file

```
(function () {
    "use strict";

    var app = WinJS.Application;
    var activation = Windows.ApplicationModel.Activation;
    WinJS.strictProcessing();

    app.onactivated = function (args) {
        if (args.detail.kind === activation.ActivationKind.launch) {
            if (args.detail.previousExecutionState
                    != activation.ApplicationExecutionState.suspended) {

                args.setPromise(WinJS.UI.processAll().then(function () {
                    ViewModel.writeMessage("App Launched");
                    ViewModel.search("");
                }));
            }
        }
    };

    app.start();
})();
```

When the app is launched, I call the ViewModel.search method to search for the empty string—this has the effect of matching all of the names and displaying the complete set when the app is first started. You can see in Figure 21-1 the layout of the app and the data and messages that it displays when first launched.

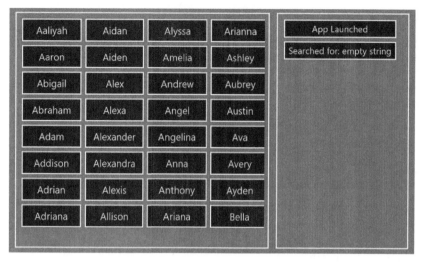

Figure 21-1. The initial layout and data of the example app

Adding the App Images

I have added some files to the `images` folder of the project, as shown in Figure 21-2. I have used the files whose names start with `tile` to set the fields in the Application UI section of the app manifest, just as I did in Chapter 4. These images contain the magnifying-glass icon shown in the figure. The other file, `user.png`, contains a person icon, and I'll use this file when I use Windows to display the results of my searches later in the chapter. You can see both icons in the figure (I have added the black background to make the icons visible—the actual files are transparent). I have included these files in the source code download for this book, which you can get from `apress.com`.

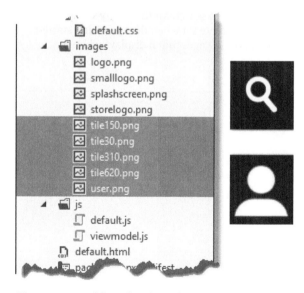

Figure 21-2. Adding the tile and user icons to the example app

Testing the Example App

As I mentioned in the introduction, this chapter isn't about how you implement search in your app—instead, it is about how you integrate that search capability into Windows so that your users have a consistent and rich search experience. The way I perform the search in my example app is pretty basic and you can see how it works by using the Visual Studio JavaScript Console window. Start the app (making sure to use the Start Debugging menu item) and go to the JavaScript Console window. Enter the following at the prompt:

```
ViewModel.search("jac")
```

(The JavaScript Console will also say Undefined—you can ignore this.) When you hit Enter, you will see that the set of names displayed by the left-hand ListView will be restricted to those that contain the search term jac, as shown in Figure 21-3. The right-hand ListView will display a new message, reporting the search term that was requested.

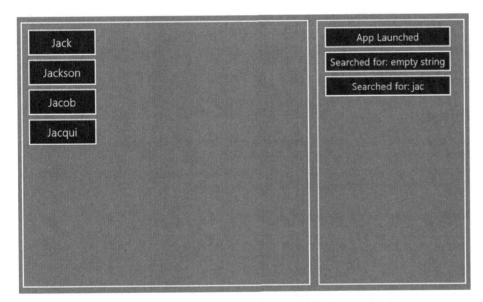

Figure 21-3. Testing the app search capability

You have to use the JavaScript Console to perform the search because I have not added any search elements or controls to the layout—this will be provided by the operating system when I integrate the app search capabilities into the wider Windows search experience. In the sections that follow, I'll show you how to perform that integration and explain the different approaches you can take.

Implementing the Search Contract

The first step is to update the app manifest to declare that you intend to support the search contract. To do this, double-click on the package.appxmanifest file in the Visual Studio Solution Explorer window and select the Declarations tab. Select Search from the Available Declarations menu and press the Add button. You will see Search is added to the Supported Declarations list, as shown in Figure 21-4. You can ignore the Properties section of the page—these are useful only if you want to use a separate app to handle search, and in this chapter, I'll show you how to directly add search support to an app.

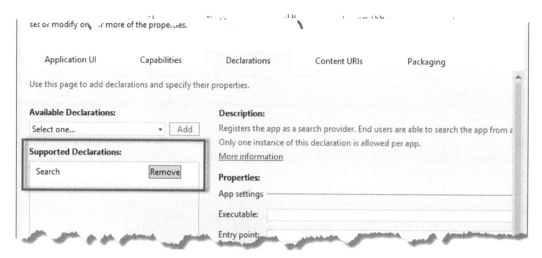

Figure 21-4. Declaring support for the search contract

Handle the Activation Event

Windows notifies your app that it needs to perform a search operation by sending an activated event. This is the same event that is sent when your app is launched, and to differentiate between the two situations, you must read the kind property of the event. Dealing with the activation of a contract requires a different approach to the onactivated function in your app, as shown in Listing 21-5.

Listing 21-5. Dealing with contract activation in the default.js file

```
(function () {
    "use strict";

    var app = WinJS.Application;
    var activation = Windows.ApplicationModel.Activation;
    WinJS.strictProcessing();

    app.onactivated = function (args) {

        var searchTerm;
        var promise;

        switch (args.detail.kind) {
            case activation.ActivationKind.search:
                ViewModel.writeMessage("Search Activation");
                searchTerm = args.detail.queryText;
                break;
            case activation.ActivationKind.launch:
                ViewModel.writeMessage("Launch Activation");
```

```
            searchTerm = "";
            break;
    }

    if (args.detail.previousExecutionState
        != activation.ApplicationExecutionState.suspended) {
        ViewModel.writeMessage("App was not resumed");
        promise = WinJS.UI.processAll();
    } else {
        ViewModel.writeMessage("App was resumed");
        promise = WinJS.Promise.as(true);
    }

    args.setPromise(promise.then(function () {
        ViewModel.search(searchTerm);
    }));
};

app.start();
})();
```

To explain how this works, I will walk through the code in detail and show you the range of scenarios it caters for. It is not at all complicated, but there are some fine details to consider, and if you understand how to deal with this contract, you will find working with other contracts simpler and easier.

Launching the App

The first thing to do is start the app. It doesn't matter how you do this—you can use the Start Debugging item from the Visual Studio Debug menu or, if you have previously run the example, using the tile on the Start screen. When the app launches, you will see the messages in the right-hand ListView control shown in Figure 21-5.

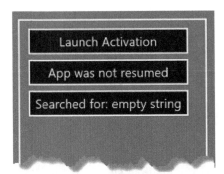

Figure 21-5. Messages that are shown when the app is launched normally

In this situation, my switch statement in the onactivated handler function will read the detail.kind property and get the launch value. In this situation, I set the search string to the empty string (""), as follows:

```
...
switch (args.detail.kind) {
    case activation.ActivationKind.search:
        ViewModel.writeMessage("Search Activation");
        searchTerm = args.detail.queryText;
        break;
    case activation.ActivationKind.launch:
        ViewModel.writeMessage("Launch Activation");
        searchTerm = "";
        break;
}
...
```

This gives me one of the two things I need: the search term. To get the Promise, I need to look at the previous execution state. Since the app has been started afresh, the previous state will be notRunning. For every state except suspended, I want to call the WinJS.UI.processAll method so as to perform the initial setup for the app:

```
...
if (args.detail.previousExecutionState
    != activation.ApplicationExecutionState.suspended) {
    ViewModel.writeMessage("App was not resumed");
    promise = WinJS.UI.processAll();
} else {
    ViewModel.writeMessage("App was resumed");
    promise = WinJS.Promise.as(true);
}
...
```

The effect is that the search will match all data items (so all of the names are displayed initially) and the app is initialized so that the WinJS UI controls are activated. You can see how I write messages throughout the code to show which conditions I am dealing with, and that is how I end up with the messages shown in Figure 21-4.

Performing a Search

Launching the app is all well and good, but you already knew how to do that. To see something new, select the Search Charm, either by typing Win+Q or by activating the charm bar and selecting the Search icon, as shown in Figure 21-6.

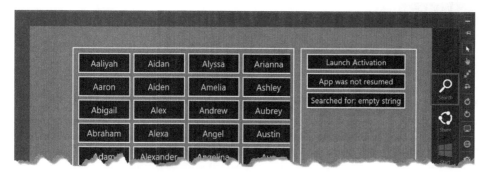

Figure 21-6. Selecting the Search Charm

When you activate the Search Charm, a new display, called the *search pane*, is overlaid on the app, allowing you to perform searches. There is a text entry box for the search term, and beneath this you will see a series of icons. These icons represent the range of search targets, which include the SearchContract example app, as shown in Figure 21-7. (You may have to scroll down the list to see the app.)

■ **Tip**   If the search pane reports that the app can't be searched, you will need to stop the Visual Studio debugger, uninstall the SearchContract app, and start the Visual Studio debugger again. Windows doesn't always respond properly to manifest changes during development, but this isn't a problem for apps that are installed via the Windows Store. (I show you the process for publishing your app to the store in Part 5 of this book.)

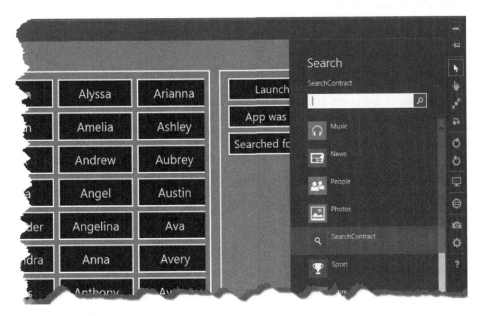

Figure 21-7. The search pane

You will notice that the SearchContract app is already selected in the list, which indicates to the user that the search request will be passed to the app for processing.

Enter jac and the search term and hit Enter or click the icon to the right of the text entry to perform the search. The app will perform the search for the specified term and display the matching names, but the search pane will remain visible.

Click anywhere on the app to close the search pane and you will see that the messages shown in the right-hand ListView control have been updated, as follows:

```
Launch Activation
App was not resumed
Searched for: empty string
Search Activation
App was not resumed
Searched for: jac
```

It is the new entries, which I have marked in bold, that are of interest. When you submitted the search, Windows sent the app another activated event, but this time the args.detail.kind property was set to search. When performing a *search activation,* as it is known, the system includes the string that the user is searching for as the value for the detail.queryText property. This is the term that I searched for in my onactivated handler when I received a search activation event:

```
...
switch (args.detail.kind) {
    case activation.ActivationKind.search:
        ViewModel.writeMessage("Search Activation");
        searchTerm = args.detail.queryText;
        break;
    case activation.ActivationKind.launch:
        ViewModel.writeMessage("Launch Activation");
        searchTerm = "";
        break;
}
...
```

Of course, the app is running at this point, and so I don't need to call the WinJS.UI.processAll method because all of my UI controls are already applied and working properly. I still want to have a Promise object to work with, and so I use the Promise.wrap method (which I described in Chapter 9) to create a Promise that will be fulfilled immediately, as follows:

```
...
if (args.detail.previousExecutionState
    != activation.ApplicationExecutionState.suspended) {
    ViewModel.writeMessage("App was not resumed");
    promise = WinJS.UI.processAll();
} else {
    ViewModel.writeMessage("App was resumed");
    promise = WinJS.Promise.as(true);
}
...
```

The app will receive additional activated events whose kind is search each time the user performs additional searches. For this reason, I have been careful to structure my code so that I don't make any assumptions about the number or kind of events I will be dealing with.

Searching When the App Isn't running

The last scenario I want to explore requires the app to have been closed. Either stop the debugger or press Alt+F4 in the app to close the app. Without restarting the app, select the Search Charm from the Start screen.

When you select the Search Charm from the Start screen, the scope of the search is set to the names of the apps installed on the device (the visual cue for this is that Apps is selected in the list under the text entry box). Enter jac as the search term and press Enter to perform the search. You will see the results in Figure 21-8 (unless you happen to have an app whose name contains jac).

Figure 21-8. The general-purpose Windows search

Now click on the icon for the SearchContract app in the list. (The app will be the first item on the list if you have been following the examples in this chapter, because Windows orders the apps based on use—you might be able to make this out from the figure.)

Clicking on the app entry in the list changes the scope of the search to the example app. The app will be launched, and the names shown in the left-hand ListView will be those that match the search term. Dismiss the search pane by clicking on the app layout, and take a look at the messages displayed in the right-hand ListView, which will be as follows:

```
Search Activation
App was not resumed
Searched for: jac
```

The important point to note is that the app didn't receive a launch activation event—only the search activation was sent by the system. If the app isn't running when the user performs a search aimed at the app, then the system will start the app, but it won't send the same event as when the app is started via its tile or the Visual Studio debugger.

Knowing this, I need to ensure that I recognize when I get a search activation event and the app wasn't previously running so that I can initialize the app properly—which, for this simple app, just means calling the WinJS.UI.processAll method and then making the search. You can now understand why I separated out the check for the previous execution state from the code that checks on the kind of event I received:

```
...
if (args.detail.previousExecutionState
    != activation.ApplicationExecutionState.suspended) {
    ViewModel.writeMessage("App was not resumed");
    promise = WinJS.UI.processAll();
} else {
    ViewModel.writeMessage("App was resumed");
    promise = WinJS.Promise.as(true);
}
...
```

Summarizing the Search Contract Activation Scenarios

It is important to make sure that you know when to initialize your app and when you can obtain a search term via the queryText property. You have seen the various scenarios in the previous sections, and for future quick reference I have summarized the permutations in Table 21-2.

Table 21-2. Summary of Search Contract Activation Scenarios

Activation Kind	Previous State	Initialize App	queryText **Search Term**
launch	Any except suspended	Yes	N/A
launch	suspended	No	N/A
search	Any except running	Yes	Yes
search	running	No	Yes

Working with the Search Pane

The technique I showed you in the previous sections is the basic implementation of the search contract, and once you have a search capability in your app, most of the work is in making sure that you handle the activation events correctly.

You can also create a tailored search experience by working directly with the search pane, which is available through the objects in the Windows.ApplicationModel.Search namespace. The key object in this namespace is SearchPane, which allows you to access and integrate with the Windows search pane. The SearchPane object defines the methods and properties shown in Table 21-3.

Table 21-3. Properties and Methods Defined by the SearchPane Object

Name	Description
getForCurrentView()	Returns a SearchPane object that you can work with
setLocalContentSuggestionSettings (settings)	Specifies if and how local files are included in the search
show() show(query)	Shows the search pane to the user, optionally with an initial query string
placeholderText	Gets or sets the text shown in the search pane text entry when there is no query
queryText	Returns the current query from the text entry box
searchHistoryContext	Gets or sets a value that can be used to differentiate between types of searches in an app
searchHistoryEnabled	Gets or sets whether previous searches are stored and used to make suggestions to the user
visible	Returns true when the search pane is visible to the user, false when it is not

In addition, the SearchPane object supports several events, which I have described in Table 21-4. These events are triggered at key moments in the search process and allow you to respond in a more sophisticated way than is possible using the basic contract implementation.

Table 21-4. Events Defined by the SearchPane Object

Name	Description
querychanged	Triggered when the user changes the content of the text entry box in the search pane
querysubmitted	Triggered when the user submits a search
resultsuggestionchosen	Triggered when the user selects a search suggestion provided by the app
suggestionsrequested	Triggered when Windows wants the app to provide search suggestions
visibilitychanged	Triggered when the search pane is shown and hidden

In the sections that follow, I'll show you some advanced search techniques that use these methods, properties, and events, including how to trigger the search process from the app layout, and make different kinds of suggestions that Windows can use to help the user during the search process.

■ **Note** Unless I note otherwise, the objects that I refer to in this section are all in the `Windows.ApplicationModel.Search` namespace.

Activating Search

Users don't always understand how Windows 8 search works, which is a shame because the idea of triggering application-specific searches from a system-wide pane is a neat one. If search is a key part of your app's functionality, you may need to provide the user with a control in the app layout that will open the search pane. To demonstrate this, I have added a `button` element to the markup in the `default.html` file, as shown in Listing 21-6.

Listing 21-6. Adding a button that will open the search pane

```
...
<body>
    <div id="NameItemTemplate" data-win-control="WinJS.Binding.Template">
        <div class="ListItem">
            <div class="ListData" data-win-bind="innerText: name"></div>
        </div>
    </div>

    <div id="MessageTemplate" data-win-control="WinJS.Binding.Template">
        <div class="message" data-win-bind="innerText: message"></div>
    </div>

    <div id="nameContainer" class="listContainer">
        <div id="nameList" data-win-control="WinJS.UI.ListView"
            data-win-options="{itemTemplate: NameItemTemplate,
                itemDataSource: ViewModel.filteredNames.dataSource}">
        </div>
```

```
        </div>

        <div id="buttonContainer" class="listContainer">
            <button id="showSearch">Show Search</button>
        </div>

        <div id="messageContainer" class="listContainer">
            <div id="messageList" data-win-control="WinJS.UI.ListView"
                data-win-options="{itemTemplate: MessageTemplate,
                    itemDataSource: ViewModel.messages.dataSource,
                    layout: {type: WinJS.UI.ListLayout}}">
            </div>
        </div>
    </body>
...
```

This doesn't create the most elegant of app layouts, but it is sufficient for my purposes. You can see the result in Figure 21-9.

Figure 21-9. Adding the Show Search button to the app layout

I have added the statements shown in Listing 21-7 to the default.js file to respond to the button being clicked.

Listing 21-7. Responding to the button being clicked

```
(function () {
    "use strict";

    var app = WinJS.Application;
    var activation = Windows.ApplicationModel.Activation;
    var search = Windows.ApplicationModel.Search;
    WinJS.strictProcessing();

    app.onactivated = function (args) {
        var searchTerm;
        var promise;

        switch (args.detail.kind) {
            case activation.ActivationKind.search:
                ViewModel.writeMessage("Search Activation");
```

```
                searchTerm = args.detail.queryText;
                break;
            case activation.ActivationKind.launch:
                ViewModel.writeMessage("Launch Activation");
                searchTerm = "";
                break;
        }

        if (args.detail.previousExecutionState
            != activation.ApplicationExecutionState.suspended) {
            ViewModel.writeMessage("App was not resumed");
            promise = WinJS.UI.processAll().then(function () {
                showSearch.addEventListener("click", function (e) {
                    search.SearchPane.getForCurrentView().show(ViewModel.searchTerm);
                });
            });
        } else {
            ViewModel.writeMessage("App was resumed");
            promise = WinJS.Promise.as(true);
        }

        args.setPromise(promise.then(function () {
            ViewModel.search(searchTerm);
        }));
    };

    app.start();
})();
```

The first step in working with the SearchPane object is to call the getForCurrentView method, which returns a SearchPane object on which you can perform operations. This means that if you want to show the search pane, as I do in the example, you must use:

```
...
search.SearchPane.getForCurrentView().show(ViewModel.searchTerm);
...
```

You will create an exception if you try to use a method or property on a SearchPane object that you have not obtained through the getForCurrentView method. In the listing, I respond to the click event from the newly added button by showing the search pane with the show method. I am able to set the initial query string in the search pane by passing a string to the show method, which allows me to ensure that the search pane is consistent with the data shown in the left-hand ListView of the app layout.

The standard Windows search pane will be shown if you run the example app and click the Show Search button. The Search example app will be automatically selected as the scope for the search, just as it was when you showed the search pane via the Search Charm earlier in the chapter.

Providing Query Suggestions

The feature I like most when working with the search pane is the ability to suggest results directly in the pane. This lets the user perform *progressive searches* on your app, where the range of possible matches is updated each time the text in the query box changes.

When the search pane is visible and the user is typing in a search term, the SearchPane object will trigger the suggestionsrequested event, which is an invitation for you to provide suggestions to the user. You can see how I have done this in the example app in Listing 21-8, where I have added a handler function for this event to the default.js file.

Listing 21-8. Adding support for the suggestionsrequested event

```
(function () {
    "use strict";

    var app = WinJS.Application;
    var activation = Windows.ApplicationModel.Activation;
    var search = Windows.ApplicationModel.Search;
    WinJS.strictProcessing();

    app.onactivated = function (args) {
        var searchTerm;
        var promise;

        switch (args.detail.kind) {
            case activation.ActivationKind.search:
                ViewModel.writeMessage("Search Activation");
                searchTerm = args.detail.queryText;
                break;
            case activation.ActivationKind.launch:
                ViewModel.writeMessage("Launch Activation");
                searchTerm = "";
                break;
        }

        if (args.detail.previousExecutionState
            != activation.ApplicationExecutionState.suspended) {
            ViewModel.writeMessage("App was not resumed");
            promise = WinJS.UI.processAll().then(function () {
                var sp = search.SearchPane.getForCurrentView();
                showSearch.addEventListener("click", function (e) {
                    sp.show(ViewModel.searchTerm);
                });
                sp.addEventListener("suggestionsrequested", function (e) {
                    var query = e.queryText;
                    var suggestions = ViewModel.search(query, true);
                    suggestions.forEach(function (item) {
                        e.request.searchSuggestionCollection
                            .appendQuerySuggestion(item.name);
                    });
                });
            });
        } else {
            ViewModel.writeMessage("App was resumed");
            promise = WinJS.Promise.as(true);
        }
```

```
        args.setPromise(promise.then(function () {
            ViewModel.search(searchTerm);
        }));
    };

    app.start();
})();
```

Notice that I call the addEventListener method on the object that I get back from the SearchPane.getForCurrentView method. To be able to offer suggestions, I have had to update the viewmodel.js file so that my search method can perform searches that update the ListView control as well as searches that just generate suggestions. You can see the new version of the search method in Listing 21-9.

Listing 21-9. Updating the search method to generate suggestions

```
...
ViewModel.search = function (term, suggestions) {
    ViewModel.writeMessage("Searched for: " + (term == "" ? "empty string" : term));
    term = term.toLowerCase();
    var target = suggestions ? [] : ViewModel.filteredNames;
    target.length = 0;
    ViewModel.allNames.forEach(function (item) {
        if (item.name.toLowerCase().indexOf(term) > -1) {
            target.push(item)
        }
    });
    if (!suggestions) {
        ViewModel.searchTerm = term;
    }
    return target;
};
...
```

If the suggestions argument is present and true, then the method will generate and return an array of matches without updating the data source used by the ListView. This allows me to add support for suggestions without having to modify any of the existing calls to the search method.

For this section, it will be easier to show you the results and then explain how all of the objects involved fit together. To see the effect of these changes, start the app, open the search pane, and type jac. As you enter each letter, you will see a list of possible matches displayed beneath the text entry box, as shown in Figure 21-10. Windows will display up to five suggestions provided by your app.

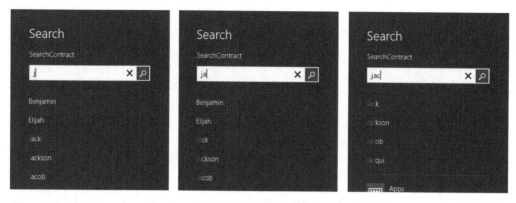

Figure 21-10. Suggestions displayed in the search pane

The list is refined each time you type an additional letter. By the time you have typed in all three letters, four suggestions are shown, all of which contain the term jac. The ListView in the example app isn't affected as you type—but if you click on any of these suggestions, the system will trigger a search activation, which will have the effect of searching for the term.

Understanding the Suggestions Example

Getting to the point where you can provide the system with suggestions requires a long chain of objects, but bear with me—it isn't as complicated as it appears at first. A SearchPaneSuggestionsRequestedEventArgs object is passed to the handler function for the suggestionrequired event. Aside from having a ridiculously long name, this object defines two useful read-only properties I have described in Table 21-5.

Table 21-5. Read-only Properties of the SearchPaneSuggestionsRequestedEventArgs Object

Name	Description
queryText	Returns the text that the user has entered into the search text box
request	Returns a SearchPaneSuggestionsRequest object, used to pass suggestions

The queryText property will be updated each time the user modifies the search text. It is common to receive a series of events as the user narrows his search—starting, perhaps, with a queryText value of j and then ja and then jac. You read the value of the queryText property and use SearchPaneSuggestionsRequest object returned by the request property to provide the system with suggestions that can be presented to the user. The SearchPaneSuggestionsRequest defines the methods and properties that I have described in Table 21-6.

Table 21-6. Methods and Properties of the SearchPaneSuggestionsRequest Object

Name	Description
getDeferral	Returns an object that can be used to provide suggestions asynchronously—see the Making Suggestions Asynchronously section later in this chapter for details

Name	Description
isCanceled	Returns true if the request has been canceled since the event was triggered and false otherwise. This can be used to avoid generating suggestions unnecessarily
searchSuggestionCollection	Returns a SearchSuggestionCollection object, which can be used to provide suggestions to the system

We have arrived at the important object in this chain, which is the SearchSuggestionCollection object, which is available via the request.searchSuggestionCollection property of the event object passed to the handler function. The SearchSuggestionCollection object defines four methods and one property, which I have summarized in Table 21-7.

Table 21-7. Methods and Properties of the SearchSuggestionCollection Object

Name	Description
appendQuerySuggestion(text)	Provides Windows with a suggestion—call this method multiple times to provide multiple suggestions
appendQuerySuggestions(text[])	Provides multiple query suggestions in a single call
appendResultSuggestion(args)	Appends a single results suggestion—see the Providing Results Suggestions section below for details of the arguments to this method
appendSearchSeparator(label)	Adds a separator to the results
size	Returns the number of suggestions in the collection

The simplest method to use is appendQuerySuggestion, which takes a string as its argument and presents it to the user as a possible query in the search pane. This is the method I used in the example, as you can see in Listing 21-10, where I have repeated the key statements.

Listing 21-10. Providing query suggestions for the user

```
...
sp.addEventListener("suggestionsrequested", function (e) {
    var query = e.queryText;
    var suggestions = ViewModel.search(query, true);
    suggestions.forEach(function (item) {
        e.request.searchSuggestionCollection.appendQuerySuggestion(item.name);
    });
});
...
```

■ **Tip** I call the appendQuerySuggestion method for every suggestion that I get back from the ViewModel. search method. That works for my example app because there isn't any significant cost in searching 200 names. However, Windows will display no more than five suggestions, so if your results are expensive to generate, you can save resources by generating only five matches.

Adding Separators to Suggestions

The SearchSuggestionCollection.appendSearchSeparator method allows you to add some structure to your suggestions. If you interleave calls to appendSearchSeparator with calls to the appendQuerySuggestion method, you can create a structured set of suggestions. However, there are still only five slots for suggestions on the search pane, so every separator you add to the suggestions means that you can offer one less result. Listing 21-11 shows the changes I have made to the suggestionsrequested handler function in the default.js file to demonstrate the use of the appendSearchSeparator method.

Listing 21-11. Using the appendSearchSeparator method to add structure to suggestions

```
...
sp.addEventListener("suggestionsrequested", function (e) {
    var query = e.queryText;
    var suggestions = ViewModel.search(query, true);
    var lastLetter = null;
    suggestions.forEach(function (item) {
        if (item.firstLetter != lastLetter) {
            e.request.searchSuggestionCollection.appendSearchSeparator(item.firstLetter);
            lastLetter = item.firstLetter;
        }
        e.request.searchSuggestionCollection.appendQuerySuggestion(item.name);

    });
});
...
```

There is no fixed structure for search suggestions and so you can apply separators in any way that makes sense in your app. In this example, I separate names based on their first letter (in doing this I rely on the fact that the names returned by the ViewModel.search method are sorted alphabetically). You can see the result in Figure 21-11.

Figure 21-11. The effect of adding separators to search suggestions

To see the effect in the sample app, you need to find a search string that matches names that start with different letters. In the example, I used the string aa, which matches Aaliyah, Aaron and Isaac. You can see in the figure that these names have been separated using the values that I passed to the appendSearchSeparator method.

■ **Tip**   I recommend that you think carefully before using separators when offering search results because they take up valuable space that could be used to offer additional suggestions to the user. Use separators only when presenting suggestions without them would not make sense to the user.

Providing Result Suggestions

You can make a *result suggestion* when the term the user is searching for exactly matches a data item in your app. This provides the user with an overview of the item and helps him decide if he has found what he is looking for. You can see an example in Figure 21-12, where I have searched for alex. Alex is a name in the list I am working with and part of other names, such as Alexa and Alexander, which is why you see a mix of query suggestions (the kind of suggestion I have been making so far) and result suggestions.

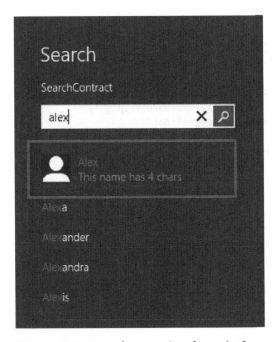

Figure 21-12. A result suggestion shown in the search pane

Result suggestions are made using the SearchSuggestionCollection.appendResultSuggestion method, which requires the arguments described in Table 21-8. These additional arguments are used to provide the additional information about the item that you can see in the figure.

Table 21-8. Arguments Required by the appendResultSuggestion Method

Name	Description
text	A summary of the matched item (used as the top line of text in the search pane)
detailText	Additional details that the user might find useful (used as the bottom line of text)
tag	A tag that uniquely identifies the suggested result (this is passed back to your app if the user accepts the suggestion)
image	An image that will be displayed as part of the suggestion
altText	Alternative text for the image

All arguments are required. For this example, I added a simple image to the sample project as images/user.png and this is the image shown alongside the suggested Alex result. You can see how I created the suggestion in Listing 21-12, which shows the changes I made to the default.js file.

Listing 21-12. Adding support for result suggestions

```
...
sp.addEventListener("suggestionsrequested", function (e) {
    var query = e.queryText;
    var suggestions = ViewModel.search(query, true);
    var lastLetter = null;
    suggestions.forEach(function (item) {
        if (query.toLowerCase() != item.name.toLowerCase()) {
            e.request.searchSuggestionCollection.appendQuerySuggestion(item.name);
        } else {
            var imageSource = Windows.Storage.Streams.RandomAccessStreamReference.
                createFromUri(Windows.Foundation.Uri("ms-appx:///images/user.png"));
            e.request.searchSuggestionCollection.appendResultSuggestion(
                item.name,
                "This name has " + item.name.length + " chars",
                item.name, imageSource, item.name);
        }
    });
});
...
```

My data isn't a perfect fit for this model—and that isn't unusual. I find that data items are either too complex to be used as a result suggestion or too simple, causing me to have to add some padding data. In this example, the data is too simple.

For the text and detailText arguments I have used the matched name and a string that reports how many characters are in the name—this isn't useful data, but it is the kind of padding that you end up with. You can set the detailText argument to the empty string if you really have nothing useful to say, but this has the effect of creating a slightly odd-looking suggestion.

I am going to skip over the tag argument for a moment and look at the image argument instead. I included the image I want to use as part of the project, but the image argument must be a Windows.Storage.Streams.IRandomAccessStreamReference object.

I introduce you to the Windows support for working with files in Chapter 22, so for now I am going to present the code required for the image argument as a black-box incantation. The incantation required to load an image from the app package is similar to the technique I showed you when I loaded an app data file, but the Windows.Foundation.Uri object is passed to the Windows.Storage.Streams.

`RandomAccessStreamReference.createFromUri` method to create the kind of object that is needed to load an image for the suggestion:

```
...
Windows.Storage.Streams.RandomAccessStreamReference.createFromUri(
    Windows.Foundation.Uri("ms-appx:///images/user.png"));
...
```

■ **Caution**   Don't forget that there are three /// characters in the URL that specifies the image file—a common mistake is to use just two. This doesn't create an error but you won't see the image displayed as part of the result suggestion.

Responding When a Suggestion Is Chosen

You can see in the listing that I have also used the name for the tag argument. This argument must uniquely identify the data item that you are suggesting. The system doesn't care what this value is—it just passes it back to you if the user clicks on the suggestion. When this happens, the SearchPane object triggers a resultsuggestionchosen event and passes the tag value you provided back to your app via the tag property of the event object. Listing 21-13 shows the addition of a handler function for the resultsuggestionchosen event in which I pass the tag value to the ViewModel.search method to reflect the user's selection.

Listing 21-13. Adding an event handler for the resultsuggestionchosen event

```
...
sp.addEventListener("suggestionsrequested", function (e) {
    var query = e.queryText;
    var suggestions = ViewModel.search(query, true);
    var lastLetter = null;
    suggestions.forEach(function (item) {
        if (query.toLowerCase() != item.name.toLowerCase()) {
            e.request.searchSuggestionCollection.appendQuerySuggestion(item.name);
        } else {
            var imageSource = Windows.Storage.Streams.RandomAccessStreamReference
                .createFromUri(Windows.Foundation.Uri("ms-appx:///images/user.png"));
            e.request.searchSuggestionCollection.appendResultSuggestion(
                item.name,
                "This name has " + item.name.length + " chars",
                item.name, imageSource, item.name);
        }
    });
});
sp.addEventListener("resultsuggestionchosen", function (e) {
    ViewModel.search(e.tag);
});
...
```

Working with the Suggestion History

Windows maintains a history of the suggested results and queries that a user accepts and gives them preference when the same search is performed again. To see how this works, start the app and search for jo. You will see that the suggestions that are presented in the search pane are:

```
Joel
John
Jonathan
Jordan
Jose
```

Click on `Jordan` to complete the search—you will see that the `ListView` control in the app layout is updated to match your search and that the search box is updated to show `Jordan`. Clear the search box and type jo again. This time the order the names are presented in is different:

```
Jordan
Joel
John
Jonathan
Jose
```

This can be a useful aid for the user and the search history is persistent, meaning that it will offer better suggestions to the user as he makes more selections.

You can disable the suggestion history by setting the `SearchPane.searchHistoryEnabled` property to false. This prevents the user's selection from being added to the history and ensures that your suggestions are presented to the user in the order you supplied them. You can see how I have used the searchHistoryEnabled property in Listing 21-14.

Listing 21-14. Disabling search history

```
...
if (args.detail.previousExecutionState
    != activation.ApplicationExecutionState.suspended) {
    ViewModel.writeMessage("App was not resumed");
    promise = WinJS.UI.processAll().then(function () {
        var sp = search.SearchPane.getForCurrentView();
        sp.searchHistoryEnabled = false;
        showSearch.addEventListener("click", function (e) {
            sp.show(ViewModel.searchTerm);
        });
        sp.addEventListener("suggestionsrequested", function (e) {
            // ... code removed for brevity...
        });
        sp.addEventListener("resultsuggestionchosen", function (e) {
            ViewModel.search(e.tag);
        });
    });
} else {
    ViewModel.writeMessage("App was resumed");
```

```
    promise = WinJS.Promise.as(true);
}
...
```

If you start the app and run the search for jo again, you will see that Jordan isn't given a preferential position in the suggestions list.

■ **Tip**   If your app supports different ways of searching your data or supports searching different data sets, you can use the `SearchPane.searchHistoryContext` property to keep separate search histories for each. Assign this property a value that represents the kind of search the user is about to perform and Windows will take into account only the selection he has made the next time the same value for the `searchHistoryContext` property is used.

Making Suggestions Asynchronously

So far I have generated all of my suggestions synchronously, which is fine because all of my data is stored in memory and is immediately available.

You will need to take a different approach if the code you rely on to generate suggestions returns a `Promise` instead of giving you the data directly. You will often find this is the case when your data is contained in files or in a `WinJS.UI.IListDataSource` object, which returns `Promise` objects from many of its methods and produces the data when the `Promises` are fulfilled.

To demonstrate the problem, I have added a `ViewModel.asyncSuggest` method to my `viewmodel.js` class. This method uses the same data I have been working with throughout this chapter, but it presents the result via a `Promise`, which is fulfilled only when the search is complete. To make this a more realistic demonstration, the search is performed as a series of small operations interleaved with calls to the `setImmediate` method to allow the JavaScript runtime to perform other operations. You can see the addition in Listing 21-15.

■ **Tip**   See Chapter 9 for details of the `WinJS.Promise` object and the `setImmediate` method.

Listing 21-15. An asynchronous search method

```
...
ViewModel.asyncSuggest = function (term) {
    return new WinJS.Promise(function (fDone, fError, fProgress) {
        var index = 0;
        var blockSize = 10;
        var matches = [];
        term = term.toLowerCase();

        function searchBlock() {
            for (var i = index; i < index + blockSize; i++) {
                if (ViewModel.allNames[i].name.toLowerCase().indexOf(term) > -1) {
                    matches.push(ViewModel.allNames[i].name);
                }
            }
            index += blockSize;
            if (index < ViewModel.allNames.length) {
```

```
                    setImmediate(searchBlock);
                } else {
                    fDone(matches);
                }
            }
        }
        setImmediate(searchBlock);
    });
}
...
```

This method returns a `WinJS.Promise` object that is fulfilled when all of the names have been searched for the query term. The search itself is performed in blocks of 10 names, and the `setImmediate` method is called after each block so that the JavaScript runtime can perform other pending work, such as process events.

To use an asynchronous method to generate suggestions, you must call the `SearchPaneSuggestionRequest.getDeferral` method. The `SearchPaneSuggestionRequest` object is available through the `request` property of the object passed to the `suggestionsrequested` event handler function. The `getDeferral` method returns a `SearchPaneSuggestionsRequestDeferral` object, which defines one method: `complete`. You call the `complete` method when the `Promise` returned by your asynchronous suggestion generating method is fulfilled. Listing 21-16 shows how I have applied this technique to the `suggestionsrequested` handler in the example.

Listing 21-16. Using an asynchronous method to generate suggestions

```
...
sp.addEventListener("suggestionsrequested", function (e) {
    var deferral = e.request.getDeferral();
    ViewModel.asyncSuggest(e.queryText).then(function (suggestions) {
        e.request.searchSuggestionCollection.appendQuerySuggestions(suggestions);
        deferral.complete();
    });
});
...
```

It is important to remember to call the `complete` method when the `Promise` is fulfilled. There are no errors reported if you forget to do this, but the user won't be shown the suggestions that you have provided.

Summary

In this chapter I have shown you how to implement the first of the Windows contracts, which allow an app to integrate with system-wide features. I showed you the search contract, and by implementing this contract, an app is able to seamlessly participate in the searches, offering its content and data alongside that of other apps.

I also showed you how to customize the search experience by working directly with the search pane. Using the search pane, I showed you how to offer query and result suggestions to help the user find what he is looking for in your app. The Windows support for search is very flexible and I recommend you take the time to integrate it into your app in a useful and meaningful way. In the next chapter, I'll show you how to work with files in Windows apps. This is an important area of functionality, which I cover fully in the next three chapters.

CHAPTER 22

Working with Files

This is the first of two chapters focused on user files, which is to say files that the user creates, changes, and stores and that are different from the app data and files I described in Chapter 21.

In this chapter, I am going to show you how to operate on files and folders directly to perform basic file operations, such as copying and deleting files. I am then going to show you the Windows app features for taking a more sophisticated view of files, including sorting lists of files, filtering the contents of folders, performing complex file searches, creating virtual folders to group related files together, and monitoring folders so that you are notified when new files are added.

These techniques allow me to set the scene for the next chapter, which shows how you can integrate your app, and its file- and folder-related capabilities into the wider Windows experience. So, in short, everything in this chapter is about dealing with the file system *inside* your app, while the next chapter is about presenting those capabilities to the user. Table 22-1 provides the summary for this chapter.

Table 22-1. Chapter Summary

Problem	Solution	Listing
Copy files	Use the StorageFile.copyAsync method	22-5–22-7
Ensure that files are copied in order	Chain the calls to the copyAsync method using the WinJS. Promise.then method	22-8
Delete files	Call the StorageFile.deleteAsync method	22-9
Sort and filter files	Use a basic file query or AQS	22-10–22-13
Use common queries	Use the properties of the CommonFileQuery object	22-14
Group files by common attributes	Use the virtual folders feature	22-15–22-17
Monitor a folder for new files	Listen for the contentschanged event	22-18

Creating the Example App

For this chapter, I have created a new example project called UserFiles. I need some example files to work with, so I created an images/flowers folder and added some JPG images to work with. These are the same images I used in Chapter 21 and I have included them in the source code download that accompanies this book (available from apress.com). You can see the list of file names in Figure 22-1, which shows the Solution Explorer window for the UserFiles project.

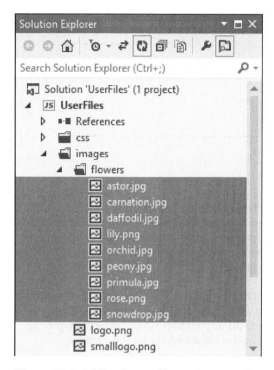

Figure 22-1. *Adding image files to the example app*

The rest of the project is a simple app. You can see the contents of the default.html file in Listing 22-1. There are two panels in the layout—one contains a series of buttons that will trigger the code for the examples in this chapter and the other contains a WinJS.UI.ListView control that I use to display messages. The WinJS.Binding.Template control is used to display the messages in the ListView.

Listing 22-1. *The default.html file for the UserFiles project*

```
<!DOCTYPE html>
<html>
<head>
    <meta charset="utf-8" />
    <title>UserFiles</title>
    <!-- WinJS references -->
    <link href="//Microsoft.WinJS.1.0/css/ui-dark.css" rel="stylesheet" />
    <script src="//Microsoft.WinJS.1.0/js/base.js"></script>
    <script src="//Microsoft.WinJS.1.0/js/ui.js"></script>
    <!-- UserFiles references -->
    <link href="/css/default.css" rel="stylesheet" />
    <script src="/js/viewmodel.js"></script>
    <script src="/js/default.js"></script>
</head>
```

```
<body>
    <div id="template" data-win-control="WinJS.Binding.Template">
        <div class="message" data-win-bind="innerText: message"></div>
    </div>

    <div id="buttonsContainer" class="container">
        <button id="copyFiles">Copy Files</button>
        <button id="copySeq">Copy Files (Ordered)</button>
        <button id="deleteFiles">Delete Files</button>
        <button id="sortFiles">Sort Files</button>
        <button id="filterBasic">Filter (Basic)</button>
        <button id="filterAQS">Filter (AQS)</button>
        <button id="commonQuery">Common Query</button>
        <button id="groupType">Group (Type)</button>
    </div>

    <div id="listContainer" class="container">
        <div id="list" data-win-control="WinJS.UI.ListView"
            data-win-options="{
                itemDataSource: ViewModel.State.messages.dataSource,
                itemTemplate: template,
                layout: {type:WinJS.UI.ListLayout}
            }">
        </div>
    </div>
</body>
</html>
```

You can see the CSS I have defined in the `css/default.css` file to manage the layout of these elements in Listing 22-2.

Listing 22-2. The contents of the css/default.css file

```
body {
    display: -ms-flexbox;
    -ms-flex-direction: row;
    -ms-flex-align: center; -ms-flex-pack: center;
}

.container {
    height: 80%; margin: 10px; padding: 10px;
    border: medium solid white;
}

#buttonsContainer button, .message {
    display: block; font-size: 20pt;
    width: 100%; margin-top: 10px;
}

#listContainer {width: 30%;}
#list { height: 100%;}
```

I have defined some basic app state and some utility functions in the js/viewmodel.js file, which you can see in Listing 22-3. These support the messages displayed in the ListView control.

Listing 22-3. The viewmodel.js file for the example app

```
(function () {

    WinJS.Namespace.define("ViewModel", {
        State: WinJS.Binding.as({
            messages: new WinJS.Binding.List()
        })
    });

    WinJS.Namespace.define("App", {
        writeMessage: function (msg) {
            ViewModel.State.messages.push({ message: msg });
        },
        clearMessages: function () {
            ViewModel.State.messages.length = 0;
        }
    });

    App.writeMessage("Ready");
})();
```

Finally, you can see the js/default.js file in Listing 22-4. This is where I will add the code for the examples by responding to the click event for the button elements in the default.html file, but for the moment this file contains just the basic app plumbing.

Listing 22-4. The initial default.js file for the example app

```
(function () {

    var $ = WinJS.Utilities.query;
    var app = WinJS.Application;
    var activation = Windows.ApplicationModel.Activation;
    var storage = Windows.Storage;
    var search = Windows.Storage.Search;

    var imageFileNames = ["astor.jpg", "carnation.jpg", "daffodil.jpg",
        "lily.png","orchid.jpg", "peony.jpg", "primula.jpg", "rose.png", "snowdrop.jpg"];

    app.onactivated = function (args) {
        if (args.detail.previousExecutionState !=
            activation.ApplicationExecutionState.suspended) {

            args.setPromise(WinJS.UI.processAll().then(function() {
                $('#buttonsContainer > button').listen("click", function (e) {
                    App.clearMessages();
                    switch (e.target.id) {
                        // ...code for examples will go here...
                    }
```

```
            });
        }));
    }
};
app.start();
})();
```

I have defined an array called `imageFileNames` that contains the names of the files in the `images/flowers` folder. In the sections that follow, I'll add code to the `switch` statement to respond to individual buttons. If you start the example app now, you'll see the basic layout shown in Figure 22-2.

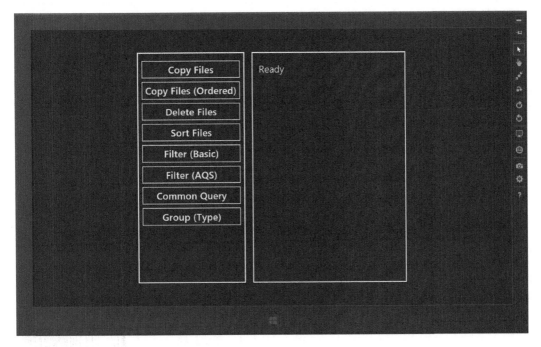

Figure 22-2. The layout of the example app

Performing Basic File Operations

In the sections that follow, I'll show you how to perform some basic file operations. This will allow me to demonstrate the differences in using the `Windows.Storage` objects to deal with user, rather than app, files and to provide some of the detail around the limitations that are placed on apps when working with the file system.

■ **Tip**   One basic file operation I have not included in this chapter is reading the content of a file. You can see how this is done in Chapter 21 (where I demonstrated reading the contents of an app data file) and again in Chapter 23 (where I show you how to use file content in app layouts).

Copying Files

In this section I am going to show you how to copy the flower image files that are included in the app package to the user's `My Pictures` folder. You can see the additions I have made to the `switch` statement in the `default.js` file in Listing 22-5. The code for working with files in Windows apps is pretty verbose, so I am only going to show the modification I make for each example.

■ **Note**   Unless I explicitly note otherwise, the new objects I describe in this chapter are all in the `Windows.Storage` namespace, which I have aliased to `storage` in the example.

Listing 22-5. Adding support for copying files from the app package to the file system

```
...
switch (e.target.id) {
    case 'copyFiles':
        storage.KnownFolders.picturesLibrary.createFolderAsync("flowers",
            storage.CreationCollisionOption.replaceExisting)
        .then(function(folder) {
            imageFileNames.forEach(function (filename) {
                storage.StorageFile.getFileFromApplicationUriAsync(
                    Windows.Foundation.Uri("ms-appx:///images/flowers/" + filename))
                .then(function (file) {
                    file.copyAsync(folder).then(function () {
                        App.writeMessage("Copied: " + filename);
                    }, function (err) {
                        App.writeMessage("Error: " + err);
                    });
                });
            });
        });
        break;
}
...
```

This is much more complicated than it looks because of the use of `Promise` objects as the results from most file-related methods. I'll walk through this code step by step and explain what's going on. Once you understand the basic structure, you'll find the rest of the examples in this section easier to parse.

Locating the Folder

The first thing I want to do is locate my target folder. Windows apps are placed under tight restrictions when it comes to working with the file system and there are only certain locations you can write to without the user's explicit permission (this permission is expressed through a file picker, which I demonstrate in Chapter 23). I won't introduce you to the file pickers until Chapter 23, which means that I am restricted to a very small set of predefined locations, which are accessible through the `KnownFolder` object. This object defines the properties shown in Table 22-2, which relate to common Windows file locations.

■ **Tip** Even accessing the set of locations defined by the KnownFolder object is restricted. Apps that want to read and write to these locations must make a declaration in their manifest, which I demonstrate later in the chapter.

Table 22-2. Properties Defined by the KnownFolder Object

Name	Description
documentsLibrary	Returns the user's Documents folder
homeGroup	Returns the home group folder
mediaServerDevices	Returns the media server content folder
musicLibrary	Returns the user's Music folder
picturesLibrary	Returns the user's Pictures folder
videosLibrary	Returns the user's Videos folder

In the example, I copy the files from the app package into the user's Pictures folder, as shown in Listing 22-6.

Listing 22-6. Working with the user's Pictures folder

```
...
storage.KnownFolders.picturesLibrary.createFolderAsync("flowers",
    storage.CreationCollisionOption.replaceExisting)
...
```

Each property returns a StorageFolder object that represents the location on the file system. Once I get the StorageFolder that represents the Pictures folder, I call the createFolderAsync method to create a flowers folder. This will be the location into which I copy my image files. In Chapter 21, I showed you the basic methods that the StorageFolder object defined to create or locate StorageFile objects, but StorageFolder also defines useful methods for working with other folders as well. Table 22-3 describes the most useful of these methods.

Table 22-3. StorageFolder Methods for Working with Folders

Name	Description
createFolderAsync(name) createFolderAsync(name, option)	Creates a new subfolder using the specified option for collision
deleteAsync()	Deletes the folder represented by the StorageFolder object
getFolderAsync(name)	Returns a StorageFolder representing the specified subfolder
getFoldersAsync()	Returns an array of StorageFolder objects representing the top-level subfolders
renameAsync(name) renameAsync(name, option)	Renames the folder using the specified option for collisions

When using the createFoldersAsync and renameAsync methods, you can provide an optional argument using a value defined by the CreationCollisionOption object, which I have summarized in Table 22-4.

Table 22-4. Values Defined by the CreationCollisionOption Enumeration

Value	Description
generateUniqueName	Appends a number to the name you have specified for the file to avoid collision with any existing files
replaceExisting	Replaces any existing file with a new, empty file
failIfExists	Returns an error if a file with the name you have specified already exists
openIfExists	Opens any existing file

In the example, I used the replaceExisting option, which will delete any existing folder called flowers and replace it with a new, empty folder for my use. The Promise returned by the createFolderAsync method passes a StorageFolder object to the then method, which represents the flowers folder I am interested in.

■ **Caution** Deleting folders is, of course, destructive. You should ensure that you don't have a folder called flowers in your Pictures folder before running this example app; otherwise you will lose your files.

Copying the Files

Now that I have a StorageFolder object that represents the target for my files, I can start to copy them. I do this through the StorageFile object, which represents a single file. First, I obtain a StorageFile for each of the files in my application package and then call the copyAsync method for each of them in turn, as shown in Listing 22-7.

Listing 22-7. Copying each file from the app package to the target folder

```
...
switch (e.target.id) {
    case 'copyFiles':
        storage.KnownFolders.picturesLibrary.createFolderAsync("flowers",
            storage.CreationCollisionOption.replaceExisting)
        .then(function(folder) {
            imageFileNames.forEach(function (filename) {
                storage.StorageFile.getFileFromApplicationUriAsync(
                    Windows.Foundation.Uri("ms-appx:///images/flowers/" + filename))
                .then(function (file) {
                    file.copyAsync(folder).then(function () {
                        App.writeMessage("Copied: " + filename);
                    }, function (err) {
                        App.writeMessage("Error: " + err);
                    });
                });
            });
        });
        break;
}
...
```

This is a good example of the verbose code that arises when you use a number of asynchronous methods to perform related operations. It can take awhile to work out which functions are operating on a given Promise object—although it does become easier as you get used to writing Windows apps.

The code I have highlighted in the listing enumerates each of the file names I defined in the imageFileNames array and uses the StorageFile.getFileFromApplicationUriAsync method to get a StorageFile object representing each image in turn. This is the technique I showed you in Chapter 21, relying on the Windows.Foundation.Uri object.

The StorageFile object is the complement to the StorageFolder object and represents a single file on the file system. Once I have a StorageFile object, I can call the copyAsync method. The argument for this method is the StorageFolder object, which represents the location the file should be copied to. I provide the flowers folder I created in the previous section. I have used the then method on the Promise returned by the copyAsync method to write success and error messages that will be displayed in the ListView control in the app layout. I have summarized the commonly used StorageFile methods in Table 22-5.

Table 22-5. Commonly Used Methods in the StorageFile Object

Name	Description
copyAndReplaceAsync(file)	Replaces the StorageFile provided as the argument with a copy of the current file (i.e., the one represented by the StorageFile on which the copyAndReplaceAsync method was called)
copyAsync(folder) copyAsync(folder, name) copyAsync(folder, name, option)	Copies the file to the specified StorageFolder. You can optionally provide a name to use for the new file and a value from NameCollisionOption to deal with conflicts
deleteAsync() deleteAsync(option)	Deletes the file, with an optional argument to specify what kind of deletion is performed—see the Deleting Files section later in this chapter for details.
getFileFromApplicationUriAsync(Uri)	Returns a StorageFile representing content in the app package. The path to the file is specified using a Windows.Foundation.Uri object
moveAndReplaceAsync(file)	Moves the file so that it replaces the file specified by the StorageFile argument
renameAsync(name)	Renames the file

Enabling the Capability in the Manifest

If you run the example app at this point and click the Copy Files button, you'll see a message displayed in Visual Studio like the one shown in Figure 22-3.

Figure 22-3. An error displayed when trying to access the file system

As I mentioned earlier, apps have very restricted access to the file system. If you want to access a location that is not provided by the user via a file picker (which I explain in Chapter 23), then you must use one of the locations defined by the KnownFolders object. You must also declare that your app is capable of accessing that location in your app manifest. If you don't do this, you'll see the error shown in the figure as soon as your app tries to access the file system.

To declare the capability, open the manifest by double-clicking on the package.appxmanifest file in the Visual Studio Solution Explorer window, and navigate to the Capabilities tab. You will see that the list of capabilities includes items for the KnownFolders locations, which I have highlighted in Figure 22-4. As you can see in the figure, I have checked the Pictures Library capability, which corresponds to the KnownFolders.picturesLibrary location. (The Internet (Client) capability is checked by default when you create a new Windows app project.)

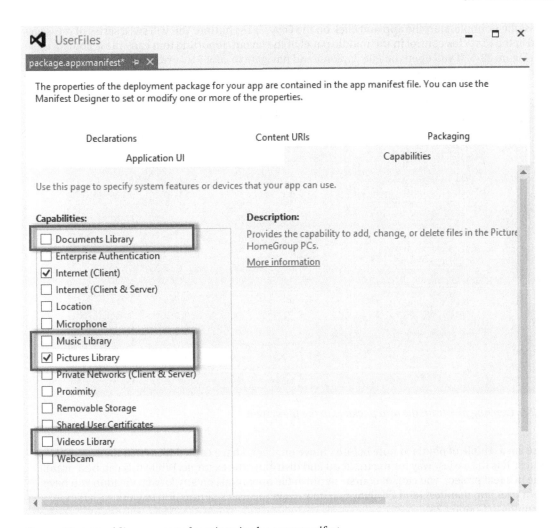

Figure 22-4. Enabling access to locations in the app manifest

You must enable the capability for each location that you want to work with. This will give your app access to that location and add an entry to your app's permissions pane (which is available via the Settings Charm) and displayed to the user if you distribute your app via the Windows Store.

■ **Tip** You should check only the capabilities that you need. The idea is to give the user the information they need to make an informed choice about how much they trust your app before they install it on their device. In practice, users don't pay much attention to this information on any platform and will download and install pretty much anything that looks interesting. Even so, it is good practice to require the minimum capabilities you need.

By adding the code to respond to the button click and declaring the capability in the manifest, I have reached the point where I can copy files from the project onto the device file system.

To test the example, start the app and click on the Copy Files button. You will see a series of messages displayed in the ListView control in the middle panel of the layout, reporting that each file is copied, as shown in Figure 22-5. If you open the File Explorer and navigate to your Pictures library, you will see a flowers folder that contains the sample images.

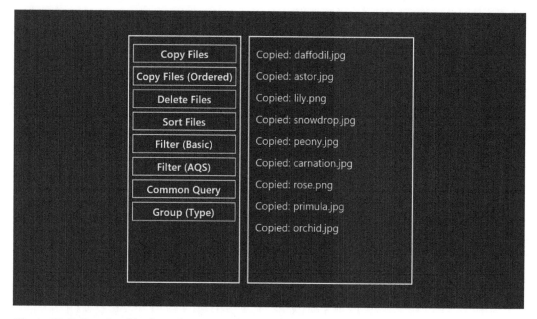

Figure 22-5. Copying files from the app package to the file system

There are a couple of points to note before I move on. First, I have copied files from the app package only because it is the easiest way for me to set up and distribute the example. While this can be a useful technique in a real project, you can, of course, perform file operations on any known location you have declared in your app manifest (and I'll show you how to get the user's permission to work with files in other locations in Chapter 23).

The second point to note is that because of the collision options I specified when using the createFolderAsync method, clicking the Copy Files button will delete the flowers folder, create a new one, and copy the files again.

Ensuring the Copy Order

If you click the Copy Files button repeatedly, you will see that the messages displayed in the ListView control are shown in different orders. You can see the effect in Figure 22-6, where I have shown the order of the messages of three clicks of the button.

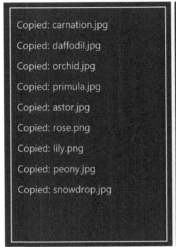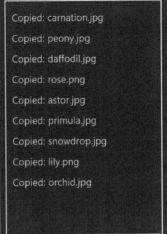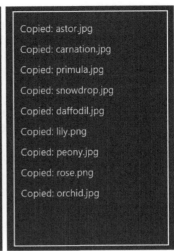

Figure 22-6. Variations in the message order

In Chapter 9, when I explained how Promise objects work, I said that JavaScript maintains a single queue of work to be done and that using Promises defers work by placing it in that queue for later processing—this is what the setImmediate method does.

However, when you are working with the Windows API (including the Windows.Storage), your work can be done in parallel because the objects in that part of the API are implemented using languages that have support for performing tasks in parallel. The details of this are hidden away from JavaScript, which doesn't have the built-in language support for parallel tasks, but it does mean that the order in which operations complete can differ.

If you don't care about the order in which operations are performed and completed, then you don't have to take any special action. If you do care, then you need to change the way that you call the asynchronous methods, so that you copy one file only when the previous operation has finished, as shown in Listing 22-8. I have added this code so that it is executed when the Copy Files (Ordered) button is clicked.

Listing 22-8. Forcing copying operations to be performed in a given sequence

```
...
switch (e.target.id) {
    case 'copyFiles':
        // ...statements removed for brevity...
        break;
    case 'copySeq':
        var index = 0;
        function copyFile(index, folder) {
            return storage.StorageFile.getFileFromApplicationUriAsync(
                Windows.Foundation.Uri("ms-appx:///images/flowers/" +
                    imageFileNames[index]))
            .then(function(file) {
                return file.copyAsync(folder).then(function () {
                    App.writeMessage("Copied: " + imageFileNames[index]);
                }).then(function() {
```

```
                    index++;
                    if (index < imageFileNames.length) {
                        return copyFile(index, folder);
                    }
                })
            });
        }
        storage.KnownFolders.picturesLibrary.createFolderAsync("flowers",
            storage.CreationCollisionOption.replaceExisting)
        .then(function (folder) {
            copyFile(index, folder).then(function () {
                App.writeMessage("All files copied");
            });
        });
        break;
}
...
```

In this listing, I chain the copy operations together using the techniques that I described in Chapter 21, which has the effect of copying the images in the order in which they are defined in the imageFileNames array. This is another tortuous-looking piece of code, but the basic pattern—of defining a function that returns a Promise and that calls itself recursively—is just the same as the chaining examples from Chapter 9.

You should force the order of asynchronous operations only when consistency is important—Windows is capable of performing many kinds of operations in parallel, and this technique forces serialization and therefore can seriously affect performance.

Deleting Files

Now that you have seen a couple of file operation examples, you will find the rest of this section much simpler to understand. If you have not yet gotten your head around the idea of working with files using asynchronous methods, you should consider revisiting Chapter 9—you will find the examples increasingly difficult to follow if you proceed before you have a good grasp of how Promise objects work.

In this section, I am going to demonstrate how to delete files. This is pretty simple, but I want to emphasize the commonality of approach—once you understand how one file operation works, you can very quickly create others. In Listing 22-9, you can see the code I have added to the default.js file to respond to the Delete Files button being clicked.

Listing 22-9. Deleting files

```
...
switch (e.target.id) {
    // ...statements omitted for brevity...
    case 'deleteFiles':
        storage.KnownFolders.picturesLibrary.getFolderAsync("flowers")
        .then(function (folder) {
            folder.getFilesAsync().then(function (files) {
                if (files.length == 0) {
                    App.writeMessage("No files found");
                } else {
                    files.forEach(function (storageFile) {
```

```
                    storageFile.deleteAsync(storage.StorageDeleteOption.default);
                    App.writeMessage("Deleted: " + storageFile.name);
                });
            }
        });
    })
    break;
}
...
```

In this listing, I have used the getFilesAsync method to get an array of StorageFile objects representing the files in the flowers directory. If the array is empty, then I know that there are no files in the folder and I display an appropriate message in the ListView control. If there are StorageFile objects in the array, then I enumerate the array contents using the forEach method and call the deleteAsync method, which deletes the file. The argument to this method is a value from the StorageDeleteOption object, which specifies the kind of deletion that is performed. I have described these values in Table 22-6.

Table 22-6. Values Defined by the StorageDeleteOption Object

Name	Description
default	Deletes the file as though it were deleted from the desktop using the Explorer. This means that for most locations, the file will be moved to the recycle bin, but will be permanently deleted for network and other locations. The file is also permanently deleted if it is in an app data folder, as described in Chapter 21. This is the value used if the deleteAsync method is called without an argument
permanentDelete	Permanently deletes the file

For the example, I specified the default value, which means that if you start the app and click the Delete Files button, you will be able to find the deleted files in the Windows Recycle Bin.

■ **Tip** You'll notice that I use the StorageFile.name property when I write the message to the ListView in this example. The StorageFile object defines a number of properties that you can use to get information about a file—I'll explain this in more detail in the next section.

Sorting and Filtering Files

The array of StorageFile objects that I called the StorageFolder.getFilesAsync method in the previous example has two defining characteristics. The first is that I got *all* of the files in the folder and the second was the object in the array in alphabetical order, based on the name of the file.

In this section, I'll show you how to perform *file queries* that allow you to be more selective about the files you retrieve and order the results in different ways. The new objects in this section are in the Windows.Storage.Search namespace, which I have aliased to search in the examples.

There are two reasons for sorting and filtering files. The first is general utility in your app—you may want to perform an operation only on files that meet some kind of criteria, and filtering and sorting the files you get from the StorageFolder is an excellent way of doing this. The other reason to sort and filter files is that these techniques underpin some of the key touch points that allow you to integrate your app into the wider Windows platform and present a consistent model of dealing with files to your users—a topic I return to in Chapter 23.

Sorting Files

In Windows app terms, sorting the order in which files are selected is a simple form of a file query. In later sections, I'll show you features that are much more the kind of thing you would associate with the word query, but starting with sorting lets me introduce the objects that are required and explain how they fit together. To get started, Listing 22-10 shows the additions I have made to the default.js file to respond when the Sort Files button is clicked. (If you have recently deleted the files, you'll need to click the Copy Files button again so that there are files in the flowers folder to process.)

Listing 22-10. Sorting files with a file query

```
...
switch (e.target.id) {
    // ...statements omitted for brevity...
    case 'sortFiles':
        var options = new search.QueryOptions();
        options.sortOrder.clear();
        options.sortOrder.push({
            ascendingOrder: false,
            propertyName: "System.ItemNameDisplay"
        });
        storage.KnownFolders.picturesLibrary.getFolderAsync("flowers")
        .then(function (folder) {
            folder.createFileQueryWithOptions(options).getFilesAsync()
            .then(function (files) {
                if (files.length == 0) {
                    App.writeMessage("No files found");
                } else {
                    files.forEach(function (storageFile) {
                        App.writeMessage("Found: " + storageFile.name);
                    });
                }
            });
        });
        break;
}
...
```

You control the way that files are selected and sorted using a QueryOptions object, and creating one of these is the first action I take in the listing. I created this object without any constructor arguments, which uses the default settings.

The QueryOptions.sortOrder property returns an array of objects that are applied in sequence to sort the files in the folder. Each object has a propertyName property, which specifies the property of the file that the sort is performed on and an ascendingOrder property, which specifies the direction of the sort.

In the example, you can see that I have started by calling the QueryOptions.sortOrder.clear method. This is because the default QueryOptions object is created with a sortOrder object that sorts the files in ascending order based on their name. If you don't call the clear method, any custom sorting you define will be applied only after the default.

■ **Tip** The sortOrder property is read-only. This means that you need to create your sorting instructions by changing the contents of the array that the property returns, rather than assigning a new array.

After clearing the default sort, I add my own, as follows:

```
...
options.sortOrder.push({
    ascendingOrder: false,
    propertyName: "System.ItemNameDisplay"
});
...
```

This statement adds a new object to the sortOrder array that sorts the files by name in reverse order, a simple variation on the default ordering. The value of the propertyName property value, System. ItemNameDisplay, is one of the extensive set of file properties that Windows defines. There are 125 of these properties, which is too many for me to list here. Instead, I have listed in Table 22-7 the ones that are commonly used. For each entry in the list, I have included details of what the property would show for the snowdrop.jpg file from the example app once it is copied into the Pictures library and has a complete path of C:\Users\adam\Pictures\flowers\snowdrop.jpg.

In addition to the 125 basic properties, including the ones in the table, there are hundreds of more specific ones available. For example, there is a whole set of System.Music properties that you can find on audio files and System.Media properties for video files. You can get details of the complete list at http:// msdn.microsoft.com/en-us/library/windows/desktop/ff521735(v=vs.85).aspx.

■ **Tip**   These are string values, even though they look like references to objects in the System namespace. You must enclose these values in quotes when you assign them to the propertyName property.

Table 22-7. Some Commonly Used File Properties

Property	Description	Example
System.ItemNameDisplay	The name of the file	snowdrop.jpg
System.ItemType	The type of the item. For files this will be the file extension. Other file system objects, such as directories, will be described with a user-readable response (such as Folder).	.jpg
System.ItemTypeText	A user-friendly description of the file type	JPG File
System.ItemDate	The primary date for the item. The exact date that is returned varies on the file type. For photos, for example, it would be the date on which the photo was taken.	Fri Mar 16 11:32:26 UTC 2007
System.DateCreated System. DateModified	The creation or modification dates for the file	Fri Jul 27 09:25:10 UTC+0100 2012
System.Size	The size of the file in bytes	641378
System.ItemPathDisplay	The full path of the file	C:\Users\adam\Pictures\ flowers\snowdrop.jpg
System.ItemFolderPathDisplay	The path of the folder that contains the file	C:\Users\adam\Pictures\ flowers

Once I have defined and configured my QueryOptions object, I call the getFilesAsync method of the StorageFolder object whose content I am interested in and that returns an array of StorageFile objects sorted in the order I have specified.

581

> ■ **Tip**   It is important to use a valid file system property name when applying sorting. The app will be terminated without warning if you provide an invalid name.

In the example, I enumerate the contents of the sorted array and display the name of each file. To get the name, I have used one of the descriptive properties defined by the StorageFile object, which I have summarized in Table 22-8. Once again, I have illustrated the value that each property returns for the snowdrop.jpg file.

Table 22-8. Properties Defined by the StorageFile Object

Property	Description	Example
contentType	The MIME type of the file	image/jpeg
dateCreated	The date the file was created	Fri Jul 27 09:25:10 UTC+0100 2012
displayName	The user-friendly name of the file	snowdrop
displayType	The user-friendly type description	JPG File
fileType	The file extension	.jpg
name	The name of the file (with extension)	snowdrop.jpg
path	The full path of the file	C:\Users\adam\Pictures\flowers\snowdrop.jpg

Some of these properties provide user-friendly values that you can include directly in the app layout, while others are more technical and detailed and are intended for use in your code.

There is a good mapping between the file system properties and the ones that are available through the StorageFile property, but not all 125 file system properties are available. If you do want to get a particular value, then you can use the StorageFile.properties.retrievePropertiesAsync method as shown in Listing 22-11.

Listing 22-11. Getting a file system property value from a StorageFile object

```
...
file.properties.retrievePropertiesAsync(["System.ItemType"]).then(function (props) {
    var value = props["System.ItemType"];
});
...
```

I haven't incorporated this technique into the example because the StorageFile properties are sufficient for my needs. If you start the app and click the Sort Files button, you will see the files listed in descending name order (i.e., reverse alphabetical order), as shown in Figure 22-7.

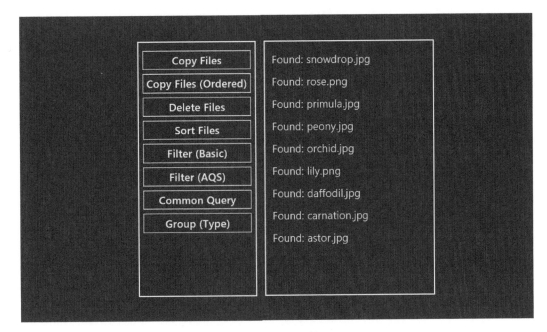

Figure 22-7. Applying a custom sort order when listing files

Filtering Files

In addition to sorting, you can also use the QueryOptions object to filter the StorageFile objects that you get from the getFilesAsync method. The QueryOptions object defines a number of properties to support filtering, which I have described in Table 22-9.

Table 22-9. Properties of the QueryOptions Object Used to Filter Files

Name	Description
applicationSearchFilter	Gets or sets an app-defined Advanced Query Syntax (AQS) string used to filter the files
fileTypeFilter	An array of file extensions that will be included in the results
folderDepth	Specifies if the query should include subfolders
indexerOption	Specifies whether previously indexed data will used
userSearchFilter	Sets a user-defined Advanced Query Syntax (AQS) string used to filter the files

These filtering properties fall into two categories—*basic* and *AQS*—and I'll explain both in the sections that follow. The three basic filtering properties are fileTypeFilter, folderDepth and indexOption. You can see these properties in use in Listing 22-12, which lists the code I added to the default.js file to respond to the Filter (Basic) button being clicked.

Listing 22-12. Performing basic filtering

```
...
switch (e.target.id) {
```

```
// ...statements omitted for brevity...
case 'filterBasic':
    var options = new search.QueryOptions();
    options.fileTypeFilter.push(".doc", ".jpg", ".pdf");
    options.folderDepth = search.FolderDepth.shallow;
    options.indexerOption = search.IndexerOption.useIndexerWhenAvailable;
    storage.KnownFolders.picturesLibrary.getFolderAsync("flowers")
    .then(function (folder) {
        folder.createFileQueryWithOptions(options).getFilesAsync()
        .then(function (files) {
            if (files.length == 0) {
                App.writeMessage("No files found");
            } else {
                files.forEach(function (storageFile) {
                    App.writeMessage("Found: " + storageFile.name);
                });
            }
        });
    });
    break;
}
...
```

This example is similar in structure to the sorting example I showed you previously, except that I am using the basic filtering properties. You can, of course, combine sorting and the filtering properties—I am showing them separately only because it makes it simple to explain the property values.

Filtering File Types

In the listing, I start with the QueryOptions.fileTypeFilter property, which filters out any files that don't have the file prefixes that you specify. This is another instance where you need to modify the contents of the array that you get from the property, rather than assigning a new array.

In the example, I have used the push method, which is defined by JavaScript arrays, to specify that I want files with the .doc, .jpg, and .pdf file extensions. My example app has only .jpg and .png files, so the effect is to exclude the .png files from the query, but I have specified multiple values to show you how it is done. The default value for this property is an empty array, which indicates that no files should be excluded on the basis of their file extension.

■ **Tip**   File extensions are specified with a leading period—i.e,. .pdf and not pdf.

Setting Search Depth

The QueryOptions.folderDepth property is set using one of the values defined by the FolderDepth object, which I have described in Table 22-10.

Table 22-10. Values Defined by the Windows.Storage.Search.FolderDepth Object

Name	Description
shallow	Only files in the StorageFolder are included in the query results
deep	Files in the StorageFolder and its subfolders are included in the query results

I have selected the shallow value in the listing, which limits the files I will receive through the getFilesAsync method to those in the flowers directory (although, of course, there are no subdirectories for me to operate on with my sample files). Be careful when using the deep value—you can end up querying a lot of files, which can be a time- and resource-consuming operation.

Using Previous Indexed Data

Windows indexes the user's content to speed up searches, avoiding the need to work through the file system to get details of file properties and content. The problem is that the indexing is done as a background task and very recent changes to the files may not be reflected in the index—in essence, indexed data is a trade-off between faster searches and accuracy. You can specify whether indexed data is used for your query using the QueryOptions.indexerOption property, which is set to a value from the IndexerOption object. I have described the available values in Table 22-11.

Table 22-11. Values Defined by the Windows.Storage.Search.IndexerOption Object

Name	Description
useIndexerWhenAvailable	The default option, which uses indexed data if it is available and accesses the file system directly when it isn't
onlyUseIndexer	Uses only indexed data, meaning that recent changes may not be reflected in the files you get from the query
doNotUseIndexer	Accesses the file system directly, which is more accurate but slower (and potentially consumes more power from the device)

I used the useIndexerWhenAvailable value in the example. Indexed data has most impact when you are interested in the content of files, and accessing the file system means searching through each file in turn. Using previously indexed data significantly speeds up this kind of search.

Reviewing the Filter Results

The effect of the values I selected for the various filter properties is that my query selects JPG, DOC and PNG files which are in the folder which is being searched and that Windows should use cached file data if it is available. You can see the results in Figure 22-8.

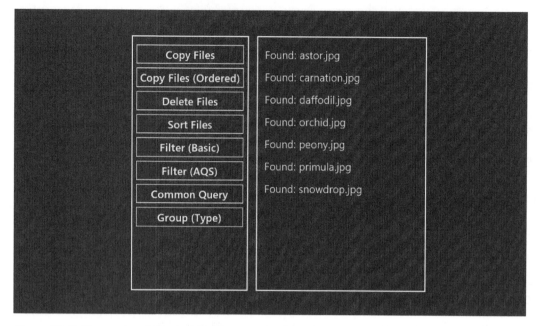

Figure 22-8. *The results of filtering the files*

Using the Advanced Query Syntax Properties

The *Advanced Query Syntax* (AQS) allows complex queries to be expressed, beyond what can be managed using the other QueryOptions properties. There are two properties which you can use to specify an AQS query: the applicationSearchFilter property is for AQS queries which you define in your app and the userSearchFilter property is for queries defined by the user. There is no enforcement of this separation and both query strings are combined automatically when querying the file system anyway.

Listing 22-13 shows the additions to the switch statement in the default.js file that I added to respond when the Filter (AQS) button is clicked. This code performs a reasonably simple AQS query.

Listing 22-13. *Performing an AQS query*

```
...
switch (e.target.id) {
    // ...statements omitted for brevity...
    case 'filterAQS':
        var options = new search.QueryOptions();
        options.folderDepth = search.FolderDepth.deep;
        options.applicationSearchFilter
            = 'System.ItemType:=".jpg" AND System.Size:>300kb AND folder:flowers';
        storage.KnownFolders.picturesLibrary.createFileQueryWithOptions(options)
            .getFilesAsync().then(function (files) {
                if (files.length == 0) {
                    App.writeMessage("No files found");
                } else {
                    files.forEach(function (storageFile) {
```

```
                    App.writeMessage("Found: " + storageFile.name);
              });
          }
      });
      break;
}
...
```

For this example, I have called the `getFilesAsync` method on the `StorageFolder` object that represents the `Pictures` library. This allows me to specify the flowers folder as part of the AQS query, as follows:

```
System.ItemType:=".jpg" AND System.Size:>300kb AND folder:flowers
```

This is a typical AQS query, which contains two search terms and a constraint. The search terms are based on the file system properties I described previously. I am querying for files whose `System.ItemType` property is `.jpg` and whose `System.Size` property is greater than 300kb. The terms and constraints are combined with the `AND` keyword, which must always by uppercase (you can also use `OR` and `NOT` in queries).

Notice that each search property is followed by a colon and then the comparison symbol, like this:

```
System.ItemType:=".jpg" AND System.Size:>300kb AND folder:flowers
```

The *constraint* is expressed using the `folder` keyword and limits the query to files whose path contains a folder called flowers. (This matches any folder in the path called flowers and not just the immediate parent folder).

If you run the app and click the `Filter (AQS)` button, the AQS query will be used to filter the files in the `Pictures` library, producing the results shown in Figure 22-9.

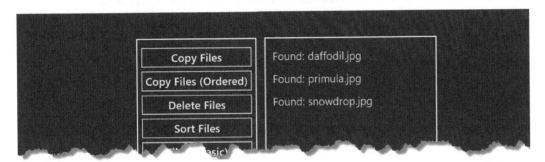

Figure 22-9. Filtering files using AQS

AQS can also be used in the Windows search pane. I don't think I have ever seen a user use AQS, but it can be a helpful way of testing your queries during app development. Figure 22-10 shows the AQS query from the previous Listing 22-used in the search pane. You may see more results if your file system contains extra copies of the image in the Visual Studio project (I cleaned up my files to get this result).

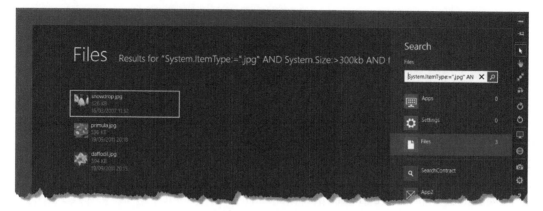

Figure 22-10. Using an AQS query in the Windows search pane to locate files

In my example, I have used AQS queries which are based on file properties and paths, but you can also use AQS to search for file contents, simply by including a phrase in quotes as part of the query. So, for example, if you wanted to find all PDF files which contained the phrase "I like apples", your query would be:

```
System.ItemType:=".pdf" AND "I like apples"
```

AQS can be used to create incredibly precise queries and a good starting place to learn more about AQS can be found at `http://msdn.microsoft.com/en-us/library/aa965711(v=VS.85).aspx`.

Using the Convenience Queries

The `CommonFileQuery` object defines six commonly-used queries, which you can use to create pre-configured `QueryOptions` objects. Listing 22-14 shows the additions I made to the `switch` statement in the `default.js` file to respond when the `Common Query` button is clicked.

Listing 22-14. Using the CommonFileQuery object

```
...
switch (e.target.id) {
    // ...statements omitted for brevity...
    case 'commonQuery':
        var options = new search.QueryOptions(
            search.CommonFileQuery.orderByName, [".jpg", ".png"]);
        storage.KnownFolders.picturesLibrary.getFolderAsync("flowers")
                .then(function (folder) {
                    folder.createFileQueryWithOptions(options).getFilesAsync()
                    .then(function (files) {
                        if (files.length == 0) {
                            App.writeMessage("No files found");
                        } else {
                            files.forEach(function (storageFile) {
                                App.writeMessage("Found: " + storageFile.name);
                            });
                        }
```

```
                    });
                });
            break;
    }
    ...
```

To use a convenience query, you pass a value from the `CommonFileQuery` object as a constructor argument to the `QueryOptions` object. You must also supply an array of file extensions, which are used to set the `fileTypeFilter` property.

In the example, I have used the `CommonFileQuery.orderByName` property, which configures the `QueryOptions` object to include all files in the `StorageFolder`, and order them by name in alphabetical order. I have filtered the files so that only jpg and png file extensions are accepted (there are only files of this type in the example folder, but you get the idea). I have described all six `CommonFileQuery` values in Table 22-12. Some of these queries only make sense when applied to music files, since they rely on `System.Music` file properties.

Table 22-12. Values Defined by the Windows.Storage.Search.CommonFileQuery Object

Name	Description
defaultQuery	A shallow query which sorts files by name in ascending order
orderByName	A deep query which sorts files by name in ascending order
orderByTitle	A deep query which sorts files by the `System.Title` property in ascending order
orderByMusicProperties	A deep query which sorts files using four file properties found in music files: `System.Music.DisplayArtist`, `System.Music.AlbumTitle`, `System.Music.TrackNumber`, and `System.Title`. This query can only be used in the `KnownFolder` locations.
orderBySearchRank	A deep query which sorts files using three file properties found in music files: `System.Search.Rank`, `System.DateModified` and `System.ItemNameDisplay`
orderByDate	A deep query which sorts files by the `System.ItemDate` property in descending order

Working with Virtual Folders

The `StorageFolder` object leads a double life. Earlier in the chapter, I showed you the `StorageFolder` methods that you can use to locate or create new folders on the file system. This is the conventional use of folders and is pretty much what you'd expect from an object called `StorageFolder`.

However, `StorageFolder` objects can also be used in the result of a file query, where they represent *virtual folders* used to group files together by common characteristic or sort order. Listing 22-15 shows how I have used this feature to group my example image files into virtual folders by year in response to the `Group (Type)` button being clicked.

Listing 22-15. Grouping files into virtual folders

```
...
switch (e.target.id) {
    // ...statements omitted for brevity...
    case 'groupType':
        storage.KnownFolders.picturesLibrary.getFolderAsync("flowers")
```

```
        .then(function (flowersFolder) {
            flowersFolder.getFoldersAsync(search.CommonFolderQuery.groupByType)
            .then(function (typeFolders) {
                var index = 0;
                (function describeFolders() {
                    App.writeMessage("Folder: " + typeFolders[index].displayName);
                    typeFolders[index].getFilesAsync().then(function (files) {
                        files.forEach(function (file) {
                            App.writeMessage("--File: " + file.name);
                        });
                        if (index < typeFolders.length -1) {
                            index++;
                            describeFolders();
                        }
                    });
                })();
            });
        });
        break;
}
...
```

The code in this listing is a little convoluted because I want to display the output in a particular order but operations I am performing are asynchronous. The easiest way to explain what's happening is to break the code into two sections. I suggest you run the app and click the Group (Type) button. You'll see the results shown in Figure 22-11.

■ **Note**   You'll need to click the Copy Files button first if you have deleted the example files.

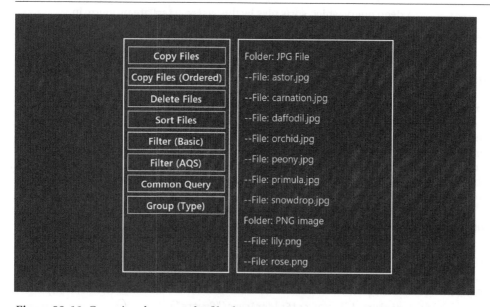

Figure 22-11. Grouping the examples files by type

Grouping the Files

The process for grouping files into virtual folders is pretty simple and you can see the important statements in Listing 22-16. This is a subset of the statements from the complete listing, just so I can focus on the grouping feature.

Listing 22-16. Grouping files

```
...
storage.KnownFolders.picturesLibrary.getFolderAsync("flowers")
    .then(function (flowersFolder) {
        flowersFolder.getFoldersAsync(search.CommonFolderQuery.groupByType)
        .then(function (typeFolders) {
            // ...code removed...
        });
});
...
```

I obtain the flowers folder by calling the getFolderAsync method on the StorageFolder object returned by the KnownFolders.picturesLibrary property, just as I have done in the previous example.

This gives me a StorageFolder object that represents the flowers folder. To group the files that the folder contains, I call the getFoldersAsync method and pass in one of the values defined by the CommonFolderQuery object. The CommonFolderQuery object defines a number of values that allow you to group files in different way, as summarized by Table 22-13.

Table 22-13. Values Defined by the Windows.Storage.Search.CommonFolderQuery Object

Name	Description
groupByYear	Groups files using the year component of the System.ItemDate property
groupByMonth	Groups files using the month component of the System.ItemDate property
groupByArtist	Groups files using the System.Music.DisplayArtist property
groupByAlbumArtist	Groups files using the System.Music.AlbumArtist property
groupByComposer	Groups files using the System.Music.Composer property
groupByGenre	Groups files using the System.Music.Genre property
groupByPublishedYear	Groups files using the System.Media.Year property
groupByRating	Groups files using the System.Rating property
groupByTag	Groups files using the System.Keywords property
groupByAuthor	Groups files using the System.Author property
groupByType	Groups files using the System.ItemTypeText property

In the example, I have used the groupByType value which, as its name suggests, groups the files by file extension. The result of calling the getFoldersAsync method with a CommonFolderQuery value is a Promise object that passes an array of StorageFolder objects to the then function when it is fulfilled.

Each StorageFolder object represents one of the values found for the group property. In the example, I have grouped the files by type and there are two types of example files—JPG and PNG files. I will receive one StorageFolder which contains all of the JPG files and one that contains all of the PNG files.

Processing the Grouped Files

Once I get my array of virtual StorageFolder objects, I need to display the results in the app layout. This is the second section of the example code, which I have shown in Listing 22-17.

Listing 22-17. Displaying the contents of each virtual folder

```
...
.then(function (typeFolders) {
    var index = 0;
    (function describeFolders() {
        App.writeMessage("Folder: " + typeFolders[index].displayName);
        typeFolders[index].getFilesAsync().then(function (files) {
            files.forEach(function (file) {
                App.writeMessage("--File: " + file.name);
            });
            if (index < typeFolders.length -1) {
                index++;
                describeFolders();
            }
        });
    })();
});
...
```

You use the getFilesAsync method to get the files in each virtual folder. I have called the method without arguments, but you can filter or sort the files using the QueryOptions object, as described earlier in the chapter.

The problem that this code solves is that the getFilesAsync method returns a Promise that provides the array of files, but I need to ensure that I have called the App.writeMessage method for all of the files in one virtual folder before moving on to the next one.

To solve this, I have used a slight variant on the techniques I introduced in Chapter 21, by defining a self-executing function that calls itself as it iterates through the virtual folders. The result of this code is that I serialize the processing of the virtual folders and the files they contain so that I can ensure that the descriptive messages are displayed in the right order, producing the results you saw in Figure 22-11 at the start of this section.

Monitoring a Folder for New Files

The last feature I am going to show you is the ability to monitor a folder for new files. To demonstrate this, I have added the code in Listing 22-18 to the default.js file. Unlike the other examples in this chapter, the code in this addition isn't triggered in response to a button click, but is executed as part of the onactivated function.

Listing 22-18. Monitoring a file

```
...
app.onactivated = function (args) {
    if (args.detail.previousExecutionState
        != activation.ApplicationExecutionState.suspended) {
```

```
    args.setPromise(WinJS.UI.processAll().then(function () {

        storage.KnownFolders.picturesLibrary.getFolderAsync("flowers")
        .then(function (folder) {
            var query = folder.createFileQuery();
            query.addEventListener("contentschanged", function (e) {
                App.writeMessage("New files!");
            });

            setTimeout(function () {
                query.getFilesAsync();
            }, 1000);
        });

        $('#buttonsContainer > button').listen("click", function (e) {
            App.clearMessages();
            switch (e.target.id) {
                // ... statements removed for brevity
            }
        });
    }));
    }
};
...
```

The starting point for monitoring a folder is to get a StorageFolder object that represents it. I will be monitoring the flowers folder again, so I start by calling getFolderAsync on the StorageFolder returned by the KnownFolders.picturesLibrary property.

The next step is to create a StorageFileQueryResult object, which you get by calling the createFileQuery method on the StorageFolder you want to monitor.

The StorageFileQueryResult object emits the contentschanged event when a new file is added to the monitored directory. In the example, I provide a function to handle this event that displays a message to the user in the ListView control in the app layout.

The final step is to call the StorageFileQueryResult.getFilesAsync method, which starts monitoring the folder. I call this method after a one-second delay using the setTimeout function—this is because the contentschanged feature isn't especially reliable and I have found this to be the best way of increasing the odds of getting things working (although it still fails for me from time to time and I don't get notifications when I should).

To test this feature in the example, start the app, click the Delete Files button to remove files from the flowers folder, and then click Copy Files to add new files to the monitored folder. After a few seconds you will see a message in the app layout, just like the one in Figure 22-12.

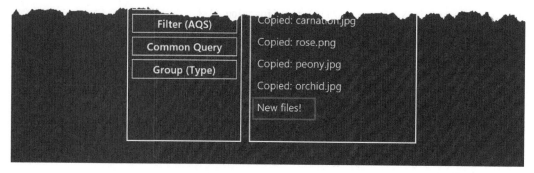

Figure 22-12. Monitoring a folder for new files

There are some serious limitations to this technique. First, the contentschanged event is triggered only when a new file is added to the folder. You won't receive the event when a file is deleted or modified. Second, there can be a delay of several seconds between a new file being added and the event being triggered. Third, this isn't a robust feature and the contentschanged event isn't always triggered when it should be and is often triggered several times for a single change. But if you can live with these issues, then monitoring a folder can be a useful way to ensure that your app keeps the user apprised of the latest content.

Summary

In this chapter, I showed you how to work with files and folders, starting with basic functions such as copying and deleting files. I then showed you how to sort, filter, and query for files, how to create virtual folders to group related files together, and how to monitor a folder for new files.

What all of these features and techniques have in common is that they are implemented inside your app, out of sight from the user. But since we are dealing with the user's files and content, it is important that we express file- and folder-handling features in a way that is clear, obvious, and consistent with other apps and with Windows itself. In the next chapter, I'll show you how to do just that, using the extensive set of integration features that Windows provides for working with the device file system.

CHAPTER 23

■ ■ ■

Integrating File Services

In this chapter, I build upon the techniques in Chapter 22 to show you how to expose file operations to the user. I show you how to use file pickers to solicit file and folder selections from the user, how to cache locations so that your app retains access to them, and how to use the file system as a data source for the WinJS data-driven UI controls, such as `FlipView` and `ListView`. Table 23-1 provides the summary for this chapter.

Table 23-1. *Chapter Summary*

Problem	Solution	Listing
Display the contents of a file using an `img` element	Use the `URL.createObjectURL` method	23-4
Ask the user to select one or more files	Use the `FileOpenPicker` object	23-5–23-7
Ask the user to select a save location	Use the `FileSavePicker` object	23-8–23-9
Ask the user to select a folder	Use the `FolderPicker` object	23-10
Generate a thumbnail from a file	Use the `StorageFile.getThumbnailAsync` method	23-11
Maintain access to a file or location	Use the access cache feature	23-12–23-14
Create a file source that contains files	Use the `StorageDataSource` object	23-15–23-18

Creating the Example Application

For this chapter, I have created an example application called `FileServices` that follows the single-page content model and uses the `WinJS.Navigation` namespace, driven by buttons on the app's NavBar. The examples in this chapter don't easily fit onto a single layout, and so this approach will let me show you multiple content pages in the same app. You can see the changes I have made to the `default.html` file in Listing 23-1.

Listing 23-1. *The default.html file from the FileServices project*

```
<!DOCTYPE html>
<html>
<head>
    <meta charset="utf-8" />
```

```
    <title>FileServices</title>
    <!-- WinJS references -->
    <link href="//Microsoft.WinJS.1.0/css/ui-dark.css" rel="stylesheet" />
    <script src="//Microsoft.WinJS.1.0/js/base.js"></script>
    <script src="//Microsoft.WinJS.1.0/js/ui.js"></script>
    <!-- FileServices references -->
    <link href="/css/default.css" rel="stylesheet" />
    <script src="/js/default.js"></script>
</head>
<body>
    <div id="contentTarget">
        <div>
            <h1 class="message">Select a page from the NavBar</h1>
        </div>
    </div>

    <div id="navbar" data-win-control="WinJS.UI.AppBar"
        data-win-options="{placement:'top'}">
        <button data-win-control="WinJS.UI.AppBarCommand"
            data-win-options="{id:'displayFile', label:'Display File',
                icon:'\u0031', section:'selection'}">
        </button>
        <button data-win-control="WinJS.UI.AppBarCommand"
            data-win-options="{id:'pickers', label:'Pickers',
                icon:'\u0032', section:'selection'}">
        </button>
        <button data-win-control="WinJS.UI.AppBarCommand"
            data-win-options="{id:'access', label:'Access Cache',
                icon:'\u0033', section:'selection'}">
        </button>
        <button data-win-control="WinJS.UI.AppBarCommand"
            data-win-options="{id:'dataSources', label:'Data Sources',
                icon:'\u0034', section:'selection'}">
        </button>
    </div>
</body>
</html>
```

The div element whose id is contentTarget will be the target for other pages of content, which are imported into the document in response to the NavBar buttons being clicked. You can see the NavBar commands set out in the default.html file and I'll add the files they relate to as I go through the chapter. The initial content is a message referring the user to the NavBar, as shown in Figure 23-1.

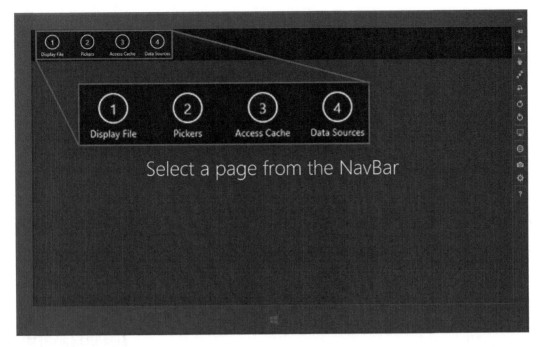

Figure 23-1. The layout of the example app

You can see the contents of the /css/default.css file in Listing 23-2. This file contains the common styles that are used across the example app and I'll supplement this with element-specific additions inline as part of the content pages for the examples.

Listing 23-2. The contents of the css/default.css file

```
body {display: -ms-flexbox; -ms-flex-direction: column;
    -ms-flex-align: center; -ms-flex-pack: center;     }

#contentTarget { display: -ms-flexbox; -ms-flex-direction: row;
    -ms-flex-align: center; -ms-flex-pack: center; text-align: center;}

.container {border: medium solid white; margin: 10px; padding: 10px;}
.container button {font-size: 25pt; margin: 10px; display: block; width: 300px;}

*.imgElem {height: 500px;}
*.imgTitle { color: white; background-color: black;font-size: 30pt; padding-left: 10px;}
```

There are no new techniques or features in the CSS—the styles and properties are only used to lay out the elements in the examples. The contents of the /js/default.js file are very simple for this project and contain only the setup and navigation code—all of the interesting features will be in the individual files that I add in each section of the chapter. You can see the contents of the default.js file in Listing 23-3.

Listing 23-3. The contents of the default.js file

```
(function () {
```

```
    var app = WinJS.Application;
    var activation = Windows.ApplicationModel.Activation;

    WinJS.Navigation.addEventListener("navigating", function (e) {
        WinJS.UI.Animation.exitPage(contentTarget.children).then(function () {
            WinJS.Utilities.empty(contentTarget);
            WinJS.UI.Pages.render(e.detail.location,
                contentTarget, WinJS.Navigation.state)
                .then(function () {
                    return WinJS.UI.Animation.enterPage(contentTarget.children)
                });
        });
    });

    app.onactivated = function (args) {
        if (args.detail.previousExecutionState
            != activation.ApplicationExecutionState.suspended) {
            args.setPromise(WinJS.UI.processAll().then(function() {
                navbar.addEventListener("click", function (e) {
                    var navTarget = "pages/" + e.target.winControl.id + ".html";
                    WinJS.Navigation.navigate(navTarget);
                    navbar.winControl.hide();
                });
            }));
        }
    };

    app.start();
})();
```

Declaring the File Location Capability

The last step to get the basic example to work is to enable access to the Pictures library. To do this, I opened the package.appxmanifest file, switched to the Capabilities tab and checked the Pictures Library capability, as shown in Figure 23-2.

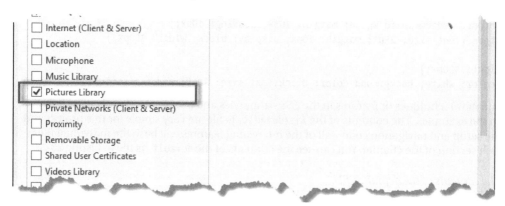

Figure 23-2. Enabling access to the Pictures library

I'll be returning to the manifest later in the chapter to declare additional capabilities, but access to the `Pictures` library is enough to get started with.

Displaying an Image File

For the first example in this chapter, I am going to start with something pretty simple: displaying an image file in the app layout. This is a nice entry point because it lets me build on the file system capabilities I showed you in Chapter 22 and demonstrate how they relate to the HTML layout in a JavaScript Metro app.

■ **Note**   Unless I state otherwise, the objects that I use in this chapter are in the `Windows.Storage` namespace.

For this section, I have added a file to the project called `pages/displayFile.html`. This is an all-in-one file that contains the markup, CSS, and JavaScript in a single file, and you can see the contents in Listing 23-4.

Listing 23-4. The content of the displayFile.html file

```
<!DOCTYPE html>
<html>
<head>
    <title></title>
    <style type="text/css">
        #imgElem { height: 500px; }
    </style>
    <script>
        var storage = Windows.Storage;
        var search = Windows.Storage.Search;
        WinJS.UI.Pages.define("/pages/displayFile.html", {
            ready: function (element, data) {
                storage.KnownFolders.picturesLibrary
                    .getFilesAsync(search.CommonFileQuery.orderByName)
                    .then(function (files) {
                        if (files.length == 0) {
                            imgElem.style.display = "none";
                            titleElem.innerText = "No Files Found!";
                        } else if (files[0].contentType.indexOf("image") != 0) {
                            imgElem.style.display = "none";
                            titleElem.innerText = "Not an image file";
                        } else {
                            imgElem.src = URL.createObjectURL(files[0]);
                            titleElem.innerText = files[0].displayName;
                        }
                    });
            }
        });
    </script>
</head>
<body>
```

```
    <div class="container">
        <img id="imgElem" />
        <div id="titleElem" class="imgTitle"></div>
    </div>
</body>
</html>
```

The simple layout of this content consists of an `img` element that I'll use to display the file and a `div` element that I'll use to display the file name. If you start the app and use the NavBar to navigate to this file by clicking the `Display File` command, you'll see something similar to Figure 23-3.

▪ **Tip**   You'll see a `No Files Found` message if there are no files in your Pictures library. Simply restart the app and click the `Copy Sample Files` button before selecting the `Display File` NavBar command to remedy the situation.

Figure 23-3. Displaying the first file found in the Pictures library

I say that you'll see something similar to the figure because the code in this example does a deep query of the files in the `Pictures` library and displays the contents of the first file. (I described file queries in Chapter 22.) For my machine, the file that is found is the `astor.jpg` file from the set of sample images I used in the previous chapter, but it could be an entirely different image on your machine.

▪ **Tip**   You'll see a `Not an image file` message if the first file in the `Pictures` library isn't an image that the browser can display. Windows doesn't enforce an image-only policy for the `Pictures` library, so I check the file type before displaying the file.

The `script` element code in the `displayFile.html` file will be familiar. I call the `getFilesAsync` method on the `StorageFolder` returned by the `KnownFolders.picturesLibrary` property, specifying the

CommonFileQuery.orderByName value to order the files and set the folder depth. The key part of this example is the following statement:

```
imgElem.src = URL.createObjectURL(files[0]);
```

The Promise returned by the getFilesAsync method yields an array of StorageFile objects representing the file in the pictures library. The problem is that the img element that I am using in the layout doesn't know how to display the contents of StorageFile objects, because they are a Windows concept and not part of HTML.

The URL.createObjectURL method solves my problem by acting as a bridge between the file and my HTML markup. The URL object is part of the W3C File API specification, which is a draft standard affiliated with HTML5. It is implemented by the browser, which is why I am able to call the method without using a namespace.

The createObjectURL method takes a file and returns a URL that can be used to access that file in HTML elements, which is why I have assigned the result of the createObjectURL call in the example to the src attribute of my img element. If you use the Visual Studio DOM Explorer window to look at the HTML in the example app, you will see that the img element ends up looking like this:

```
<img id="imgElem" src="blob:9A3CB2C5-9526-49E3-A8C3-6F0FFC3DCD66"></img>
```

■ **Tip** The URL returned by the createObjectURL method is specific to the system it was created on—you can't share this URL with other devices.

Using the File and Folder Pickers

An app can freely access only file system locations that are defined by the KnownFolders object and that are declared in the capabilities section of the app manifest. In order to access other locations, you need explicit permission from the user, which is obtained using the file and folder pickers. Using a picker, you can ask the user to specify a file to open or save to, or pick a folder.

To demonstrate the use of the pickers, I have added a new file to the Visual Studio project called pages/pickers.html, the contents of which are shown in Listing 23-5. This content is shown when the Pickers command in the NavBar is clicked. To begin with, this file contains code to demonstrate just one of the pickers, and I'll make additions for the others shortly.

Listing 23-5. The initial contents of the pages/pickers.html file

```
<!DOCTYPE html>
<html>
<head>
    <title></title>
    <style>
        #pickerImgElem {display: none}
    </style>
    <script>
        var $ = WinJS.Utilities.query;
        var storage = Windows.Storage;
        var search = Windows.Storage.Search;
        var pickers = Windows.Storage.Pickers;
```

```
                var loadedFile = null;

                WinJS.UI.Pages.define("/pages/pickers.html", {
                    ready: function () {
                        $('.container button').listen("click", function (e) {
                            if (this.id == "open") {
                                var openPicker = Windows.Storage.Pickers.FileOpenPicker();
                                openPicker.fileTypeFilter.push(".png", ".jpg");
                                openPicker.suggestedStartLocation =
                                    pickers.PickerLocationId.picturesLibrary;
                                openPicker.viewMode = pickers.PickerViewMode.thumbnail;
                                openPicker.pickSingleFileAsync().then(function (pickedFile) {
                                    if (pickedFile != null) {
                                        loadedFile = pickedFile;
                                        pickerImgElem.style.display = "block";
                                        pickerImgElem.src = URL.createObjectURL(pickedFile);
                                        pickerTitleElem.innerText = pickedFile.displayName;
                                        save.disabled = false;
                                    } else {
                                        pickerImgElem.style.display = "none";
                                        pickerTitleElem.innerText = "No file selected";
                                    }
                                });
                            }
                        });
                    }
                });
        </script>
    </head>
    <body>
        <div class="container">
            <button id="open">Open File Picker</button>
            <button id="save" disabled>Save File Picker</button>
            <button id="folder">Folder Picker</button>
        </div>
        <div class="container">
            <img id="pickerImgElem" class="imgElem" />
            <div id="pickerTitleElem" class="imgTitle">Select an image file</div>
        </div>
    </body>
</html>
```

This example contains three buttons, which I'll use to activate the pickers. There is also an img and div element that I'll use to display selected files. The code for this file demonstrates the use of the file open picker, which allows the user to select one or more files. Since this is the first time that I have shown you a picker, I'll walk through how it is presented to the user and then explain how the code works.

Using the Example

When you first select the command on the NavBar, you will see a very basic layout. The img element is hidden from view and only the buttons and a message are displayed, as shown in Figure 23-4.

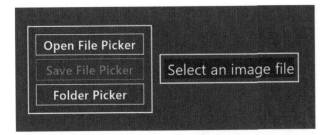

Figure 23-4. The initial layout of the pickers.html file

Click the Open File Picker button to display the picker, which you can see in Figure 23-5. The picker fills the screen, allows the user to navigate around the file system, and shows thumbnails of the files in the current folder.

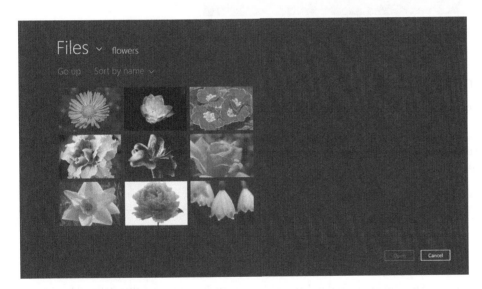

Figure 23-5. The file open picker

Navigate to the flowers folder, which is shown in the figure, and select one of the images (the image will be checked). The Open button is activated—click it to select the file. The file picker disappears and the selected image is shown in the app layout, as you can see in Figure 23-6.

Figure 23-6. Displaying an image selected with the file picker

Understanding the Code

Now that you have seen how the file picker is presented to the user, I will explain how the code in the example created the behavior you saw. When you need the user to select one or more files, you use the FileOpenPicker object, which is in the Windows.Storage.Pickers namespace. To use the picker you create a new instance of the object and then set values for the properties it defines. You can see a list of the FileOpenPicker properties in Table 23-1.

Table 23-1. Properties Defined by the FileOpenPicker

Name	Description
commitTextButton	Sets the text for the button that selects the file or files, which defaults to Open
fileTypeFilter	Returns an array of file type filters. This is a read-only property, and you set filters by adding and removing the items in the array
suggestedStartLocation	Sets the initial folder displayed by the picker, using a value defined by the Windows.Storage.Pickers.PickerLocationId object
viewMode	Sets the view mode for the picker, using a value from the Windows.Storage.Pickers.PickerViewMode object

I have repeated the statements that create and conFigure 23-the FileOpenPicker in Listing 23-6. You can see that I have added the png and jpg extensions to the fileTypeFilter array and that I have not set a value for the commitTextButton property, relying instead on the default value of Open.

Listing 23-6. Creating and configuring the picker

```
...
var openPicker = Windows.Storage.Pickers.FileOpenPicker();
openPicker.fileTypeFilter.push(".png", ".jpg");
openPicker.suggestedStartLocation = pickers.PickerLocationId.picturesLibrary;
```

```
openPicker.viewMode = pickers.PickerViewMode.thumbnail;
...
```

You use the suggestedStartLocation property to indicate the initial folder that should be displayed in the picker. This is only a suggestion and the picker may display another value—this can happen when the picker was used before and it has remembered the last location or because the location you specify isn't available. You set the initial location to a value from the Windows.Storage.Pickers.PickerLocationId object, which I have listed in Table 23-2. In the example, I used the picturesLibrary value, so that the picker opened the Pictures location initially.

Table 23-2. Values Defined by the PickerLocationId Object

Name	Description
documentsLibrary	The Documents library
computerFolder	The Computer folder
desktop	The desktop
downloads	The downloads folder
homeGroup	The HomeGroup folder
musicLibrary	The Music library
picturesLibrary	The Pictures library
videosLibrary	The Videos library

The viewMode property is set using a value from the Windows.Storage.Pickers.PickerViewMode object, and it allows you to specify how files and folders are displayed by the picker. There are two defined values, which I have shown in Table 23-3.

Table 23-3. Values Defined by the PickerViewMode Object

Name	Description
list	Displays files and folders in a list
thumbnail	Displays files and folders using thumbnail images

I used the thumbnail value in the example, which is ideal when you are expecting to work with image files, as I am for my example app. The user can't change the view in the picker, so you must be sure to pick a sensible value for the content you expect to work with.

Picking the File

The FileOpenPicker object defines two methods that you call when you are ready to display the picker and let the user make a selection. The methods are described in Table 23-4.

Table 23-4. Methods from the FileOpenPicker Object

Name	Description
pickSingleFileAsync()	Displays the picker and allows the user to select a single file
pickMultipleFilesAsync()	Displays the picker and allows the user to select one or more files

In the example, I used the `pickSingleFileAsync` method, which allows the user to select a single file. This method returns a `Promise` that is fulfilled when the user makes a selection and that yields a `StorageFile` object via the then method. (As a reminder, you can read all about `Promise` objects and the then method in Chapter 9.) If the user cancels the picker without making a selection, the object passed to the then method function will be `null`. In Listing 23-7, I have repeated the code from the example that displays the picker and processes the user's selection.

Listing 23-7. Displaying the picker and processing the user's selection

```
...
openPicker.pickSingleFileAsync().then(function (pickedFile) {
    if (pickedFile != null) {
        loadedFile = pickedFile;
        pickerImgElem.style.display = "block";
        pickerImgElem.src = URL.createObjectURL(pickedFile);
        pickerTitleElem.innerText = pickedFile.displayName;
        save.disabled = false;
    } else {
        pickerImgElem.style.display = "none";
        pickerTitleElem.innerText = "No file selected";
    }
});
...
```

In order to display the selected file, I used the `URL.createObjectURL` method and assigned the result to the `src` property of the `img` element in the layout. Working with the `pickMultipleFilesAsync` method is similar, except that the then method is passed an array of `StorageFile` objects when the user makes a selection.

■ **Tip** In this example, I restricted the type of files that the user could select, meaning that I can safely display the contents of the file in an `img` element. Later in this chapter, I'll show you how to deal with files that are not images.

Using the File Save Picker

Now that you have seen how one of the pickers works, I can introduce the others without having to go into the same level of detail. Listing 23-8 shows the additions I have made to the pickers.html file to respond when the `Save File Picker` button is clicked. This code uses the `Windows.Storage.Pickers.FileSavePicker` object, which allows the user to select a location and save a file.

Listing 23-8. Saving a file with the File Save Picker

```
...
<script>
    var $ = WinJS.Utilities.query;
    var storage = Windows.Storage;
    var search = Windows.Storage.Search;
    var pickers = Windows.Storage.Pickers;
```

```
var loadedFile = null;

WinJS.UI.Pages.define("/pages/pickers.html", {
    ready: function () {
        $('.container button').listen("click", function (e) {
            if (this.id == "open") {
                // ...statements omitted for brevity...
            } else if (this.id == "save") {
                var savePicker = Windows.Storage.Pickers.FileSavePicker();
                savePicker.defaultFileExtension = loadedFile.fileType;
                savePicker.fileTypeChoices.insert(loadedFile.displayType,
                    [loadedFile.fileType]);
                savePicker.suggestedFileName = "New Image File";
                savePicker.suggestedStartLocation =
                    pickers.PickerLocationId.documentsLibrary;
                savePicker.pickSaveFileAsync().then(function (saveFile) {
                    if (saveFile) {
                        loadedFile.copyAndReplaceAsync(saveFile).then(function () {
                            pickerImgElem.style.display = "none";
                            pickerTitleElem.innerText = "Saved: " + saveFile.name;
                        });
                    }
                });
            }
        });
    }
});
</script>
...
```

To test this code, start the app, click the Open File Picker button, and select an image file. When the image file is displayed, the Save File Picker button will be enabled, allowing you to save the image file you loaded to a new location. When you click the Save File Picker button, the picker will be shown, as illustrated by Figure 23-7.

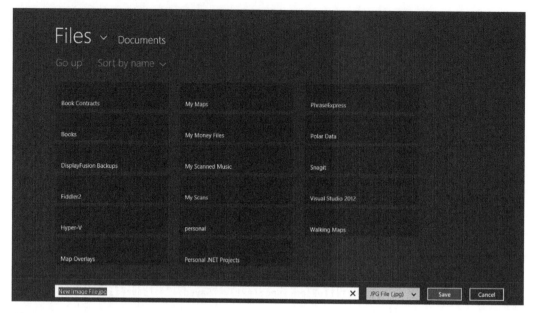

Figure 23-7. Saving a file with the picker

The appearance of the save picker is similar to the open picker, except that the user is able to specify a name and a type for the file that is going to be saved. I have set the initial location for the picker to be the Documents library, which is why there are so many different folders listed. You create a new picker by creating a new FileSavePicker object and configure it through the object's properties. I have listed the properties in Table 23-5, some of which are shared with the FileOpenPicker.

Table 23-5. Properties Defined by the FileSavePicker

Name	Description
commitButtonText	Sets the text for the button that saves the file—this is Save by default
defaultFileExtension	Sets the file type that will be selected by default
fileTypeChoices	Returns a read-only array whose contents can be changed to define the set of file types that the user can select when saving the file
suggestedFileName	Sets the file name that will be suggested to the user
suggestedSaveFile	Sets the StorageFile that will be suggested to the user
suggestedStartLocation	Sets the initial location for the picker, specified as a value from the PickerLocationId object—see Table 23-2 for the supported values

In the example, I have used the properties to constrain the user's choices so that they can select the location and name of the file, but will only be able to select the type of file loaded with the open picker. This is because I don't want to get into the world of file type conversion, and want to demonstrate just how the picker works.

Picking the File

You call the pickSaveFileAsync method when you are ready to show the picker to the user. This method returns a Promise that passes a StorageFile object representing the user's choice to the then method function. If the user clicks the Cancel button, then null is passed to the then function.

The picker only solicits a location from the user—it is the responsibility of the app to do something with it. For the example, I copy the previous loaded file to the picked location. I have repeated the code that does this in Listing 23-9.

Listing 23-9. Processing the location picked by the user

```
...
savePicker.pickSaveFileAsync().then(function (saveFile) {
    if (saveFile) {
        loadedFile.copyAndReplaceAsync(saveFile).then(function () {
            pickerImgElem.style.display = "none";
            pickerTitleElem.innerText = "Saved: " + saveFile.name;
        });
    }
});
...
```

Using the Folder Picker

The third picker allows the user to select a folder. By now you will understand the pattern for configuring and using the pickers, so I have added a new technique to this example, just to make things more interesting.

So far, I have assumed that the user only wants to work with image files. This is a convenient shortcut because it works nicely with the use of the img element in the app layout. The reality, of course, is that most apps will need to work with different kinds of files, and so in this example I show you how to display a thumbnail image for any file you might encounter. Listing 23-10 shows the additions to the pickers.html file for using the folder picker when the Folder Picker button is clicked (and working with thumbnails).

▪ **Note** Displaying the thumbnail isn't the same as reading the contents of the file, of course. As I demonstrated in the earlier examples, working with the contents of image files is easy, because you can rely on the built-in support that IE10 has for displaying images using HTML img elements. In Chapter 22, I showed you how to read the contents of files and mentioned the support for dealing with binary content, which you may need, depending on the types of files your app operates on.

Listing 23-10. Additions to the pickers.html file to add support for the folder picker

```
...
<script>
    var $ = WinJS.Utilities.query;
    var storage = Windows.Storage;
    var pickers = Windows.Storage.Pickers;
```

```
    var loadedFile = null;

    WinJS.UI.Pages.define("/pages/pickers.html", {
        ready: function () {
            $('.container button').listen("click", function (e) {
                if (this.id == "open") {
                    // ...statements omitted for brevity...
                } else if (this.id == "save") {
                    // ...statements omitted for brevity...
                } else {
                    var folderPicker = Windows.Storage.Pickers.FolderPicker();
                    folderPicker.suggestedStartLocation =
                        pickers.PickerLocationId.picturesLibrary;
                    folderPicker.fileTypeFilter.push("*");
                    folderPicker.pickSingleFolderAsync().then(function (selectedFolder) {
                        if (selectedFolder != null) {
                            selectedFolder.getFilesAsync().then(function (files) {
                                files[0].getThumbnailAsync(
                                    storage.FileProperties.ThumbnailMode.singleItem, 500)
                                .then(function (thumb) {
                                    pickerImgElem.style.display = "block";
                                    pickerImgElem.src = URL.createObjectURL(thumb);
                                    pickerTitleElem.innerText = files[0].displayName;
                                });
                            });
                        }
                    });
                }
            });
        }
    });
</script>
...
```

The technique for using the folder picker is similar to the previous examples. You create a Windows.Storage.Pickers.FolderPicker object and configure it through its properties, which I have listed in Table 23-6.

Table 23-6. Properties Defined by the FolderPicker

Name	Description
commitButtonText	Sets the text used for the button that selects a folder, which defaults to Choose this folder
fileTypeFilter	Returns a read-only array whose contents are the file extensions of files that will be displayed to the user in the picker
suggestedStartLocation	Sets the initial location for the picker, specified as a value from the PickerLocationId object—see Table 23-2 for the supported values
viewMode	Sets the view mode for the picker, using a value from the Windows.Storage.Pickers.PickerViewMode object

In the example, I set the initial location to be the Pictures library and used an asterisk (the *
character) to specify that all types of files should be shown to the user.

■ **Tip** The FolderPicker object will throw an exception if the fileTypeFilter array doesn't contain at least
one item, and so you must either list out the file types you want displayed or use an asterisk.

The pickSingleFolderAsync method displays the picker and allows the user to select a folder. You can
see how the picker appears to the user in Figure 23-8, which shows the contents of a folder containing the
manuscript for an earlier chapter in this book.

Figure 23-8. Using the Folder Picker to select a folder

The FolderPicker looks a lot like the FileOpenPicker, but the user cannot select individual files and
the button text makes it clear that a folder is being picked. The pickSingleFolderAsync method returns a
Promise that is fulfilled when the user picks a folder. The user's pick is passed to the then method function
as a StorageFolder object (which I introduced in Chapter 22).

Working with Thumbnail Images

I have repeated the code from the previous example that processes the StorageFolder in Listing 23-11.
When the user selects a folder, I call the getFilesAsync method to get the files in the folder.

Listing 23-11. Working with thumbnails

```
...
folderPicker.pickSingleFolderAsync().then(function(selectedFolder) {
    if (selectedFolder != null) {
```

```
        selectedFolder.getFilesAsync().then(function (files) {
            files[0].getThumbnailAsync(storage.FileProperties.ThumbnailMode.singleItem,
                500)
            .then(function (thumb) {
                pickerImgElem.style.display = "block";
                pickerImgElem.src = URL.createObjectURL(thumb);
                pickerTitleElem.innerText = files[0].displayName;
            });
        });
    }
});
...
```

I take the first `StorageFile` object in the folder and call the getThumbnailAsync method. This method generates an image that can be used to visually reference the file. For images files, the thumbnail will be the file contents and for other files, the thumbnail will usually be the app icon of the default app used by the system to open the file type.

The getThumbnailAsync method takes two arguments. The first argument is a value from the `Windows.Storage.FileProperties.ThumbnailMode` object and it specifies the kind of thumbnail that will be generated. I have listed and described the ThumbnailMode values in Table 23-7.

Table 23-7. Values defined by the ThumbnailMode object

Name	Description
picturesView	Creates a medium image, using a wide aspect ratio
videosView	Creates a medium image, using a wide aspect ratio
musicView	Creates a small image, using a square aspect ratio
documentsView	Creates a small image, using a square aspect ratio
listView	Creates a small image, using a square aspect ratio
singleItem	Creates a large image, using the original aspect ratio of the file

In the example, I select the first file in the folder that the user picks and use the singleItem value when I create the thumbnail, which means that I will receive a large image that has the original aspect ratio of the file (which is important when displaying image files). The second argument is the size you would like the longest edge thumbnail to be—I have specified 500, which means that the longest edges of my thumbnail will be 500 pixels.

When the Promise returned by the getThumbnailAsync method is fulfilled, I create a URL for the thumbnail using the URL.createObjectURL method, like this:

```
...
pickerImgElem.src = URL.createObjectURL(thumb);
...
```

The createObjectURL method accepts a range of different object types, including the `Windows.Storage.FileProperties.StorageItemThumbnail` object yielded by the getThumbnailAsync method.

To demonstrate generating thumbnails for non-image files, I selected the folder in my Music library that contained the manuscript files. Selecting a folder with the folder picker is a two-stage process.

First, you click the Choose this folder button once you have navigated to the folder you want to pick. This makes a provisional pick, but performs a subtle UI update where the folder is displayed at the bottom edge of the screen and the text of the button changes to OK, as shown in Figure 23-9.

Figure 23-9. *Provisionally picking a folder*

You can see the effect of picking a non-image file in Figure 23-10. I have picked the Microsoft Word file that contains the text for the manuscript chapter, which is displayed using the thumbnail image associated with Word files.

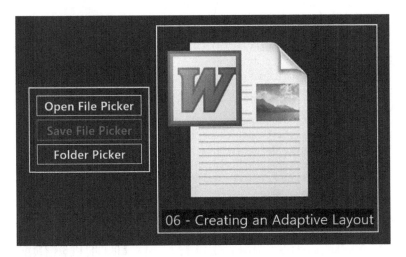

Figure 23-10. *The thumbnails for a Word file*

Caching Location Access

As you have seen several times, Metro apps work under strict access restrictions when it comes to the file systems. Your app can freely access the locations defined by the KnownFolders object, but only if each location you want to access is declared as a capability in the app manifest. If you need to work on files in a different location, then you need to use the pickers to get explicit access granted by the user.

This model works fine if your app allows users to create some content and then save it to a single file—in this situation, it makes perfect sense to use the picker, because the location that each file should be opened or saved from could be different.

But many Metro apps will need persistent access to a location once the user has picked it, and to manage this, you must use the objects in the Windows.Storage.AccessCache namespace. To get started, I have added a new file to the example Visual Studio project called access.html, which you can access by using the Access Cache NavBar command in the example app. You can see the content in Listing 23-12.

Listing 23-12. *The initial content for the access.html file*

```
<!DOCTYPE html>
<html>
<head>
```

```
<title></title>
<style>
    #accessImgElem {display: none;}
</style>
<script>
    var $ = WinJS.Utilities.query;
    var storage = Windows.Storage;
    var pickers = Windows.Storage.Pickers;
    var access = Windows.Storage.AccessCache;

    WinJS.UI.Pages.define("/pages/access.html", {
        ready: function () {
            $('#accessButtons button').listen("click", function (e) {
                if (this.id == "pick") {
                    var folderPicker = pickers.FolderPicker();
                    folderPicker.fileTypeFilter.push("*");
                    folderPicker.suggestedStartLocation =
                        pickers.PickerLocationId.musicLibrary;
                    folderPicker.pickSingleFolderAsync().then(function (folder) {
                        if (folder != null) {
                            var token = access.StorageApplicationPermissions
                                .futureAccessList.add(folder);
                            storage.ApplicationData.current.
                                localSettings.values["folder"] = token;
                            accessTitleElem.innerText = "Selected: " +
                                folder.displayName;
                        }
                    });
                } else {
                    var token = storage.ApplicationData.current.
                        localSettings.values["folder"];
                    var folder = access.StorageApplicationPermissions
                            .futureAccessList.getFolderAsync(token)
                            .then(function (folder) {
                        return folder.getFilesAsync().then(function (files) {
                            files[0].getThumbnailAsync(
                                storage.FileProperties.ThumbnailMode.singleItem,
                                    500).then(function (thumb) {
                                accessImgElem.src = URL.createObjectURL(thumb);
                                accessImgElem.style.display = "block";
                                accessTitleElem.innerText = files[0].displayName;
                            });
                        });
                    });
                }
            });
        }
    });
</script>
</head>
<body>
```

```
<div id="accessButtons" class="container">
    <button id="pick">Pick Folder</button>
    <button id="load">Load File</button>
</div>
<div class="container">
    <img id="accessImgElem" class="imgElem" />
    <div id="accessTitleElem" class="imgTitle">Ready</div>
</div>
</body>
</html>
```

The idea behind this example is to show two related file operations. There are two button elements in the layout and to test the example, start the app, select the appropriate common on the NavBar and click the Pick Folder button. The app will display the folder picker so that you can select a location. Pick any folder that is not in the Pictures library (because the app has declared access to Pictures in the manifest and so already has access to that location).

Click the Load File button after you have picked a folder. The app displays the name of the first file in the selected folder—but it doesn't display the thumbnail yet, as shown in Figure 23-11.

Figure 23-11. Selecting a folder using the example app

Now, to see what's different about this example, restart the app by selecting Restart from the Visual Studio Debug menu. (It is important to *restart*, rather than *refresh* the app.)

Click the Load File button (but not the Pick Folder button) and you will see that the thumbnail and the name of the first file in the previously picked folder are displayed, as shown in Figure 23-12. I have picked a folder in the Documents library, to which the app has no access normally.

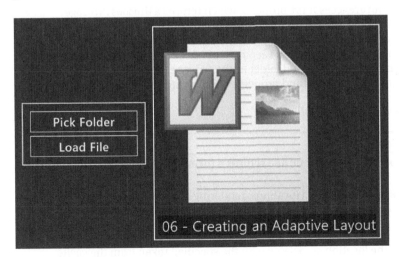

Figure 23-12. Using a cached file location

There are two things that are significant about this example. The first is that the picked location was stored persistently, and the second is that the *permission* to access the location was persistent as well. The app didn't have to go back to the user and display the picker to get the location (and permission to access it) again.

Using the Access Cache

There are two parts to this process—caching access to the location and retrieving the cached data. I have repeated the key statements from the example that handle the caching part of the process in Listing 23-13.

Listing 23-13. Caching access to a file system location

```
...
folderPicker.pickSingleFolderAsync().then(function (folder) {
    if (folder != null) {
        var token = access.StorageApplicationPermissions.futureAccessList.add(folder);
        storage.ApplicationData.current.localSettings.values["folder"] = token;
        accessTitleElem.innerText = "Selected: " + folder.displayName;
    }
});
...
```

The `Windows.Storage.AccessCache` namespace (which I have aliased to access in the example) contains the `StorageApplicationPermissions` object. This object defines two properties, as described in Table 23-8.

Table 23-8. Properties Defined by the StorageApplicationPermissions Object

Name	Description
futureAccessList	Returns an object used to store locations for future reference
mostRecentlyUsedList	Returns an object used to store recently used locations

In the example, I have used the `futureAccessList` property, which returns a `Windows.Storage.AccessCache.StorageItemAccessList` object. I store my location by calling the add method, passing in the `StorageFile` or `StorageFolder` object whose location I want to use again in the future.

The add method returns a string token that I need to keep note of—I use the app settings feature I described in Chapter 20 to persistently store the picked folder as the folder setting. The `StorageItemAccessList` object defines the methods and properties I have listed in Table 23-9.

Table 23-9. Members of the StorageItemAccessList Object

Name	Description
add(StorageFolder) add(StorageFile)	Adds a location to the cache and returns a token that must be kept for future use
clear()	Removes all of the cached locations, rendering any stored tokens useless
getFileAsync(token)	Gets the StorageFile associated with the specified token
getFolderAsync(token)	Gets the StorageFolder associated with the specified token
remove(token)	Removes the location associated with the specified token from the cache

Name	Description
entries	Returns an array of the tokens in the cache
maximumItemsAllowed	Returns the maximum number of items that can be cached

When it comes time for me to display the thumbnail and name of the file, I retrieve the token I stored in the app settings and pass it to the getFolderAsync method. This method returns a Promise that, when fulfilled, yields a StorageFolder object that corresponds to the cached location. I have repeated the statements from the example that get the token and retrieve the location in Listing 23-14.

Listing 23-14. Retrieving a location from the access cache

```
...
var token = storage.ApplicationData.current.localSettings.values["folder"];
var folder = access.StorageApplicationPermissions.futureAccessList.getFolderAsync(token)
.then(function (folder) {
    // ...statements that process StorageFolder omitted for brevity...
});
...
```

By using the access cache, I am able to preserve the permission that the user gives me to access locations so that I don't have to use a picker every time the app starts—I can just get the locations I need once and then continue to use them.

There are a few considerations, of course. First, and most important, I must not abuse the trust of the user by performing unexpected operations on locations my app has been granted access to. As a rule of thumb, I continue to use cached locations to perform nondestructive operations, such as reading files, monitoring folders for changes, or creating new files. I prompt the user for explicit permission if I need to perform any kind of change to the file system—including renaming, moving, and (especially) deleting files.

Prompting the user not only gives them the chance to say no, but it also means that they clearly understand that it was *my* app that made a given set of changes, avoiding nasty surprises when they try to find files that have been filed away to different places or, worse, have been deleted.

The second consideration when using the access cache is to make sure that there are no more than 1,000 locations in the cache. A thousand locations sounds like a lot, but the cached entries can quickly mount up, especially if your app is used frequently and operates on individual files rather than folders. There are two ways of dealing with this—you can manually manage the contents of the futureAccessList. entries array and ensure that it doesn't exceed the maximumItemsAllowed value. Each entry is represented by an AccessListEntry item, whose token property returns the token required to access the cached location via the getFileAsync and getFolderAsync methods.

As an alternative, you can use the StorageApplicationPermissions.mostRecentlyUsedList. This works just like the futureList, but it contains only the 25 most recently used locations. When you add the 26th item, the item that has been used least is automatically removed, freeing you from the need to manage the contents directly.

Using File Data Sources

In Chapters 14, 15, and 16, I explained how you could use data sources with the data-driven WinJS UI controls FlipView, ListView, and SemanticZoom. In those chapters, I used the WinJS.Binding.List object as the data source, even when I was demonstrating how to display images.

A better approach is to create data sources that are driven directly by file system queries, allowing you to operate on files that the user stored on the device. To demonstrate this, I have added the pages/

dataSources.html file to the example Visual Studio project, the contents of which you can see in Listing 23-15.

Listing 23-15. The contents of the dataSources.html file

```
<!DOCTYPE html>
<html>
<head>
    <title></title>
    <style type="text/css">
        #flip {background-color: black; width: 500px; height: 500px;}
    </style>
    <script>
        var storage = Windows.Storage;
        var search = Windows.Storage.Search;

        WinJS.Namespace.define("Converters", {
            img: function (src, srcprop, dest, destprop) {
                if (src.thumbnail == null) {
                    src.addEventListener("thumbnailupdated", function (e) {
                        dest[destprop] = URL.createObjectURL(src.thumbnail);
                    });
                } else {
                    dest[destprop] = URL.createObjectURL(src.thumbnail);
                }
            },
            general: function (src, srcprop, dest, destprop) {
                dest[destprop] = src[srcprop];
            }
        });

        Converters.img.supportedForProcessing = true;
        Converters.general.supportedForProcessing = true;

        WinJS.UI.Pages.define("/pages/dataSources.html", {
            ready: function () {
                storage.KnownFolders.picturesLibrary.getFolderAsync("flowers")
                .then(function (folder) {
                    var options = new search.QueryOptions();
                    options.fileTypeFilter = [".png"];
                    options.folderDepth = search.FolderDepth.deep;

                    var query = folder.createFileQueryWithOptions(options);
                    flip.winControl.itemDataSource
                        = new WinJS.UI.StorageDataSource(query, {
                            mode: storage.FileProperties.ThumbnailMode.picturesView,
                            requestedThumbnailSize: 400,
                            thumbnailOptions:
                                storage.FileProperties.ThumbnailOptions.resizeThumbnail,
                            synchronous: false
                        });
```

```
            });
        }
    });
    </script>
</head>
<body>
    <div id="imgTemplate" data-win-control="WinJS.Binding.Template">
        <div>
            <img data-win-bind="src: img Converters.img">
            <div class="imgTitle" data-win-bind="innerText: displayName
                Converters.general"></div>
        </div>
    </div>

    <div class="container">
        <div id="flip" data-win-control="WinJS.UI.FlipView"
            data-win-options="{itemTemplate: imgTemplate}">
        </div>
    </div>
</body>
</html>
```

This example queries the Pictures library for PNG image files, producing a data source that is then used with a FlipView control so that the user can page through their images. You can see the layout of the app in Figure 23-13, which you can load in the example app by using the Data Sources NavBar command.

Figure 23-13. The layout of the dataSources.html page

The layout is simple, but there is a surprising amount going on in this short example, so I'll go through the code in detail.

Creating the Data Source

The easy part is creating the data source itself, which is done using the WinJS.UI.StorageDataSource object. You start by creating a QueryOptions object, which I introduced in Chapter 22, and pass it to the StorageFolder.createFileQueryWithOptions method. This returns a StorageFolderQueryResult object, which you pass as an argument to the StorageDataSource constructor. I have repeated the statements from the example that set up the StorageDataSource object in Listing 23-16.

Listing 23-16. Creating the StorageDataSource object

```
...
var options = new search.QueryOptions();
options.fileTypeFilter = [".png"];
options.folderDepth = search.FolderDepth.deep;

var query = folder.createFileQueryWithOptions(options);
flip.winControl.itemDataSource = new WinJS.UI.StorageDataSource(query, {
    mode: storage.FileProperties.ThumbnailMode.picturesView,
    requestedThumbnailSize: 400,
    thumbnailOptions: storage.FileProperties.ThumbnailOptions.resizeThumbnail,
    synchronous: false
});
...
```

In this example, I have created a QueryOptions object that performs a deep folder query and limits its matches to PNG files. I assign the StorageDataSource object to the itemDataSource property of the FlipView control, which means that the files matches by the QueryOptions will be displayed by the UI control.

There are two arguments to the StorageDataSource constructor: the QueryOptions object and an object that has four specific properties. These properties are described in Table 23-10.

Table 23-10. Properties of the Object Passed to the StorageDataSource Object

Name	Description
mode	A value from the Windows.Storage.FileProperties.ThumbnailMode object that specifies what kind of thumbnail images should be produced by the data source—the values defined by ThumbnailMode are described in Table 23-7
requestedThumbnailSize	The size, in pixels, of the longest edge of the thumbnail images
thumbnailOptions	A value from the Windows.Storage.FileProperties.ThumbnailOptions object that provides additional instructions for processing the thumbnail image. The values for the ThumbnailOptions object are described in Table 23-11
synchronous	When true, this property ensures that thumbnails are loaded before the items in the data source are passed to the UI control. The default is false

For the example, I have used the ThumbnailMode.picturesView value to get a wide aspect ratio thumbnail image and specified a size of 400 pixels. I used the ThumbnailOptions.resizeThumbnail value, which is described in Table 23-11, and set the synchronous property to false, which means that I need to cater for data source items whose thumbnails have not been loaded—I'll explain how to do this shortly.

Table 23-11. Values Defined by the Windows.Storage.FileProperties.ThumbnailOptions Object

Name	Description
none	No options—use this value if you want to disable the default behavior
returnOnlyIfCached	Returns a thumbnail only if it is already cached
resizeThumbnail	Resizes the image to the specified size
useCurrentScale	This is the default value and it resizes the thumbnail image to account for the device screen pixel density (which I described in Chapter 6)

Generating the Template Data

Creating the data source is only part of the process—I also need to use the WinJS data binding feature to populate the template used by the FlipView control. This isn't as simple as it might be because the objects returned by the file system query cannot be extended with new properties, something that the WinJS. Binding.converter method attempts as it tries to make the properties of data objects observable.

Instead, I have to use an open value converter, which lets me map functions more loosely. I described this technique in Chapter 8, and dealing with objects that can't be extended is one situation in which it can be useful. First, I add the data-win-bind attribute to the elements in the HTML template, as shown in Listing 23-17, where I have repeated the template elements from the example.

Listing 23-17. Adding the data-win-bind attribute to the HTML template elements

```
...
<div id="imgTemplate" data-win-control="WinJS.Binding.Template">
    <div>
        <img data-win-bind="src: img Converters.img">
        <div class="imgTitle" data-win-bind="innerText: displayName
            Converters.general"></div>
    </div>
</div>
...
```

To support the template, I have defined two open converters, which I have repeated in Listing 23-18.

Listing 23-18. The open data converters to support the HTML template

```
WinJS.Namespace.define("Converters", {
    img: function (src, srcprop, dest, destprop) {
        if (src.thumbnail == null) {
            src.addEventListener("thumbnailupdated", function (e) {
                dest[destprop] = URL.createObjectURL(src.thumbnail);
            });
        } else {
            dest[destprop] = URL.createObjectURL(src.thumbnail);
        }
    },
    general: function (src, srcprop, dest, destprop) {
        dest[destprop] = src[srcprop];
    }
});
```

```
Converters.img.supportedForProcessing = true;
Converters.general.supportedForProcessing = true;
```

The simplest converter, called `Converters.general`, simply sets the value of the specified attribute to the specified data object value. The second, called `Converters.img`, requires a little more explanation. This is a simple solution to the problem of not being able to use file system objects as the source of data binding values. The general converter simply uses the value of the source property to set the value of the destination property, with no transformation or formatting, and acts as a bridge between the `Windows.Storage` and the `WinJS.Binding` namespaces.

The `Converters.img` converter takes care of two problems. First, it uses the `URL.createObjectURL` method to create URLs that refer to file thumbnail images so that I can use them with HTML `img` elements.

The second problem is that Windows only generates file thumbnails when they are needed. This means that if you are paging through files in the data source (which is what the user will be doing with the `FlipView` control in the example), then you will encounter data objects whose thumbnails are not yet loaded.

The source for data when using the `StorageDataSource` object will be a `Windows.Storage.BulkAccess.FileInformation` object. The `Windows.Storage.BulkAccess` namespace provides objects that you can use to perform large-scale efficient file-system operations, which is generally useful for creating data source providers, but generally not that useful for regular app development (which is why I don't go into any detail about that namespace outside of this section).

The thumbnail image is available through the `FileInformation.thumbnail` property, but this will return `null` if Windows has yet to generate and cache a suitable image. To get around this, I listen for the `thumbnailupdated` event, which the `FileInformation` object will emit when Windows does generate the thumbnail. The result is that the HTML elements will be updated, even if it takes Windows a moment to generate the thumbnails that are required. All of this fits together to provide a data source that can be used with the data-driven WinJS UI controls, built on the objects and techniques that I introduced in Chapter 22.

Summary

In this chapter, I have shown you some of the ways that you can integrate the underlying support for working with the file system into your app. I showed you how to create URLs that refer to the contents of image files, how to present the user with open file, save file, and folder pickers, and how to cache access to locations so that you can provide service to the user without constantly badgering them to give you access to file system locations. Along the way, I also showed you how to generate thumbnail images and how to create data sources that query the file system and present the results in a way that can be consumed by the WinJS data-driven UI controls. In the next chapter, I'll show you how to implement the Metro contracts that relate to the file system.

■ ■ ■

CHAPTER 24

The File Activation & Picker Contracts

In this chapter, I show you how to implement three of the contracts that allow Windows apps to integrate file-related functionality into Windows. I show you how to register an app to handle particular types of file with the *file activation contract* and how to provide storage services to other apps using the *save picker* and *open picker contracts*. Implementing these contracts, like all contracts, is optional—but if your app works with files in any way, you should look at them carefully to see if they offer integration that would make using your app simpler and easier for the user. Table 24-1 provides the summary for this chapter.

Table 24-1. Chapter Summary

Problem	Solution	Listing
Add your app as a handler for a file type	Implement the file activation contract	24-1–24-10
Add your app as a save location for a file type	Implement the save picker contract	24-11–24-14
Add your app as a location from which files can be opened	Implement the open picker contract	24-15–24-16

Creating the Example App

The example app for this chapter will offer some basic functionality, which I will then enhance by implementing the file contracts. I am going to build a simple photo album app, which in its initial incarnation will let the user select image files from the file system to add to the album. A thumbnail of each image will be shown in a `ListView` UI control (which I described in Chapter 15). I will cache the file locations that the user picks using the objects in the `Windows.Storage.AppCache` namespace (which I described in Chapter 23), which will make the user's file picks persistent.

I used the `Blank App` template to create a new Visual Studio project called `PhotoAlbum`. You can see the contents of the `default.html` file in Listing 24-1.

Listing 24-1. The default.html file from the PhotoAlbum app

```
<!DOCTYPE html>
<html>
<head>
```

```
    <meta charset="utf-8" />
    <title>PhotoAlbum</title>
    <!-- WinJS references -->
    <link href="//Microsoft.WinJS.1.0/css/ui-dark.css" rel="stylesheet" />
    <script src="//Microsoft.WinJS.1.0/js/base.js"></script>
    <script src="//Microsoft.WinJS.1.0/js/ui.js"></script>
    <!-- PhotoAlbum references -->
    <link href="/css/default.css" rel="stylesheet" />
    <script src="/js/setup.js"></script>
    <script src="/js/app.js"></script>
    <script src="/js/default.js"></script>
</head>
<body>
    <div id="imageTemplate" data-win-control="WinJS.Binding.Template">
        <div class="imgContainer">
            <img class="listImg" data-win-bind="src: img" />
            <span class="listTitle" data-win-bind="innerText: title"></span>
        </div>
    </div>

    <div id="contentTarget"></div>
</body>
</html>
```

This app will use the standard content navigation model to bring pages of content into the app layout using the WinJS.Navigation namespace. Unlike the other examples where I have used WinJS.Navigation, the content transitions will be triggered by the app in response to the file contracts. The default.html file also includes the elements for a WinJS.Binding.Template, which I will use to display thumbnails for image files throughout the app. The template displays the image and a label containing the file name.

The content files can be found in the pages folder, and I have started with just one page of content, called pages/albumView.html, which I will load when the app starts. This will provide the basic album features, and you can see the contents of this file in Listing 24-2.

Listing 24-2. The contents of the albumView.html file

```
<!DOCTYPE html>
<html>
<head>
    <title></title>
    <script>
        WinJS.UI.Pages.define("/pages/albumView.html", {
            ready: function () {
                WinJS.Utilities.query("button").listen("click", function (e) {
                    if (this.id == "openButton") {
                        App.pickFiles();
                    } else {
                        App.clearCache();
                    }
                });
            }
        });
```

```
    </script>
</head>
<body>
    <div id="listView" data-win-control="WinJS.UI.ListView"
        data-win-options="{ itemTemplate: imageTemplate,
            itemDataSource: ViewModel.fileList.dataSource}">
    </div>
    <div id="buttonContainer">
        <button id="openButton">Open</button>
        <button id="clearButton">Clear</button>
    </div>
</body>
</html>
```

Aside from the ListView control that will display the image thumbnails, this file contains two buttons. The Open button displays the file open picker (described in Chapter 23) so that the user can open image files within the app. The Clear button removes the images from the ListView and clears the location cache, resetting the app to its initial state. You can see the styles I defined for these elements in Listing 24-3, which shows the contents of the css/default.css file. There are no special features or app-specific techniques in the CSS.

Listing 24-3. The contents of the default.css file

```
#contentTarget {
    width: 100%; height: 100%;
    display: -ms-flexbox; -ms-flex-direction: column;
    -ms-flex-align: center; -ms-flex-pack: center;}

#listView { border: medium solid white; margin: 10px;
    height: 80%; width: 80%; padding: 20px;}

#buttonContainer button { font-size: 20pt; width: 100px;}

.imgContainer { border: thin solid white; padding: 2px;}

.listTitle { font-size: 18pt; max-width: 180px;
    text-overflow: ellipsis; display: block; white-space: nowrap;
    margin: 0 0 5px 5px; height: 35px;}

.listImg {height: 200px; width: 300px;}
.title { font-size: 30pt;}
```

Defining the JavaScript

I want to keep the default.js file as simple as possible for this project because it will be the file that changes most in this chapter and I don't want to have to repeatedly list code that is part of the basic, non-contract functionality. To this end, I have created a couple of JavaScript files that perform the basic setup for the app and provide the functions needed to manage the album of images. The first of these files, /js/setup.js, is shown in Listing 24-4.

Listing 24-4. The contents of the setup.js file

```
(function () {

    WinJS.Namespace.define("ViewModel", {
        fileList: new WinJS.Binding.List()
    });

    WinJS.Navigation.addEventListener("navigating", function (e) {
        WinJS.UI.Animation.exitPage(contentTarget.children).then(function () {
            WinJS.Utilities.empty(contentTarget);
            WinJS.UI.Pages.render(e.detail.location, contentTarget,
                WinJS.Navigation.state)
                .then(function() {
                    WinJS.Binding.processAll(document.body, ViewModel);
                }).then(function () {
                    return WinJS.UI.Animation.enterPage(contentTarget.children)
                });
        });
    });
})();
```

This file creates the ViewModel.fileList object, which I use as the data source for the ListView control so that I can display the image thumbnails. I also set up the event handler for the navigating event, which loads content into the main page. The functions I mentioned are in the /js/app.js file, the contents of which are shown in Listing 24-5.

Listing 24-5. The contents of the app.js file

```
(function () {

var storage = Windows.Storage;
var access = storage.AccessCache;
var cache = access.StorageApplicationPermissions.futureAccessList;
var pickers = storage.Pickers;

WinJS.Namespace.define("App", {

    loadFilesFromCache: function () {
        return new WinJS.Promise(function (fDone, fErr, fProg) {
            if (cache.entries.length > 0) {
                ViewModel.fileList.length = 0;
                var index = cache.entries.length - 1;
                (function processEntry() {
                    cache.getFileAsync(cache.entries[index].token)
                        .then(function (file) {
                            App.processFile(file, false);
                            if (--index != -1) {
                                processEntry();
                            } else {
                                fDone();
                            }
```

```
                        });
                    })();
                } else {
                    fDone();
                }
            });
        },

        processFile: function (file, addToCache) {
            ViewModel.fileList.unshift({
                img: URL.createObjectURL(file),
                title: file.displayName,
                file: file
            });
            if (addToCache !== false) {
                cache.add(file);
            }
        },

        pickFiles: function () {
            var picker = pickers.FileOpenPicker();
            picker.fileTypeFilter.replaceAll([".jpg", ".png"]);
            picker.pickMultipleFilesAsync().then(function (files) {
                if (files != null) {
                    files.forEach(function (file) {
                        App.processFile(file);
                    });
                }
            });
        },

        clearCache: function () {
            cache.clear();
            ViewModel.fileList.length = 0;
        }
    });
})();
```

I am not going to go through this code in detail because it builds on functionality I have described and demonstrated in previous chapters and that I am using just as a foundation to demonstrate the file contracts.

That said, a couple of techniques in this listing that are minor variations on those I showed you in earlier chapters are worth pointing out. First, I use the pickMultipleFilesAsync method on the FileOpenPicker object so that the user can select multiple files at ones. This is not a complex feature and the only difference from working with pickSingleFileAsync is that the Promise the method returns yields an array of StorageFile objects via the then method (instead of a single StorageFile object).

The second variation is that I don't store the tokens returned by the futureAccessList.add method. Instead, I work with the items in the entries array, using the token property to get the strings I need to get StorageFile objects from the getFileAsync method. (I enumerate the cached locations in reverse so that the most recently added images are shown at the top of the ListView display.) The final file is js/default. js, which is shown in Listing 24-6.

Listing 24-6. The initial contents of the default.js file

```
(function () {

    var app = WinJS.Application;
    var activation = Windows.ApplicationModel.Activation;
    var appstate = activation.ApplicationExecutionState;
    var storage = Windows.Storage;

    app.onactivated = function (args) {

        if (args.detail.previousExecutionState != appstate.suspended) {
            args.setPromise(WinJS.UI.processAll().then(function () {
                if (ViewModel.fileList.length == 0) {
                    App.loadFilesFromCache();
                }

                switch (args.detail.kind) {
                    default:
                        WinJS.Navigation.navigate("/pages/albumView.html");
                        break;
                }
            }));
        }
    };
    app.start();
})();
```

I have kept this as simple as possible, relying on the objects in the ViewModel and App namespaces I created in the viewmodel.js file to implement the basic functionality of the photo album, which I demonstrate in the next section. The switch statement may look a little odd, since it only has a default block, but I'll be adding handlers for different kinds of activation events as I go through the chapter.

Testing the Example App

To test the example, start the app and click the Open button. Navigate to a folder where you have some image files (I used the Pictures/flowers folder I created in earlier chapters) and select one or more images with the picker. Click the Open button in the picker to open the files and you will see thumbnails displayed in the app layout, as shown in Figure 24-1.

Figure 24-1. *Loading images into the example app*

Stop the app by selecting Stop Debugging from the Visual Studio Debug menu and then launch the app again. You will see that the images you loaded previously are displayed again, thanks to the file locations cached in the futureAccessList object.

This has been a long setup for the example app, but it gives me a good foundation for implementing the file contracts, which I can now do with the minimum of additional code.

Adding the Images

I use a number of images in this example app, all of which can be found in the images folder of the Visual Studio project. The first two images are called jpgLogo.png and pngLogo.png and I'll use them when I implement the file activation contract. You can see these images in Figure 24-2. These two files show the same image, but on different backgrounds.

Figure 24-2. *The images that will be used in the file activation contract*

I have also replaced all of the default images that Visual Studio creates in the images folder with ones that have the same dimensions, but show the same icon as the images in the figure.

For the logo.png, slashscreen.png, and storelogo.png files, the images I have added to the project show a white icon on a transparent background, which means they are impossible to show on a white page—but if you imagine one of the images shown in Figure 24-2 without the color background, you'll get the idea.

I have removed the smalllogo.png file and replaced it with a 30 by 30 pixel file called small.png, which shows the same icon in white, but with a black background, which looks the same as the left-hand image in Figure 24-2. I then updated the app manifest to specify the small.png file for the Small logo field, as shown in Figure 24-3.

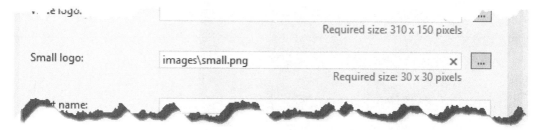

Figure 24-3. *Changing the small logo file*

This name change is important because it works around an odd bug—I'll explain the problem when I implement the file activation contract later in the chapter.

■ **Tip**   You can find all of these image files in the source code download that accompanies this book, which is available freely from apress.com.

Creating the Helper App

Some of the contracts that I implement in this chapter provide services to other apps and I need a helper app to demonstrate these features. This app is called FileHelper and it is very simple, using the file pickers I introduced in Chapter 23 to load and save a single image file. You can see the contents of the default. html file for the FileHelper project in Listing 24-7.

Listing 24-7. *The contents of the FileHelper default.html file*

```
<!DOCTYPE html>
<html>
<head>
    <meta charset="utf-8" />
    <title>FileHelper</title>

    <!-- WinJS references -->
    <link href="//Microsoft.WinJS.1.0/css/ui-dark.css" rel="stylesheet" />
    <script src="//Microsoft.WinJS.1.0/js/base.js"></script>
    <script src="//Microsoft.WinJS.1.0/js/ui.js"></script>

    <!-- FileHelper references -->
    <link href="/css/default.css" rel="stylesheet" />
    <script src="/js/default.js"></script>
</head>
<body>
    <div class="container">
        <button id="open">Open</button>
```

```
            <button id="save" disabled>Save</button>
        </div>
        <div class="container">
            <img id="thumbnail" src="/images/logo.png"/>
        </div>
    </body>
</html>
```

The layout for this app is built around two button elements and an img element. The Open button uses the file open picker to load a single image file, which is displayed using the img element. You can see the CSS that I have used to style these elements in Listing 24-8, which shows the content of the css/default. css file.

Listing 24-8. The default.css file from the FileHelper project

```
body, div.container {display: -ms-flexbox;-ms-flex-direction: row;
    -ms-flex-align: center; -ms-flex-pack: center; }
div.container {margin: 10px; height: 80%; -ms-flex-direction: column;}
button {font-size: 25pt; width: 200px; margin: 10px;}
#thumbnail {width: 600px; border: medium white solid;}
```

The only other file in this project is default.js, in which I respond to the button clicks by showing the pickers so that the user can load and save an image file. You can see the content of the default.js file in Listing 24-9.

Listing 24-9. The contents of the default.js file from the FileHelper project

```
(function () {
    "use strict";

    var app = WinJS.Application;
    var activation = Windows.ApplicationModel.Activation;
    var storage = Windows.Storage;
    var pickers = Windows.Storage.Pickers;

    var pickedFile = null;

    app.onactivated = function (args) {
        if (args.detail.previousExecutionState
            != activation.ApplicationExecutionState.suspended) {

            args.setPromise(WinJS.UI.processAll().then(function() {
                WinJS.Utilities.query('button').listen("click", function (e) {
                    if (this.id == "open") {
                        var openPicker = new pickers.FileOpenPicker();
                        openPicker.fileTypeFilter.replaceAll([".png", ".jpg"]);
                        openPicker.pickSingleFileAsync().then(function (file) {
                            pickedFile = file;
                            save.disabled = false;
                            thumbnail.src = URL.createObjectURL(file);
                        });
                    } else {
```

```
                var savePicker = new pickers.FileSavePicker();
                savePicker.defaultFileExtension = pickedFile.fileType;
                savePicker.fileTypeChoices.insert(pickedFile.displayType,
                    [pickedFile.fileType]);
                savePicker.suggestedFileName = "New Image File";
                savePicker.pickSaveFileAsync().then(function (saveFile) {
                    if (saveFile) {
                        pickedFile.copyAndReplaceAsync(saveFile);
                    }
                });
            }
        });
    }));
    }
};
app.start();
})();
```

There are no new techniques in this listing and I use the pickers just as I did in Chapter 23. The helper app exists only to help me demonstrate the implementation of the file contracts in the PhotoAlbum app. You can see the helper app in Figure 24-4, which shows one of the sample images I used in earlier chapters.

Figure 24-4. The FileHelper app

Implementing the File Activation Contract

The file activation contract lets you declare that your app is willing and able to work with files of a certain type. To see what I mean, go the desktop and use the File Explorer to find a PNG or JPG file—the flower images from the previous chapters are ideal. Right-click on the file and select the Open with menu and you'll see a list of apps, both desktop and Windows Store apps, which can open the file. You can see the apps that will open a PNG file on my desktop PC in Figure 24-5.

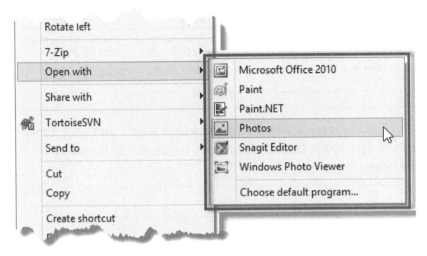

Figure 24-5. The apps that are able to open a PNG file on my system

As the figure shows, I am able to open a PNG file using Microsoft Office, Paint, Paint.NET, the Photos app, Snagit Editor (which I use for screenshots), and Windows Photo Viewer. In this section, I am going to show you how to add your app to that list and demonstrate how you respond when your app is the one chosen to open a file.

Declaring the File Type Associations

You declare the file types that you want to support in the app manifest. Open the package.appxmanifest file from the Solution Explorer and switch to the Declarations tab.

Select File Type Associations from the Declarations list and click the Add button. Visual Studio will present you with a form to fill out with the details of the file association. For this example, I need two file associations—one for PNG file and one for JPG files. Table 24-2 describes the meaning of the fields that need to be populated and provides the values for each association. Click the Add button when you have finished populating the first form using the values in the First Form column to create a second association. Fill out the form using the values in the Second Form column and then type Control+S to save the changes to the manifest. When you are done, you will see two entries in the declarations list, as shown in Figure 24-6.

Table 24-2. Meaning of and Values for the File Type Association Declaration Fields

Field	Description	First Form	Second Form
Display name	The description of the file shown when the app is the default for handling the type	PNG Image	JPG Image
Logo	The thumbnail used when the app is the default for handling the file type	images\ pngLogo.png	images\ jpgLogo.png
Info tip	Specifies the text displayed when the user hovers the mouse over a file and the app is the default for handling the file type	PNG Image	JPG Image
Name	An app-specific name for the association	png	jpg

Field	Description	First Form	Second Form
Edit flags	Flags that indicate the security status that will be shown to the user when opening files	Check the Open is safe option	Check the Open is safe option
File type	The extension of the file that will be associated with the app	.png	.jpg

■ **Tip**   You can support multiple file extensions as part of the same declaration by clicking the Add New button, which will add a new Supported File Type section to the form. I have used two declarations because I want different images and descriptive text for each file type.

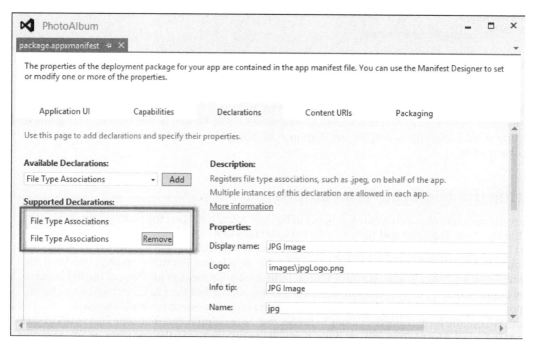

Figure 24-6. Adding file type association declarations to the app manifest

When you start an app with Visual Studio, the app package is installed onto the device and this includes creating the Windows file associations. Even though I have only partially implemented the contract, you can already see the effect of the file associations: start the app and then navigate to the desktop (the simplest way is to type Control+D). Open the Explorer and find any PNG or JPG file. If you right-click on the file and select the Open with menu, you will see that the PhotoAlbum app has been added to the list, as shown in Figure 24-7. (The name displayed is taken from the Display name field from the Application UI section of the manifest—I changed this value to add a space between the words Photo and Album.)

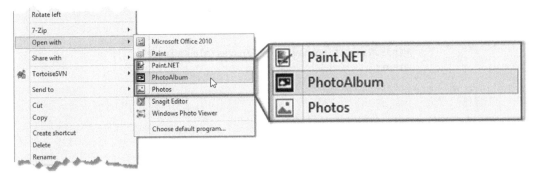

Figure 24-7. The app associated with the file type in Explorer

■ **Note**   When I created the example app, I made a point of changing the name used for the file specified in the Small logo manifest field. There is an odd bug where if you don't change the file name, Windows will display the logo.png file from your project images folder, which typically has a transparent background so that it can be used on Start screen tiles (a topic I discuss in depth in Chapter 19). The transparent background prevents the app from being displayed properly on the Open with list. To avoid this issue, ensure that you change the name of the 30 by 30 pixel file so that it is used, presenting the user with an image that has a solid background color.

Handling the File Activation Event

The last step is to respond when the user selects the app to open a file, which is signaled using an activated event whose kind property is set to ActivationKind.file. You can see the changes I have made to the onactivated function in the default.js file in Listing 24-10 to support this kind of event.

Listing 24-10. Responding to the file activation event

```
(function () {

    var app = WinJS.Application;
    var activation = Windows.ApplicationModel.Activation;
    var appstate = activation.ApplicationExecutionState;
    var storage = Windows.Storage;

    app.onactivated = function (args) {
        if (args.detail.previousExecutionState != appstate.suspended) {
            args.setPromise(WinJS.UI.processAll().then(function () {

                var promise = ViewModel.fileList.length == 0 ?
                    App.loadFilesFromCache() : WinJS.Promise.wrap(false);

                promise.then(function () {
                    switch (args.detail.kind) {
                        case activation.ActivationKind.file:
                            args.detail.files.forEach(function (file) {
```

```
                          App.processFile(file);
                    });
                default:
                    WinJS.Navigation.navigate("/pages/albumView.html");
                    break;
            }
        });

        return promise;
    }));
    }
};
app.start();
})();
```

The bold statements respond to the file activation event. The detail.files property of the event object contains an array of StorageFile objects, each of which has been selected by the user to be opened by the app. In this listing, I use the forEach method to enumerate the contents of the array and call the App. processFile method (which I defined in the app.js file) for each StorageFile, which has the effect of adding the thumbnails to the ListView control and caching the file locations so that the app works persistently.

■ **Note**   Notice that the case block that handles the file activation event falls through to the default block. This means that the albumView.html file will be used to provide content for the file event as well as for regular launch events. You can learn more about launch events in Chapter 19.

To test the handling of the event, start the app, navigate to the desktop, and right-click on a PNG or JPG file. Select the Open with menu item and click Photo Album from the list. A thumbnail of the file you opened will be added to the ListView in the layout, shown along with the file's displayName value.

■ **Tip**   If you don't get the right results, then right-click the Photo Album app icon on the start screen, select Uninstall, and then start the app from Visual Studio again. Windows doesn't always pick up changes when the app is restarted, and uninstalling the app package fixes the problem.

Making the App the Default Handler

There is one more aspect of the file activation handler I want to describe. For that, you need to make the app the default handler for the file type. From the Windows desktop, use the File Explorer to find and right-click on a PNG file, select the Open with ➤ Choose default program menu item. You will see a popup like the one shown in Figure 24-8. (The app is shown with the logo I defined in the Application UI section of the manifest. I used the same icon I used for the file associations, but with a transparent background.) Select the Photo Album item to make the example app the default handler and then repeat this process for a JPG file.

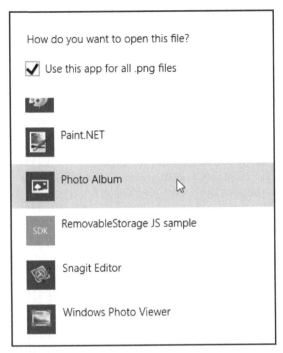

Figure 24-8. Making the app the default handler for PNG files

This doesn't change the way the app behaves, but it does mean that Windows will use the images I added to the app earlier in the chapter, and which were specified as part of the file association declaration, as the file icon when showing the user PNG and JPG files. You can see how this appears in Explorer in Figure 24-9.

Figure 24-9. The file icons from the file association declaration used in Windows Explorer

Because I am working with image files, Windows will show the file contents whenever it can, but the icons are used more broadly, including when searching for files on the Start screen, for other file types. The figure shows the File Explorer in its List view.

Implementing the App-to-App Picking Contracts

The app-to-app picking contracts allow other apps to load and save files through your app, rather than the local file system. This is useful if your app provides some kind of value above and beyond what the user can get from storing files in the regular way—a good example would be an app that supports Dropbox- or SkyDrive-style file replication or provides access to files that are stored in a remote location.

I need something simpler to demonstrate the file picker contracts, and so my example app will store files in local app data folder. This doesn't add any value to the user, but it does mean I can focus on the contract without too many distractions and diversions.

In the sections that follow, I'll show you how to implement the app-to-app picking contracts: the *save picker contract* and the *open picker contract*.

Implementing the Save Picker Contract

The *save picker contract* allows others apps to save files to your app, as though it were a file system location like a folder. As with most of the contracts, you must make a declaration in the app manifest and handle a specific type of activation event. This contract is slightly different from ones you have seen so far, because you also are required to prepare your app's layout so that the app can show the content in the picker. I'll explain how it all works in the sections that follow.

Declaring Support for the Contract

The first step is to declare that the app implements the contract in the manifest. This tells Windows that your app should be presented to the user as a location to which files can be saved. Open the package. appxmanifest file from the Visual Studio Solution Explorer window and click the tab for the Declaration section.

Select File Save Picker from the Available Declarations list and click the Add button. If you want your app to be able to handle any kind of file (which would make sense in the Dropbox/SkyDrive scenario), then check the Supports any file type option. The PhotoAlbum example app will support only JPG and PNG files, so enter .png in the File type text box, click the Add New button to get another box, and enter .jpg in the second File type text box. Type Control+S to save the changes. Your manifest should look like the one in Figure 24-10.

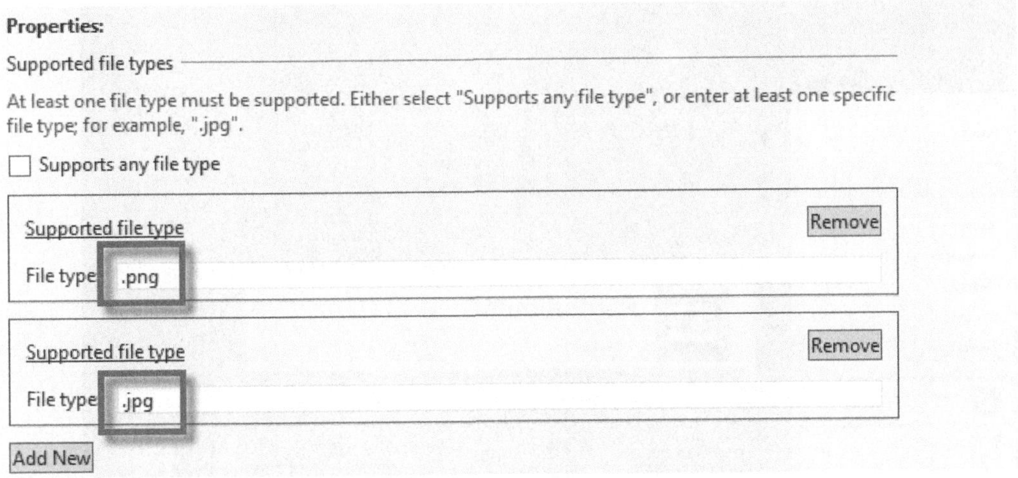

Properties:

Supported file types

At least one file type must be supported. Either select "Supports any file type", or enter at least one specific file type; for example, ".jpg".

☐ Supports any file type

Supported file type	Remove
File type .png	

Supported file type	Remove
File type .jpg	

Add New

Figure 24-10. Adding the file save picker contract declaration to the app manifest

Testing the Save Picker Declaration

Just making the manifest declaration defines the app as a save location, even though I have yet to implement the activation event that is part of the contract. Seeing how this works now will make it easier to understand the rest of the work that the app has to do to implement this contract.

Testing the save picker contract declaration requires the use of the FileHelper app that I created at the start of this chapter as well as the PhotoAlbum itself and requires a couple of steps.

First, start the PhotoAlbum app. The app doesn't need to be running to be a save location, but Visual Studio installs the app when it is started, and this registers the file types defined in the manifest declaration with Windows. Click the Open button and pick some images, just so there is some content in the app.

Second, start the FileHelper app I created at the start of the chapter, click the Open button, and pick an image file—ideally one that you didn't pick a moment ago. Click the Save button. The app will present the file save picker. If you click on the arrow next to the Files link, you'll see a list of save destinations, including Photo Album as shown in Figure 24-11.

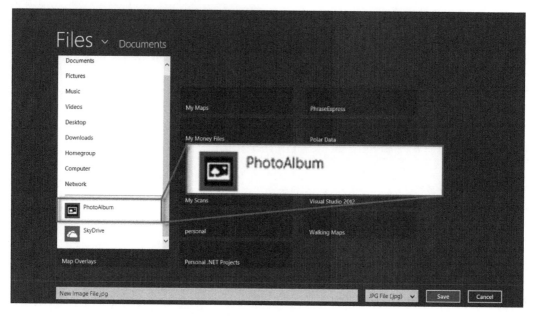

Figure 24-11. The app shown as a save location in the picker

If you select Photo Album from the list, you'll see something similar to the layout shown in Figure 24-12. This is a strange mix of the PhotoAlbum app layout displayed within the file picker.

The work required to finish implementing the contract is two-fold: I need to update the app so that a more useful layout is displayed in the picker and to support saving the file from the FileHelper app. I'll show you how to do both in the next section.

Figure 24-12. The app layout displayed in the save picker

Handling the Activated Event

Windows sends an activated event when the user selects the app as a save location. The detail.kind property of the event is set to ActivationKind.fileSavePicker, and this is the cue to change the layout of the app so that it fits within the picker and presents the user with some meaningful content. You can see how I have responded to the event in the PhotoAlbum app in Listing 24-11, which shows changes I have made to the /js/default.js file.

Listing 24-11. Responding to the activation event for the save picker contract in default.html

```
(function () {

    var app = WinJS.Application;
    var activation = Windows.ApplicationModel.Activation;
    var appstate = activation.ApplicationExecutionState;
    var storage = Windows.Storage;

    app.onactivated = function (args) {

        if (args.detail.previousExecutionState != appstate.suspended) {
            args.setPromise(WinJS.UI.processAll().then(function () {

                if (ViewModel.fileList.length == 0) {
                    App.loadFilesFromCache();
                }

                switch (args.detail.kind) {
                    case activation.ActivationKind.fileSavePicker:
                        var pickerUI = args.detail.fileSavePickerUI;
                        WinJS.Navigation.navigate("/pages/savePickerView.html",
                            pickerUI);
                        break;
                    case activation.ActivationKind.file:
                        args.detail.files.forEach(function (file) {
                            App.processFile(file);
                        });
                    default:
                        WinJS.Navigation.navigate("/pages/albumView.html");
                        break;
                }
            }));
        }
    };
    app.start();
})();
```

In addition to these changes, I have added a new file to the project called pages/savePickerView.html, which I display when I get the activation event for the file save picker contract.

Notice that when I call the WinJS.Navigation.navigate method, I pass the value of the detail.fileSavePickerUI property from the activation event. This object lets me respond when the user saves a file and by passing it to the navigate method I'll be able to deal with the object in the savePickerView.html file, which is shown in Listing 24-12.

■ **Note**   To be clear, I am able to pass the object like this because the function I defined in the `js/setup.js` file passes the value of the `WinJS.Navigation.state` property to the `WinJS.UI.Pages.render` method. You can learn more about the `WinJS.Navigation.state` property and `WinJS.UI.Pages.render` method in Chapter 7.

Listing 24-12. The content of the pages/savePickerView.html file

```html
<!DOCTYPE html>
<html>
<head>
    <title></title>
    <style>
        #saveListView { width: 75%; height: 275px;}
    </style>
    <script>
        var storage = Windows.Storage;
        WinJS.UI.Pages.define("/pages/savePickerView.html", {
            ready: function (element, pickerUI) {
                pickerUI.title = "Save to Photo Album";
                pickerUI.addEventListener("targetfilerequested", function (e) {
                    var deferral = e.request.getDeferral();
                    storage.ApplicationData.current.localFolder
                        .createFileAsync(pickerUI.fileName,
                            storage.CreationCollisionOption.replaceExisting)
                        .then(function (file) {
                            e.request.targetFile = file;
                            App.processFile(file);
                            deferral.complete();
                        });
                });
            }
        });
    </script>
</head>
<body>
    <div class="title">Add to the
        <span class="title" data-win-bind="innerText: fileList.length"></span>
        images in your album</div>
    <div id="saveListView" data-win-control="WinJS.UI.ListView"
        data-win-options="{
            itemTemplate: imageTemplate,
            itemDataSource: ViewModel.fileList.dataSource,
            maxRows: 1
        }">
    </div>
</body>
</html>
```

There are two parts to this file. The markup is self-contained and presents the user with a helpful message and a single row of image thumbnails to show the content already in the album. When the activated event is received, I use this markup as the app layout, and the data bindings and the `ListView` control provide the content to the user. You can see the result in Figure 24-13. (I got these results by restarting the `PhotoAlbum` app, switching to the `FileHelper` app, and clicking the Save button so that I could select `PhotoAlbum` from the list of file locations.)

Figure 24-13. Presenting the user with content suitable for the picker

You can use any layout you like in this situation as long as it fits inside the letterbox area of the file picker. Whatever you present should be useful—and that usually means giving the user some indication of what's already available. To my mind, value to the user takes priority of a strictly accurate view of the content. In the figure, you'll see that I have decided to show the images that are part of the album, rather than focusing on just those that have been stored in the app in its role as a save location.

Configuring the Picker

Presenting the user with content in the picker is only part of the task. I also have to configure the picker itself and respond when the user clicks the save button. In Listing 24-13, I have repeated the code from the `savePickerView.html` file that does both.

Listing 24-13. The code from the savePickerView.html file that deals with the picker

```
...
ready: function (element, pickerUI) {
    pickerUI.title = "Save to Photo Album";
    pickerUI.addEventListener("targetfilerequested", function (e) {
        var deferral = e.request.getDeferral();
        storage.ApplicationData.current.localFolder
            .createFileAsync(pickerUI.fileName,
                storage.CreationCollisionOption.replaceExisting)
            .then(function (file) {
                e.request.targetFile = file;
                App.processFile(file);
                deferral.complete();
            });
```

```
        });
    }
    ...
```

The `pickerUI` variable that I receive in my ready function is the value of the `detail.fileSavePickerUI` property from the activation event. This property returns a `Windows.Storage.Pickers.Provider.FileSavePickerUI` object, which you use to configure the picker presented to the user. The `FileSavePickerUI` object defines the properties described in Table 24-3.

Table 24-3. Properties Defined by the Windows.Storage.Pickers.Provider.FileSavePickerUI Object

Name	Description
allowedFileTypes	Returns a read-only list of the file types that can be saved
fileName	Returns the file name that the user has specified in the picker
title	Sets the title of the picker when it is displayed to the user

In the example, I have used the `title` property to specify the string `Save to Photo Album`, which you can see in Figure 24-13. This property is useful when there is some kind of hierarchy to the storage that you are providing because you can use it to indicate the location that the file will be saved to. The `FileSavePickerUI` object also defines two events, one of which I used in the example. You can see details of these events in Table 24-4.

Table 24-4. Events Defined by the Windows.Storage.Pickers.Provider.FileSavePickerUI Object

Name	Description
filenamechanged	Triggered when the user changes the name of the file in the picker
targetfilerequested	Triggered when the user clicks the Save button in the picker

It is the `targetfilerequested` event that I am interested in for this chapter because it signals to the app that the user wants to save a file. The handler for the `targetfilerequested` event is passed a `Windows.Storage.Pickers.Provider.targetFileRequestedEventArgs` object. This object defines just one property called `request`, which is needed to complete the contract. The `request` property returns a `Windows.Storage.Pickers.Provider.TargetFileRequest` object, which defines the properties shown in Table 24-5.

Table 24-5. Properties Defined by the Windows.Storage.Pickers.Provider.TargetFileRequest Object

Name	Description
getDeferral()	Returns a `targetFileRequestDeferral` object, whose complete method you call once you have handled the file save request
targetFile	This property is set to the `StorageFile` that the calling app should use to store its contents.

There are a lot of objects involved for what is a simple operation. When you receive the `targetfilerequested` event, you call the `request.getDeferral` method to tell Windows to wait while you perform an asynchronous operation.

You then create or obtain the `StorageFile` object that will be passed to the other app so that it can write its contents. In the example, I call the `createFileAsync` method on the `StorageFolder` object that represents the local app data folder (as described in Chapter 20). For the name of the file, I read the `FileSavePickerUI.fileName` property. You assign the `StorageFile` to the `request.targetfile` property and call the complete method on the object you got when you called getDeferral earlier—this tells Windows that you are done and that the StorageFile can now be passed to the app that wants to save data.

Updating the Data

One further step is required to complete the implementation of the contract, and it involves keeping your app layout up-to-date.

If your app isn't running when the user selects it as a save location, the app is started and sent the file activation event. As soon as the save operation is complete, the app is terminated.

However, if your app is running when the user selects it as a save location, a second instance of the app is created, with completely separate global namespace and variables. The second instance is terminated as soon as the save operation is completed, but it leaves a problem: How does the instance of your app that is left running find out about the newly saved file?

You cannot rely on a view model to solve this problem, because the view model is a global variable and each instance of the app has its own copy. You have to solve this problem with some kind of shared storage, through which you can discover the file. For my app, this means that I have to monitor the local app data folder and load any new files I discover there. You can see how I have done this using the folder monitoring technique I showed you in Chapter 22, in Listing 24-14, which shows the additions I have made to the default.js file in the PhotoAlbum app.

Listing 24-14. Monitoring the local app data folder for changes

```
(function () {

    var app = WinJS.Application;
    var activation = Windows.ApplicationModel.Activation;
    var appstate = activation.ApplicationExecutionState;
    var storage = Windows.Storage;

    var query = storage.ApplicationData.current.localFolder
        .createFolderQuery();
    query.addEventListener("contentschanged", function () {
        App.loadFilesFromCache();
    });
    query.getFoldersAsync();


    app.onactivated = function (args) {

        if (args.detail.previousExecutionState != appstate.suspended) {
            args.setPromise(WinJS.UI.processAll().then(function () {

                if (ViewModel.fileList.length == 0) {
                    App.loadFilesFromCache();
                }

                switch (args.detail.kind) {
                    case activation.ActivationKind.fileSavePicker:
                        var pickerUI = args.detail.fileSavePickerUI;
                        WinJS.Navigation.navigate("/pages/savePickerView.html",
```

645

```
                                pickerUI);
                        break;
                    case activation.ActivationKind.file:
                        args.detail.files.forEach(function (file) {
                            App.processFile(file);
                        });
                    default:
                        WinJS.Navigation.navigate("/pages/albumView.html");
                        break;
                }
            }));
        }
    };
    app.start();
})();
```

Whenever I receive the contentschanged event, I call the App.loadFilesFromCache function, which is defined in the /js/app.js file (shown earlier in this chapter). With this addition, you can save files to the PhotoAlbum app from the FileHelper app and see them appear immediately. For this simple app, it is easier to reload all of the files than to figure out what's new. With this addition, I have a nice implementation of the save picker contract and can receive and store files from other apps.

Now when you save the file from the FileHelper app, you can switch to the PhotoAlbum app and see the image that you have saved displayed in the app layout. You can see the effect in Figure 24-14, which shows the addition of an image to the app layout.

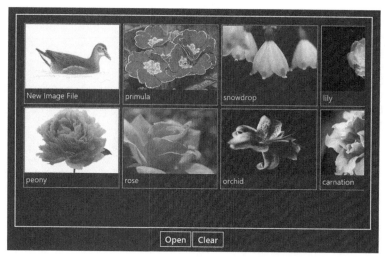

Figure 24-14. Saving an image to the example app through the save picker contract

Implementing the Open Picker Contract

Now that you've seen the save picker contract, its complement—the open picker contract—will be easy to understand by comparison. As with all contracts, start by adding a declaration to the apps manifest. Open the package.appxmanifest file from the Visual Studio Solution Explorer window and click the tab for the Declarations section.

Select File Open Picker from the Available Declarations list and click the Add button. I am going to support JPG and PNG files in the example, so enter .jpg in the existing File type text box, click the Add New button, and enter .png in the newly created File type text box. Type Control+S to save the changes. The manifest should look like the one shown in Figure 24-15.

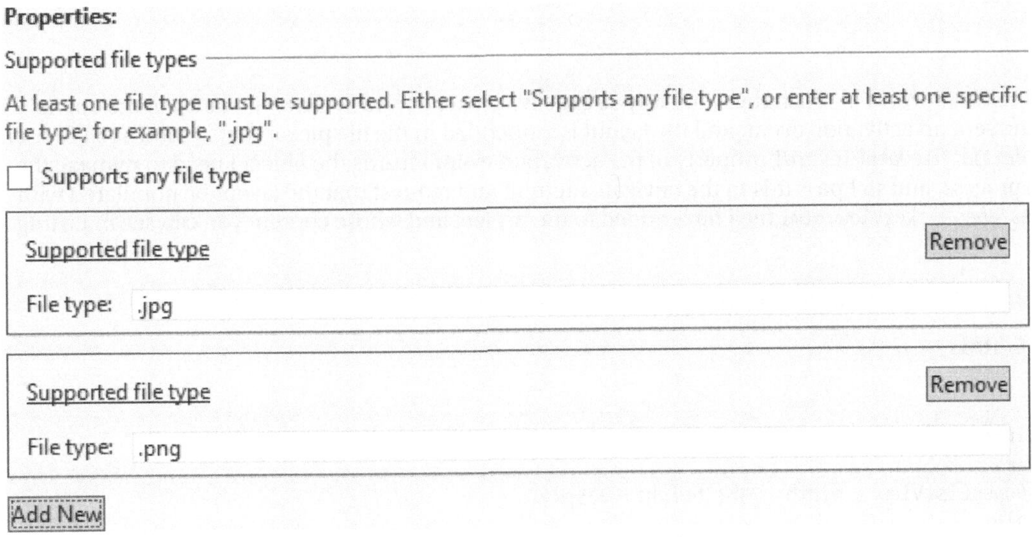

Properties:

Supported file types ──

At least one file type must be supported. Either select "Supports any file type", or enter at least one specific file type; for example, ".jpg".

☐ Supports any file type

┌───┐
│ Supported file type   [Remove]   │
│   │
│ File type: .jpg   │
└───┘

┌───┐
│ Supported file type   [Remove]   │
│   │
│ File type: .png   │
└───┘

[Add New]

Figure 24-15. Adding the declaration for the file open picker contract

Handling the Activation Event

Windows sends an activation event when the user selects the app as a location from which to open files. The detail.kind property of the activation event is set to ActivationKind.fileOpenPicker and, just like when dealing with the save picker event, this is the cue to change the layout of the app so that it fits within the picker and presents the user with some meaningful content. You can see how I have responded to the activation event in the PhotoAlbum app in Listing 24-15, which shows the changes I have made to the switch statement in the default.html file.

Listing 24-15. Responding to the open picker activation event in the default.html file

```
...
switch (args.detail.kind) {
    case activation.ActivationKind.fileOpenPicker:
        var pickerUI = args.detail.fileOpenPickerUI;
        WinJS.Navigation.navigate("/pages/openPickerView.html",
            pickerUI);
        break;
    case activation.ActivationKind.fileSavePicker:
        var pickerUI = args.detail.fileSavePickerUI;
        WinJS.Navigation.navigate("/pages/savePickerView.html",
            pickerUI);
        break;
    case activation.ActivationKind.file:
```

```
                args.detail.files.forEach(function (file) {
                    App.processFile(file);
                });
            default:
                WinJS.Navigation.navigate("/pages/albumView.html");
                break;
        }
    }
    ...
```

This contract works in much the same way as the save picker contract. A new instance of the app is started and sent an activation event, and the layout is embedded in the file picker that is shown to the user.

The detail.fileOpenPickerUI property of the activation event returns the object I need to manage the file open process, and so I pass this to the navigate method and request that the layout be populated with the /pages/openPickerView.html file I have added to the project and whose content you can see in Listing 24-16.

Listing 24-16. The contents of the /pages/openPickerView.html file

```
<!DOCTYPE html>
<html>
<head>
    <title></title>
    <style>
        #openListView { width: 75%; height: 275px;}
    </style>
    <script>
        var storage = Windows.Storage;
        var provider = Windows.Storage.Pickers.Provider;

        WinJS.UI.Pages.define("/pages/openPickerView.html", {
            ready: function (element, pickerUI) {

                var previousSelection = [];

                openListView.winControl.selectionMode = (pickerUI.selectionMode ==
                    provider.FileSelectionMode.single) ? WinJS.UI.SelectionMode.single
                    : WinJS.UI.SelectionMode.multi;

                openListView.addEventListener("selectionchanged", function (e) {

                    previousSelection.forEach(function (id) {
                        pickerUI.removeFile(id);
                    });
                    previousSelection.length = 0;

                    var newSelection = openListView.winControl.selection.getItems()
                        .then(function (items) {
                            items.forEach(function (item) {
                                pickerUI.addFile(item.data.file.path,
                                    item.data.file);
                                previousSelection.push(item.data.file.path);
                            });
```

```
                        });
                    });
                }
            });
        </script>
    </head>
    <body>
        <div class="title">Select images from the album</div>
        <div id="openListView" data-win-control="WinJS.UI.ListView"
            data-win-options="{
                itemTemplate: imageTemplate,
                itemDataSource: ViewModel.fileList.dataSource,
                tapBehavior: WinJS.UI.TapBehavior.directSelect,
                maxRows: 1
            }">
        </div>
    </body>
</html>
```

The layout defined by the file is very similar to the one I used for the save picker contract— a WinJS. UI.ListView UI control shows the images currently in the album. The user will select files to pick them.

To see this layout, you need to go through a specific sequence of events. First, restart the PhotoAlbum app—open picker apps don't need to be running to work, but you need to restart the app so that Visual Studio notifies Windows that your app has declared support for the open picker contract.

Now switch to the FileHelper app and click the Open button to display an open picker. Click the arrow next to the location title and you will see PhotoAlbum listed as a source of files, as shown in Figure 24-16.

Figure 24-16. The example app shown as a source for files to open

If you select the PhotoAlbum item from the list, you will trigger the activation event, which will cause the new layout to be displayed, as shown in Figure 24-17.

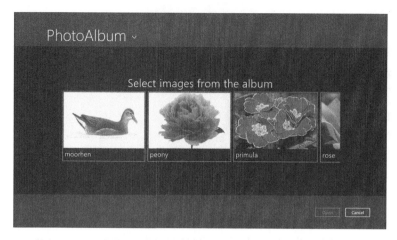

Figure 24-17. Opening a file using the open picker contract

Select one of the files and click the Open button and you will see the image you picked displayed in the FileHelper app.

From the perspective of the PhotoAlbum app, the object returned by the detail.fileOpenPickerUI property of the activation event is a Windows.Storage.Pickers.Provider.FileOpenPickerUI object and it works slightly differently to the corresponding object for the save picker contract. To demonstrate how it works, I will break down the object and talk about its properties, methods, and events in turn.

The properties defined by the FileOpenPickerUI object are shown in Listing 24-6 and they are used to get information about the picker that is being shown to the user and to set some basic configuration options.

Table 24-6. Properties Defined by the FileOpenPickerUI Object

Name	Description
allowedFileTypes	Gets a read-only array of the file types that can be opened by the app
selectionMode	Indicates whether the user can open one file or multiple files in the picker
title	Sets the title of the picker shown to the user

The selectionMode property has the most impact on the layout that you present to the user because it indicates whether the app that is trying to open a file will accept one file or multiple files. This property returns one of the values defined by the Windows.Storage.Pickers.Provider.FileSelectionMode object, which I have listed in Table 24-7.

Table 24-7. Values Defined by the FileSelectionMode Object

Name	Description
single	The user can select a single file
multiple	The user can select multiple files

It is important to ensure that the layout that you present to the user in the open file picker honors the FileSelectionMode value—otherwise you will confuse the user by either letting them pick more files that can be opened or restricting them to one when they should be able to pick multiple files.

I use the selectionMode property in the example to change the selectionMode property of the ListView control. Even though the property names are the same, the objects that define the values are different, so I have to map from one to the other, like this:

```
...
openListView.winControl.selectionMode = (pickerUI.selectionMode ==
    provider.FileSelectionMode.single) ? WinJS.UI.SelectionMode.single
        : WinJS.UI.SelectionMode.multi;
...
```

The ListView control triggers the selectionchanged event when the user selects or deselects items, and I respond using the methods defined by the FileOpenPickerUI to reflect the files that the user has picked. These methods are described in Table 24-8.

Table 24-8. Methods Defined by the FileOpenPickerUI Object

Name	Description
addFile(id, file)	Adds a StorageFile to the picker, associating it with the specified ID
containsFile(id)	Returns true if a file with the specified ID has already been added to the picker and false otherwise
removeFile(id)	Removes the file with the specified ID from the picker

When you call the addFile method, you pass in a StorageFile representing the user's selection and a unique ID to represent the file. You can then use this ID to check if the file is already part of the selection or to remove it from the selection. There is no method to enumerate the files in the picker, which is a problem because the selectionchanged event doesn't indicate what changed in the selection. This means that I have to clear the picked files each time the user changes the ListView selection and add new entries for each selected item to make sure that I don't leave any files in the picker that have been deselected.

No explicit action is required other than to call the addFile method. The StorageFile objects that you pass to addFile are given to the app which is opening files for the user, so your only obligation is to ensure that the StorageFile objects correspond to the user's picks. You can get more insight into the pick process by listening for the events that the FileOpenPickerUI defines, which I have described in Table 24-9.

Table 24-9. Events Defined by the FileOpenPickerUI Object

Name	Description
closing	Triggered when the user closes the file picker
fileremoved	Triggered when the user removes a file from the picker selection

Summary

In this chapter, I have shown you how to implement three of the key contracts: file activation, save picker, and open picker. These contracts allow you to integrate your app into Windows so that you can handle files on behalf of the user and provide storage services to other apps. In the next chapter, I will show you the sharing contract, which is a key Windows 8 feature.

CHAPTER 25

■ ■ ■

The Sharing Contract

The *sharing contract* allows users to share data items between apps. This is one of the key features of Windows apps and it allows the user to create ad hoc workflows using apps that have no knowledge of each other and that only share data formats in common.

Two apps are required to participate in the sharing contract. The app that is the *share source* possesses one or more items of data that the user wants to share. Windows presents the user with a list of apps, known as *share targets*, that are capable of processing that data, and the user picks the one they want to receive the items from the share source. In this chapter, I'll show you how to create both participants in the contract and demonstrate how you can streamline repeated operations to make sharing simpler for the user. Table 25-1 provides the summary for this chapter.

Table 25-1. Chapter Summary

Problem	Solution	Listing
Create a share source	Respond to the datarequested event emitted by the DataTransferManager object	25-4
Report a share source error	Call the failWithDisplayText method	25-5
Create a share data package	Use the DataPackage object	25-6
Describe the data in a package	Define values for the DataPackage object	25-7–25-8
Create a share target	Declare the Share Target contract in the manifest and respond to the activated event	25-9–25-13
Allow the user to repeat common sharing operations	Create quick links	25-14–25-15

Creating the Example App

I am going to start by creating a *share source*, which is an app that offers data to be consumed by another app. I have created a simple helper app called ShareHelper. I'll introduce the basic app without any support for sharing and then show how to implement the share source functionality. Listing 25-1 shows the default.html file from the ShareHelper app.

Listing 25-1. The default.html file from the ShareHelper app

```
<!DOCTYPE html>
<html>
<head>
    <meta charset="utf-8" />
    <title>ShareHelper</title>
    <!-- WinJS references -->
    <link href="//Microsoft.WinJS.1.0/css/ui-dark.css" rel="stylesheet" />
    <script src="//Microsoft.WinJS.1.0/js/base.js"></script>
    <script src="//Microsoft.WinJS.1.0/js/ui.js"></script>
    <!-- ShareHelper references -->
    <link href="/css/default.css" rel="stylesheet" />
    <script src="/js/default.js"></script>
</head>
<body>
    <div id="imageTemplate" data-win-control="WinJS.Binding.Template">
        <div class="imgContainer">
            <img class="listImg" data-win-bind="src: img" />
            <span class="listTitle" data-win-bind="innerText: title"></span>
        </div>
    </div>
    <div id="listView" data-win-control="WinJS.UI.ListView"
        data-win-options="{
            itemTemplate: imageTemplate,
            tapBehavior: WinJS.UI.TapBehavior.directSelect,
            maxRows: 2
        }">
    </div>
</body>
</html>
```

The layout in this app consists of a large ListView control, using the same kind of item template that I have employed in other recent examples. The idea here is to present the user with a set of images from which they can make a selection and then use the sharing contract to share those images with the PhotoAlbum app, which will then add the shared images to the album.

With such a simple layout, the CSS required for the ShareHelper app is largely focused on the elements in the templates, as you can see in Listing 25-2, which shows the contents of the css/default.css file.

Listing 25-2. The css/default.css file from the ShareHelper app

```
body {
    display: -ms-flexbox;
    -ms-flex-direction: column;   -ms-flex-pack: center;}

#listView { width: 100%; height: 100%; padding: 10px;}

.imgContainer { border: thin solid white; padding: 2px; }

.listTitle { font-size: 18pt; max-width: 180px;
    text-overflow: ellipsis; display: block; white-space: nowrap;
    margin: 0 0 5px 5px; height: 35px;}
```

```
.listImg {width: 300px; height: 200px;}
```

The next step in creating the helper app is to load some images and populate the ListView control. You can see how I have done this in Listing 25-3, which shows the js/default.js file. I perform a deep query of the Pictures library and show all of the image files that I find there.

Listing 25-3. The contents of the default.js file from the ShareHelper app

```
(function () {

    var app = WinJS.Application;
    var activation = Windows.ApplicationModel.Activation;
    var appstate = activation.ApplicationExecutionState;
    var storage = Windows.Storage;

    app.onactivated = function (args) {
        if (args.detail.previousExecutionState != appstate.suspended) {
            args.setPromise(WinJS.UI.processAll().then(function () {
                var list = new WinJS.Binding.List();
                listView.winControl.itemDataSource = list.dataSource;

                storage.KnownFolders.picturesLibrary
                    .getFilesAsync(storage.Search.CommonFileQuery.orderByName)
                    .then(function (files) {
                        files.forEach(function (file) {
                            list.unshift({
                                img: URL.createObjectURL(file),
                                title: file.displayName, file: file
                            });
                        });
                    });
            }));
        }
    };
    app.start();
})();
```

This is a rudimentary app and I make some assumptions in the name of brevity, the most important of which is that I assume that all of the files in the Pictures library are image files.

The last step to create the helper app is to declare the need to access the Pictures library in the manifest. Open the package.appxmanifest file, navigate to the Capabilities section and check the Pictures Library option, as shown in Figure 25-1.

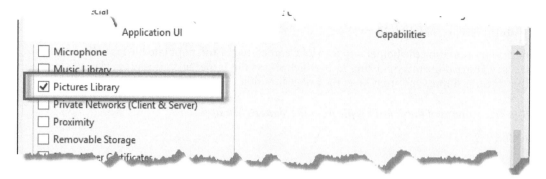

Figure 25-1. *Declaring access to the Pictures library*

If you start the app, you'll see the images in your Pictures folder displayed in the ListView, as shown in Figure 25-2.

Figure 25-2. *The basic functionality of the ShareHelper app*

Create a Share Source

Although the share source is a key part of the share contract, no changes to the app manifest are made. Instead, everything is handled in JavaScript when the app starts. To demonstrate this, I have made the changes to the /js/default.js file in the ShareHelper app shown in Listing 25-4.

Listing25- 4. *Creating a share source in the ShareHelper app*

```
(function () {

    var app = WinJS.Application;
    var activation = Windows.ApplicationModel.Activation;
    var appstate = activation.ApplicationExecutionState;
    var storage = Windows.Storage;
    var share = Windows.ApplicationModel.DataTransfer;
```

```
app.onactivated = function (args) {
    if (args.detail.previousExecutionState != appstate.suspended) {
        args.setPromise(WinJS.UI.processAll().then(function () {
            var list = new WinJS.Binding.List();
            listView.winControl.itemDataSource = list.dataSource;

            storage.KnownFolders.picturesLibrary
                .getFilesAsync(storage.Search.CommonFileQuery.orderByName)
                .then(function (files) {
                    files.forEach(function (file) {
                        list.unshift({
                            img: URL.createObjectURL(file),
                            title: file.displayName, file: file
                        });
                    });
                });

            share.DataTransferManager.getForCurrentView()
                .addEventListener("datarequested", function (e) {

                var deferral = e.request.getDeferral();

                listView.winControl.selection.getItems().then(function (items) {
                    if (items.length > 0) {
                        var datapackage = e.request.data;

                        var files = [];
                        items.forEach(function (item) {
                            files.push(item.data.file);
                        });
                        datapackage.setStorageItems(files);

                        datapackage.setUri(new Windows.Foundation.Uri(
                            "http://apress.com"));

                        datapackage.properties.title = "Share Images";
                        datapackage.properties.description
                            = "Images from the Pictures Library";
                        datapackage.properties.applicationName = "ShareHelper";
                    } else {
                        e.request.failWithDisplayText(
                            "Select the images you want to share and try again");
                    }
                });
                deferral.complete();
            });
        }));
    }
};
app.start();
})();
```

The code I have highlighted in the listing does two things: it registers the app as a source of sharing data and it responds when the user activates the Share Charm. I'll explain each activity in the sections that follow.

Registering as a Share Source

The technique required to tell Windows that your app is a source of sharing data doesn't require any manifest declarations and isn't done through activation events. Instead, you must work through the `DataTransferManager` object that is in `Windows.ApplicationModel.DataTransfer` namespace. (I have aliased this namespace to share in the example.) The `DataTransferManager` object defines the events I have described in Table 25-2.

■ **Note**   In this chapter, all of the new objects that I introduce are in the `Windows.ApplicationModel.DataTransfer` namespace unless I note otherwise.

Table 25-2. Events Defined by the DataTransferManager Object

Name	Description
datarequested	Triggered when the user activates the Share Charm
targetapplicationchosen	Triggered when the user selects the share target app

To register a handler function for these events, you must call the `addEventListener` method on the object that is returned by the `DataTransferManager.getForCurrentView` method. (This is another one of those objects whose structure makes more sense if you are a .NET programmer, but it works perfectly well in JavaScript as long as you remember to call getForCurrentView.)

Responding to the Event

I am interested in the `datarequested` event for this example, which is triggered when the user activates the Windows Share Charm and is my cue to prepare the data that is to be shared. The object passed to the handler for the `datarequested` event is a little odd, in that the `request` property, and not the `detail` property, contains the information required to service the sharing operation.

The `request` property returns a `DataRequest` object, which you use to create a *package* of data that will be shared with another app. I have summarized the methods and properties defined by the `DataRequest` objects in Table 25-3.

Table 25-3. Methods and Properties Defined by the DataRequest Object

Name	Description
failWithDisplayText(message)	Cancels the sharing operation and displays the specified message to the user
getDeferral()	Returns an object that can be used to signal that the shared data is ready when it is prepared using asynchronous methods
data	Returns a `DataPackage` object used to send the shared data
dealine	Returns the `Date` that represents the deadline by which a deferred operation must be complete (after which the share fails)

The first thing you need to do when you receive the datarequested event is call the getDeferral method if you will be performing any asynchronous method calls. If you don't call getDeferral, then Windows will think that you haven't provided any data when the execution of your handler function is complete.

The getDeferral method returns a DataRequestDeferral object that defines the complete method. This is the only method that DataRequestDeferral defines, and you call it when you have created your data package and are ready for it to be presented to the user.

For my example app, I have defined some code that creates an outline of the handler for the event, as shown in Listing 25-5.

Listing 25-5. Dealing with the datarequested object

```
...
share.DataTransferManager.getForCurrentView().addEventListener("datarequested",
    function (e) {

    var deferral = e.request.getDeferral();

    listView.winControl.selection.getItems().then(function (items) {
        if (items.length > 0) {
            // ...statements to prepare shared data go here...
        } else {
            e.request.failWithDisplayText(
                "Select the images you want to share and try again");
        }
    });
    deferral.complete();
});
...
```

I call the getDeferral method because I need to get the selection from the ListView control using the asynchronous getItems method and I call the failWithDisplayText method if the user hasn't selected any images to share. If the user activates the Share Charm without selecting any images in the ListView control, they will see the message passed to the failWithDisplayText method. This is the basic pattern for setting the app up as a provider of shared data, leaving the preparation and packaging of the data itself. I show you how to do this in the next section.

Packaging the Shared Data

If your app has data that can be shared, then you must populate the DataPackage object obtained from the DataRequest.data property so that a share target can be located and passed your data. The DataRequest object is obtained by reading the request property of the object passed to the datarequested event handler function.

The DataPackage is very flexible and can be used to share all sorts of data. I have summarized the most useful methods for adding data to the DataPackage in Table 25-4.

Table 25-4. Methods for Adding Data to the DataPackage Object

Name	Description
setBitmap(bitmap)	Adds the specified bitmap to the data package
setData(format, dataobject)	Adds a custom data object, identified with the specified format
setHtmlFormat(html)	Adds the specified HTML data to the data package. HTML content must be passed to the HtmlFormatHelper.createHtmlFormat method before this method to add the required headers. The HtmlFormatHelper object is in the Windows.ApplicationModel.DataTransfer namespace.
setRtf(richtext)	Adds the specified data in the Rich Text Format to the data package
setStorageItems(files[])	Adds the specified StorageFile or StorageFolder objects to the data package
setText(string)	Adds the specified text to the data package
setUri(uri)	Adds the Windows.Foundation.Uri object to the data package

You use the methods shown in the table to add data to the package that will be shared with another app. Your package can contain different types of data, but if you call the same method twice, the data that you pass on the second occasion will replace the data already in the package.

■ **Tip**   You don't have to specify the contents of your data package in advance—you can decide at the moment when the datarequested event arrives. This means you can share different kinds of data based on the state of your app—for example, I might share image files when the user selects single images in the ListView control, share a list of file names if multiple files are selected, and share something else entirely if the user has navigated to a different part of the app. A big part of the flexibility in the share contract comes from being able to select content for sharing based on the task the user is performing.

You can see in Listing 25-6 how I have used the setStorageItems method to add files to the data package, corresponding to the images that the user has selected in the ListView. I have also used the setUri method to provide the user with a link they can follow for more information—I have used the URL apress.com as a placeholder in my example.

Listing 25-6. Packaging the data for sharing

```
...
share.DataTransferManager.getForCurrentView()
    .addEventListener("datarequested", function (e) {

    var deferral = e.request.getDeferral();

    listView.winControl.selection.getItems().then(function (items) {
        if (items.length > 0) {
            var datapackage = e.request.data;

            var files = [];
            items.forEach(function (item) {
                files.push(item.data.file);
            });
```

```
        datapackage.setStorageItems(files);

        datapackage.setUri(new Windows.Foundation.Uri("http://apress.com"));

        datapackage.properties.title = "Share Images";
        datapackage.properties.description = "Images from the Pictures Library";
        datapackage.properties.applicationName = "ShareHelper";

    } else {
        e.request.failWithDisplayText(
            "Select the images you want to share and try again");
    }
    });
    deferral.complete();
});
...
```

▪ **Note** I have deliberately introduced a problem in the way I have used the setUri method on this data package. Later in the chapter I'll come back and explain the problem and why it is some commonly encountered—so, don't use the setUri method until you have read the rest of this chapter.

Describing the Data

The DataPackage object defines a property called properties, which returns a DataPackagePropertySet object (the object and member names in this section can be a little bewildering since the term *property* appears so often).

You use DataPackagePropertySet to provide additional information about the sharing operation and its data, and I have described the properties defined by this object in Table 25-5.

Table 25-5. Properties Defined by the DataPackagePropertySet

Name	Description
applicationListingUri	Sets the URI of the app's location in the store
applicationName	Sets the name of the share source app
description	Sets a description of the data that can be displayed to the user
fileTypes	Sets the types of file in the package as an array of file extensions
size	Sets the number of items that are in the data package
thumbnail	Sets a thumbnail that can be displayed to the user
title	Sets a title for the data package that can be displayed to the user

These properties are not set for you, even though some of them—such as applicationListUri and fileTypes—seem like they should. On the other hand, you are not required to provide values for any of these properties, so you only have to deal with the ones that will help the user make sense of the sharing operation.

In my example, I have set values for three of the properties, as shown in Listing 25-7. I'll use these values to display details of the sharing operation when I make the PhotoAlbum app a sharing target later in this chapter, and you can see how they are used by Windows in the next section.

Listing 25-7. Using properties to describe the data package

```
...
datapackage.properties.title = "Share Images";
datapackage.properties.description = "Images from the Pictures Library";
datapackage.properties.applicationName = "ShareHelper";
...
```

■ **Tip**   You can also use the `insert` method to add a custom property to the data package. I'll show you an example of this in the Adding a Custom Property section later in the chapter.

Testing the Share Source App

To test the sharing of data, start the `ShareHelper` app using the `Start Debugging` item from the Visual Studio Debug menu and select one or more images in the `ListView`.

Open the Charm Bar and select the Share Charm (you can activate the Share Charm directly using Win+H). You will see the Share flyout, which will contain a list of the apps that can process the data package prepared by the `ShareHelper` app, as shown in Figure 25-3.

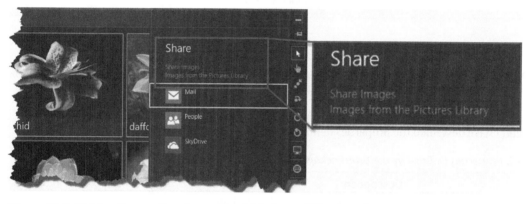

Figure 25-3. Picking the app that data with which data will be shared

I have expanded part of the Share flyout so that you can see the effect of the properties I specified for the data package and how they are displayed to the user to describe the data.

In the figure, there are three apps that can receive the data from the `ShareHelper` app: `Mail`, `People`, and `SkyDrive`. You may see other entries if you have installed additional apps on your system, but notice that all of the apps listed are Windows Store apps—the sharing contract only works on apps and doesn't include traditional Windows desktop programs.

Understanding a Common Sharing Problem

Windows selects apps to handle shared data based on the set**<XXX>** methods called when the sharing data package is created. I called `setStorageItems` and `setUri`, so Windows is looking for apps that can handle files or URLs.

The key word is *or*—apps only have to declare support for any *one* of the types of data in the package to be a suitable target for sharing. Apps are free to take the data they can support from a shared package and ignore everything else.

In the case of the built-in Windows app, the Mail app (an e-mail client) will use the files as attachments in a new e-mail message, the People app (a social media tool) will share the URL with my social media contacts, and the SkyDrive app will save the image files to cloud storage.

This is the problem I created back in Listing 25-6. I used the setUri to add a URL to the package that provides some additional information to the user, but isn't directly related to the content that the user is trying to share. However, if the user chooses the People or Mail app as the sharing target, then the image files—the real content—will be discarded and the link will be treated with more importance than it is due. The user's contacts will be sent a URL without any of the context provided by the images the user was trying to share—a pretty confusing outcome for the user and the recipients of the message, and sadly, this is a common mistake when sharing data.

You can see the problem if you select the Mail app from the Share flyout. The Mail app will be displayed in a small flyout, allowing you to complete the e-mail by selecting a recipient and adding some text, as shown in Figure 25-4.

■ **Tip**   You will need to perform this test on the local machine because the Mail app won't start properly in the Visual Studio simulator.

Figure 25-4. Sharing data with the Mail app

The image files that the user is trying to share have been ignored and, worse, the Mail app has gone to the URL, located the images that it contains, and presented them in a FlipView to the user. This is just plain confusing, because the user selected image files but is now being offered a choice of completely different images that have been obtained from a URL that my example app quietly added to the data package.

Avoiding the Problem

To avoid this problem, it is important to make sure that each and every type of data that you add to the package is self-contained and valuable to the user. My preference is to add multiple types of data to the package only when they are equivalent—so if, for example, I was sharing the text of this chapter, I might add the RTF formatted manuscript, the plain-text equivalent, and a URL to the content on my SkyDrive storage.

My baseline thought when working out how to share data is to ask myself, what would the user *expect* to happen? You should revisit your package contents if you can't immediately correlate the items in your data package to the user's reasonable expectations.

If you do need to add supplementary information to the data package in support of the data that the user has selected, you should define a custom property. Custom properties are not used to select suitable share target apps, and they can be ignored by any app that doesn't know of their significance. You add a custom property to the data package by using the DataPackagePropertySet.insert method, passing the name you want to give the property and its value. You can see how I have replaced the setUrimethod with a custom property called referenceURL in Listing 25-8.

Listing 25-8. Adding a custom property with the insert method

```
...
var datapackage = e.request.data;

var files = [];
items.forEach(function (item) {
    files.push(item.data.file);
});
datapackage.setStorageItems(files);

// This statement is now commented out
//datapackage.setUri(new Windows.Foundation.Uri("http://apress.com"));

datapackage.properties.title = "Share Images";
datapackage.properties.description = "Images from the Pictures Library";
datapackage.properties.applicationName = "ShareHelper";
datapackage.properties.insert("referenceURL", "http://apress.com");
...
```

If you restart the ShareHelper app, select some images in the ListView, and activate the Share Charm again, you will see only the Mail and SkyDrive apps on the list of targets—this is because the People app can't handle files in a shared data package and so won't be selected by Windows as a target for the data. If you select the Mail app, you'll see that the image files selected by the user have been added to the message as attachments, as shown in Figure 25-5.

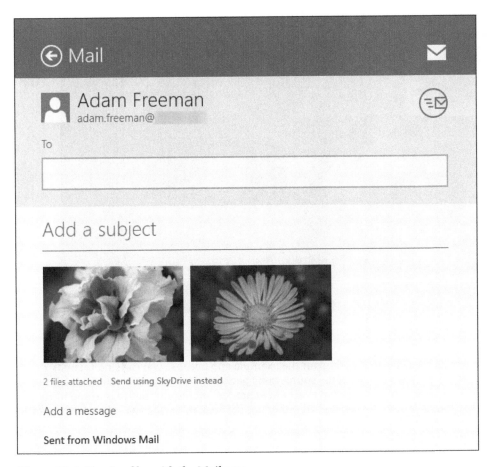

Figure 25-5. *Sharing files with the Mail app*

Creating the Share Target

In this section, I am going demonstrate the other side of the sharing contract by making the PhotoAlbum app I created in Chapter 24 into a share target and allowing it to receive data packages that contain files.

As a reminder, the basic functionality of the PhotoAlbum app lets the user pick image files to be displayed in a simple album, which is shown as a series of thumbnail images displayed in WinJS.UI. ListView control.

In the previous chapter, I built on this foundation to implement the file activation, save picker, and open picker contracts, showing the different ways that an app can integrate into the operating system—a theme I'll continue in this chapter with the share contract. As a reminder, Figure 25-6 shows you what the PhotoAlbum looks like when displaying images.

Figure 25-6. The PhotoAlbum example app

I am not going to relist the code and markup for the example app because you can find them in Chapter 24 or download the project as part of the source code pack from Apress.com. I know it can be frustrating to have to flick backward and forward to another chapter, but the alternative is to spend 10 pages listing code that you have already seen and I'd rather use the space showing you new contracts and features.

Updating the Manifest

Unlike share sources, share targets have to declare their capabilities in the manifest. This makes sense because share sources need to be free to share whatever data the user is working on, whereas share targets are going to have predetermined ways of dealing with a set range of data types.

For this chapter, I am going to enhance the PhotoAlbum app so that it is able to deal with data packages that contain .jpg and .png files. To do this, open the package.appxmanifest file from the Visual Studio Solution Explorer window and navigate to the Declarations section. Select Share Target from the Available Declarations list and click the Add button. As with the other contracts, a form for additional details is displayed, as shown in Figure 25-7. The red warnings are shown because I have yet to populate the form.

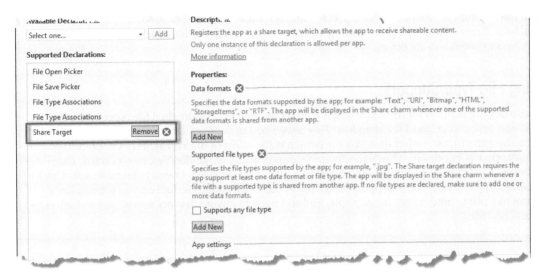

***Figure 25-7.** Adding the Share Target declaration to the manifest*

Declaring a Data Format

You can declare your support for the share target in one of two ways. The first is to use a data format, which you do by clicking the Add New button in the Data formats section of the manifest form. When you click the button, you are presented with a Data format field into which you can enter a data format that your app will support.

The Data format fields take values that correspond to the methods in the DataPackage object, which I described earlier in the chapter. Table 25-6 provides a quick reference between the methods in the DataPackage object that the share source can use and the corresponding Data format values that the share target has to declare in the manifest to be able to receive that kind of package.

■ **Tip** Remember that Windows will include your app in the list of share targets presented to the user if the data package being shared contains at least one of the types you have declared. You don't need to declare the exact combination of Data format values to receive a package that contains multiple types. Equally, you should not declare support for any data type that your app can't do something useful with.

***Table 25-6.** Data Format Values for Share Target Manifests and the DataPackage Methods They Relate To*

DataPackage Method	Data format Field Value
setBitmap	Bitmap
setHtmlFormat	HTML
setRtf	RTF
setStorageItems	StorageItems
setText	Text
setUri	URI

If you want to support more than one type of data, say, files and URLs, click Add New again to create additional Data format fields and enter the appropriate value from the table. Type Control+S to save the manifest changes when you are done.

Declaring File Type Support

You can also declare support for the share target contact by specifying individual file types using the Supported file types section of the manifest. This allows you to support data packages that contain types of file your app can process, rather than any file (which is the effect of the StorageItems data format).

The difference is important. The Mail app, for example, wants to handle files, but it doesn't care what they are because every file is a suitable attachment for an e-mail message. I need to be more selective for the PhotoAlbum app because I only support image files—there is nothing useful I can do with an Excel spreadsheet in a photo album app, for example, and so I need to ensure that my app is only a share target for PNG and JPG files.

■ **Tip**   I am showing you how the two sections of the manifest declaration work separately, but you can use both sections in the same declaration to support a mix of data types and file types. You must specify at least one file type or data format for this contact, but otherwise you are free to mix and match as you see fit.

To set up the manifest declaration for the PhotoAlbum app, click the Add New button to create a new File type field and enter the .png file extension (including the period). Click the Add New button again and enter .jpg in the File type field. The manifest should look like the one shown in Figure 25-8. When you have added the first file type, the red warning marks will disappear, telling you that your manifest declaration is valid.

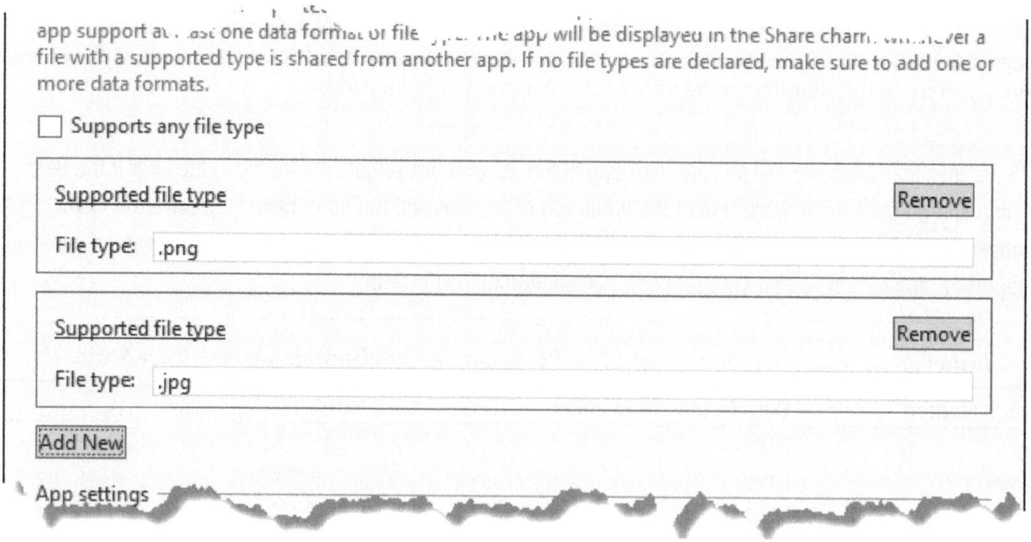

Figure 25-8. Adding support for specific file types in the PhotoAlbum manifest

Windows will add your app to the list of share targets if the data package contains at least one file that matches the types you have specified. That means that you may receive packages that contain some files that you can't process—it is your responsibility to find the files in the package that you *can* handle and ignore the rest. (You can see how I do this later in the chapter.)

Responding to the Activation Event

Windows uses an activated event to notify you when your app is selected as the share target for a data package. The detail.kind property of the activation event is set to ActivationKind.shareTarget. In Listing 25-9, you can see the additions I have made to the /js/default.js file in the PhotoAlbum project to respond to this event.

Listing 25-9. Responding to the activated event

```
...
switch (args.detail.kind) {
    case activation.ActivationKind.shareTarget:
        WinJS.Navigation.navigate("/pages/shareTargetView.html",
            args.detail.shareOperation);
        break;
        // ... statements for other activation types removed for brevity...
    default:
        WinJS.Navigation.navigate("/pages/albumView.html");
        break;
}
...
```

The args.detail.shareOperation property returns a Windows.ApplicationModel.DataTransfer. ShareTarget.ShareOperation object, which provides access to the data package and provides methods by which I can signal my progress to Windows as I deal with the data package. I pass the ShareOperation object to the WinJS.Navigation.navigate method so that it is available in the content file that I have created to deal with shareTarget activation events, which is called shareTargetView.html and which I added to the pages folder in the PhotoAlbum Visual Studio project. I'll show you the contents of this file in the sections that follow.

■ **Note** One important point to note is that a new instance of your app is launched to deal with shareTarget events. This means that if your app is already running, then a second instance will be created. You will need to provide some kind of coordination so that the instance of your app that was started by the user reflects the updates made by the instance started by Windows to deal with the share data package. For this example, I will be copying the files shared by the user into the local app data folder, which the PhotoAlbum app monitors for changes.

Processing the Share Operation

In Listing 25-10, you can see the contents of the shareTargetView.html file, which I created to add support for the share target contract to the PhotoAlbum app. Two of the key functions in the script element are placeholders, which I will complete later in this section.

Listing 25-10. The initial contents of the shareTargetView.html file

```
<!DOCTYPE html>
<html>
<head>
    <title></title>
    <style>
        body {background-color: #303030;}
        #shareListView {
            width: 90%; height: 275px; border: medium solid white;
            margin: 20px 10px;}
        .addButton { font-size: 18pt; margin: 10px; width: 175px}
        .titleSmall { font-size: 20pt;}
    </style>
    <script>
        var storage = Windows.Storage;
        var share = Windows.ApplicationModel.DataTransfer;
        var localFolder = storage.ApplicationData.current.localFolder;

        function processPackage(data) {
            // ...this function will return a Promise which is fulfilled when
            // ...the contents of the package are processed. The Promise yields
            // ...a WinJS.Binding.List containing objects for use with the HTML template
        }

        function copySelectedFiles(files) {
            // ...this function will return a Promise that is fulfilled when
            // ...all of the shared image files have been copied
        }

        WinJS.UI.Pages.define("/pages/shareTargetView.html", {
            ready: function (element, shareOperation) {

                processPackage(shareOperation.data).then(function (list) {
                    if (list.length == 0) {
                        shareOperation.reportError("No images files were shared");
                        return;
                    }

                    shareOperation.reportStarted();

                    shareListView.winControl.itemDataSource = list.dataSource;

                    WinJS.Utilities.query("button.addButton").listen("click",
                        function (e) {

                        if (this.id == "addAll") {
                            shareListView.winControl.selection.selectAll();
                        }
                        var filesToProcess = [];
                        shareListView.winControl.selection.getItems()
```

```
                                .then(function (items) {
                                    items.forEach(function (item) {
                                        filesToProcess.push(item.data.file);
                                    });
                                });

                            copySelectedFiles(filesToProcess).then(function () {
                                shareOperation.reportDataRetrieved();
                                shareOperation.reportCompleted();
                            });;;
                        });
                    });
                }
            });
    </script>
</head>
<body>
    <div class="title" id="shareTitle"></div>
    <div class="titleSmall">Shared by: <span id="appName"></span></div>
    <div class="titleSmall">(For info: <a id="infoAnchor"></a>)</div>
    <div id="shareListView" data-win-control="WinJS.UI.ListView"
        data-win-options="{
            itemTemplate: imageTemplate,
            tapBehavior: WinJS.UI.TapBehavior.directSelect,
            maxRows: 1
        }">
    </div>
    <div>
        <button class="addButton" id="addAll">Add All</button>
        <button class="addButton" id="addSelected">Add Selected</button>
    </div>
</body>
</html>
```

Even with the incomplete functions, there are still some important things going on in this file. The best way for me to explain them is to show you what the finished page looks like and then work back. Figure 25-9 shows the shareTargetView.html file being used by Windows to handle a share data package.

■ **Note** You won't be able to re-create this figure at the moment, because the key functions in the default.js file are not yet implemented.

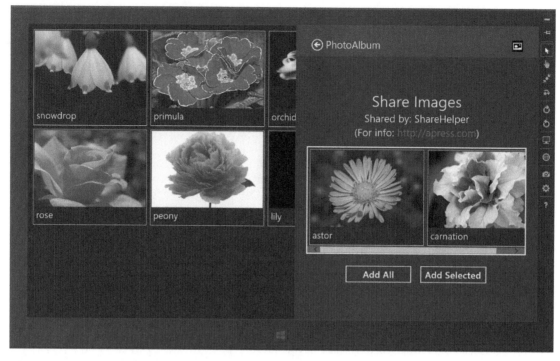

Figure 25-9. The PhotoAlbum app receiving a share data package

Windows displays the share target app in a 650-pixel pane (645 of which is available for the app to use). For my example app, I am using a layout that contains some title information (which I will populate using the properties from the share data package), a ListView (which I will populate with the StorageFile objects the data package), and two button elements.

The buttons allow the user to further refine their choice of files in the package. Clicking the Add All button will copy all of the files from the data package into the local app data folder and add them to the album. Clicking the Add Selected button will operate on just those images that the user selects in the ListView.

I like to provide the user with the option to further filter the contents of data packages because I don't know anything about the app that the data came from. This creates an extra step in the sharing process, which is a bad thing, but many apps seem not to let the user fine-tune their selections before sharing, which is even worse. I justify adding the extra step to the process by supporting the quick link feature, which I describe later in this chapter.

Reporting Progress

The ShareOperation object defines a number of methods that you use to keep Windows informed as you process the data package, as described in Table 25-7.

Table 25-7. Methods Defined by the ShareOperation Object

Name	Description
reportStarted()	Reports that the app has started to process the data from the package
reportDataRetrieved()	Reports that the app has copied the data it needs from the package
reportError(msg)	Reports the specified error message to the user
reportSubmittedBackgroundTask()	Indicates that the data in the package will be copied using a background task
reportCompleted()	Indicates that the target app has finished the sharing operation

You can see how I have used these methods in the ready function for the shareTargetView.html page in Listing 25-11, where I have repeated the code and highlighted the key statements.

Listing 25-11. Using the ShareOperation methods when processing the share package

```
...
ready: function (element, shareOperation) {

    processPackage(shareOperation.data).then(function (list) {
        if (list.length == 0) {
            shareOperation.reportError("No images files were shared");
            return;
        }

        shareListView.winControl.itemDataSource = list.dataSource;
        WinJS.Utilities.query("button.addButton").listen("click", function (e) {
            shareOperation.reportStarted();
            if (this.id == "addAll") {
                shareListView.winControl.selection.selectAll();
            }
            var filesToProcess = [];
            shareListView.winControl.selection.getItems().then(function (items) {
                items.forEach(function (item) {
                    filesToProcess.push(item.data.file);
                });
            });

            copySelectedFiles(filesToProcess).then(function () {
                shareOperation.reportDataRetrieved();
                shareOperation.reportCompleted();
            });;;
        });
    });
}
...
```

You should call the reportStarted method only when no further user interaction with your app is required—this is because Windows may dismiss your app and allow the share operation to continue in the background, allowing the user to carry on working with the share source app.

For my example, that means that I can't call `reportStarted` until the user has clicked one of the buttons, indicating which files they want to import. I call the `reportStarted` method as soon as I have parsed the content in the package and call the `reportDataRetrieved` and `reportCompleted` methods after I have copied the content into the local app data folder.

I call the `reportError` method if the `WinJS.Binding.List` object that I get from the `processPackage` function doesn't contain any files I can operate on. In an ideal world, I shouldn't need to do this, because Windows will have matched the contents of the package to the file types in the manifest declaration, but I add this check to my share target apps to deal with badly written apps. Some share source apps set the value of the `fileTypes` property in the data package (described earlier in this chapter) incorrectly—this value overrides the types of the files that are really being used, which causes Windows to send my app packages that don't contain any useful files.

■ **Note**   The way that errors are presented to the users is a little odd. The share target app is immediately closed when the `reportError` method is called. The user is then presented with a notification message that tells them there has been a problem. They can see the message you passed to the `reportError` method only if they click on the notification.

Processing the Data Package

The `ShareOperation.data` property returns a `DataPackageView` object, which is a read-only version of the data package. You use this object to learn about the package you have been sent and get the data it contains. Table 25-8 shows the methods that the `DataPackageView` object defines.

Table 25-8. Methods Defined by the DataPackageView Object

Name	Description
`contains(format)`	Returns true if the data package contains the specified data format
`getBitMapAsync()`	Returns a `Promise` that yields the Bitmap data
`getDataAsync(format)`	Returns a `Promise` that yields the specified data format
`getHtmlFormatAsync()`	Returns a `Promise` that yields the HTML data
`getRtfAsync()`	Returns a `Promise` that yields the RTF data
`getStorageItemsAsync()`	Returns a `Promise` that yields the `StorageFile` and `StorageFolder` objects in the package
`getTextAsync()`	Returns a `Promise` that yields the text data
`getUriAsync()`	Returns a `Promise` that yields the URL

The methods that retrieve data from the package are all asynchronous and return a `WinJS.Promise` object that yields the data of the appropriate type when it is fulfilled.

The `contains` method lets you check to see if the package contains a given data type. You can pass one of the string values from Table 25-6 to this method or use one of the values from the `StandardDataFormats` object, which I have listed in Table 25-9.

Table 25-9. Values Defined by the StandardFormats Object

Name	Description
Bitmap	Specifies bitmap data
Html	Specifies HTML data
Rtf	Specifies RTF data
StorageItems	Specifies StorageFile/StorageFolder objects
Text	Specifies text
Uri	Specifies a URL

You can see how I have used the contains and getStorageItemsAsync methods in Listing 25-12, which shows how I have implemented the processPackage function in the shareTargetView.html file.

Listing 25-12. Completing the processPackage method

```
...
function processPackage(data) {
    if (data.contains(share.StandardDataFormats.storageItems)) {
        return data.getStorageItemsAsync().then(function (files) {
            var fileList = new WinJS.Binding.List();
            files.forEach(function (file) {
                if (file.fileType == ".jpg" || file.fileType == ".png") {
                    fileList.unshift({
                        img: URL.createObjectURL(file),
                        title: file.displayName,
                        file: file
                    });
                }
            });
            appName.innerText = data.properties.applicationName;
            shareTitle.innerText = data.properties.title;
            var refLink = data.properties["referenceURL"]
            infoAnchor.innerText = infoAnchor.href = refLink == null ? "N/A" : refLink;
            return fileList;
        });
    };
}
...
```

I start by using the contains method to make sure that there are files or folders in the data package—this is the only kind of data I support in my example app and there is no point processing the package further otherwise.

I call the getStorageItemsAsync method and inspect the fileType property of each of the objects that are passed to the then method, which allows me to filter out folders and files of the wrong type. I add an object to a WinJS.Binding.List for each image file I find with properties that mean I can display it in the ListView UI control using the HTML template in the default.html file (this is the same template I used for all of the PhotoAlbum examples in Chapter 24 as well).

The DataPackageView.properties property returns an object you can use to get the properties that were added to the data package by the sharing source app. I read the value of the applicationName and title properties and check to see if the custom property that the ShareHelper app adds to packages is present. I use the values to set the contents of some of the HTML elements in the layout.

■ **Tip** You must be careful to make sure that your asynchronous method calls are complete before telling Windows that you have finished the sharing operation. In this example, I do this by returning a Promise from the processPackage function that is fulfilled only when I have received and processed the results from the getStorageItemsAsync method.

Copying the Data

All that remains is to copy the data from the sharing package to the local app data folder, which I do by implementing the copySelectedFiles function, as shown in Listing 25-13.

Listing 25-13. Implementing the copySelectedFiles function

```
...
function copySelectedFiles(files) {
    var promises = [];
    files.forEach(function (file) {;
        var promise = localFolder.createFileAsync(file.name,
            storage.CreationCollisionOption.replaceExisting)
            .then(function (newfile) {
                return file.copyAndReplaceAsync(newfile).then(function () {
                    App.processFile(newfile);
                });
            });
        promises.push(promise);
    });
    return WinJS.Promise.join(promises)
}
...
```

There are no new techniques in this function—you can read about the basic file operations in Chapter 22 and see how to use the Promise.join method in Chapter 9. The completed copySelectedFiles function copies all of the files that the user has selected from the data package to the local app data folder and returns a Promise that is fulfilled only when all of the copy operations are complete (which I do to ensure that I don't call the ShareOperation methods until I know I am done with the contents of the data package).

There are two reasons I copy the files instead of using the locations I receive in the data package. The first is that it makes it easier for me to ensure that the new additions to the album are reflected if there is another instance of the example app running. This is the same problem I faced when implementing the app-to-app picker contract in Chapter 24 and I have solved it the same way—by copying the files I am working with into a location that is being monitored for new files by the PhotoAlbum app. I admit that this is a bit of a hack, but there are very few occasions when Windows creates two instances of your app simultaneously and, try as I might, I have been unable to find a better way to communicate between them. The second reason I copy the files is that I don't know what the share source app intends to do with them when the share operation is over. I need to make a copy to ensure that the images are available to the user.

Testing the Share Target Implementation

The implementation of the share target contract is complete and you can now share image files with the PhotoAlbum app. You already know how to do that with the ShareHelper app, but one of the nice things about the sharing contract is that you can receive a compatible data package from any app. To that end, go to the desktop and use the File Explorer to locate an image file that is outside of the Pictures library.

Right-click on the file, select Open with from the popup menu, and pick Photos from the list (this is the default image viewer app included with Windows 8, and selecting it from the desktop means that you don't have to worry about the default app for the image file type, which may well be the PhotoAlbum app if you followed the examples in Chapter 24).

Activate the sharing charm and select Photo Album from the list of target apps. You will see the layout from the shareTargetView.html file shown in Figure 25-10. Click the Add All button and start the PhotoAlbum app—you will see the image you shared displayed.

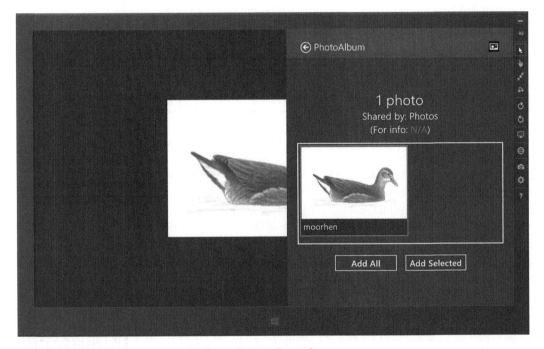

Figure 25-10. Sharing an image file from the Windows Photos app

There is one final point to note before I move on. The reason I asked you to locate an image file outside of the Pictures library is that I wanted to demonstrate the way that packaging up StorageFile objects transfers implied permission to access those files to the target app. Everything just works the way it should—you don't have to worry about ensuring that the target app has been granted permission to read the folder that contains the file, for example.

Of course, with that implied permission is the implied trust that you won't do something unexpected with the data. And you should be sure not to delete or modify the original file without getting explicit permission from the user.

Creating a Quick Link

A *quick link* is a preconfigured action that allows the user to perform a streamlined sharing action using details or decisions that they made previously. In my PhotoAlbum app, I asked the user to pick the images in the data package they want to copy and import. Forcing the user to make the same decision every time they share files with the PhotoAlbum is repetitive and annoying, especially since there is a good chance that they already took the time to pick the images they wanted in the share source app.

To streamline my app, I am going to create a quick link that allows the user to import all of the files without having to interact with my app layout at all. There are two stages to working with quick links— creating them and receiving them—and I'll show you both in the sections that follow.

Creating a Quick Link

You create a quick link by passing a QuickLink object, which can be found in the Windows. ApplicationModel.DataTransfer.ShareTarget namespace, to the ShareOperation.reportCompleted method. You configure the QuickLink object so that it contains all of the information your app needs to repeat the sharing operation that the user has just performed. The QuickLink object defines the properties shown in Table 25-10.

Table 25-10. Properties Defined by the QuickLink Object

Name	Description
id	A value that your app will use to recognize the operation that the user wants to repeat
supportedDataFormats	An array of the data formats that the repeatable operation supports
supportedFileTypes	An array of the file types that the repeatable operation supports
thumbnail	A thumbnail that will be displayed alongside the quick link when it is presented to the user. This property must be set to a stream object, and you can see how this is done in Listing 25-14.
title	The title that will be shown to the user to identify the quick link

You can see how I have created a QuickLink for the PhotoAlbum app in Listing 25-14, which shows the changes I have made to the ready function in the shareTargetView.html file.

Listing 25-14. Creating a quick link at the end of a share operation

```
...
WinJS.Utilities.query("button.addButton").listen("click", function (e) {

    if (this.id == "addAll") {
        shareListView.winControl.selection.selectAll();
    }
    var filesToProcess = [];
    shareListView.winControl.selection.getItems()
        .then(function (items) {
            items.forEach(function (item) {
                filesToProcess.push(item.data.file);
            });
        });
```

```
copySelectedFiles(filesToProcess).then(function () {
    shareOperation.reportDataRetrieved();

    if (e.target.id == "addAll") {
        var qlink = new share.ShareTarget.QuickLink();
        qlink.id = "all";
        qlink.supportedFileTypes.replaceAll([".png", ".jpg"]);
        qlink.title = "Add all files";
        qlink.thumbnail = storage.Streams.RandomAccessStreamReference.
            createFromUri(Windows.Foundation.Uri("ms-appx:///images/logo.png"));
        shareOperation.reportCompleted(qlink);

    } else {
        shareOperation.reportCompleted();
    }
});
});
...
```

I want to create a quick link only if the user has picked all of the images from the data package because there is no way in which I can usefully repeat picking individual images in the future. Other kinds of apps could sensibly offer a range of quick links—if you were writing an e-mail app, for example, you might create QuickLink objects so that the user could quickly send e-mails to previous recipients.

You can see the effect of these changes, but it takes a moment to do so. Start the PhotoAlbum app (to make sure the latest version is running). Then start the ShareHelper app, select images using the ListView control, activate the Share Charm, and select PhotoAlbum from the list. Click on the Add All button.

Remaining within the ShareHelper app, activate the Share Charm again and you will see a new item on the share flyout, as shown in Figure 25-11. This is the quick link and, in the case of the example, it allows the user to add all of the files they selected for sharing in a single step. I haven't added the code to the PhotoAlbum app to process the quick link yet—I'll do that in the next section—but the figure shows you how the quick link is presented to the user.

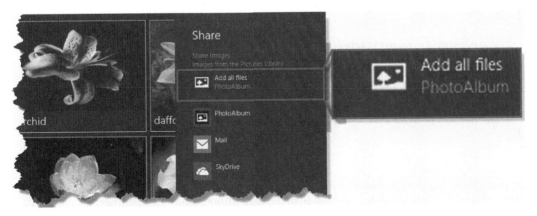

Figure 25-11. A quick link added to the share flyout

Just to recap, quick links are used to allow the user to repeat share operations that are performed frequently. This is why I had you activate the Share Charm twice: the first time defined the operation that was shown as the quick link the second time.

Picking the quick link just loads the standard share target layout at the moment, but in the next section I'll show you how to recognize when your quick link has been picked so that you can streamline the share operation.

Receiving a Quick Link

You can determine if the user has picked one of your quick links by reading the ShareOperation.quickLinkId property when your app is activated. The value that this property returns is the value you assigned to the QuickLink.id property, allowing you to determine which share operation the user wants to repeat. My example app only has one quick link id—all—and you can see how I respond to it being picked by the user in Listing 25-15.

Listing 25-15. Detecting when a quick link has been picked by the user

```
...
ready: function (element, shareOperation) {

    processPackage(shareOperation.data).then(function (list) {
        if (list.length == 0) {
            shareOperation.reportError("No images files were shared");
            return;
        } else if (shareOperation.quickLinkId == "all") {
            shareOperation.reportStarted();
            var files = [];
            list.forEach(function (listItem) {
                files.push(listItem.file);
            });
            copySelectedFiles(files).then(function () {
                shareOperation.reportDataRetrieved();
                shareOperation.reportCompleted();
            });
        } else {

            shareOperation.reportStarted();

            shareListView.winControl.itemDataSource = list.dataSource;
            WinJS.Utilities.query("button.addButton").listen("click", function (e) {
                // ...statements removed for brevity...
            });
        }
    });
}
...
```

When the user picks the quick link, I process all of the files without prompting the user for any input. The result is a simplified sharing operation that doesn't even present the user with an interface—the files are just seamlessly added to the photo album.

Summary

In this chapter, I showed you how to implement the two parts of the sharing contract, allowing you to enable the smooth flow of data from one app to another. The share source app is responsible for packaging up data and making it available to Windows, which acts as a broker to find suitable share target apps that can process the shared data. Sharing is one of the key Windows interactions and I encourage you to add it to your app—and to do so in such a way that you support the widest range of data formats and file types. The more opportunities you give to the user to share in your app, the more deeply your app will become embedded in their workflows.

In the next chapter, I demonstrate some of the other contracts that Windows 8 supports.

CHAPTER 26

■ ■ ■

The AutoPlay, Protocol Activation and Print Contracts

In this chapter, I show you how to implement another three contracts that you can use to more tightly integrate your apps into Windows: the AutoPlay contract, the Protocol Activation contract, and the Print contract. Table 26-1 provides the summary for this chapter.

Table 26-1. Chapter Summary

Problem	Solution	Listing
Respond to removable storage	Declare support for the AutoPlay contract and respond to the activated event	26-1–26-2
Add support for protocol activation	Declare support for the Protocol Activation contract and respond to the activated event	26-3–26-4
Add support for printing	Handle the printtaskrequested event emitted by the PrintManager object	26-5–26-8
Customize content for printing	Use the CSS media query feature or use JavaScript to adapt the existing app layout	26-9–26-11
Create print-specific content	Respond to the printtaskrequested event by loading new content using the Navigation API	26-12–26-13

Revisiting the Example App

For this chapter, I am going to continue using the PhotoAlbum app that I created in Chapter 24 and extended in Chapter 25. As a reminder, the basic functionality of this app lets the user pick image files to be displayed in a simple album (which is just a series of thumbnail images displayed in WinJS.UI.ListView control).

I built on this foundation to implement the file activation, save picker and open picker, and sharing contracts, showing the different ways that an app can integrate into the operating system—a theme I'll continue in this chapter by adding support for more contracts. As a reminder, Figure 26-1 shows you what the PhotoAlbum looks like when displaying images.

Figure 26-1. The PhotoAlbum example app

■ **Note**   Once again, I am not going to relist the code and markup for the example because you can find them in Chapter 24 or download the project as part of the source code pack from Apress.com.

Implementing the AutoPlay Contract

The AutoPlay contract allows your app to respond automatically when new storage is attached to the Windows 8 device. AutoPlay has fallen out of favor in recent years because it has been used as a means to infect PCs with malware, but has been revamped for Windows 8 and is likely to be used more widely, especially on slate/tablet devices where users favor simplicity over security (in general, I have found that users will favor pretty much *anything* over security, given the chance).

Like all contracts, implementing AutoPlay is optional, but is worthwhile, especially if your app deals with media files in any way. As you'll see, the AutoPlay contract builds on the File Activation contract I showed you in Chapter 24 and only a little additional effort is required once you have the file activation implementation in place.

Updating the Manifest

There are two manifest changes required for the AutoPlay contract. First, I need to declare that my app wants access to removable storage. To do this, open the package.appxmanifest file from the Visual Studio Solution Explorer window, click the Capabilities tab, and check the Removable Storage item in the capabilities list, as shown in Figure 26-2.

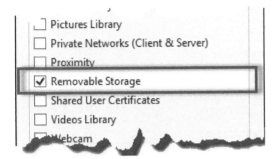

Figure 26-2.Eenabling the Removable Storage capability in the app manifest

In addition, I must also tell Windows how my app wants to be integrated into the AutoPlay feature, which requires moving to the Declarations tab of the manifest.

Select AutoPlay Content from the Available Declarations list and click the Add button. Fill in the properties section to match Figure 26-3, clicking the Add New button to create new Launch action sections.

Properties:

Launch actions ───

Launch action		Remove
Verb:	addpictures	
Action display name:	Add to Photo Album	
Content event:	ShowPicturesOnArrival	

Launch action		Remove
Verb:	addmixed	
Action display name:	Add to Photo Album	
Content event:	MixedContentOnArrival	

Launch action		Remove
Verb:	addstorage	
Action display name:	Add to Photo Album	
Content event:	StorageOnArrival	

Add New

Figure 26-3. Declaring support for the AutoPlay contract

It can be hard to read text in images, so I have listed the required values for the manifest form fields in Table 26-2.

Table 26-2. Settings for the AutoPlay Declaration of the Example App

Verb	Action Display Name	Content Event
addpictures	Add to Photo Album	ShowPicturesOnArrival
addmixed	Add to Photo Album	MixedContentOnArrival
addstorage	Add to Photo Album	StorageOnArrival

The Content event value is the name of the Windows event you want your app to be notified about. For my example, I am interested in the ShowPicturesOnArrival, MixedContentOnArrival, and StorageOnArrival events. These are *not* JavaScript events and the entries in the declaration act as the mapping between the internals of Windows and your app—I'll show you how these events are presented to your app shortly. Make sure that you capitalize the event names as I have shown—your contract implementation will fail if you adopt the JavaScript all-lowercase convention. Table 26-3 contains a list of the most commonly encountered Windows AutoPlay events.

Table 26-3. Windows AutoPlay Events

Name	Description
WPD\ImageSource	Triggered when the user connects a camera to the device
WPD\AudioSource	Triggered when the user connects a music player to the device
WPD\VideoSource	Triggered when the user connects a video camera to the device
StorageOnArrival	Triggered when a new drive or storage device is connected
ShowPicturesOnArrival	Triggered when the user connects a storage device that has a DCIM, AVCHD, or PRIVATE\ACHD folder. This is commonly the case when connecting storage that has been removed from a camera (as opposed to connecting the camera directly). Also triggered when the user has configured AutoPlay to respond to individual media types and the connected device contains image files
PlayMusicFilesOnArrival	Triggered when the user has configured AutoPlay to respond to individual media types and the connected device contains music files
PlayVideoFilesOnArrival	Triggered when the user *has configured AutoPlay to respond to individual media types and the connected device contai*ns video files
MixedContentOnArrival	Triggered when the user has configured AutoPlay to respond to individual media types but no specific content type is found

It takes some playing around with Windows to figure out the circumstances in which each kind of event is triggered. I find it easier to register interest in a wide range of events, which is why I have created declarations for each of the events I can expect if the user attaches a storage device that contains images.

The verb value is an app-specific string that you will use to identify the Windows event. My example app can only add files to the album, which is why my verbs are addpictures, addmixed, and addstorage and why the Action Display Name, which is the description given to the user of the action that the app will perform by AutoPlay, is set to Add to Photo Album in every case. A more sophisticated app might present multiple actions for each event—offering, for example, to play, copy, print, or compress the files on the storage device.

Responding to the Activation Event

The detail.kind property of the activation event for the AutoPlay contract is set to ActivationKind.file. This is the same value that is used for the file association contract. You differentiate between the contracts that the event relates to by reading the value of the detail.verb property, which will be set to open for file association and to the value you assigned to the verb field of the manifest declaration for AutoPlay. For my example, this means that I can expect the verb property to be open for file association and addpictures, addmixed, or addstorage for the AutoPlay contract, depending on which Windows event was triggered.

To respond to the AutoPlay verb values, I have made the changes to the PhotoAlbum default.js file shown in Listing 26-1.

Listing 26-1. Updating the default.js file to support AutoPlay

```
(function () {

    var app = WinJS.Application;
    var activation = Windows.ApplicationModel.Activation;
    var appstate = activation.ApplicationExecutionState;
    var storage = Windows.Storage;

    var query = storage.ApplicationData.current.localFolder.createFolderQuery();
    query.addEventListener("contentschanged", function () {
        App.loadFilesFromCache();
    });
    query.getFoldersAsync();

    app.onactivated = function (args) {
        if (args.detail.previousExecutionState != appstate.suspended) {
            args.setPromise(WinJS.UI.processAll().then(function () {

                if (ViewModel.fileList.length == 0) {
                    App.loadFilesFromCache();
                }

                switch (args.detail.kind) {
                    case activation.ActivationKind.fileOpenPicker:
                        var pickerUI = args.detail.fileOpenPickerUI;
                        WinJS.Navigation.navigate("/pages/openPickerView.html",
                            pickerUI);
                        break;
                    case activation.ActivationKind.fileSavePicker:
                        var pickerUI = args.detail.fileSavePickerUI;
                        WinJS.Navigation.navigate("/pages/savePickerView.html",
                            pickerUI);
                        break;
                    case activation.ActivationKind.file:
                        switch (args.detail.verb) {
                            case 'addpictures':
                            case 'addmixed':
                            case 'addstorage':
                                WinJS.Navigation.navigate("/pages/autoplayView.html",
```

```
                                args.detail.files);
                            break;
                        case 'open':
                            args.detail.files.forEach(function (file) {
                                App.processFile(file);
                            });
                            WinJS.Navigation.navigate("/pages/albumView.html");
                            break;
                    }
                    break;
                default:
                    WinJS.Navigation.navigate("/pages/albumView.html");
                    break;
                }
            }));
        }
    };
    app.start();
})();
```

When dealing with a file activation event, I now look at the value of the verb event property. If the value is open, I know I am dealing with the file association contract and I call the App.processFile function for every file contained in the array from the detail.files property, just as I did in the previous chapter.

When I get one of the other verb values, I know I am dealing with the AutoPlay contract and I respond by navigating to a new content page I have added to the project pages folder called autoPlayView.html. When calling the WinJS.Navigation.navigate method, I pass the value of the detail.files property so that I can use it in the content file (you can learn more about this technique in Chapter 7). You can see the contents of the autoPlayView.html file in Listing 26-2.

Listing 26-2. The contents of the autoPlayView.html file

```
<!DOCTYPE html>
<html>
<head>
    <title></title>
    <style>
        #apListView { width: 75%; height: 275px;}
        #addButton { font-size: 20pt; margin-top: 10px;}
    </style>
    <script>
        var storage = Windows.Storage;
        var provider = Windows.Storage.Pickers.Provider;
        var localFolder = storage.ApplicationData.current.localFolder;

        WinJS.UI.Pages.define("/pages/autoPlayView.html", {
            ready: function (element, folders) {

                var list = new WinJS.Binding.List();
                apListView.winControl.itemDataSource = list.dataSource;

                var addFile = function (file) {
```

```
                    list.push({
                        img: URL.createObjectURL(file),
                        title: file.displayName,
                        file: file
                    });
                };

                folders.forEach(function (folder) {
                    folder.getFilesAsync(storage.Search.CommonFileQuery.orderByName)
                        .then(function (files) {
                            files.forEach(addFile);
                        });
                });

                addButton.addEventListener("click", function (e) {
                    apListView.winControl.selection.getItems().then(function (items) {
                        items.forEach(function (item) {
                            localFolder.createFileAsync(item.data.file.name,
                                storage.CreationCollisionOption.replaceExisting)
                                .then(function (newfile) {
                                    item.data.file.copyAndReplaceAsync(newfile)
                                        .then(function () {
                                            App.processFile(newfile);
                                        });
                                });
                        });
                    });
                    WinJS.Navigation.navigate("/pages/albumView.html");
                });
            }
        });
    </script>
</head>
<body>
    <div class="title">Select images to add to the album</div>
    <div id="apListView" data-win-control="WinJS.UI.ListView"
        data-win-options="{
            itemTemplate: imageTemplate,
            tapBehavior: WinJS.UI.TapBehavior.directSelect,
            maxRows: 1
        }">
    </div>
    <button id="addButton">Add Selected Images</button>
</body>
</html>
```

The layout presented by this file is based around a ListView control in which I display the images that I find on the storage device, allowing the user to select the ones that should be imported to the photo album. There is also a button, which the user clicks to signify that they have picked the files they want.

■ **Note**   I could have used a standard open file picker to let the user select the files they want to import from the storage device, but there is no way to disable the picker navigation controls. This means that the user can navigate away from the storage device and pick files from anywhere. This isn't always a problem for all apps, but I want to constrain the user's choice for this example, which is why I have used a custom layout.

The code in this file is a recitation of the techniques I used in previous chapters with a few tweaks to suit the AutoPlay contract. The value of the detail.files property from the activation event is passed as the folders parameter to the ready function—I changed the name because the array that the detail.files property returns actually contains StorageFolder objects when the event is triggered for the AutoPlay contract. There is usually just one folder and it is the root of the removable storage device. I process all of the items in the array, just as a precaution for removable devices that behave differently (Microsoft is maddeningly vague on whether multiple folders will ever be sent to the app.)

To be safe, I query each folder in the array and build up details of the files I find in a WinJS.Binding.List object, which I use as the data source for the ListView control. I don't want to mix the contents of the storage device with the rest of the images in the app at this point, which is why I define the List locally to this file, rather than using the one in the view model.

■ **Tip**   Windows will filter the files that are returned from the query so only those that match the AutoPlay manifest declarations are included in the results.

I get the selected ListView items when the user clicks the Add Selected Images button and copy the files into the local app data folder. Copying the files allows me to show the images as part of the album, even when the AutoPlay storage device has been disconnected or removed.

Once the file operations are under way, I navigate to the /pages/albumView.html file so that the user can see the effect of their additions.

Testing the Contract Implementation

Now that you have seen how I implemented the contract, it is time to see it in action. First, start the app so that the latest version is installed on the Windows device. The app doesn't need to be running to deal with AutoPlay events, so you can stop or terminate the app at this point if you wish.

The next step is to prepare the Windows 8 machine. This isn't a step that the user will take, but I want to demonstrate a particular effect. Open the AutoPlay control panel, and ensure that the Use AutoPlay for all media and devices option is checked and that the option for Removable drive is set to Ask me every time, as shown in Figure 26-4.

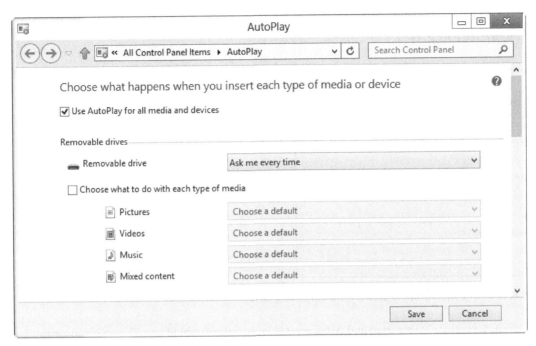

Figure 26-4. Configuring AutoPlay to test the contract implementation

Next, insert some removable storage that contains a JPG or PNG file, such as a USB stick or a memory card from a camera. I used a USB stick for my testing, but pretty much any removable storage device will do. You will see a toast message pop-up, just like the one shown in Figure 26-5.

Figure 26-5. The AutoPlay toast

Click on the toast to tell Windows what action you want to perform on the storage device. Windows will present a set of options like the ones shown in Figure 26-6. You may see different options depending on the apps you have installed. I have highlighted the action you should select, which shows the example app and the message I specified in the manifest earlier.

Figure 26-6. *Selecting the AutoPlay action for a removable drive*

Click the Add to Photo Album item and Windows will launch the example app. The activation event will load the autoPlayView.html file as the layout, the storage device will be queried for file contents, and the image files that are found are presented to the user in the ListView control, as shown in Figure 26-7.

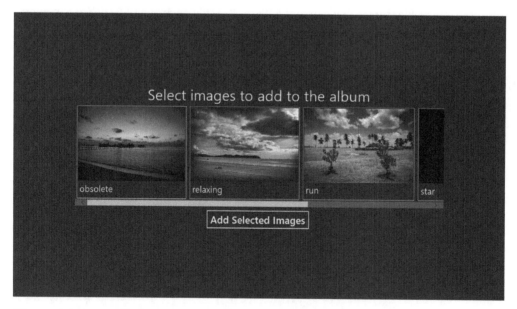

Figure 26-7. *Responding to AutoPlay events by presenting the images found on the removable storage device*

Selecting images and clicking the Add Selected Images button will copy the images to the local app data folder and switch the layout to the pages/albumView.html file.

Hints for Testing

Plugging and unplugging storage devices can become a tedious process when you are testing your implementation of the AutoPlay contract. There are a couple things you can do to make the process simpler. The first is to change the setting in the AutoPlay control panel for the kind of device that you are working with, as shown in Figure 26-8. You can see that the example app is included in the list of apps that can be selected as the default to be used when a new storage device is attached.

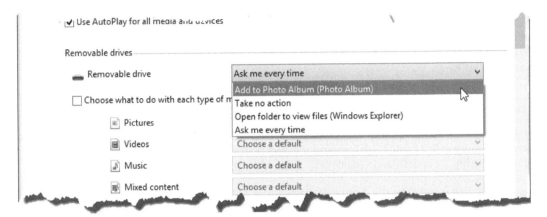

Figure 26-8. Setting the example app as the default AutoPlay action for removable drives

You can avoid having to deal with the hardware entirely by plugging it in once and then using File Explorer to trigger the AutoPlay action each time you want to test. Right-click on the device in the File Explorer window and select Open AutoPlay from the pop-up menu, as shown in Figure 26-9.

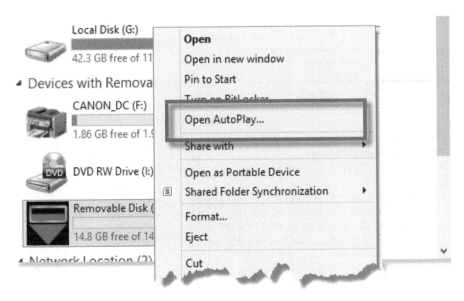

Figure 26-9. Triggering the AutoPlay action without removing and attaching the storage device

693

These techniques make testing AutoPlay contract implementation a much more pleasant experience, especially if you are handling a wide range of different events and verbs.

Implementing the Protocol Activation Contract

The protocol activation contract lets your app handle standard URL protocols, such as `mailto`, which is used to start the process of creating and sending an e-mail. This contract can also be used to handle custom protocols, which can be used to perform basic communication between apps or to hand off a task between your website and a Windows app (you embed a link with a specific protocol in the web page that activates the app when the user clicks on the link).

In this section, I am going to demonstrate how to handle a custom protocol and use it to pass data from one app to another.

Creating the Helper App

First, I need to create the helper app that will present the user with the link that uses my custom protocol. I have created a new app called `ProtocolHelper` and this app is so simple that everything—the HTML, the CSS, and the JavaScript—is contained in the `default.html` file, which is shown in Listing 26-3.

Listing 26-3. The default.html file from the ProtocolHelper app

```
<!DOCTYPE html>
<html>
<head>
    <meta charset="utf-8" />
    <title>ProtocolHelper</title>
    <link href="//Microsoft.WinJS.1.0/css/ui-dark.css" rel="stylesheet" />
    <script src="//Microsoft.WinJS.1.0/js/base.js"></script>
    <script src="//Microsoft.WinJS.1.0/js/ui.js"></script>
    <style type="text/css">
        body { display: -ms-flexbox; -ms-flex-direction: column;
            -ms-flex-align: center; -ms-flex-pack: center}
        body > * { margin: 20px; width: 60%}
        #linkElem { display: block; font-size: 30pt;
            text-align: center; color: white;}
    </style>
    <script>
        var storage = Windows.Storage;
        storage.KnownFolders.picturesLibrary
            .getFilesAsync(storage.Search.CommonFileQuery.orderByName)
            .then(function (files) {
                files[0].getThumbnailAsync(storage.FileProperties.
                    ThumbnailMode.singleItem, 500).then(function (thumb) {
                    imgElem.src = URL.createObjectURL(thumb);
                    linkElem.href = "photoalbum:" + files[0].path;
                });
            });
    </script>
</head>
```

```
<body>
    <img id="imgElem" />
    <a id="linkElem">Protocol Link</a>
</body>
</html>
```

This app performs a deep query of the Pictures library and displays a thumbnail of the first image that it finds. The layout also contains an a element, whose href attribute contains a URL with a custom protocol, as follows:

```
<a id="linkElem" href="photoalbum:C:\Users\adam\Pictures\flowers\astor.jpg">Protocol Link</a>
```

The protocol is set to photoalbum and the rest of the URL contains the path of the file that the helper app has located and displayed. You can see how the helper app appears when it is run in Figure 26-10.

■ **Note**   To ensure that the helper app can find the file, you will need to check the Pictures Library capability in the manifest.

Figure 26-10. The layout of the ProtocolHelper app

Clicking on the Protocol Link will cause Windows to look for an app that can handle the custom protocol. There is no such app at the moment, of course, so you will see a message like the one shown in Figure 26-11. In the next section, I'll show you how to add protocol activation support in the PhotoAlbum app.

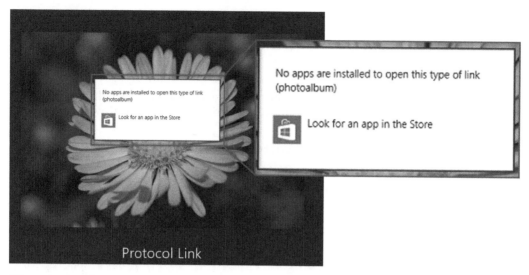

Figure 26-11. The message displayed when there is no app to handle a URL protocol

Adding Protocol Activation Support

Now that I have an app that contains a link with the photoalbum protocol, I can turn back to the PhotoAlbum app and add support for handling that protocol, which means that when you click on the link in the helper app, PhotoAlbum will be activated and given the task of figuring out what to do.

Adding the Manifest Declaration

The first step is to update the manifest. Open the package.appxmanifest file from the Visual Studio Solution Explorer window and navigate to the Declarations tab. Select Protocol from the Available Declarations list and click Add. Text fields will be displayed for you to enter the details of the protocol you want to support. Enter photoalbum into the Name field and type Control+S to save the changes to the manifest. (You can ignore the Logo and Display name fields for this example—they are used to differentiate between apps that can support the same protocol, which doesn't occur in this situation.) You can see the completed manifest section in Figure 26-12.

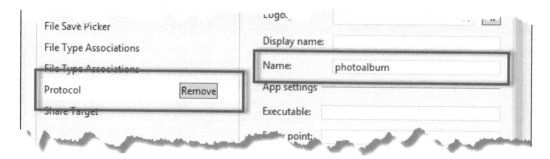

Figure 26-12. Declaring support for the protocol activation contract

Responding to the Activation Event

The detail.kind property of the activation event for protocol activation is set to ActivationKind.protocol.
You can see how I have responded to this event in the PhotoAlbum default.js file in Listing 26-4.

Listing 26-4. Responding to the protocol activation event

```
(function () {

    var app = WinJS.Application;
    var activation = Windows.ApplicationModel.Activation;
    var appstate = activation.ApplicationExecutionState;
    var storage = Windows.Storage;

    var query = storage.ApplicationData.current.localFolder.createFolderQuery();
    query.addEventListener("contentchanged", function () {
        App.loadFilesFromCache();
    });
    query.getFoldersAsync();

    app.onactivated = function (args) {
        if (args.detail.previousExecutionState != appstate.suspended) {
            args.setPromise(WinJS.UI.processAll().then(function () {

                if (ViewModel.fileList.length == 0) {
                    App.loadFilesFromCache();
                }

                switch (args.detail.kind) {
                    case activation.ActivationKind.protocol:
                        if (args.detail.uri.schemeName == "photoalbum") {
                            var path = args.detail.uri.path;
                            storage.StorageFile.getFileFromPathAsync(path)
                                .then(function (file) {
                                    App.processFile(file);
                                });
                        }
                        break;
                    // ...statements removed for brevity...
                    default:
                        WinJS.Navigation.navigate("/pages/albumView.html");
                        break;
                }
            }));
        }
    };
    app.start();
})();
```

The detail.uri property of the activation event returns a Windows.Foundation.Uri object. I use the
schemeName property to work out which protocol my app has been activated for and use the path property

697

to get the path component of the URL, which in this example is the path of the file that the `ProtocolHelper` app located in the `Pictures` library. The `Windows.Foundation.Uri` object has a number of useful properties in addition to `schemeName` and `path` and I have listed them in Table 26-4, along with the value that they would return if the URL in use was `http://www.apress.com/books/index.html` (an invented but useful URL to demonstrate).

Table 26-4. Properties Defined by the Windows.Foundation.Uri Object

Name	Description	Example
absoluteUri	The entire URL	`"http://www.apress.com/books/index.html"`
displayUri	A version of the URL that can be displayed to the user	`"http://www.apress.com/books/index.html"`
domain	The domain name from the URL	`apress.com`
extension	The file name extension	`.html`
fragment	The fragment identifier	There is no fragment in the example URL
host	The URL host	`www.apress.com`
path	The URL path	`/books/index.html`
port	The IP port	`80`
query	The URL query element	There is no query in the example URL
schemeName	The protocol name	`http`

Putting everything together, you can see that I respond to activation by the `photoalbum` protocol by using the `path` component of the URL to get a `StorageFile` object by calling the `StorageFile.getFileFromPathAsync` method. I then pass the `StorageFile` to the `App.processFile` method, which adds the file to the photo library.

Declaring the Capability

There is one more step: declaring in the `PhotoAlbum` manifest that the app requires access to the `Pictures` library.

This isn't a requirement of protocol activation, but it is needed to make my app work the way I want it to. The strength of protocol activation is that it is quick and simple to implement and there are already a lot of useful protocols defined, such as `mailto`.

The downside is that there is no transfer of trust or manifest declarations between apps, which means that protocol activation is best suited to simple data or when you are confident that both apps have the same access to the device. For my example, this means that the `PhotoAlbum` app needs to be able to access the file that is sent as part of the protocol activation process, meaning access is needed to the `Pictures` library (because, as you will remember, the `ProtocolHelper` app, the cause of the activation event, finds and displays the first image in the `Pictures` library location).

Open the `package.appxmanfest` file in Visual Studio, navigate to the `Capabilities` tab, and check the `Pictures Library Access` capability. For a more sophisticated approach, you will need to use the *sharing contract*, which I described in Chapter 25.

Testing the Contract Implementation

To test support for the protocol activation contract, start the `PhotoAlbum` app so that the latest changes are installed on your device. As with many of the other contracts, the app doesn't have to be running for the contract to work, but the process of starting the app within Visual Studio forces Windows to process the manifest and register the app's support for the contract. You can terminate the PhotoAlbum app at this point if you want and the test will still work.

Next, start the ProtocolHelper app and click the Protocol Link anchor element. Windows will send the PhotoAlbum app the protocol activation event, which will have the effect of passing the path of a file from one app to the other, resulting in the image being added to the album.

Implementing the Printing Contract

The ability to print content from your app is important, even though users print less often and view and read more content on screens than just a few years ago. It can be tempting to assume that your users won't need to print and to skip this contract, but in making that decision you are forcing the user to consume your content in a particular way and ignoring their preferences.

I find working with printers a painful business—although it is relatively easy to handle in Windows apps—but whenever I am thinking of skipping support for printing, I remind myself of my book sales figures. There is a better than 50% chance that you are reading this chapter in a printed copy of this book. There are endless reasons you might prefer a printed copy—perhaps you like to read on the train while you commute, you like to have the book open so you can follow the examples as you code on screen, or you like to buy one copy and share it with your team. Whatever the reason, Apress doesn't ignore your preferences by making you buy an e-book and, similarly, you shouldn't ignore your users' preferences by skipping on the ability to print. In this section, I'll explain how the Windows support for printing works by adding support for printing images from the PhotoAlbum example app.

Printing from a Windows app is based around sending the app's current layout to the printer, which means that it is simple to get basic printing working, but that more effort is required to produce something useful. I'll start by showing you the basic printing mechanism and then show you how to create content that is used just for printing.

■ **Note**   You will, as you might expect, need a printer to follow this section of the chapter. You don't have to actually print anything, but you need to have a device that Windows recognizes as a printer so that it appears in the Devices Charm.

Implementing Basic Printing

The printing contract doesn't require a manifest declaration. Instead, you register a function to handle the printtaskrequested event when it is emitted by the PrintManager object that can be found in the Windows. Graphics.Printing namespace. This event signals that the user has initiated a print request and you can prepare your app accordingly.

To demonstrate how the contract operates, I have added printing support to the albumView.html file, which is the content that PhotoAlbum app uses to display the images that it has catalogued. You can see the changes I have made in Listing 26-5, and I'll walk through the objects that I have used in the sections that follow.

■ **Note**   The new objects I introduce in this part of the chapter are all in the Windows.Graphics.Printing namespace unless otherwise indicated. I have aliased this namespace to print in the code examples.

Listing 26-5. Adding basic printing support to the albumView.html file

```
<!DOCTYPE html>
<html>
<head>
    <title></title>
    <script>
        var print = Windows.Graphics.Printing;

        WinJS.UI.Pages.define("/pages/albumView.html", {
            ready: function () {

                print.PrintManager.getForCurrentView()
                    .addEventListener("printtaskrequested", function (e) {

                        if (ViewModel.fileList.length > 0) {
                            var printTask = e.request.createPrintTask(
                                "PrintAlbum", function (printEvent) {
                                printEvent.setSource(
                                    MSApp.getHtmlPrintDocumentSource(document));
                                });
                            printTask.options.orientation =
                                print.PrintOrientation.landscape;
                        };
                    });

                WinJS.Utilities.query("button").listen("click", function (e) {
                    if (this.id == "openButton") {
                        App.pickFiles();
                    } else {
                        App.clearCache();
                    }
                });
            }
        });
    </script>
</head>
<body>
    <div id="listView" data-win-control="WinJS.UI.ListView"
        data-win-options="{
            itemTemplate: imageTemplate,
            itemDataSource: ViewModel.fileList.dataSource,
            tapBehavior: WinJS.UI.TapBehavior.directSelect
        }">
    </div>
    <div id="buttonContainer">
        <button id="openButton">Open</button>
        <button id="clearButton">Clear</button>
    </div>
</body>
</html>
```

When the printtaskrequested event is triggered, the handler function is passed an object whose request property returns a PrintTaskRequest. Your objective is to create and configure a PrintTask object, setting the content that will be printed and configuring the print process.

Creating the Print Task

You create a PrintTask object by calling the PrintTaskRequest.createPrintTask method. The arguments are a title for the task and a handler that will be invoked if the user goes ahead and selects the print task. This may seem duplicative, but it makes sense when you correlate the steps required to support the print contract. To see what I mean, start the PhotoAlbum app, bring up the Charm Bar and activate the Devices Charm (you can activate the charm directly using Win+K if you prefer).

When you activate the Devices Charm, Windows sends you the printtaskrequested event and this is your chance to decide if your app is able to print at the moment. You can see how I have handled this in Listing 26-6, where I have repeated part of the code from the printtaskrequested event handler.

Listing 26-6. Deciding whether to print when receiving the printtaskrequested event

```
...
print.PrintManager.getForCurrentView().addEventListener("printtaskrequested",
    function (e) {
        if (ViewModel.fileList.length > 0) {
            var printTask = e.request.createPrintTask("PrintAlbum",
                function (printEvent) {
                printEvent.setSource(MSApp.getHtmlPrintDocumentSource(document));
            });
            printTask.options.orientation = print.PrintOrientation.landscape;
        };
    });
...
```

If there are no images in the album, then I have nothing to print. So, when I get the printtaskrequested, I check to see if there are objects in the WinJS.Binding.List that I use to track the app's content and only call the createPrintTask method if there are images.

What you saw when you activated the Device Charm will have depended on how many images you previously added to the app. You can see the two different outcomes in Figure 26-13. The screen on the left of the figure shows the user the list of available printers and is shown when the app calls createPrintTask. The screen on the right of the figure shows the message presented to the user when no call to createPrintTask is made, indicating that there is nothing to print at the moment.

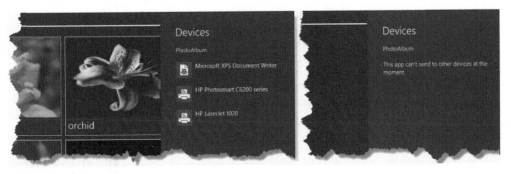

Figure 26-13. The effect of calling the createPrintTask method when receiving the printtaskrequested event

As you can see from the figure, I have a couple of old HP printers to choose from and, of course, what you see in the list will be different.

Configuring the Print Task

Once you have created the PrintTask object, you can configure it to present the user with sensible initial values for the print task. You do this through the PrintTask.options property, which returns a PrintTaskOptions object. There are a lot of options you can configure for the print task, but I am not going to list them here. First, many of them are pretty niche settings that most apps won't care about and second, the user can set them anyway at the next stage in the print process (which I'll get to shortly).

Instead, I have listed a sample of four of the configuration options in Table 26-5. Two of them are useful in a lot of situations and the other two illustrate the level of control that you can have over the print task.

Table 26-5. Commonly Used Configuration Properties of the PrintTaskOptions Object

Name	Description
numberOfCopies	Sets the number of copies for the print task
minCopies	Sets the fewest number of copies that can be printed
maxCopies	Sets the most copies that can be printed
orientation	Sets the orientation of the print task

Many of the configuration options take values that are defined by objects in the Windows.Graphics.Printing namespace. So, for example, the orientation property is set to one of the values defined by the PrintOrientation object, which you can see in Table 26-6.

Table 26-6. Values Defined by the PrintOrientation Object

Name	Description
default	The default orientation for the printer
portrait	The standard portrait orientation
landscape	The standard landscape orientation
portraitFlipped	The rotated portrait orientation
landscapeFlipped	The rotated landscape orientation

I don't want you to feel that I am needlessly skipping over this section. I want to get to the meat of the printing contract, which is preparing your app's content so that you get a good print result. There is so much detail you can set on a print task that I'd run out of room if I listed everything out full, and most of these settings are never used. Instead, you can see how I have applied one of the genuinely useful setting options in Listing 26-7, where I set the orientation of the print task.

Listing 26-7. Setting the orientation of the print task

```
...
print.PrintManager.getForCurrentView().addEventListener("printtaskrequested",
    function (e) {
        if (ViewModel.fileList.length > 0) {
            var printTask = e.request.createPrintTask("PrintAlbum",
```

```
            function (printEvent) {
                printEvent.setSource(MSApp.getHtmlPrintDocumentSource(document));
            }
        );
        printTask.options.orientation = print.PrintOrientation.landscape;
    };
});
...
```

■ **Note**   I am taking something of a shortcut here—something that I don't recommend in a real app. If you look at the values in Table 26-6, you will see that they correspond to the orientations I showed you in Chapter 6. As you see shortly, Windows app printing works by printing the layout of the app—this means that you will usually want to set the orientation of the print task to match the orientation of the device.

Specifying the Content to Print

When you create a PrintTask, you specify a function that will be called when the user selects a device from the Device Charm. That function is passed a PrintTaskSourceRequestedArgs object, which defines the setSource method.

The setSource method is used to specify the content that will be printed and for JavaScript Windows apps, this means that you must use the MSApp.getHtmlPrintDocumentSource method, as highlighted in Listing 26-8, where I have repeated the statements from the PhotoAlbum app.

Listing 26-8. Setting the print source

```
...
print.PrintManager.getForCurrentView().addEventListener("printtaskrequested",
    function (e) {
        if (ViewModel.fileList.length > 0) {
            var printTask = e.request.createPrintTask("PrintAlbum",
                function (printEvent) {
                    printEvent.setSource(MSApp.getHtmlPrintDocumentSource(document));
                }
            );
            printTask.options.orientation = print.PrintOrientation.landscape;
        };
    });
...
```

The getHtmlPrintDocumentSource method will only take a DOM Document object, which means that you are limited to printing the current content of the app or the content of an iframe element. That means that you have to be creative to print something useful for the document, which is a topic I'll return to shortly.

First, however, let us complete the printing process with the default content from the app. Start the app, ensure that there are some images in the album, and activate the Devices Charm. Clicking one of the printers in the list will trigger the function I passed to the createPrintTask method, which will set the source for the print task—Windows takes this information and presents it to the user, as I have shown in Figure 26-14.

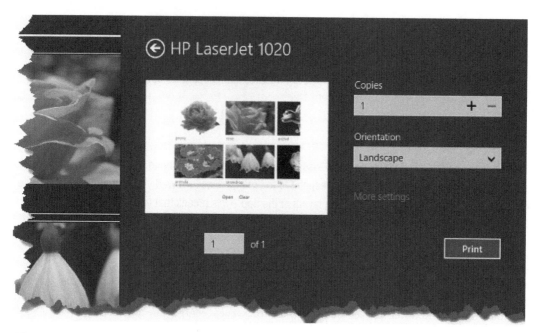

Figure 26-14. Finalizing the print task

Windows shows the user a preview of the content and the opportunity to change the settings for the print task (the More settings link allows the user to see and change the more arcane configuration options I mentioned earlier). If you go ahead and print this document, you'll end up with what's shown in Figure 26-15. (I captured this using a printer driver that saves images, which allows me to show you the results without having to print out to paper and then scan the page back in again.)

Figure 26-15. The print output

I added the border shown in this figure because one of the changes that Windows makes is to change the background color in the print task so that not all of the user's ink/toner is consumed printing the image.

That's the only change I made—otherwise, the print output matches the layout of the app at the moment the print task was created. This is good, because it means supporting basic printing in an app is simple, and bad, because it means that everything in the layout—including buttons and scrollbars—is sent to the printer. In the sections that follow I'll show you different techniques to take control of the content you send to the printer.

Manipulating the App Layout for Printing

The first approach to improving your printing results is to temporarily manipulate the layout of the app specifically for the print job. You can do this using CSS or, of course, JavaScript, and I show you both in this section of the chapter.

Using CSS to Manipulate the App Layout

A little-known, and event less often used, CSS feature is the ability to create styles that are applied only to certain types of media. This means that I can easily add a `style` element to my `albumView.html` document that changes the layout of the content when it is printed. You can see a simple example in Listing 26-9, where I have created a style that hides the Open and Clear buttons and performs some other minor layout tweaks for printing.

Listing 26-9. Using CSS to style elements when they are printed

```
...
<head>
    <style media="print">
        #buttonContainer { visibility: hidden }
        .listTitle { text-align: center; max-width: none;
            border: thin solid black; margin: 0px }
        .listImg { height: 180px; width: 270px }
    </style>
    <title></title>
    <script>
        // ...JavaScript statements removed for brevity...
    </script>
</head>
...
```

The key to this technique is to add the `media` attribute to the `style` element and set the value to `print`. This ensures that the styles are applied only when the layout is being printed, allowing you to tweak your app layout to improve the printing results. You can see the changes in Figure 26-16. (Once again, I have added a border to this figure.)

Figure 26-16. Using CSS to change the style of the layout for printing

As you can see in the figure, I have hidden the buttons and changed the formatting of the labels that are displayed for each image. The styles I have defined in this example apply relatively minor changes, but the effect can be as sweeping as you like.

Using JavaScript to Manipulate the App Layout

You make more profound changes by using JavaScript to change the layout of the app, although it requires more effort than using CSS. In particular, you need to take into account the way that some UI controls, including the ListView that I am using in the example app, rely on data sources that communicate changes to the UI control using events. As a demonstration, I have modified the PhotoAlbum app so that at most two images per row are printed, avoiding the issue you can see in Figure 26-16 where the third image in each row is only partially visible. To start with, I have created a new function, called adaptLayout, in the js/app. js file that toggles the number of elements in the WinJS.Binding.List object that is the data source for the ListView UI control. You can see this function in Listing 26-10.

Listing 26-10. The adaptLayout function in the app.js file

```
(function () {

var storage = Windows.Storage;
var access = storage.AccessCache;
var cache = access.StorageApplicationPermissions.futureAccessList;
var pickers = storage.Pickers;

var dataCache = [];

WinJS.Namespace.define("App", {

    adaptLayout: function (prepareForPrint) {
        var flist = ViewModel.fileList;
```

```
        if (prepareForPrint == true) {
            dataCache = flist.splice(4, flist.length -4);
        } else {
            dataCache.forEach(function (item) {
                flist.push(item);
            });
            dataCache.length = 0;
        }
    },
    // ...other functions removed for brevity...
});

})();
```

If this function is called with `true` as the argument, the number of items in the `List` is reduced to four. The items are removed when the function is called again with an argument of `false`, restoring the layout to its previous state.

I have also updated the `script` element in the `albumView.html` file to use this function for printing, as shown in Listing 26-11.

Listing 26-11. Altering the printing layout using JavaScript

```
...
<script>
    var print = Windows.Graphics.Printing;

    WinJS.UI.Pages.define("/pages/albumView.html", {
        ready: function () {

        print.PrintManager.getForCurrentView()
            .addEventListener("printtaskrequested", function (e) {
                if (ViewModel.fileList.length > 0) {
                    var printTask = e.request.createPrintTask("PrintAlbum",
                        function (printEvent) {
                            var deferral = printEvent.getDeferral();
                            App.adaptLayout(true);
                                setImmediate(function() {
                                    printEvent.setSource(
                                        MSApp.getHtmlPrintDocumentSource(document));
                                    deferral.complete();
                            })
                        });
                    printTask.options.orientation = print.PrintOrientation.landscape;
                    printTask.addEventListener("completed", App.adaptLayout);
                };
            });

        WinJS.Utilities.query("button").listen("click", function (e) {
            if (this.id == "openButton") {
                App.pickFiles();
            } else {
```

```
                        App.clearCache();
                    }
                });
            }
        });
    </script>
    ...
```

I call the `App.adaptLayout` function when my `PrintTask` is activated by the user. The problem I have is that the `adaptLayout` function makes changes to the `List` object that communicates those changes with the `ListView` UI control using events. Those events will be executed after my function has been executed, which means that I need to delay passing my app layout to Windows with the `setSource` method until after those events are processed, which is why I use the `setImmediate` method (which defers the execution of work and which I described fully in Chapter 9):

```
...
var printTask = e.request.createPrintTask("PrintAlbum", function (printEvent) {
    var deferral = printEvent.getDeferral();
    App.adaptLayout(true);
    setImmediate(function() {
        printEvent.setSource(MSApp.getHtmlPrintDocumentSource(document));
        deferral.complete();
    })
})
...
```

Since I am deferring the call to the `setSource` method, I won't be able to give Windows the content to print before the execution of my function finishes. Fortunately, the `PrintTaskSourceRequestedArgs` object defined a `getDeferral` method that returns an object whose `complete` method I can call when I have set the content asynchronously. (You can learn more about deferrals in Chapter 19, where I explain their use with the life-cycle events.) The result is that I modify the contents of the `List` and then defer the call to the `setSource` method until after those changes are reflected in the `ListView` control.

Unlike the CSS technique, using JavaScript affects the layout of the app in a way that the user can see, which means that it is important to restore the layout to its original state when the print task is finished or canceled by the user. The `PrintTask` object defines some useful events, which I have described in Table 26-7, which can be used to track the printing progress.

Table 26-7. Events Defined by the PrintTask Object

Name	Description
completed	Triggered when the task is complete or canceled by the user
previewing	Triggered when the preview is displayed to the user
progressing	Triggered to provide detailed progress information as the task is performed
submitting	Triggered when the content is being sent to the printer

For the purposes of restoring the layout, I am interested in the `completed` event, which I respond to by calling the `App.adaptLayout` function. I have provided this function as an argument to the `addEventListener` method, which means that it will be passed the event object, which has the effect of restoring the layout (because any value other than Boolean true is taken as a request to restore the images to the `List`):

```
...
printTask.addEventListener("completed", App.adaptLayout);
...
```

You can see the result of these changes on the printed result in Figure 26-17.

Figure 26-17. Using JavaScript to change the layout of the app for printing

Creating Print-Specific Content

You can improve the print result you get by adapting the existing layout of the app, but to get complete control over the print process, you need to create content that will be used just for printing. To demonstrate this approach, I have added a new feature to the script element of the albumView.html file that displays print-specific content when the user selects a single item in the ListView control before activating the Devices Charm. You can see the changes that support this feature in Listing 26-12.

Listing 26-12. Adding support for print-specific content

```
...
<script>
    var print = Windows.Graphics.Printing;

    WinJS.UI.Pages.define("/pages/albumView.html", {
        ready: function () {

            print.PrintManager.getForCurrentView().onprinttaskrequested = function(e) {
                if (ViewModel.fileList.length > 0) {
                    var printTask = e.request.createPrintTask("PrintAlbum",
```

```
                function (printEvent) {
                var deferral = printEvent.getDeferral();

                listView.winControl.selection.getItems().then(function (items) {
                    if (items.length == 1) {
                        WinJS.Navigation.navigate("/pages/printView.html", {
                            event: printEvent,
                            deferral: deferral,
                            item: items[0]
                        });
                        printTask.addEventListener("completed", function () {
                            WinJS.Navigation.navigate("/pages/albumView.html");
                        });
                    } else {
                        App.adaptLayout(true);
                        setImmediate(function () {
                            printEvent.setSource(
                                MSApp.getHtmlPrintDocumentSource(document));
                            deferral.complete();
                        });
                        printTask.addEventListener("completed", App.adaptLayout);
                    }
                });
            });
            printTask.options.orientation = print.PrintOrientation.landscape;
        };
    };

    WinJS.Utilities.query("button").listen("click", function (e) {
        if (this.id == "openButton") {
            App.pickFiles();
        } else {
            App.clearCache();
        }
    });
    }
});
</script>
...
```

If one item has been selected in the ListView, then I call the Navigation API to display a new page I added to the pages folder called printView.html. I pass an object to the navigate method that contains references to the PrintTaskSourceRequestedArgs object, the object returned by the getDeferral method, and the item from the ListView data source that the user has selected. These details will be available to the ready function I define in the script element of the printView.html file, which you can see in Listing 26-13.

■ **Note**   I register a handler for the PrintTask.completed event that navigates the app back to the albumView. html page when the print task is completed or canceled. One side effect of this is that I have also had to change the way I register interest in the printtaskrequested event emitted by the PrintManager object. An exception is thrown if you try to add a second listener for the `printtaskrequested` event using the `addEventListener` method, and since the code in the `ready` function is executed when the app navigates back to the `albumView.html` file, I need to replace the existing listener by assigning a new function to the `onprinttaskrequested` property—this ensures that there is at most one listener and no exception is encountered.

Listing 26-13. The contents of the printView.html file

```
<!DOCTYPE html>
<html>
<head>
    <title></title>
    <style>
        #imgContainer.printContainer  { background-color: white;
            display: -ms-flexbox; -ms-flex-direction: column;
            -ms-flex-align: center; -ms-flex-pack: center;
            margin: 10px; padding: 10px; border: medium solid black;
            text-align: center; height: 90%;}
        .printContainer #imgElem {max-height: 90%;}
        .printContainer #imgTitle { font-size: 30pt; color: black; }
    </style>
    <script>
        WinJS.UI.Pages.define("/pages/printView.html", {
            ready: function (element, details) {

                imgElem.src = URL.createObjectURL(details.item.data.file);
                imgTitle.innerText = details.item.data.file.displayName;

                details.event.setSource(MSApp.getHtmlPrintDocumentSource(document));
                details.deferral.complete();
            }
        });
    </script>
</head>
<body>
    <div id="imgContainer" class="printContainer">
        <img id="imgElem" />
        <span id="imgTitle"></span>
    </div>
</body>
</html>
```

This file contains a very simple layout that displays the selected image, and its name. The code in the script element uses the selected item from the `ListView` data source to configure the elements in the layout and then calls the `setSource` method to provide Windows with the content to print. Finally, the complete method of the deferral object is called, indicating to Windows that the asynchronous task is complete and that the user can be shown the content preview. You can see the print result produced by this file in Figure 26-18.

Figure 26-18. Using dedicated content for printing

As you can see from the figure, a little additional effort allows you to create content that is specifically intended for printing and is free of the constraints that come from trying to adapt a layout that is intended mainly to be displayed on a screen.

Summary

In this chapter, I have shown you how to implement three more contracts: AutoPlay, Protocol Activation, and Printing. All three have their place in providing a first-class app experience and you should consider implementing all of them to more tightly integrate your apps into the wider Windows experience. In the next chapter, I show you how to take control of the tile that is created for your app on the Windows Start screen.

CHAPTER 27

■ ■ ■

Working with App Tiles

In Chapter 4, I showed you how to set the image that an app uses for its tile on the Windows Start screen. This is the basic action for tiles, but apps can go a lot further and create *live* tiles, which present useful information via the Start screen, even when the app isn't running. In this section, I'll show you how to create a live tile and the different ways that you can update it from your app.

There are two basic reasons to use live tiles: because you want the user to run your app more frequently or because you want the user to run your app less frequently. If you have an app that aims to attract users' attention, then you want to draw users' eyes to your app tile and remind them that you are there. This is true for games, for example, where you want to draw the users in and remind them that your game is more interesting or exciting than whatever it was that they intended to do via the Start menu instead. In these situations, you have a responsibility to create tiles that are attractive, but not distracting – something that is in your interest because Windows 8 allows the user to disable live tiles for apps that are annoying. Some of the early apps in the Windows Store had live tile designs that were so aggressive in their styling that I found myself moving the tiles so that I couldn't see them.

If you have an app that aims to improve the user's productivity or working life, then you want to use the tile to provide the user with a timely summary of key information so that they can easily get the critical facts *without* having to start your app, wait for initialization, navigate to the right section, and so on. In short, you help the users by giving them the information they need without launching your app. This requires some careful thought about what the user cares about and provides the means for the user to change the kind of information that is displayed on the tile.

For this kind of app, your responsibility is to create a tile whose contents are timely, obvious, and accurate, which means updating the tile when the app state is changed.

I think about live app tiles in the same way that I think about UI animations: they are a good thing when used sparingly, but they can quickly because annoying and distracting (and you should always provide a way to disable them). Don't misjudge the importance of your app to your user and don't turn their Start screen into a Vegas slot machine. Table 1 provides the summary for this chapter.

Table 1. Chapter Summary

Problem	Solution	Listing
Create a live tile notification	Select and populate a template and pass the content to Windows.	1-4
Select a tile template	Use one of the values defined by the `Windows.UI.Notifications.TileTemplateType` object.	5
Populate a basic tile template	Use the objects in the `Windows.Data.Xml.Dom` namespace to locate the text element in the template and set their content.	6

Problem	Solution	Listing
Update the tile	Create a `TileNotification` object from the populated XML template. Create a `TileUpdater` object and pass the `TileNotification` to the update method.	7
Update square and wide sizes in one go	Populate square and wide XML templates and merge them together.	8-10
Populate templates that support images	Locate the image elements in the XML and set the `src` attributes.	11-12
Clear a tile of notifications	Create a `TileUpdater` object and call the `clear` method.	13-14
Create a badge notification	Select and populate the glyph or number template and pass the content to Windows.	15-17
Display a sequence of notifications in rotation	Use the tile notification queue.	18-21
Update a single notification in the queue	Reuse a tag value when issuing the update.	22
Schedule notifications	Use a `ScheduledTileNotification` object and specify the start and expiry times using JavaScript `Date` objects.	23-25
Determine if notifications will be displayed on the app tile	Create a `TileUpdate` object and read the value of the `setting` property.	26-27

Creating the Example for this Chapter

I have created a new Visual Studio project called `LiveTiles` for this chapter. The starting point is pretty basic because I just need the layout to contain buttons that will perform different kinds of tile updates, starting with a basic live tile. Listing 1 shows the `default.html` file for the app, which contains a single button. I'll add new elements as I go through the chapter and demonstrate different techniques.

Listing 1. The default.html file from the LiveTiles Project

```
<!DOCTYPE html>
<html>
<head>
    <meta charset="utf-8" />
    <title>LiveTiles</title>

    <!-- WinJS references -->
    <link href="//Microsoft.WinJS.1.0/css/ui-dark.css" rel="stylesheet" />
    <script src="//Microsoft.WinJS.1.0/js/base.js"></script>
    <script src="//Microsoft.WinJS.1.0/js/ui.js"></script>

    <!-- LiveTiles references -->
    <link href="/css/default.css" rel="stylesheet" />
    <script src="/js/default.js"></script>
</head>
<body>
    <div id="container">
        <button id="basicTile">Basic Live Tile</button>
```

```
        </div>
    </body>
</html>
```

The CSS for this example app is similarly simple, and you can see the contents of the /css/default.css file in Listing 2. There are no new techniques in this CSS, which only positions the button from the HTML in the center of the screen.

Listing 2. *The Contents of the /css/default.css File*

```
body { display: -ms-flexbox;-ms-flex-direction: row;-ms-flex-align: stretch;
    -ms-flex-pack: center;}
#container { display: -ms-flexbox; -ms-flex-direction: column; -ms-flex-align: stretch;
    -ms-flex-pack: center;}
#container button {font-size: 30pt; width: 400px; margin: 10px;}
```

You can see the initial layout of the app in Figure 1. It is, as promised, very simple, and I'll add additional buttons later in the chapter to demonstrate other features.

Figure 1. *The initial layout of the example app*

Defining the JavaScript

As Listing 3 shows, I have started with a simple default.js file. This app is all about tiles, and I don't have any background work or app state to worry about. I don't even have to make the usual call to the WinJS.Binding.processAll method because I don't have a view model or any data bindings to deal with.

Listing 3. *A Simple Default.js File*

```
(function () {
    "use strict";

    var app = WinJS.Application;
    var activation = Windows.ApplicationModel.Activation;
    var $ = WinJS.Utilities.query;
    WinJS.strictProcessing();

    var textMessages = ["Today: Pick up groceries",
                        "Tomorrow: Oil change",
                        "Wed: Book vacation",
                        "Thu: Renew insurance"];

    app.onactivated = function (args) {
```

```
        if (args.detail.kind === activation.ActivationKind.launch) {
            args.setPromise(WinJS.UI.processAll().then(function () {
                $("#container > button").listen("click", function (e) {
                    switch (this.id) {
                        case "basicTile":
                            // TODO - code for tile goes here
                            break;
                    }
                });
            }));
        }
    };
    app.start();
})();
```

I locate the button elements in the document and listen for the click event, using the id value of the clicked button to work out what I need to do in each case. There is only one button in the layout at the moment, but I will add more.

Setting the Tile Images

Since this is a chapter about tiles, I have added files to the images folder of the Visual Studio project so that I can create a basic static tile. The files are called tile30.png, tile150.png, and tile310.png, and you can see how I have applied these images in the Application UI section of the manifest in Figure 2.

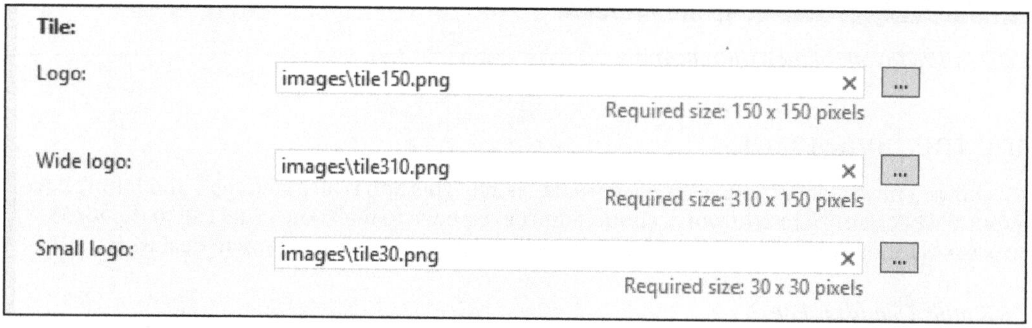

Tile:

Logo:	images\tile150.png	×	...
	Required size: 150 x 150 pixels		
Wide logo:	images\tile310.png	×	...
	Required size: 310 x 150 pixels		
Small logo:	images\tile30.png	×	...
	Required size: 30 x 30 pixels		

Figure 2. Setting the images for the app tile

■ **Tip**   When you are working with tiles and changing the setting the app uses, you may find that the tile icons are not displayed on the Start screen. I find that right-clicking the app, clicking Uninstall on the App Bar, and starting the app again often fixes the problem. Sometimes the app tile doesn't show up at all – in this case, type the first few letters of the app name to perform a search and then press the escape key to return to the main Start screen; the tile usually appears. If all else fails, uninstall the app from both the simulator and the development machine, restart, and launch the app from Visual Studio without ever starting the simulator.

Testing the Example App

There isn't a great deal of functionality at the moment, but if you start the app from Visual Studio and then switch to the Start screen, you will be able to see the static tile for the example app. You can use the Larger and Smaller AppBar commands to toggle between the normal and wide button configurations, which you can see in Figure 3.

Figure 3. *The square and wide static tiles for the example app*

As the figure shows, the images I have added to the project and applied in the manifest show an alarm bell; I selected this image for the example app because it is going to create tile updates as though it were a reminder program. I am not going to create the reminder logic, but I needed a theme for the updates and reminders are ideal.

Creating a Live Tile

The basic principle to creating a live tile consists of three steps:

1. Select an XML template.

2. Populate the template with your data.

3. Pass the populated XML to Windows to update the tile.

The API for doing all of this is pretty awkward, but that awkwardness can be wrapped up in helper functions reasonably simply, and once you are up and running, the process becomes relatively easy. To start, I'll create the basic kind of live tile, which just contains text information, and then move on to more complex alternatives. Listing 4 shows the changes to the default.js file that create a live tile when the button in the app layout is clicked.

Listing 4. *Creating a Live Tile*

```
(function () {
    "use strict";

    var app = WinJS.Application;
    var activation = Windows.ApplicationModel.Activation;
    var wnote = Windows.UI.Notifications;
    WinJS.strictProcessing();

    var textMessages = ["Today: Pick up groceries",
                        "Tomorrow: Oil change",
                        "Wed: Book vacation",
```

```
                              "Thu: Renew insurance"];

    function getTemplateContent(template) {
        return wnote.TileUpdateManager.getTemplateContent(template);
    }

    function populateTemplateText(xml, values) {
        var textNodes = xml.getElementsByTagName("text");
        var count = Math.min(textNodes.length, values.length);
        for (var i = 0; i < count; i++) {
            textNodes[i].innerText = values[i];
        }
        return xml;
    }

    function updateTile(xml) {
        var notification = new wnote.TileNotification(xml);
        var updater = wnote.TileUpdateManager.createTileUpdaterForApplication();
        updater.update(notification);
    }

    app.onactivated = function (args) {
        if (args.detail.kind === activation.ActivationKind.launch) {
            args.setPromise(WinJS.UI.processAll().then(function () {
                WinJS.Utilities.query("#container > button").listen("click",
                    function (e) {
                        switch (this.id) {
                            case "basicTile":
                                var template = wnote.TileTemplateType.tileSquareText03;
                                var xml = getTemplateContent(template);
                                updateTile(populateTemplateText(xml, textMessages));
                                break;
                        }
                    });
            }));
        }
    };
    app.start();
})();
```

I have broken the work into three helper functions that I can use in later examples, without having to work directly with the Windows.UI.Notifications namespace, which is where the tile related functionality can be found. I'll break down the process in the sections that follow.

Getting the Template Content

The set of templates available for live tiles is defined by the Windows.UI.Notifications.TileTemplateType enumeration. There are 45 different kinds of template available, and they offer a mix of sizes (for square and wide tiles) and differing amounts of text, with or without images. If you look at the API documentation for TileTemplateType (which is at http://msdn.microsoft.com/en-us/library/windows/apps/windows.ui.

notifications.tiletemplatetype.aspx), then you'll see an example of each different template. I am going to start with the TileTemplateType.tileSquareText03 template, which is a text-only template that displays four lines of text. You can see the XML for this template in Listing 5.

Listing 5. *The XML for the tileSquareText03 Template*

```
<tile>
    <visual>
        <binding template="TileSquareText03">
            <text id="1"></text>
            <text id="2"></text>
            <text id="3"></text>
            <text id="4"></text>
        </binding>
    </visual>
</tile>
```

The goal is to set the contents of each text element – I'll be using the four strings I defined in the textMessages array in the /js/default.js file, which represent forthcoming alerts from my fake reminder app.

Getting the content of the XML template requires passing a value from the TileTemplateType enumeration to the getTemplateContent method defined by Windows.UI.Notifications.TileUpdateManager. There are some pretty long namespaces and object names in this area, so I have defined an alias for the Windows.UI.Notifications namespace and put the call to get the XML content into the getTemplateContent helper function.

The getTemplateContent method returns a Windows.Data.Xml.Dom.XmlDocument object, which provides DOM manipulation for XML content. Manipulating XML is very similar to working with HTML content, although as you'll see in the next section, you don't have to do much manipulation when working with live tiles.

■ **Tip** Along with the Windows.Data.Xml.Dom namespace, you will find that apps can also use the Windows. Data.Html and Windows.Data.Json namespaces as well. They provide objects for processing HTML and JSON content and can be useful if you want to process HTML outside of the current DOM or go beyond the basic JSON support that is available in Internet Explorer 10.

Populating the Content of the XML text Element

Having obtained the XML template, I now need to populate the content of the text elements. I have defined the populateTemplateText function, which takes a template and an array of string values and sets the content of the text elements using the innerText property.

Although the text elements in the template have id attributes, the XmlDocument.getElementById method doesn't work properly, and so the next best option is to locate all of the text elements using the getElementsByTagName method. This gives me the set of text elements in the order in which they appear in the XML document, and I rely on this ordering to set the content of the text elements using the innerText property, just as I would with HTML elements. The result is a populated XML template, as shown in Listing 6.

Listing 6. The Populated XML Template

```
<tile>
    <visual>
        <binding template="TileSquareText03">
            <text id="1">Today: Pick up groceries</text>
            <text id="2">Tomorrow: Oil change</text>
            <text id="3">Wed: Book vacation</text>
            <text id="4">Thu: Renew insurance</text>
        </binding>
    </visual>
</tile>
```

Updating the Tile

The last step is to update the tile by passing the populated XML to the system, which is done through the awkward sequence of API calls you can see in Listing 7, which repeats the updateTile helper function from a few pages ago.

Listing 7. Updating the Tile with the Populated XML

```
...
function updateTile(xml) {
    var notification = new wnote.TileNotification(xml);
    var updater = wnote.TileUpdateManager.createTileUpdaterForApplication();
    updater.update(notification);
}
...
```

First, I need to create a TileNotification object, passing in the populated XML as the constructor argument. For a simple tile, you just need to create the object, but I'll show you how to configure it for different scenarios later in the chapter. Next, I create a TileUpdater object by calling the TileUpdateManager.createTileUpdaterForApplication method. The TileUpdater object provides a range of different ways to update a tile. For the moment, I am just using the most basic, which is to call the update method, passing in the TileNotification object created in the previous step. I'll show you more sophisticated arrangements shortly. The result is that when you click the button in the layout, the static tile is made live and displays my fake appointment data, as shown in Figure 4.

■ **Caution**   The Visual Studio simulator doesn't support live tiles. To test live tiles, you have to use a real Windows 8 device.

Figure 4. *A basic live tile*

You can see that the small icon is used in live tile updates to help the user identify the app associated with the tile. You can also see that the update I have made is not especially useful – there isn't a lot of space in a square tile, and it can be hard to provide meaningful information to the user when relying on text.

■ **Tip**   You can't rely on the user seeing your tile updates. First, your app tile might not be on the part of the Start screen that is displayed initially, and the user may not scroll so that it becomes visible. Second, the user can disable live tiles using the Start screen App Bar. This means that you should use live tiles to display information that is also available within the app itself, rather than treating the tile as a part of the core app functionality.

Creating a More Useful Live Tile

My basic tile update has another problem, which is that it doesn't affect the wide tile. To address the lack of utility and to support all of the tile formats, I am going to take a different approach, as shown in Listing 8, which highlights additions I have made to the default.js file to update the narrow and wide tile formats together.

Listing 8. Creating a More Useful Tile Update

```
(function () {
    "use strict";

    var app = WinJS.Application;
    var activation = Windows.ApplicationModel.Activation;
    var wnote = Windows.UI.Notifications;
    WinJS.strictProcessing();

    var textMessages = ["Today: Pick up groceries",
                        "Tomorrow: Oil change","Wed: Book vacation",
                        "Thu: Renew insurance", "Sat: BBQ"];

    function getTemplateContent(template) {
        return wnote.TileUpdateManager.getTemplateContent(template);
    }

    function populateTemplateText(xml, values) {
        var textNodes = xml.getElementsByTagName("text");
```

721

```
            var count = Math.min(textNodes.length, values.length);
            for (var i = 0; i < count; i++) {
                textNodes[i].innerText = values[i];
            }
            return xml;
        }

        function updateTile(xml) {
            var notification = new wnote.TileNotification(xml);
            var updater = wnote.TileUpdateManager.createTileUpdaterForApplication();
            updater.update(notification);
        }

        function combineXML(firstXml, secondXML) {
            var wideBindingElement = secondXML.getElementsByTagName("binding")[0];
            var importedNode = firstXml.importNode(wideBindingElement, true);
            var squareVisualElement = firstXml.getElementsByTagName("visual")[0];
            squareVisualElement.appendChild(importedNode);
            return firstXml;
        }

        app.onactivated = function (args) {
            if (args.detail.kind === activation.ActivationKind.launch) {
                args.setPromise(WinJS.UI.processAll().then(function () {
                    WinJS.Utilities.query("#container > button").listen("click",
                        function (e) {
                            switch (this.id) {
                                case "basicTile":
                                    var squareTemplate =
                                        wnote.TileTemplateType.tileSquareBlock;
                                    var squareXML = populateTemplateText(
                                        getTemplateContent (squareTemplate),
                                            [textMessages.length, "Reminders"]);

                                    var wideTemplate =
                                        wnote.TileTemplateType.tileWideBlockAndText01;
                                    var wideData = textMessages.slice(0, 4)
                                    wideData.push(textMessages.length, "Reminders");
                                    var wideXml = populateTemplateText(
                                        getTemplateContent(wideTemplate),wideData);

                                    updateTile(combineXML(squareXML, wideXml));
                                    break;
                            }
                        });
                }));
            }
        };
        app.start();
    })();
```

To perform a tile update that affects both the square and wide tile, you need to select and populate two different templates and combine their contents. To make the square update more readable, I have used a different template, tileSquareBlock, which has two text elements – a large one displayed above a short one (I selected the template by looking at the API documentation for the TileTemplateType enumeration, which contains pictures of how each of the templates will appear). Figure 5 shows the description and image that Microsoft provides for this template.

TileSquareBlock | tileSquareBlock   1   One string of large block text over a single, short line of bold, regular text.

Figure 5. The description for the tileSquareBlock template

I won't display details of individual reminders because as the last demonstration showed, there isn't space on a narrow tile, so I call the populateTemplateText method with summary information, like this:

```
...
var squareXML = populateTemplateText(getTemplateContent (squareTemplate),
    [textMessages.length, "Reminders"]);
....
```

The order of the text elements in the template matches the order in which they appear in the template, which makes setting the content for templates pretty simple. For the wide tile, I have selected the tileWideBlockAndText01 template and you can see how Microsoft describes this in Figure 6.

TileWideBlockAndText01 | 14   Four strings of regular, unwrapped text on the left; large block text over a single, short
tileWideBlockAndText01   string of bold, regular text on the right.

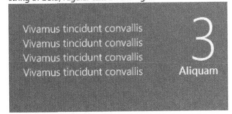

Figure 6. The description for the tileWideBlockAndText01 template

You can see the XML for this template in Listing 9. Once again, the order of the text elements is consistent with the order in which they are displayed, so the first four text elements correspond to the text on the left of the tile and the last two correspond to the text on the right.

Listing 9. The XML for the Wide Tile Template

```
<tile>
    <visual>
```

```
        <binding template="TileWideBlockAndText01">
            <text id="1"></text>
            <text id="2"></text>
            <text id="3"></text>
            <text id="4"></text>
            <text id="5"></text>
            <text id="6"></text>
        </binding>
    </visual>
</tile>
```

I populate the template by copying the first four items from the data array and pushing two new items into the array. In a real project, you would need to cater for there being fewer data items than text elements, but I have skipped over this detail for the sake of simplicity. The next step is to combine the two templates together to form the basis of a single update. This requires some manipulation of the XML – I find the binding element in the XML for the wide template and insert it into the XML for the square template, producing the combined fragment of XML shown in Listing 10.

Listing 10. Combining XML Fragments to Update Different Tile Sizes

```
<tile>
    <visual>
        <binding template="TileSquareBlock">
            <text id="1">5</text>
            <text id="2">Reminders</text>
        </binding>
        <binding template="TileWideBlockAndText01">
            <text id="1">Today: Pick up groceries</text>
            <text id="2">Tomorrow: Oil change</text>
            <text id="3">Wed: Book vacation</text>
            <text id="4">Thu: Renew insurance</text>
            <text id="5">5</text>
            <text id="6">Reminders</text>
        </binding>
    </visual>
</tile>
```

Passing the XML to Windows is done in the same way and updates both sizes of tile. You can see the result in Figure 7. To see the live tile, you will need to restart the example app, click the Basic Tile button in the app layout and then switch to the Start screen. You can switch between tile sizes by selecting the tile and selecting the Larger or Smaller buttons from the Start screen App Bar.

Figure 7. The square and wide tile updates for the example app

The right choice of template for your app is essential. You need to find a way of conveying information to the user that is helpful and (optionally) will encourage them to open and use your app.

Using Templates with Images

Not all apps benefit from displaying just text in their tile. To that end, there are templates that display images or a mix of images and text. There are also *peek* templates that alternate between two displays, typically all images and then text or a mixture of text and images. Listing 11 shows the XML for the tileSquarePeekImageAndText02 template, which contains a mix of text and image elements.

Listing 11. The XML of a Mixed Text and Image Template

```
<tile>
    <visual>
        <binding template="TileSquarePeekImageAndText02">
            <image id="1" src=""/>
            <text id="1"></text>
        </binding>
    </visual>
</tile>
```

You can see how I am building up a small library of helper functions for dealing with tiles and I need to add support for dealing with image elements. You can see the changes I have made to the default.js file in Listing 12.

Listing 12. Adding support for populating image elements

```
(function () {
    "use strict";

    var app = WinJS.Application;
    var activation = Windows.ApplicationModel.Activation;
    var wnote = Windows.UI.Notifications;
    WinJS.strictProcessing();

    var textMessages = ["Today: Pick up groceries", "Tomorrow: Oil change",
                        "Wed: Book vacation", "Thu: Renew insurance", "Sat: BBQ"];

    var images = ["/images/lily.png", "/images/astor.png", "/images/carnation.png",
        "/images/daffodil.png", "/images/snowdrop.png"];

    function getTemplateContent(template) {
        return wnote.TileUpdateManager.getTemplateContent(template);
    }

    function populateTemplate(xml, textValues, imgValues) {
        if (textValues) {
            var textNodes = xml.getElementsByTagName("text");
            var count = Math.min(textNodes.length, textValues.length);
            for (var i = 0; i < count; i++) {
                textNodes[i].innerText = textValues[i];
```

```
            }
        }
        if (imgValues) {
            var imgNodes = xml.getElementsByTagName("image");
            var count = Math.min(imgNodes.length, imgValues.length);
            for (var i = 0; i < count; i++) {
                imgNodes[i].attributes.getNamedItem("src").innerText = imgValues[i]
            }
        }
        return xml;
    }

    function updateTile(xml) {
        var notification = new wnote.TileNotification(xml);
        var updater = wnote.TileUpdateManager.createTileUpdaterForApplication();
        updater.update(notification);
    }

    function combineXML(firstXml, secondXML) {
        var wideBindingElement = secondXML.getElementsByTagName("binding")[0];
        var importedNode = firstXml.importNode(wideBindingElement, true);
        var squareVisualElement = firstXml.getElementsByTagName("visual")[0];
        squareVisualElement.appendChild(importedNode);
        return firstXml;
    }

    app.onactivated = function (args) {
        if (args.detail.kind === activation.ActivationKind.launch) {
            args.setPromise(WinJS.UI.processAll().then(function () {
                WinJS.Utilities.query("#container > button").listen("click",
                    function (e) {
                        switch (this.id) {
                            case "basicTile":
                                var squareTemplate =
                                    wnote.TileTemplateType.tileSquarePeekImageAndText02;
                                var squareXML =
                                    populateTemplate(getTemplateContent(squareTemplate),
                                        [textMessages.length, "Reminders"], images);
                                var wideTemplate =
                                    wnote.TileTemplateType.tileWidePeekImageCollection02;
                                var wideData = textMessages.slice(0, 4)
                                wideData.unshift(textMessages.length + " Reminders");
                                var wideXml =
                                    populateTemplate(getTemplateContent(wideTemplate),
                                        wideData, images);
                                updateTile(combineXML(squareXML, wideXml));
                                break;
                        }
                    });
            }));
        }
```

```
    };
    app.start();
})();
```

I have replaced the populateTemplateText function with populateTemplate, which deals with both text and image elements. To demonstrate the use of images, I added some files to the images folder in the Visual Studio project. I used the flower pictures from previous chapters, and you can see the additions I have made shown in the Solution Explorer in Figure 8. You can get these images as part of the source code download that accompanies this book at apress.com or use your own images (in which case, you will need to change the file names in the /js/default.js file).

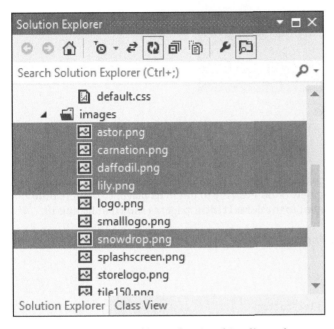

Figure 8. Adding image files to the Visual Studio project

■ **Tip**   Notice that I set the value of the src attribute in image elements via the attributes property, rather than using the setAttribute method defined by the XmlElement object. This is because the Windows 8 DOM support is inconsistent, and calling getElementsByNameTag will sometimes return a collection of XmlElement objects and sometimes return a collection of IXmlNode objects instead. The IXmlNode object doesn't define the setAttribute method, so I have to locate the src attribute and set its contents using the innerText property.

When updated, the tiles display images initially and then switch to the text display with an animation. A few seconds later, the process is repeated and so it goes on. I find this kind of live tile slightly annoying, but it may be just what you need for your app. You can see the different states for the tile in Figure 9. Notice that the template I used for the wide size has five images. I didn't have to resize the images to display them this way; it was done for me automatically as part of the tile update.

Figure 9. Using tile templates that contain images

Clearing a Tile

There will be times when you need to clear the contents of a tile, typically because the information that is displayed is now out of date and there is nothing new or noteworthy to put in its place. To demonstrate clearing the file, I have added a new button element to the default.html page, as shown in Listing 13.

Listing 13. Adding a Button to the Layout to Clear the Tile

```
...
<body>
    <div id="container">
        <button id="basicTile">Basic Live Tile</button>
        <button id="clearTile">Clear Tile</button>
    </div>
</body>
...
```

Clearing the tile is simple, as shown in Listing 14, which details the changes I have made to the default.js file.

Listing 14. Adding Support for Clearing the Tile

```
(function () {
    "use strict";

    var app = WinJS.Application;
    var activation = Windows.ApplicationModel.Activation;
    var wnote = Windows.UI.Notifications;
    WinJS.strictProcessing();

    var textMessages = ["Today: Pick up groceries", "Tomorrow: Oil change",
```

```
                        "Wed: Book vacation", "Thu: Renew insurance", "Sat: BBQ"];

    var images = ["/images/lily.png", "/images/astor.png", "/images/carnation.png",
        "/images/daffodil.png", "/images/snowdrop.png"];

    // ...helper functions removed for brevity...

    function clearTile() {
        wnote.TileUpdateManager.createTileUpdaterForApplication().clear();
    }

    app.onactivated = function (args) {
        if (args.detail.kind === activation.ActivationKind.launch) {
            args.setPromise(WinJS.UI.processAll().then(function () {
                WinJS.Utilities.query("#container > button").listen("click",
                    function (e) {
                        switch (this.id) {
                            case "basicTile":
                                // ...statements removed for brevity...
                                break;
                            case "clearTile":
                                clearTile();
                                break;
                        }
                    });
            }));
        }
    };
    app.start();
})();
```

To clear the tile, you create a TileUpdater object by calling the TileUpdateManager.
createTileUpdaterForApplication method and call the clear method on it. Clearing a tile returns it to the
static state, displaying the app images defined in the manifest.

Using Badges

Badges are a small indicator displayed on a tile and can be used as an alternative or a complement to the
full live tile updates I showed you in the previous sections. The steps required to add a badge are similar to
those required for a regular update, in that you select an XML template, populate the content and pass it to
Windows as an update.

Badges appear in the lower-right corner of the app tile and can either be a number from 1 to 99 or one
of a small number of icons that are defined by Windows (known as *badge glyphs*). This is a pretty limited
way of expressing information, but it can be useful in certain situations. I find the ability to display
numbers useful, but have yet to find a real project in which the glyphs have been helpful since the
selection is so limited (and you cannot define your own).

I have added two new button elements to the default.html file for the example project so that I can
demonstrate the use of badges. The additions are shown in Listing 15.

Listing 15. Adding a new button element to the default.html file

```
...
<body>
    <div id="container">
        <button id="basicTile">Basic Live Tile</button>
        <button id="numericBadge">Numeric Badge</button>
        <button id="glyphBadge">Glyph Badge</button>
        <button id="clearTile">Clear Tile</button>
    </div>
</body>
...
```

You can see the additions I have made to the `default.js` file to support the badges in Listing 16. I have listed the complete code for this file because I want to emphasize just how similar the technique for badges is to the one for tiles.

Listing 16. Adding Support for Badges to the default.js File

```
(function () {
    "use strict";

    var app = WinJS.Application;
    var activation = Windows.ApplicationModel.Activation;
    var wnote = Windows.UI.Notifications;
    WinJS.strictProcessing();

    var textMessages = ["Today: Pick up groceries", "Tomorrow: Oil change",
                        "Wed: Book vacation", "Thu: Renew insurance", "Sat: BBQ"];

    var images = ["/images/lily.png", "/images/astor.png", "/images/carnation.png",
        "/images/daffodil.png", "/images/snowdrop.png"];

    function getTemplateContent(template) {
        return wnote.TileUpdateManager.getTemplateContent(template);
    }

    function getBadgeTemplateContent(template) {
        return wnote.BadgeUpdateManager.getTemplateContent(template);
    }

    function populateTemplate(xml, textValues, imgValues) {
        if (textValues) {
            var textNodes = xml.getElementsByTagName("text");
            var count = Math.min(textNodes.length, textValues.length);
            for (var i = 0; i < count; i++) {
                textNodes[i].innerText = textValues[i];
            }
        }
        if (imgValues) {
            var imgNodes = xml.getElementsByTagName("image");
            var count = Math.min(imgNodes.length, imgValues.length);
```

```
        for (var i = 0; i < count; i++) {
            imgNodes[i].attributes.getNamedItem("src").innerText = imgValues[i]
        }
    }
    return xml;
}

function populateBadgeTemplate(xml, value) {
    var badgeNode = xml.getElementsByTagName("badge")[0];
    badgeNode.attributes.getNamedItem("value").innerText = value;
    return xml;
}

function updateTile(xml) {
    var notification = new wnote.TileNotification(xml);
    var updater = wnote.TileUpdateManager.createTileUpdaterForApplication();
    updater.update(notification);
}

function updateBadge(xml) {
    var notification = new wnote.BadgeNotification(xml);
    var updater = wnote.BadgeUpdateManager.createBadgeUpdaterForApplication();
    updater.update(notification);
}

function combineXML(firstXml, secondXML) {
    var wideBindingElement = secondXML.getElementsByTagName("binding")[0];
    var importedNode = firstXml.importNode(wideBindingElement, true);
    var squareVisualElement = firstXml.getElementsByTagName("visual")[0];
    squareVisualElement.appendChild(importedNode);
    return firstXml;
}

function clearTile() {
    wnote.TileUpdateManager.createTileUpdaterForApplication().clear();
    wnote.BadgeUpdateManager.createBadgeUpdaterForApplication().clear();
}

app.onactivated = function (args) {
    if (args.detail.kind === activation.ActivationKind.launch) {
        args.setPromise(WinJS.UI.processAll().then(function () {
            WinJS.Utilities.query("#container > button").listen("click",
                function (e) {
                    switch (this.id) {
                        case "basicTile":
                            var squareTemplate =
                                wnote.TileTemplateType.tileSquarePeekImageAndText02;
                            var squareXML =
                                populateTemplate(getTemplateContent(squareTemplate),
                                    [textMessages.length, "Reminders"], images);
                            var wideTemplate =
```

```
                                        wnote.TileTemplateType.tileWidePeekImageCollection02;
                            var wideData = textMessages.slice(0, 4)
                            wideData.unshift(textMessages.length + " Reminders");
                            var wideXml =
                                populateTemplate(getTemplateContent(wideTemplate),
                                wideData, images);
                            updateTile(combineXML(squareXML, wideXml));
                            break;
                        case "clearTile":
                            clearTile();
                            break;
                        case "numericBadge":
                            var template = getBadgeTemplateContent(
                                wnote.BadgeTemplateType.badgeNumber);
                            var badgeXml = populateBadgeTemplate(template,
                                textMessages.length);
                            updateBadge(badgeXml);
                            break;
                        case "glyphBadge":
                            var template = getBadgeTemplateContent(
                                wnote.BadgeTemplateType.badgeGlyph);
                            var badgeXml = populateBadgeTemplate(template, "alert");
                            updateBadge(badgeXml);
                            break;
                    }
                });
            }));
        }
    };
    app.start();
})();
```

All of the objects for badges are in the Windows.UI.Notifications namespace, alongside those used for tiles. You obtain the template you want to use by passing a value from the BadgeTemplateType enumeration to the BadgeUpdateManager.getTemplateContent method. I have shown the two different template types in Table 2.

Table 2. *The Values Defined by the BadgeTemplateType Enumeration*

Value	Description
badgeGlyph	Use when you want to display an icon badge
badgeNumber	Use when you want to display a numeric badge

The content for both templates is the same, although it is important to use the right template in case they change in future releases. You can see the XML that is returned by the getTemplateContent method in Listing 17.

Listing 17. *The XML content of the badge template*

```
<badge value=""/>
```

This is a very simple template. If you want to display a numeric badge, then you set the value to the number you want to display, between 1 and 99. If you set the value outside of this range, the value will be displayed as 99+ (the number 99 followed by a plus symbol).

If you want to display a glyph badge, then you set the value attribute to the name of the glyph that you want. In the example, I use the alert value. There is no JavaScript object that enumerates the values, but you can see a list of them at http://msdn.microsoft.com/en-us/library/windows/apps/hh761458.aspx. There are 11 glyphs and they cover some common messages that an app might want to convey to the user.

Once you have populated the template, you create a notification and pass it to a badge updater, as demonstrated by the updateBadge function in the example. You don't need to worry about different tile sizes when working with badges – a single badge update will affect both square and wide tiles. You can see the numeric and glyph badges applied to the example app's tile in Figure 10. I have shown the badges applied to the static and live tiles.

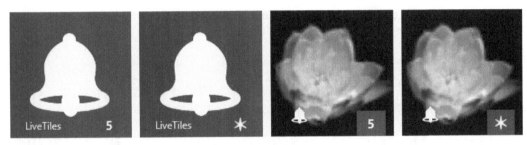

Figure 10. Applying a badge to static and live app tiles

Finally, clearing a badge update requires a call to the clear method on a badge updater. You can see a demonstration in the clearTile function in the example, which now removes the live tile update and the badge, returning the tile to its initial static state.

Advanced Tile Features

The tile techniques I showed you in the preceding sections will cover the needs of most apps. For more specialized situations, there are some advanced features that you can use to get greater control over your app tile. In the sections that follow, I'll show you to use these features. To demonstrate these features, I have created a new Visual Studio project called AdvancedTiles. The initial layout in default.html is shown in Listing 18 and consists of three simple button elements.

Listing 18. The Initial Content of the default.html File

```
<!DOCTYPE html>
<html>
<head>
    <meta charset="utf-8" />
    <title>AdvancedTiles</title>

    <!-- WinJS references -->
    <link href="//Microsoft.WinJS.1.0/css/ui-dark.css" rel="stylesheet" />
    <script src="//Microsoft.WinJS.1.0/js/base.js"></script>
    <script src="//Microsoft.WinJS.1.0/js/ui.js"></script>
```

```
        <!-- AdvancedTiles references -->
        <link href="/css/default.css" rel="stylesheet" />
        <script src="/js/tiles.js"></script>
        <script src="/js/default.js"></script>
    </head>
    <body>
        <div id="container">
            <button id="multiple">Multiple Notifications</button>
            <button id="update">Update Notification</button>
            <button id="clear">Clear Tile</button>
        </div>
    </body>
</html>
```

The button elements are set up for the first example in this part of the chapter. You can see the contents of the /css/default.css for this project in file in Listing 19.

Listing 19. *The contents of the default.css file*

```
body { display: -ms-flexbox; -ms-flex-direction: row; -ms-flex-align: stretch;
    -ms-flex-pack: center;}
#container {display: -ms-flexbox; -ms-flex-direction: column; -ms-flex-align: stretch;
    -ms-flex-pack: center;}
#container button {font-size: 30pt; width: 500px; margin: 10px;}
```

You can see the initial layout of this app in Figure 11. I'll be adding additional buttons later in this chapter.

Figure 11. *The layout of the example app*

I have put the tile helper functions from earlier in the chapter into a file called /js/tiles.js, and made them available via the Tiles namespace. You can see the contents of the tiles.js file in Listing 20.

Listing 20. *The Contents of the /js/tiles.js File*

```
(function () {

    var wnote = Windows.UI.Notifications;

    WinJS.Namespace.define("Tiles", {
```

```
        getTemplateContent: function (template) {
            return wnote.TileUpdateManager.getTemplateContent(template);
        },
        getBadgeTemplateContent: function (template) {
            return wnote.BadgeUpdateManager.getTemplateContent(template);
        },
        populateTemplate: function (xml, textValues, imgValues) {
            if (textValues) {
                var textNodes = xml.getElementsByTagName("text");
                var count = Math.min(textNodes.length, textValues.length);
                for (var i = 0; i < count; i++) {
                    textNodes[i].innerText = textValues[i];
                }
            }
            if (imgValues) {
                var imgNodes = xml.getElementsByTagName("image");
                var count = Math.min(imgNodes.length, imgValues.length);
                for (var i = 0; i < count; i++) {
                    imgNodes[i].attributes.getNamedItem("src").innerText = imgValues[i]
                }
            }
            return xml;
        },
        populateBadgeTemplate: function (xml, value) {
            var badgeNode = xml.getElementsByTagName("badge")[0];
            badgeNode.attributes.getNamedItem("value").innerText = value;
            return xml;
        },
        updateTile: function (xml) {
            var notification = new wnote.TileNotification(xml);
            var updater = wnote.TileUpdateManager.createTileUpdaterForApplication();
            updater.update(notification);
        },
        updateBadge: function (xml) {
            var notification = new wnote.BadgeNotification(xml);
            var updater = wnote.BadgeUpdateManager.createBadgeUpdaterForApplication();
            updater.update(notification);
        },
        combineXML: function (firstXml, secondXML) {
            var wideBindingElement = secondXML.getElementsByTagName("binding")[0];
            var importedNode = firstXml.importNode(wideBindingElement, true);
            var squareVisualElement = firstXml.getElementsByTagName("visual")[0];
            squareVisualElement.appendChild(importedNode);
            return firstXml;
        },
        clearTile: function () {
            wnote.TileUpdateManager.createTileUpdaterForApplication().clear();
            wnote.BadgeUpdateManager.createBadgeUpdaterForApplication().clear();
        }
    });
})();
```

735

I will call on these functions when I want to build on the earlier example and just list out the differences. You can see the initial content for the /js/default.js file in Listing 21.

Listing 21. The Initial Content for the default.js File

```
(function () {
    "use strict";

    var app = WinJS.Application;
    var activation = Windows.ApplicationModel.Activation;
    var wnote = Windows.UI.Notifications;
    WinJS.strictProcessing();

    var dataObjects = [
        { name: "Projects", quant: 6, key: "projects" },
        { name: "Clients", quant: 2, key: "clients" },
        { name: "Milestones", quant: 4, key: "milestones" }
    ];

    app.onactivated = function (args) {
        if (args.detail.kind === activation.ActivationKind.launch) {
            args.setPromise(WinJS.UI.processAll().then(function () {

                WinJS.Utilities.query("#container > button").listen("click",
                    function (e) {
                        switch (this.id) {
                            case "clear":
                                Tiles.clearTile();
                                break;
                        }
                    });
            }));
        }
    };
    app.start();
})();
```

The Clear Tile button is already wired up and called the Tile.clearTile method to reset the tile to its static state and remove any badges. In the sections that follow, I'll add the code for the other buttons.

Finally, I added the same tile images to the project as I used in the previous example app and updated the app manifest, as shown in Figure 12.

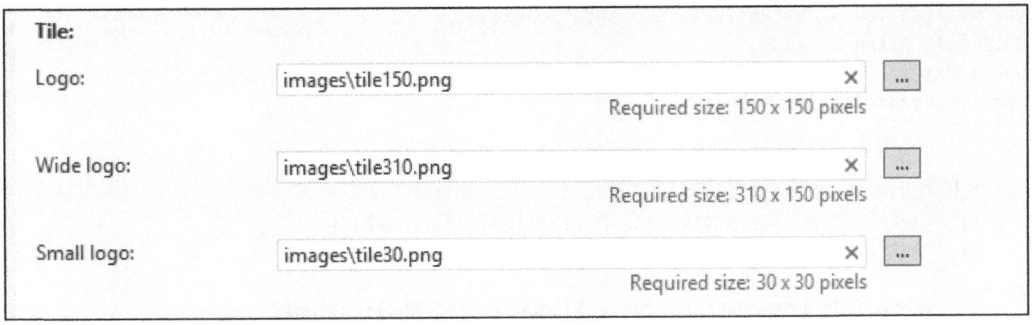

Tile:			
Logo:	images\tile150.png	×	...
	Required size: 150 x 150 pixels		
Wide logo:	images\tile310.png	×	...
	Required size: 310 x 150 pixels		
Small logo:	images\tile30.png	×	...
	Required size: 30 x 30 pixels		

Figure 12. Setting the manifest image files

Using the Notification Queue

The first advanced feature I am going to describe is the *notification queue*, which lets you use the tile to display up to five updates in rotation. This can be useful when your app needs to show a sequence of related messages or images to the user – although, since individual messages are displayed for about 5 seconds, you can't rely on users seeing all of the messages in the queue when they visit the Start screen. This means that you should select the content you display carefully so that each message is self-contained and meaningful, and is helpful or enticing in its own right. In the example app, I have defined some data that might summarize a user's project commitments:

```
...
var dataObjects = [
    { name: "Projects", quant: 6, key: "projects" },
    { name: "Clients", quant: 2, key: "clients" },
    { name: "Milestones", quant: 4, key: "milestones" }];
...
```

Each data object has three properties: a name, a quantity and a key. The first two are the data items that will be displayed to the user, and the key property will let me differentiate messages in the queue – something that becomes important when you want to refresh a notification. You can see the changes I have made to the default.js file to use the notification queue in Listing 22.

Listing 22. Using the Notification Queue

```
(function () {
    "use strict";

    var app = WinJS.Application;
    var activation = Windows.ApplicationModel.Activation;
    var wnote = Windows.UI.Notifications;
    WinJS.strictProcessing();

    var dataObjects = [
        { name: "Projects", quant: 6, key: "projects" },
        { name: "Clients", quant: 2, key: "clients" },
        { name: "Milestones", quant: 4, key: "milestones" }];

    function updateTileQueue(xml, tag) {
```

```
            var notification = new wnote.TileNotification(xml);
            notification.tag = tag;
            var updater = wnote.TileUpdateManager.createTileUpdaterForApplication();
            updater.update(notification);
        }

        app.onactivated = function (args) {
            if (args.detail.kind === activation.ActivationKind.launch) {
                args.setPromise(WinJS.UI.processAll().then(function () {

                    wnote.TileUpdateManager.createTileUpdaterForApplication()
                        .enableNotificationQueue(true);

                    WinJS.Utilities.query("#container > button").listen("click",
                        function (e) {
                            switch (this.id) {
                                case "clear":
                                    Tiles.clearTile();
                                    break;
                                case "multiple":
                                    dataObjects.forEach(function (item) {
                                        var xml = Tiles.getTemplateContent(
                                            wnote.TileTemplateType.tileSquareBlock);
                                        Tiles.populateTemplate(xml, [item.quant, item.name]);
                                        updateTileQueue(xml, item.key);
                                    });
                                    break;
                            }
                        });
                }));
            }
        };
        app.start();
    })();
```

You have to explicitly enable the notification queue, which is done by creating a TileUpdater object and calling the enableNotificationQueue method, passing true as the method argument. You only need to do this once, which is why I perform this task during the initialization phase in the app.

When the Multiple Notifications button is clicked, I call the forEach method to enumerate the data object. For each object, I get and populate the template XML, just as I did earlier in the chapter. (I am only going to create notifications for the square tile size, but the process of combining templates is just the same as in the first part of the chapter).

■ **Tip**   The notification queue will hold up to five notifications; if you add any more than five, the most recent additions will push out the older items.

The difference arises when I come to update the tile. I create the TileNotification object using the populated XML and then I assign a value to the tag property. All of this happens in the updateTileQueue function and it allows the system to differentiate between the different notifications it has to display. As you'll learn shortly, you can replace single notifications by reusing the tag values. The result is that I put three notifications into the queue, and the tile will rotate through them, switching from one to the other every five seconds or so. You can see the three notifications displayed in Figure 13.

Figure 13. Showing multiple notifications in a tile

■ **Note** Once again, you will need to run this example app on the local machine because the Visual Studio simulator doesn't support live tiles or notifications.

I can't really capture the way that this works by showing the individual notifications and I suggest that you run the example app and look at the Start screen to see how the items in the notification queue are presented.

Updating a Notification

You can update a notification by issuing an update that reuses a tag name. So, for example, if I took on a new client, then I would want to update the client notification that it correctly reflected the additional business. Listing 23 shows how to do this in response to the Update Notification button being clicked.

Listing 23. Updating a Notification by Reusing a Tag

```
...
switch (this.id) {
    case "clear":
        Tiles.clearTile();
        break;
    case "multiple":
        dataObjects.forEach(function (item) {
            var xml = Tiles.getTemplateContent(
                wnote.TileTemplateType.tileSquareBlock);
            Tiles.populateTemplate(xml, [item.quant, item.name]);
            updateTileQueue(xml, item.key);
        });
        break;
    case "update":
        var dob = dataObjects[1];
        dob.quant++;
        var xml = Tiles.getTemplateContent(
```

```
                    wnote.TileTemplateType.tileSquareBlock);
            Tiles.populateTemplate(xml, [dob.quant, dob.name]);
            updateTileQueue(xml, dob.key);
            break;
    }
    ...
```

I increment the numerical property and issue an update via the updateTileQueue function. It is important that you take care to use the right tag value. If you reuse a tag, the update will replace the existing item, preserving the order of the queue. If you use a tag value that is not already in the queue, then Windows will see this as a new notification and append it to the end of the queue, which means that you can end up with two notifications that appear to show conflicting data.

Scheduling Notifications

You can schedule when notifications appear on the tile and how long until they will be removed from the queue. The ability to schedule notifications in the future is useful for making sure that information that isn't immediately useful is presented to the user at a time when the app may be suspended or have been terminated. However, you can't rely on the user looking at your app tile when this happens, so for important information you should use a more direct approach, such as a *toast notification*, which I describe in Chapter 28.

The ability to schedule the point at which a notification is removed from the queue is more useful and allows you avoid presenting the user with stale data if they don't run your app for a while. I have added a new button to the default.html file to send a scheduled notification, as shown in Listing 24.

Listing 24. Adding A Button Element to Support Scheduled Notifications

```
...
<body>
    <div id="container">
        <button id="multiple">Multiple Notifications</button>
        <button id="update">Update Notification</button>
        <button id="schedule">Schedule Notification</button>
        <button id="clear">Clear Tile</button>
    </div>
</body>
...
```

Listing 25 shows the changes I have made to the default.js file to respond to this button and schedule a notification.

Listing 25. Scheduling a Tile Notification

```
(function () {
    "use strict";

    var app = WinJS.Application;
    var activation = Windows.ApplicationModel.Activation;
    var wnote = Windows.UI.Notifications;
    WinJS.strictProcessing();

    var dataObjects = [
```

```
        { name: "Projects", quant: 6, key: "projects" },
        { name: "Clients", quant: 2, key: "clients" },
        { name: "Milestones", quant: 4, key: "milestones" }];

function updateTileQueue(xml, tag) {
    var notification = new wnote.TileNotification(xml);
    notification.tag = tag;
    var updater = wnote.TileUpdateManager.createTileUpdaterForApplication();
    updater.update(notification);
}

function scheduleTileQueue(xml, tag, start, end) {
    var notification = new wnote.ScheduledTileNotification(xml, start);
    notification.tag = tag;
    notification.expirationTime = end;
    var updater = wnote.TileUpdateManager.createTileUpdaterForApplication();
    updater.addToSchedule(notification);
}

app.onactivated = function (args) {
    if (args.detail.kind === activation.ActivationKind.launch) {
        args.setPromise(WinJS.UI.processAll().then(function () {

            wnote.TileUpdateManager.createTileUpdaterForApplication()
                    .enableNotificationQueue(true);

            WinJS.Utilities.query("#container > button").listen("click",
                function (e) {
                    switch (this.id) {
                        case "clear":
                            Tiles.clearTile();
                            break;
                        case "multiple":
                            // ...statements removed for brevity...
                            break;
                        case "update":
                            // ...statements removed for brevity...
                            break;
                        case "schedule":
                            var xml = Tiles.getTemplateContent(
                                wnote.TileTemplateType.tileSquareBlock);
                            Tiles.populateTemplate(xml, [10, "Days Left"]);
                            var start = new Date(new Date().getTime() + (20 * 1000));
                            var end = new Date(start.getTime() + (30 * 1000));
                            scheduleTileQueue(xml, "daysleft", start, end);
                            break;
                    }
                });
        }));
    }
};
```

```
    app.start();
})();
```

Creating the notification is exactly the same as for the other techniques: you obtain and populate the XML content as normal. The difference comes when you apply the update to the tile, which I do through the `scheduleTileQueue` function shown in the listing.

The key to this technique is the `ScheduledTileNotification` object, which you create by passing the populated XML and the time at which the tile should start showing the update to the constructor. The time is expressed as a `Date` object, and in the example I have specified that the update should start being shown 20 seconds into the future (this is a ridiculously short time for a real app, but ideal for an example because you get to see the change not long after clicking the button). The `ScheduledTileNotification` object defines a set of properties for configuring the notification as shown in Table 3.

Table 3. The Properties Defined by the ScheduledTileNotification Object

Name	Description
content	Gets the XML content for the notification.
deliveryTime	Gets the time at which the notification will be displayed (as a `Date` object).
expirationTime	Gets or sets the time at which the notification will be removed from the display.
id	When set, uniquely identifies an update. The schedule for updates can be managed through the `TileUpdater` object.
tag	Identifies the notification so that subsequent updates can replace existing content.

You can see from the listing that I have set the expiration time to be 30 seconds after the notification is first displayed. The time values for the `ScheduledTileNotification` object are absolute, meaning that your `Date` objects should be defined with days, months, and years (rather than being expressed just an elapsed period). You can see the effect of these changes if you start the example app, click the `Schedule Notification` button, and switch to the Start screen.

The exact effect you see will depend on the state of the tile when the notification starts to be shown. If there are already notifications in the queue, then the scheduled notification will be displayed as part of the regular rotation. After the expiry time is reached, the scheduled notification will be removed from the queue, and just the original notifications will be shown.

Things are slightly different if the tile is static (i.e., there are no notifications in the queue). The notification is shown as the only content of the tile and the tile resets to its static state when the expiry time is reached. You can see the effect on the notifications for the example in Figure 14.

Figure 14. Adding a scheduled notification to the tile

Determining if Notifications are Enabled

The last technique I am going to show you in this chapter is determining if the app tile will display live updates. The setting for the app tile is represented by the values in the `Windows.UI.Notifications.NotificationSetting` object, which I have listed in Table 4.

Table 4. *The Values Defined by the NotificationSetting Object*

Value	Description
enabled	Live tile updates will be displayed
disabledForApplication	The user has disabled live updates for this app
disabledForUser	The user has disabled live updates for all apps
disabledByGroupPolicy	Live updates have been disabled by group policy (commonly used in enterprise deployments)
disabledByManifest	This value does not apply to live tiles, but is part of the enumeration because the same values are used elsewhere – see Chapter 28 for details.

I have added a final `button` to the `default.html` file to determine the app tile setting, as shown in Listing 26.

Listing 26. *Adding a Button to Check the Status of Live Tile Updates*

```
...
<body>
    <div id="container">
        <button id="multiple">Multiple Notifications</button>
        <button id="update">Update Notification</button>
        <button id="schedule">Schedule Notification</button>
        <button id="check">Check Status</button>
        <button id="clear">Clear Tile</button>
    </div>
</body>
...
```

Listing 27 shows the additions I have made to the `default.js` file to determine the status. For simplicity, I write the result to the Visual Studio `JavaScript Console` window, which means that you will need to start the app using the debugger to see the messages.

Listing 27. *Checking if Live Updates Will be Visible to the User*

```
(function () {
    "use strict";

    var app = WinJS.Application;
    var activation = Windows.ApplicationModel.Activation;
    var wnote = Windows.UI.Notifications;
    WinJS.strictProcessing();

    var dataObjects = [
        { name: "Projects", quant: 6, key: "projects" },
        { name: "Clients", quant: 2, key: "clients" },
```

```
                { name: "Milestones", quant: 4, key: "milestones" }];

        // ...functions removed for brevity...

        function getValueFromEnum(val) {
            for (var prop in wnote.NotificationSetting) {
                if (wnote.NotificationSetting[prop] == val) {
                    return prop;
                }
            }
        }

        app.onactivated = function (args) {
            if (args.detail.kind === activation.ActivationKind.launch) {
                args.setPromise(WinJS.UI.processAll().then(function () {

                    wnote.TileUpdateManager.createTileUpdaterForApplication()
                            .enableNotificationQueue(true);

                    WinJS.Utilities.query("#container > button").listen("click",
                        function (e) {
                            switch (this.id) {
                                case "clear":
                                    Tiles.clearTile();
                                    break;
                                case "multiple":
                                    // ...statements removed for brevity...
                                    break;
                                case "update":
                                    // ...statements removed for brevity...
                                    break;
                                case "schedule":
                                    // ...statements removed for brevity...
                                    break;
                                case "check":
                                    var setting =
                                        wnote.TileUpdateManager.
                                        createTileUpdaterForApplication().setting;
                                    console.log("Live tile updates are " +
                                        getValueFromEnum(setting));
                                    break;
                            }
                        });
                }));
            }
        };
        app.start();
    })();
```

You can see which of these values applies by creating a TileUpdater object (by calling the TileUpdateManager.createTileUpdaterForApplication method) and reading the value of the setting

744

property. You can change the setting by selecting the app tile and clicking a button in the App Bar. The two options are shown in Figure 15. They will switch between the enabled and disabledForApplication settings.

Figure 15. Enabling and disabling tile notifications for a single app

Generating notifications when they are not enabled for the tile doesn't cause any problems – the notifications are simply discarded. This means that you only need to check the setting value if you want to remind the user that tile notifications are available. Be sensitive to the significance of the setting value – if the user has disabled notifications for just your app (the disabledForApplication value), then it is possible that your notifications are annoying or don't provide value for the user. If the user has disabled live tiles for all apps (the disabledForUser value), then they are unlikely to make an exception for your app. If you encounter the disabledByGroupPolicy value, then just move on – there is no point reminding the user that notifications are available because they are unlikely to be able to override the setting. This is common in large enterprise deployments in which many system functions are disabled in the name of security and ease-of-administration.

Summary

Live tiles, when used thoughtfully, can be a powerful addition to an app's core functionality, either freeing the user from having to launch the app or drawing them in so that they do. In this chapter, I have shown you how to use live app tiles, starting with the basic technique of selecting and populating a single template and moving on to demonstrate how to combine multiple templates and how to use badges.

For the most part, these basic techniques will be all that you need, but I also showed you some advanced features for more demanding apps. These included using the notification queue to display a rotating sequence of messages, updating the content for individual notifications in the queue, and taking control of when notifications are scheduled. I finished the chapter by showing you how to figure out if live tile updates are displayed. It may seem odd to put this technique last, but it is not needed in most situations because notifications are simply discarded if the live tile has been disabled. Tiles are not the only notification mechanism available for Windows apps – as you'll learn in the next chapter when I show you how to use *toast*, as well as introduce the system launcher feature.

CHAPTER 28

■ ■ ■

Using Toast and the System Launcher

In this chapter, I show you how to use *toast notifications*, which are a more direct and intrusive mechanism for attracting the user's attention. Toast notifications are a complement to the more subtle tile notifications and badges I showed you in the previous chapter and are used for more important or urgent information. Like any kind of notification, toasts should be used thoughtfully and sparingly – too few notifications and your user won't get the cues and reminders they expect, and too many will fatigue and annoy the user. When in doubt, allow the user to configure the circumstances under which toast notifications are made, using the settings features and techniques I described in Chapter 27.

I also describe the *system launcher* feature in this chapter, which allows you to launch the user's choice of app to handle files and URLs that your app can't process. This is a simple but useful feature, and it is worth understanding how to use it. Table 1 provides the summary for this chapter.

Table 1. Chapter Summary

Problem	Solution	Listing
Show toast notifications	Enable the toast capable option in the manifest and pass a populated XML template to Windows	1-8
Configure the period for which a toast notification is shown to the user	Set the value of the duration attribute in the XML template	9-11
Configure the audio played when a toast notification is shown	Set the value of the audio and loop attributes in the XML template	12-14
Respond when a toast is activated	Set a value for the launch attribute and handle the activated event emitted by the notification	15-17
Respond when a toast is dismissed	Handle the dismissed event	18
Defer a toast notification	Schedule the notification for a future time	19-20
Determine if toast notifications are enabled	Read the value of the setting property	21-22
Launch an app to handle a file or URL	Use the app launcher feature	23-27

Using Toast Notifications

Toast notifications are a more direct and attention-grabbing way of notifying the user. A toast pops up on the screen, typically accompanied by a sound effect, and has the effect of interrupting the user's concentration and flow of work. For that reason, you should use toast notifications sparingly and only display them for matters which are important and require immediate action. In the sections that follow, I'll walk you through the process of creating and displaying toast notifications and show you how to respond when the user interacts with them.

Creating the Example Application

The example application I created for this chapter is called Toast, and I have followed the same basic format as for the example in the last chapter – a single-page app that will display buttons that, when pressed, will trigger notifications. You can see the initial additions I have made to the default.html file in Listing 1, which includes the button elements for the toast notification examples in this chapter.

Listing 1. The Initial default.html for the Toast Example Application

```
<!DOCTYPE html>
<html>
<head>
    <meta charset="utf-8" />
    <title>Toast</title>

    <!-- WinJS references -->
    <link href="//Microsoft.WinJS.1.0/css/ui-dark.css" rel="stylesheet" />
    <script src="//Microsoft.WinJS.1.0/js/base.js"></script>
    <script src="//Microsoft.WinJS.1.0/js/ui.js"></script>

    <!-- Toast references -->
    <link href="/css/default.css" rel="stylesheet" />
    <script src="/js/default.js"></script>
</head>
<body>
    <div id="container">
        <button id="toast">Show Toast</button>
        <button id="schedule">Schedule Toast</button>
        <button id="check">Check Status</button>
    </div>
</body>
</html>
```

You can see the css/default.css file in Listing 2, which shows the styles I have used to create the layout for the app.

Listing 2. The css/default.css File from the Toast Project

```
body, #container { display: -ms-flexbox; -ms-flex-direction: row;
    -ms-flex-align: stretch; -ms-flex-pack: center;}
#container {-ms-flex-direction: column;}
#container button {font-size: 30pt;width: 400px; margin: 10px;}
```

The markup and the CSS are combined to create a simple layout for the app, which you can see in Figure 1. The layout is so simple because all of the effort in this example will go into producing and managing toast notifications.

Figure 1. *The layout for the Toast example app*

For this chapter, I don't need to worry about saving app state or dealing with suspension or termination, so I have started with a simple default.js file, as shown in Listing 3.

Listing 3. *The Initial default.js File for the Toast Example Application*

```
(function () {
    "use strict";

    var app = WinJS.Application;
    var activation = Windows.ApplicationModel.Activation;
    var wnote = Windows.UI.Notifications;
    WinJS.strictProcessing();

    var toastMessages = ["7pm Leave Office", "8pm: Meet Jacqui at Lucca's Bar",
        "9pm: Dinner at Joe's"];
    var toastImage = "/images/reminder.png";

    app.onactivated = function (args) {
        if (args.detail.kind === activation.ActivationKind.launch) {
            args.setPromise(WinJS.UI.processAll().then(function () {
                WinJS.Utilities.query("#container > button").listen("click",
                    function (e) {
                        switch (this.id) {
                            case "toast":
                                // code will go here
                                break;
                        }
                    });
            }));
        }
    };
    app.start();
})();
```

749

This is pretty much the same starting point I used for the live tiles chapter. The switch statement in the code is set up to respond when the Show Toast button is pressed (which has an id attribute value of toast), and I'll add other case statements for the remaining buttons later in the chapter.

■ **Note**   The objects that provide the toast notification functionality are part of the Windows.UI.Notifications namespace, which I have aliased to wnote in the example for brevity. Unless I state otherwise, all the objects I refer to in this chapter are part of this namespace.

I have defined different reminder data for this example and added an image to the project called images/reminder.png, which is shown in Figure 2.

Figure 2. The reminder.png image added to the project for use in toast notifications

You'll see the image again when I display the toast notification later in the chapter. Along with the reminder.png file, I have added the same set of alarm-bell icons to the images folder that I used in the previous section and applied these files in the Application UI section of the app manifest, as shown in Figure 3.

■ **Tip**   You can get all of the image files as part of the free source code download for this book, which is available from apress.com.

Tile:

Logo:	images\tile150.png	✕	...
	Required size: 150 x 150 pixels		
Wide logo:	images\tile310.png	✕	...
	Required size: 310 x 150 pixels		
Small logo:	images\tile30.png	✕	...
	Required size: 30 x 30 pixels		

Figure 3. Applying the icon images in the manifest

One important difference when working with toast notifications is that you have to explicitly declare that you will be using them in your app manifest. To do this, look for the Notifications section on the manifest Application UI tab. Set Toast capable to Yes, as shown in Figure 4.

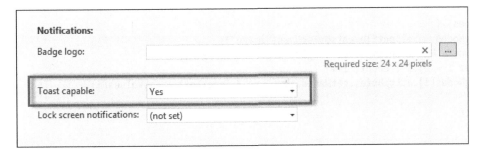

Figure 4. *Enabling toast notifications*

■ **Caution**   Windows will silently discard your toast notifications if you forget to declare that you will be using toast notifications in the manifest.

Creating a Basic Toast Notification

The process for creating a toast notification is remarkably similar to that for creating a live tile notification: you select an XML template, populate the contents, and pass it to the system so it can be displayed to the user. You can see the code I added to the default.js file to create a basic toast notification in Listing 4.

Listing 4. Creating a Basic Toast Notification

```
(function () {
    "use strict";

    var app = WinJS.Application;
    var activation = Windows.ApplicationModel.Activation;
    var wnote = Windows.UI.Notifications;
    WinJS.strictProcessing();

    var toastMessages = ["7pm Leave Office", "8pm: Meet Jacqui at Lucca's Bar",
        "9pm: Dinner at Joe's"];
    var toastImage = "/images/reminder.png";

    function getTemplateContent(templateName) {
        var template = wnote.ToastTemplateType[templateName];
        return wnote.ToastNotificationManager.getTemplateContent(template);
    }

    function populateTemplate(xml, textValues, imgValues) {
        if (textValues) {
            var textNodes = xml.getElementsByTagName("text");
```

```
                    var count = Math.min(textNodes.length, textValues.length);
                    for (var i = 0; i < count; i++) {
                        textNodes[i].innerText = textValues[i];
                    }
                }
                if (imgValues) {
                    var imgNodes = xml.getElementsByTagName("image");
                    var count = Math.min(imgNodes.length, imgValues.length);
                    for (var i = 0; i < count; i++) {
                        imgNodes[i].attributes.getNamedItem("src").innerText = imgValues[i]
                    }
                }
                return xml;
            }

            function showToast(xml) {
                var notification = wnote.ToastNotification(xml);
                var notifier = wnote.ToastNotificationManager.createToastNotifier();
                notifier.show(notification);
                return notification;
            }

            app.onactivated = function (args) {
                if (args.detail.kind === activation.ActivationKind.launch) {
                    args.setPromise(WinJS.UI.processAll().then(function () {
                        WinJS.Utilities.query("#container > button").listen("click",
                            function (e) {
                                switch (this.id) {
                                    case "toast":
                                        var xml = getTemplateContent("toastImageAndText04");
                                        populateTemplate(xml, toastMessages, [toastImage]);
                                        showToast(xml);
                                        break;
                                }
                            });
                    }));
                }
            };
            app.start();
        })();
```

If you run the app and click the Show Toast button, you will see the toast pop up in the top-right corner of the screen, and you can see what the toast produced by the example looks like in Figure 5.

■ **Note**   The Visual Studio simulator doesn't support toast notifications, just like it doesn't support live tiles. To test this example and all the other examples in this chapter, you will have to use a real Windows 8 device, such as your development machine.

Figure 5. A toast notification

I selected a toast notification template that contains image and some lines of text, but the system has added the bell logo, which I have used for my app configuration in the manifest again, just as I did in Chapter 27. By default, you will hear a chime when the toast is displayed, and the toast will disappear again after a few seconds.

Up to three notifications can be shown at once and they can come from multiple apps or from the same app. The first toast notification is aligned to the right side of the screen, and there is a small gap from the top of the screen, and subsequent notifications are stacked beneath the first. If there are more than three notifications to be displayed, a queue is used, and new notifications are displayed as old ones fade away. In the sections that follow, I'll explain how the code in the example works and how it leads to the toast shown in the figure.

Getting and Populating the Toast Template

The first step in creating a toast notification is selecting a template. The eight supported templates are enumerated by the Windows.UI.Notifications.ToastTemplateType object and contain a mix of text-only and text-and-image options. You can see samples of the templates in the documentation for the ToastTemplateType object at http://msdn.microsoft.com/en-us/library/windows/apps/windows.ui. notifications.toasttemplatetype.aspx. You can get the XML content of a toast template by passing a value from the ToastTemplateType object as the argument to the Windows.UI.Notifications. ToastNotficationManager.getTemplateContent method. I have added a helper function to do this in the example, which I have also called getTemplateContent. As a variation on the approach I used in the last chapter, this function takes a string value containing the name of a template as its argument and returns the appropriate XML, as shown in Listing 5.

Listing 5. The getTemplateContent Function from the Example App

```
...
function getTemplateContent(templateName) {
    var template = wnote.ToastTemplateType[templateName];
    return wnote.ToastNotificationManager.getTemplateContent(template);
}
...
```

In the example, I have chosen the toastImageAndText04 template, which contains an image and three non-wrapping lines of text. The first line is shown in bold in this template, and if the text lines are too long to be displayed, Windows will shorten them and apply an ellipsis (...). You can see the XML for this template in Listing 6.

Listing 6. The XML for the toastImageAndText04 Template

```
<toast>
    <visual>
        <binding template="ToastImageAndText04">
```

```
                    <image id="1" src=""/>
                    <text id="1"></text>
                    <text id="2"></text>
                    <text id="3"></text>
                </binding>
            </visual>
    </toast>
```

The process for populating the XML template is identical to the process for tile – and, in fact, I copied the populateTemplate function for this example from the last chapter. There is only one size of toast template, which means that you don't have to worry about combining XML fragments. In the example, I use three simple text strings and the image I mentioned earlier to populate the template, and you can see the result in Listing 7.

Listing 7. The Populated Toast Template for the Example App

```
<toast>
    <visual>
        <binding template="ToastImageAndText04">
            <image id="1" src="/images/reminder.png"/>
            <text id="1">7pm Leave Office</text>
            <text id="2">8pm: Meet Jacqui at Lucca's Bar</text>
            <text id="3">9pm: Dinner at Joe's</text>
        </binding>
    </visual>
</toast>
```

Showing the Toast Notification

Once you have populated the XML template, you can show the toast notification to the user. In the example, I have created the showToast function to take care of this.

The first step is to create a ToastNotification object, passing in the populated XML as the constructor argument. You then create a ToastNotifier object that is responsible for doing the actual work – you get this object by calling the ToastNotificationManager.createToastNotifier method. The final step is to call the show method on the ToastNotifier object, passing in the ToastNotification object to show the toast to the user. I have repeated the showToast function in Listing 8.

Listing 8. The showToast function from the Example App

```
...
function showToast(xml) {
    var notification = wnote.ToastNotification(xml);
    var notifier = wnote.ToastNotificationManager.createToastNotifier();
    notifier.show(notification);
    return notification;
}
...
```

Configuring the Toast Notification

You can change the behavior of the toast notification by adding attributes to the template XML. In the sections that follow, I'll explain these options and demonstrate the code required to apply them.

Configuring the Duration

There are two settings available for controlling the period for which the toast notification is displayed to the user: short and long. The default is short, which means that the toast is shown for 7 seconds. The long duration shows the notification for 25 seconds.

You can specify which setting will be used by adding a duration attribute to the toast element in the template XML and setting it to either long or short (these are the only two supported values). To support setting the duration, I added a setToastDuration function to the default.js file in the example, as shown in Listing 9.

Listing 9. Adding the setToastDuration Function to the default.js file

```
...
function getTemplateContent(templateName) {
    var template = wnote.ToastTemplateType[templateName];
    return wnote.ToastNotificationManager.getTemplateContent(template);
}

function setToastDuration(xml, duration) {
    var attribute = xml.createAttribute("duration");
    attribute.innerText = duration;
    xml.getElementsByTagName("toast")[0].attributes.setNamedItem(attribute);
}

// ...other functions omitted for brevity...
...
```

I then call this function from the click event handler function for the button element in the onactivated function. You can see how I have applied this change to the default.js file in Listing 10.

Listing 10. Calling the setToastDuration Function

```
...
app.onactivated = function (args) {
    if (args.detail.kind === activation.ActivationKind.launch) {
        args.setPromise(WinJS.UI.processAll().then(function () {
            WinJS.Utilities.query("#container > button").listen("click",
                function (e) {
                    switch (this.id) {
                        case "toast":
                            var xml = getTemplateContent("toastImageAndText04");
                            populateTemplate(xml, toastMessages, [toastImage]);
                            setToastDuration(xml, "long");
                            showToast(xml);
                            break;
                    }
```

```
                        });
            }));
        }
    };
    ...
```

You can see the addition of the `duration` attribute to the template XML in Listing 11.

Listing 11. Adding the Duration Attribute to the Toast Element in the XML

```
<toast duration="long">
    <visual>
        <binding template="ToastImageAndText04">
            <image id="1" src="/images/reminder.png"/>
            <text id="1">7pm Leave Office</text>
            <text id="2">8pm: Meet Jacqui at Lucca's Bar</text>
            <text id="3">9pm: Dinner at Joe's</text>
        </binding>
    </visual>
</toast>
```

You should use the `long` setting only if the content of the notification is particularly important and the impact of missing the notification is serious. As examples, Microsoft cites missed telephone calls and upcoming appointment reminders as being suitable for the `long` option. My problem with this approach is that it makes me decide what is important for the user, so I tend to make this a configurable option for my apps, using the settings features that I described in Chapter 20.

Configuring the Audio Alert

The other behavior you can configure via an XML attribute is the audio alert which is played when the toast notification is displayed. You do this by adding an `audio` attribute, which has an `src` attribute to specify the audio that is played and a `loop` attribute to specify how it is played. The options for both attributes are very constrained, presumably to enforce some kind of consistency and ensure that users come to associate the small range of audio options with toast notifications. There are nine different values that you can use for the `src` attribute, as described in Table 2. As you'll see, Microsoft has been very proscriptive about when they should be used.

Table 2. The Supported Values for the src Attribute of the Audio Element in a Toast Template

Value	Description
ms-winsoundevent:Notification.Default	This is the default sound for toast notifications
ms-winsoundevent:Notification.IM	Use when a new instant message arrives
ms-winsoundevent:Notification.Mail	Use this sound when a new email arrives
ms-winsoundevent:Notification.Reminder	Use this sound when a calendar item is due
ms-winsoundevent:Notification.SMS	Use this sound when a new text message arrives
ms-winsoundevent:Notification.Looping.Alarm	Use this sound when a timed alarm arises
ms-winsoundevent:Notification.Looping.Alarm2	An alternative sound for alarms
ms-winsoundevent:Notification.Looping.Call	Use when there is an incoming phone call
ms-winsoundevent:Notification.Looping.Call2	An alternative sound for phone calls

The Default, IM, Mail, Reminder, and SMS sounds are short and are played once when the notification is first shown. The Alarm, Alarm2, Call, and Call2 sounds are longer and are repeated for as long as the notification is visible.

Some care is required when using the values in the table to specify a sound effect for a toast notification. If you want to use the Alarm, Alarm2, Call, or Call2 sounds, then you need to ensure that the loop attribute on the audio element is set to true and the duration attribute on the toast element is set to long. If you don't set both attributes correctly, then the user will hear the default sound (equivalent to specifying the Notification.Default value).

However, if you want to use the Default, IM, Mail, Reminder, or SMS sounds when the duration attribute is set to long, then you must ensure that loop is set to false. If loop is true, then the user will hear the Alarm sound, irrespective of the value you specify.

■ **Tip** If you don't want any sound to accompany your toast notification, use an audio element that has a silent attribute set to true.

For my example app, I want to use the Reminder sound, which means that I want to generate the XML that is shown in Listing 12, ensuring that the value of the loop attribute is false.

Listing 12. Adding an Audio Element to the Toast Notification XML

```
<toast duration="long">
    <visual>
        <binding template="ToastImageAndText04">
            <image id="1" src="/images/reminder.png"/>
            <text id="1">7pm Leave Office</text>
            <text id="2">8pm: Meet Jacqui at Lucca's Bar</text>
            <text id="3">9pm: Dinner at Joe's</text>
        </binding>
    </visual>
    <audio src="ms-winsoundevent:Notification.Reminder" loop="false"/>
</toast>
```

To add the audio element to the XML in the example, I have defined the setToastAudio function, which you can see in Listing 13. This function will disable sound for the toast notification if the silent argument is true and will otherwise set the src and loop attributes using the provided values.

Listing 13. The setToastAudio Function for the Example App

```
...
function getTemplateContent(templateName) {
    var template = wnote.ToastTemplateType[templateName];
    return wnote.ToastNotificationManager.getTemplateContent(template);
}

function setToastDuration(xml, duration) {
    var attribute = xml.createAttribute("duration");
    attribute.innerText = duration;
    xml.getElementsByTagName("toast")[0].attributes.setNamedItem(attribute);
}
```

```
function setToastAudio(xml, silent, sound, loop) {
    var audioElem = xml.createElement("audio");
    if (silent) {
        audioElem.setAttribute("silent", "true");
    } else {
        audioElem.setAttribute("src", sound);
        audioElem.setAttribute("loop", loop);
    }
    xml.getElementsByTagName("toast")[0].appendChild(audioElem);
}

// ...other functions omitted for brevity...
...
```

You can see how I call this function from the default.js button click handler function in Listing 14, which creates the XML I showed you in Listing 12.

Listing 14. Calling the setToastAudio Function

```
...
app.onactivated = function (args) {
    if (args.detail.kind === activation.ActivationKind.launch) {
        args.setPromise(WinJS.UI.processAll().then(function () {
            WinJS.Utilities.query("#container > button").listen("click",
                function (e) {
                    switch (this.id) {
                        case "toast":
                            var xml = getTemplateContent("toastImageAndText04");
                            populateTemplate(xml, toastMessages, [toastImage]);
                            setToastDuration(xml, "long");
                            setToastAudio(xml, false,
                                "ms-winsoundevent:Notification.Reminder", false);
                            showToast(xml);
                            break;
                    }
                });
        }));
    }
};
...
```

The effect of these changes is that my toast is accompanied by the standard sound associated with reminders.

Dealing with Toast Activation and Dismissal

I am not quite done adding attributes to the XML. There is one more attribute that you can use, and I'll explain what it is and how it works in this section. Before I do that, I need to explain the (short and simple) lifecycle of a toast notification.

Once you pass the populated XML to the ToastNotifier.show method, and the notification is presented to the user, there are three possible outcomes. The first outcome is that the user *activates* the notification by clicking or touching it. The second outcome is that the user dismisses the notification, either by making a swiping the notification toward the right edge of the screen or clicking the X icon that appears when the mouse is over the notification window, which I have shown in Figure 6 (the red highlight in this image is my addition and is not presented to the user).

Figure 6. The icon for dismissal appearing on a toast notification

The third outcome is that the user just ignores the notification. After the period specified by the duration attribute, the system will dismiss the notification on behalf of the user by making the popup slowly fade away. You can respond to these outcomes by listening to the set of events that the ToastNotification object emits. There are three events, which I have summarized in Table 3.

Table 3. The Events Emitted by the ToastNotification Object

Name	Description
activated	Triggered when the notification is clicked or touched by the user
dismissed	Triggered when the notification times out or is dismissed by the user
failed	Triggered when Windows was unable to display the notification

In the sections that follow, I'll show you how to deal with the activated and dismissed events. The failed event is triggered when Windows can't show the toast notification to the user. I know of only found two things that cause the failed event: trying to issue more than 4,096 notifications from an app and trying to schedule a toast notification for a past date. I'll show you how to schedule toast notifications later in the chapter, but I have so rarely encountered any problems with toast notifications that I am not going to demonstrate handling the failed event.

Dealing with Activation

The activated event is triggered when the user clicks or touches the notification while it is being displayed. The target property of the object passed to the handler function returns the ToastNotification object that the user activated, which is useful if you are using a single function in an app that generates multiple notifications. The ToastNotification.content property returns the XML that was used to create the notification, and you need to correlate this value with your app data to figure out which notification was activated. To help with this, you can apply the launch attribute to the toast element in your XML – this attribute can be set to any string value that makes it easier to identify a notification. I have added two functions to the example to set and read the launch attribute, as shown in Listing 15.

Listing 15. Functions to Set and Read the Launch Attribute on the Toast Element

```
...
function getTemplateContent(templateName) {
    var template = wnote.ToastTemplateType[templateName];
```

```
        return wnote.ToastNotificationManager.getTemplateContent(template);
}

function setToastLaunchValue(xml, val) {
    var attribute = xml.createAttribute("launch");
    attribute.innerText = val;
    xml.getElementsByTagName("toast")[0].attributes.setNamedItem(attribute);
}

function getToastLaunchValue(xml) {
    var attribute =
        xml.getElementsByTagName("toast")[0].attributes.getNamedItem("launch");
    return attribute ? attribute.value : null;
}

function setToastDuration(xml, duration) {
    var attribute = xml.createAttribute("duration");
    attribute.innerText = duration;
    xml.getElementsByTagName("toast")[0].attributes.setNamedItem(attribute);
}
...
```

These functions use standard XML DOM manipulation to set or read the value of the attribute. If I set the value in the XML before I show the notification, then I can more readily identify which notification has been activated, as shown in Listing 16.

Listing 16. Using the Launch Attribute to Identify a Notification

```
...
app.onactivated = function (args) {
    if (args.detail.kind === activation.ActivationKind.launch) {
        args.setPromise(WinJS.UI.processAll().then(function () {

            var notificationId = 0;

            WinJS.Utilities.query("#container > button").listen("click",
                function (e) {
                    switch (this.id) {
                        case "toast":
                            var xml = getTemplateContent("toastImageAndText04");
                            populateTemplate(xml, toastMessages, [toastImage]);
                            setToastDuration(xml, "long");
                            setToastAudio(xml, false,
                                "ms-winsoundevent:Notification.Reminder", false);
                            setToastLaunchValue(xml, "notification" + notificationId++);
                            var notification = showToast(xml);
                            notification.addEventListener("activated", function (e) {
                                var id = getToastLaunchValue(e.target.content)
                                console.log("Toast notification " + id
                                    + " was activated");
                            });
```

```
                            break;
                    }
                });
            }));
    }
};
...
```

In this listing, I assign a launch value to each notification using the setToastLaunchValue function and read the value using the getToastLaunchValue function. If you launch the app, click the Show Toast button, and then click the toast notification popup, you will see a message similar to this one on the Visual Studio JavaScript Console window, indicating that the notification was activated:

```
Toast notification notification0 was activated
```

Dealing with Toast Activation Causing App Activation

You can only use the ToastNotification activated event to respond to toast activations when your app is running or suspended. If your app has been terminated or closed by the user since the notification was shown, then Windows will activate your app and pass the value you assigned to the launch attribute of the notification XML to your app using the detail.arguments property of the object passed to the onactivated handler function. In Listing 17, I show you how you can respond to this information.

Listing 17. Receiving Details of Toast Activation via the onactivated Function

```
...
app.onactivated = function (args) {
    if (args.detail.kind === activation.ActivationKind.launch) {
        args.setPromise(WinJS.UI.processAll().then(function () {

            if (typeof args.detail.arguments == "string"
                    && args.detail.arguments.indexOf("notification") == 0) {
                // respond to notification being activated
            }

            var notificationId = 0;

            WinJS.Utilities.query("#container > button").listen("click",
                function (e) {
                    switch (this.id) {
                        case "toast":
                            var xml = getTemplateContent("toastImageAndText04");
                            populateTemplate(xml, toastMessages, [toastImage]);
                            setToastDuration(xml, "long");
                            setToastAudio(xml, false,
                                "ms-winsoundevent:Notification.Reminder", false);
                            setToastLaunchValue(xml, "notification" + notificationId++);
                            var notification = showToast(xml);
                            notification.addEventListener("activated", function (e) {
                                var id = getToastLaunchValue(e.target.content)
                                console.log("Toast notification " + id
                                    + " was activated");
```

```
                    });
                    break;
                }
            });
        }));
    }
};
...
```

Dealing with Dismissal

The ToastNotification object triggers the dismissed event when the use explicitly dismisses the popup, or when the user ignores it entirely and it times out. You can find out what happened by reading the value of the reason property of the event passed to the handler function. This property will return one of the values enumerated by the ToastDismissalReason object, which I have summarized in Table 4.

Table 4. The Values Defined by the ToastDismissalReason Enumeration

Name	Description
userCanceled	The user explicitly canceled the notification
applicationHidden	The application called the ToastNotifier.hide method
timedOut	The notification timed out

Listing 18 shows additions to the default.js file to deal with the dismissed event.

Listing 18. Handling the Notification dismissed Event

```
...
switch (this.id) {
    case "toast":
        var xml = getTemplateContent("toastImageAndText04");
        populateTemplate(xml, toastMessages, [toastImage]);
        setToastDuration(xml, "long");
        setToastAudio(xml, false, "ms-winsoundevent:Notification.Reminder", false);
        setToastLaunchValue(xml, "notification" + notificationId++);
        var notification = showToast(xml);
        notification.addEventListener("activated", function (e) {
            var id = getToastLaunchValue(e.target.content);
            console.log("Toast notification " + id + " was activated");
        });
        notification.addEventListener("dismissed", function (e) {
            var id = getToastLaunchValue(e.target.content);
            if (e.reason == wnote.ToastDismissalReason.userCanceled) {
                console.log("The user dismissed toast notification " + id);
            } else if (e.reason == wnote.ToastDismissalReason.timedOut) {
                console.log("Toast notification " + id + " timed out");
            }
        });
        break;
```

```
}
...
```

■ **Tip** You can only learn when a notification has been dismissed if your app is running. The system will not launch your app to tell you that the user has not responded or has cancelled a notification.

Scheduling a Toast Notification

You can schedule toast notifications to be shown to the user at a future time, potentially when your app is no longer running or is suspended. This is useful for time-specific notifications, such as calendar reminders where you want to make sure that the user gets the notification, but you can't be sure that they will be using your app at the critical moment.

You schedule toast notifications by creating a ScheduledToastNotification object, as illustrated by Listing 19, which shows the scheduleToast function I added to the default.js file to help schedule notifications.

Listing 19. The scheduleToast function Added to the default.js File of the Example App

```
...
function getToastLaunchValue(xml) {
    var attribute =
        xml.getElementsByTagName("toast")[0].attributes.getNamedItem("launch");
    return attribute ? attribute.value : null;
}

function scheduleToast(xml, time, interval, count) {
    var notification = wnote.ScheduledToastNotification(xml, time, interval, count);
    var notifier = wnote.ToastNotificationManager.createToastNotifier();
    notifier.addToSchedule(notification);
}

function setToastDuration(xml, duration) {
    var attribute = xml.createAttribute("duration");
    attribute.innerText = duration;
    xml.getElementsByTagName("toast")[0].attributes.setNamedItem(attribute);
}
...
```

The four arguments you pass to the function to create a ScheduledToastNotification object are the populated XML template, a Date object specifying the future time at which the notification will be shown, the snooze duration, and the number of times the notification will snooze.

A scheduled toast notification snoozes when the user doesn't explicitly activate it or dismiss within the period specified by the duration property (which I described earlier in the chapter). Windows will show the notification after the snooze interval, which is specified in milliseconds, has elapsed – this gives the user another chance to respond. This process is repeated for the number of times specified by the final argument. You can see how I schedule a notification in response to the Schedule Toast button being pressed in Listing 20.

Listing 20. *Scheduling a Toast Notification*

```
...
app.onactivated = function (args) {
    if (args.detail.kind === activation.ActivationKind.launch) {
        args.setPromise(WinJS.UI.processAll().then(function () {

            if (typeof args.detail.arguments == "string"
                    && args.detail.arguments.indexOf("notification") == 0) {
                // respond to notification being activated
            }

            var notificationId = 0;

            WinJS.Utilities.query("#container > button").listen("click",
                function (e) {
                    switch (this.id) {
                        case "toast":
                            // ...statements removed for brevity...
                            break;
                        case "schedule":
                            var xml = getTemplateContent("toastImageAndText04");
                            populateTemplate(xml, toastMessages, [toastImage]);
                            var scheduleDate = new Date(new Date().getTime()
                                + (10 * 1000));
                            scheduleToast(xml, scheduleDate, 60000, 2);
                            break;
                    }
                });
        }));
    }
};
...
```

In this example, I schedule the notification 10 seconds in the future (so that you don't have to wait too long when experimenting with the example). I tell Windows to snooze the notification for 60 seconds and to allow the notification to snooze twice (which means that the user will be shown the notification three times in total – once when the scheduled time is reached and twice after the notification has snoozed).

■ **Caution**   Windows enforces limits on the snooze interval and the number of snoozes allowed. The interval must be at least 1 minute and cannot be more than 1 hour. The number of snoozes must be between 1 and 5 inclusive.

Determining Whether Toast Notifications Are Enabled

You can determine whether toast notifications will be displayed by creating a ToastNotifier object (via the ToastNotificationManager) and reading the setting property. In Listing 21, you can see the final case statement I added to the default.js file to respond to the Check Status button being pressed.

Listing 21. Checking the Status for Toast Notifications

```
...
switch (this.id) {
    case "toast":
        // ...statements omitted for brevity...
        break;
    case "schedule":
        // ...statements omitted for brevity...
        break;
    case "check":
        var notifier = wnote.ToastNotificationManager.createToastNotifier();
        var value = getToastSettingValueFromEnum(notifier.setting);
        console.log("Toast setting: " + value);
        break;
}
...
```

The setting property will return one of the values enumerated by the NotificationSetting object, and to render the value into a readable form I have added the getToastSettingValueFromEnum function to the example, as shown in Listing 22.

Listing 22. The getToastSettingValueFromEnum Function

```
...
function setToastDuration(xml, duration) {
    var attribute = xml.createAttribute("duration");
    attribute.innerText = duration;
    xml.getElementsByTagName("toast")[0].attributes.setNamedItem(attribute);
}

function getToastSettingValueFromEnum(val) {
    for (var prop in wnote.NotificationSetting) {
        if (wnote.NotificationSetting[prop] == val) {
            return prop;
        }
    }
}

// ...other functions omitted for brevity...
...
```

You can see the values that the NotificationSetting object defines in Table 5. These are the same values I described in Chapter 27 when showing you how to determine whether live tile notifications will be shown to the user.

Table 5. The Values Defined by the NotificationSetting Object

Value	Description
enabled	Toast notifications will be shown to the user.
disabledForApplication	The user has disabled toast notifications for this app.

Value	Description
disabledForUser	The user has disabled toast notifications for all apps.
disabledByGroupPolicy	Toast notifications have been overridden by group policy (commonly used in enterprise deployments).
disabledByManifest	The manifest for the app does not permit toast notifications – see the start of this chapter for details of how to enable toast notifications in the manifest.

Using the App Launcher

There will be occasions when you want to notify the user of something important about data that your app can't process directly. For example, I might have an app that monitors the Pictures library for new files, but that has the capability to display only a limited range of formats. I want to notify the user when there are new files, even if I can't display them in the app directly.

This is a contrived example because Internet Explorer will happily display most types of image file – but it lets me build an example app to demonstrate the *app launcher*, which you can use to invoke other apps to process your data for you. While image formats might not be a problem, the techniques I describe in this section can be applied whenever you are dealing with data that you can't process directly.

Although this example app is simple, it is quite long given the simplicity of the feature I am going to demonstrate. I make no apology for this: it allows me to demonstrate how different features can be used together – in this case, the objects in the Windows.Storage and Windows.Storage.Search namespace (described in Chapter 21 through 23), the file activation contract (described in Chapter 24), toast notifications (this chapter), and the new addition – the app launcher. The more examples I can show you in this book, the greater the chance that you can find something you need when you have a problem to solve in the future.

Creating the Example App

The example app for this section is called FileWatcher and it presents the problem that I described previously – it monitors the Pictures library and notifies the user when new files are added. I have written the app so that it can display only JPG files. You can see the content of the default.html file for this project in Listing 23.

Listing 23. The Contents of the default.html File

```
<!DOCTYPE html>
<html>
<head>
    <meta charset="utf-8" />
    <title>FileWatcher</title>

    <!-- WinJS references -->
    <link href="//Microsoft.WinJS.1.0/css/ui-dark.css" rel="stylesheet" />
    <script src="//Microsoft.WinJS.1.0/js/base.js"></script>
    <script src="//Microsoft.WinJS.1.0/js/ui.js"></script>

    <!-- FileWatcher references -->
    <link href="/css/default.css" rel="stylesheet" />
```

```
    <script src="/js/toast.js"></script>
    <script src="/js/default.js"></script>
</head>
<body>
    <div id="imgContainer">
        <img id="imgElem" src="ms-appx:///images/logo.png"/>
    </div>
    <button id="startButton">Start</button>
</body>
</html>
```

The layout for this app is based around an img element and a button. I'll start monitoring the Pictures library when the button is clicked and use the img element to display JPG images when the user activates my toast notification. You can see the CSS I used to style the layout in Listing 24, which shows the css/default.css file.

Listing 24. *The Contents of the default.css File*

```
body { display: -ms-flexbox; -ms-flex-direction: column;
    -ms-flex-align: center; -ms-flex-pack: center;}

#imgContainer { border: medium solid white;
    width: 512px; height: 382px;
    margin: 20px; text-align: center;}

img {height: 382px; max-width: 512px;}
button {font-size: 24pt; margin: 10px;}
```

Adding the Images

I have added a file to the images directory called logo.png, which you can see I have used in the src attribute of the img element in the default.html file. This image shows a white icon on a transparent background, and you can see the image in Figure 7, which shows the layout of the app.

Figure 7. *The initial layout of the FileWatcher app*

I have also replaced the image files used by the manifest with files that contain the same icon, but are sized to the required dimensions. You can get all these image files as part of the free source code download, which is available from apress.com.

Defining the JavaScript Code

This app will generate toast notifications, so I have taken the functions I need from the first part of this chapter and put them in a file called js/toast.js. I have not made any changes to the functions, other than to place them in a namespace called Toast. You can see the contents of the toast.js file in Listing 25.

Listing 25. *The toast.js File*

```
(function () {
    "use strict";

    var wnote = Windows.UI.Notifications;

    WinJS.Namespace.define("Toast", {

        getTemplateContent: function(templateName) {
            var template = wnote.ToastTemplateType[templateName];
            return wnote.ToastNotificationManager.getTemplateContent(template);
        },

        populateTemplate: function (xml, textValues, imgValues) {
            if (textValues) {
                var textNodes = xml.getElementsByTagName("text");
                var count = Math.min(textNodes.length, textValues.length);
                for (var i = 0; i < count; i++) {
                    textNodes[i].innerText = textValues[i];
                }
            }
            if (imgValues) {
                var imgNodes = xml.getElementsByTagName("image");
                var count = Math.min(imgNodes.length, imgValues.length);
                for (var i = 0; i < count; i++) {
                    imgNodes[i].attributes.getNamedItem("src").innerText = imgValues[i]
                }
            }
            return xml;
        },

        showToast: function(xml) {
            var notification = wnote.ToastNotification(xml);
            var notifier = wnote.ToastNotificationManager.createToastNotifier();
            notifier.show(notification);
            return notification;
        }

    });
})();
```

I only need a few of the functions because this app will only create basic toast notifications. The main code for this app, contained in the default.js file that is shown in Listing 26, uses a file query to monitor the Pictures library and displays a toast notification when new files are added. When the user activates the notification, the img element in the layout will display the new file – that is, as long as it is a JPG file. For the purposes of this example, I am pretending that my app can't handle other file formats in the same way. In the listing, you will see a comment that is acting as a placeholder for the code that will handle other file types.

Listing 26. The Initial Contents of the js/default.js File

```
(function () {
    "use strict";

    var app = WinJS.Application;
    var activation = Windows.ApplicationModel.Activation;
    var storage = Windows.Storage;

    var fileList = [];

    app.onactivated = function (args) {
        if (args.detail.kind === activation.ActivationKind.launch) {
            args.setPromise(WinJS.UI.processAll().then(function () {

                startButton.addEventListener("click", function (e) {
                    startButton.disabled = true;
                    var query = storage.KnownFolders.picturesLibrary.createFileQuery(
                        storage.Search.CommonFileQuery.orderByName);

                    query.addEventListener("contentschanged", function (e) {

                        query.getFilesAsync().then(function (files) {
                            files.forEach(function (file) {
                                if (fileList.indexOf(file.path) == -1) {
                                    fileList.push(file.path);
                                    displayToastForFile(file);
                                }
                            });
                        });
                    });

                    setTimeout(function () {
                        query.getFilesAsync().then(function (files) {
                            files.forEach(function (file) {
                                fileList.push(file.path);
                            });
                        });
                    }, 1000);
                });
            }));
        }
    };
```

```
function displayToastForFile(file) {
    var messages = ["Found new file", file.displayName];
    var xml = Toast.getTemplateContent("toastImageAndText04");
    Toast.populateTemplate(xml, messages, ["ms-appx:///images/logo.png"]);
    var notification = Toast.showToast(xml);
    notification.addEventListener("activated", function (e) {
        if (file.fileType == ".jpg") {
            imgElem.src = URL.createObjectURL(file);
        } else {
            // ... code to process other file types will go here...
        }
    });
}

app.start();
})();
```

The contentschanged event that I receive when a new file is added to the Pictures library doesn't provide me with details of the newly added files, so I keep an array of the file paths and use it to work out which files in the library are new. You may want to monitor a different location if you have a large number of files in your Pictures library because the array will get quite large.

Updating the Manifest

Two manifest changes are required for this app to work. Open the package.appxmanifest file and navigate to the Capabilities tab. Check the Pictures Library option, as shown in Figure 8. This is required to allow the app to monitor the Pictures library for new files.

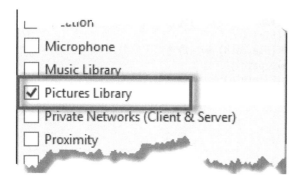

Figure 8. *Enabling access to the Pictures library*

The second change is to declare that the app will generate toast notifications. Navigate to the Application UI section of the manifest and set the Toast capable option to Yes, as shown in Figure 9. (You can also set the logo for the app as well, although this isn't a requirement. I have reused the logos I created for the PhotoAlbum app in Chapter 24.)

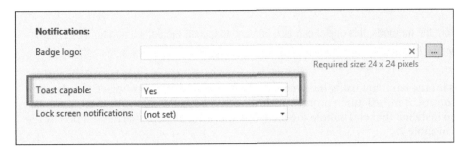

Figure 9. *Enabling Toast Notification for the Example App*

Testing the Example App

Start the example app and click the Start button to begin monitoring the Pictures library for new files. You will see a toast notification if you copy a new file to the Pictures library, as shown in Figure 10. (It can take a few seconds for the new file to be reported to the app.)

■ **Note** You will need to run this app on a real Windows 8 device such as the local development machine because the notification won't be displayed in the Visual Studio simulator.

Figure 10. *A toast notification reporting a newly discovered file*

If you activate the notification by clicking or touching it, then the app will display the image using the img element in the markup, but only if it is a JPG file. If it isn't, then nothing will happen. I'll remedy this in the next section.

Using the App Launcher

Launching the default app for a file is done through the Windows.System.Launcher object, which defines the methods shown in Table 6.

Table 6. *The Methods Defined by the Windows.System.Launcher Object*

Name	Description
launchFileAsync(file)	Launches the default app for the specified file
launchfileAsync(file, options)	Launches the default app for the specified file using the options provided
launchUriAsync(url)	Launches the default app for the specified URL
launchUriAsync(url, options)	Launches the default app for the specified URL using the options provided

■ **Tip**   As you can see from the methods, this object can also be used to launch the default app for a URL. I am going to focus on file activation in this chapter, but the process for URL activation follows the same pattern.

You specify options for the launcher using the Windows.System.LauncherOptions object. This lets you get some fine-grained control over the launch process, including instructing Windows as to what should happen if there is no app installed that can handle the file type. You can see the properties defined by the LauncherOptions object in Table 7.

Table 7. The Properties Defined by the Windows.System.LauncherOptions Object

Name	Description
contentType	Sets the data type of the file being opened.
displayApplicationPicker	When set to true, Windows will display the Open With dialog that will prompt the user to choose an app rather than launching the default app.
fallbackUri	Specifies a URL that will be presented to the user if there are no installed apps that can process the file. This is an opportunity to present the user with a store front or catalogue of suitable apps.
preferredApplicationDisplayName	Sets the name of the app in the Windows Store that the user should be directed toward if there are no apps installed that can handle the file type.
treatAsUntrusted	When set to true, Windows will treat the file as being potentially dangerous.

You can see how I use the Launcher and LauncherOptions object in my example app in Listing 27, which shows the changes I have made to the displayToastForFile function in the default.js file. I use the launchFileAsyc method with a LauncherOptions object, configured to present the user with the list of apps that can process the image file.

Listing 27. Adding Support for Launching Default Apps

```
...
function displayToastForFile(file) {
    var messages = ["Found new file", file.displayName];
    var xml = Toast.getTemplateContent("toastImageAndText04");
    Toast.populateTemplate(xml, messages, ["ms-appx:///images/logo.png"]);
    var notification = Toast.showToast(xml);
    notification.addEventListener("activated", function (e) {
        if (file.fileType == ".jpg") {
            imgElem.src = URL.createObjectURL(file);
        } else {
            var options = new Windows.System.LauncherOptions();
            options.displayApplicationPicker = true;
            Windows.System.Launcher.launchFileAsync(file, options);
        }
    });
}
app.start();
...
```

If you start the app, click the Start button and copy any file that isn't a JPG file to the Pictures library and you'll be presented with the same kind of toast notification I showed you in the previous section. The difference is that when you activate the toast, you'll see a list of Windows Store apps that have implemented the file activation contract (and desktop apps that have implemented the equivalent desktop feature). Select one of the apps, and the file you added to the library will be opened.

This feature works without you having to know what apps are available for a given file type or which app the user has selected as the default. To see how this works, copy in a completely different type of file – such as a Word DOCX file – and you will see that Windows will take care of the details. Even better, Microsoft has streamlined the process for locating a suitable app when there isn't one installed. To see how this works, take an existing file and change the file extension to .xxxxx (or any extension for which the system doesn't have a suitable app). When you activate the toast notification in the sample app, you'll be presented with a helpful warning and an invitation to locate the software you need, as illustrated in Figure 11.

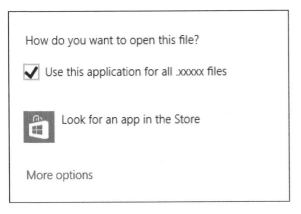

Figure 11. *Helping the user locate an app to deal with a file type*

This is a simple feature, but it allows you to build apps that can operate on files whose format they don't support directly. This feature also leverages the file and protocol activation contracts, allowing you to build complementary apps that *can* process specific file formats.

Summary

In this chapter, I showed you how to attract the user's attention using toast notifications. Used sparingly and thoughtfully, this is an important feature that can enhance the value of your app to the user. Used excessively, and you create an app that is annoying, intrusive, and that interrupts the users' concentration for notifications they don't value. I also showed you how to use the app launcher, which allows you to launch the default app for a file or URL without knowing which app is configured as the default, or even if there is a suitable app installed. In the next chapter, I show you how to use the Windows support for sensors to bring data about the real world into your app.

CHAPTER 29

Working with Sensors

Windows 8 supports a sensor framework that you can use to get information about the conditions in which the device is operating. I describe most frequently encountered sensors in this chapter, starting with the location sensor, with which you can determine where in the world the device is being used.

Windows will try and determine the device location even if there is no special location-sensing hardware in the device, such as a GPS receiver. The other sensors I describe in this chapter do require special hardware, such as light and acceleration sensors, although this kind of equipment is increasingly common, especially in laptops and tablets.

I show you how to read the data from the different sensors in this chapter, but how you use this data to the advantage of the user is very app-specific. As a consequence, the examples generally just display the sensor data as text.

As you read this chapter, you'll encounter a few places where I have noted that certain features don't work for the sensors in my test hardware. This isn't uncommon because there is a lot of variability in the quality of sensors and their device drivers, and so careful testing is required.

When using sensors, be careful not to make bold inferences about what the user is doing based on the data you receive. For example, when using the light level sensor, don't assume that it is nighttime just because the light-level is low – this could have happened because the device is being stored in a bag or just because the sensor is being obscured. Always allow the user to override the changes to the app's behavior made based on sensor data and, where possible, try to draw together data from different sources before making an assumption about the current conditions – for example, by combining light levels with the current time and location, you can avoid assuming it is night during the working day. Table 1 provides the summary for this chapter.

Table 1. *Chapter Summary*

Problem	Solution	Listing
Determine the location of the device	Use the `Geolocator.getGeopositionAsync()` method	1–9
Track changes in the location	Handle the `positionchanged` event	10
Determine the ambient light level	Use the `LightSensor` object	11–13
Get details of how the device is tilted	Use the `Inclinometer` object	14
Detect device movement	Use the `Accelerometer` object	15
Determine the device heading	Use the `Compass` object	16

Creating the Example App

I am going to create a single example app that will allow me to demonstrate each of the sensors I cover in this chapter. I'll do this by following a pattern I have used elsewhere in this book, which is to create an app that uses a NavBar to navigate to content pages, each of which covers a major feature. I created a new Visual Studio project called Sensors, and you can see the content of the default.html file in Listing 1. This file contains the target element into which I'll load the content pages and the NavBar, with commands for each page.

Listing 1. *The Contents of the default.html File*

```html
<!DOCTYPE html>
<html>
<head>
    <meta charset="utf-8" />
    <title>Sensors</title>
    <link href="//Microsoft.WinJS.1.0/css/ui-dark.css" rel="stylesheet" />
    <script src="//Microsoft.WinJS.1.0/js/base.js"></script>
    <script src="//Microsoft.WinJS.1.0/js/ui.js"></script>
    <link href="/css/default.css" rel="stylesheet" />
    <script src="/js/default.js"></script>
</head>
<body>
    <div id="contentTarget">
        <h1 class="message">Select a page from the NavBar</h1>
    </div>
    <div id="navbar" data-win-control="WinJS.UI.AppBar"
        data-win-options="{placement:'top'}">

        <button data-win-control="WinJS.UI.AppBarCommand"
            data-win-options="{id:'geolocation', label:'Location',
                icon:'\u0031', section:'selection'}">
        </button>
        <button data-win-control="WinJS.UI.AppBarCommand"
            data-win-options="{id:'light', label:'Light',
                icon:'\u0032', section:'selection'}">
        </button>
        <button data-win-control="WinJS.UI.AppBarCommand"
            data-win-options="{id:'tilt', label:'Tilt',
                icon:'\u0033', section:'selection'}">
        </button>
        <button data-win-control="WinJS.UI.AppBarCommand"
            data-win-options="{id:'acceleration', label:'Acceleration',
                icon:'\u0034', section:'selection'}">
        </button>
        <button data-win-control="WinJS.UI.AppBarCommand"
            data-win-options="{id:'direction', label:'Direction',
                icon:'\u0035', section:'selection'}">
        </button>
    </div>
</body>
</html>
```

The HTML file contains buttons that will navigate all of the content pages I use in this chapter, but I won't add the files until the start of each section. You can see the styles I have defined to manage the layout of the elements in this example in Listing 2, which shows the contents of the /css/default.css file.

Listing 2. The contents of the /css/default.css File

```
body {display: -ms-flexbox; -ms-flex-direction: column;
    -ms-flex-align: stretch; -ms-flex-pack: center;      }
#contentTarget {display: -ms-flexbox; -ms-flex-direction: row;
    -ms-flex-align: stretch; -ms-flex-pack: center;}
.container { border: medium solid white; margin: 10px; padding: 10px;}
.containerHeader {text-align: center;}

#buttonsContainer button {font-size: 20pt; margin: 20pt; display: block; width: 80%;}

*.imgElem {height: 500px;}
*.imgTitle { color: white; background-color: black;font-size: 30pt; padding-left: 10px;}

.messageItem {display: block; font-size: 20pt; width: 100%; margin-top: 10px;}
#messageContainer {width: 60%;}
.messageList {height: 80vh;}

.label { margin: 20px; width: 600px;}
.label span { display: inline-block; width: 250px; text-align: right;}
h1.warning { display: none; text-align: center;}
```

And, finally, I have defined the code in Listing 3, which shows the contents of the /js/default.js file. I am focusing on devices in this chapter, and so I am not worried about managing different lifecycle events – as a consequence, the JavaScript code performs a very basic app initialization to set up the navigation for the content pages, which I will add to the pages folder in the Visual Studio project.

Listing 3. The Contents of the /js/default.js File

```
(function () {

    var app = WinJS.Application;
    var activation = Windows.ApplicationModel.Activation;

    WinJS.Navigation.addEventListener("navigating", function (e) {
        WinJS.UI.Animation.exitPage(contentTarget.children).then(function () {
            WinJS.Utilities.empty(contentTarget);
            WinJS.UI.Pages.render(e.detail.location,
                contentTarget, WinJS.Navigation.state)
                .then(function () {
                    return WinJS.UI.Animation.enterPage(contentTarget.children)
                });
        });
    });

    app.onactivated = function (args) {
        if (args.detail.previousExecutionState
                != activation.ApplicationExecutionState.suspended) {
```

```
                args.setPromise(WinJS.UI.processAll().then(function () {
                    navbar.addEventListener("click", function (e) {
                        var navTarget = "pages/" + e.target.winControl.id + ".html";
                        WinJS.Navigation.navigate(navTarget);
                        navbar.winControl.hide();
                    });
                }));
        }
    };

    app.start();
})();
```

If you start the app and display the NavBar, you will see the layout shown in Figure 1 – although clicking on the NavBar command bars will generate an error because I have not yet added the files that are loaded when they are activated.

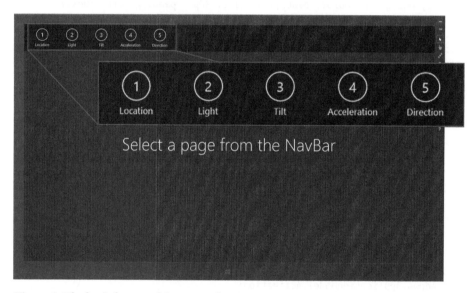

Figure 1. *The basic layout of the example app*

■ **Note**   To keep this example as simple as possible, I have written each content page as though it were the only one that will be displayed. That means that you will have to restart the example app before displaying the data from a different sensor.

Working with Geolocation

Geolocation is an increasingly important feature for app development because it provides the basis for tailoring the user experience based where the user happens to be. Many Windows 8 devices will be equipped with GPS hardware, but Windows can also attempt to determine the current location for devices that *don't* have GPS by combining information taken from a range of alternative sources – including the device IP address and the names of nearby wireless networks, for example – a technique, which can be surprisingly accurate. In the sections that follow, I'll show you how to use the geolocation feature and how to test geolocation using the Visual Studio simulator.

■ **Note** Geolocation is an example of a feature that you can access using a Windows-specific API or through an HTML5 API. I find that the Windows APIs tend to offer fine-grained features that are more consistent with the capabilities of a Windows device, which is only to be expected since the HTML5 APIs are intended for very broad use. I will be using the Windows geolocation API in this chapter.

Preparing the Geolocation Example

To demonstrate the geolocation feature, I have added a file to the pages folder of the Visual Studio project called geolocation.html. You can see the contents of this file in Listing 4.

Listing 4. The Contents of the geolocation.html File

```
<!DOCTYPE html>
<html>
<head>
    <title></title>
    <script src="/pages/geolocation.js"></script>
</head>
<body>
    <div id="template" data-win-control="WinJS.Binding.Template">
        <div class="messageItem" data-win-bind="innerText: message"></div>
    </div>

    <div id="buttonsContainer" class="container">
        <button>Get Location</button>
        <button id="start">Start Tracking</button>
        <button id="stop" disabled>Stop Tracking</button>
    </div>

    <div id="messageContainer" class="container">
        <h1 class="containerHeader">Messages</h1>
        <hr />
        <div id="messageList" class="messageList" data-win-control="WinJS.UI.ListView"
            data-win-options="{ itemTemplate: template,
                layout: {type: WinJS.UI.ListLayout}}">
        </div>
    </div>
</body>
</html>
```

This file defines a layout with three buttons in a left-hand panel that will activate different geolocation features and a large right-hand panel that I'll use to display update messages. I have put the JavaScript for this example into a separate file called /pages/geolocation.js, which you can see in Listing 5. At the moment, this file contains a handler function that listens for when the button elements are clicked and placeholder functions that will be executed when the events are received – I'll populate these functions in the sections that follow as I show you different aspects of the geolocation feature. I have also added the code that lets me easily display messages in the app layout.

Listing 5. The Initial Contents of the /pages/geolocation.js File

```
(function () {
    var geo = Windows.Devices.Geolocation;

    var messages = new WinJS.Binding.List();
    function writeMessage(msg) {
        messages.push({ message: msg });
    }

    function getFromCode(src, code) {
        for (var propName in src) {
            if (code == src[propName]) { return propName; }
        }
    }

    WinJS.UI.Pages.define("/pages/geolocation.html", {
        ready: function () {
            messageList.winControl.itemDataSource = messages.dataSource;

            WinJS.Utilities.query("#buttonsContainer button").listen("click",
                function (e) {
                switch (e.target.innerText) {
                    case "Get Location":
                        getLocation();
                        break;
                    case "Start Tracking":
                        startTracking();
                        break;

                    case "Stop Tracking":
                        stopTracking();
                        break;
                }
            });
        }
    });

    function getLocation() {
        // ...code will be added here...
    }

    function startTracking() {
        // ...code will be added here...
    }

    function stopTracking() {
```

```
        // ...code will be added here...
    }
})();
```

Enabling Location Access in the Manifest

Access to the device location must be enabled in the manifest, which is done by opening the package. appxmanifest file, navigating to the Capabilities section, and checking the Location option, as shown in Figure 2.

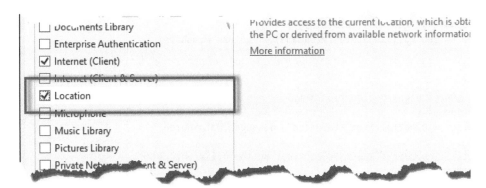

Figure 2. Enabling location access in the manifest

■ **Caution** You will generate an error if you try and access the device location without enabling the Location capability in the manifest.

Getting a Location Snapshot

The simplest way to get the current location of the device is to take a snapshot, which means that you ask the system for the current location, the system provides it, and then you are done. The alternative is to track the current location, which means that the system provides your app with updates as the location changes. I'll show you how location tracking works later in the chapter, but taking a location snapshot is relatively simple and lets me introduce the objects that support the geolocation feature, which are defined in the Windows.Devices.Geolocation namespace.

■ **Note** Unless I note otherwise, all of the new objects I refer to in this section can be found in the Windows. Devices.Geolocation namespace, which I have aliased to the variable geo in the examples.

To add support for taking a location snapshot, I implemented the getLocation function in the /pages/ geolocation.js file, as shown in Listing 6.

Listing 6. Implementing the getLocation Function to Take a Location Snapshot

```javascript
(function () {
    var geo = Windows.Devices.Geolocation;
    var geoloc;

    var messages = new WinJS.Binding.List();
    function writeMessage(msg) {
        messages.push({ message: msg });
    }

    function getStatus(code) {
        for (var propName in geo.PositionStatus) {
            if (code == geo.PositionStatus[propName]) { return propName; }
        }
    }

    WinJS.UI.Pages.define("/pages/geolocation.html", {
        ready: function () {
            messageList.winControl.itemDataSource = messages.dataSource;

            WinJS.Utilities.query("#buttonsContainer button").listen("click",
                function (e) {
                switch (e.target.innerText) {
                    case "Get Location":
                        getLocation();
                        break;
                    case "Start Tracking":
                        startTracking();
                        break;
                    case "Stop Tracking":
                        stopTracking();
                        break;
                }
            });

            geoloc = new geo.Geolocator();
            writeMessage("Status: " + getStatus(geoloc.locationStatus));
            geoloc.addEventListener("statuschanged", function (e) {
                writeMessage("Status: " + getStatus(geoloc.locationStatus));
            });
        }
    });

    function getLocation() {
        geoloc.desiredAccuracy = geo.PositionAccuracy.high;
        geoloc.getGeopositionAsync().then(function (pos) {
            writeMessage("Snapshot - Lat: " + pos.coordinate.latitude
                + " Lon: " + pos.coordinate.longitude
                + " (" + pos.coordinate.timestamp.toTimeString() + ")");
        });
```

```
    }
    function startTracking() { /* ...code will go here... */}
    function stopTracking() { /* ...code will go here... */}
})();
```

Although there are only a small number of additions, there is quite a lot going on in this code, so I'll break things down step-by-step in the sections that follow.

Creating and Configuring the Geolocator Object

The first step in getting the location is to create and then configure a Geolocator object. One object can be used to get the location multiple times, so I have created a Geolocation object in the ready function that is executed when the content page is loaded – this will allow me to use one Geolocator object throughout this example. No constructor arguments are used when you create a new Geolocator object, as shown in Listing 7, where I have repeated the statement from the geolocation.js file.

Listing 7. Creating a new Geolocator Object

```
...
geoloc = new geo.Geolocator();
...
```

The next step is to configure the Geolocator object. When taking a location snapshot, there is only one setting, which is accessed through the desiredAccuracy property. This property must be set to one of the values defined by the PositionAccuracy enumeration, which I have described in Table 2.

Table 2. The Values Defined by the PositionAccuracy Object

Name	Description
default	Accuracy is less important than minimizing the resource and financial costs
high	Accuracy is important, even if it costs money or consumed device resource

The default and high values don't specify how accurately the location should be determined. Instead, they specify how the device should go about getting the location. The default value will favor less-accurate information that can be obtained quickly, easily, and free-of-charge. The high value will get the most accurate position that the device can produce, and it will use all of the resources it has to get that accuracy, even if it means consuming a lot of battery power or using services that can cost the user money (such as location services from cell service providers).

■ **Tip** Notice that you can't specify the technique used to obtain the location or even figure out the different options that the device has to get it. All you can do is set the level of accuracy you would like and leave the rest to Windows.

The decision about which value to use for the desiredAccurcy property is typically best made by the user, not least because of the financial considerations. It is bad enough to find that a badly written app has used up all your battery charge, but it is unbearable to find that it has been costing you money while doing so. You can see how I have specified the high accuracy option in my example in Listing 8, where I have repeated the statement from the geolocation.js file.

Listing 8. Configuring the Accuracy of the Geolocator Object

```
...
geoloc.desiredAccuracy = geo.PositionAccuracy.high;
...
```

I am not worried about the cost of getting the location because I'll be using the Visual Studio simulator to provide location data to the app.

Monitoring the Geolocation Status

The Geolocator object defines the statuschanged event, which provides notifications about the state of the geolocation feature. The status of a Geoloctor object is obtained through the locationStatus property and will be one of the values defined by the PositionStatus enumeration, which I have listed in Table 3.

Table 3. The Values Defined by the PositionStatus Object

Name	Description
ready	Location data is available
initializing	The provider for location data is initializing (I usually see this when working with GPS hardware that is still trying to find satellites)
noData	There is no location data available
disabled	Location data has been disabled
notInitialized	No request to obtain the location has been made yet
notAvailable	The location feature is not available in the current version of Windows

I handle the statuschanged event by reading the value of the locationStatus property and displaying a message in the ListView control in the right-hand panel of the app layout. If you start the app, you will be prompted to allow the app to access the location data, as shown in Figure 3.

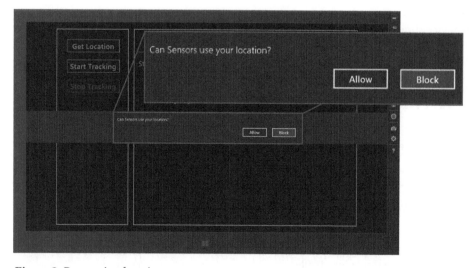

Figure 3. Requesting location access

If you click the Block button, Windows will deny your app access to the location data, and the statuschanged event will fire to indicate that the locationStatus property has changed to disabled, as shown in Figure 4.

Figure 4. *The effect of disabling access to the location data*

If you get the disabled value in your app, then you will know that you won't be able to access the location data. At this point, depending on your app, you might be able to carry on and offer some kind of reduced functionality to the user or you might need to display a message that encourages the user to grant your app the access it needs. What you should *not* do is ignore the disabled value and just try to read location data anyway – you won't get any data, and it won't be obvious to the user that the lack of location access is the reason why your app produces odd results.

To enable access to the location data, activate the Settings Charm, click the Permissions link, and change the position of the Location toggle switch. When you reload the app, you will see that the status is displayed as ready, indicating that there is location data available, as shown in Figure 5.

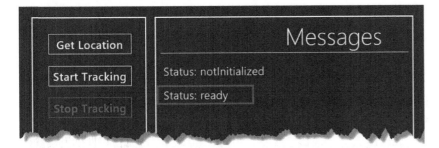

Figure 5. *The effect of enabling access to the location data*

Getting the Location

Clicking the Get Location button in the app layout calls the getLocation function in the geolocation.js file, and it is this function that generates a snapshot of the location. In Listing 9, I have repeated the getLocation implementation.

Listing 9. *The Implementation of the getLocation Function*

```
...
function getLocation() {
    geoloc.desiredAccuracy = geo.PositionAccuracy.high;
```

```
        geoloc.getGeopositionAsync().then(function (pos) {
            writeMessage("Snapshot - Lat: " + pos.coordinate.latitude
                + " Lon: " + pos.coordinate.longitude
                + " (" + pos.coordinate.timestamp.toTimeString() + ")");
        });
    }
    ...
```

Once I have configured the Geolocator object, I call the getGeopositionAsync method. This method returns a Promise that, when fulfilled, will yield a snapshot of the current location. The snapshot is passed to the then function as a Geoposition object, which defines the two properties I have described in Table 4.

Table 4. The Properties Defined by the Geoposition Object

Name	Description
civicAddress	Returns a CivicAddress object, used to describe the street address of the location
coordinate	Returns a Geocoordinate object, used to describe the coordinates of the location

The CivicAddress object is something of a disappointment because Windows doesn't populate the object with details of the address. The idea is that third-party additions to Windows can provide this service, but they are not widely used, so you can't expect to find one installed on the user's device.

GOING BEYOND GETTING THE LOCATION

The Windows location sensor is pretty good at giving you the longitude and latitude of the device, but that's about it, and you can't even rely on the CivicAddress object being populated automatically. If you want to go beyond getting basic coordinates, then you will need to use one of the many mapping web services that are available. I like openstreetmap.org, which has an excellent reverse geocoding service (which translates coordinates into street addresses) and accurate mapping data. Best of all, the services are free to use and don't require you to embed API keys into your app (which is a pain to manage when keys are changed or expire).

If you are less bothered by API keys than I am, then you might like to consider the Bing Map AJAX control, which makes it pretty easy to get addresses and display maps in a Windows app. There are usage limitations, and fees are charged for high request volumes, but the maps are pretty good and there are some code examples for app development. You can find more details at http://bingmapsportal.com. There is, of course, an equivalent library from Google, which works every bit as well the Bing option and also requires API keys and fees for high usage. You can get details of the Google APIs at https://developers.google.com/maps.

I am going to focus on the Geocoordinate object, which *is* properly populated and defines the properties I have described in Table 5.

Table 5. The Properties Defined by the Geocoordinate Object

Name	Description
accuracy	The accuracy of the location data, in meters
altitude	The altitude of the location, in meters
altitideAccuracy	The accuracy of the altitude value, in meters

Name	Description
heading	The heading in degrees relative to true north
latitude	The latitude in degrees
longitude	The longitude in degrees
speed	The speed at which the device is moving
timestamp	The time at which the location was determined

Not all of the properties in a Geocoordinate object will be populated – this can be because the device doesn't have hardware capable of providing details of altitude, for example, or because some of the properties are only available when the location is being tracked, as opposed to taking a snapshot. In the example, when the Promise returned by the getGeopositionAsync method is fulfilled, I use the latitude, longitude, and timestamp properties to display a message in the right-hand panel of the app layout.

Testing the Location Snapshot

Now that you have seen how the various objects fit together, it is time to test the example app's ability to take a snapshot of the location data. The easiest way to do this is to use the Visual Studio simulator, which has the ability to simulate location data. Before starting the app, click the Set location button on the simulator window, check the Use simulated location option, and enter a latitude value of 38.89 and a longitude value of -77.03, as shown in Figure 6 (this is the location of the White House).

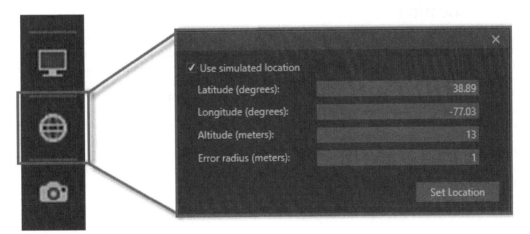

Figure 6. Entering simulated location data

Click the Set Location button to apply the simulated location and then start the example app. Click the Get Location button to generate a location snapshot and display a message in the app layout. You can see the result of using the simulated data for this test in Figure 7.

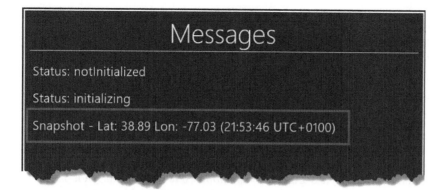

Figure 7. *Generating a location snapshot*

You don't have to use simulated data. If you don't check the Use simulated location option in the simulator popup, then the app will read the location data from Windows instead. I have used simulated data because I want to create a result that you can repeat consistently, but I recommend playing around with the real data as well – especially if you have a device that doesn't have GPS support. Although variable, the accuracy of non–GPS location data can be pretty amazing – using just wireless network names, my PC can determine its location to within about 200 feet of my house.

Tracking the Location

The next feature to show you is the ability to track the location as it changes. If you want to monitor the location of the device, you could call the getGeopositionAsync method periodically, but that turns out to be a difficult process to get right. You don't want to snapshot the location too frequently because the device may not be moving, and you will be consuming device resources (and possibly the user's money) needlessly. If you snapshot too infrequently, you will miss the moment when the device moves and end up with a partial data track.

To make it easier to track the location, the Geolocator object defines the positionchanged event, which is triggered when the location of the device moves beyond a threshold you have defined. You can see how I have added support for location tracking to the example app in Listing 10, which shows my implementation of the startTracking and stopTracking functions and a new function to write a message displaying the location.

Listing 10. The Implementation of Location Tracking

```
...
function startTracking() {
    geoloc.movementThreshold = 100;
    geoloc.addEventListener("positionchanged", displayLocation);
    writeMessage("Tracking started");
    start.disabled = !(stop.disabled = false);
}

function stopTracking() {
    geoloc.removeEventListener("positionchanged", displayLocation);
    writeMessage("Tracking stopped");
    start.disabled = !(stop.disabled = true);
```

```
}

function displayLocation(e) {
    writeMessage("Track - Lat: " + e.position.coordinate.latitude
        + " Lon: " + e.position.coordinate.longitude
        + " (" + e.position.coordinate.timestamp.toTimeString() + ")");

}
...
```

You set the threshold for movement by setting a value for the Geolocator.movementThreshold property. When the device moves farther than the number of meters you specify, the positionchanged event will be triggered.

■ **Tip**   One meter is about 3 feet and 3 inches. It is possible to specify a movement threshold that is below the accuracy to which the device can determine its location, in which case the positionchanged event will be triggered whenever the location changes.

In the startTracking function, I set the threshold to 100 meters (about 110 yards) and then use the addEventListener method to set up an event listener for the positionchanged event, specifying that the displayLocation function, which is also defined in the listing, be used to handle the event. To stop tracking, I simply call the removeEventListener function to unregister the displayLocation as an event listener.

The event object that is passed to the handler function defines a position property that returns a Geoposition object, and I use its coordinate property to display details of the new location.

To test location tracking, start the app, navigate to the geolocation.html page via the NavBar, and click the Start Tracking button. Now click the Visual Studio simulator's Set location button, enter new coordinates, and click the Set Location button. A new message will be displayed in the app layout each time you set a new coordinate, as long as the new location is at least 100 meters away from the old location. You can see the effect of tracking the location in Figure 8.

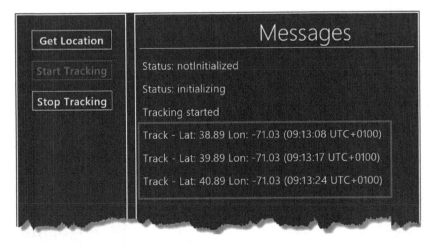

Figure 8. Tracking the location using the positionchanged event

Using the Light Sensor

Light sensors are increasingly common these days and are used to vary the amount of power used to illuminate a device screen, so as to minimize battery consumption (the screen is often the largest consumer of device power, and dimming the screen in low-light situations saves a lot of power and makes the screen less tiring to use). For an app, the most common use of a light sensor is to try and figure out when the device is outdoors or when the user has gone to sleep, both of which can be correlated to other information (such as the time or the location) to change the behavior of the app. A few years ago, I had a PDA that used its light sensor to offer unusual options such as a dawn alarm and a reminder if I spent too many hours indoors – it wasn't always successful, but it was fun to play with.

■ **Note**   Unlike the location sensor, which will generate a location even if the device doesn't have dedicated location hardware, the light sensor (and the other sensors I describe in this chapter) require actual hardware. The hardware is pretty common, and for testing the example project, I used my Dell Inspiron Duo that I mentioned in Chapter 6. The Duo has a touch screen and a range of hardware sensors, which make it ideal for testing apps. I don't want to sound like an advert for Dell (which I have very little love for), but the Duo is available pretty cheaply, especially used, and I find it invaluable for testing apps before deployment, especially when it comes to making sure that my touch screen interactions make sense and feel natural.

To demonstrate the light sensor, I have added a file to the pages folder of the project called light.html, the contents of which you can see in Listing 11.

Listing 11. The Contents of the light.html File

```
<!DOCTYPE html>
<html>
<head>
    <title></title>
    <script>
        WinJS.UI.Pages.define("/pages/light.html", {
            ready: function () {
                var sensor = Windows.Devices.Sensors.LightSensor.getDefault();
                if (sensor == null) {
                    WinJS.Utilities.query(".message").setStyle("display", "none");
                    WinJS.Utilities.query(".warning").setStyle("display", "block");
                } else {
                    //displaySensorReading(sensor.getCurrentReading().illuminanceInLux);
                    sensor.addEventListener("readingchanged", function (e) {
                        displaySensorReading(e.reading.illuminanceInLux);
                    });
                }
            }
        });

        function displaySensorReading(reading) {
            level.innerText = reading;
            var conditionText = "Unknown";
```

```
            if (reading > 10000) {
                conditionText = "Outdoors";
            } else if (reading > 300) {
                conditionText = "Office";
            } else if (reading > 50) {
                conditionText: "Home";
            } else {
                conditionText = "Dark";
            }
            condition.innerText = conditionText;
        }

    </script>
</head>
<body>
    <div id="lightContainer" class="container">
        <h1 class="message warning">No Light Sensor Installed</h1>
        <h1 class="message">Light level: <span id="level">(None)</span></h1>
        <h1 class="message">Condition: <span id="condition">(None)</span></h1>
    </div>
</body>
</html>
```

The light sensor is represented by the Windows.Devices.Sensors.LightSensor object, and you get a reference to the sensor through the getDefault method, like this:

```
...
var sensor = Windows.Devices.Sensors.LightSensor.getDefault();
...
```

If the value returned by the getDefault method is null, then the current device does not contain a light sensor. In the example, I check for the null result and display a message if the sensor isn't present.

Taking a Snapshot of the Light Level

Once you have obtained the sensor object, you can take a snapshot of the sensor value by calling the getCurrentReading method, as shown in Listing 12.

Listing 12. Taking a Snapshot of the Light Level

```
...
displaySensorReading(sensor.getCurrentReading().illuminanceInLux);
...
```

The getCurrentReading method returns a Windows.Devices.Sensors.LightSensorReading object, which defines the two properties I have described in Table 6.

Table 6. The Properties Defined by the LightSensorReading Object

Name	Description
illuminanceInLux	Returns the light level, expressed in lux
timestamp	Returns a Date object representing the time that the sensor reported the reading

The illuminanceInLux property returns the light level expressed in lux. Wikipedia has a nice description of the lux unit and a table that describes some helpful lux ranges. You can see the article at http://en.wikipedia.org/wiki/Lux. I have used a simplified set of these lux ranges to make a guess at the conditions in which the device is operating, including being outdoors, inside a house, and inside an office – you can see my mappings in the displaySensorReading function in the light.html file.

■ **Caution**   You will notice that the call to the getCurrentReading method is commented out in Listing 11, which shows the contents of the light.html file. If I call the getCurrentReading method to take a snapshot of the light level, I find that tracking the level (which I describe in the next section) won't work anymore. This may just be a characteristic of the light sensor in my Dell Duo, but I don't have access to any other sensors to make sure.

Tracking the Light Level

Taking a snapshot of the light level can be useful, but generally you will want to receive notifications as the light level changes. The LightSensor object defines the readingchanged event, which is triggered when the light level changes. The event passed to the handler function defines a property called reading, which returns a LightSensorReading object containing details of the light level. You can see how I have added a handler function for this event in Listing 13, and how I display the light level (and my guess at the condition the device is operating in) by calling my displaySensorReading function.

Listing 13. Tracking the Light Level Through the readingchanged Event

```
...
sensor.addEventListener("readingchanged", function (e) {
    displaySensorReading(e.reading.illuminanceInLux);
});
...
```

Testing the Light Sensor Example

You can see the layout of the light.html page and the light level at the moment I tested the example app in Figure 9.

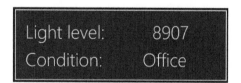

Figure 9. Using the light sensor

I recommend caution when making decisions about app behavior based on the light level because there are no firm correlations between the light level and the conditions in which the device is operating. In the figure, you can see that my light level was 8907 lux, which I categorized as being in an office. This isn't a bad guess, but I took that snapshot while the device was at my house in a room with a glass wall just before dusk. My point is that the same light level can exist in a range of different systems, and it pays to be flexible when responding to readings from the light sensor – for example, it might be helpful if an app changed my network settings to my office configuration at 8900 lux, but some kind of override is essential since I happen to be working at home today. This is true with all of the sensors that I describe in this chapter – the sensor data can be useful and it can make your app more helpful and flexible, but you should be adaptable in the way that you respond to the readings and always provide an override for the user for when the data causes you to make bad inferences.

Using the Inclinometer

An inclinometer measures the angle at which the device has been tilted. Inclinometers are usually used in gaming, to allow the device to be used as a controller. As you'll soon see, using the inclinometer is very similar to using the light sensor, since most of the objects that represent sensors have a broadly similar design. To demonstrate the use of the inclinometer, I have added a file called tilt.html to the pages folder of the example project, the contents of which you can see in Listing 14.

Listing 14. The Contents of the tilt.html File

```
<!DOCTYPE html>
<html>
<head>
    <title></title>
    <style>
        #box { background-color: red; width: 200px; margin: 100px; height: 200px;}
    </style>
    <script>
        WinJS.UI.Pages.define("/pages/tilt.html", {
            ready: function () {
                var sensor = Windows.Devices.Sensors.Inclinometer.getDefault();
                if (sensor == null) {
                    WinJS.Utilities.query(".label").setStyle("display", "none");
                    WinJS.Utilities.query(".warning").setStyle("display", "block");
                } else {
                    displaySensorReading(sensor.getCurrentReading());

                    setInterval(function () {
                        displaySensorReading(sensor.getCurrentReading());
                    }, 100);
                    //sensor.addEventListener("readingchanged", function (e) {
                    //    displaySensorReading(e.reading);
                    //});
                }
            }
        });
        function displaySensorReading(reading) {
            pitch.innerText = reading.pitchDegrees.toFixed(1);
            roll.innerText = reading.rollDegrees.toFixed(1);
            yaw.innerText = reading.yawDegrees.toFixed(1);
            box.style.transform =  "rotate(" + (360 - reading.rollDegrees) + "deg)";
        }
    </script>
</head>
```

```
<body>
    <div id="tiltContainer" class="container">
        <h1 class="label warning">No Inclinometer Installed</h1>
        <h1 class="label">Pitch: <span id="pitch">(None)</span></h1>
        <h1 class="label">Roll: <span id="roll">(None)</span></h1>
        <h1 class="label">Yaw: <span id="yaw">(None)</span></h1>
    </div>
    <div id="boxContainer" class="container">
        <div id="box"></div>
    </div>
</body>
</html>
```

The inclinometer is represented by the Windows.Devices.Sensors.Inclinometer object; just as with the light sensor, you have to call the getDefault method to get an object that you can read data from, like this:

```
...
var sensor = Windows.Devices.Sensors.Inclinometer.getDefault();
...
```

If the value returned by the getDefault method is null, then the device doesn't have an inclinometer installer.

Getting the Device Tilt

You can take a snapshot of the current device tilt by calling the getCurrentReading method, which returns a Windows.Devices.Sensors.InclinometerReading object that defines the properties shown in Table 7.

Table 7. The Properties Defined by the InclinometerReading Object

Name	Description
pitchDegrees	Gets the rotation, in degrees, around the x-axis
rollDegrees	Gets the rotation, in degrees, around the y-axis
yawDegrees	Gets the rotation, in degrees, around the z-axis
timestamp	Returns a Date object representing the time that the sensor reported the reading

The Inclinometer object defines a readingchanged event, but I can't get it to trigger on my device. To work around this, I have commented out the event handling code and replaced it with a call to setInterval, which I use to repeatedly poll the sensor for the tilt values. As part of the process of displaying the reading values, I apply a transformation to a div element in the layout, so as to display a square that "self-levels" as the device is rotated – this is the same kind of transformation that I described in Chapter 18. You can see the layout of the app in Figure 10 (bear in mind that this screenshot was taken while the device was being tilted).

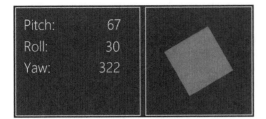

Figure 10. *Tracking and displaying the device tilt*

Using the Accelerometer

The accelerometer measures acceleration, and is often used alongside location data to determine how and when the device is being moved – for example, if location tracking reports that the device is moving a 6 miles per hour, and the accelerometer reports regular pulses of acceleration, then an exercise-related app might start recording data just in case the user forgot to record their daily run. The accelerometer can also be used to determine how the device is oriented because the acceleration toward the earth will be 1g when the device is at rest.

To demonstrate the use of the accelerometer, I have added a new file called acceleration.html to the pages folder of the Visual Studio project. You can see the contents of this file in Listing 15.

Listing 15. *The Contents of the acceleration.html File*

```
<!DOCTYPE html>
<html>
<head>
    <title></title>
    <script>
        WinJS.UI.Pages.define("/pages/acceleration.html", {
            ready: function () {
                var sensor = Windows.Devices.Sensors.Accelerometer.getDefault();
                if (sensor == null) {
                    WinJS.Utilities.query(".label").setStyle("display", "none");
                    WinJS.Utilities.query(".warning").setStyle("display", "block");
                } else {
                    displaySensorReading(sensor.getCurrentReading());
                    sensor.addEventListener("readingchanged", function (e) {
                        displaySensorReading(e.reading);
                    });
                }
            }
        });

        function displaySensorReading(reading) {
            x.innerText = reading.accelerationX.toFixed(2);
            y.innerText = reading.accelerationY.toFixed(2);
            z.innerText = reading.accelerationZ.toFixed(2);
        }
    </script>
</head>
```

```
<body>
    <div class="container">
        <h1 class="label warning">No Accelerometer Installed</h1>
        <h1 class="label">Accelerate X: <span id="x">(None)</span></h1>
        <h1 class="label">Accelerate Y: <span id="y">(None)</span></h1>
        <h1 class="label">Accelerate Z: <span id="z">(None)</span></h1>
    </div>
</body>
</html>
```

You will recognize the pattern by now. The accelerometer device is represented by the `Windows.Devices.Sensors.Accelerometer` object, and you must call the `getDefault` method to get an object that represents the sensor, as follows:

```
...
var sensor = Windows.Devices.Sensors.Accelerometer.getDefault();
...
```

If the result from the `getDefault` method is null, then there is no accelerometer hardware in the device.

Getting the Device Acceleration

You can get a snapshot of the forces measured by the accelerometer by calling the `getCurrentReading` method, which returns a `Windows.Devices.Sensors.AccelerometerReading` object. This object defines the properties I have described in Table 8.

Table 8. *The Properties Defined by the InclinometerReading Object*

Name	Description
accelerationX	The g-force acceleration along the x-axis
accelerationY	The g-force acceleration along the y-axis
accelerationZ	The g-force acceleration along the z-axis
timestamp	Returns a Date object representing the time that the sensor reported the reading

I read the value of these properties in the `displaySensorReading` function, which produces the layout and data shown in Figure 11.

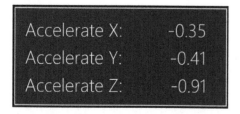

Figure 11. *Measuring acceleration*

You can track the device acceleration by listening for the readingchanged event, which is emitted by the Accelerometer object. The reading property of the event object passed to the handler function returns an AccelerometerReading object, and you can see how I have handled this event in the acceleration.html file.

■ **Note** The Accelerometer also defines the shaken event. Some accelerometer hardware can detect when the device is quickly shaken, and this gesture will trigger the shaken event. The accelerometer hardware in my test device doesn't support the shaken gesture and usually interprets changes in the device orientation (which I described in Chapter 6). Be careful when relying on this event because it may not be fired and requiring users to shake devices may result in unexpected configuration changes, as I experience with my Dell Duo.

Using the Compass

The compass allows you to determine the direction in which the device is being pointed. Using the compass requires magnetometer hardware, which measures the strength and direction of magnetic fields. The compass is most useful when orienting mapping data so that it corresponds to the real world – as an example, I do a lot of long-distance walking and running and my hand-held (non-Windows) GPS device uses its compass to ensure that the topology maps correspond to the direction I am facing, making it far easier for me to figure out where I am.

To demonstrate the compass sensor, I have added a new file called direction.html to the pages folder of the Visual Studio project, and you can see the contents of the file in Listing 16.

Listing 16. The Contents of the direction.html File

```
<!DOCTYPE html>
<html>
<head>
    <title></title>
    <style>
        #compass {
            width: 200px; height: 200px; text-align: center;
            display: -ms-flexbox; -ms-flex-direction: column;-ms-flex-pack: center;}
        #cspan { display: block; font-family: "Segoe UI Symbol"; font-size: 100pt;}
    </style>
    <script>
        WinJS.UI.Pages.define("/pages/direction.html", {
            ready: function () {
                var sensor = Windows.Devices.Sensors.Compass.getDefault();
                if (sensor == null) {
                    WinJS.Utilities.query(".label").setStyle("display", "none");
                    WinJS.Utilities.query(".warning").setStyle("display", "block");
                } else {
                    displaySensorReading(sensor.getCurrentReading());
                    sensor.addEventListener("readingchanged", function (e) {
                        displaySensorReading(e.reading);
                    });
                }
```

```
            }
        });

        function displaySensorReading(reading) {
            heading.innerText = reading.headingMagneticNorth;
            cspan.style.transform = "rotate("
                + (360 - reading.headingMagneticNorth) + "deg)";
        }
    </script>
</head>
<body>
    <div id="compassContainer" class="container">
        <div id="compass">
            <span id="cspan">&#8657;</span>
        </div>
    </div>
    <div class="container">
        <h1 class="label warning">No Compass Installed</h1>
        <h1 class="label">Heading: <span id="heading">(None)</span></h1>
    </div>
</body>
</html>
```

The compass works just like the other sensors I have described in this chapter. The compass is represented by the Windows.Devices.Sensors.Compass object, and you must call the getDefault method to obtain an object in order to read the sensor data, as follows:

```
...
var sensor = Windows.Devices.Sensors.Compass.getDefault();
...
```

If the getDefault method returns null, then the device doesn't have compass sensor hardware.

Getting the Device Direction

You can get a snapshot of the direction that the device is facing by calling the getCurrentReading method, which returns a Windows.Devices.Sensors.CompassReading object. This object defines the properties shown in Table 9.

Table 9. The Properties Defined by the CompassReading Object

Name	Description
headingMagneticNorth	Returns the magnetic-north heading in degrees
headingTrueNorth	Returns the true-north heading in degrees
timestamp	Returns a Date object representing the time that the sensor reported the reading

Not all compass hardware packages are capable of producing both magnetic and true north headings – the sensor in my test device only produces magnetic bearings, for example. In the example, I pass the CompassReading object to the displaySensorReading function, which displays the numeric heading and applies a rotation to a div element in order to show an arrow that always points north. You can see the layout and the sensor data in Figure 12.

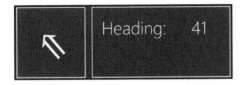

Figure 12. Displaying data from the compass

You can track the heading as it changes by listening to the readingchanged event, which is triggered by the Compass object when the direction reported by the compass sensor changes. I use this event in the example to keep the example layout up to date.

Summary

In this chapter, I have shown you how your app can take advantage of the Windows 8 sensor framework to get data about the real world. Like all advanced features, sensor data needs to be used carefully, but you can create flexible and innovative apps that adapt to their environment by using the data you receive. In the next part of this book, I'll show you how to prepare and publish your app to the Windows Store.

PART 5

Selling Apps

In this part of the book, I show you how to integrate your app into the Windows Store so that you can sell your app and provide in-app upgrades.

CHAPTER 30

■ ■ ■

Creating an App to Publish

In this part of the book, I show you how to publish an app in the Windows Store. I am going to start right from the beginning and build an app that I'll take from the point of creation through to submitting it for review by Microsoft. Along the way, I'll show you how to apply the features that drive your business model and make sure that the app conforms to the Windows Store policies. In this chapter, I am going to take you through the steps that are required before you start and then create an app that I'll take through to publication in the chapters that follow.

Deciding On Your App

Obviously, the place to start is deciding what your app is going to do. For this chapter, I am going to create a photo viewer app. This isn't something that any real users would want to pay for (not least because there is already such an app included in Windows 8), but it is an ideal example for this part of the book because the functionality is simple and self-contained and will let me focus on the different parts of the publishing process.

Deciding On Your Business Model

When creating an app, the first thing to do is decide on the business model that you want to use. The Windows Store supports a range of different ways of selling your app, including giving it away for free, trial versions, charging a flat fee, charging a subscription, in-app advertising, and selling in-app upgrades.

For my example app, I am going to offer a free time-limited trial to draw users in and then charge them $5 for the basic app. But my Windows 8 riches are going to come in the form of in-app upgrades, some of which will be licensed forever and some of which will be sold on a subscription basis.

■ **Note** I am not going to demonstrate in-app advertising because it isn't directly related to the Windows 8 store. Microsoft has an Advertising SDK that makes it easy to include ads in an app, which you can get from http:// advertising.microsoft.com/windowsadvertising/developer. If you want to use another ad provider, you will need to check carefully that the ad content and mechanism for getting the ads doesn't break the app certification requirements (which I show you how to test in Chapter 33).

In Table 30-1, I have listed out the different purchasable features of my app, how much they cost, and what they will do. The free trial of the app will support all of the features for 30 days.

Table 30-1. Example App Features and Costs

Name	Description	Price
Basic App	Will display PNG image files found in the top-level folder of the Pictures library	$4.99 (perpetual)
File Types Upgrade	Will display JPG images, as well as PNG images	$4.99 (perpetual)
Depth Upgrade	Will display all images from the Pictures library and not just those in the top-level folder	$4.99 (perpetual)
Thumbnails Upgrade	Will allow the user to see their images as thumbnails	$1.99 every 30 days
The Works	All of the app features, plus support for printing	$9.99 every 30 days

Once again, let me emphasize that I won't actually be selling this app—I just need a vehicle to show you how to sell yours. So, while my app and its upgrades are simultaneously dull and expensive, they will allow me to demonstrate how to create and combine a range of business models in a single app.

Getting Ready

There are a couple of things I need to do before I start creating my app. The first is to create a Windows Store Developer Account, which allows you to publish apps to the store and receive any income from them. You can create an account as an individual or on behalf of a corporation, and Microsoft changes an annual fee for the account (currently $49 for individuals and $99 for corporations). You will need a Microsoft account to open a Windows Store developer account, but you should already have one from when you downloaded Visual Studio.

■ **Tip** Microsoft includes Windows Store accounts as part of its developer products, such as TechNet and MSDN. You might not have to pay directly for an account if you have already purchased one of these services.

You start the process of creating an account by selecting Open Developer Account from the Store menu in Visual Studio. The process for getting an account requires filling out a few forms and setting up payment details so you can receive the profits from your app sales. Once you have created an account, you'll see the dashboard as shown in Figure 30-1. This dashboard provides details of your store account, including your apps and payments.

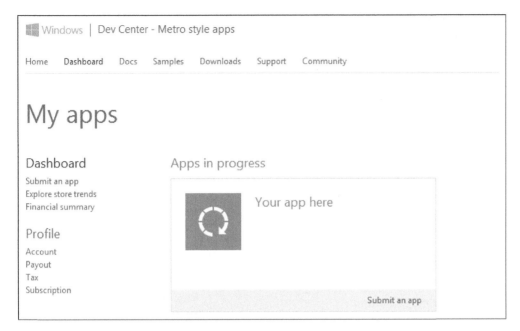

Figure 30-1. *The Windows Store Dashboard*

Reserving the App Name

You can reserve the name of your app in the Windows Store before you start developing it. A reservation lasts for a year, during which time only you can publish an app with that name. It is a sensible idea to reserve a name so that you can go ahead and create artwork, websites, and marketing collateral without worrying that someone else will take the name while you are developing the app.

You can reserve a name by selecting the Reserve App Name item from the Visual Studio Store menu or by clicking on the Submit an app link in the Windows Store dashboard (which is where the Reserve App Name menu takes you anyway). The dashboard presents the different steps required to publish an app, but the only one I care about at the moment is the first, which is the App name step, as shown in Figure 30-2.

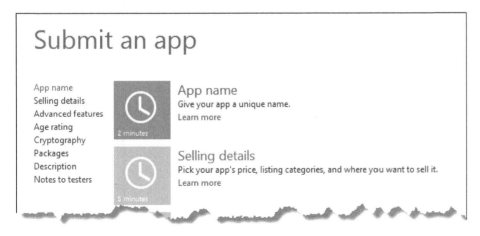

Figure 30-2. *The Windows Dashboard showing the first steps in the app publishing process*

Click on the App name item and enter the name you want to reserve. For my app, I have reserved the name Simple Photo Album, as shown in Figure 30-3.

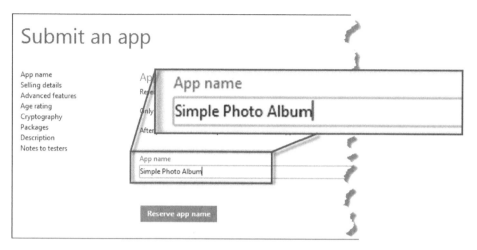

Figure 30-3. Selecting the name for the app

The name that you reserve is the one that the app will be listed by in the store and is separate from the name of your Visual Studio project. I'll show you how to associate the Visual Studio project with the dashboard in Chapter 33, but I haven't even created my Visual Studio project yet).

■ **Note** Although I go through the complete publishing process in this part of the book, I am not going to sell my app in the store—it doesn't do anything interesting and I can't imagine that anyone would want to give me the fees for the upgrades. This means that my reservation on the Simple Photo Album name may have lapsed by the time you read this chapter and that someone else may have used it.

Once you have reserved your app name, the dashboard updates the first step in the publishing process to reflect your selection, as shown in Figure 30-4.

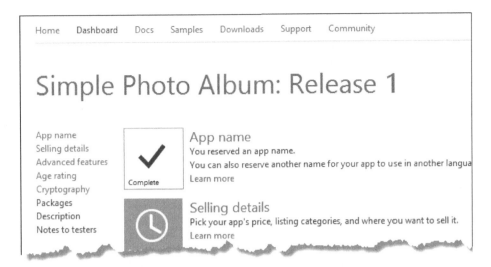

Figure 30-4. Completing the first step in the app publishing process

That's all the preparation that's required for the moment. Having reserved the name, I can now create my Visual Studio project and start building my app.

Creating the Visual Studio Project

I have created a new Visual Studio project using the Blank App template. I called the project PhotoApp, just to demonstrate that you can separate the name of the project from the name that the app will be known by in the store and by its users. You can see the appearance of the finished app in Figure 30-5.

Figure 30-5. The layout of the example app

The left-hand panel contains some button and ToggleSwitch controls that allow the user to choose which images are displayed and whether thumbnails are shown. The right-hand panel contains a large FlipView control that is always visible and can be used to page through the images that have been loaded. At the bottom of the right-hand panel is a ListView control that displays thumbnails of the available images. The visibility of the thumbnails and the selection of images will be controlled by the capabilities that the user has purchased. I'll show you the various components of the app layout later in this chapter.

Creating the Business Model Code

If you are creating an app that you are going to give away entirely for free, then you can just start building out your functionality by applying the techniques I have shown you throughout this book. You don't have to worry about gathering payments or enabling features or any other kind of interaction with the store. But if you are planning to charge for your app, or for some of its features, you need to give careful thought to the structure of your app. I find that the best approach is to bake some core business-model-related functionality into the app right from the start, so that I can build the app functionality and then come back and implement my business plan later.

To this end, the first file I added to the PhotoApp project was called store.js, which I put into the js folder. You can see the contents of this file in Listing 30-1.

Listing 30-1. The contents of the /js/store.js file

```
(function() {

    WinJS.Namespace.define("ViewModel.Store", {
        events: WinJS.Utilities.eventMixin,

        checkCapability: function(name) {
            var available = true;
            setImmediate(function () {
                ViewModel.Store.events.dispatchEvent("capabilitycheck",
                    { capability: name, enabled: available });
            });
            return available;
        }
    });

})();
```

This file is very simple at the moment, but it will become my main focus in Chapter 31 when I add support for integrating my app into the Windows Store. I have created a new namespace called ViewModel. Store, into which I have added a checkCapability function. Other parts of the app will call this function to see if the user has purchased the right to perform certain actions—in Chapter 32, I'll implement the code that checks this against my product tiers and upgrades, but for the moment every request returns true, indicating that a capability is available. This will allow me to build out the functionality of my app before I implement my business model code.

The checkCapability function sends out a capabilitycheck event when it is called—I'll use this event in Chapter 32 to respond when the user tries to use a feature that they have not yet purchased. I have implemented the event using the WinJS.Utilties.eventMixin, which is a helpful object that you can use to add event support to regular JavaScript objects. It defines the standard addEventListener and removeEventListener methods that you find on DOM element objects and the dispatchEvent method, which allows you to send out an event of an arbitrary type to registered listeners. Using the eventMixin object is simpler and less error-prone than writing my own event handling code and by making the object available through the `ViewModel.Store.event` property, I have provided a point where other parts of my app can come and register for events.

■ **Tip**   You don't have to create a new instance of the `eventMixin` object. One instance is shared between any part of an app that wants to use the object, and the `eventMixin` code keeps the listeners for different kinds of event separate. You can see how Microsoft implements this feature by looking at the `base.js` file in the Visual Studio project references.

Creating the View Model State

My next step is to create the code that will let me maintain the state of the app, which I have done by adding a new file called `viewmodel.js` to the `js` folder. You can see the contents of the file in Listing 30-2.

Listing 30-2. The contents of the viewmodel.js file

```
(function () {

    WinJS.Namespace.define("ViewModel", {
        State: WinJS.Binding.as({
            pictureDataSource: new WinJS.Binding.List(),
            fileTypes: false,
            depth: false,
            thumbnails: false,
        }),
    });

    WinJS.Namespace.define("Converters", {
        display: WinJS.Binding.converter(function(val) {
            return val ? "block" : "none";
        })
    });

})();
```

The `ViewModel.State` namespace contains the `WinJS.Binding.List` object that I will use as a data source to display pictures using the WinJS `FlipView` and `ListView` UI controls. I have also defined a set of observable properties that I'll use to keep track of which features the user has currently enabled in the app—this is different from whether or not the user has licensed them. I need to keep track of both the user's entitlement to use a feature and whether it is currently switched on, and the properties in the `ViewModel.State` namespace track the latter.

■ **Tip**   This approach requires me to check that the user is entitled to use a feature before enabling the corresponding property in the `ViewModel.State` namespace. This is what the `ViewModel.Store.checkCapability` function is for, and you will be able to see how I handle this shortly, when I show you the contents of the `/js/default.js` file.

Defining the Layout

To create the layout I showed you in Figure 30-5, I added the elements shown in Listing 30-3 to the
default.html file. This app doesn't require any navigation or content pages because it requires such a
simple layout.

Listing 30-3. Defining the markup for the example app in the default.html file

```
<!DOCTYPE html>
<html>
<head>
    <meta charset="utf-8" />
    <title>PhotoApp</title>
    <!-- WinJS references -->
    <link href="//Microsoft.WinJS.1.0/css/ui-dark.css" rel="stylesheet" />
    <script src="//Microsoft.WinJS.1.0/js/base.js"></script>
    <script src="//Microsoft.WinJS.1.0/js/ui.js"></script>
    <!-- PhotoApp references -->
    <link href="/css/default.css" rel="stylesheet" />
    <script src="/js/viewmodel.js"></script>
    <script src="/js/store.js"></script>
    <script src="/js/default.js"></script>
</head>
<body>
    <div id="flipTemplate" data-win-control="WinJS.Binding.Template">
        <div class="flipItem">
            <img class="flipImg" data-win-bind="src: image" />
            <div class="flipTitle" data-win-bind="innerText: title"></div>
        </div>
    </div>
    <div id="listTemplate" data-win-control="WinJS.Binding.Template">
        <div class="listItem">
            <img class="listImg" data-win-bind="src: image" />
        </div>
    </div>

    <div id="buttonContainer" class="container">
        <div id="fileTypes" data-win-control="WinJS.UI.ToggleSwitch"
            data-win-bind="winControl.checked: State.fileTypes"
            data-win-options="{title: 'Show JPG',  labelOn: 'Yes', labelOff: 'No'}">
        </div>
        <div id="depth" data-win-control="WinJS.UI.ToggleSwitch"
            data-win-bind="winControl.checked: State.depth"
            data-win-options="{title: 'All Folders',  labelOn: 'Yes', labelOff: 'No'}">
        </div>
        <div id="thumbnails" data-win-control="WinJS.UI.ToggleSwitch"
            data-win-bind="winControl.checked: State.thumbnails"
            data-win-options="{title: 'Show Thumbnails',labelOn: 'Yes', labelOff: 'No'}">
        </div>
        <button id="refresh">Refresh</button>
        <button id="upgrade">Buy/Upgrade</button>
    </div>
```

```
<div id="imageContainer" class="container">
    <div id="flipView" data-win-control="WinJS.UI.FlipView"
        data-win-options="{ itemTemplate: flipTemplate,
            itemDataSource: ViewModel.State.pictureDataSource.dataSource}">
    </div>
    <div id="listView" data-win-control="WinJS.UI.ListView"
        data-win-bind="style.display: State.thumbnails Converters.display"
        data-win-options="{ itemTemplate: listTemplate,
            tapBehavior: invokeOnly,
            itemDataSource: ViewModel.State.pictureDataSource.dataSource}">
    </div>
</div>
</body>
</html>
```

The markup can be broken into three categories. The first category is the control elements that go into the left-hand panel (which is represented by the div element whose id attribute is buttonsContainer). Aside from the standard HTML button element, I also apply the WinJS.UI.ToggleSwitch control, which I described in Chapter 11. You can see the control buttons in detail in Figure 30-6 and you will notice that these closely represent the capabilities that I will be selling to the user as upgrades.

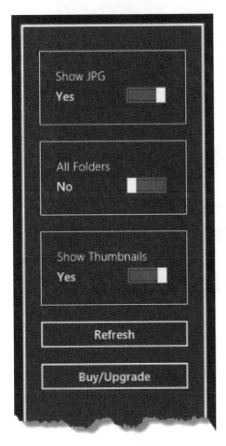

Figure 30-6. The control elements

I need some way of letting the user buy the basic functionality while in the trial period or upgrading to the full set of features, which is why I have added the Buy/Upgrade button. You can see how I have linked the checked property of the ToggleSwitch controls to the observable values in the ViewModel.State namespace.

The next section of markup is contained in the div element whose id attribute is imageContainer. I use a FlipView control as the main image display and a ListView control to display the thumbnails. I covered these WinJS UI controls in Chapters 14 and 15, and my use of them in this app is very straightforward and standard.

The final section of markup is the templates for the ListView and FlipView controls. These use the WinJS.Binding.Template functionality that I described in Chapter 8. Both templates have an img element and, in the case of the template for the FlipView control, I use a div element to display the name of the currently displayed file. You can see how the controls and the templates are combined to form the right-hand panel of the app layout in Figure 30-7.

Figure 30-7. The right-hand panel of the example app

Defining the CSS

The CSS for this example is pretty simple—I rely heavily on the flex box layout to create an app that will adapt to different screen resolutions and device orientations and layouts. You can see the styles I have defined in the /css/default.css file in Listing 30-4.

Listing 30-4. The contents of the /css/default.css file

```
body {display: -ms-flexbox; -ms-flex-direction: row;}

div.container { border: medium solid white; padding: 20px; margin: 20px;
    display: -ms-flexbox; -ms-flex-direction: column; -ms-flex-align: stretch;
    -ms-flex-pack: center;}

div[data-win-control='WinJS.UI.ToggleSwitch'] { border: thin solid white;
    padding: 20px; margin: 10px 0;}

#buttonContainer {-ms-flex-pack: start;}
#buttonContainer button { margin: 10px 0;}

#imageContainer {-ms-flex: 2;}
#flipView {-ms-flex: 2;}
#listView { -ms-flex: 1; max-height: 200px; min-height: 200px; border: thin solid white;
    display: none;}

.flipItem {display: -ms-flexbox;-ms-flex-direction: column;-ms-flex-align: center;
    -ms-flex-pack: center; width: 100%; height: 100%;}
.flipImg { position: relative; top: 0; left: 0; height: calc(100% - 70px); z-index: 15;}
.flipTitle { font-size: 30pt;}
.listItem img { width: 250px; height: 200px;}

@media print {
    #buttonContainer, #listView { display: none;}
}

@media screen and (-ms-view-state: snapped) {
    #buttonContainer { display: none;}
}

@media screen and (-ms-view-state: fullscreen-portrait) {
    body { -ms-flex-direction: column-reverse;}
    #buttonContainer { -ms-flex-direction: row; -ms-flex-pack: distribute;}
    #buttonContainer button {display: none;}
}
```

I have used the media queries to change the app layout when printing and when the app is in the portrait orientation and the snapped layout. The different layouts don't directly relate to Windows Store integration, but I have added the variations in layout for completeness.

Defining the JavaScript Code

The /js/default.js file contains the code that ties together the different parts of the layout and displays the images. You can see the contents of this file in Listing 30-5.

Listing 30-5. The contents of the default.js file

```
(function () {
    "use strict";

    WinJS.Binding.optimizeBindingReferences = true;

    var app = WinJS.Application;
    var activation = Windows.ApplicationModel.Activation;
    var storage = Windows.Storage;
    var search = storage.Search;

    app.onactivated = function (args) {
        if (args.detail.kind === activation.ActivationKind.launch) {
            if (args.detail.previousExecutionState !==
                activation.ApplicationExecutionState.suspended) {

                refresh.addEventListener("click", function (e) {
                    loadFiles();
                });

                WinJS.Utilities.query("#buttonContainer > div").listen("change",
                    function (e) {
                    if (ViewModel.Store.checkCapability(e.target.id)) {
                        ViewModel.State[e.target.id] = e.target.winControl.checked;
                        if (e.target.id == "thumbnails") {
                            listView.winControl.itemDataSource
                                = ViewModel.State.pictureDataSource.dataSource;
                        } else {
                            setImmediate(loadFiles);
                        }

                    } else {
                        e.target.winControl.checked = false;
                    }
                });

                listView.addEventListener("iteminvoked", function (e) {
                    flipView.winControl.currentPage = e.detail.itemIndex;
                });
                flipView.addEventListener("pageselected", function (e) {
                    var index = flipView.winControl.currentPage;
                    listView.winControl.ensureVisible(index);

                });
            }
            args.setPromise(WinJS.UI.processAll().then(function() {
                return WinJS.Binding.processAll(document.body, ViewModel)
                    .then(function () {
                        setupPrinting();
                        loadFiles();
```

```javascript
                });
            }));
        }
    };

    function setupPrinting() {
        Windows.Graphics.Printing.PrintManager.getForCurrentView().onprinttaskrequested =
            function (e) {
                if (ViewModel.Store.checkCapability("print")
                        && ViewModel.State.pictureDataSource.length > 0) {
                    var printTask = e.request.createPrintTask("PrintAlbum",
                        function (printEvent) {
                            printEvent.setSource(
                                MSApp.getHtmlPrintDocumentSource(document));
                    });
                    printTask.options.orientation
                        = Windows.Graphics.Printing.PrintOrientation.landscape;
                };
            };
    }

    function loadFiles() {
        var options = new search.QueryOptions();
        options.fileTypeFilter.push(".png");

        if (ViewModel.State.fileTypes) {
            options.fileTypeFilter.push(".jpg", ".jpeg");
        }
        if (ViewModel.State.depth) {
            options.folderDepth = search.FolderDepth.deep;
        } else {
            options.folderDepth = search.FolderDepth.shallow;
        }
        storage.KnownFolders.picturesLibrary.createFileQueryWithOptions(options)
            .getFilesAsync().then(function (files) {
                var list = ViewModel.State.pictureDataSource;
                list.dataSource.beginEdits();
                list.length = 0;
                files.forEach(function (file) {
                    list.push({
                        image: URL.createObjectURL(file),
                        title: file.displayName
                    });
                });
                list.dataSource.endEdits();
            })
    };

    app.start();
})();
```

The important thing to note in this example is the way that the properties in the ViewModel.State namespace control the way that the app behaves. In the loadFiles function, for example, the types of file that are located and the depth at which files are searched for are driven by the ViewModel.State.fileTypes and ViewModel.State.depth properties, as follows:

```
...
if (ViewModel.State.fileTypes) {
    options.fileTypeFilter.push(".jpg", ".jpeg");
}
if (ViewModel.State.depth) {
    options.folderDepth = search.FolderDepth.deep;
} else {
    options.folderDepth = search.FolderDepth.shallow;
}
...
```

These properties are set by the ToggleSwitch controls in the app layout, but the values are changed only after a successful call to the ViewModel.Store.checkCapability function, like this:

```
...
if (ViewModel.Store.checkCapability(e.target.id)) {
    ViewModel.State[e.target.id] = e.target.winControl.checked;
    if (e.target.id == "thumbnails") {
        listView.winControl.itemDataSource= ViewModel.State.pictureDataSource.dataSource;
    } else {
        setImmediate(loadFiles);
    }
} else {
    e.target.winControl.checked = false;
}
...
```

For simplicity I have set the id of each ToggleSwitch control to be the name of the capability that I want to check for and used the same property names in the ViewModel.State namespace. Implementing business model code can get complicated, and driving as much commonality between the components of your app and the products and upgrades you sell makes life a lot easier.

That said, for the most part, this is code that uses the techniques I have shown you throughout this book. I don't want to go through the code in detail, because I have already described how the various features work. In case something catches your eye and you can't place it, I have listed in Table 30-2 the key features from the code and where you can find them described in this book.

Table 30-2. Key Code Techniques from the Example

Description	Reference
Handling the app life-cycle events	Chapter 19
Using the WinJS.Utilities.query method to select elements using CSS selectors	Chapter 18
Binding data properties to HTML element attributes	Chapter 8
Defining WinJS templates	Chapter 8
Using the FlipView control and its events	Chapter 14
Using the ListView control and its events	Chapter 15

Description	Reference
Locating and filtering files	Chapter 22
Implementing printing	Chapter 26

Updating the Manifest

The last step in creating the basic app is to update the manifest. In order to get access to the files in the Pictures library, I need to open the package.appxmanifest file, navigate to the Capabilities section, and check the Pictures Library option, as shown in Figure 30-8.

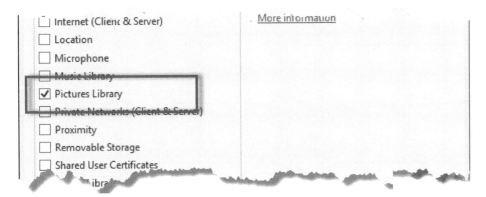

Figure 30-8. Enabling access to the Pictures library in the manifest

I also added some new files to the images folder to use for the tile and the splash screen. All of the files that I added show the same icon, drawn in white on a transparent background. You can see the icon in Figure 30-9, where it is shown on a black background so that it is visible on the page.

Figure 30-9. The icon used for the example app

The files I added were named tile<size>.png, where <size> is the width of the image in pixels. You can see how I have applied the images to the app in Figure 30-10, which shows the Application UI section of the manifest and the changes I have made.

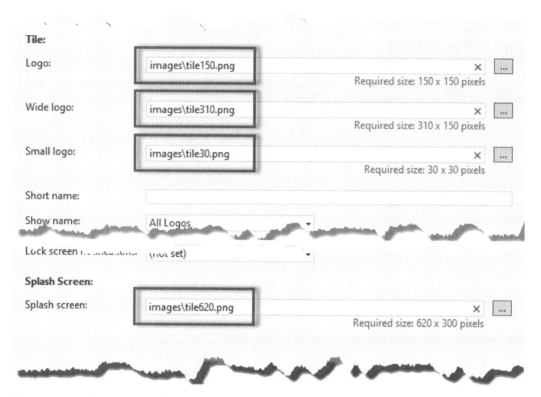

Figure 30-10. Changing the tile and splash screen images used by the app

Testing the Example App

All that remains in this chapter is to test the example app. Start the app using the Start Debugging item from the Visual Studio Debug menu. By default, the properties in the ViewModel.State namespace are set to false, which means that you will see the basic app layout, as shown in Figure 30-11.

Figure 30-11. *The basic app layout*

What you see when you run the app will depend on the contents of your Pictures Library, of course. When the app first starts, it will show only PNG files in the root Pictures directory, which will limit the content that is displayed. In the basic mode, you can navigate through the images by swiping the FlipView or clicking on its navigation buttons.

By enabling the ToggleSwitch controls you broaden the scope of the images that are displayed so that JPG files and files deeper in the Pictures Library are included. And, of course, the ListView control is displayed, showing thumbnails of the available images.

The Refresh button will clear the contents of the data source and reload the files from the disk. The Buy/Upgrade button doesn't do anything at the moment, but I'll wire it up in Chapter 32 so that the user can make a purchase.

Summary

In this chapter, I started the process for creating and publishing an app, beginning by reserving the name for my app and then building the basic functionality that will be offered to the user. Right from the start, I added support to check that the user has purchased access to the key functions of the app, and I'll implement the policy behind those checks in the next chapter, where I will also show you how to integrate your app into the Windows Store.

■ ■ ■

CHAPTER 31

Windows Store Integration

In this chapter, I will show you how to integrate your app with the Windows Store and implement your app business model. I'll show you the objects that provide access to the store functionality and how to use them to simulate different licensing scenarios before your app is published to the store. I show you how to determine what capabilities your user is entitled to and how to enforce that model to stop the app being used without a suitable license.

You will find that the techniques for integrating with the Windows Store are reasonably straightforward, but that enforcing a business model and simulating different scenarios can be quite tricky and require lots of testing.

General Advice on App Licensing

Before I start implementing and enforcing a business model for my example app, I want to offer some general advice. It is perfectly reasonable and fair to expect your users to pay to use your app, but you need to be realistic about the value of the functionality you offer and the world in which you are operating.

You must accept that your app will be pirated widely. It will start showing up in unexpected places within a few hours of being published, and any license enforcement and rights management will be broken pretty much immediately. Users (lots of them if you have an especially compelling app) will benefit from your hard work without paying you a cent.

If this is your first app, you'll go through a common set of emotions: shock, frustration, outrage, and a sense of injustice. You may be so upset that you update your app to add more elaborate licensing schemes or require periodic checks against some additional validation service. This is the worst thing you can do.

Each time you add extra layers of rights-management and licenses, you make your app harder to use. But you don't actually make it harder to copy because there is no scheme in existence that can withstand the focused attention of someone who wants a free copy. The only people you punish are your legitimate users, who now have to jump through hoops to get your app working. In a competitive marketplace, you want to remove as many barriers as possible to attract users to your app – and each barrier to use that you add makes competing apps more appealing.

A much more sensible approach is to accept that people will always copy your software and take some time to consider why this might be.

You might be wondering what makes me feel that I can tell you to just let all those criminals rip you off – but this is something that I spend a lot of time thinking about because it affects me every day.

Books and Apps Have a Lot in Common

My books appear on file-sharing sites within a few hours of being published. This has happened for years, and I have come to understand that not the problem it first appears to be.

First, in purely practical terms, there is no way that I could stop my books being shared, even if I wanted to. Second, I have come to realize that people download illicit copies for a range of reasons, and some of them can be beneficial to my sales figures over the long-term. Here are the broad categories that I think about for my books:

1. Collectors
2. Quick-fixers
3. Budgeteers
4. Pain-avoiders

Collectors share my books because they can – they take pleasure in collecting large libraries of books, music, apps, games, and whatever else they are interested in. These people don't represent lost sales to me because they would never have bought a copy in the first place and they never will.

Quick-fixers are people who have a particular problem they want to solve and they copy one of my books to see whether it contains the solution. These people don't represent a lost sale, either, because the solution to a single specific problem doesn't represent $20–$50 of value to them. But these people *do* represent potential future customers – they might remember they found my book useful and buy a copy (or a copy of another one of my titles) for a topic they want to learn about in more depth.

Budgeteers are people who might prefer to buy a copy, but can't afford to. Books can be expensive, and it doesn't matter how important they are if money is tight. These people are *also* potential customers because they might be broke now, but that won't always be the case. They might start buying books when they have more money, and I'd like them to have positive feelings about my titles when they do.

Pain-avoiders are those readers who want the content, but can't get it in a format that suits them. They want their content in a particular way or delivered in a particular manner, and I and Apress don't give it to them. So they turn to file sharing because it gives them what they need in the way they need. These people are potential customers, either when my titles are available in the way they want or when their needs change.

So, to recap, there is one group of people who copy my books because they can and will never buy a copy, and *three* categories of people who copy my books today but might be great customers in the future. They might also recommend my books to other people, who might pay for a copy (this happens more often than you might imagine).

Collectors are a lost cause to me, so I don't lose any sleep over them. The other kinds of file copiers are people I want to cultivate and let them experience my content in the hope that I'll make some money from them in the future. I can honestly say that I have never put any of my books on a file-sharing site, but I'd be sorely tempted to do so because I think it helps secure future income.

Just as important, making my books harder to use doesn't make any of the file copiers buy a book. The quick-fixers will find a solution elsewhere, the budgeteers won't have any more spare cash, so they'll just copy someone else's book, and the pain-avoiders still can't get the content in the way that they want. They'll never know if they like my writing style because they'll never see it – and I won't get any sales from them now or in the future.

Focusing on What Matters

Instead of trying to punish copiers, I try to consider what they want. Need a quick fix? I add summary tables at the start of each chapter to make it easier to find a specific solution. Don't have any cash? I wrote *Windows Revealed* books, which cost a few bucks and get you up and running with the basics quickly.

Need a particular format of e-book? I work with Apress, which offers a range of different, DRM-free formats.

My response to file sharers is to try and make my books more *appealing* and more *useful*, not harder to use. And, if I am successful, I please my paying readers because they want to locate solutions quickly, have access to a range of e-book formats, and get cheap and effective quick-start titles for new topics, too.

Rather than waste my time getting upset, I am quietly proud that my books are shared so widely and am continually hopeful that the people who copy my books today will pay good money for books tomorrow.

My advice to you is to follow a similar approach with your Windows Store apps. Think about why people copy them and try to add value for those people who might buy in the future, while adding value for the people who have bought in the present. You can't stop file copying, so you may was well embrace it and consider it to be the free market exposure it truly is.

I don't *want* people to copy my books, but if they are not going to buy a copy, I'd much rather that they copied on of my titles than one of the competitors, and what's true for books is just as true for apps.

Dealing with a Basic Store Scenario

The process for implementing an app's business model is a little odd, in that you create a series of XML files that represent different licensing scenarios and then implement the code in your app that deal with them. These files, called *scenario files,* stand in for that data that your app will have access to when it is published in the store and has been downloaded or purchased by the user. In this section, I will create a very basic scenario file to introduce the format, show you how to access the data that the scenario represents, and respond to it in the app.

Creating the Scenario File

I have added a new folder to the project called store, in which I will place the scenario files. My first scenario describes the situation in which the user has downloaded the app but has not purchased any in-app upgrades or subscriptions. For my business model, this means that I am interested in representing three scenarios:

1. The user has purchased a perpetual license for the basic app functionality.
2. The user has downloaded a free-trial that has not yet expired.
3. The user has downloaded a free-trial that has expired.

To represent and test these scenarios, I have created a new file in the store folder called initial.xml, the contents of which you can see in Listing 1.

Listing 1. The Contents of /store/initial.xml

```xml
<?xml version="1.0" encoding="utf-16" ?>
<CurrentApp>
  <ListingInformation>
    <App>
      <AppId>e4bbe35f-0509-4cca-a27a-4ec43bed783c</AppId>
      <LinkUri>http://apress.com</LinkUri>
      <CurrentMarket>en-US</CurrentMarket>
      <AgeRating>3</AgeRating>
      <MarketData xml:lang="en-us">
```

```
        <Name>Simple Photo Album</Name>
        <Description>An app to display your photos</Description>
        <Price>4.99</Price>
        <CurrencySymbol>$</CurrencySymbol>
        <CurrencyCode>USD</CurrencyCode>
      </MarketData>
    </App>
  </ListingInformation>
  <LicenseInformation>
    <App>
      <IsActive>true</IsActive>
      <IsTrial>false</IsTrial>
      <ExpirationDate>2012-09-30T00:00:00.00Z</ExpirationDate>
    </App>
  </LicenseInformation>
</CurrentApp>
```

There are two sections in this file, contained in the CurrentApp element. The ListingInformation element contains details of the app's listing on the Windows Store, while the LicenseInformation element contains the details of the license under which the user has obtained the software. I'll explain both elements in the sections that follow.

■ **Caution**   Windows is very particular about the content of the scenario file. Make sure that there is no content after the CurrentApp element is closed, including blank lines. If the app crashes when starting, try to reload the app from Visual Studio, and if that doesn't work, then look carefully at your scenario file to see whether you have added anything that Windows doesn't expect.

Understanding the Listing Section

The ListingInformation section of the scenario file contains a description of the app, and provides you with details about how the app was displayed to the user in the store. I don't pay much attention to this section of the scenario file, although I will add to it in Chapter 32 when I create definitions for the in-app upgrades and subscriptions that I want to offer. In Table 1, I describe the various elements and the effect they have during store integration and testing.

Table 1. The Elements in the ListingInformation Section of the Scenario File

Element	Description
App	Declares the region of the file that describes the app – in Chapter 32, I'll add additional content to the ListingInformation that describes in-app upgrades.
AppId	Defines the unique ID that is assigned to the app when it is published in the Windows Store. During integration, any correctly formatted value can be used (see the note after this table for further details).
LinkUri	Defines a URL that refers to the app's page in the Windows Store. The URL isn't used during integration.

Element	Description
CurrentMarket	Defines the local market from which the user has obtained the app. The Windows Store is localized for a long list of countries, and this element identifies the regional variant of the Windows Store that has been used. For my testing, I have set this to be en-US, which indicates the English language variant of the Windows Store available to users in the U.S.
AgeRating	Specifies the minimum age for which the app is suitable. I have set this to 3, which means that the app is safe to use for users who are 3 years old and up. Other values are 7, 12, and 16, but this value isn't used during integration.
MarketData	Denotes the section of the document that details how the app is described and sold in the user's region.
Name	The name of the app.
Description	The description of the app.
Price	The price for which the app is sold, which I have set to 4.99 in my example.
CurrencySymbol	The currency in which the price is charged. This is $ in my example, representing dollars.
CurrencyCode	The code for the currency in which the price is charged. This is USD in my example, representing the U.S. dollar.

Although you need to create values for these elements in a scenario file, the values in the ListingInformation section are taken from the information you provide when you publish the app, which I demonstrate in Chapter 33. It doesn't matter what values you use for testing – they are required, but the values are just placeholders for the real data, and you don't have to use the same values that you plan to provide for the real Windows Store deployment.

■ **Note** A common problem during Windows Store integration is to use a badly-formatted value for the AppId element. I find that the easiest approach is to take the value from the app manifest. Open the manifest, navigate to the Packaging tab and copy the value from the Package name field.

Understanding the Licensing Section

The LicenseInformation element contains details of all of the licenses that the user has obtained for the app and its upgrades. For my initial example, I have only defined a test license for the app itself, which I have repeated in Listing 2. It is this section that I will change to create the different scenarios I want to cater for.

Listing 2. The License Information from the initial.xml scenario file

```
...
<LicenseInformation>
  <App>
    <IsActive>true</IsActive>
    <IsTrial>false</IsTrial>
    <ExpirationDate>2012-09-30T00:00:00.00Z</ExpirationDate>
  </App>
</LicenseInformation>
...
```

I describe the elements in this section of the scenario file in Table 2.

Table 2. The Elements in the LicenseInformation Section of the Scenario File

Element	Description
App	Declares the region of the file that describes the app – in Chapter 32, I'll add additional content that describes in-app upgrades.
IsActive	The content of this element will be set to true if the user has a value license. The exact meaning of a true value will vary based on the business model for the app, but it can mean that the app is free, that the user has purchased a perpetual license, has a current subscription, or that the user has downloaded a free-trial which has not yet expired. A false value means that the user does not have a value license.
IsTrial	The content of this element will be true when the app is being used during a trial period and false otherwise.
ExpirationDate	The date on which the trial period for the app expires.

For my initial scenario, I have set the IsActive element to true and the IsTrial element to false – this combination represents the situation in which the user has purchased the basic functionality of the app.

Using the License Information

Now that I have defined the scenario file, I can use it in my app. I want to keep the management of the licenses separate from the rest of the code in the app, as far as is possible, so that I can change the business model in just one place. There is a lot of flexibility in the way that you can sell apps and in-app upgrades in the Windows Store, and you might not get the pricing and mix of optional features right the first time – so it makes sense to code on the basis that you will be making changes and you want to make that process as simple as possible.

To get started, I have made some additions to the /js/store.js file, as shown in Listing 3. There are only a few new lines of code, but there is a lot of new objects and technique to cover, so I'll break down the additions step-by-step in the sections that follow.

Listing 3. Adding to the /js/store.js File

```
(function() {
    var storage = Windows.Storage;

    var licensedCapabilities = {
        basicApp: false,
    }

    WinJS.Namespace.define("ViewModel.Store", {
        events: WinJS.Utilities.eventMixin,

        checkCapability: function (name) {
            var available = licensedCapabilities[name] != undefined
                ? licensedCapabilities[name] : true;
            setImmediate(function () {
                ViewModel.Store.events.dispatchEvent("capabilitycheck",
                    { capability: name, enabled: available });
            });
```

```
            return available;
        },

        currentApp: Windows.ApplicationModel.Store.CurrentAppSimulator,

        loadLicenseData: function () {
            var url = new Windows.Foundation.Uri("ms-appx:///store/initial.xml");
            return storage.StorageFile.getFileFromApplicationUriAsync(url)
                .then(function (file) {
                    return ViewModel.Store.currentApp.reloadSimulatorAsync(file);
                });
        },

    });

    ViewModel.Store.currentApp.licenseInformation.addEventListener("licensechanged",
        function () {
            var license = ViewModel.Store.currentApp.licenseInformation;
            licensedCapabilities.basicApp = license.isActive;
        });

})();
```

Tracking Capabilities Entitlement

The first addition I have made to the store.js file is to define an object called licensedCapabilities that I will use to track the user's entitlement to the various areas of functionality in the app – although initially I am only tracking the basic functionality of the app, as follows:

```
...
var licensedCapabilities = {
    basicApp: false,
}
...
```

It is important to track the user's entitlement to use the features of your app separately from the license information in the scenario file, even if the capabilities of your app match neatly to the in-app upgrades you are going to sell, as is the case for my contrived example app.

This is for two reasons: first, you may need to make changes later and you want to make your code too dependent on the licenses you define initially. Second, you rarely get a perfect match, so, as an example, I am intending to offer an upgrade called The Works (as described in Chapter 30) that will allow the user access to all of the app features, and so there isn't a direct mapping between the license for this upgrade and the app functionality – you can see how I handle this slight mismatch in Chapter 32.

The addition of the licensedCapabilities object allows me to update the Windows.Store. checkCapabilities method so that it starts to reflect the user's entitlements, as follows:

```
...
checkCapability: function (name) {
    var available = licensedCapabilities[name] != undefined ? licensedCapabilities[name]
        : true;
    setImmediate(function () {
```

```
        ViewModel.Store.events.dispatchEvent("capabilitycheck",
            { capability: name, enabled: available });
    });
    return available;
},
...
```

I have marked the key statement in bold. If there is a property in the licensedCapabilities that corresponds to the capability that is being checked, then I use the licensedCapabilities value to respond to the checkCapability call.

Notice the differences in the default values. In the licensedCapabilities object, I set the value of the basicApp property to be false, which will deny the user access to the capability by default. However, in the checkCapability method, I return true if there isn't a corresponding value in the licensedCapabilities object. I have done this so that capabilities I have defined always require a license, but if I forget to define a capability I don't break the user's experience by disabling a feature that they can't activate even if they are willing to pay for it.

■ **Tip** This may strike you as oddly cautious, but I have written a few of these Windows Store implementations and they get very complicated – erring on the side of generosity makes for a better experience if you forget to wire up an app capability.

Getting the Data for the Current App

The objects that are used for managing Windows Store integration are in the Windows.ApplicationModel. Store namespace. The key object is called CurrentApp, and it provides access to the license information obtained the Windows Store and defines methods that allow you to initiate the app and upgrade purchasing processes. Table 3 shows the methods and properties that the CurrentApp object defines and that I will use in this chapter to manage the example app.

Table 3. The Methods and Properties defined by the CurrentApp Object

Name	Description
getAppReceiptAsync()	Returns an XML string containing transaction details for the purchase of the app
getProductReceiptAsync(name)	Returns an XML string containing transaction details for the purchase of the in-app upgrade with the specified name
loadListingInformationAsync()	Returns a ListingInformation object, from the Windows. ApplicationModel.Store namespace, which contains the contents of the ListingInformation element from the scenario file (or the real Windows Store data for deployed apps)
requestAppPurchaseAsync(receipt)	Initiates the purchase process for the app, specifying whether a receipt is specified
requestProductPurchaseAsync(name, receipt)	Initiates the purchase process for the specified in-app upgrade, specifying whether a receipt is required
licenseInformation	Returns a LicenseInformation object from the Windows. ApplicationModel.Store namespace, which contains details of the licenses the user has obtained for the app and its upgrades

I'll be using the key methods and the property throughout this chapter and I'll introduce the other objects from the Windows.ApplicationModel.Store namespace as I use them. However, there is a problem with the CurrentApp object – it only works when the user has downloaded the app from the store after it has been published.

For integration and testing purposes, you must use the CurrentAppSimulator object, which is also contained in the Windows.ApplicationModel.Store namespace. The CurrentAppSimulator object defines all of the methods and properties that CurrentApp defines, but works on scenario files. You work with the CurrentAppSimulator object until you are ready to publish your app, at which point you replace the references in your app so that you are working with the CurrentApp object.

I want to make the transition from integration to publishing as simple as possible, so I have defined a single reference to the CurrentAppSimulator class so I only have one change to make later. You can see the reference I added to the ViewModel.Store namespace, as follows:

```
...
WinJS.Namespace.define("ViewModel.Store", {
    events: WinJS.Utilities.eventMixin,

    checkCapability: function (name) {
        // ...code removed for brevity...
    },

    currentApp: Windows.ApplicationModel.Store.CurrentAppSimulator,

    loadLicenseData: function () {
        // ...code removed for brevity...
    },

});
...
```

I will refer to the ViewModel.Store.currentApp property any time I need to use the CurrentApp/CurrentAppSimulator functionality, and just make one change when I am ready to publish (which I'll demonstrate in Chapter 33).

The CurrentAppSimulator object defines an additional method over and above those defined by CurrentApp. This method, called getFileFromApplicationUriAsync, takes a StorageFile object representing a scenario file as its argument. The method loads the XML elements in the file and uses them to simulate a licensing scenario, so you can implement your business model before you publish your app to the store.

To load the scenario file, I have defined a function called loadLicenseData in the ViewModel.Store namespace, as follows:

```
...
WinJS.Namespace.define("ViewModel.Store", {
    events: WinJS.Utilities.eventMixin,

    checkCapability: function (name) {
        // ...code removed for brevity...
    },

    currentApp: Windows.ApplicationModel.Store.CurrentAppSimulator,

    loadLicenseData: function () {
        var url = new Windows.Foundation.Uri("ms-appx:///store/initial.xml");
```

```
        return storage.StorageFile.getFileFromApplicationUriAsync(url)
            .then(function (file) {
                return ViewModel.Store.currentApp.reloadSimulatorAsync(file);
            });
    },

});
...
```

I obtain a StorageFile object using a URL and then call the reloadSimulatorAsync method to load the data from my /store/initial.xml file.

Responding to License Changes

The last addition I made to the /js/store.js file was to add a handler function for the licensechanged event. This event is triggered when there is a change in the license information (such as when the user makes a purchase) and when a scenario file is loaded using the CurrentAppSimulator object. Here is the handler function I defined:

```
...
ViewModel.Store.currentApp.licenseInformation.addEventListener("licensechanged",
    function () {
        var license = ViewModel.Store.currentApp.licenseInformation;
        licensedCapabilities.basicApp = license.isActive;
    }
);
...
```

The CurrentApp.licenseInformation property returns a LicenseInformation object. The object defines the licensechanged event, for which I have added the handler.

When the event is triggered, I read the value of the CurrentApp.licenseInformation property again to get the LicenseInformation object, which defines the properties I have described in Table 4.

Table 4. The Properties Defined by the LicenseInformation Object

Name	Description
isActive	Corresponds to the content of the LicenseInformation.App.IsActive element from the scenario file.
isTrial	Corresponds to the content of the LicenseInformation.App.isTrial element from the scenario file.
ExpirationDate	Corresponds to the content of the LicenseInformation.App.ExpirationDate element from the scenario file.
ProductLicenses	Returns details of the license for in-app upgrades – I'll come back to these in Chapter 32.

As you can see from the table, the elements in the scenario file correspond directly to the properties defined by the LicenseInformation object, which makes it relatively easy to create and test a range of different license situations. In my handler function, I set the value of the basicApp property in the licenseCapabilities object to the value of the LicenseInformation.isActive property. This means that calls to the ViewModel.Store.checkCapability method for the basicApp capability will return true if the user has a valid license.

Loading the Scenario Data

To load my scenario data, I have added a call to the `loadLicenseData` method from the `/js/default.js` file, as shown in Listing 4.

Listing 4. Ensuring that the License Information is Loaded when the App Starts

```
...
app.onactivated = function (args) {
    if (args.detail.kind === activation.ActivationKind.launch) {
        if (args.detail.previousExecutionState !==
            activation.ApplicationExecutionState.suspended) {
            // ...code removed for brevity...
        }
        args.setPromise(WinJS.UI.processAll().then(function() {
            return WinJS.Binding.processAll(document.body, ViewModel)
                .then(function () {
                    return ViewModel.Store.loadLicenseData().then(function () {
                        setupPrinting();
                        loadFiles();
                    });
                });
        }));
    }
};
...
```

I call the `ViewModel.Store.loadLicenseData` method as part of the chain of `Promise` objects that will be fulfilled before the splash screen is removed when the app is launched. This ensures that my license data is loaded before the app functionality is shown to the user.

Enforcing the License Policy

At this point, I have built up my support for the Windows Store so that my `checkCapabilities` method will return `true` if there is a valid license for the app itself in the scenario file, but testing this feature is pretty disappointing because I don't enforce the license anywhere in the app. In this section, I am going to start fleshing out the code that enforces different aspects of my business model, stating by only allowing the user access to the basic functions of the app if they have purchased a license or if they are using a free trial.

Triggering the Capability Check

The first thing I need to do is call the `checkCapability` method to see if the user is entitled to the `basicApp` capability. I have done this in the `/js/default.js` file, as shown in Listing 5.

Listing 5. Checking to See if the User has an Entitlement to the Basic App Functionality

```
...
app.onactivated = function (args) {
    if (args.detail.kind === activation.ActivationKind.launch) {
        if (args.detail.previousExecutionState !==
```

```
            activation.ApplicationExecutionState.suspended) {
                // ...code removed for brevity...
            }
        args.setPromise(WinJS.UI.processAll().then(function() {
            return WinJS.Binding.processAll(document.body, ViewModel)
                .then(function () {
                    return ViewModel.Store.loadLicenseData().then(function () {
                        setupPrinting();
                        loadFiles();
                        ViewModel.Store.checkCapability("basicApp");
                    });
                });
            }));
        }
    };
    ...
```

You will notice that although I call the checkCapability method, I don't do anything with the result. I am relying on the event capabilitycheck event that is triggered whenever the checkCapability method is called. I will handle this event in the code that enforces the policy for the basic app capability, which I have defined in a new file called /js/storeInteractions.js. I added a new script element to the default.html file for the storeInteractions.js file, as shown in Listing 6.

Listing 6. *Adding a New Script Element to the default.html File*

```
...
<head>
    <meta charset="utf-8" />
    <title>PhotoApp</title>

    <!-- WinJS references -->
    <link href="//Microsoft.WinJS.1.0/css/ui-dark.css" rel="stylesheet" />
    <script src="//Microsoft.WinJS.1.0/js/base.js"></script>
    <script src="//Microsoft.WinJS.1.0/js/ui.js"></script>

    <!-- PhotoApp references -->
    <link href="/css/default.css" rel="stylesheet" />
    <script src="/js/viewmodel.js"></script>
    <script src="/js/store.js"></script>
    <script src="/js/storeInteractions.js"></script>
    <script src="/js/default.js"></script>
</head>
...
```

I have defined a new file because the code that enforces this kind of policy tends to be verbose and repetitive, and I want to keep it separate from the code in the store.js file. You can see the contents of the storeInteractions.js file in Listing 7.

Listing 7. *The Initial Contents of the storeInteractions.js File*

```
(function () {
```

```
    var pops = Windows.UI.Popups;

    ViewModel.Store.events.addEventListener("capabilitycheck", function (e) {
        if (e.detail.capability == "basicApp") {
            if (ViewModel.Store.currentApp.licenseInformation.isTrial &&
                e.detail.enabled) {
                // user has a trial period which has not expired
            } else if (!e.detail.enabled) {
                // user has a trial period which has expired
            }
        }
    });

    function buyApp() {
        // code to purchase the app will go here
        return WinJS.Promise.wrap(true);
    }
})();
```

The handler function for the capabilitycheck event will be invoked as a consequence of the call to the ViewModel.Store.checkCapability method I added to default.js. I am interested in two scenarios in this code file. The first is that the user is using a free trial of the app that has not yet expired, and the second is that the free trial *has* expired. You can see in the listing how I combine the details from the event object and the LicenseInformation object to work out when I am dealing with these scenarios.

■ **Note** The third of my scenarios for the basic app functionality is that the user has purchased a license. In this situation, I don't do anything because I want to stay out of the way of my paying customers. Well, at least until they try to use a feature that requires an upgrade, but I'll come back to that in Chapter 32.

In the sections that follow, I'll fill in each of the three sections of the event handler function that currently contain comments.

Dealing with Valid Trial Periods

I want to take the opportunity to remind users that they are partway through a trial period of my app and give them the opportunity to buy a license when they start the app. You can see how I do this in Listing 8, in which I show the additions I have made to the storeInteractions.js file.

Listing 8. Prompting the User to Purchase the App

```
(function () {
    var pops = Windows.UI.Popups;

    ViewModel.Store.events.addEventListener("capabilitycheck", function (e) {
        if (e.detail.capability == "basicApp") {
            if (ViewModel.Store.currentApp.licenseInformation.isTrial
                    && e.detail.enabled) {

                var daysLeft = Math.ceil(
```

```
                    (ViewModel.Store.currentApp.licenseInformation.expirationDate
                        - new Date()) / (24 * 60 * 60 * 1000));
                var md = new pops.MessageDialog("You have " + daysLeft
                    + " days left in your free trial");
                md.title = "Free Trial";
                md.commands.append(new pops.UICommand("OK"));
                md.commands.append(new pops.UICommand("Buy Now"));
                md.defaultCommandIndex = 0;
                md.showAsync().then(function (command) {
                    if (command.label == "Buy Now") {
                        buyApp();
                    }
                });

            } else if (!e.detail.enabled) {
                // user has a trial period which has expired
            }
        }
    });

    function buyApp() {
        // code to purchase the app will go here
        return WinJS.Promise.wrap(true);
    }
})();
```

I work out how many days the user has left in their trial period and display this information using a Windows.UI.Popups.MessageDialog, which I described in Chapter 13. The MessageDialog has an OK button that dismisses the popup and a Buy Now button that calls the buyApp function (which I'll implement shortly).

Testing the Scenario

I need to modify my scenario file to test this new code, creating a situation in which the user has a trial period that has not expired. You can see how I changed the /store/initial.xml file to create the circumstances I want in Listing 9.

Listing 9. *Changing the Scenario in the initial.xml File*

```
...
<LicenseInformation>
  <App>
    <IsActive>true</IsActive>
    <IsTrial>true</IsTrial>
    <ExpirationDate>2012-09-30T00:00:00.00Z</ExpirationDate>
  </App>
</LicenseInformation>
...
```

I have changed the value of the IsTrial element to true and ensured that the ExpirationDate element contains a date that is a few days in the future. I am writing this chapter on September 22, 2012, and so the date I have specified in the listing is 8 days into the future. You will need to change the data when you test this example.

When you start the app, you will see a message that tells you how many days are left in the trial, as shown in Figure 1.

Figure 1. *Showing the user how much time remains in the trial period*

Clicking the OK button dismisses the dialog and lets the user continue using the app. Clicking on the Buy Now button calls the buyApp function I defined in the storeInteractions.js file, which will start the purchasing process when I implement it in the next section. With this new functionality, I can remind the user that they only have a trial period and give them an early opportunity to purchase the app.

Dealing with Expired Trial Periods

I want to stop the user from using the app when the trial period has expired and only offer them the opportunity to make a purchase. I do this using another MessageDialog, as shown in Listing 10.

Listing 10. *Dealing with Expired Trial Periods*

```
(function () {

    var pops = Windows.UI.Popups;

    ViewModel.Store.events.addEventListener("capabilitycheck", function (e) {
        if (e.detail.capability == "basicApp") {
            if (ViewModel.Store.currentApp.licenseInformation.isTrial
                    && e.detail.enabled) {
                var daysLeft = Math.ceil(
                    (ViewModel.Store.currentApp.licenseInformation.expirationDate
                    - new Date()) / (24 * 60 * 60 * 1000));
                var md = new pops.MessageDialog("You have " + daysLeft
                    + " days left in your free trial");
```

```
            md.title = "Free Trial";
            md.commands.append(new pops.UICommand("OK"));
            md.commands.append(new pops.UICommand("Buy Now"));
            md.defaultCommandIndex = 0;
            md.showAsync().then(function (command) {
                if (command.label == "Buy Now") {
                    buyApp();
                }
            });

        } else if (!e.detail.enabled) {
            var md = new pops.MessageDialog("Your free trial has expired");
            md.commands.append(new pops.UICommand("Buy Now"));
            md.showAsync().then(function () {
                buyApp().then(function (purchaseResult) {
                    if (!purchaseResult) {
                        ViewModel.Store.checkCapability("basicApp");
                    }
                });
            });
        }
    }
});

function buyApp() {
    // code to purchase the app will go here
    return WinJS.Promise.wrap(true);
}
})();
```

The dialog that I display to the user informs them that the trial has expired and offers them a Buy Now button. When the button is clicked, I call the buyApp function, which will be responsible for initiating the purchasing process. This function returns a Promise object that is fulfilled when the process is complete and that yields true if the purchase was successful and false if the purchase wasn't made (which can happen for lots of reasons, including the user cancelling the transaction, failing to provide a valid form of payment, or because the Windows Store is unreachable – devices with no connectivity cannot make purchases).

■ **Tip**   When building apps that have a free trial, I like to add a grace period. This came after I wanted to use a trial app on a long haul flight a few years ago, only to find that it had expired and that my lack of connectivity meant that I couldn't upgrade, even though I was willing to do so. Instead, I got annoyed with the hard-stop that the developers had decided on and never purchased the app. So, for my own projects, I generally add a button that will extend the trial by an extra few days so that they have an opportunity to make a purchase. I only allow one extension, after which the app stops working.

If the purchase is successful, then I dismiss the dialog so that the user can use the app. I call the ViewModel.Store.checkCapability method if the purchase isn't completed, which evaluates the license again, leading to the same dialog to be displayed until the user terminates the app or is able to complete the purchase. I use the checkCapability method so that the capabilitycheck event is triggered, allowing other parts of my app to remain informed about what's going on.

Testing the Scenario

To test this scenario, I have to specify a past date in the /store/initial.xml scenario file, as shown in Listing 11. To get the effect I want, I have to set the isActive element to false and ensure that the isTrial element is set to true.

Listing 11. Creating an Expired Trial Scenario in the initial.xml File

```
...
<LicenseInformation>
  <App>
    <IsActive>false</IsActive>
    <IsTrial>true</IsTrial>
    <ExpirationDate>2011-09-30T00:00:00.00Z</ExpirationDate>
  </App>
</LicenseInformation>
...
```

When you start the app, you will see the dialog shown in Figure 2.

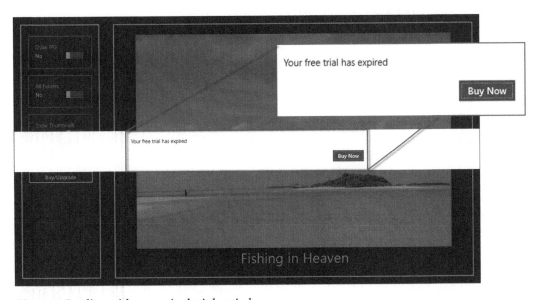

Figure 2. Dealing with an expired trial period

At the moment, the Promise returned by the buyApp function returns true, which signifies a successful purchase from the store. Click the Buy Now button and the dialog will be dismissed and you can use the app.

To simulate a failed purchase, change the buyApp function so that the Promise yields false, as shown in Listing 12.

Listing 12. Simulating a Failed Purchase

```
...
function buyApp() {
    // code to purchase the app will go here
    return WinJS.Promise.wrap(false);
}
...
```

Restart the app and you will see the same dialog box. Clicking the Buy Now button will briefly dismiss the dialog, but it will reappear a moment later, preventing the app from being used.

Adding Support for Buying the App

Most of the work in purchasing the app is taken care of by Windows and the Windows Store. All I have to do is indicate that I want to initiate the process, which I do through the CurrentApp object. You can see how I have implemented the buyApp function in the storeInteractions.js file in Listing 13 to use this aspect of the CurrentApp functionality.

Listing 13. Implementing the buyApp Function

```
...
function buyApp() {
    var md = new pops.MessageDialog("placholder");
    return ViewModel.Store.currentApp.requestAppPurchaseAsync(false).then(function () {
        if (ViewModel.Store.currentApp.licenseInformation.isActive) {
            md.title = "Success"
            md.content = "Your purchase was succesful. Thank you.";
            return md.showAsync().then(function () {
                return true;
            });
        } else {
            return false;
        }
    }, function () {
        md.title = "Error"
        md.content = "Your purchase could not be completed. Please try again.";
        return md.showAsync().then(function () {
            return false;
        });
    });
}
...
```

The key part is the call to the requestAppPurchaseAsync method, which initiates the purchase process. The argument to this method is a boolean value indicating whether a receipt should be generated for the transaction – I have specified false, meaning no receipt is required.

The requestAppPurchaseAsync method returns a WinJS.Promise that completes normally if the purchase is successful and invokes the error function if not (see Chapter 9 for an explanation of the different functions that are passed to the Promise.then method).

The success and error relate to the process itself, so you need to check the license status in your success function to ensure that the purchase was successful. I respond to the outcome of the purchase by using another MessageDialog to report the result. My buyApp function returns a Promise that yields true if the purchase was successful and false if it was not.

When using the CurrentAppSimulator object, calling the requestAppPurchaseAsync method displays a dialog that allows you to simulate different outcomes of the purchase request. To see this dialog, start the app and click the Buy Now button. Figure 3 shows the dialog and the options you can pick to simulate the outcome.

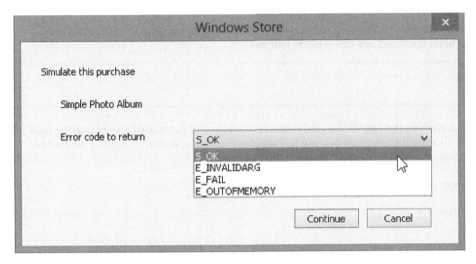

Figure 3. Simulating the app purchase process

The S_OK option will simulate a successful purchase, while the other values simulate different kinds of error. I don't differentiate between different kinds of error in my example and treat all failed purchases the same way.

Testing a Failed Purchase

If you select one of the error conditions and click the Continue button, you will see the error message shown in Figure 4. Clicking the Close button dismisses the dialog and, because the app still isn't licensed, causes the app to display the expired warning again.

Figure 4. Notifying the user that a purchase has failed

Testing a Successful Purchase

Testing a successful purchase is a little more involved because it is important to check that the license information is properly updated. To begin, start the app and before doing anything else, enter the following statements into the Visual Studio JavaScript Console:

```
console.log("Active: " + ViewModel.Store.currentApp.licenseInformation.isActive);
console.log("Trial: " + ViewModel.Store.currentApp.licenseInformation.isTrial);
```

These statements produce the following output, which indicates that the app doesn't have a valid license and that it has been obtained as a free trial, as follows:

```
Active: false
Trial: true
```

Click the Buy Now button on the app dialog and simulate a successful purchase by selecting the S_OK value from the list and clicking the Continue button. You will see the dialog shown in Figure 5 and when you click the Close button, you will be able to use the app.

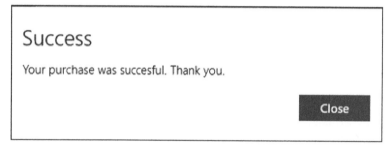

Figure 5. Confirmation of a successful app purchase

Now reenter those commands into the JavaScript Console window and you will see that the license information has changed, indicating that the user has licensed the app as follows:

```
Active: true
Trial: false
```

The licensechanged event is triggered automatically when the user acquires a license, which means that my handler function in the /js/store.js file will reevaluate the available licenses and update the properties used to respond to calls to the ViewModel.Store.checkCapability function, ensuring that the app state remains consistent with the licenses that the user has acquired.

■ **Note**   It is important to understand that the scenario file doesn't change – only the state of the license information inside the running app. If you restart the app, the scenario described in the /store/initial.xml file will be reloaded, re-creating the situation in which the user doesn't have a license, and the free trial period has expired.

Summary

In this chapter, I have introduced you to the `Windows.ApplicationModel.Store` namespace and used some of the objects it contains to implement part of my example business model. I have added support to my app for enforcing trial periods and for purchasing the app from the store to gain a perpetual license and tested this functionality using a scenario file. In the next chapter, I'll show you how to sell and manage in-app upgrades.

CHAPTER 32

Selling Upgrades

In this chapter, I show you how to use the Windows Store to sell upgrades to your users from within your app. I demonstrate how to create entries in the simulator file that describe the upgrades, how to get information about which upgrades have been purchased, and how to start the Windows Store process to purchase upgrades.

Defining the Products in the Scenario File

The technique for creating in-app upgrades starts with definitions in a scenario file. For this chapter, I have created a new file in the store folder called upgrades.xml, the contents of which you can see in Listing 1.

Listing 1. The Contents of the upgrades.xml File

```xml
<?xml version="1.0" encoding="utf-16" ?>
<CurrentApp>
  <ListingInformation>
    <App>
      <AppId>e4bbe35f-0509-4cca-a27a-4ec43bed783c</AppId>
      <LinkUri>http://apress.com</LinkUri>
      <CurrentMarket>en-US</CurrentMarket>
      <AgeRating>3</AgeRating>
      <MarketData xml:lang="en-us">
        <Name>Simple Photo Album</Name>
        <Description>An app to display your photos</Description>
        <Price>4.99</Price>
        <CurrencySymbol>$</CurrencySymbol>
        <CurrencyCode>USD</CurrencyCode>
      </MarketData>
    </App>
    <Product ProductId="fileTypes">
      <MarketData xml:lang="en-us">
        <Name>JPG Files Upgrade</Name>
        <Price>4.99</Price>
        <CurrencySymbol>$</CurrencySymbol>
        <CurrencyCode>USD</CurrencyCode>
      </MarketData>
```

```
      </Product>
    </ListingInformation>
    <LicenseInformation>
      <App>
        <IsActive>true</IsActive>
        <IsTrial>false</IsTrial>
        <ExpirationDate>2012-09-30T00:00:00.00Z</ExpirationDate>
      </App>
      <Product ProductId="fileTypes">
        <IsActive>true</IsActive>
      </Product>
    </LicenseInformation>
</CurrentApp>
```

I have added just one in-app upgrade to the upgrades.xml file. In the parlance of the Windows Store, an in-app upgrade is referred to as a *product*, as opposed to an *app*, which defines the base functionality. To define a new product, you must add an element in both the ListingInformation and LicenseInformation sections of the scenario file, as I have done in the example.

> ■ **Note** For this scenario file, I want the basic functionality of the app available on a trial period that has not expired. You can see how I have done this in the LicenseInformation.App element, but you will have to change the date in the ExpirationDate element to specify a date that is in the future to get the right effect.

Defining Product Details

You define the details of the product using a Product element and specify the name of the product using the ProductId attribute like this:

```
...
<Product ProductId="fileTypes">
...
```

This is the name by which the upgrade will be known to your app and isn't displayed to the user. I have specified the fileTypes name, which is consistent with the capabilities I have been building up in my app. The elements that are contained in the Product element have the same meaning as when applied in the App element, and they describe the upgrade and specify its cost and currency. In this example, I have described the fileTypes product as the JPG Files Upgrade and set its price at $4.99.

Defining the Product License

You set the license state for the scenario by adding a Product element to the LicenseInformation section of the XML file. You must ensure that the value of the ProductId attribute matches the one you used to describe the upgrade and you must include an IsActive element, which is set to true to indicate that the user a valid license and false otherwise.

You can also use an ExpirationDate element for products that you intend to sell on a subscription basis. The date you specify will be the point at which the subscription elapses (or has elapsed, if you specify a date in the past).

Defining the Remaining Products

Now that I have shown you how a single product is defined, I will add entries to the scenario file for the other upgrades my app will support. You can see the additions, which are quite lengthy, in Listing 2.

Listing 2. Defining Scenario Entries for the Remaining Products

```xml
<?xml version="1.0" encoding="utf-16" ?>
<CurrentApp>
  <ListingInformation>
    <App>
      <AppId>e4bbe35f-0509-4cca-a27a-4ec43bed783c</AppId>
      <LinkUri>http://apress.com</LinkUri>
      <CurrentMarket>en-US</CurrentMarket>
      <AgeRating>3</AgeRating>
      <MarketData xml:lang="en-us">
        <Name>Simple Photo Album</Name>
        <Description>An app to display your photos</Description>
        <Price>4.99</Price>
        <CurrencySymbol>$</CurrencySymbol>
        <CurrencyCode>USD</CurrencyCode>
      </MarketData>
    </App>
    <Product ProductId="fileTypes">
      <MarketData xml:lang="en-us">
        <Name>JPG Files Upgrade</Name>
        <Price>4.99</Price>
        <CurrencySymbol>$</CurrencySymbol>
        <CurrencyCode>USD</CurrencyCode>
      </MarketData>
    </Product>
    <Product ProductId="depth">
      <MarketData xml:lang="en-us">
        <Name>All Folders Upgrade</Name>
        <Price>4.99</Price>
        <CurrencySymbol>$</CurrencySymbol>
        <CurrencyCode>USD</CurrencyCode>
      </MarketData>
    </Product>
    <Product ProductId="thumbnails">
      <MarketData xml:lang="en-us">
        <Name>Thumbnails Upgrade</Name>
        <Price>1.99</Price>
        <CurrencySymbol>$</CurrencySymbol>
        <CurrencyCode>USD</CurrencyCode>
      </MarketData>
    </Product>
    <Product ProductId="theworks">
      <MarketData xml:lang="en-us">
        <Name>The Works Upgrade + Printing</Name>
        <Price>9.99</Price>
```

```
      <CurrencySymbol>$</CurrencySymbol>
      <CurrencyCode>USD</CurrencyCode>
    </MarketData>
  </Product>
</ListingInformation>
<LicenseInformation>
  <App>
    <IsActive>true</IsActive>
    <IsTrial>false</IsTrial>
    <ExpirationDate>2012-09-30T00:00:00.00Z</ExpirationDate>
  </App>
  <Product ProductId="fileTypes">
    <IsActive>true</IsActive>
  </Product>
  <Product ProductId="thumbnails">
    <IsActive>false</IsActive>
    <ExpirationDate>2011-09-30T00:00:00.00Z</ExpirationDate>
  </Product>
</LicenseInformation>
</CurrentApp>
```

My scenario file now contains listing information for all of the upgrades that I sell and license information for two of them. The fileTypes upgrade is correctly licensed, but the license for the thumbnails upgrade, which I sell on a subscription basis, has expired.

As a reminder, I have listed the upgrades and their product IDs in Table 1.

Table 1. App Upgrades

ID	Name	Description	Price
fileTypes	File Types Upgrade	Will display JPG images, as well as PNG images	$4.99 (perpetual)
depth	Folders Upgrade	Will display all images from the Pictures library, not just those in the top-level folder	$4.99 (perpetual)
thumbnails	Thumbnails Upgrade	Will allow users to see their images as thumbnails	$1.99 every 30 days
theworks	The Works	All of the app features, plus support for printing	$9/99 every 30 days

Omitting details of a product from the LicenseInformation section of the scenario file is equivalent to their not being a license for it – you can also achieve this effect by adding a Product element but setting the IsActive element to false.

Switching to the New Scenario File

In order to use my new scenario file, I need to update the code in the /js/store.js file, as shown in Listing 3. Typically, you will build up a library of different scenario files to support thorough testing. For my own projects, I find that I can end up with up to 20 different scenario files before I have a complete set of tests that cover all of the license permutations. Fortunately, for my relatively simple example app, I won't need anywhere near that number of files.

Listing 3. *Changing the store.js File to Load the New Scenario*

```
...
loadLicenseData: function () {
    var url = new Windows.Foundation.Uri("ms-appx:///store/upgrades.xml");
    return storage.StorageFile.getFileFromApplicationUriAsync(url)
        .then(function (file) {
            return ViewModel.Store.currentApp.reloadSimulatorAsync(file);
        });
},
...
```

■ **Tip**   I find that if I am getting unexpected results, it is often because I have forgotten to load the right file.

Using the License Information

My goal now is to use the license information I have defined to set the user's entitlement to the different features in the app. I do this through the CurrentApp object (or the CurrentAppSimulator object during development). You can see the changes I have made to the /js/store.js file to take advantage of the new license information in Listing 4.

Listing 4. *Using the Product License Information in the /js/store.js File*

```
(function() {
    var storage = Windows.Storage;

    var licensedCapabilities = {
        basicApp: false,
        fileTypes: false,
        depth: false,
        thumbnails: false,
        print: false,
    }

    WinJS.Namespace.define("ViewModel.Store", {
        events: WinJS.Utilities.eventMixin,

        checkCapability: function (name) {
            var available = licensedCapabilities[name] != undefined
                ? licensedCapabilities[name] : true;
            setImmediate(function () {
                ViewModel.Store.events.dispatchEvent("capabilitycheck",
                    { capability: name, enabled: available });
            });
            return available;
        },

        currentApp: Windows.ApplicationModel.Store.CurrentAppSimulator,
```

```
        loadLicenseData: function () {
            var url
                = new Windows.Foundation.Uri("ms-appx:///store/upgrades.xml");
            return storage.StorageFile.getFileFromApplicationUriAsync(url)
                .then(function (file) {
                    return ViewModel.Store.currentApp.reloadSimulatorAsync(file);
                });
        },
    });


    ViewModel.Store.currentApp.licenseInformation.addEventListener("licensechanged",
        function () {
            var license = ViewModel.Store.currentApp.licenseInformation;
            licensedCapabilities.basicApp = license.isActive;

            var products = license.productLicenses;
            if (products.lookup("theworks").isActive) {
                licensedCapabilities.fileTypes = true;
                licensedCapabilities.depth = true;
                licensedCapabilities.thumbnails = true;
                licensedCapabilities.print = true;
            } else {
                licensedCapabilities.fileTypes = products.lookup("fileTypes").isActive;
                licensedCapabilities.depth = products.lookup("depth").isActive;
                licensedCapabilities.thumbnails = products.lookup("thumbnails").isActive;
            }
        });
})();
```

Processing the Product Licenses

The other change I have made in the store.js file is to expand the code in the event handler for the licensechanged event so that it processes the licenses for the upgrade products and sets the properties in the licensedCapabilities event.

The LicenseInformation object defines a productLicenses property (I obtain the LicenseInformation object from the CurrentApp.licenseInformation property). The object returned by the productLicenses property allows you to look up individual products using the lookup method, like this:

```
...
products.lookup("theworks")
...
```

The argument to the lookup method is the ProductId attribute value from the Product element in the scenario file. In the fragment above, I have requested the license for the upgrade called theworks.

The lookup method returns a ProductLicense object that contains details of the license status of the requested product. The ProductLicense object defines the properties described in Table 2.

Table 2. The Properties Defined by the ProductLicense Object

Name	Description
productId	Returns the value from the ProductId attribute in the scenario file, identifying the product unique within the scope of the app.
isActive	Returns the value of the IsActive element in the scenario file. This value will be true if the user has a valid license for the upgrade and false otherwise.
expirationDate	Returns the value of the ExpirationDate element in the scenario file. This property will return the date that the subscription for an upgrade lapses.

The nice thing about the lookup method is that will return a ProductLicense object even when there is no corresponding Product element in the scenario file – the isActive property will be set to false, indicating that there is no value license. This means that I can safely look up the product called theworks and get a response that I can use to make decisions about which app capabilities should be enabled. My approach to processing the product licenses is to start by seeing whether the user has purchased a license for theworks. If so, then I enable all of the capabilities defined by the licensedCapabilities object, as follows:

```
...
var products = license.productLicenses;
if (products.lookup("theworks").isActive) {
    licensedCapabilities.fileTypes = true;
    licensedCapabilities.depth = true;
    licensedCapabilities.thumbnails = true;
    licensedCapabilities.print = true;
} else {
    licensedCapabilities.fileTypes = products.lookup("fileTypes").isActive;
    licensedCapabilities.depth = products.lookup("depth").isActive;
    licensedCapabilities.thumbnails = products.lookup("thumbnails").isActive;
}
...
```

If the user has not got a valid license for the works, then I look up each of the other products in turn and set the state of the corresponding capability. This means, for example, that the print capability will only be enabled if the user has theworks, providing a simple demonstration of how I have separated the app capabilities from the upgrade products.

Testing the License Information

You can test the license information by starting the app and entering the following statement into the Visual Studio JavaScript Console window:

```
["fileTypes", "depth", "thumbnails", "print"].forEach(function(cap) {
    console.log(cap + ": " + ViewModel.Store.checkCapability(cap));
});
```

Hit Return and you should see the following output, which indicates which app capabilities the user is entitled to use based on the license information in the scenario file:

```
fileTypes: true
depth: false
thumbnails: false
print: false
```

As you would expect, the fileTypes capability is enabled, and all of the others are disabled. You can see this information being applied in the app. Dismiss the dialog that tells you how many days are left in the trial period and try and change the position of the ToggleSwitch controls. You will only be able to move the one that is labeled Show JPG because the others are related to capabilities to which the user isn't entitled. Similarly, if you activate the Devices Charm, you will see the message shown in Figure 1 because the print capability isn't available to the user.

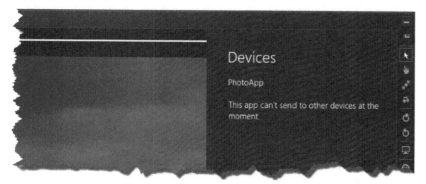

Figure 1. Activating the Devices Charm when the print capability isn't licensed

Correcting the License Entitlements

Now that I have shown you how to check the license information for individual products, I need to go back and correct the code in the /js/store.js file. When the app is within the trial period, I want users to be able to use all of the app capabilities, just as if they had purchased the basic app and subscribed to the theworks upgrade. You can see the change I have made to store.js in Listing 5.

Listing 5. Allowing the User Access to All Capabilities During the Trial Period

```
...
ViewModel.Store.currentApp.licenseInformation.addEventListener("licensechanged",
    function () {
        var license = ViewModel.Store.currentApp.licenseInformation;
        licensedCapabilities.basicApp = license.isActive;

        var products = license.productLicenses;
        if (products.lookup("theworks").isActive
                || (license.isActive && license.isTrial)) {

            licensedCapabilities.fileTypes = true;
            licensedCapabilities.depth = true;
            licensedCapabilities.thumbnails = true;
            licensedCapabilities.print = true;
        } else {
```

```
        licensedCapabilities.fileTypes = products.lookup("fileTypes").isActive;
        licensedCapabilities.depth = products.lookup("depth").isActive;
        licensedCapabilities.thumbnails = products.lookup("thumbnails").isActive;
    }
});
...
```

I have used the license information about the basic app to create equivalence between an unexpired trial period and licenses for the basic app plus theworks upgrade.

You will recall that the upgrade.xml scenario file specifies that the app is within a trial period, so if you restart the app once you have updated the store.js file, you should have access to all of the capabilities.

Selling Upgrades

Now that my app enforces product licenses, I can prompt the user to purchase upgrades. How you do this depends on the nature of your app. I recommend that you think this through carefully because there is a fine line that separates prompting users in a helpful and polite manner and bombarding them with constant demands for money.

For this chapter, I will use a simple approach that is to prompt the user to upgrade when they try to use a feature that is not licensed.

■ **Tip**   I am going to prompt the user to upgrade because I want to focus on the upgrade mechanism, but I wouldn't do this in a real app because it annoys the user. When I prompt the user to upgrade the first time, I usually provide an option to disable any further prompts for the same feature. I suggest that you consider a similar approach. You can make a persistent record of the user's preferences using the app data feature, which I described in Chapter 20.

You will recall that the Windows.Store.checkCapability method triggers the capabilitycheck event when the user tries to use a capability. I responded to this event in the /js/storeInteractions.js file in Chapter 31 to enforce my business model for the basic app so that I could sell the app to the user and enforce the trial period. I will use a similar technique to manage the process for upgrades. In the sections that follow, I'll walk through the changes and additions I have made.

Dispatching State Events

I will start by adding support for dispatching events from the ViewModel.State namespace. My approach to selling upgrades is to prompt the user in response to changes in the app layout, and I want to make sure that I correctly update the state of the app layout when the user successfully purchases an upgrade. That means that I need some way to signal that the data in the ViewModel.State namespace has been changed, and to do this, I have made some additions in the /js/viewmodel.js file, as shown in Listing 6.

Listing 6. Adding Support for Emitting Events from the ViewModel.State Namespace

```
(function () {

    WinJS.Namespace.define("ViewModel", {
```

```
        State: WinJS.Binding.as({
            pictureDataSource: new WinJS.Binding.List(),
            fileTypes: false,
            depth: false,
            thumbnails: false,
            events: WinJS.Utilities.eventMixin,
            reloadState: function () {
                ViewModel.State.events.dispatchEvent("reloadstate", {});
            }
        }),
    });

    WinJS.Namespace.define("Converters", {
        display: WinJS.Binding.converter(function(val) {
            return val ? "block" : "none";
        })
    });

})();
```

The individual properties in the ViewModel.State namespace are observable, but I need some way to indicate that a fundamental change in the app state has occurred and that the data in the app should be refreshed. To this end, I have added an events property to which I have assigned the WinJS.Utilities. eventMixin object and a reloadState function that, when called, triggers an event called reloadstate. You will see how I use the function and respond to the event in the sections that follow.

Managing the Purchasing Process

I start the upgrade purchasing process when the user tries to activate a capability to which they are not entitled. I detect this situation by handling the capabilitycheck event, extending the code I added in Chapter 31 to handle the app purchasing process. You can see the changes I have made to the /js/ storeInteractions.js file that extend purchases to include upgrades in Listing 7.

Listing 7. Adding Support for Selling In-app Upgrades

```
(function () {

    var pops = Windows.UI.Popups;

    ViewModel.Store.events.addEventListener("capabilitycheck", function (e) {
        if (e.detail.capability == "basicApp") {
            // ...statements removed for brevity...

        } else if (e.detail.capability == "print" && !e.detail.enabled) {
            var md = new pops.MessageDialog("Printing is only available to subscribers");
            md.commands.append(new pops.UICommand("Subscribe"));
            md.commands.append(new pops.UICommand("Cancel"));
            md.showAsync().then(function (command) {
                if (command.label != "Cancel") {
                    buyUpgrade("theworks");
                }
```

```
        });

    } else if (!e.detail.enabled) {
        var md = new pops.MessageDialog("You need to buy an upgrade to use this "
            + " feature or subscribe to unlock all features");
        md.commands.append(new pops.UICommand("Upgrade"));
        md.commands.append(new pops.UICommand("Subscribe"));
        md.commands.append(new pops.UICommand("Cancel"));
        md.showAsync().then(function (command) {
            if (command.label != "Cancel") {
                var product = command.label
                    == "Upgrade" ? e.detail.capability : "theworks";
                buyUpgrade(product).then(function (upgradeResult) {
                    if (upgradeResult) {
                        var val = ViewModel.State[e.detail.capability];
                        if (val != undefined) {
                            ViewModel.State[e.detail.capability] = !val;
                        }
                        ViewModel.State.reloadState();
                    }
                });
            }
        });
    }
});

function buyApp() {
    // ...statements removed for brevity...
}

function buyUpgrade(product) {
    var md = new pops.MessageDialog("");
    return ViewModel.Store.currentApp.requestProductPurchaseAsync(product, false)
    .then(function () {
        if (ViewModel.Store.currentApp.licenseInformation.productLicenses
                .lookup(product).isActive) {
            md.title = "Success"
            md.content = "Your upgrade was succesful. Thank you.";
            return md.showAsync().then(function () {
                return true;
            });
        } else {
            return false;
        }
    }, function () {
        md.title = "Error"
        md.content = "Your upgrade could not be completed. Please try again.";
        return md.showAsync().then(function () {
            return false;
        });
    });
```

```
    }
})();
```

You will recall that the capabilitycheck event is triggered when the ViewModel.Store.checkCapability method is called. If the capability being asked for isn't basicApp, then I know that it is associated with one of the upgrades I want to sell. I explain how I sell different categories of upgrade in the sections that follow.

Selling Capabilities Indirectly

My app contains the print capability (which I only sell as part of my theworks product) that unlocks everything in the app. This is an example of an indirect upgrade, where the product I sell doesn't just activate the capability that the user wants right now. I deal with requests for the print capability separately from other kinds of upgrade, as follows:

```
...
} else if (e.detail.capability == "print" && !e.detail.enabled) {
    var md = new pops.MessageDialog("Printing is only available to subscribers");
    md.commands.append(new pops.UICommand("Subscribe"));
    md.commands.append(new pops.UICommand("Cancel"));
    md.showAsync().then(function (command) {
        if (command.label != "Cancel") {
            buyUpgrade("theworks");
        }
    });
}
...
```

I show a simple message to the user that explains that the capability they have requested is only available to subscribers and give them the opportunity to purchase a subscription, as shown in Figure 2.

Figure 2. Prompting the user to subscribe when printing is requested

Windows 8 doesn't provide a means for me to prevent the Devices pane being displayed when the Devices Charm is activated, so I display my message so users can see it when they dismiss the pane. If the user clicks the Subscribe button, then call the buyUpgrade function, which initiates the upgrade process (and that I'll describe shortly). I call the buyUpgrade function with theworks as the argument, indicating that the user wants to purchase the subscription product.

Selling Capabilities Directly

For the other capabilities in the app, I want to offer the user the choice between buying just the feature they have tried to use or subscribing and unlocking all of the features, which I do as follows:

```
...
} else if (!e.detail.enabled) {
    var md = new pops.MessageDialog("You need to buy an upgrade to use this "
        + " feature or subscribe to unlock all features");
    md.commands.append(new pops.UICommand("Upgrade"));
    md.commands.append(new pops.UICommand("Subscribe"));
    md.commands.append(new pops.UICommand("Cancel"));
    md.showAsync().then(function (command) {
        if (command.label != "Cancel") {
            var product = command.label
                == "Upgrade" ? e.detail.capability : "theworks";
            buyUpgrade(product).then(function (upgradeResult) {
                if (upgradeResult) {
                    var val = ViewModel.State[e.detail.capability];
                    if (val != undefined) {
                        ViewModel.State[e.detail.capability] = !val;
                    }
                    ViewModel.State.reloadState();
                }
            });
        }
    });
}
...
```

I achieve the effect I want by adding a Subscribe button to the MessageDialog and varying the argument that I pass to the buyUpgrade function. You can see the dialog that I present to the user in Figure 3.

Figure 3. Selling upgrade and subscriptions to the user

If the user clicks the Upgrade button, then I start the process for buying the product that unlocks that capability. If the user clicks the Subscribe button, then I start the process for buying the theworks product.

If the user makes a successful purchase, then I try and update the ViewModel.State property associated with the capability, if there is one. This completes the UI interaction that the user started by activating a ToggleSwitch, meaning that the result of upgrading is immediate. Some of the upgrades that the user can license require the data to be reloaded, so I call the ViewMode.State.reloadState method that I defined in the /js/viewmodel.js file in Listing 6.

Refreshing the App State

The last step I need to perform is to ensure that the app state reflects the capabilities that the user has licensed. The simplest way to do this is to reload the files from the Pictures library so that the app displays all the images that the user is entitled to. You can see how I refresh the app state in response to the reloadstate event in Listing 8, which shows the changes I have made to the onactivated function in the / js/default.js file.

Listing 8. Refreshing the State of the App

```
...
args.setPromise(WinJS.UI.processAll().then(function() {
    return WinJS.Binding.processAll(document.body, ViewModel)
        .then(function () {
            return ViewModel.Store.loadLicenseData().then(function () {

                ViewModel.State.events.addEventListener("reloadstate", function (e) {
                    loadFiles();
                    listView.winControl.itemDataSource
                        = ViewModel.State.pictureDataSource.dataSource;
                });

                setupPrinting();
                loadFiles();
                ViewModel.Store.checkCapability("basicApp");
            });
        });
}));
...
```

To handle the event, I call the loadFiles function, which locates the files that the user is entitled to see. I also refresh the data source used for the ListView control that displays the thumbnail images, like this:

```
...
listView.winControl.itemDataSource = ViewModel.State.pictureDataSource.dataSource;
...
```

A quirk of the ListView control is that it won't display content properly if it is initialized while it is hidden and then shown to the user – you just get an empty-looking control. A quick and simple fix is to set the itemDataSource property, which triggers an update and generates new content elements. I don't change the data source – I just assign it to the control property again so that the content is displayed properly when the user purchases the capability to view thumbnails.

Buying the Upgrade

The buyUpgrade function is responsible for initiating the purchase process and responding to the result. The currentApp object defines the requestProductPurchaseAsync method, which initiates the Windows Store upgrade process (or the purchase simulation when the CurrentAppSimulator object is being used). The arguments for this method are the ProductId value for the product that the purchase relates to and a boolean value indicating whether a receipt is required:

```
...
ViewModel.Store.currentApp.requestProductPurchaseAsync(product, false)
...
```

I receive the product that should be purchased as the argument to the buyUpgrade function and I specify false, indicating that I don't want a receipt. The requestProductPurchaseAsync method returns a Promise that is fulfilled when the purchasing process is complete. The success handler function is executed when the purchase is successful, and the error handler if not. I show the user a message confirming the outcome of the purchase, as follows:

```
...
function buyUpgrade(product) {
    var md = new pops.MessageDialog("");
    return ViewModel.Store.currentApp.requestProductPurchaseAsync(product, false)
    .then(function () {
        if (ViewModel.Store.currentApp.licenseInformation.productLicenses
                .lookup(product).isActive) {
            md.title = "Success"
            md.content = "Your upgrade was succesful. Thank you.";
            return md.showAsync().then(function () {
                return true;
            });
        } else {
            return false;
        }
    }, function () {
        md.title = "Error"
        md.content = "Your upgrade could not be completed. Please try again.";
        return md.showAsync().then(function () {
            return false;
        });
    });
}
...
```

My buyUpgrade function returns a Promise that is fulfilled when the user dismisses the message dialog and that yields true if the purchase was successful and false otherwise, allowing me to build chains of actions, such as refreshing the app state.

Testing the Scenario

If you start the app and slide the Show Thumbnails ToggleSwitch to the Yes position, you will be prompted to upgrade or subscribe. Click the Upgrade button and you will see the dialog for simulating purchases, as shown in Figure 4.

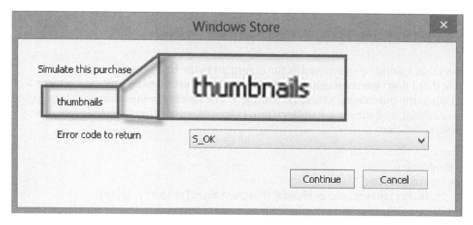

Figure 4. Simulating the purchase of an upgrade

This is the same dialog that simulates app purchases and it has the same choice of results. The dialog displays the name of the product that is being purchased, which I have highlighted in the figure.

Ensure that the S_OK option is selected and click the Continue button to simulate a successful purchase. When you dismiss the dialog that confirms the successful purchase, you will see that the app layout is updated to show the thumbnails and that the ToggleSwitch has been moved to the Yes position, as shown in Figure 5.

Figure 5. The effect of purchasing a license for the thumbnails capability

The other capabilities are still unlicensed, which means that you will be prompted again if you slide one of the other ToggleSwitch controls or activate the Devices Charm.

Testing a Subscription Upgrade

Restart the app so that the licensing information is reset to the contents of the scenario file and slide the Show Thumbnails ToggleSwitch again. This time, when prompted, click the Subscribe button. You will see the purchase simulator dialog again, but this time the product being purchased is reported as theworks, as shown in Figure 6.

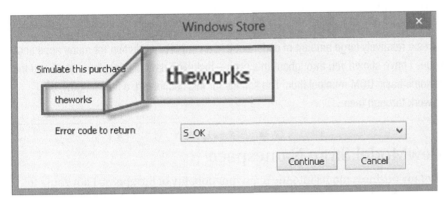

Figure 6. Simulating the purchase of an upgrade that unlocks multiple capabilities

Simulate a successful purchase by selecting the S_OK option and clicking the Continue button. The thumbnails will be displayed just as they were before, but this time the other features of the app have been unlocked as well – so, for example, if you slide the All Folders ToggleSwitch to the Yes position, a deep query will be used to locate the files in your Pictures library, as shown in Figure 7.

Figure 7. The effect of purchasing an upgrade that applies to multiple capabilities

Creating an In-App Store-Front

My final addition to my example app is to wire up the Buy/Upgrade button in order to create a store-front for the various products I want to sell to the user. So far, all of my sales prompts have been triggered by the user trying to perform a specific action, but I'd also like to give the user the opportunity to make purchases at any time, for any reason. In the sections that follow, I'll make a series of additions to the app so that the user can click the button, see the options available, and make purchases.

■ **Note**   This addition requires a relatively large amount of code, but it is an important addition for many apps and requires many of the techniques I have shown you throughout this book – including data binding, templates, and the Flyout control – as well as some basic DOM manipulation. The listings for this section are a little lengthy, but I suggest making the effort to work through them.

Enhancing the ViewModel.Store Namespace

I don't want to leak details of my business model into the main functionality of the app, so I am going to make some additions to the ViewModel.Store namespace to represent products and initiate purchases without exposing the Windows.ApplicationModel.Store namespace directly. You can see the additions I have made to the /js/store.js file in Listing 9.

Listing 9. Expanding the Capabilities of the ViewModel.Store Namespace

```
(function() {
    var storage = Windows.Storage;

    var licensedCapabilities = {
        basicApp: false,
        fileTypes: false,
        depth: false,
        thumbnails: false,
        print: false,
    }

    WinJS.Namespace.define("ViewModel.Store", {
        events: WinJS.Utilities.eventMixin,

        checkCapability: function (name) {
            //  ...statements omitted for brevity...
        },

        currentApp: Windows.ApplicationModel.Store.CurrentAppSimulator,

        loadLicenseData: function () {
            //  ...statements omitted for brevity...
        },

        isBasicAppPurchased: function () {
            var license = ViewModel.Store.currentApp.licenseInformation;
```

```
                return license.isActive && !license.isTrial;
        },

        isFullyUpgraded: function() {
            return ViewModel.Store.currentApp.licenseInformation.productLicenses
                .lookup("theworks").isActive;
        },

        getProductInfo: function () {
            var products = [
                { id: "p1", name: "Product 1", price: "$4.99", purchased: true },
                { id: "p2", name: "Product 2", price: "$1.99", purchased: false },
                { id: "p3", name: "Product 3", price: "$10.99", purchased: false },
                { id: "p4", name: "Product 4", price: "$0.99", purchased: false }];
            return products;
        },

        requestAppPurchase: function() {
            ViewModel.Store.events.dispatchEvent("apppurchaserequested");
        },

        requestUpgradePurchase: function (productId) {
            ViewModel.Store.events.dispatchEvent("productpurchaserequested",
                { product: productId });
        }
    });

    ViewModel.Store.currentApp.licenseInformation.addEventListener("licensechanged",
        function () {
            //  ...statements omitted for brevity...
        });
})();
```

The functions that I have added to the ViewModel.Store namespace fall into three categories: two that provide information needed to manage the button element, one that provides a catalogue of the products available, and two that initiate the purchase process. I'll explain each in the following sections.

Providing Information for the Layout

One aspect of integrating with the Windows Store (or any other commerce platform, for that matter) is the number of different possible states that the app can be in and the need to cater for all of them. You can see this reflected in miniature in the getStoreLabel, isBasicAppPurchased and isFullyUpgraded functions, all of which I use to manage the presentation of the Buy/Upgrade button in the app layout.

If the user is partway through a free trial period, then I want the button to offer them the chance to buy the app. The Windows Store won't allow the user to purchase an in-app upgrade until the basic app has been purchased, so I need to make sure that I offer the user the right transaction in order to present a sensible and useful user experience.

The isBasicAppPurchased allows me to tell when I need to sell the user the basic app and when I need to sell upgrades. At the other end of the end of the spectrum, I want to disable the button element when the user purchased theworks upgrade because there is nothing left to sell. To that end, I have created the isFullyUpgraded function, which returns true when there are no longer any products left to pitch to the user.

■ **Tip** Notice that I don't expose any details of what defines the basic app functionality or what products have to be purchased to create the condition of being fully upgraded. I am keen to keep a strong sense of separation between the different parts of the app and not build knowledge of the business model anywhere outside of the store.js file, so that I can make adjustments more easily in the future.

Providing Product Information

The getProductInfo function provides details of the upgrades available for the app. The function returns an array of objects, each of which contains properties representing the store product id (that will correspond to the entries in the scenario file), the name that should be displayed to the user, the price of the upgrade, and whether or not the product has already been purchased, as follows:

```
...
getProductInfo: function () {
    var products = [
        { id: "p1", name: "Product 1", price: "$4.99", purchased: true },
        { id: "p2", name: "Product 2", price: "$1.99", purchased: false },
        { id: "p3", name: "Product 3", price: "$10.99", purchased: false },
        { id: "p4", name: "Product 4", price: "$0.99", purchased: false }];
    return products;
},
...
```

My initial implementation of this function uses static dummy data. I do this a lot when I am working with the Windows Store because it allows me to make absolutely sure that I don't build in any dependency on the objects in the Windows.ApplicationModel.Store namespace or on the actual products that are for sale within the app. Once again, I do this to make long-term maintenance as easy as possible. I'll return to this function once I have got the in-app store front feature working and add support for generating real data.

Providing Support for Making Purchases

The last two functions I added to the ViewModel.Store namespace provide support for other parts of the app to initiate app and upgrade purchases. I use this feature in the layout I create shortly to display the products to the user:

```
...
requestAppPurchase: function() {
    ViewModel.Store.events.dispatchEvent("apppurchaserequested");
},

requestUpgradePurchase: function (productId) {
    ViewModel.Store.events.dispatchEvent("productpurchaserequested",
        { product: productId });
}
...
```

The storeInteractions.js file contains the code that handles the purchasing process and I don't want to tightly couple that functionality to the store.js file, so I signal the request for purchases using two new events: apppurchaserequested and productpurchaserequested. I'll handle these events in the next section.

Defining the Store Interactions

To get the back-end processes sorted out, I need to handle the two new events I created in the store.js file in the storeInteractions.js file, which already contains all of the code I need to sell to the user. You can see the additions I have made to the storeInteractions.js file in Listing 10.

Listing 10. Responding to the New Purchase Events in the storeInteractions.js File

```
(function () {

    var pops = Windows.UI.Popups;

    ViewModel.Store.events.addEventListener("capabilitycheck", function (e) {
        // ...statements omitted for brevity...
    });

    ViewModel.Store.events.addEventListener("apppurchaserequested", function () {
        buyApp().then(function (result) {
            if (result) {
                ViewModel.State.reloadState();
            }
        });
    });

    ViewModel.Store.events.addEventListener("productpurchaserequested", function (e) {
        buyUpgrade(e.detail.product).then(function (result) {
            if (result) {
                ViewModel.State.reloadState();
            }
        });
    });

    function buyApp() {
        // ...statements omitted for brevity...
    }

    function buyUpgrade(product) {
        // ...statements omitted for brevity...
    }

})();
```

On receipt of an event, I call my existing buyApp or buyUpgrade functions and call the ViewModel.State.reloadState method after a successful purchase to ensure that the app layout reflects the newly acquired capabilities.

Defining the Markup and Styles

I am going to present the user with the in-app store using a WinJS.UI.Flyout control, which I described in Chapter 12. The store will contain details of each product returned by the ViewModel.Store. getProductInfo method, and I'll generate the HTML elements I require using a WinJS.Binding.Template object, which I described in Chapter 8. You can see the changes I have made to the default.html file in Listing 11 to add the Flyout and the template.

Listing 11. Adding the Flyout and the Template to the default.html File

```
...
<body>
    <div id="flipTemplate" data-win-control="WinJS.Binding.Template">
        <div class="flipItem">
            <img class="flipImg" data-win-bind="src: image" />
            <div class="flipTitle" data-win-bind="innerText: title"></div>
        </div>
    </div>

    <div id="listTemplate" data-win-control="WinJS.Binding.Template">
        <div class="listItem">
            <img class="listImg" data-win-bind="src: image" />
        </div>
    </div>

    <div id="productTemplate" data-win-control="WinJS.Binding.Template">
        <div class="pname" data-win-bind="innerText: name"></div>
        <div class="pprice" data-win-bind="innerText: price"></div>
    </div>

    <div id="storeFlyout" data-win-control="WinJS.UI.Flyout"
        data-win-options="{placement: 'right'}">
        <div class="title">Upgrades</div>
        <div id="productContainer">
            <div class="pname subtitle">Name</div>
            <div class="pprice subtitle">Price</div>
            <div class="pbuy subtitle">Buy</div>
        </div>
        <div id="cancelContainer">
            <button>Cancel</button>
        </div>
    </div>

    <!-- other markup removed for brevity -->
</body>
...
```

This new markup is very simple. I will generate the elements in the productTemplate template for each product and add them to the productContainer element in the Flyout (along with some supplementary elements that I will generate in code). I added a new style sheet to the project called /css/store.css to contain the styles I use for the Flyout and template elements and you can see the contents of this new file in Listing 12.

Listing 12. Defining styles for the Flyout and template elements

```
.title {font-size: 20pt;text-align: center;}
#productContainer {display: -ms-grid;}
.pname, .pprice, .pbuy, .purchased {margin: 10px;}
.pname {-ms-grid-column: 1;}
.pprice {-ms-grid-column: 2; text-align: right;}
.pbuy, .purchased { text-align: center; -ms-grid-column: 3;}
#cancelContainer {text-align: center}
```

I rely on the CSS grid layout to position the elements; and part of the grid information is applied via the style sheet, and part is applied in code when I generate the elements from the template in the default. js file, which I'll describe in the following section. I added a script element to the head section of the default.html file to include the new file in the app, as shown in Listing 13.

Listing 13. Adding a Script Element for the store.css file to the default.html File

```
...
<head>
    <meta charset="utf-8" />
    <title>PhotoApp</title>

    <!-- WinJS references -->
    <link href="//Microsoft.WinJS.1.0/css/ui-dark.css" rel="stylesheet" />
    <script src="//Microsoft.WinJS.1.0/js/base.js"></script>
    <script src="//Microsoft.WinJS.1.0/js/ui.js"></script>

    <!-- PhotoApp references -->
    <link href="/css/default.css" rel="stylesheet" />
    <link href="/css/store.css" rel="stylesheet" />
    <script src="/js/viewmodel.js"></script>
    <script src="/js/store.js"></script>
    <script src="/js/storeInteractions.js"></script>
    <script src="/js/default.js"></script>
</head>
...
```

Writing the Code

I have all of the basic plumbing in place for my in-app store and all that remains is to add the code to the / js/default.js file that will bring the various parts together. You can see the additions I have made in Listing 14.

Listing 14. The Additions to the default.js file Required to Implement the In-app Store

```
(function () {
    "use strict";

    WinJS.Binding.optimizeBindingReferences = true;

    var app = WinJS.Application;
    var activation = Windows.ApplicationModel.Activation;
```

```javascript
var storage = Windows.Storage;
var search = storage.Search;

app.onactivated = function (args) {
    if (args.detail.kind === activation.ActivationKind.launch) {
        if (args.detail.previousExecutionState !==
            activation.ApplicationExecutionState.suspended) {

            // ...statements removed for brevity...
        }

        args.setPromise(WinJS.UI.processAll().then(function() {
            return WinJS.Binding.processAll(document.body, ViewModel)
                .then(function () {
                    return ViewModel.Store.loadLicenseData().then(function () {

                        ViewModel.State.events.addEventListener("reloadstate",
                            function (e) {
                            loadFiles();
                            listView.winControl.itemDataSource
                                = ViewModel.State.pictureDataSource.dataSource;
                            configureUpgradeButton();
                        });

                        upgrade.addEventListener("click", function () {
                            if (ViewModel.Store.isBasicAppPurchased()) {
                                showStoreFront();
                            } else {
                                ViewModel.Store.requestAppPurchase();
                            }
                        });

                        setupPrinting();
                        loadFiles();
                        configureUpgradeButton();
                        ViewModel.Store.checkCapability("basicApp");
                    });
                });
        }));
    }
};

function configureUpgradeButton() {
    if (ViewModel.Store.isFullyUpgraded()) {
        upgrade.disabled = "true"
    } else if (ViewModel.Store.isBasicAppPurchased()) {
        upgrade.innerText = "Upgrade";
    } else {
        upgrade.innerText = "Purchase";
    }
}
```

```javascript
function showStoreFront() {
    var products = ViewModel.Store.getProductInfo();
    var rowNum = 2;
    WinJS.Utilities.empty(productContainer);
    products.forEach(function (product) {
        productTemplate.winControl.render(product).then(function (newDiv) {
            if (!product.purchased) {
                var button = document.createElement("button");
                button.innerText = "Buy";
                button.setAttribute("data-product", product.id);
                WinJS.Utilities.addClass(button, "pbuy");
                newDiv.appendChild(button);
            } else {
                var div = document.createElement("div");
                div.innerText = "Purchased";
                WinJS.Utilities.addClass(div, "purchased");
                newDiv.appendChild(div);
            }
            while (newDiv.children.length > 0) {
                var celem = newDiv.children[0];
                celem.style.msGridRow = rowNum;
                productContainer.appendChild(celem);
            }
        });
        rowNum++;
    });
    WinJS.Utilities.query("button.pbuy", productContainer).listen("click",
            function(e) {
        var productId = e.target.getAttribute("data-product");
        ViewModel.Store.requestUpgradePurchase(productId);
    });

    WinJS.Utilities.query("#cancelContainer button").listen("click", function () {
        storeFlyout.winControl.hide();
    });

    storeFlyout.winControl.show(upgrade);
}

function setupPrinting() {
    // ...statements removed for brevity...
}

function loadFiles() {
    // ...statements removed for brevity...
};

app.start();
})();
```

There is a lot of new code here, but it is pretty simple stuff. I'll break it down into two sections to make the explanation simpler to follow.

Managing the Button Element

My first task is to make sure that the button element that the user clicks to display the store is displayed correctly, which I have done through the addition of the configureUpgradeButton function, as follows:

```
...
function configureUpgradeButton() {
    if (ViewModel.Store.isFullyUpgraded()) {
        upgrade.disabled = "true"
    } else if (ViewModel.Store.isBasicAppPurchased()) {
        upgrade.innerText = "Upgrade";
    } else {
        upgrade.innerText = "Purchase";
    }
}
...
```

You can see how I have used the methods I added in the ViewModel.Store namespace to work out what to do with the button. If the app has been fully upgraded and there is nothing left to sell, then I disable the button. If the user has purchased the app, then I set the text in the button to Upgrade, and if the user has yet to buy the basic capability, I set the text to Purchase. You can see these different states later in the chapter when I test my in-app store capability.

I also use the isBasicAppPurchased method to figure out what to do when the user clicks the button. If the user has not purchased the basic app yet, then I call the ViewModel.Store.requestAppPurchase method, which will lead to the app purchase process being started, as follows:

```
...
upgrade.addEventListener("click", function () {
    if (ViewModel.Store.isBasicAppPurchased()) {
        showStoreFront();
    } else {
        ViewModel.Store.requestAppPurchase();
    }
});
...
```

If the user *has* already purchased the app, then I call the showStoreFront function, which I describe in the next section.

Populating the Flyout

The showStoreFront function is responsible for populating the Flyout control and configuring it so that the user can start the purchase process for an upgrade. The code for this function is verbose because I supplement the elements generated from the template with either a button to initiate the purchase for a product or a div element that I use to indicate that the upgrade has already been purchased. If you ignore that part of the function, the rest of the code becomes a lot easier to understand, like this:

```
...
function showStoreFront() {
```

```
    var products = ViewModel.Store.getProductInfo();
    var rowNum = 2;
    WinJS.Utilities.empty(productContainer);
    products.forEach(function (product) {
        productTemplate.winControl.render(product).then(function (newDiv) {
            // ...statements to supplement template elements omitted...
        });
        rowNum++;
    });
    WinJS.Utilities.query("button.pbuy", productContainer).listen("click",
            function(e) {
        var productId = e.target.getAttribute("data-product");
        ViewModel.Store.requestUpgradePurchase(productId);
     });

    WinJS.Utilities.query("#cancelContainer button").listen("click", function () {
        storeFlyout.winControl.hide();
    });

    storeFlyout.winControl.show(upgrade);
}
...
```

I add elements to the Flyout for each product and set up a handler for the click event from the buttons that start the upgrade process. Once I have populated and configured the Flyout control, I call the show method to display it to the user. You can see how the store appears in the next section when I test the new functionality.

Testing the In-App Store Feature

I am ready to test the new functionality I added for the in-app store, although you will notice that I am still working with my static dummy product data. Only when I am happy with the way that the in-app store works will I make the switch to real data. I need to start by configuring my scenario file. I am still using the upgrades.xml file I created earlier in the chapter, and in Listing 15 you can see the initial set up for the LicenseInformation.App section, which is the part that I will be changing for these tests.

Listing 15. *The License Configuration for the Basic App Purchase Test*

```
...
<LicenseInformation>
  <App>
    <IsActive>true</IsActive>
    <IsTrial>true</IsTrial>
    <ExpirationDate>2012-09-30T00:00:00.00Z</ExpirationDate>
  </App>
  <Product ProductId="fileTypes">
    <IsActive>true</IsActive>
  </Product>
  <Product ProductId="thumbnails">
    <IsActive>false</IsActive>
    <ExpirationDate>2011-09-30T00:00:00.00Z</ExpirationDate>
```

```
    </Product>
</LicenseInformation>
</CurrentApp>
...
```

I want to simulate a trial period that has not expired, so I set the isActive and isTrial elements to true and specified a date in the ExpirationDate element that is, for me, in the future. You'll have to use a different date to get the right effect.

Testing Basic App Purchasing

Start the app and after you dismiss the reminder about how many days are left in the trial, you will see that button in the layout is labeled Purchase. If you click this button, you will see the purchase simulator dialog, which will show that the basic app is being purchased.

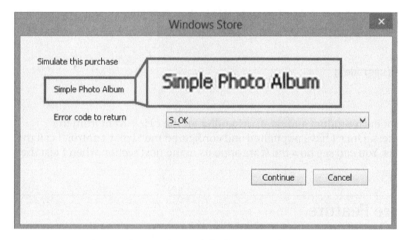

Figure 8. *Simulating the purchase of the basic app functionality*

Simulate a successful purchase by ensuring that the S_OK option is selected and clicking the Continue button. When you dismiss the message that confirms your purchase, you will see that the button label has changed to Upgrade.

Testing Upgrade Purchasing

Without restarting the app, click the button again and you will see the in-app store, as shown in Figure 9. I have used a very basic layout, but you can see how I have displayed the dummy product data to offer upgrade to the user.

Click one of the Buy buttons and you will see the purchase simulator dialog, albeit for a product that doesn't exist in the scenario file.

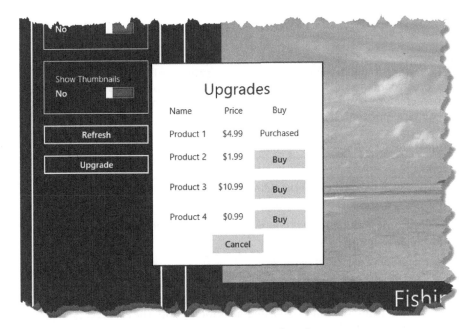

Figure 9. The in-app store displaying dummy product data

Adding the Real Product Data

Now that I know my in-app store works, I can add the real product data, which I do by revising the code in the /js/store.js file. You can see the changes I have made in Listing 16.

Listing 16. Using Real Product Data

```
...
getProductInfo: function () {
    return ViewModel.Store.currentApp.loadListingInformationAsync()
    .then(function (info) {

        var products = [];
        var cursor = info.productListings.first();
        do {
            var prodInfo = cursor.current;

            products.push({
                id: prodInfo.value.productId,
                name: prodInfo.value.name,
                price: prodInfo.value.formattedPrice,
                purchased: ViewModel.Store.currentApp.licenseInformation.productLicenses
                    .lookup(prodInfo.value.productId).isActive
            });
        } while (cursor.moveNext());
        return products;
    });
```

```
},
...
```

The `CurrentApp` and `CurrentAppSimjulator` objects define the `loadListingInformationAsync`. This method returns a `Promise` that, when fulfilled, yields a `Windows.ApplicationModel.Store.ListingInformation` object, which contains the listing information about your app and its upgrades in the Windows Store – this information corresponds to the `ListingInformation` section of the scenario file. The `ListingInformation` object defines the properties I have described in Table 3.

Table 3. The Properties Defined by the ListingInformation Object

Name	Description
ageRating	Corresponds to the App.AgeRating element
description	Corresponds to the Description element
formattedPrice	Returns the price, formatted with the currency symbol (such as $4.99)
name	Corresponds to the Name element
productListings	Returns a list of ProductListing objects

It is the `productListings` property that interests me for the in-app store because it returns a list of `ProductListing` objects, each of which describes one of the upgrades for my app. The `ProductListing` object defines the properties I have described in Table 4.

Table 4. The Properties defined by the ProducListing Object

Name	Description
productId	Corresponds to the ProductId attribute of the Product element
name	Corresponds to the Name element
formattedPrice	Returns the price for the upgrade, formatted with the currency symbol

The object that the `ListingInformation.productListings` property returns presents the `ProductListing` objects as a list, which is why I have used a `do...while` loop. For each product listing, I create an object with the properties I require for my in-app store `Flyout` and look up the license information for each one to see if whether has already been purchased.

The result from my revised `getProductInfo` method is a `Promise` that yields an array of descriptive objects when it is fulfilled; this means I need to update the `showStoreFront` function in the `default.js` file to expect the `Promise`, as shown in Listing 17.

Listing 17. Revising the showStoreFront Function in the Default.js file

```
function showStoreFront() {
    ViewModel.Store.getProductInfo().then(function (products) {
        var rowNum = 2;
        WinJS.Utilities.empty(productContainer);
        products.forEach(function (product) {
            productTemplate.winControl.render(product).then(function (newDiv) {
                if (!product.purchased) {
                    var button = document.createElement("button");
                    button.innerText = "Buy";
                    button.setAttribute("data-product", product.id);
```

```
                    WinJS.Utilities.addClass(button, "pbuy");
                    newDiv.appendChild(button);
                } else {
                    var div = document.createElement("div");
                    div.innerText = "Purchased";
                    WinJS.Utilities.addClass(div, "purchased");
                    newDiv.appendChild(div);
                }
                while (newDiv.children.length > 0) {
                    var celem = newDiv.children[0];
                    celem.style.msGridRow = rowNum;
                    productContainer.appendChild(celem);
                }
            });
            rowNum++;
        });
        WinJS.Utilities.query("button.pbuy", productContainer).listen("click",
                function (e) {
            var productId = e.target.getAttribute("data-product");
            ViewModel.Store.requestUpgradePurchase(productId);
        });
        WinJS.Utilities.query("#cancelContainer button").listen("click", function () {
            storeFlyout.winControl.hide();
        });

        storeFlyout.winControl.show(upgrade);
    });
}
```

With this change, my in-app store feature will display real product data, which is obtained from the scenario file when the CurrentAppSimulator object is used and from the Windows Store data when the CurrentApp object is used.

Testing the In-App Store with Real Data

The final tests are to check that the real product data is displayed properly and that the button in the layout is disabled when the user buys the theworks upgrade. Start by updating the upgrades.xml scenario file so that the app starts with a license for the basic app. Set the IsActive element to true and the IsTrial element to false, as shown in Listing 18.

Listing 18. Updating the Scenario File for the Final Test

```
...
<LicenseInformation>
  <App>
    <IsActive>true</IsActive>
    <IsTrial>false</IsTrial>
    <ExpirationDate>2012-09-30T00:00:00.00Z</ExpirationDate>
  </App>
  <Product ProductId="fileTypes">
    <IsActive>true</IsActive>
```

```
    </Product>
    <Product ProductId="thumbnails">
      <IsActive>false</IsActive>
      <ExpirationDate>2011-09-30T00:00:00.00Z</ExpirationDate>
    </Product>
  </LicenseInformation>
...
```

Start the app and click the button that will be labeled Upgrade; you will see the in-app store showing real product data, as illustrated by Figure 10.

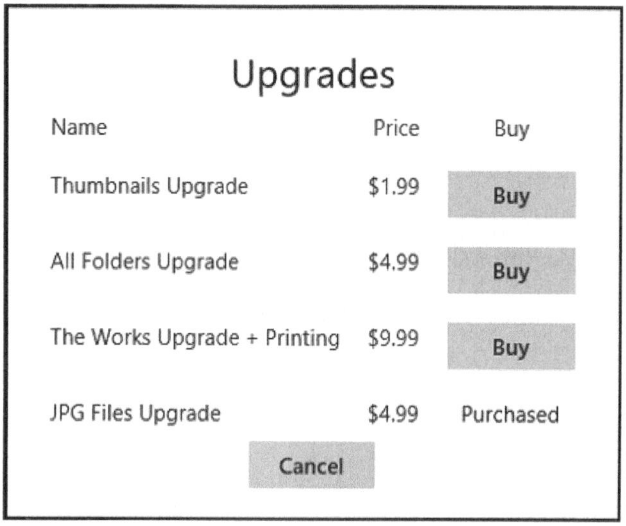

Figure 10. *The in-app store showing real product data*

You can see that the JPG Files Upgrade is shown as purchased, which matches the data in the LicenseInformation section of the scenario file. Click the Buy button for The Works Upgrade and you will see the purchase simulator dialog. If you simulate a successful purchase and dismiss the confirmation dialog, you will see that the Upgrade button has now been disabled to indicate that no further upgrades are available.

Summary

In this chapter, I have shown you how to take advantage of the Windows Store support for selling in-app upgrades. I demonstrated how to sell upgrades for single and multiple app capabilities and how to determine which capabilities the user has purchased. I also demonstrated how to create an in-app store, which allows the user to purchase upgrades at any time. In the next chapter, which is the last in this book, I show you how to prepare and publish your app to the Windows Store.

CHAPTER 33

■ ■ ■

Publishing to the Windows Store

In this chapter, I complete the process I started in Chapter 30 and prepare my app so that it can be submitted to the Windows Store for certification and listing. I show you how to prepare the app listing on the Windows Store Dashboard, how to test your app to find problems, and how to upload your app to Microsoft so that it can be tested.

Preparing the App Listing

Now that I have a working and tested app, I need to return to the Windows Store Dashboard and complete some more steps in the publishing process. You can open the Dashboard by selecting Open Developer Account from the Visual Studio Store menu.

In Chapter 30, I completed the first step of the publishing process by reserving a name for the app; you will see that this step is shown as complete in the Windows Store, as shown in Figure 1.

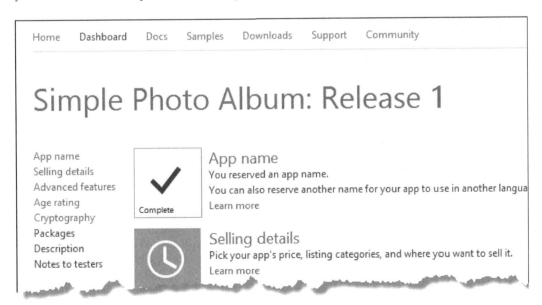

Figure 1. The Windows Store Dashboard showing the completed first step

In the sections that follow, I'll complete some more of the steps so that I can prepare the app for final checks, testing, and changes.

Completing the Selling Details Section

Click the Selling Details link to set the pricing information for the basic app. I am going to charge $4.99 for my example app and offer a 30-day trial (you can see how I have configured this in Figure 2).

Figure 2. *Setting the selling details for the app*

Check the markets in which you want to sell the app. I used the Select all link to select all of the markets in which the Windows Store operates in order to sell my app as widely as possible. Microsoft will automatically price my app at the local equivalent of my dollar price. Click the Save button to store the selling details; you will be returned to the list of steps.

Completing the Advanced Features Section

Click the Advanced Features link to set up the listing information for the in-app upgrades. (This section can also be used to configure notification services, which I haven't covered in this book because they require server capabilities to work).

Use the web form to create the set of upgrades that you want to offer. It is important to ensure that the Product ID field corresponds to one of the products you have been testing with the scenario file; otherwise, you will create an app capability that the user won't be able to license. You can see the set of upgrades I have created for my example app in Figure 3. Click the Save button to save these settings and return to the main list.

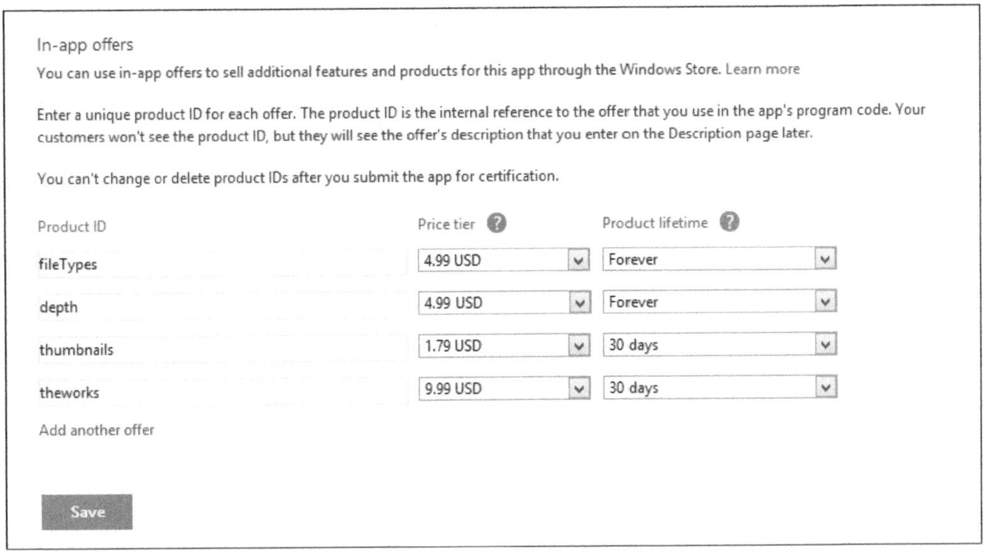

In-app offers

You can use in-app offers to sell additional features and products for this app through the Windows Store. Learn more

Enter a unique product ID for each offer. The product ID is the internal reference to the offer that you use in the app's program code. Your customers won't see the product ID, but they will see the offer's description that you enter on the Description page later.

You can't change or delete product IDs after you submit the app for certification.

Product ID	Price tier	Product lifetime
fileTypes	4.99 USD	Forever
depth	4.99 USD	Forever
thumbnails	1.79 USD	30 days
theworks	9.99 USD	30 days

Add another offer

Save

Figure 3. Creating the in-app upgrades

Completing the Age Rating Section

Click the Age rating and rating certificates link and select the age group for which your app is suitable. The Windows Store Dashboard provides information about the intended audience and app capabilities for each age group. Select the most suitable group, bearing in mind that the app intended for younger users won't be able to access devices and sensors. I have selected the 12+ category, as shown in Figure 4. Click the Save button to save these settings and return to the main list.

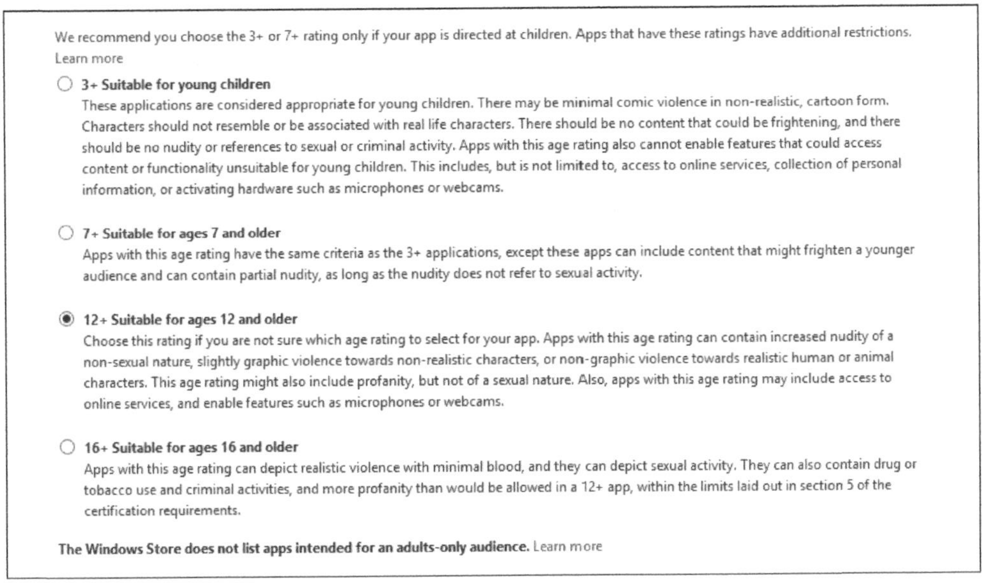

We recommend you choose the 3+ or 7+ rating only if your app is directed at children. Apps that have these ratings have additional restrictions. Learn more

○ **3+ Suitable for young children**
These applications are considered appropriate for young children. There may be minimal comic violence in non-realistic, cartoon form. Characters should not resemble or be associated with real life characters. There should be no content that could be frightening, and there should be no nudity or references to sexual or criminal activity. Apps with this age rating also cannot enable features that could access content or functionality unsuitable for young children. This includes, but is not limited to, access to online services, collection of personal information, or activating hardware such as microphones or webcams.

○ **7+ Suitable for ages 7 and older**
Apps with this age rating have the same criteria as the 3+ applications, except these apps can include content that might frighten a younger audience and can contain partial nudity, as long as the nudity does not refer to sexual activity.

◉ **12+ Suitable for ages 12 and older**
Choose this rating if you are not sure which age rating to select for your app. Apps with this age rating can contain increased nudity of a non-sexual nature, slightly graphic violence towards non-realistic characters, or non-graphic violence towards realistic human or animal characters. This age rating might also include profanity, but not of a sexual nature. Also, apps with this age rating may include access to online services, and enable features such as microphones or webcams.

○ **16+ Suitable for ages 16 and older**
Apps with this age rating can depict realistic violence with minimal blood, and they can depict sexual activity. They can also contain drug or tobacco use and criminal activities, and more profanity than would be allowed in a 12+ app, within the limits laid out in section 5 of the certification requirements.

The Windows Store does not list apps intended for an adults-only audience. Learn more

Figure 4. Selecting the age rating for the app

Completing the Cryptography Section

Click the Cryptography link and specify whether or not your app uses cryptography. Quite a few countries, including the United States, limit the use or export of cryptography, so it is especially important to make an accurate declaration for this section. I have checked the No option, as shown in Figure 5, because my example app doesn't use cryptography in any form.

This app is considered to use encryption even if another entity performs the encryption, such as the operating system, an external library, a third-party product, or a cryptographic processor.

Does this app call, support, contain, or use cryptography or encryption? *

○ Yes

⦿ No

☑ I confirm that this app is widely distributable to all jurisdictions without government review, approval, license or technology-based restriction. *

Figure 5. Declaring the use of cryptography

That is the last of the changes needed at the most, so when you click the Save button, you should see that the first five steps have been completed, as shown in Figure 6. I'll come back and complete the remaining steps later.

App name
You reserved an app name.
You can also reserve another name for your app to use in another language or to change your app's name.
Learn more

Complete

Selling details
Your app will sell for 4.99 and is scheduled for release after it passes certification.
Learn more

Complete

Advanced features
Number of in-app offers: 4
Configure push notifications and Live Services and define in-app offers.
Learn more

Complete

Age rating and rating certificates
Windows Store age rating: 12+ Suitable for ages 12 and older
Learn more

Complete

Cryptography
Declaration complete.
Learn more

Complete

Packages
Upload your app to the Windows Store.
Learn more

Figure 6. Progressing through the publication process

Associating the App with the Store

The next step is to update the Visual Studio project so that it is associated with the Windows Store listing. To do this, select the Associate App with the Store menu item from the Visual Studio Store menu. Once you have provided your developer credentials, you will be able to pick from the app listings you have created, as shown in Figure 7.

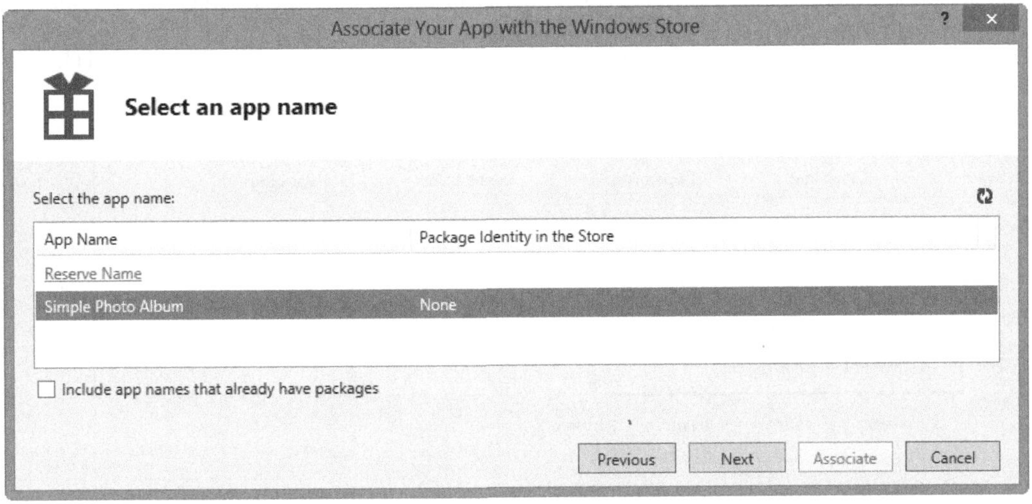

Figure 7. Selecting a listing for an app

Select a listing and click the Next button. I have selected my Simple Photo Album listing, but because you will be unable to create a listing with the exact same name, you will see the listings you have created.

You will be presented with details of values that will be taken from the Windows Store listing and used in the app manifest, as shown in Figure 8.

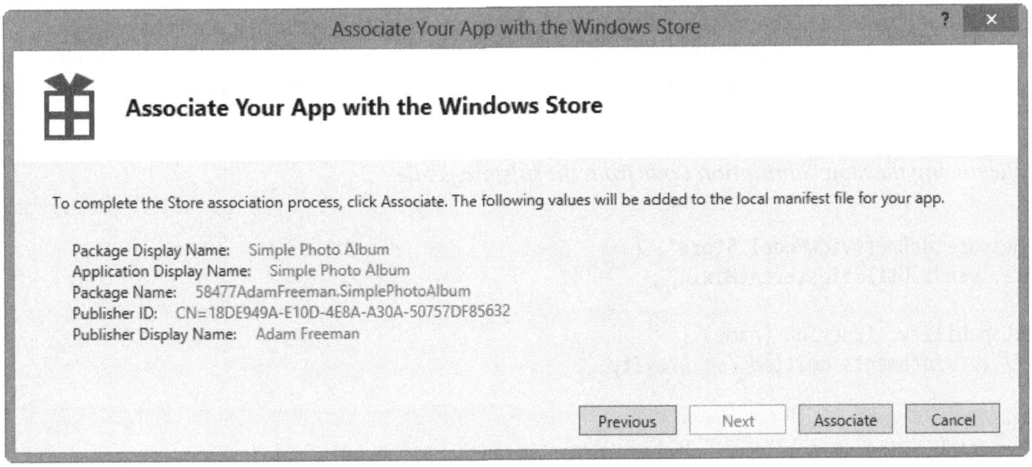

Figure 8. The list of store values that will be used in the manifest

Click the Associate button to associate the Visual Studio project with the Windows Store listing. Your manifest will be updated so that key fields in the project match the information you provided in the listing.

Providing a Store Logo

At this point, you need to add a logo that will be displayed alongside your app in the Windows Store, which is provided as a 50 x 50 pixel file. I have used the same logo as for the tile and splash screen, which I added to the images folder of the project in a file called store50.png.

To apply the store logo, open the package.appxmanifest file, navigate to the Packaging tab, and change the value of the Logo field, as shown in Figure 9.

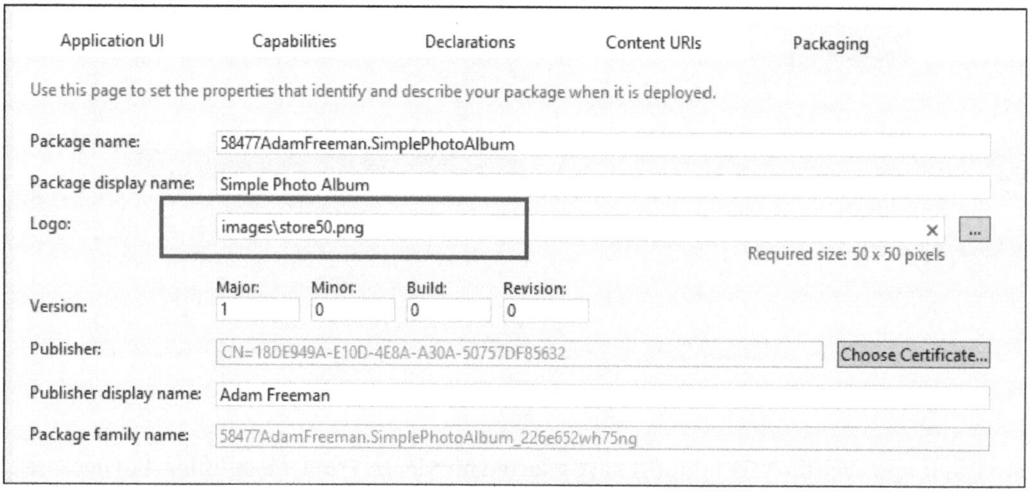

Figure 9. Changing the store logo

Removing the Store Simulation Code

It is important to remove the CurrentAppSimulator object from the app and replace it with CurrentApp before you publish. You can see the changes I have made in the /js/store.js file to prepare the app for publishing in Listing 1. I find it helpful to be able to easily move back to the testing code for dealing with bug reports, so I have commented out the simulation code rather than removing it.

Listing 1. Removing the Store Simulation Code from the /js/store.js File

```
...
WinJS.Namespace.define("ViewModel.Store", {
    events: WinJS.Utilities.eventMixin,

    checkCapability: function (name) {
        // ...statements omitted for brevity...
    },

    //currentApp: Windows.ApplicationModel.Store.CurrentAppSimulator,
    currentApp: Windows.ApplicationModel.Store.CurrentApp,
    loadLicenseData: function () {
```

```
        //var url
        //    = new Windows.Foundation.Uri("ms-appx:///store/upgrades.xml");
        //return storage.StorageFile.getFileFromApplicationUriAsync(url)
        //    .then(function (file) {
        //        return ViewModel.Store.currentApp.reloadSimulatorAsync(file);
        //    });
        return WinJS.Promise.wrap("true");
    },

    isBasicAppPurchased: function () {
        var license = ViewModel.Store.currentApp.licenseInformation;
        return license.isActive && !license.isTrial;
    },

    isFullyUpgraded: function() {
        return ViewModel.Store.currentApp.licenseInformation.productLicenses
            .lookup("theworks").isActive;
    },

    getProductInfo: function () {
        // ...statements omitted for brevity...
    },

    requestAppPurchase: function() {
        ViewModel.Store.events.dispatchEvent("apppurchaserequested");
    },

    requestUpgradePurchase: function (productId) {
        ViewModel.Store.events.dispatchEvent("productpurchaserequested",
            { product: productId });
    }
});
...
```

Because I am not removing the loadLicenseData function, I need to return a result that will allow the call from the /js.default.js file to work. To this end, I used the Promise.wrap method, which I described in Chapter 9.

■ **Tip** You can also remove the scenario files at this point because they won't be used by the published app.

Building the App Package

The next step is to build the package that will be uploaded to the Windows Store. To begin, select Create App Packages from the Visual Studio Store menu. The Create App Packages wizard will be shown, and the first question asks you if you want to create a package for the Windows Store, as shown in Figure 10.

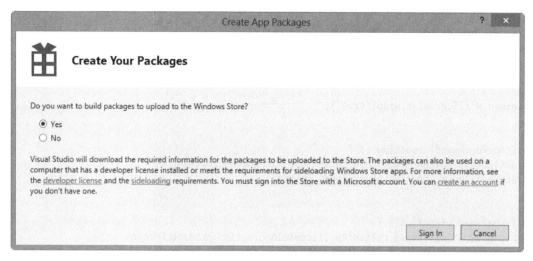

Figure 10. *The Create App Package Wizard*

Select Yes and click the Sign In button. Provide your developer account credentials and then select the listing you want the app package to be associated with from the list, as shown in Figure 11.

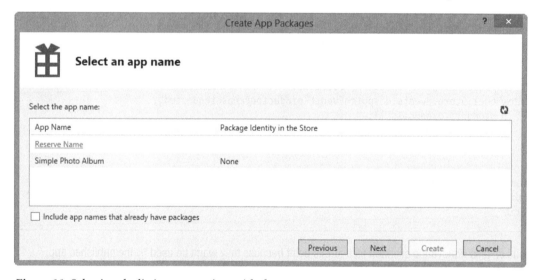

Figure 11. *Selecting the listing to associate with the store*

This ensures that the latest information in your listing is used to build the app package. Click the Next button and you will be able to set the location where the package will be created, set the version information, and specify which processor architectures your app will run on.

I have accepted the default values, as shown in Figure 12. This means that the package will be created in the AppPackages folder within my project folder, the version will be 1.0.0, and my app will be able to run on any platform.

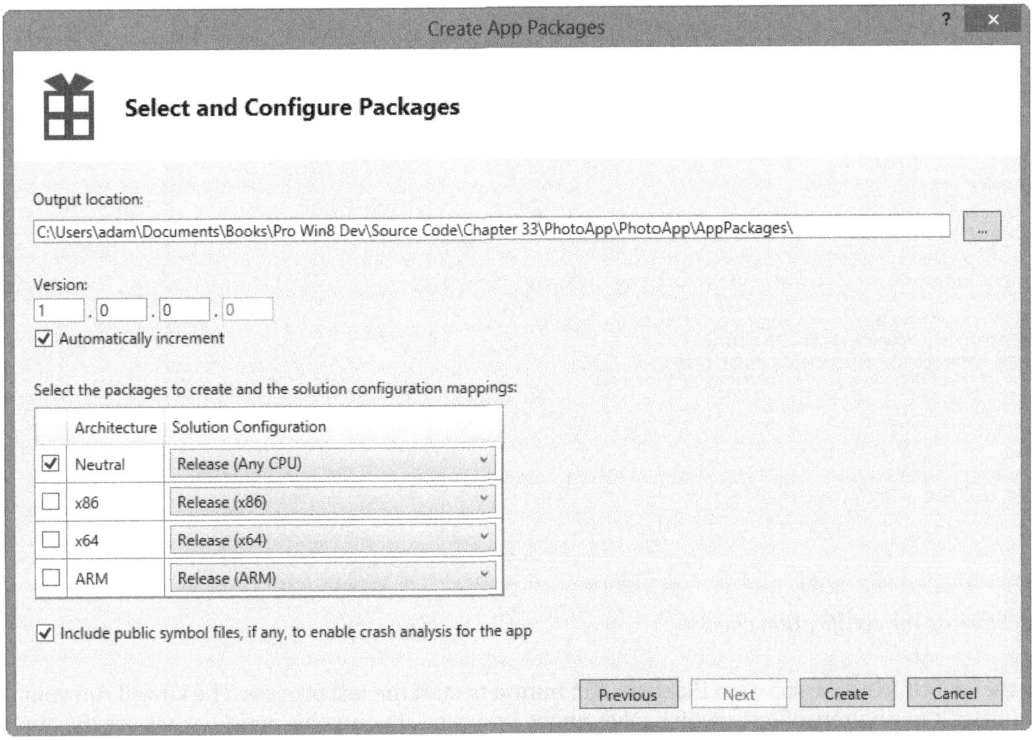

Figure 12. Setting the version and architecture option

Click the Create button to generate the app package. When the package has been created, you will be offered the chance to run the Windows App Certification Kit, as shown in Figure 13. Microsoft subjects its apps to a range of tests before they are approved for sale in the Windows Store, and you can head off potential problems by running the certification kit, which will check your app for some of the same problems that Microsoft looks for.

▓ **Tip** You can download the certification kit as part of the Windows 8 SDK if you don't have it already installed. The SDK is available at http://msdn.microsoft.com/en-us/windows/hardware/hh852363.aspx.

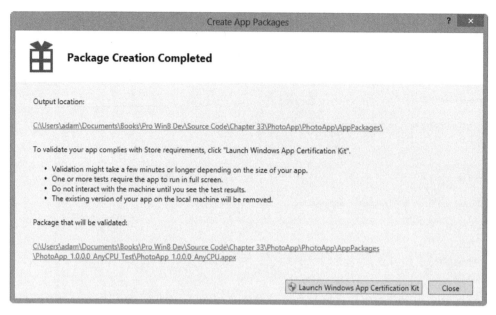

Figure 13. Starting the certification check

Click the Launch Windows App Certification Kit button to start the test process. The kit will run your app and subject it to a battery of tests, which takes about 5 minutes. During this period, you'll see the app running momentarily and then disappear – don't try and interact with the app while it is being tested.

When the test is complete, you'll see the results and be offered the chance to see a detailed report. The report contains details of any problems that were found and offers some basic suggestions as to how they can be resolved.

My example app doesn't have any issues, so after a few minutes I see the summary screen shown in Figure 14.

Figure 14. The summary showing a successful certification test

Completing the App Listing

Now that the app package is complete and tested, it is time to return to the Windows Store Dashboard and complete the app listing (you can return to the Dashboard by selecting Open Developer Account from the Visual Studio Store menu).

Completing the Packages Section

Click the Package link and upload the app package to the Windows Store. If you accepted the default location when you created the package, then you will be able to find the file you need in the AppPackages folder of your Visual Studio project. The package file has a file extension of appxupload and you can just drag it to the web page, as shown in Figure 15. Click the Save button to return to the main listing page when you have uploaded your package file.

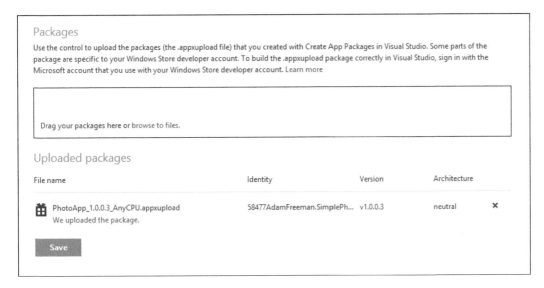

Figure 15. Uploading the package to the store

Completing the Description Section

Click the Description link and enter the details of your app. This information is presented to the user when they are browsing or searching the Windows Store and well-thought-out information can make your app easier to find – something that is important given how competitive the app market can be. In particular, I suggest you pay attention to providing good quality screenshots (which you can take with the Visual Studio simulator) and give careful thought to the keywords you specify.

At the end of the list of information that is required are descriptions of the upgrades that you offer in your app, as shown in Figure 16. Make sure that you provide descriptions of those that will have some meaning to the user.

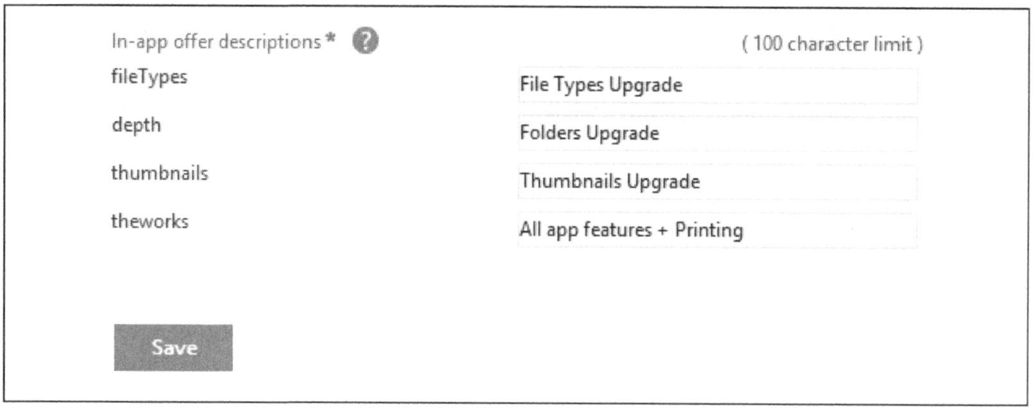

In-app offer descriptions * ❓	(100 character limit)
fileTypes	File Types Upgrade
depth	Folders Upgrade
thumbnails	Thumbnails Upgrade
theworks	All app features + Printing

Save

Figure 16. Providing descriptions of upgrades

When you have filled out all of the required details and uploaded your images, click the Save button to return to the main listing page.

Completing the Notes for Testers Section

Click the Notes for Testers section to provide any information that the Microsoft testers will need to validate your app. This is important information to include because the testers have a limited amount of attention and interest in your app, and you need to make sure that they can get your app working quickly and easily. When you have entered your testing hints, click the Save button to return the main listing page.

Submitting Your App

The main listing page should show that all of the steps are now complete. When you are ready to submit your app, click the Submit for certification button, as shown in Figure 17.

Figure 17. Submitting the app for certification

Your app will be submitted for certification and you will see details of its progress through the testing process, as shown in Figure 18. It takes several days for an app to go through certification, but Microsoft will e-mail you as your app passes through each stage in the process.

Figure 18. Tracking your app through the certification process

If your app passes all of the tests and reviews without any problems, it will be listed on the Windows Store and be available for users to purchase and download.

Summary

In this chapter, I have shown you the process for preparing and submitting your app for certification and listing in the Windows Store. It is important to test your app thoroughly before submitting it to Microsoft because it can take several days before you get back details of any problems.

And that's the end of this book. I started by showing you how you can use your existing web app knowledge to build a simple Windows app and then built on that foundation to show you more complex and sophisticated features and techniques, culminating in integration with the Windows Store and submitting an app for certification and publication. I wish you every success with your apps and hope that you have enjoyed reading this book every bit as much as I have enjoyed writing it.

Index

CPSIA information can be obtained at www.ICGtesting.com
Printed in the USA
LVOW010745120113

315486LV00009B/428/P